Beginning ATL 3 COM Programming

Dr Richard Grimes
George Reilly
Alex Stockton
Julian Templeman
Karli Watson

Wrox Press Ltd. ®

Beginning ATL 3 COM
Programming

© 1999 Wrox Press

Published by Wrox Press Ltd, Arden House, 1102 Warwick Road, Acocks Green,
Birmingham, B27 6BH, UK
Printed in Canada
ISBN 1-861001-20-7

Trademark Acknowledgements

Wrox has endeavored to provide trademark information about all the companies and products mentioned in this book by the appropriate use of capitals. However, Wrox cannot guarantee the accuracy of this information.

Credits

Authors
Dr Richard Grimes
George Reilly
Alex Stockton
Julian Templeman
Karli Watson

Technical Editors
Jon Hill
Karli Watson

Technical Reviewers
This Edition
Dr Richard Grimes
Davide Marcato
Kenn Scribner

Previous Edition
Michael Hupp
Sing Li
Christian Nagel
Michael O'Keefe
M. G. "Ravi" Ravichandran
Dean Rowe
Jim Springfield
Julian Templeman

Managing Editor
Chris Hindley

Development Editor
John Franklin

Figures
David Boyce
William Fallon

Design/Layout
Tom Bartlett
Mark Burdett
Jonathan Jones
John McNulty
William Fallon
David Boyce

Cover
Chris Morris

Index
Andrew Criddle
Robin Smith

COMDude Cartoon
Alex Hughes

About the Authors

Richard Grimes started programming eons ago on 8-bit computers and hasn't looked back since. He has spent an interesting time as a research scientist (the little known "Grimes' effect" is his creation), underpaid time as a computer trainer and done time as a distributed object developer.

ATL took hold of Richard while he was part of a team developing a COM-based workflow system and its elegance has had a lasting effect on him. Although his is not an obsessively pure COM existence, he finds that an ATL-assisted COM lifestyle gives him more time to enjoy his garden.

Richard writes and advises on COM and ATL, and can be contacted via e-mail at atl.dev@grimes.demon.co.uk.

Alex Stockton is an author and past editor for Wrox Press, as well as creator of the World of ATL web site (http://www.worldofatl.com/). Alex is barely old enough to remember the dark days before COM and has never seen a punch card in his whole life. His first PC was a Pentium Pro 180.

George Reilly has spent eleven years working with C&C++ and has developed in Windows since C7 and the SDK. He is an ActiveX expert, a member of Microsoft's IIS team and a founder member of all the IIS/ISAPI discussion forums.

Julian Templeman lives in London with his wife and three children, two cats, a dog, two PCs, a Mac and a PDP-11. He trains and consults in C++, Windows programming, Java and COM/ActiveX. In such spare time as he has, he writes articles and reviews for programming journals, and contributes as an author and technical reviewer to Wrox Press.

Karli Watson is an author and editor for Wrox Press with a penchant for multicolored clothing. He started out with the intention of becoming a world famous nanotechnologist, so perhaps one day you might recognize his name as he receives a Nobel Prize. Until then, he will have to put up with his ongoing quest to learn every computer language in existence, except FORTRAN. Karli is also a snowboarding enthusiast, and wishes he had a cat.

Author Acknowledgements

Richard Grimes
My thanks go to the guys at Wrox whose hard work and attention to detail made sure that this book reached the shelves in time. Also to Roy Bailey and Lee Spring who taught me that ATL could be applied in ways I didn't know was possible. Then there are the contributions of the technical reviewers who reined in my late-night ramblings. Finally, thanks are due to John Franklin for making sure the project stayed alive.

Alex Stockton
Thanks to the many kind people at Wrox Press who toil away behind the scenes.

Thanks also to the ATL development team for their excellent work in producing the library that is the subject of this book, as well as for the direct support they've provided.

Julian Templeman
My thanks are due to all at Richford's, for providing a stimulating and relaxed working environment. I've learnt a lot from my colleagues there, and have valued their suggestions and comments (especially the helpful ones!).

The team at Wrox has been unfailingly supportive. Special thanks go to John Franklin, for managing the project, and Jon Hill, for turning my prose into something readable.

Karli Watson
Thanks to all here at Wrox, particularly John Franklin for giving me this opportunity, and Jon Hill for getting late night food in occasionally. Also, thanks to Donna for putting up with colorful working hours, and to my housemates for drinking solidarity.

Table of Contents

Chapter 3: Building And Calling A COM Object Using ATL   63

Chapter 5: Automation And Error Handling   171

Chapter 6: DCOM, Marshaling, And Threading 229

Chapter 7: ATL Window Classes   283

Chapter 8: Connectable Components   317

Chapter 9: Properties, Persistence and Collections   365

Introduction

Welcome to *Beginning ATL 3 COM Programming*. With this book, you'll learn how to use Visual C++ and ATL to program COM components. You'll see how ATL wraps up the difficult and repetitive parts of COM to enable you to get the most from your coding time.

The aim of the Active Template Library development team at Microsoft is to give programmers the tools with which to produce tight, optimized COM code. Our aim with this book is to give you the best start we can down that road.

Who This Book Is For

This book is for fairly experienced C++ developers who want to get to grips with COM programming using the Active Template Library. The *Beginning* in the title of this book refers to *COM* and it refers to *ATL*. It does not refer to *Programming*. If you're new to programming, put this book down and check out Ivor Horton's best-selling *Beginning Visual C++* instead. You'll probably be able to find it on a shelf near this book.

We don't expect you to know anything about COM. We're going to explain the essentials of COM, how to use it, and how to get the most out of it. But if you *do* already know something about COM, that's a bonus. You'll still learn a lot about the way that ATL works, and you'll be one step ahead of the COM neophytes.

We don't expect you to know anything about ATL. ATL is the prime focus of the book. If you've never touched ATL, or if you've been using it for a short while but still have many unanswered questions, this is the book for you. If you've written your own COM_INTERFACE_ENTRY()-style macro to handle virtual base classes, you're probably better off with *Professional ATL COM Programming* (1-861001-40-1)!

About The New Edition

This book is a revised edition of *Beginning ATL COM Programming*, which was first published in January 1998. ATL and COM have both moved on since then, so as well as the corrections and clarifications you would expect from the second edition of a book, we have introduced new sections that address the new features of ATL 3.0 and talk about advances like COM+.

ATL 3 marks the blossoming of ATL as a technology. It covers the entire spectrum of COM applications, from ActiveX controls through ASP and MMC to OLE DB providers. As a C++ framework, it represents the most efficient way to write COM components. However, ATL 3 is more than that. It contains windowing classes that make Win32 development straightforward, without obscuring the code like an application framework does. This means that Win32 applications written with ATL can be small and fast, and we treat this aspect of ATL's operation in Chapter 7.

Although it's a buzzword in the industry, COM+ is a difficult subject to tackle in an introductory book about ATL, because even version 3.0 predates a lot of COM+'s history. At heart, however, COM+ *are* COM components: they should still implement IUnknown; they should still be created with a standard class object; they should still be described by a type library; they should still be self registering. ATL provides all of these requirements, and this book concentrates on these fundamentals of COM, giving information about COM+ when it's salient to do so. In this way, we've tried to make the book form a foundation for your studies into COM *and* COM+. The things you learn here are not about to change.

How To Read This Book

First, particularly if you're in a bookstore, read the whole of this introduction to determine whether this book is the right one for you. The previous section described the intended audience of the book. Now you know whether you have the right skills to act as the foundation for the tutorial ahead. The next section will quickly let you know whether you have the requisite software to get any benefit from the book.

This book is designed to be read while you're at your computer. You'll get more out of the book if you have Visual C++ running as you progress through the book, giving you a chance to experiment with the examples.

This book is complementary to the existing documentation (and the source code) supplied with Visual C++. We don't try to replace Microsoft's documentation, nor do we duplicate it. We don't expect you to have read any of the Microsoft-supplied documentation before starting this book, but checking the online help for function prototypes and quick reminders will be increasingly useful as you start to use the knowledge gained from this book to strike out on your own path.

What You Need To Use This Book

To get the most out of this book, you need Visual C++ 6.0, the latest version of Microsoft's C++ compiler, and a computer on which to run it. The absolute minimum requirements for Visual C++ 6.0 are a PC with 32Mb of RAM and a 486/66 MHz processor or higher, running Windows 95/98 or Windows NT 4.0, but the more you can add above any of these baselines, the better.

You will get extra benefit by having access to a selection of other software:

Windows NT Service Pack 5

Since the initial release of Windows NT 4.0, Microsoft has made a number of service packs available, featuring bug fixes and enhancements to the operating system. However you're using Windows NT, it makes sense to take advantage of these updates, which you can freely download from Microsoft's web site. The Windows NT service packs are of particular interest to COM developers — we certainly recommend that you install service pack 5, which is the latest release at the time of writing.

Visual Studio Service Pack 3

The latest service pack released for Visual Studio (including Visual C++, Visual Basic, etc.) is service pack 3, and it always makes sense to install the latest version Once again, you can download the service pack free of charge from the Microsoft web site.

DCOM9x For Windows 9x, Version 1.3

If you're using Windows 9x, you should install the latest version of the COM library in the form of either DCOM95 or DCOM98. DCOM95 enhances COM on Windows 95 by allowing COM objects to communicate across a network. Windows 98 has this facility by default, but DCOM98 adds the usual enhancements and bug fixes.

Microsoft Visual Basic 6.0

If you have Visual Basic, you'll be able to run the small number of Visual Basic examples contained in this book. These examples are always used as clients once we've already seen a C++ client in action, so they're a bonus for readers with Visual Basic. If you don't have Visual Basic, you won't be missing out.

Users of Visual C++ 5.0

This book covers ATL version 3.0, which is only available with the Visual C++ 6.0 product. The version of ATL that shipped with Visual C++ 5.0 was 2.1, and there are sufficient differences between them to make compatibility a problem. If you have Visual C++ 5.0, we suggest that you seek out a copy of *Beginning ATL COM Programming* (1-861000-11-1), which treats ATL 2.1 by design. We have not tested the examples in this book for compatibility with ATL 2.1. *Caveat emptor*.

Conventions and Terminology Used

We use a number of different styles of text and layout in the book to help differentiate between the different kinds of information. Here are examples of the styles we use and an explanation of what they mean:

> **These boxes hold important, not-to-be forgotten, mission-critical details that are directly relevant to the surrounding text.**

Background information, asides, references and extra details appear in text like this. For example,

> *'Click' or 'left-click' means click once with the primary mouse button,*
> *'Double-click' means double-click with the primary mouse button*
> *and 'right-click' means click once with the secondary mouse button.*

❑ **Important Words** are in a bold type font.

❑ Words that appear on the screen, such as menu options, are in a similar font to the one used on screen, for example the File | New... menu. The levels of a cascading menu are separated by a pipe character (|).

❑ Keys that you press on the keyboard, like *Ctrl* and *Enter*, are in italics.

❑ All filenames are in this style: Videos.mdb.

❑ Function names look like this: sizeof().

❑ Template classes look like this: CComObject<>.

❑ Code that is new, important or relevant to the current discussion will be presented like this:

```
int main()
{
    cout << "Beginning ATL COM Programming";
    return 0;
}
```

❑ Whereas code you've seen before, or which has little to do with the matter at hand, looks like this:

```
void main()
{
    cout << "Beginning ATL COM Programming";
    return 0;
}
```

Tell Us What You Think

We have tried to make this book as accurate and enjoyable for you as possible, but what really matters is what the book actually does for you. Please let us know your views, whether positive or negative, either by returning the reply card in the back of the book or by contacting us at Wrox Press at feedback@wrox.com.

Source Code and Keeping Up-to-date

We try to keep the prices of our books reasonable, and so to replace an accompanying disc we make the source code for the book available on our web site at http://www.wrox.com. One-time registration there entitles you to code downloads, errata sheets, and lifetime support for all Wrox Press titles.

If you don't have access to the Internet, we can provide a disk for a nominal fee to cover postage and packing.

Errata & Updates

We've made every effort to make sure there are no errors in the text or the code. However, to err is human and as such we recognize the need to keep you, the reader, informed of any mistakes as they're spotted and corrected.

While you're visiting our web site, please make use of our errata page, which is dedicated to fixing any small errors in the book, or offering new ways around a problem and its solution. Errata sheets are available for all our books — please download them, or take part in the continuous improvement of our tutorials and upload a 'fix' or a pointer to the solution.

For those without access to the Net, we'll gladly send errata sheets by return of mail if you send a letter to:

Wrox Press Inc.,
29 South LaSalle Street,
Suite 520,
Chicago,
IL 60603
USA

Wrox Press Ltd,
Arden House,
1102 Warwick Road,
Acock's Green,
Birmingham B27 6BH
UK

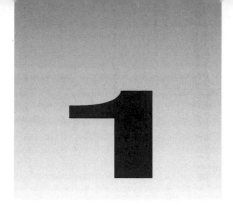

An Introduction To COM

The Holy Grail of computing is to put applications together quickly and cheaply from reusable, maintainable code — preferably, code written by someone else. For many years now, experience and research have shown that object-oriented languages have a marked effect on the ability of software developers to write this kind of code. The ability to abstract concepts from a problem, and to turn them into classes and objects in a way that is fundamentally supported by the programming language, is a powerful draw for software engineers. The benefits of object-oriented techniques are there for all to see.

On its own, however, an object-oriented programming language is not sufficient for widespread reuse. As soon as we go beyond the idea of having a single developer or group of developers, the real world comes crashing in. The first problem we see is that developers throughout the world are programming in *different* languages.

As much as some well-known Californian companies would like us to simplify things by standardizing around a single programming language, it's never going to happen. The reasons for the diversity of languages in the world today are complex, beyond one company's control, and in many cases well founded. Some languages are better suited than others to a particular problem domain; some programmers have a natural preference for a particular language because it more closely reflects the way they think; some languages relate well to particular hardware. New languages and tools replace old ones because they're based on new ideas or take advantage of processor power that wasn't previously available. The popularity of a language responds to fashion and hype, and even to the quantity of good books teaching the subject. We live, and will continue to live, in a world of many tongues.

Now, a multitude of languages has its benefits, but the problem it presents to us is that it fragments the marketplace for reusable components. A Java class is of little use to a C++ developer, and a chunk of Visual Basic code won't help a COBOL programmer. If I write a system in C++ today, will that effort be superceded five years from now by the arrival of a new programming language, as yet undreamed? It was issues like these that drove the authors of the **Component Object Model** (**COM**) to their solution, which is to use language-neutral, *binary* components. Subject to a few considerations, this methodology allows developers to write components in whatever language they choose. It's the compiled code that matters, not the source code.

Of course, COM is neither the first nor the only way of reusing compiled code. C-style DLLs, for example, have been used extensively in Windows programming for a very long time, and their advantages are manifold:

❑ They allow parts of an application to be swapped out or upgraded without the need for recompilation

❑ Code can be loaded on a just-in-time basis, so that it doesn't take up any memory if it's never needed

❑ Code can be shared between processes, which can be more memory-efficient than linking it statically (that is, compiling it into the application)

Given this list of important features, it will come as no surprise that COM components can themselves be packaged as DLLs. However, if it were as simple as that, you'd be looking at a very thin book indeed. Happily for us, C-style DLLs also have a number of disadvantages that COM must address:

❑ Although they are callable from most languages, relatively few languages let you create them.

❑ They expose only simple functions — they are not object-oriented.

❑ Traditionally, DLLs have been loaded by filename, which means that if the location or the name of a DLL changes, the application will not be able to load it.

❑ It is difficult to provide different versions of a DLL on the same system, because doing so can cause conflicts between different vendors' products.

As you read on, you'll discover how COM overcomes all of these problems, and provides a number of other facilities we've yet to mention. We should begin, though, by getting a firmer grasp of exactly what COM *is*.

A One Sentence Description Of COM

COM is a complicated topic, but we can write a simple one-sentence description that outlines its most important features:

> *"COM is a specification and a set of services that allow you to create modular, object-oriented, customizable and upgradeable, distributed applications using a number of programming languages."*

Let's look more closely at that overlong sentence and its implications to get a fuller picture of the kinds of facilities offered by COM.

❑ **COM is a specification**
The COM specification describes the standards that you need to follow in order to create interoperable COM components. This standard describes what COM components should look like and how they should behave.

❑ **COM is a set of services**
The specification is backed up by a set of services or APIs. These services are provided by the **COM library**, which is part of the operating system on Win32 platforms, and available as a separate package for other operating systems.

❑ **COM allows modular programming**
COM components can be packaged as DLLs or EXEs — COM provides the communication mechanism to allow components in different modules to talk to each other.

❑ **COM is object-oriented**
COM components are true objects in the usual sense: they have identity, state and behavior. In certain circumstances, COM components can be treated polymorphically.

❑ **COM enables easy customization and upgrades to your applications**
COM components link with each other dynamically, and COM defines standard ways of locating components and identifying their functionality, so individual components are swappable without having to recompile the entire application.

❑ **COM enables distributed applications**
COM provides a communication mechanism that enables components to interact across a network. More importantly, COM provides location transparency to applications (if desired) that enables them to be written without regard to the location of their components. The components can be moved without requiring any changes to the application.

❑ **COM components can be written in many programming languages**
COM is a binary standard. Any language that can cope with the binary standard can create or use COM components. The number of languages and tools that support COM is sizable, with C, C++, Java, JScript, Visual Basic, VBScript, Delphi, PowerBuilder, and MicroFocus Cobol forming just part of the list.

COM is not about any particular type of application. It's not about controls (that's ActiveX); it's not about compound documents (that's OLE); it's not about data access (that's OLE DB and ADO); and it's not about games and graphics (that's DirectX). But COM is the object model that underlies *all* these technologies. An understanding of COM is vital to programming any of these technologies successfully.

The Component Object Model

The component object model is built around the notions of **components** (often called **coclasses**), **objects**, and **interfaces**. These three different entities are defined and related as follows:

❑ Loosely, as we have just been discussing, a coclass (named from *component object class*) is a piece of binary code that implements some kind of functionality. Coclasses can be distributed in DLLs, or in executable files. It is possible for a single module (DLL or executable) to contain more than one coclass.

❑ A COM object is an *instance* of a coclass that gets loaded into memory. (By the same token, one might say that a coclass is a 'blueprint' for a COM object.) It is not unreasonable (indeed, it is quite common) for more than one object of a given coclass to be active at a time.

❑ COM interfaces are the means — the *only* means — by which other components and other programs get access to the functionality of a COM component. An interface is a set of definitions of logically-related methods that will control one aspect of the component's operation. Each component can have one or more interfaces.

You should have a good understanding of the concepts behind terms like "class" and "object" from your experience of object-oriented programming with C++. These concepts are not altered by COM, but you should be careful not to assume that there is a complete, one-to-one mapping that encapsulates all the secondary meanings of these terms. A coclass can be defined in C++ using a single C++ class, but it could also be defined with many C++ classes, or without any C++ classes at all (COM classes can be created in plain old C, for example). Remember that COM is a language-neutral protocol.

These definitions are accurate, but they probably haven't done a great deal to straighten things out in your mind — for a start, they're written in terms of one another. Let's start again with a closer look at the most important of the three: the COM interface.

The Importance Of Interfaces

Depending on the context in which it's being used, the word "interface" can have slightly different meanings. In the broadest possible terms, a COM interface is a group of definitions of methods that are usually related in the operations they perform. The methods in an interface can be called by using a pointer to that interface, and doing so results in the execution of the code in a COM object.

A "human" component, for example, might have interfaces called IMouth *and* IHand. *These interfaces would group different methods — for example,* IMouth *might contain methods called* Eat(), Talk(), *and* Kiss(), *and* IHand *might contain* Write(), Point() *and* Scratch().

Choosing our words a little more carefully, we can say that an interface is an abstraction. The definition of an interface includes the *syntax* of the methods it contains (return types, parameter types and calling conventions), and the *semantics* of how to use them. To see how the latter can be important, consider that there are often restrictions placed upon implementers and users of an interface that just can't be described in code. A requirement such as the need to call an Init() method on the interface before calling any other method needs to be clearly documented, and forms the semantic part of the interface definition.

More carefully still, an interface actually has a very specific structure: it is an array of pointers to the implementations of the functions it contains — this is the binary standard that we mentioned earlier. Because the implementation of each function in the interface is accessed by a pointer in an array, the precise order of the items in that array is an important part of the interface's definition. Pictorially, we have a situation like this:

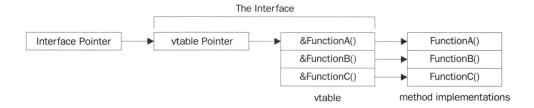

The array of function pointers associated with an interface is usually known as a **vtable** *because it has the same structure as that produced by most compilers for the virtual function table of a C++ class.*

Notice that the definition of an interface does *not* include an implementation of its methods. When a component says that it's going to implement an interface, it's up to that component to do so in a way that is both appropriate to itself and in accordance with the semantics defined for that interface. This separation leads to more robust design: interfaces can be reused in different situations, and a component that makes a particular interface available can be swapped with another component that makes available (**exposes**) the same interface. As a client, if you know that you need the functions of a particular interface, all you need to do is find an object that implements it.

We began this chapter by talking about the desire to build reusable components, but from the point of view of the user (usually called the **client**), the important aspect is not what the component *is*, but what it can *do*. Because interfaces are the only way of making a component do anything at all, we can say that the functionality of a component *is defined by* the interfaces it exposes. For example, if you want to say that a coclass is both a lawyer and a philanthropist (and if you don't feel that's an oxymoron), you can do so by having it expose interfaces called (say) ILawyer and IPhilanthropist.

By convention, the names of all interfaces start with 'I'. For fun, you can give your interfaces names like IAmTheWalrus, IRobot, ICLAVDIVS, or IDo, but you may find that the joke soon wears thin.

The COM specification includes details of a number of **standard interfaces** that Microsoft has defined. By implementing one of these interfaces, a component states that it supports some kind of functionality, or that it will work in some given situation. For example, a coclass that implements ISupportErrorInfo is able to return rich error information, while a component implementing IDataObject is capable of allowing data to be pasted or dropped into another application.

Interfaces As Contracts

As we've explained, COM enforces complete encapsulation of the data and implementation of a component. You can only call methods on the interfaces exposed by a component; you never get direct access to its data.

This fact is what makes interfaces so fundamental, and when we link it to our earlier assertion about COM allowing easy customization and upgrading of applications, we can reach a couple of important conclusions:

❑   An interface, once defined, must never change. Published interfaces are **immutable**.

❑   Once a component has said that it exposes an interface, any future version of that component should also support that interface, to avoid existing clients from malfunctioning.

The interfaces that a component exposes represent a 'contract' between the component and its clients. A consequence of the second of these points when taken in the context of the first is that changes made to the contract in order to 'update' a component will surely break any existing clients, and so any revisions must be made with care. We'll return to this subject in the next chapter.

Creating A COM Component

We've come this far without a single mention of the Active Template Library, and given the title of the book, that may have come as something of a surprise. Microsoft designed ATL to make COM programming in C++ as simple as possible, while at the same time keeping the library extremely efficient through the use of advanced optimization techniques. The vast majority of this book will be given over to an examination of ATL, but to appreciate exactly how it helps, some groundwork is required. Here and in the following chapter, we're going to look at what COM programming looks like in 'plain' C++. Once you understand how that works, learning about ATL later on will come much more naturally.

COM programming splits roughly into two parts: **server** and **client**. The former is generally regarded as being the more difficult, and involves the actual creation of COM components. Assisting with this process is the purpose for which ATL is primarily intended, and we'll be looking at server programming in the next chapter, and indeed for much of the rest of the book. Client programming, on the other hand, is comparatively simple: it involves writing code that makes use of the components that you or a third party have created. By studying it in this chapter, we'll come across issues that will need to be faced later on, when we start writing COM components of our own.

That decision made, we find ourselves with something of a problem: if we want to use a COM component, and we're not going to write it, we need to get it from somewhere else. You are doubtless already familiar with the hazards of assuming that some 'standard' piece of code will be available on every machine you ever use, but to be sure that we're looking at the same thing, we need to find something just like that. For the purposes of this chapter, then, we're going to make limited use of one of the ATL sample projects that Microsoft provides on the MSDN CDs that ship with Visual C++ 6.0.

The ATLFire Project

The sample COM project called `ATLFire` contains a component called `AtlFireCtl` that is actually intended to demonstrate some of ATL's graphical capabilities, but by chance it also has some functionality that we can use from a simple C++ console application. To get the files you need to create the component, open up the MSDN Library and navigate to Visual C++ Documentation\Samples\ATL Samples\ATLFire. From there, click on the link that invites you to copy the project files, and opt to Copy All... on the subsequent dialog. At this point you will be given the opportunity to choose an installation path for the project, which you are free to modify to your own requirements.

Sample projects are not included as part of a standard MSDN installation, so you will probably need to have your CDs to hand in order to copy the files for this project. Alternatively, you can get the code from the MSDN web site; just point your browser at http://msdn.microsoft.com/library *and navigate from there.*

Start up Visual C++, and open ATLFire from wherever you installed it. If you decide to have a look around (and who wouldn't?), don't be put off when you come across anything unfamiliar — all will become clear in good time. For now, all we're concerned about is creating the component, so make sure that the active configuration is set appropriately for your machine, and build the project. It should go without a hitch, and when it does, you're ready to move to the next stage.

Using A COM Component

The COM component you have just created implements a single interface called IFireTabCtrl. In this interface (among other things) is a method called AboutBox() that displays a dialog box containing information about the component. Of course, what we're interested in here is not what the dialog box contains, but how to make it appear at all. Here's a list of the things our C++ COM client code must be able to do:

- ❏ Locate the component
- ❏ Create an instance of the component (that is, an object)
- ❏ Get access to the object's IFireTabCtrl interface
- ❏ Call the AboutBox() method on the IFireTabCtrl interface

That might seem to cover everything, but you should be aware that when you create an object, some machine resources get used. For those resources to be used efficiently, you will want them to be released when the object is no longer required — the alternative is that they will begin to get used up alarmingly quickly as more objects are created. The COM specification contains a mechanism to allow you to define the lifetime of an object. Furthermore, the COM library is capable of 'unloading' object servers that are no longer required, but that ability introduces the risk of an object being unloaded while it is still being used. To prevent that from happening, our client code must also be able to:

- ❏ Specify that it is currently using the object
- ❏ Say that it is no longer using the object

The rest of this section is dedicated to explaining how each of these functions is performed from client code. By the end, we'll have assembled a very simple client for the ATLFireCtl component.

Initializing COM

Even before you can perform any of the above steps, you must initialize the COM library, which allows all operations involving COM to take place. It is an absolute requirement that you should initialize COM once (and only once) on each thread from which you use it. Furthermore, when you have finished using COM, you should uninitialize the library.

The COM API function that initializes COM is called `CoInitializeEx()` (there is also an older variant of this function called `CoInitialize()`); the COM library is unloaded by calling `CoUninitialize()`. `CoInitializeEx()` takes two parameters: the first remains for legacy reasons and must always be `NULL`, while the second parameter defines the type of **apartment** being joined. That subject can wait until Chapter 6; for now we'll just use the legacy function `CoInitialize()` that omits the apartment type. `CoUninitialize()`, by the way, takes no parameters.

```
#include <windows.h>

int main()
{
   CoInitialize(NULL);

   // Code to create and use the COM object will go here

   CoUninitialize();
   return 0;
}
```

Server Location

It is one of the fundamental principles of COM that a client should never need to be aware of the location of the server it's using — not the directory, not the drive, not even the machine it's on. This is an admirable aim, but it raises a rather obvious problem: if the client doesn't know where a component is located, how on earth can it create an instance of it? Depending on the operating system, and on how the component is configured, the answer to this question lies in the **system registry**, the **MTS catalog** or the **COM+ catalog**. The client has to give the COM library enough information to identify the component, and the library will do the rest.

Identifiers

As well as names like `AtlFireCtl` and `IFireTabCtrl`, many of the entities in the COM world (coclasses, interfaces and so forth) have additional identifiers that distinguish them *uniquely* from every other entity, and these serve a number of vital functions:

❑   Because COM is language neutral, the names of coclasses and interfaces also must be language neutral. However, C++ (to take a notorious example) 'mangles' the names of the entities exported by any DLLs you create using it, and other languages do similar things. The identifiers that COM uses do not suffer from these problems.

❑   The trouble with text-based names is that it's quite possible for two programmers to give the same name to (say) two different interfaces. However, because their identifiers will be different, COM will always be able to tell them apart.

❏   In addition, there are more subtle issues like **locale** (should an interface written in the US appear in Cyrillic in Russia?), and even spoken language (should IEat be called JeMange in France?). COM's identifiers avoid these issues too.

To achieve this neutrality, COM associates the name of everything you define with strings of *numbers* that get called different things according to how they are used. For example, coclasses have *class identifiers* (**CLSIDs**); interfaces have *interface identifiers* (**IIDs**); servers have *application identifiers* (**AppIDs**); and there are a number of others that you'll come across later in the book. However, these identifiers *all* have the same format, and they are known collectively as *globally unique identifiers*, or **GUIDs**.

> *GUIDs are also known as* **UUIDs** (*universally unique identifiers*), *because they originate from DCE UUIDs that are used to define RPC interfaces. The precise reason why Microsoft decided to be cautious and call them "global" rather than "universal" is lost in the mists of time, but wherever you see UUID, you can think GUID, and vice versa.*

Technically, a GUID is a very large, statistically unique, 128-bit number (about 10^{38}) generated from the address of the Ethernet card in the current machine, the current time in 100-nanosecond intervals since 1582 (60 bits), and some other stuff. No two Ethernet cards anywhere should have the same address. If the machine has no network card, another number is synthesized that will almost certainly be unique to the machine. It is vanishingly unlikely that duplicate GUIDs will ever be created. The GUID generation algorithm is capable of coming up with 10 million numbers unique to your network card every second for almost 4,000 years before it wraps around.

GUIDs are useful because they ensure that there will be no naming clashes, without requiring a central naming authority to check everything. This means that people throughout the world can independently create their own interfaces and coclasses, without worrying that someday their components will meet up with another incompatible coclass with the same CLSID.

As well as being used to identify the various entities used by COM, GUIDs are used as index values into the store where COM keeps information about them. On older versions of Windows, this information is held in the system registry (see the next section). If a component is to be used with **Microsoft Transaction Server** (**MTS**), information about it will be held in both the registry and the MTS catalog. Information about a COM+ configured component running under Windows 2000 is stored in the COM+ catalog and the registry, although in this case there is no reliance upon the latter — it's there if legacy applications need it.

> *Microsoft Transaction Server is a run-time environment for COM objects that provides services for the objects that run inside it. Its abilities include acting as a transaction monitor and optimizing the process of creating and destroying objects in a way that's invisible to the clients that use them.*
>
> *For more information about COM, COM+, MTS and the catalogs, take a look at* Professional Visual C++MTS Programming *(1-861002-39-4). We won't go into any further depth about these catalogs here, but the principles you'll learn will remain valid throughout your COM programming career.*

The Registry

The registry provides many different services for many different people. It is a hierarchical data store that's used to hold all kinds of information, but its particular interest to COM programmers lies in the fact that it maps the identifiers of COM entities to the physical locations of the modules that contain them.

You can view and edit the registry using RegEdit.exe (Windows 95 and Windows NT) or RegEdt32.exe (Windows NT only). If you want to follow this discussion, it would be a good idea to start one of these applications up now; the screenshots below were taken in the first of the two.

The registry consists of entries called **hives**, **keys**, and **values**. The hives are the top-level folders shown by RegEdit.exe (HKEY_CLASSES_ROOT, HKEY_CURRENT_USER, HKEY_LOCAL_MACHINE, HKEY_USERS, HKEY_CURRENT_CONFIG, and on Windows 9x, HKEY_DYN_DATA). All the other folders are keys, while the values are the list entries in the right-hand pane. Each value consists of a name and some data that can be in one of a few different formats, such as string or binary data. Note also that each key can have a **default value**, and since there can only be one default value in any one key, these do not have a name.

> As far as COM is concerned, the most important hive is **HKEY_CLASSES_ROOT**, because it contains the information that's used to map CLSIDs to file locations. In fact, this is just a mapping of the **HKEY_LOCAL_MACHINE\SOFTWARE\Classes** key.

In a manner analogous to the way you would refer to the location of a file in the file system, keys in the registry are often referred to with a string that's created by concatenating the names of all the keys and sub-keys that lead to them, separated by backslashes. You can see that RegEdit.exe shows the location of the currently selected key in this form in its status bar:

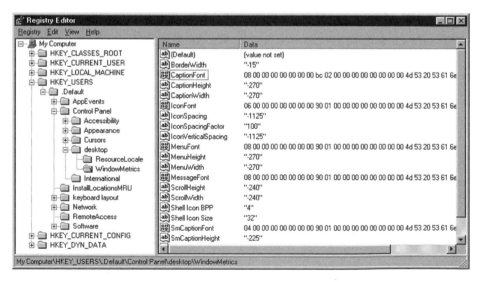

RegEdt32.exe was the original Windows NT registry editor. RegEdit.exe first appeared on Windows 95 and was later ported to NT 4.0. RegEdit.exe has a nicer user interface and good search functionality, but it can't do everything that RegEdt32.exe can. In particular, if you need to edit the security attributes on a key, you must use RegEdt32.exe.

If you open the key called `HKEY_CLASSES_ROOT\CLSID`, you'll see hundreds of CLSIDs. Open some of CLSID's sub-keys, and you'll see that almost all of the CLSIDs have an `InprocServer32` or `LocalServer32` key that contains information about the location of the server. Many of the components will have other keys too, but those are often optional or only relevant to particular types of COM component.

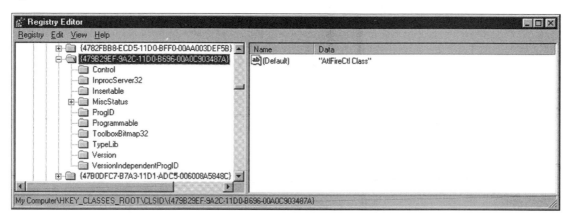

The above screenshot shows the entry in the registry for our `AtlFireCtl` component, which was made by Visual C++ at the very end of the project build process. If you find this entry yourself and look under the `InprocServer32` key, you'll find that it contains the path of the `AtlFire.dll` file that contains the component.

Creating A COM Object

Now, we know what you're thinking. Earlier, we talked about arranging a situation in which the client code never has to know the location of the coclass it wants to use, but haven't we just replaced one problem with another? We may not need to know the whereabouts of the coclass, but we *do* need to know its identifier.

During the process of building the ATLFireCtl component, Visual C++ created a header file called ATLFire.h that contains the following (slightly edited) lines, in which interface is a #define for struct:

```
typedef interface IFireTabCtrl IFireTabCtrl;

...

#ifdef __cplusplus
typedef class FireTabCtrl FireTabCtrl;
#else
typedef struct FireTabCtrl FireTabCtrl;
#endif /* __cplusplus */

...

#if defined(__cplusplus) && !defined(CINTERFACE)

    MIDL_INTERFACE("479B29EE-9A2C-11D0-B696-00A0C903487A")
    IFireTabCtrl : public IDispatch
    {
        // Lines omitted for brevity
    };

...

#endif

...

#ifdef __cplusplus

class DECLSPEC_UUID("479B29EF-9A2C-11D0-B696-00A0C903487A")
FireTabCtrl;
#endif
```

> The **MIDL_INTERFACE()** and **DECLSPEC_UUID()** macros associate a GUID with a C++ **class** or **struct**, so that you can later get the GUID using the **__uuidof()** operator. The SDK header files define practically all standard interfaces and system-implemented components in this way, and parts of ATL expect it.

At the start of this section, we explained that the client must be able to create a COM object and get access to an interface on that object, and you can see that the above listing contains definitions of both these entities (FireTabCtrl and IFireTabCtrl respectively). Once you've included this file in your client project, you can use a function provided by the COM API that takes the information we've outlined and returns a pointer to the desired interface. That function is called CoCreateInstance():

```
WINOLEAPI CoCreateInstance(
    REFCLSID     rclsid,          // Class identifier (CLSID) of the object
    LPUNKNOWN    pUnkOuter,       // Outer unknown pointer
    DWORD        dwClsContext,    // Execution Context
    REFIID       riid,            // Reference to the interface identifier
    LPVOID FAR* ppv               // Indirect pointer to requested interface
    );
```

WINOLEAPI is a synonym for STDAPI, *a macro defined in* objbase.h *that expands to* extern "C" HRESULT __stdcall.

Taking things from the top, the return value of this function is of type HRESULT, a 32-bit integer value containing a status code to indicate any problems that occurred during execution. HRESULTs are the cornerstone of error handling in COM, and we'll be looking at them in more detail in the next chapter.

Moving on, we can deal with four of the five parameters to CoCreateInstance() fairly quickly. The first is the CLSID of the component to be instantiated, which the COM library will use to find out the physical location of the server, and ask it to create an object of the desired type. The second parameter is used for **aggregation**, a technique for reusing COM components from within other components. We'll look at aggregation in detail later in the book, but for now we'll assume that we're not going to use it, in which case this parameter can safely be set to NULL.

Skipping the third parameter for a moment, the fourth parameter to CoCreateInstance() identifies the interface to which we want a pointer, while the fifth will be filled by the function when it returns to the caller. It will contain a pointer to the interface requested.

Execution Context

In the above discussion, we've made a very obvious point of not talking about the third parameter to CoCreateInstance(), which merits some further discourse. Briefly, it specifies the **execution context** for the object, which can be set with one or more of the flags in the CLSCTX enumeration:

```
typedef enum tagCLSCTX
{
    CLSCTX_INPROC_SERVER      = 0x1,
    CLSCTX_INPROC_HANDLER     = 0x2,
    CLSCTX_LOCAL_SERVER       = 0x4,
    CLSCTX_INPROC_SERVER16    = 0x8,
    CLSCTX_REMOTE_SERVER      = 0x10,
    CLSCTX_INPROC_HANDLER16   = 0x20,
    CLSCTX_INPROC_SERVERX86   = 0x40,
    CLSCTX_INPROC_HANDLERX86  = 0x80,
    CLSCTX_ESERVER_HANDLER    = 0x100
} CLSCTX;
```

Here, a 'local' server is one that runs on the same machine as the client, but in a different process. Typical combinations of these values also have named constants to represent them. There's CLSCTX_SERVER *(which unites the* CLSCTX_xxx_SERVER *values), and* CLSCTX_ALL *(which combines* CLSCTX_SERVER *with* CLSCTX_INPROC_HANDLER*). You can also OR individual values together manually.*

What does all this mean? Well, you know that COM components can be implemented in two types of code modules: DLLs and EXEs. In addition, they can run on machines remote to the client. In most cases, the client doesn't care where the object is located, so it will use the CLSCTX_ALL context that indicates to COM that it should decide which server context to use. (COM will use the most efficient method, which effectively means going down the list of execution contexts from top to bottom.) If you know the code module that will be used, it is more efficient to specify it and prevent COM from making the search.

Requesting an "inproc" (in-process) server means that the components will be implemented in a DLL, which in most cases will be loaded into the memory space of the client, making access to the components very efficient:

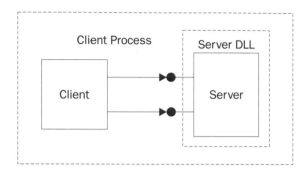

When the component is in-process, the client's memory is not protected against any actions taken by the DLL, and a badly written DLL could cause the client to crash. In addition, COM applies security only when process boundaries are crossed, so in-process components running on Windows NT will use the security context of the client process.

If, on the other hand, the server is implemented as an EXE, Windows will allow it to execute in its own, protected memory space. This trades off performance for robustness, because cross-process calls are slower than in-process calls, but it doesn't need to affect the client code. COM loads **proxy-stub DLLs** into the process spaces of the client and server, so that they can communicate:

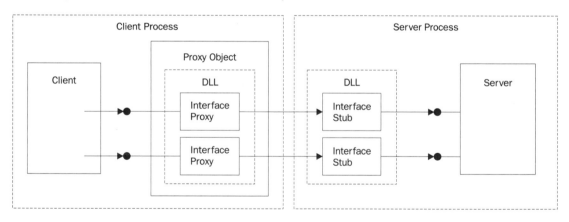

In this situation, the client can call functions directly on a **proxy object** loaded into its address space. Each proxy object looks just like the object the client is attempting to connect to. As the client accesses interfaces, COM will use an interface proxy that looks like the interface on the server object, so the client doesn't need to know whether it's actually talking directly to a server in its own address space, or to a proxy. Similarly, a server is always called by code in *its* own process space called a **stub**. It doesn't need to know whether it's being called directly by the client, or whether it's a stub that's making the call. The proxy and stub hide all the details required to make the call across the process boundary.

*As a bonus, if the server runs under NT it can have a different security account to the client —
without the client code having to log on to that other account.*

This second scenario can be extended to cover the circumstances when the server is located not just in
another process, but on another machine. In that case, all that needs to change is how the proxy and stub
communicate with each other — cross-network, rather than cross-process. Once again, the client code
doesn't need to change because it's *always* acting on an in-process object, but there is something else that
we should take account of: performance.

> **When you're talking specifically about the issues involved with COM operating across
> a network, the term** Distributed COM **or** DCOM **is often used.**

In-process calls are quicker than cross-process calls, which in turn are quicker than cross-network calls.
Since it's quite reasonable for a given coclass to have versions that involve each of these possibilities, COM
allows the client to specify the context of the server it wants to use (whether it's in-process, local, remote,
or whether it doesn't care). The means by which it does this is through the dwClsContext parameter of
CoCreateInstance().

In simple terms, COM will use the server with the best performance that matches a context specified in
this parameter; so in-process servers take precedence over local servers when both contexts are allowed. In
our particular case, we only have an in-process server, so when we call CoCreateInstance() we'll use
CLSCTX_INPROC_SERVER.

The Interface Pointer

Putting together everything we've considered so far, and adding a couple of features that will be our
subject in this section, our client code for the ATLFireCtl component now looks like this:

```
#include <windows.h>

#include "..\AtlFire.h"         // The client project will reside in
                                // a subdirectory of the server project

int main()
{
   CoInitialize(NULL);

   IFireTabCtrl* pFTC = NULL;
   CoCreateInstance(__uuidof(FireTabCtrl),
                    NULL,
                    CLSCTX_INPROC_SERVER,
                    __uuidof(IFireTabCtrl),
                    reinterpret_cast<void**>(&pFTC));

   // Code to use the COM object will go here

   CoUninitialize();
   return 0;
}
```

The only things in this code that we haven't already examined are the declaration of a variable of type IFireTabCtrl* and the precise form of the final parameter to CoCreateInstance(). For the first, you already know that the methods of an interface are accessed through a pointer to that interface, and IFireTabCtrl is defined in ATLFire.h.

For the second, the reason why the type of the final parameter to CoCreateInstance() is void** is simply that the function must be multi-purpose. With correct use of casting, the address of a pointer to any interface can be used as an argument to CoCreateInstance().

Using The Object

To recap, our client code now initializes the COM library and then locates and creates the component we requested. In pFTC, we have a pointer to the IFireTabCtrl interface. In terms of pure functionality, all that remains is to call the AboutBox() method using this pointer, like so:

```
IFireTabCtrl* pFTC = NULL;
CoCreateInstance(__uuidof(FireTabCtrl),
                 NULL,
                 CLSCTX_INPROC_SERVER,
                 __uuidof(IFireTabCtrl),
                 reinterpret_cast<void**>(&pFTC));

pFTC->AboutBox();
```

However, that's not *quite* the end of the matter. As I stated earlier, it is the client's responsibility to make sure that the objects it's using are around for as long as it needs to use them, but no longer. In short, the lifetime of a COM object is entirely in the hands of its clients.

Object Lifetime

To exercise control over the lifetime of an object, we need a mechanism that allows the object to be loaded when it's needed, and unloaded when it isn't. This system needs to be able to cope with multiple clients using an object simultaneously, and it needs to hide as many implementation details from the client as possible.

COM's solution is interface-based reference counting. Each interface on an object keeps track of the number of clients using it; this number is referred to as the **reference count** for that interface. When its reference count reaches zero, the interface can unload itself; when the reference counts for all the interfaces on an object reach zero, the object can unload itself. All the client needs to do is tell the interface when it's being used (so that it can increment its reference count), and inform the interface again when it's finished with it (so that it can decrement the reference count). In this way, the client doesn't need to know how many other clients are using the object.

The methods to increment and decrement the reference count of an interface are called **AddRef()** and **Release()** respectively. Every COM interface you ever write or use will have these methods.

Any function that returns an interface pointer — including `CoCreateInstance()` — should ensure that the interface has a reference counted on it, so that it doesn't disappear before the client gets a chance to use it. Similarly, any time an interface pointer is copied, there must be an accompanying call to `AddRef()`. When the interface pointer has been finished with, clients should call `Release()`, and that's the final line we need to add to our extremely simple client:

```
    pFTC->AboutBox();
    pFTC->Release();

    CoUninitialize();
    return 0;
};
```

If the object is ever to unload, the number of calls to `AddRef()` should be matched by the same number of calls to `Release()` on any particular interface (remember that the call to `AddRef()` in our code is buried in the call to `CoCreateInstance()`). Clients should never dereference an interface pointer once it has been `Release()`'d as many times as the client has `AddRef()`'d.

Note that components often use a single reference count for all the interfaces on an object. They ensure that all interfaces are available for as long as this reference count is greater than zero, then unload the whole object when it reaches zero. However, this is an implementation detail: clients cannot assume that reference counting is anything other than per-interface.

Assembling The Client

You now have all the code you need in order to assemble a simple client for the `ATLFireCtl` component. To do so, create a new, empty **Win32 Console Application** project in Visual C++; the one we used was called `SimpleClient` and stored in a subdirectory of the `ATLFire` project.

Create a new source code file, add it to the project, and then enter the program that we've been putting together over the course of this chapter:

```
#include <windows.h>

#include "..\AtlFire.h"          // The client project will reside in
                                 //   a subdirectory of the server project

int main()
{
    CoInitialize(NULL);

    IFireTabCtrl* pFTC = NULL;
    CoCreateInstance(__uuidof(FireTabCtrl),
                     NULL,
                     CLSCTX_INPROC_SERVER,
                     __uuidof(IFireTabCtrl),
                     reinterpret_cast<void**>(&pFTC));

    pFTC->AboutBox();
    pFTC->Release();

    CoUninitialize();
    return 0;
}
```

With that, you're in a position to compile and execute the project. When you do so, you should see something like this:

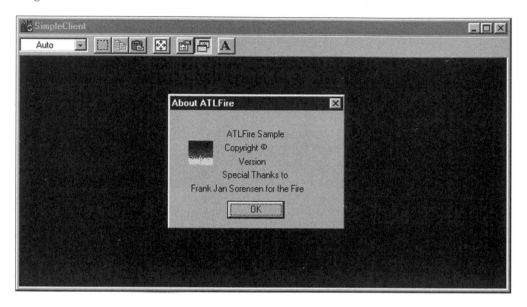

It's not much to look at, but the few lines of C++ code we've written hide a great deal of complexity, and it's easy to forget that this program would look exactly the same regardless of the location of the component whose interface we have used. Keep your mind on that point, and the example should seem at least a little more impressive!

The Next Stage

By intention, this chapter has been a gentle introduction to COM, but the principles of the sample code we developed are all sound, and they will reappear time and again as we deal with more involved examples. Despite the considerable amount of basic COM theory we've already covered, there's still plenty more to come — in fact, you can probably divine some of the things we need to look at by considering the obvious shortcomings of the client code:

❑ We've successfully called a single method of a single COM object, but you were doubtless expecting rather more functionality than that. In general, a COM component can have very many interfaces, and it would be ridiculous if we had to destroy and recreate objects every time we wanted to call a method on another interface.

❑ There is absolutely no error checking — we just assume that everything will work out all right in the end. However, you've already seen the importance of making calls in the correct sequence, and when you add to that the potential for communication between client and server to break down for reasons beyond the programmer's control (a network failure, for example), it's clear that there are many things that could go wrong.

In the next chapter, we'll approach the task of addressing these issues on two fronts. We're going to explain how to write a simple COM component, and we'll write a more robust client for that component. This chapter should have given you an idea of what things a coclass needs to be able to do; the chapter to come will show you exactly how it achieves them.

Summary

It may not seem like it, but you've already learned about many of COM's fundamental features and a number of techniques that will hold true whenever you program using COM. In brief, you've seen that:

- ❑ COM is a specification and a set of services that allow you to create modular, object-oriented, customizable and upgradeable, distributed applications.

- ❑ COM is based around the notions of components, objects and interfaces. A COM object is an instance of a COM component, and an interface is a group of functions through which a client can communicate with an object. The functionality of a component is defined by the interfaces it implements.

- ❑ COM is location-independent. A client does not need to know the whereabouts of a component it wants to use.

- ❑ On Windows 9x and Windows NT, the registry is used to store the locations of COM components. The system uses the registry to discover the location of components dynamically.

- ❑ Any thread that wants to use COM must call `CoInitializeEx()` before it does so, and `CoUninitialize()` when it has finished.

- ❑ COM objects can be created by calling `CoCreateInstance()`. Thereafter, the client is responsible for ensuring that the object remains in memory for as long as it needs it, but no longer.

If you can keep all of these points in mind as we move into the next chapter, you should find that the reasons *why* things are as they are become progressively clearer.

Writing A COM Component

In Chapter 1, we constructed a client program that called one method of a pre-written COM component. Assumptions were made and details were glossed over for the sake making the basics of COM programming as clear as possible. In this chapter, however, we need to probe deeper and explain things more carefully. We're going to examine *how* a COM component performs the tasks that a client may require of it, write a brand new COM component in C++, and develop a new client that uses it. Specifically, we're going to look at:

❑ How to call methods on more than one interface of a single object

❑ How error checking is managed in COM

❑ How to develop a COM component in C++, with no help from ATL

❑ How to write a robust COM client application

The Active Template Library is predominantly a technology for creating COM components (although it can be used to create clients, as we'll see further on in this book), and for that reason the features we'll be considering in this chapter are those that ATL tends to provide help with. A good understanding of the concepts covered in this chapter will prepare you well for what's in store later on.

Getting Access To Another Interface

Despite the example in Chapter 1, it's true to say that in general, a COM component will implement and expose more than one interface. You've seen how a client gets a pointer to its *first* interface — by passing the IID to CoCreateInstance() — but that's the extent of our exploration so far. To this point, we've said nothing about getting access to another interface, although the things you have learned place considerable restrictions on what the technique could be.

You already know that the only way to communicate with a component is to use its interfaces, and so the only possible way for a client to get a pointer to a different interface, is to call a method of the interface to which it already has a pointer. The logical consequence of this conclusion is that *all* COM interfaces must include a method that can return pointers to other interfaces on the same object. The name of this method is QueryInterface(), and it looks like this:

```
HRESULT QueryInterface(REFIID iid, void** ppvObject);
```

Here, `riid` is a reference to an IID (hence `REFIID`), and `ppvObject` is an indirect pointer to the returned interface. If you're really concentrating hard, you may have noticed that these are the same as the last two parameters to `CoCreateInstance()`.

Because it has a long name, because it crops up very frequently in discussions about COM, and because programmers like to make things sound more complicated than they really are, `QueryInterface()` *is often abbreviated to* `QI()` *by the cognoscenti.*

> Combining this information with our work in the last chapter, we now have three methods that we know all interfaces must contain: **QueryInterface()**, **AddRef()**, and **Release()**. This means that the simplest possible interface would be one that included these methods and no others. In fact, so important to COM is this interface that it has a standard name and definition — indeed, it's the most fundamental of all the standard interfaces defined in the COM specification. Its name is **IUnknown**.

IUnknown

When we said in Chapter 1 that the `AtlFireCtl` component exposed just a single interface (`IFireTabCtrl`), we were being slightly economical with the truth. It is one of the rules of COM that along with any other interfaces they may implement, *all* components must implement `IUnknown` — if a component doesn't implement `IUnknown`, it's not a COM component. However, when the interfaces exposed by a given component are listed, it is common for `IUnknown` to be left out, on the understanding that it is always present.

`IUnknown` is the only interface that a component must *implement. The intended use of the component will determine the other interfaces that it implements.*

`QueryInterface()`, `AddRef()`, and `Release()` are known collectively as the `IUnknown` methods, because they form the entire definition of the `IUnknown` interface. In order to allow reference counting and navigation among interfaces, all COM interfaces must support the `IUnknown` methods. In fact, more than merely supporting these methods, all COM interfaces must inherit from `IUnknown`. If an interface doesn't derive (directly or indirectly) from `IUnknown`, it's not a COM interface.

Interface Inheritance

Interface inheritance is not necessarily the same as the class inheritance (sometimes called **implementation inheritance**) we have in C++. The former just means that the signatures and semantics of the methods in the first portion of the vtable for the derived interface are the same as the signatures and semantics of the methods in the base interface. Often, a component will implement the base interface and a derived interface using a single implementation of the methods common to both interfaces, but this is entirely the decision of the implementer of the object.

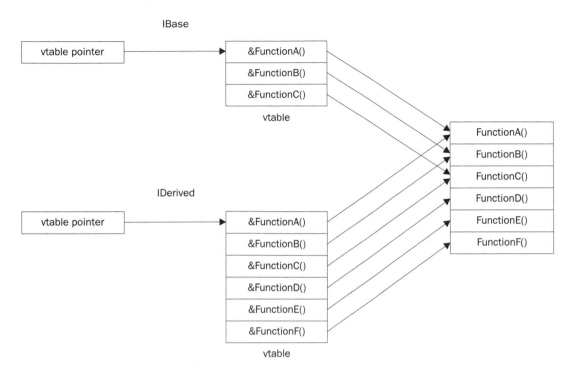

Although COM allows interface inheritance to any depth, it is always *single* inheritance. There is no multiple interface inheritance in COM for a fairly simple reason: two sets of methods can't both be first in the vtable, and there's no standard way of choosing one set of methods over another.

> Note that COM *does* not *support implementation inheritance. There is no way of having one coclass derive from another in order to reuse its implementation. However, COM does support other mechanisms for reusing coclass implementations, including* **aggregation**, *which is discussed in Chapter 4.*

Rules for Implementing QueryInterface()

Later in the chapter, we'll need to implement the QueryInterface() method in our COM component, so we should take a little time to understand precisely what it needs to be able to do.

You must always remember that QueryInterface() is the method that represents the link between multiple interfaces and a single object. It is vital that QueryInterface() maintains the appearance and behavior of a single COM object, even if the COM object is actually implemented using many C++ objects. These are the semantics of the method, and they are designed to ensure not only that COM works, both mechanically and conceptually, but also that it does so in a way that is simple for the client programmer to use.

Identity

The first rule concerns the **identity** of a 'live' COM object. You have already discovered that all COM components must implement the IUnknown interface, and we know that clients can only ever use an object through pointers to its interfaces. This means that the value of an IUnknown pointer is the only possible mechanism for comparing the identities of objects; if the IUnknown pointers are the same, the objects are the same.

The constraint that this places on the implementation of QueryInterface() is that it must always return the same IUnknown pointer for a given object, no matter when (during the lifetime of that object) it's called, and no matter which interface's implementation of QueryInterface() is called.

> *Note that the IUnknown pointer must always be obtained by calling* QueryInterface() *directly, never by casting another interface pointer to* IUnknown. *We'll examine this point more closely when we start to look at how coclasses can be implemented in C++.*

The constraint of always returning the same interface pointer in response to a QueryInterface() request *doesn't* apply to interfaces other than IUnknown. This allows objects to implement interfaces dynamically if they wish, to free the implementations when they're no longer being used, and then to recreate them when they're needed again. This can be useful if a resource that the interface is used to access is easy to acquire but expensive to maintain. Such an interface is typically called a **tear-off**.

The remaining rules cover two main aspects of QueryInterface()'s behavior: how (or whether) it is allowed to change over the lifetime of an object, and how (or whether) it is allowed to change between implementations on different interfaces of the same object. The first aspect is covered by the concept of predictability; the second is governed by the rules of reflexivity, symmetry, and transitivity.

Predictability

Once an object says that it supports an interface, it must continue to support that interface throughout its life — there are no deadbeat dads in the COM world. This does *not* mean that it has to return the same interface pointer each time (except in the case of IUnknown), just that (barring catastrophes) it returns some valid interface pointer.

In addition, if an object says that it *doesn't* support an interface at some point in its life, it can't then change its mind and start supporting that interface. If it rejects a request once, it must always reject requests for pointers to that interface.

In short, the set of interfaces for a particular object must be static over time. This rule enforces stability and simplifies client code by ensuring that an object's behavior doesn't change unpredictably over time.

> *Note that the set of interfaces supported by a particular object does not have to be the same as that supported by other objects of the same coclass.*

Reflexivity

Calls to `QueryInterface()` must be **reflexive**. This just means that querying an interface for itself will always succeed.

> *Note that the new interface pointer is only guaranteed to be the same as the original pointer if the interface in question is* `IUnknown`.

Symmetry

Calls to `QueryInterface()` must be **symmetrical**. This means that if you can successfully query an interface `IA` for a second interface `IB`, you can also successfully query the interface `IB` for `IA`.

Transitivity

Calls to `QueryInterface()` must be **transitive**. This means that if you can successfully query `IA` for `IB`, and you can successfully query `IB` for `IC`, then you can successfully query `IA` for `IC`.

Summary

The result of all these rules is that:

- ❏ `IUnknown` is the root of a COM object's identity
- ❏ The set of interfaces supported by a particular object is consistent over time
- ❏ The set of interfaces supported by an object is the same no matter which interface's implementation of `QueryInterface()` you use

Checking And Handling Errors

The second issue that we highlighted at the start of the chapter as requiring further treatment was that of error handling, which has hardly featured at all in our discussions so far. However, the ability to report that an error has occurred (and even that one has not occurred) is an extremely important part of COM programming, and it throws up some interesting problems.

The mechanism that COM uses for handling errors can have no language or platform dependence, so COM objects cannot transmit errors to their clients using standard C++ or Win32-style exceptions. These exceptions cannot cross process boundaries, and different languages handle exceptions in different ways. Whatever system is used must be completely generic, and therefore fairly simple in implementation. This happy compromise is achieved through the use of `HRESULT`s.

HRESULT

When you've seen a few COM interfaces, you'll notice that 99% of them return `HRESULT`s from all of their methods. Furthermore, a number of the COM API functions return them too. It's not a requirement of COM that *all* methods should return `HRESULT`s, but there are two very good reasons for doing so:

- ❏ It's a consistent way of returning status information from a method
- ❏ It allows the COM library to return errors to the caller of the method

The COM library will intervene in a method call if it goes across an apartment, process or machine boundary, and there are a number of errors that can occur during this procedure.

> An **apartment** is a conceptual unit within a process in which COM method calls can be made, and interface pointers passed about, without the intervention of proxies and stubs. For more information, see Chapter 6.

If your methods return HRESULTs, COM can return information about these errors back to the caller. If your methods don't return HRESULTs, the caller can't find out what went wrong.

> As we saw in the last chapter with the CoCreateInstance() function, the net result of COM methods returning HRESULTs is that any 'real' return values have to come back via method parameters.

At heart, an HRESULT is simply a 32-bit number containing a structured error code:

31	30	29	28	27	16	15	0
S	R	C	N	r	Facility	Return Code	

S (bit 31) is the **severity** code, indicating success or failure of the method call. The predefined severity constants are SEVERITY_SUCCESS (zero) and SEVERITY_ERROR (one). The bits labeled R, C, N, and r are reserved, while the **facility** is used to group related status codes together. The predefined facilities are given in Appendix A, along with some more detail about the specifics of HRESULTs.

There are a good many standard HRESULTs, and you can find a complete list of them in the winerror.h header file. This table lists a few of the more important ones, but if you need to get text descriptions of any of the others, you can use the Errlook.exe tool that's provided with Visual C++.

Symbolic constant	Value	Meaning
S_OK	0x00000000	Success. Sometimes used to represent the fact that had we not been dealing in COM, the function would have returned a Boolean TRUE value.
NOERROR	0x00000000	Old synonym for S_OK.
S_FALSE	0x00000001	Success (0x1). Used to contrast with S_OK when the function has executed correctly but would have returned Boolean FALSE.
E_UNEXPECTED	0x8000FFFF	Catastrophic failure.
E_NOTIMPL	0x80004001	This method is not implemented.
E_OUTOFMEMORY	0x8007000E	Could not allocate required memory.
E_INVALIDARG	0x80070057	One or more arguments are invalid.

Symbolic constant	Value	Meaning
E_NOINTERFACE	0x80004002	Returned by QueryInterface() if the object doesn't support the interface that has been requested.
E_POINTER	0x80004003	Function has been given an invalid pointer.
E_HANDLE	0x80070006	Function has been given an invalid handle.
E_ABORT	0x80004004	Operation aborted.
E_FAIL	0x80004005	Unspecified failure.
E_ACCESSDENIED	0x80070005	General 'access denied' error.

This table contains entries from two particular groups of COM-related HRESULT values (those starting with S_ and E_), but there are many others. Common prefixes include CO_, OLE_, DV_, DRAGDROP_, CLASS_, REGDB_, MK_, DISP_, and RPC_. Most of these HRESULTs are error codes, but there are dozens of success codes too.

> *The COM specification says that the success codes returned by an interface are part of the interface definition. This means that you must document the success codes that interface methods may return, and once you have done this you cannot return any other success codes. Conversely, COM interface methods are allowed to return any error code they see fit.*

HRESULT Tips

Whether you're writing code that sets HRESULTs (servers) or receives and acts upon them (clients), there are a few things that you should try to remember:

❑ When testing to see if a function succeeded or failed, never say if(hr == S_OK). It is much safer to say if(SUCCEEDED(hr)) or if(FAILED(hr)), and then to check for more specific HRESULTs as appropriate. Although you may think that you know all of the possible error codes returned from a component (especially if you wrote it yourself), COM might return additional error codes (such as network failures) when running a component on a different thread, process, or computer. Conversely, success codes are part of the contract that an interface represents and, once specified, may not be augmented.

❑ If you want to return a Win32 error code from one of your methods (typically, you would obtain one of these with GetLastError()), convert it to an HRESULT with the HRESULT_FROM_WIN32() macro. If you *receive* an HRESULT with a facility code of FACILITY_WIN32, use HRESULT_CODE() to extract the Win32 error code.

❑ Note that S_OK is 0 and S_FALSE is 1, the inverses of the usual C++ values for Boolean true and false, so take care when using them. Note also that some clients fail to differentiate between S_OK and S_FALSE, seeing them both as successful return codes.

❑ Try not to return E_FAIL from your functions: it's frustratingly unspecific to users of the component. We'll take a look at how to return more helpful errors in Chapter 5.

❑ You may see SCODEs being used as the return values of methods and APIs in some older code and books. SCODEs are obsolete and you can treat SCODE as a synonym for HRESULT.

❑ Remember that HRESULTs are not just used for errors; there are various success codes too.

Writing A COM Component

With some knowledge of these last two issues under our belts, we can finally begin to think about what it will take to write our own COM components. From our discussions so far, you know that a COM component is essentially the implementation of a number of COM interfaces. It follows, then, that the first thing we must do is to decide and define the interfaces our component should implement. Straight away, we run into something of a problem.

Regardless of the programming language chosen, the one thing a component writer absolutely must have is an unambiguous definition of the interfaces they are implementing. Thankfully, although COM is language-independent, it does have a language all of its own for this very purpose. The **Interface Definition Language (IDL)** is used to provide complete definitions of COM interfaces, and it's important for three reasons that will be explained in the following sections:

❑ It allows us to associate the methods of an interface with its IID

❑ It allows us to specify details of the interface in a form that can be machine-processed to produce marshaling code

❑ It allows us to instruct clients and servers on how they should allocate and deallocate memory

The Interface Definition Language

IDL is relatively simple because it's a lot like the declarative parts of C++, with the addition of **attributes**. An interface definition doesn't include an implementation, so IDL doesn't need the control structures that would be necessary for that.

> *IDL attributes are used to alter the specific meaning of the statements being described. They are not related in any way to the COM+ attributes that you may come across.*

To get a feel for how it works, let's look at the IDL definition for IUnknown (you can find this in the file Microsoft Visual Studio\VC98\Include\Unknwn.idl):

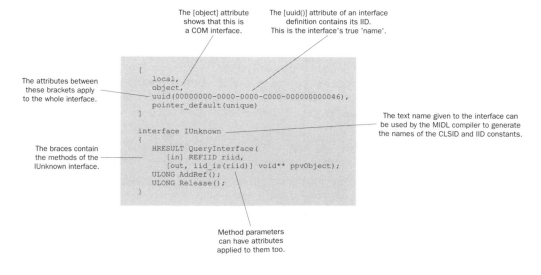

The [object] attribute shows that this is a COM interface.

The [uuid()] attribute of an interface definition contains its IID. This is the interface's true 'name'.

The attributes between these brackets apply to the whole interface.

```
[
    local,
    object,
    uuid(00000000-0000-0000-C000-000000000046),
    pointer_default(unique)
]

interface IUnknown
{
    HRESULT QueryInterface(
        [in] REFIID riid,
        [out, iid_is(riid)] void** ppvObject);
    ULONG AddRef();
    ULONG Release();
}
```

The text name given to the interface can be used by the MIDL compiler to generate the names of the CLSID and IID constants.

The braces contain the methods of the IUnknown interface.

Method parameters can have attributes applied to them too.

If you ignore the block of code between the brackets at the top for now, you can see that IUnknown has been defined using the interface keyword, followed by the name of the interface. The interface methods are then listed *in vtable order* within the interface body (which is defined by the braces). It looks a lot like the definition of a C++ class.

Any pair of brackets in an IDL file contains attributes that apply to the items immediately following them. Here, the first pair of brackets contains attributes pertaining to the whole interface. We won't look at all the possible attributes (you'll see more as you progress through the book), but the most important ones here are [object] and [uuid()].

When you're defining COM interfaces, [object] should be used. The reason for this is that IDL can also be used to define RPC interfaces, and this attribute helps to distinguish between COM and RPC interfaces. However, it is not *required*, because an IDL file used for RPC interfaces will also have an associate ACF file.

The [uuid()] attribute is used to identify the interface uniquely. The number in parentheses is the interface's IID. You can see that it's in same format you'd find in the system registry, minus the braces. This IID will ultimately be associate with the C++ interface name using a MIDL_INTERFACE() macro, as explained in the last chapter.

The IID of the interface is the most important of its associated identifiers. It *is* the name of the interface. The 'name' that appears after the interface keyword in the IDL definition is just used to generate class names and symbolic constants when the IDL is used to create C++ code, as we saw with IFireTabCtrl.

Marshaling

You've now seen something of how IDL allows the definition of interfaces and the methods they contain, but it has other responsibilities too. In the last chapter, you saw how COM uses proxies and stubs to manage communication between code executing in different processes or on different machines, but we paid little attention to how this trick is performed. It turns out that IDL plays a significant role in the proceedings.

The process by which arguments are sent across apartment, process, or machine boundaries is called **marshaling**. The proxy accepts function calls from the client and packages up the arguments in order to transmit them to the stub in the receiver's address space. The stub receives the arguments from the proxy, unmarshals them, and makes the necessary calls against the server's interface in its own process. It then takes the results of the calls and passes them back to the proxy, so that it, in turn, can pass them on to the client.

The proxy and stub code is usually created automatically, by compiling an IDL interface definition with the **Microsoft IDL (MIDL) compiler**, of which we shall see more later on. The MIDL compiler uses the interface definition to generate marshaling code that can then be compiled into a proxy-stub DLL by a standard C compiler.

> Note that the MIDL compiler produces source code, *not binary code like a C++ compiler. Note also that as a final incentive for your interface methods to return HRESULTs, MIDL is unable to produce marshaling code for interfaces whose methods do not comply with this recommendation.*

Memory Management

The other service provided by the IDL definition of a COM interface is in the field of memory management. As you can see from the code for IUnknown given above, attributes can be applied to the parameters of an interface's methods (take a look at IUnknown::QueryInterface()). These attributes give important information about memory management to implementers and clients of an interface, as well as ensuring that the marshaling code knows what it should be doing.

The most important and frequently used parameter attributes are [in] and [out]. These attributes denote the direction of travel of data, relative to the method. This means if you're passing data into a method, the parameter should be specified with the [in] attribute; if data is being returned from a method via a parameter (as we have to do for methods that return HRESULTs), it should be specified as an [out] parameter.

> *Note that attributes applying to a single item can be combined as a comma-separated list within a single pair of brackets. If a parameter is* [in] *and* [out], *you would specify it as* [in, out].

This means that if you wanted to pass a long into a method, you would declare it like so:

```
HRESULT MethodName([in] long lInput);
```

All [out] parameters must be specified as *pointers to* the data type being transmitted, so if you wanted to get a long out of a method, you would declare it like this:

```
HRESULT AnotherMethodName([out] long* plOutput);
```

When data is passed by value, as in this case, you aren't required to perform any special memory allocation. However, when the data *isn't* passed by value, the attributes carry with them important rules:

Attribute	Description
[in]	The parameter should be allocated by the caller. The method being called should do nothing to free the parameter.
[out]	The parameter should be allocated by the method being called.
[in, out]	The parameter should be allocated by the caller. The method being called may free and reallocate the parameter.

> **In all cases, the parameter should ultimately be freed by the caller.**

In the cases of [out] and [in, out] parameters, the memory should be allocated and freed using the standard **COM memory allocator**, to ensure that both sides are using the same method of memory allocation. In general, this means calling CoTaskMemAlloc() to allocate memory and CoTaskMemFree() to free it:

```
LPVOID CoTaskMemAlloc(
    ULONG cb                // Size in bytes of memory block to be allocated
);

void CoTaskMemFree(
    LPVOID pv               // Pointer to memory block to be freed
);
```

Versioning

Before we leave the subject of defining interfaces (for a while, at least), there's one last important point to be made that goes back to our discussion in Chapter 1. An interface, once published, must not be changed. Ever. You must not add methods or remove methods. You must not change the signatures of the methods. You must not change calling conventions. You must not change the semantics. If you change the IID, then you've created a new interface — interfaces are identified by their IIDs.

If you find limitations in an existing interface, create a new one with a new IID. It can be as similar to or different from the original interface as you require. If appropriate, you can derive the new interface from the old one.

You should also be careful how you change your coclasses. Coclasses can be upgraded by implementing new interfaces, and as long as they continue to expose the original interfaces, everything will work as expected. You should never remove interfaces from a coclass.

It's a classic COM pattern for a client to call QueryInterface() with the intention of getting a pointer to the newest version of an interface that it knows about. Should that fail, it queries for the second most recent version of the interface, and so on, until it reaches the original interface. This gives a graceful degradation of functionality and allows for both forward and backward compatibility. It also allows for a 'robust evolution of functionality over time' — as you update your components to implement newer interfaces, up-to-date clients can immediately take advantage of the new interfaces, while older clients can still make use of the old, familiar ones.

The traditional approaches to upgrading components are either to upgrade clients and components simultaneously, or to postpone upgrading components until their clients have been upgraded. Both approaches can be horrors of logistics and administration. With immutable interfaces, and forward-only evolution of coclasses, upgrades can be much, much simpler to manage.

COM Diagrams

To supplement or summarize the information contained in an IDL file, it is common to represent a coclass and the interfaces it implements in a COM diagram like this one:

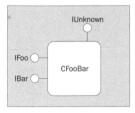

Drawings like these are often referred to as 'plug-in jack' or 'lollipop' diagrams. By convention, the IUnknown interface is drawn plugged into the top of the object, while the other interfaces are plugged into the left-hand side. The IUnknown interface is occasionally omitted from these diagrams because it's understood that all components implement IUnknown.

Creating Interfaces in C++

IDL is a fine and useful thing, but when at last we start to implement coclasses in C++, we're going to need a language-*specific* way of representing a COM interface. In C++, COM interfaces map to a special, restricted kind of abstract class. All the methods are public, pure virtual (= 0), and have no default implementation.

Furthermore, because interfaces have no member data, they have no state. Therefore, these special C++ classes do not have constructors or destructors (not even virtual destructors) — they don't need them, because they have no state to construct or destroy. The C++ definition for IUnknown is shown below:

```
class IUnknown
{
public:
    __stdcall virtual HRESULT QueryInterface(REFIID riid, void** ppvObject) = 0;
    __stdcall virtual ULONG AddRef() = 0;
    __stdcall virtual ULONG Release() = 0;
};
```

You can see that the methods appear in the same order as they did in the original IDL definition. This results in a vtable being created with exactly the structure required. To hook the vtable up to some real functions and any necessary data, we can just derive a concrete class from this abstract class and implement all the functions. When we want a COM IUnknown pointer, we can just cast from a pointer to the concrete class to get a C++ IUnknown*, and use that.

> *Note the use of the __stdcall calling convention on these methods. __stdcall didn't appear in the IDL definition of the interface because the MIDL compiler assumes __stdcall by default. However, the default C++ calling convention is __cdecl, so to ensure that the C++ and IDL definitions match, we need to use __stdcall explicitly in the C++ code. You can actually use any convention you like, but you'll need to specify the convention in the IDL definition of your interface if you decide not to use __stdcall. Most methods use __stdcall because it reduces code size and is the standard on Windows platforms.*

> Because these abstract classes are so closely related to the interfaces that they represent, they are simply called 'interfaces' and are usually defined using the **interface** macro (which is just a **#define** for **struct**), rather than **class**.

Macros

In addition to the #define for interface, the Platform SDK defines a few other macros to simplify the declarations of COM methods. These are the STDMETHOD(), STDMETHOD_() and PURE macros, which you can find in basetyps.h. These macros make it possible to have a single interface definition that works for both C and C++, but we'll use them simply because it saves typing, makes the interface definitions look cleaner, and because ATL uses them too.

The STDMETHOD() macro wraps up the __stdcall calling convention, the virtual specifier, and the HRESULT return type. STDMETHOD_() does the same job, except that it allows you to specify the method's return type as the first macro argument. PURE simply replaces = 0. We can therefore rewrite the C++ definition of IUnknown using these macros, as shown below:

```
interface IUnknown
{
    STDMETHOD(QueryInterface)(REFIID riid, void** ppvObj) PURE;
    STDMETHOD_(ULONG, AddRef)() PURE;
    STDMETHOD_(ULONG, Release)() PURE;
};
```

Interface Inheritance in C++

As you've seen, the vtables of *all* COM interfaces must start with the QueryInterface(), AddRef() and Release() methods, in that order. When we try to model this requirement in C++, we must be careful not to confuse COM (interface) inheritance with C++ (implementation) inheritance. Although it turns out that we can model COM inheritance using C++ inheritance mechanisms, this isn't a requirement. For example, we could create an interface called IWroxInterface that looks like this in IDL:

```
[
    object,
    uuid(FEB89321-6D77-11D1-B28D-00A0C94515AD)
]
interface IWroxInterface : IUnknown
{
    HRESULT Alert();
};
```

And we could describe this interface in C++ in any of the following ways (only one of which uses C++ inheritance):

```
interface IWroxInterface : public IUnknown
{
    STDMETHOD(Alert)() PURE;
};
```

```
interface IWroxInterface
{
    STDMETHOD(QueryInterface)(REFIID riid, void** ppvObj) PURE;
    STDMETHOD_(ULONG, AddRef)() PURE;
    STDMETHOD_(ULONG, Release)() PURE;

    STDMETHOD(Alert)() PURE;
};
```

```
interface IWroxInterface
{
    STDMETHOD(QueryInterface)(REFIID riid, void** ppvObj) PURE;
    STDMETHOD_(ULONG, AddRef)() PURE;
    STDMETHOD_(ULONG, Release)() PURE;

    STDMETHOD(RenamedAlert)() PURE;
};
```

The first C++ definition of the interface is the preferred one. It creates the required vtable and clearly models the relationship between the C++ classes and the COM interfaces. The second and third definitions are also fine as far as COM is concerned, as they result in the same vtable signatures, but less useful in C++ because the relationship with the IUnknown interface has been lost. From the third example, you can see that the names of the methods used in the C++ definition are not important to COM — all that matters is the vtable. Changing the names of methods isn't usually a good idea as it is likely to lead to confusion, but it can be useful in some circumstances.

The MIDL Compiler and C++

It can't have escaped your attention that the IDL and C++ definitions of the IUnknown interface bore a considerable resemblance to one another, and in those circumstances it would be a real nuisance if we had to write both of them scratch every time we wanted to create a new interface. As well as its ability to generate marshaling code, the MIDL compiler can create C++ interfaces from IDL definitions. By passing an IDL file through the MIDL compiler, we can get it to create a header file containing the C++ definitions of the interfaces contained in the IDL file, as well as symbolic constants for the IIDs.

> *The MIDL compiler was responsible for the creation of the* AtlFire.h *file that we used in our client application in the previous chapter.*

Let's create an IDL file containing the definitions of some interfaces that we will use in an ongoing example throughout the rest of the chapter. Create a new directory called ComDll to store the files for this project, make a new text file in this directory called ComDll_IDL.idl, and add the following code:

```
// ComDll_IDL.idl
import "oaidl.idl";

[
    object,
    uuid(MY_GUID1)
]
interface IWroxInterface : IUnknown
{
    HRESULT Alert();
};

[
    object,
    uuid(MY_GUID2)
]
interface IWroxSimple : IUnknown
{
    HRESULT Display();
};

[
    uuid(MY_GUID3),
    version(1.0)
]
library WroxComponentLib
{
    importlib("stdole32.tlb");

    [
        uuid(MY_GUID4)
    ]
    coclass WroxComponent
    {
        [default] interface IWroxInterface;
        interface IWroxSimple;
    };
};
```

The symbols MY_GUID1 to MY_GUID4 need to be replaced with four GUIDs freshly generated using the **GUID Generator**, which is supplied with Visual C++. To use it, run the Guidgen.exe applet in your Microsoft Visual Studio\Common\Tools directory, or use the **GUID Generator** component in the Component Gallery (Project | Add to Project | Components and Controls...):

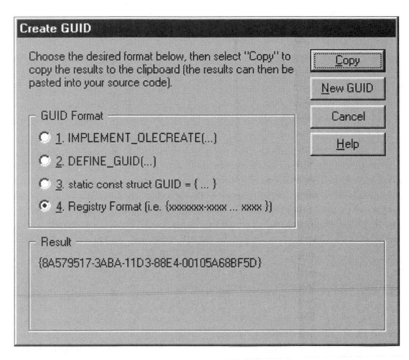

The GUID Generator lets you create GUIDs in a number of formats. The first format is only useful for MFC projects, so we won't worry about that. The second and third formats are used for defining constants to represent the GUID in C++ code. In general, these constants will be declared automatically, so you won't need to use these options very often. The final option generates GUIDs in the format used in the system registry and elsewhere, and it's the one we'll use here, but you should delete the braces once you've pasted them into the right place. A typical entry should look something like this:

```
uuid(48B51E21-5BD4-11d3-A074-00902707906A)
```

> *Internally, the GUID Generator calls the* `CoCreateGUID()` *API function to generate the GUIDs. If you should ever need to generate GUIDs programmatically, you can call this same function. If you're really interested, the source code for* `GuidGen.exe` *is shipped with Visual C++ 6 as a sample MFC dialog-based application.*

The `import` statement at the top of the file just brings in the standard types defined by the `oaidl.idl` file, which include many of the standard COM interfaces. The `import` statement in IDL is similar to C++'s `#include`, but it only allows us to use the *data types* defined in the imported file. We import this file here simply so that we can use the `HRESULT` and `IUnknown` types.

In this code, we've defined two very simple interfaces — `IWroxInterface` and `IWroxSimple` — each of which contains a single method (plus the three `IUnknown` methods). We've also defined a `library` section in the IDL file. A `library` section is used to output a **type library** (which we're not interested in at the moment), but it also allows us to specify coclasses, the names of which will be used by the MIDL compiler to produce symbolic constants for the CLSIDs.

When this file has been completed and saved, we can use the MIDL compiler to output some files. Open up a command prompt in the ComDll directory and use the following command to generate the files:

```
>MIDL ComDll_IDL.idl
```

If necessary, run Microsoft Visual Studio\VC98\Bin\VCVars32.bat *to set your environment variables to allow you to run* MIDL.exe *from a command line.*

Once you've run this command, you'll see that a number of new files have been output to the ComDll directory:

❑   ComDll_IDL.h contains the C++ interface definitions and associates GUIDs with interface and coclass names. The C++ interfaces have the same names as the simple text names given to the interfaces in the IDL file, and the IIDs are associated with these using MIDL_INTERFACE(). The CLSIDs are associated with an empty C++ class that has the same name as the coclass in the IDL, using DECLSPEC_UUID().

❑   ComDll_IDL_i.c contains the *definitions* of the GUID constants in C. This file is typically used by projects that cannot use the __uuidof() operator.

❑   ComDll_IDL_p.c contains the marshaling code for the interfaces defined in the IDL file.

❑   DllData.c contains some more code that is used when building the proxy-stub DLL.

❑   ComDll_IDL.tlb is the type library generated from the information in the IDL file.

For backward compatibility, ATL projects use constants defined in the _i.c file rather than the __uuidof() operator — there's a constant called IID_IWroxSimple, for example, that evaluates to the same thing as __uuidof(IWroxSimple). For this chapter's sample project, we'll use the ATL style. However, we'll only be using the .h and _i.c files in our project — we won't be generating the proxy-stub DLL because our simple tests won't need it, and we're not interested in the type library at this stage.

Implementing Interfaces

Now let's turn our attention to hooking up the interfaces we've just defined to some kind of functionality. Consider a C++ class called CWroxComponent that implements IWroxInterface and IWroxSimple. On this occasion, we'll see how we can implement the component using multiple inheritance. The advantage of multiple inheritance (over, say, using different classes for each of the interfaces) is that it's simple to implement the IUnknown methods just once for all the interfaces.

Create another new text file and save it in the ComDll directory as WroxComponent.h. We'll add the whole implementation of the component to the same file, so all the methods will be defined inline. Enter the following code:

```cpp
// Get all the system stuff from Windows.h
#include <windows.h>

// Include the MIDL-generated header file to get interface definitions
#include "ComDll_IDL.h"

// Define a class to implement the interfaces using multiple inheritance
class CWroxComponent : public IWroxInterface, public IWroxSimple
{
public:
    // Constructor
    CWroxComponent() : m_lRefCount(0)
    {...}
```

```
    // Destructor
    ~CWroxComponent() {...}

    // The IUnknown methods
    STDMETHOD(QueryInterface)(REFIID riid, void** ppv)
    {
        ...
    }

    STDMETHOD_(ULONG, AddRef)()
    {
        ...
    }

    STDMETHOD_(ULONG, Release)()
    {
        ...
    }

    // IWroxInterface method
    STDMETHOD(Alert)()
    {
        ...
    }

    // IWroxSimple method
    STDMETHOD(Display)()
    {
        ...
    }
private:
    long m_lRefCount;
};
```

Clearly, these are the very basics of the class, leaving us to fill in the method implementations as we go along.

The #include statements give us access to the Win32 API and to the interfaces defined in the MIDL compiler-generated header file. We make use of these interfaces by deriving our class from them. The methods for all the interfaces, including IUnknown, are laid out in the body of the class. You can see that we've declared a private member, m_lRefCount, to hold the reference count of the object, and that we've set the count to zero in the constructor's initializer list.

AddRef() and Release()

Implementing AddRef() and Release() is a simple matter of incrementing and decrementing the reference count:

```
STDMETHOD_(ULONG, AddRef)()
{
    return InterlockedIncrement(&m_lRefCount);
}

STDMETHOD_(ULONG, Release)()
{
    ULONG ul = InterlockedDecrement(&m_lRefCount);

    if(ul == 0)
        delete this;               // The object must be created with new

    return ul;
}
```

Note that we're using a single reference count for all the interfaces on the object. Although multiple inheritance makes our lives easier by allowing us to implement the IUnknown methods only once for all three interfaces exposed by our object (IUnknown, IWroxInterface and IWroxSimple), it does mean that we can't provide a different reference count for each interface. COM allows for per-*interface* reference counts, but implementing per-*object* reference counts doesn't break the expected behavior.

We have used the InterlockedIncrement() and InterlockedDecrement() APIs to increase and decrease the reference count on the component (instead of the simpler ++m_lRefCount and --m_lRefCount) because the APIs are thread safe. The prototypes of these functions come from the windows.h header file.

Note also that this implementation of Release() assumes that the object has been created on the heap (with new CWroxComponent) because it calls delete this to destroy the object when the reference count reaches zero. Calling delete this on a stack-based, static, or global object would be disastrous. In practice, COM objects are almost always created on the heap, so this is a typical implementation, but a different implementation must be used for non-heap-based COM objects.

Furthermore, be aware that we keep the return value from InterlockedDecrement() (which is the value of m_lRefCount *after* being decremented) in the local variable ul. This is so that we can return the value from Release() after the object has been deleted. It is an error to try and return the value of member variables (such as m_lRefCount) from an object that has been deleted.

Finally, do not rely on the return values from AddRef() or Release() being accurate (or even meaningful) in terms of the number of references held on a particular interface. COM provides various optimizations through the use of proxies that can affect the reference count of an interface, and COM objects are not required to implement true per-interface reference counting; they are simply required to provide AddRef() and Release() (and QueryInterface()) methods. Clients, however, must always act as if components *do* implement true per-interface reference counting, which means always calling Release() on the same interface that was AddRef()'d.

QueryInterface()

The implementation of QI() looks like this:

```
STDMETHOD(QueryInterface)(REFIID riid, void** ppv)
{
    if(riid == IID_IUnknown)
        *ppv = static_cast<IWroxInterface*>(this);
    else if(riid == IID_IWroxInterface)
        *ppv = static_cast<IWroxInterface*>(this);
    else if(riid == IID_IWroxSimple)
        *ppv = static_cast<IWroxSimple*>(this);
    else
    {
        *ppv = NULL;
        return E_NOINTERFACE;
    }

    static_cast<IUnknown*>(*ppv)->AddRef();
    return S_OK;
}
```

This implementation is straightforward: we just compare riid against the interface ID for each of the interfaces supported by our component. For the standard interface IUnknown, we use the IID_ constant defined in the system headers. For our custom interfaces, we get the IIDs from the MIDL compiler-produced header file.

If the interface is not supported, we set *ppv = NULL and return E_NOINTERFACE. If riid matches one of the supported interfaces, we return a pointer to the appropriate interface and increment the reference count. Note that we increment the reference count by calling AddRef() rather than incrementing m_lRefCount directly. This would allow the implementation to work correctly even if per-interface reference counting was employed.

There are four casts in this implementation, and the first three of them ensure that we are setting *ppv to the right pointer for the requested interface. These casts are vital, because the pointer value can change when casting to a base class from a multiply derived class.

The first cast may seem confusing because when we're asked for a pointer to IUnknown, we cast to IWroxInterface* rather than IUnknown*. The reason we cast to IWroxInterface* is that we have to disambiguate the inheritance branch for the compiler (because both IWroxInterface and IWroxSimple derive from IUnknown). This is really just an intermediate step; to make things clearer, we could include the cast from IWroxInterface* to IUnknown*, like this:

```
*ppv = static_cast<IUnknown*>(static_cast<IWroxInterface*>(this));
```

This would show explicitly that we are casting from CWroxComponent*, through IWroxInterface*, to IUnknown*. However, this extra cast actually has no effect on the pointer we return, because casting to a base type when only *single* inheritance is involved (IWroxInterface inherits singly from IUnknown) has no effect on the pointer value. As already pointed out, single inheritance is the only sort of inheritance allowed for COM interfaces.

The final cast just gives the void pointer a real type so that we can use it to call AddRef().

As you've seen, using multiple inheritance makes it very easy to implement a COM component with multiple interfaces. ATL itself uses this technique, but it's not the only way of implementing interfaces. It's quite common, for example, to see each interface implemented by a single class. If these classes are defined as nested classes within another class that controls the lifetime of the COM object, it's possible to use offsets to delegate the nested classes' IUnknown methods to the outer class. This is the method used by MFC.

Alert() and Display()

Finally, we can add some extremely simple implementations for the Alert() and Display() methods:

```
// IWroxInterface method
STDMETHOD(Alert)()
{
    MessageBox(NULL, "The Alert() method was called", "IWroxInterface", MB_OK);
    return S_OK;
}

// IWroxSimple method
STDMETHOD(Display)()
{
    MessageBox(NULL, "The Display() method was called", "IWroxSimple", MB_OK);
    return S_OK;
}
```

Vtable Layout, Casting & Identity

When writing COM clients, you need to be *very* careful how you cast interface pointers. This can be particularly important if you're writing the server at the same time as you develop the client — don't let your knowledge of the implementation of the server cause you to write bad client code.

A CWroxComponent object would be laid out something like this:

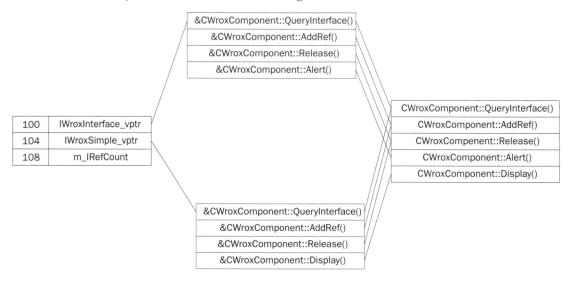

If the client was in the same apartment as the server, it could get hold of an IUnknown* (0x100), an IWroxInterface* (0x100) or an IWroxSimple* (0x104).

To see if two interfaces really *are* on the same object, you need to compare IUnknowns. However, don't be tempted just to cast interface pointers to IUnknown in order to compare them. You must always QI() for IUnknown before making a comparison. In other words, this is wrong:

```
// Wrong way to see if two interface pointers refer to the same COM object
if(static_cast<IUnknown*>(pIWroxInterface) == static_cast<IUnknown*>(pIWroxSimple))
{
    ...
}
```

In this case, we'd be comparing 0x100 with 0x104. Those numbers clearly aren't equal, and yet we know that these two interface pointers *are* from the same object. This is the right way to do it:

```
// Right way to see if two interface pointers refer to the same COM object
IUnknown* punk1 = NULL;
IUnknown* punk2 = NULL;

pIWroxInterface->QueryInterface(IID_IUnknown, reinterpret_cast<void**>(&punk1));
pIWroxSimple->QueryInterface(IID_IUnknown, reinterpret_cast<void**>(&punk2));

if(punk1 == punk2)
{
    ...
}

punk2->Release();
punk1->Release();
```

Notice the calls to Release(), *which pair up with the calls to* AddRef() *that are embedded in the implementation of* QueryInterface().

Similarly, don't be tempted to cast from IUnknown* to IWroxInterface*. Although this will work if the server and client are in the same apartment, it won't work if they're not. A separate proxy is created for each interface, and the IUnknown proxy won't implement the IWroxInterface methods. Attempting to call non-existent methods against that pointer will almost certainly result in an access violation.

[iid_is()]

This may lead you to wonder how the marshaling code knows what proxy to create — just as we saw with the CoCreateInstance() function in Chapter 1, all the interfaces are being passed as void**, which is of no help at all. The answer lies in the IDL definition of QI(), which looked like this:

```
HRESULT QueryInterface(
    [in] REFIID riid,
    [out, iid_is(riid)] void** ppvObject);
```

Notice the [iid_is()] attribute, which tells the MIDL compiler to produce generic marshaling code that marshals the pointer based on the IID passed in another parameter (in this case, riid). This means that when riid is the IID for IUnknown, ppvObject will be marshaled as if it's an indirect pointer to IUnknown — if a proxy is created, it will be a proxy for IUnknown. Similarly, when riid is the IID for IWroxInterface, ppvObject will be marshaled as if it's an indirect pointer to IWroxInterface — if a proxy is created, it will be a proxy for IWroxInterface; and so on.

You can pass interface pointers as parameters to COM methods without using the [iid_is()] attribute, and many standard interfaces have methods that do exactly that. In that case, the parameters will be marshaled as their declared types. [iid_is()] makes the declared pointer type irrelevant from a marshaling point of view.

Creating An Object

Let's pause for a moment and take stock of what we've achieved so far. After our work in the sections above, we can be reasonably confident that we have written all the C++ code necessary for the implementation of a simple COM component. However, you know that components have to be housed in modules (DLL or EXE files), and we haven't looked at that aspect of the problem at all. When we do so, you'll find that writing COM modules takes a little more effort than you might have thought.

In Chapter 1, you saw how a client calls CoCreateInstance() to specify which object it wants to create, and how COM can use the information passed as arguments to look up the location of the module to load. In the general case, though, a single module can contain the implementations of a number of components, so how does COM ask the module to create a particular object? It turns out that the COM library actually asks *another* COM object called a **class object** to create the requested object.

Class objects are designed simply to create objects of a particular coclass. Each class object is implemented in the same module as the object that it is responsible for creating. To square the circle, class objects *don't* need to be created by other COM objects.

DLL or EXE?

The means by which the COM library gets hold of a class object that matches the CLSID of the object that it really wants to create depends on whether the server module is a DLL or an EXE.

If the server is an EXE, it must register each of its class objects with the system as it starts up, using the `CoRegisterClassObject()` API. This means that the EXE server must create all the class objects when it first starts executing, and then pass `IUnknown` pointers to the system. Each class object is associated with the CLSID of the object it creates. When the EXE shuts down, it has to tell the system that the class objects will no longer be available by calling `CoRevokeClassObject()`.

If the server is a DLL, the system will call into a well-known entry point that all DLL COM servers must export called `DllGetClassObject()`. This function takes a CLSID for the object that needs to be created, and an IID parameter for an interface on the class object that should be returned in the third parameter:

```
STDAPI DllGetClassObject(REFCLSID rclsid, REFIID riid, LPVOID* ppv);
```

`DllGetClassObject()` is one of four functions that DLL COM servers must export. The names of the others are `DllCanUnloadNow()`, `DllRegisterServer()` and `DllUnregisterServer()`, and you'll be seeing them all shortly.

Class Objects

Once the system has got a pointer to an interface on the class object, it can use it to create a new object. Class objects are often known as **class factories**, because they usually implement the `IClassFactory` interface. (To be used with `CoCreateInstance()`, the class object *must* implement `IClassFactory`.)

Stripped of some advanced features, the `IClassFactory` interface looks like this:

```
interface IClassFactory : IUnknown
{
    HRESULT CreateInstance(
        [in, unique]           IUnknown*  pUnkOuter,
        [in]                   REFIID     riid,
        [out, iid_is(riid)] void**       ppvObject);

    HRESULT LockServer(
        [in]                   BOOL       fLock);
}
```

For now, we'll just concentrate on the `CreateInstance()` method. We'll discuss `IClassFactory::LockServer()` when we look at server lifetimes later on.

The `CreateInstance()` method creates a new, *uninitialized* object of this class object's class, `QI()`s it for the `riid` interface, and returns the interface pointer in `ppvObject`. In fact, `riid` and `ppvObject` are used as the parameters for `QueryInterface()`. The `pUnkOuter` parameter is the "outer `IUnknown`", which is used in aggregation, discussed in Chapter 4. (`pUnkOuter` will always be `NULL` when aggregation isn't involved). This new object is, of course, eventually destroyed when the caller (or some other client) `Release()`s the interface pointer.

Note that `CreateInstance()` does *not* take a CLSID parameter. By definition, a class object only knows how to create objects of one class, so there's no need for a CLSID at this stage.

CoGetClassObject()

Internally, `CoCreateInstance()` calls `CoGetClassObject()`:

```
STDAPI CoGetClassObject(
    REFCLSID        rclsid,         // CLSID associated with the class object
    DWORD           dwClsContext,   // Context
    COSERVERINFO*   pServerInfo,    // Machine info
    REFIID          riid,           // Reference to the identifier of the interface
    LPVOID*         ppv             // Indirect pointer to the interface
    );
```

`CoGetClassObject()` does the hard work of determining which server is responsible for the CLSID, making sure it's loaded, and then returning a pointer to the requested interface on the class object. `CoGetClassObject()` hides the differences between EXE and DLL servers.

`CoCreateInstance()` always uses `CoGetClassObject()` to get the `IClassFactory` interface from the class object. However, class objects may implement interfaces other than `IClassFactory`, so you may occasionally need to call `CoGetClassObject()` directly and ask for a different interface instead.

You may also choose to call `CoGetClassObject()` directly if you intend to create several objects of the same class. If you call `CoCreateInstance()` repeatedly, the class factory may be created and destroyed between each call. If you use `CoGetClassObject()`, you can keep the class factory alive while you call `IClassFactory::CreateInstance()` several times. Over time, this will give you better performance.

> *CoCreateInstance() always sets CoGetClassObject()'s pServerInfo parameter to NULL, so COM only searches for the class object on the current machine. However, you don't need to call CoGetClassObject() directly if all you want is for the pServerInfo parameter to be exposed to you, because COM also provides the CoCreateInstanceEx() function for just this purpose. You can find more information on CoCreateInstanceEx() in Chapter 6.*

Server Lifetime

So far, we've seen how components use reference counts to manage their own lifetimes, but how is the lifetime of the module that contains the components managed? There are two answers to that question, depending once again on whether the server is packaged as a DLL or an EXE. This difference arises because while EXEs take responsibility for unloading themselves, DLLs must be unloaded by an external force.

Unloading and Locking DLL Servers

DLLs have to rely on the client to load and unload them; the problem is that only the DLL itself can know when it's safe for it to be unloaded. The DLL will not want to be unloaded while it's serving objects, so it needs to keep a count on the number of objects that are currently 'alive'. This count should be incremented when objects are created, and decremented when they're destroyed.

The DLL should also keep track of calls to `IClassFactory::LockServer()`. Clients will call `IClassFactory::LockServer(TRUE)` to tell the server not to let itself be unloaded (by incrementing the lock count), and `IClassFactory::LockServer(FALSE)` to decrement the lock count. A client will make a call to lock the server to ensure that any subsequent objects can be created as quickly as possible, without having to reload the server.

Since both the lock count and the count of the number of active objects are simply there so that the DLL knows when it's safe to be unloaded, it's usual to see these counts combined into a single count for the whole DLL. The DLL knows that it shouldn't be unloaded when the count is greater than zero, and that it can be unloaded when the count equals zero.

COM clients should never unload DLL servers directly; instead, they should ask COM to do it by calling `CoFreeUnusedLibraries()`. This is an extremely polite API that checks with a DLL to see if it's being used, then unloads it if it isn't. `CoFreeUnusedLibraries()` discovers whether a DLL is being used by calling `DllCanUnloadNow()` — if that returns `S_OK`, the DLL can be unloaded; if it returns `S_FALSE`, it can't:

```
STDAPI DllCanUnloadNow();
```

If a client doesn't call `CoFreeUnusedLibraries()`, DLL COM servers loaded by that process will remain in memory until the client uninitializes COM with a call to `CoUninitialize()`, which the client should always do before shutting down.

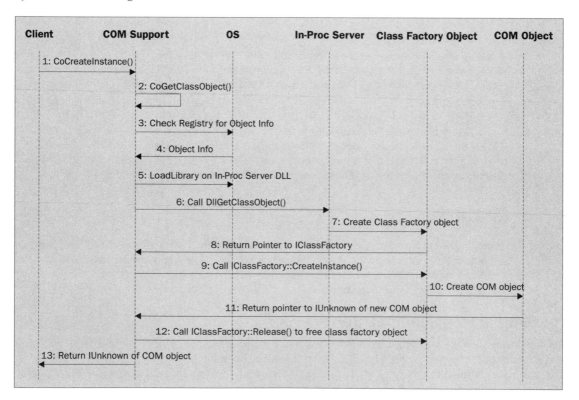

Unloading and Locking EXE Servers

Unlike passive DLLs, EXEs can be proactive and unload themselves as soon as it's safe to do so. Specifically, the EXE should exit when one of two conditions occurs:

- ❑ If the lock count (the sum of all the `IClassFactory::LockServer()` calls) is zero, then the EXE exits when the last active object is destroyed (by its last `Release()`).
- ❑ If there are no active objects, then the EXE exits when the lock count goes to zero after a call to `IClassFactory::LockServer(FALSE)`.

Note that class objects are *not* included in the count of active objects. Class objects must be automatically created and registered when the EXE server starts up. COM hangs on to the class objects until the EXE revokes them while shutting down, but the EXE won't exit until its object count goes to zero. If the server included the number of active class objects in its object count, the count would never reach zero and it would never be able to shut down!

This means that having a reference count on an out-of-process server's class factory is *not* sufficient to keep the out-of-process server running (this runs counter to the usual rules of COM, of course), so calling `IClassFactory::LockServer(TRUE)` is vital to ensuring that EXE servers remain loaded if necessary.

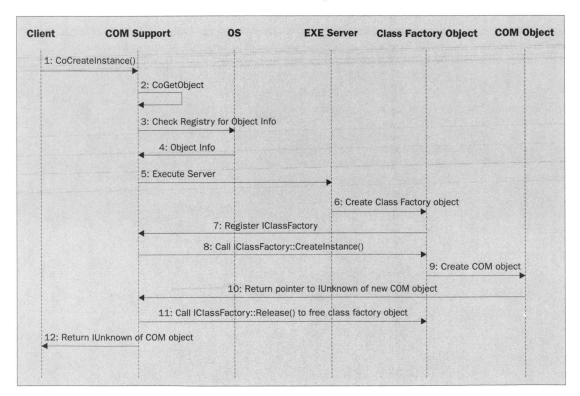

Interactive Servers

EXE COM servers can often be launched independently of COM, and may have a user interface. One example of this is Microsoft Word, which exposes a lot of its features to programmers via COM. It is important that applications like this know whether they have been launched by an interactive user or by COM, so that they can start up without the user interface when COM launches them. A local server can tell if it has been launched by COM (and not interactively by the user) by looking for /Embedding (or -embedding) on its command line.

Note also that interactive users are *also* clients of the server, and should be accorded a reference count. The server must not shut down until *all* clients are finished, although it can choose to hide its windows if all *interactive* clients are finished.

Completing A Basic COM DLL Server

Let's use the knowledge you've just gained to complete the example we began earlier in the chapter. Previously, we had a directory called ComDll in which we'd created an IDL definition of two simple interfaces. We passed this IDL file through the MIDL compiler to create C++ definitions for the interfaces and identifiers it contained. We also created a coclass implementation in the form of CWroxComponent. Now let's put this coclass into a DLL that we can compile, register and use.

First, start Visual C++ and use it to create a new, empty **Win32 Dynamic-Link Library** project called ComDll. Store the project in the ComDll directory we created previously, create a new source file called ComDll.cpp, save it in the project directory, and add it to the project. Add the following code to it:

```cpp
// ComDll.cpp

// The module's lock count
static long g_lLockCount = 0;

// Create class object as a global
#include "WroxClassFactory.h"
static CWroxClassFactory g_WroxClassFactory;

// MIDL-generated GUID Definitions
#include "ComDll_IDL_i.c"

extern "C"
BOOL WINAPI DllMain(HINSTANCE hInstance, DWORD dwReason, LPVOID /*lpReserved*/)
{
    // No implementation needed here
    return TRUE;
}

STDAPI DllGetClassObject(REFCLSID rclsid, REFIID riid, LPVOID* ppv)
{
    if(rclsid == CLSID_WroxComponent)
        return g_WroxClassFactory.QueryInterface(riid, ppv);
    else
    {
        *ppv = NULL;
        return CLASS_E_CLASSNOTAVAILABLE;
    }
}
```

```
STDAPI DllCanUnloadNow(void)
{
    return (g_lLockCount == 0) ? S_OK : S_FALSE;
}

STDAPI DllRegisterServer(void)
{
    // Registration implementation should go here
    return S_OK;
}

STDAPI DllUnregisterServer(void)
{
    // Unregistration implementation should go here
    return S_OK;
}
```

The first thing that you can see in this file is the variable that we're using for the module's lock count, g_lLockCount. This will keep track of any active objects and any calls to IClassFactory::LockServer(). We'll see where this value gets updated shortly, but you can already see how it gets used in the implementation of DllCanUnloadNow().

Next, you can see that we've included a file called WroxClassFactory.h. We haven't actually created this file yet, but when we do, it will contain the definition of CWroxClassFactory, the class object for the component we created earlier in the chapter. Beneath the #include statement, we've declared a global object of type CWroxClassFactory. This object, g_WroxClassFactory, is the class object itself.

The next #include brings in the GUID definitions from the _i.c file. This file needs to be #include'd once in any project that uses the MIDL compiler-generated GUID constants.

Next up, you can see the definition of DllMain(). This function must be provided by all DLLs, whether or not they're COM servers. In our case, we don't need to do any special initialization in it, so we can simply return TRUE for success.

> *In the last chapter, we said that any thread wanting to use COM must call CoInitialize(), so you may have been expecting to see a call to that API function here. However, DLL servers do not need to do this, since they will be loaded into a thread that must already have initialized COM.*

After that, we have DllGetClassObject().This function is used to return pointers to interfaces on the class object that creates objects of the type specified by the CLSID passed as the first parameter. You can see that we simply check the value of the CLSID against CLSID_WroxComponent, and use QueryInterface() on our global class object to return an interface pointer if appropriate. If the CLSID is for a class our server does not support, we return CLASS_E_CLASSNOTAVAILABLE.

The remaining functions are as simple as can be. DllCanUnloadNow() just returns S_OK if the lock count is zero (and S_FALSE otherwise), and we haven't provided an implementation for the registration functions at all. Of course, we *should* provide these functions, but then we'd have to get into some quite complicated registration manipulation. You can either implement these functions yourself, or wait until we see how ATL makes our lives much easier in the next chapter.

Next, we need to create a new module definition file to export the necessary functions from the DLL. Create a new text file containing the following text, save it in the project directory as ComDll.def, and add it to the project:

```
LIBRARY        "ComDll.dll"

EXPORTS
    DllCanUnloadNow       @1 PRIVATE
    DllGetClassObject     @2 PRIVATE
    DllRegisterServer     @3 PRIVATE
    DllUnregisterServer   @4 PRIVATE
```

This file just tells the linker to export the functions specified, so that they can be called from outside the DLL.

Now we'll turn our attention to the class object. Create a new file in the project directory and save it as WroxClassFactory.h. Add the following code to it:

```cpp
#include "WroxComponent.h"

class CWroxClassFactory : public IClassFactory
{
public:
    // Constructor
    CWroxClassFactory() : m_lRefCount(0) {}

    // The IUnknown methods
    STDMETHOD(QueryInterface)(REFIID riid, void** ppv)
    {
        if(riid == IID_IUnknown)
            *ppv = static_cast<IUnknown*>(this);
        else if(riid == IID_IClassFactory)
            *ppv = static_cast<IClassFactory*>(this);
        else
        {
            *ppv = NULL;
            return E_NOINTERFACE;
        }

        static_cast<IUnknown*>(*ppv)->AddRef();
        return S_OK;
    }

    STDMETHOD_(ULONG, AddRef)()
    {
        return InterlockedIncrement(&m_lRefCount);
    }

    STDMETHOD_(ULONG, Release)()
    {
        return InterlockedDecrement(&m_lRefCount);
    }
```

```
        // The IClassFactory methods
        STDMETHOD(CreateInstance)(IUnknown* punkOuter, REFIID riid, void** ppvObject)
        {
            *ppvObject = NULL;        // Initialize

            // Disallow aggregation
            if(punkOuter != NULL)
                return CLASS_E_NOAGGREGATION;
            // Create a new CWroxComponent object
            CWroxComponent* pwc = new CWroxComponent;
            if(pwc == NULL)
                return E_OUTOFMEMORY;

            // QI for riid; destroy the object if QI fails
            HRESULT hr = pwc->QueryInterface(riid, ppvObject);
            if(FAILED(hr))
                delete pwc;

            return hr;
        }

        STDMETHOD(LockServer)(BOOL fLock)
        {
            if(fLock)
                InterlockedIncrement(&g_lLockCount);
            else
                InterlockedDecrement(&g_lLockCount);
            return S_OK;
        }

private:
    long m_lRefCount;
};
```

Once we've #include'd the WroxComponent.h file that contains our coclass implementation, we begin to implement the class object. The class object implements the IClassFactory interface, so we derive our class from IClassFactory. The C++ definition for IClassFactory comes from the system headers that we've got from windows.h, via the WroxComponent.h file.

Since the class object is a COM object, it also implements IUnknown and the IUnknown methods. The implementations of these methods are very similar to the implementations that we provided for CWroxComponent, but note that we *don't* delete the object when the reference count gets to zero. We know that our class object hasn't been created on the heap (it's just stored in an automatic variable), so we don't want to call delete on it. The class object will live for as long as our DLL is loaded.

The implementation of IClassFactory::CreateInstance() is quite straightforward. We disallow aggregation (because we haven't discussed it yet), create a new instance of CWroxComponent, and call its QueryInterface() method to return the desired pointer to the caller. If QueryInterface() fails (which would happen if the object doesn't implement the requested interface), we make sure that the CWroxComponent object is deleted.

The implementation of IClassFactory::LockServer() just increments and decrements the global lock count for the module.

Now the only thing left to do is ensure that the lock count gets updated each time a CWroxComponent object is created or destroyed. Open up WroxComponent.h and add the following code to the constructor and destructor:

```
// Constructor
CWroxComponent() : m_lRefCount(0) { InterlockedIncrement(&g_lLockCount); }

// Destructor
~CWroxComponent() { InterlockedDecrement(&g_lLockCount); }
```

We can now be sure that the lock count will always be greater than zero when there are active components being served by this module.

At this stage, you can compile the ComDll project. You now have a fully working COM server, and the only thing that's stopping us from using it is the fact that it's not registered. In the last chapter, you saw how Visual C++ registered the ATLFireCtl component automatically, at the end of the build process. To understand how it did that, and why we'll use a more rudimentary technique in this example, you need to know more about exactly what registration entails.

Registering A Component

For a component to be creatable by COM, it needs to be registered. Components that will be used in MTS or COM+ need to be added to the respective catalogs using the MTS Explorer or Component Services Explorer; doing so registers the component server's location so that MTS or COM+ know where it is. Components like ours that are used outside of MTS or COM+ need to register their location in the system registry. COM servers that contain this registration code are known as **self-registering**, and although MTS and COM+ components will not use most of the entries added to the registry, they too must be self registering for reasons of backward compatibility.

Self-registering EXE servers are asked to add their entries to the registry when they are run from the command line with the -RegServer switch, and to unregister themselves when -UnRegServer is the command line parameter.

Self-registering DLL servers, on the other hand, export two functions for registering and unregistering themselves: DllRegisterServer() and DllUnregisterServer(). These are called by an external program, typically RegSvr32.exe, which is provided with the system. You can use:

```
>regsvr32.exe filename
```

to register a DLL server, and

```
>regsvr32.exe /u filename
```

to unregister it. As an absolute minimum, a server must add its CLSID as a key beneath HKEY_CLASSES_ROOT, and the location of its module as a value beneath an InprocServer32 sub-key (if it's a DLL) or a LocalServer32 sub-key (if it's an EXE). Visual C++ performs the trick of 'automatic' registration by issuing one of these two commands at the end of a successful build process.

The proxy-stub DLLs produced from MIDL compiler-generated code are also *self-registering COM DLLs. In addition to the entries under* HKEY_CLASSES_ROOT\CLSID\clsid\ InprocServer32, *proxy-stub DLLs make an entry under* HKEY_CLASSES_ROOT\ Interface\iid\ProxyStubClsid32 *that relates back to their CLSID. This allows COM to determine which proxy-stub to use for a particular interface. Note that the CLSID for a MIDL compiler-produced proxy is the same as the IID of the interface that it represents.*

Because we didn't implement the DLL registration functions, and since registry manipulation using the raw Win32 API can be quite convoluted, we're going to add the registry entries by hand. Note that because of this, this component cannot be used with MTS or COM+. However, it *is* a fully-fledged COM component, and so it *will* run on Windows 2000.

Open the IDL file that you created earlier in the chapter and copy the GUID for the coclass to the clipboard. (This GUID was denoted by MY_GUID4 when we created the IDL file). Next, fire up RegEdit.exe and right-click the HKEY_CLASSES_ROOT\CLSID key. Choose **New** | **Key** from the context menu and paste the GUID from the clipboard into the new key. Make sure that the new key begins with an opening brace and terminates with a closing brace, like all the other keys beneath HKEY_CLASSES_ROOT\CLSID.

Select the new key and double-click on the (Default) value in the right-hand pane. This allows you to edit the default value for the new key, which should contain the name of the coclass for the CLSID that we just added. Type WroxComponent into the **V**alue data box, and click **OK**.

Now add a new key beneath the key you just created, giving it the name InprocServer32. Edit the (Default) value of this key to give the location of the ComDll.dll file. Finally, right-click in the right-hand pane and add a new string value to the InprocServer32 key. Give the new value the name ThreadingModel, and use Apartment as the data. The registry entries should look something like the ones shown below:

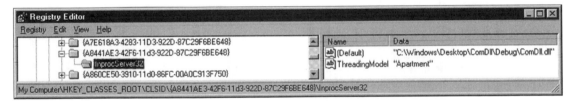

The OLE/COM Object Viewer

Now that you've compiled and registered the server, you can do a quick test to see if it's functioning by using the OLE/COM Object Viewer (OleView.exe). You'll find a shortcut to this program in the **Microsoft Visual Studio 6.0 Tools** group in your **Start** | **Programs** menu, or you can activate it from within Visual C++ via the **Tools** menu. The OLE/COM Object Viewer is a useful tool for examining the COM components on your system.

Once the OLE/COM Object Viewer is running, select **View** | **Expert Mode** so that you can see all the objects on your system. Then, expand the Object Classes folder, and All Objects beneath it. Below All Objects you should find an entry for WroxComponent; this represents the coclass that we just registered.

If you click on the text of this item to select it, the right hand pane will show the registry entries for this component on the **Registry** page. If you click on the + icon, the OLE/COM Object Viewer will create an instance of your component.

At this point, a list will appear beneath the name of the component showing all the interfaces that the OLE/COM Object Viewer knows are supported by the component. It determines this by calling `QueryInterface()` for every interface listed in the registry. In our case, we only see `IUnknown`, because we haven't registered either of our custom interfaces. If we had built and registered the proxy-stub DLL for our component, the other interfaces would also appear.

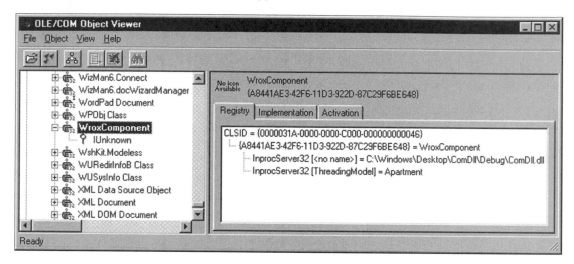

When you've got bored of seeing that your server can be instantiated with the OLE/COM Object Viewer, you can release it by right clicking on `WroxComponent` and selecting Release Instance from the context menu. Note that clicking on the - sign will *not* release the component. The OLE/COM Object Viewer lets you know when a component is active by making its name bold.

Creating A Basic Client

At long last, we're in a position to create a custom client to test this server. Unlike our example in the last chapter, this client will be able to call methods on several interfaces, and handle errors gracefully. To begin, create a new, empty **Win32 Console Application** called `Client` in a subdirectory of the `ComDll` directory. Create a new text file, save it in the `Client` project directory as `Client.cpp`, and add the file to the project. Add the following code to the file:

```
// Client.cpp
#include <windows.h>
#include <iostream>
```

Here we've just added the headers that we'll need for the code to come. The `windows.h` file gives us access to all the COM APIs and data types that we'll need, and `iostream` will enable us to use the standard library's stream classes so that we can output text to the console window.

Next, just as we did in the last chapter, we need to #include the MIDL compiler-generated header file from the `ComDll` project. This time we'll also use the `_i.c` file, but don't worry: the effects on our client code of doing this are very small. We'll simply use the CLSIDs and IIDs defined in the `_i.c` file, instead of using `__uuidof()`:

```
#include "..\comdll_idl.h"
#include "..\comdll_idl_i.c"
```

These files give us access to the interface and GUID definitions that we need to be able to create and manipulate instances of the WroxComponent coclass. After that, we can create the main() function for our project:

```
int main()
{
    CoInitialize(NULL);

    IWroxInterface* pWI = NULL;
    HRESULT hr = CoCreateInstance(CLSID_WroxComponent,
                                  NULL,
                                  CLSCTX_INPROC_SERVER,
                                  IID_IWroxInterface,
                                  reinterpret_cast<void**>(&pWI));

    if(FAILED(hr))
    {
        std::cout << "CoCreateInstance() failed : 0x" << std::hex << hr << "\n";
        CoUninitialize();
        return 0;
    }

    pWI->Alert();
```

This time around, after the inevitable call to CoInitialize(), we call CoCreateInstance() to create an instance of the WroxComponent coclass and get a pointer to IWroxInterface. Notice how we check the HRESULT returned by CoCreateInstance() for failure, and output a message, uninitialize COM, and exit the function if it did fail. If everything worked, we call the interface's Alert() method.

Since the WroxComponent implements two interfaces (plus IUnknown), we can add some code to call QueryInterface() to retrieve a pointer to the other interface:

```
    IWroxSimple* pWS = NULL;
    hr = pWI->QueryInterface(IID_IWroxSimple, reinterpret_cast<void**>(&pWS));

    if(FAILED(hr))
    {
        std::cout << "QueryInterface() failed : 0x" << std::hex << hr << "\n";
        pWI->Release();
        CoUninitialize();
        return 0;
    }

    pWS->Display();
```

Once again, we check for failure before attempting to use the pWS interface pointer. If there's a failure this time, we have to remember to Release() the pWI interface pointer before returning. If the call to QueryInterface() succeeds, we can call the IWroxSimple::Display() method.

Finally, we can Release() both the interface pointers, call CoUninitialize(), and return from the function:

```
    pWS->Release();
    pWI->Release();
    CoUninitialize();
    return 0;
}
```

At the end of all that work, you can run and test the code. If all goes well, you will see two message boxes appear telling you when the `Alert()` and `Display()` methods have been called. If anything goes wrong, an error code will be output to the console window. You can use this error code to find out what the problem is by using the error lookup utility provided with Visual C++ (<u>T</u>ools | Error Loo<u>k</u>up). Just enter the code into the Value box provided, and hit the <u>L</u>ook Up button.

Summary

This chapter has taken up the story where the first one left off. You've seen more about the things that are expected of a COM component, and more of the rules that apply to COM programming in all its forms. In particular, you now know that:

❑ All COM interfaces must include a method called `QueryInterface()` that allows client code to navigate from one of the interfaces on an object to another

❑ The three methods `QueryInterface()`, `AddRef()` and `Release()` make up the definition of the `IUnknown` interface

❑ All coclasses must implement `IUnknown`, and all other interfaces must derive from it

❑ C++ (implementation) inheritance and COM (interface) inheritance are not the same thing, but the latter can be modeled using the former

❑ In COM programming, errors are communicated back to the client by means of the `HRESULT` return type

❑ Every coclass is identified by a CLSID, and every interface is identified by an IID

❑ The interface definition language (IDL) is used to associate the methods of an interface with its IID, to produce the marshaling code that's used in proxy-stub DLLs, and to instruct client and server in how memory should be managed

❑ As well as generating marshaling code, the Microsoft IDL (MIDL) compiler can produce C++ interface definitions from the IDL that we supply for our custom interfaces

❑ Every coclass has an associated class object (sometimes called a class factory) that is responsible for creating instances of that class

❑ As well as the inevitable `DllMain()`, all DLL COM servers must export functions called `DllCanUnloadNow()`, `DllGetClassObject()`, `DllRegisterServer()`, and `DllUnregisterServer()`.

As this long list amply demonstrates, we've seen a lot of theory in this chapter, and in the example you've learned just how hard it can be to set up even the simplest of COM classes from scratch. Imagine that we wanted to create a new module that contained more objects! We'd have to:

❏ Create class objects for every coclass in the module

❏ Implement the IUnknown functions on every one of the objects

❏ Keep track of reference counts for each object and for the module itself

❏ Implement slightly different code depending on whether the module was an EXE or a DLL

❏ Write registration code

And this is without even considering some of the subtleties and more advanced features of COM that we haven't met yet. There's a lot of housekeeping to do when you're implementing COM servers!

Fortunately, as you'll see in the next chapter, ATL comes to our rescue. A combination of ATL itself and Visual C++'s Wizards make it incredibly easy to write high quality COM servers. ATL makes it possible for you to concentrate on the code that's specific to your component by providing the implementations for the class objects, the IUnknown methods, reference counting and registration. You'll see just how easy it is, starting from the very next chapter.

Building And Calling A COM Object Using ATL

In the two chapters so far you've seen a lot of the theory behind COM, and a little of how to write COM code using no more than C++ and the COM API. In this chapter, we're going to start our practical exploration of what *ATL* can do by building a simple DLL COM server, and a couple of client applications to test it. ATL programming is mainly about writing COM servers, but just to show it can be done, we'll also use ATL to write a client. While we're doing this, we'll be covering the following topics:

❑ The ATL COM AppWizard

❑ The code that the AppWizard generates

❑ The ATL Object Wizard

❑ What registry scripts are, and how they work

❑ Creating a COM client using ATL

❑ Using the #import directive

❑ Creating a COM client in Visual Basic

You'll see how easy it is to create fully functional COM servers without having to write all the code we considered in the last chapter, thanks to the combination of Wizard-generated code and the library code provided by ATL. As we progress, we'll compare the stages we go through in this example with the work that we had to do in the last chapter — ATL provides a vast array of macros and classes that provide standard implementations of common COM constructs. You'll see how the two approaches compare, and just a few of the facilities with which ATL makes COM programming easier.

Using The ATL COM AppWizard

First, we're going to create the skeleton of a new DLL server project using the ATL COM AppWizard. Close any projects that you still have open in Visual C++ from the last chapter and create a new one. Give your project the name Simple, and choose **ATL COM AppWizard** as the project type.

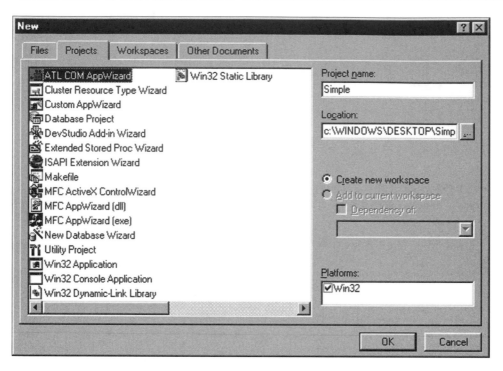

When you press OK, the Wizard will run and show you its one-and-only step:

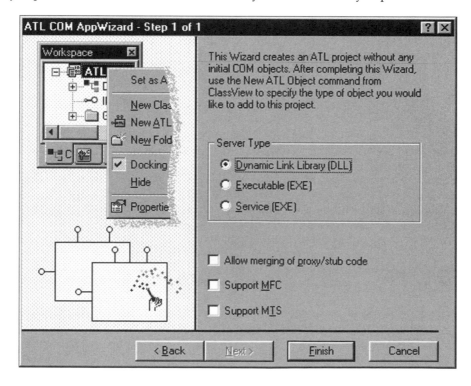

Like the other AppWizards supplied with Visual C++, the ATL COM AppWizard presents you with a number of options related to the creation of a new project. In this case, all the options fit on to a single step of the Wizard.

Server Type

The ATL COM AppWizard lets you package your COM server in one of three ways:

❑ As a DLL

❑ As an executable (an EXE file)

❑ As an NT service

We saw in the last chapter that the code necessary for creating a COM server differs depending on whether it's packaged as a DLL or an EXE. By picking one of the first two options, the AppWizard will generate the code appropriate to the module type. If you pick the final option, the AppWizard will create a project suitable for an EXE COM server, but will also add extra code to allow the executable to act as an **NT service**. A service is a special type of application that can be started automatically at boot-up (before any user logs in), and can be run under the SYSTEM account. We won't be looking at services in this book, and for now you should leave the default option intact; we're going to create a DLL server for this example.

> *For more information about NT services and using the ATL COM AppWizard to create them, see* Professional NT Services *(1-861001-30-4), also published by Wrox Press.*

In most cases, choosing a DLL server will be a good option, and creating one doesn't mean that you have to live without the benefits of process isolation or remoting that EXE servers bring. It is possible to isolate DLL servers from the client process or allow them to be accessed remotely by using **surrogates**, which are explained in Chapter 6.

Allow Merging Of Proxy/Stub Code

This option lets you choose to merge the proxy-stub code that handles marshaling into your server DLL, so that you can get just one file to redistribute. The proxy-stub code won't *actually* be compiled into your DLL unless you also manually define the symbol _MERGE_PROXYSTUB and add some of the other generated files to the build. For this simple example, we'll leave the proxy-stub generation as it is.

> *Note that this checkbox is disabled for either of the EXE server types. Proxy-stub code needs to be in a DLL so that it can run in the process of the client. Also be aware that proxy-stub code is often required even when the server itself is implemented in a DLL; we'll see why in Chapter 6.*

Support MFC

Checking the Support MFC checkbox gives you access to MFC classes, which may make writing your code easier. It is especially useful when you're writing ATL COM servers that wrap existing C++ objects that use MFC. Be aware, though, that including MFC support will increase the size of your server, and will make it necessary for clients to have the correct MFC libraries on their machines. Of course, you can choose to link to MFC statically, but then you'll get an even larger component!

Note that Microsoft doesn't provide MFC support for EXE-based servers. It *is* possible to add MFC to ATL EXE servers yourself, and if you find that you need to do this, you can consult the Microsoft Knowledge Base article Q173974. We won't go into this topic in any more detail in this book, as we won't be including MFC support in the servers we write.

Support MTS

Selecting this option (which is only available when you're building a DLL server) will equip your project with support for **Microsoft Transaction Server** (**MTS**), but in truth the changes it makes are not very significant. It links to the MTS libraries (`mtx.lib` and `mtxguid.lib`), and provides support for 'delay loading' of the MTS executive (by linking to `delayimp.lib` and using the `/delayload` linker switch). The most useful thing that this option does is to change the makefile for the proxy-stub DLLs that may be generated for the project so that they work with MTS, but even this may not affect you — it depends on the type of interfaces you use, as you'll discover later.

As we said back in Chapter 1, this book is focusing on the fundamentals of ATL. MTS is another topic to which we'll be giving no further coverage, and you should therefore leave this box unchecked too. For now, select the DLL server type option and press Finish to exit from the Wizard. As usual, you'll get a summary screen, telling you what the Wizard is intending to create:

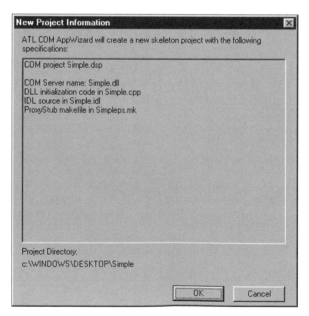

Examining The AppWizard Code

Now that we have instructed the AppWizard to generate the skeleton for our container application, let's take a look at what's been produced.

The Files

The list of files produced by the Wizard is shown in the following picture; you'll see that there are far fewer than for a typical MFC project. We have:

❑ Precompiled header files, StdAfx.h and StdAfx.cpp

❑ An IDL file, Simple.idl

❑ Resource files, Resource.h and Simple.rc

❑ A module definition file, Simple.def

❑ A C++ source file, Simple.cpp

If you look at the project directory, you will also see three more files (as well as the usual Visual C++ project stuff): Simple.h, Simpleps.mk *and* Simpleps.def. *The first is simply an empty header file, but the other two are the makefile and module definition file for the proxy-stub DLL. We'll look at creating the proxy-stub DLL in Chapter 6.*

The Precompiled Header Files

Let's take a brief look at StdAfx.h, since quite apart from including the ATL headers, it contains some interesting information:

```
// stdafx.h : include file for standard system include files,
//      or project specific include files that are used frequently,
//      but are changed infrequently

#if !defined(AFX_STDAFX_H__8D152D64_4218_11D3_922D_C9790CAEC34F__INCLUDED_)
#define AFX_STDAFX_H__8D152D64_4218_11D3_922D_C9790CAEC34F__INCLUDED_

#if _MSC_VER > 1000
#pragma once
#endif // _MSC_VER > 1000

#define STRICT
#ifndef _WIN32_WINNT
#define _WIN32_WINNT 0x0400
#endif
#define _ATL_APARTMENT_THREADED

#include <atlbase.h>
// You may derive a class from CComModule and use it if you want to override
// something, but do not change the name of _Module
extern CComModule _Module;
#include <atlcom.h>

//{{AFX_INSERT_LOCATION}}
// Microsoft Visual C++ will insert additional declarations
//      immediately before the previous line.
#endif // !defined(AFX_STDAFX_H__8D152D64_4218_11D3_922D_C9790CAEC34F__INCLUDED)
```

_WIN32_WINNT

ATL and the Windows system headers use this symbol to protect code that is only available in a particular version of Windows NT. If this symbol is defined to be greater than or equal to 0x400, then code specific to Windows NT 4.0 can be compiled into your project. If this symbol is not defined, or it is defined to be a value less than 0x400, then that code will not be compiled into your project.

In most cases, the code protected by this symbol is related to DCOM (DCOM first became available with Windows NT 4.0), and will work on Windows 9x machines with DCOM installed. To get access to only this kind of code, you can define the _WIN32_DCOM symbol instead. The implications of this situation are summarized below:

❑   If your code is destined to run only on version 4.0 or later of Windows NT, you can leave the _WIN32_WINNT symbol in StdAfx.h. In most cases the code will still work on Windows 9x machines, but you will be able to *compile* code that only works on NT.

❑   If your code is intended to run on any system with DCOM installed (Windows NT 4.0 or Windows 9x with DCOM), you should remove the #define for _WIN32_WINNT and replace it with #define _WIN32_DCOM. This allows DCOM-specific code to compile, but not NT-specific code.

❑   If your code is intended to run on versions of Windows 9x or Windows NT without DCOM installed, just remove the #define for _WIN32_WINNT. This allows the compiler to flag code that will not run on those operating systems.

_ATL_APARTMENT_THREADED

The next definition in this file is for the symbol _ATL_APARTMENT_THREADED. The definition of this symbol defines the default **threading model** of the DLL to be the **apartment model**. This does not mean that all components in the DLL will have this threading model, but that if they don't specify one explicitly, this default setting will be used. This symbol is more important for EXE servers, where it also determines the apartment type of the main thread of the process. We'll be looking at threading in Chapter 6.

_Module

The other item of interest in StdAfx.h is the declaration of a CComModule object called _Module. CComModule implements the basic functionality of a COM server (whether in a DLL or EXE), and provides basic services such as registering and instantiating the objects supported by the server, and managing their lifetimes by means of an **object map**. We'll look at CComModule in more detail later in the chapter, and object maps are covered in Chapter 4.

> Note that the CComModule object must be global and must be called _Module, since it's referenced throughout the ATL header files.

The IDL File

As you saw briefly in the last chapter, the MIDL compiler uses the IDL file to produce several things: the C++ headers for our interfaces, the type library for our server, and the marshaling source code. At this stage, the IDL only contains the bare minimum necessary for it to compile, such as the name of the type library and its GUID. Once we start adding coclasses, interfaces, and their methods, the Wizards will insert the appropriate code into the IDL file on our behalf.

```
// Simple.idl : IDL source for Simple.dll
//

// This file will be processed by the MIDL tool to
// produce the type library (Simple.tlb) and marshalling code.

import "oaidl.idl";
import "ocidl.idl";

[
    uuid(B8240741-4995-11D3-88E4-00105A68BF5D),
    version(1.0),
    helpstring("Simple 1.0 Type Library")
]
library SIMPLELib
{
    importlib("stdole32.tlb");
    importlib("stdole2.tlb");

};
```

You saw some IDL in Chapter 2, but here you can see a couple more elements of the language. First of these is the `library` block, items within which will be compiled into the type library file. Type libraries can also have IDL attributes associated with them, such as the `[uuid()]`, `[version()]` and `[helpstring()]` attributes used here.

> **A type library is a compiled version of the information contained in the `library` block of an IDL file that gets used in a number of different situations by several different tools. Examples of their use include the `#import` directive that you'll see later in this chapter, and the Visual Basic References dialog that enables the auto-completion and context-sensitive help (so-called "IntelliSense") features.**

Within the type library block, you can see that the `importlib()` statement has been used to bring in the standard COM (OLE) type libraries. It's worth making the distinction between this and the quite similar `import`. The latter is used to include actual *definitions* from another IDL file, in the same way that `#include` is used to include structure and class definitions in C++. `importlib()` is used when you don't have the original IDL, but only the type library; it inserts a reference to the type library into the IDL. This means that at runtime, clients accessing `Simple.tlb` will be able to use the information in `stdole32.tlb` and `stdole2.tlb` via these references. A consequence of this is that any libraries referenced in `importlib()` statements must be distributed with the application (or be already present on the target machine).

Environmental Support For The MIDL Compiler

Compilation of the IDL file occurs automatically when the project is built thanks to Visual C++'s inbuilt support for the MIDL compiler. Right-click on the IDL file's icon in FileView and select the Settings... item from the context menu, like this:

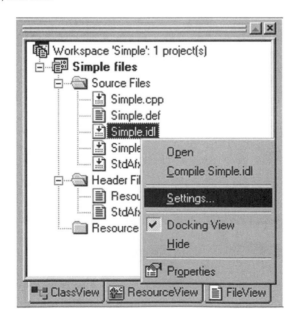

The resulting Project Settings dialog has a tab named MIDL that allows you to customize the output of the MIDL compiler when this file is processed:

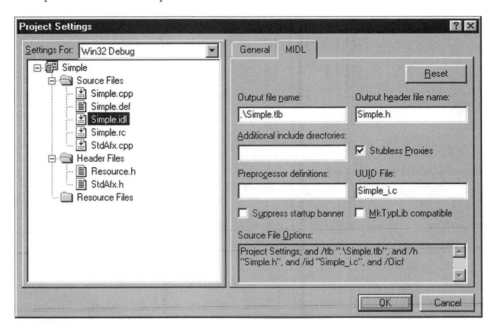

As you can see, the options are set by default to generate the .h, _i.c and .tlb files that you know about from Chapter 2. You're free to change the names of any of these files, and if for any reason you don't want one of them to be generated at all, you can simply delete its name from the edit box.

It is fairly unusual to need to alter the other settings in this dialog. The uses of the three on the left are self-evident, Stubless Proxies are a marshaling optimization that's recommended provided that the target machine for your component is DCOM-enabled, and MkTypLib compatible shouldn't be used unless you're having trouble with legacy code.

We'll be seeing the IDL file and the significance of the MIDL compiler's output again as we progress through the chapter.

The Module Definition File

Simple.def just lists the functions that need to be exported from the DLL:

```
; Simple.def : Declares the module parameters.

LIBRARY        "Simple.DLL"

EXPORTS
    DllCanUnloadNow      @1 PRIVATE
    DllGetClassObject    @2 PRIVATE
    DllRegisterServer    @3 PRIVATE
    DllUnregisterServer  @4 PRIVATE
```

You can see that all the functions you'd expect to see exported by a COM DLL server are listed. We looked at these functions in Chapter 2, and we'll see exactly how ATL implements them in the next section.

The Source File

At the top of Simple.cpp you can see that a number of header files are included:

```
#include "stdafx.h"
#include "resource.h"
#include <initguid.h>
#include "Simple.h"

#include "Simple_i.c"
```

Just as we saw with the ATLFire project in Chapter 1, Simple.h is a MIDL compiler-maintained header file that will contain the C++ definitions for all the interfaces defined in the project's IDL file (once we've added some), as well as extern declarations of constants for the GUIDs. Simple_i.c, a file of another familiar type, is generated entirely by the MIDL compiler and contains the non-extern definitions of the GUIDs. Because the MIDL compiler generates it, you won't be able to find it until you've built the whole project; you'll get a compiler error if you try to compile Simple.cpp in isolation.

The non-extern definition of a GUID actually defines *the GUID. Obviously, this must be done only once, and all other references to this GUID must be* extern.

> **MIDL compiler-generated GUID constants are made up of the name of the interface, coclass, or library prefixed with IID_, CLSID_ or LIBID_ respectively, and must be included exactly once in a file in your project.**

initguid.h is a system header file that allows you to use the DEFINE_GUID() macro to initialize GUIDs. Neither the .h nor the _i.c file produced by the MIDL compiler make use of the DEFINE_GUID() macro, so its usefulness is questionable.

Further down Simple.cpp, you can see the definition of _Module and the server's object map, which is used to list the coclasses that this server implements. The object map is currently empty because we don't have any coclasses in our project yet. We'll look at the object map again when there's more to see.

```
CComModule _Module;

BEGIN_OBJECT_MAP(ObjectMap)
END_OBJECT_MAP()
```

The remainder of `Simple.cpp` is taken up with the implementations of the DLL's exposed functions. The first function is `DllMain()`, the standard DLL entry point on Windows platforms:

```
extern "C"
BOOL WINAPI DllMain(HINSTANCE hInstance, DWORD dwReason, LPVOID /*lpReserved*/)
{
    if (dwReason == DLL_PROCESS_ATTACH)
    {
        _Module.Init(ObjectMap, hInstance, &LIBID_SIMPLELib);
        DisableThreadLibraryCalls(hInstance);
    }
    else if (dwReason == DLL_PROCESS_DETACH)
        _Module.Term();
    return TRUE;    // ok
}
```

The main purpose of this function is to initialize and free the data members used by the `CComModule` object, by calling its `Init()` and `Term()` functions. Note that the module is passed the object map as the first parameter to the `Init()` method.

The call to `DisableThreadLibraryCalls()` disables the calls that the operating system would normally make to `DllMain()` when threads attach to or detach from the DLL. This can reduce the amount of server code that will have to be kept in memory, and is entirely in keeping with the ATL team's constant quest for extreme efficiency. As you will see time and again during the book, ATL was designed to be as small and fast as possible.

The rest of the functions in `Simple.cpp` call the corresponding methods of the server's `CComModule` object:

```
STDAPI DllCanUnloadNow(void)
{
    return (_Module.GetLockCount()==0) ? S_OK : S_FALSE;
}

STDAPI DllGetClassObject(REFCLSID rclsid, REFIID riid, LPVOID* ppv)
{
    return _Module.GetClassObject(rclsid, riid, ppv);
}

STDAPI DllRegisterServer(void)
{
    // registers object, typelib and all interfaces in typelib
    return _Module.RegisterServer(TRUE);
}

STDAPI DllUnregisterServer(void)
{
    return _Module.UnregisterServer(TRUE);
}
```

We met these functions in the last chapter, and now you can see that ATL implements them by handing off the hard work to methods of the `CComModule` class. As a quick reminder, here's what they all do:

❑ `DllCanUnloadNow()` is called to determine whether a DLL is still in use. If it's OK for the DLL to be unloaded, it will return `S_OK`. In the case of our ATL server, the `CComModule` object maintains a lock count, and it is safe to unload when that reaches zero.

❑ DllGetClassObject() retrieves the class object for a coclass. Given a CLSID and an interface ID, the function will attempt to create a class object and return a pointer to the interface.

❑ DllRegisterServer() is used to tell the DLL to create registry entries for all the coclasses supported by this server, and in some circumstances for the type library as well.

❑ DllUnregisterServer() tells the DLL to remove those entries that were created using DllRegisterServer().

Building The Server

Although our server doesn't do anything at all at this stage, it's still worth building it in order to see the files that the MIDL compiler creates for us — you'll find that Simple.h, Simple.tlb and Simple_i.c are listed under the **External Dependencies** folder in FileView.

Later, after we've added an object to our project (see the next section), two more files will be generated. Simple_p.c and dlldata.c will contain source code that helps with the marshaling for this DLL.

We discussed the .h and .c files when we looked at the #includes in Simple.cpp. You shouldn't ever need to touch these, as the MIDL compiler maintains them from the information in the IDL file. The Simple.tlb file is the (currently empty) type library for the server. Once again, it falls to the MIDL compiler to maintain it.

Using The ATL Object Wizard

In order to make our server do anything useful, we need to add a coclass to it, and this is done using the ATL Object Wizard. You can start up the Object Wizard using the Insert | New ATL Object... menu item. The dialog that's displayed shows all the different types of COM object that can be added to a server:

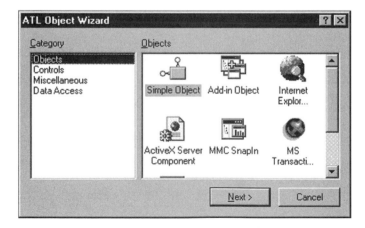

Here's a quick synopsis of the different types of component available:

Group	Object
Objects	Simple Object adds a minimal COM object.
	Add-in Object creates a COM object that can be used to extend Visual Studio.
	Internet Explorer Object creates an object that contains all the interfaces necessary for it to work with Internet Explorer, but has no user interface.
	ActiveX Server Component creates an object that can be used as part of an Active Server Page (ASP) with Internet Information Server (IIS).
	MMC SnapIn creates an object that supports the necessary interfaces to be used in the Microsoft Management Console.
	MS Transaction Server Component includes the header files needed by MTS, and makes the object non-aggregatable.
	Component Registrar Object adds an object that implements the `IComponentRegistrar` interface, which is used to register the objects in a server individually.
Controls (The first three of these have "lite" companions that implement only the interfaces needed to work within MS Internet Explorer.)	Full Control adds an object that implements all the interfaces needed by a full ActiveX control (OCX), such that it should work with any ActiveX control container.
	Composite Control adds a control that's capable of hosting other controls.
	HTML Control adds a control that includes a DHTML resource and displays an HTML page in its user interface.
	Property Page adds a property page object.
Miscellaneous	Dialog adds a class that implements a dialog.
Data Access	Provider creates classes for the OLE DB objects that a consumer (below) will use. OLE DB is a technology that allows access to any data source via a standard set of COM interfaces.
	Consumer isn't actually a COM object at all. This option creates a wrapper class that gives access to an OLE DB provider.

Many of these (such as the data access "objects") are pretty specialized, and we'll meet the Controls group later on. For the present, we just want to add a basic, simple object to the project.

Click on the Simple Object icon, and then on the Next button to bring up the Properties dialog. The Properties dialog consists of two pages: Names and Attributes.

Names

As you might expect, the Names page allows you to specify the names of various aspects of the component. The Short Name acts as the basis for all the other names on the dialog. If you fill in the Short Name with CalcEaster (we're going to be writing a simple component that calculates the date of Easter for any given year), you'll see how the remaining boxes are populated automatically.

If you want to change any of the names from their default values, you can just alter the text in the appropriate edit box. In this case, we'd like to ensure that our component has a unique Prog ID, so we'll change that to Wrox.CalcEaster. You should end up with something like this:

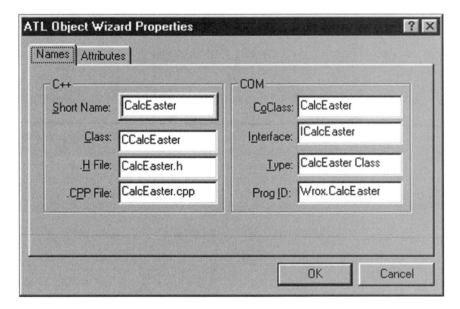

The Wizard will use the information you provide to create a C++ class with the name specified in the Class field, in header and source files named after the values in the .H File and .CPP File boxes. The C++ class will represent a coclass with the name specified in the CoClass field (this value will be used as the name of the coclass in the IDL file). The coclass will expose a single interface with the name specified in the Interface box. The values of the Type and Prog ID fields will ultimately end up in the registry:

❑   Type will be used to provide a readable description of the coclass

❑   Prog ID will be used to allow the coclass to be created via its ProgID

ProgIDs

The name of a component is its CLSID, period. Whenever clients create instances of components, they ultimately use the CLSID. However, humans find 128-bit integers hard to remember, and languages like Visual Basic and VBScript don't have 128-bit integer data types. To make life easier, Microsoft defined a textual version of a component's name, called a **programmatic identifier**, or **ProgID**.

Inevitably, ProgIDs are not guaranteed to be unique, and if you want to be absolutely sure about naming and using components you should always use CLSIDs and languages that understand them. However, if you're careful about the ProgIDs that you define, you can be *reasonably* sure that they will be unique. The recommended format for a ProgID is as follows (but remember, it *is* only a recommendation):

```
Server.Component.Version
```

The `Server` part is typically the DLL, EXE or application name (for example, `Word`), `Component` is the component you are naming (for example `Document`) and `Version` is simply a number. Another convention often used by organizations that want to keep track of all the components their developers produce is to replace the `Server` term with a `Company` term. This is the format we have chosen to use in our example by changing the ProgID of our coclass to `Wrox.CalcEaster`.

C++ clients can use the `CLSIDFromProgID()` *or* `ProgIDFromCLSID()` *API functions to get one form of identifier from the other, based on information stored in the registry. Note once again that ProgIDs are a* secondary *form of identification — all COM components must have a CLSID, but ProgIDs are optional. You can see ProgIDs in the registry, directly beneath* `HKEY_CLASSES_ROOT`.

Attributes

Once you've entered the names as shown, click on the **Attributes** tab. This tab displays a page showing several options that affect the way our control will function:

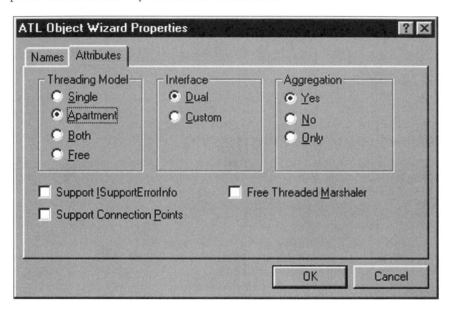

We don't need to change any of these options for our simple example — that's what default settings are for, after all — but rest assured that we'll be looking at these settings and what they mean as we progress through the book. For the determinedly curious, however, we'll just give you a quick description, and tell you when we'll be looking at them in more detail.

The **Threading Model** determines the preferred apartment type that the component will use, and also the thread synchronization code that ATL will use. Both EXE and DLL components will show these four options, but only **Apartment** and **Free** are relevant to EXE components. The various COM threading models (and how to choose the one you need) are covered in more detail in Chapter 6. For most simple components, you're quite safe sticking with the <u>A</u>partment threading model.

The **Interface** setting determines whether this component will support the IDispatch interface that's required by Automation. Leaving our selection as <u>D</u>ual ensures that it will. Automation, IDispatch and dual interfaces are covered in Chapter 5.

The **Aggregation** setting determines whether this object can be part of a composite COM object; the default value says that it can. Aggregation is covered in Chapter 4.

The three checkboxes at the bottom of the page provide some advanced options. The **Free Threaded Marshaler** option has to do with marshaling interface pointers between apartments in the same process, an advanced topic that we won't be looking at in this book. You shouldn't check this box unless you're *absolutely* sure what you're doing. Checking the **Support ISupportErrorInfo** box adds support for the `ISupportErrorInfo` interface, which will enable your object to return rich error and status information to callers. Finally, **Support Connection Points** makes the object capable of originating events. We'll look at connection points in Chapter 7, and rich error reporting in Chapter 5.

For this example, you can leave all these options as they are, and simply press the **OK** button to generate the code.

Examining The Object Wizard Code

Let's look at the things that have been generated for us by the Wizard. We have three new files, and a few changes to existing ones. The new files are:

❑ `CalcEaster.h`

❑ `CalcEaster.cpp`

❑ `CalcEaster.rgs`

The `CalcEaster.h` and `.cpp` files implement the simple COM component itself. The `.cpp` file is essentially empty apart from a `#include` for the header file, `CalcEaster.h`, which looks like this:

```
// CalcEaster.h : Declaration of the CCalcEaster

#ifndef __CALCEASTER_H_
#define __CALCEASTER_H_

#include "resource.h"        // main symbols

/////////////////////////////////////////////////////////////////////////////
// CCalcEaster
class ATL_NO_VTABLE CCalcEaster :
    public CComObjectRootEx<CComSingleThreadModel>,
    public CComCoClass<CCalcEaster, &CLSID_CalcEaster>,
    public IDispatchImpl<ICalcEaster, &IID_ICalcEaster, &LIBID_SIMPLELib>
{
public:
    CCalcEaster()
    {
    }

DECLARE_REGISTRY_RESOURCEID(IDR_CALCEASTER)

DECLARE_PROTECT_FINAL_CONSTRUCT()

BEGIN_COM_MAP(CCalcEaster)
    COM_INTERFACE_ENTRY(ICalcEaster)
    COM_INTERFACE_ENTRY(IDispatch)
END_COM_MAP()

// ICalcEaster
public:
};

#endif //__CALCEASTER_H_
```

There are several important points to note from this file. Firstly, notice that the class definition uses multiple inheritance to derive from three ATL-provided classes. As you might expect, given the name of the library, all the classes are templates. CComObjectRootEx<> handles object reference count management, CComCoClass<> defines the class object and aggregation model for the component, and IDispatchImpl<> provides the implementation of the IDispatch portion of the dual interface that was mentioned earlier.

The ATL_NO_VTABLE macro wraps __declspec(novtable), a special compiler optimization first introduced in Visual C++ 5.0 that tells the compiler to create a class without initializing the vtable in the constructor. This means that the linker can eliminate both the vtable and all the functions it points to, reducing the size of your code. It also means that you can't call any virtual functions in the constructor of such a class.

Not having a vtable is useful for classes that are only ever used as base classes, but any class that can be independently instantiated must not use ATL_NO_VTABLE. Such classes need a properly initialized vtable pointer. As you'll see, the class we've just created with the Object Wizard is only ever used as a base class, and a vtable will be generated for the most derived class.

DECLARE_REGISTRY_RESOURCEID() implements script-based registry support (described in the following section), and provides the resource ID for the registry script information. DECLARE_PROTECT_FINAL_CONSTRUCT(), on the other hand, protects against a potential problem with reference counting that is most likely to occur if the component is used in aggregation, which we'll examine in the next chapter.

The BEGIN_COM_MAP() and END_COM_MAP() macros define the **COM map**, which is how the COM interfaces in your object are exposed to clients via QueryInterface(). This means that if an interface isn't in the map, a client can't get a pointer to it. The way that COM maps work is also covered in the next chapter.

Registry Scripts

The RGS file contains a script for adding entries about our component to the registry. This script is compiled into the server as a custom "REGISTRY" resource, and used whenever the server is told to register itself.

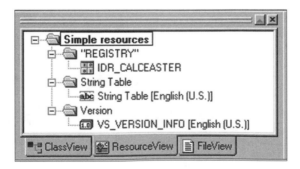

The registry script is understood by the **ATL Registrar**, which is ultimately responsible for adding the entries to the registry. Your code has to have access to the Registrar in order for this to work, and there are two ways in which this can be achieved.

The first method relies on the fact that the Registrar lives in a DLL called Atl.dll, so you'd normally make sure that Atl.dll is present and registered on any machine that wants to register this component. This may require you to distribute Atl.dll with your component.

Note that there are two versions of Atl.dll *on the Visual C++ 6 CD: one ANSI (for Windows 9x systems), the other Unicode (for Windows NT). Make sure that you install the correct one!*

The second method uses static linking. If you choose the Win32 MinDependency target when building the component, the Registrar code will be linked into the component, so that it doesn't rely on Atl.dll. In this case, of course, your component will be larger in size.

Here's the CalcEaster.rgs file for our project:

```
HKCR
{
    Wrox.CalcEaster.1 = s 'CalcEaster Class'
    {
        CLSID = s '{5DC86882-58F2-11D1-A159-04DCF8C00000}'
    }
    Wrox.CalcEaster = s 'CalcEaster Class'
    {
        CLSID = s '{5DC86882-58F2-11D1-A159-04DCF8C00000}'
        CurVer = s 'Wrox.CalcEaster.1'
    }
    NoRemove CLSID
    {
        ForceRemove {5DC86882-58F2-11D1-A159-04DCF8C00000} = s 'CalcEaster Class'
        {
            ProgID = s 'Wrox.CalcEaster.1'
            VersionIndependentProgID = s 'Wrox.CalcEaster'
            ForceRemove 'Programmable'
            InprocServer32 = s '%MODULE%'
            {
                val ThreadingModel = s 'Apartment'
            }
            'TypeLib' = s '{B8240741-4995-11D3-88E4-00105A68BF5D}'
        }
    }
}
```

Although it may look slightly unfamiliar, the syntax is relatively straightforward. Registry scripts use the following keywords:

Keyword	Description
ForceRemove	When creating the following key, ensures that any existing key has been completely removed first before adding the key back. This is useful if the key already exists, but sub-keys or values beneath it need changing.
NoRemove	Doesn't remove the following key during unregistration. (With the exception of root keys, all keys specified in the script will be removed during unregistration unless this keyword is present.)
val	The following is a named value.
Delete	Deletes the following key during registration.
s	The following value is a string.
d	The following value is a DWORD.
b	The following string value is binary data in the form of hexadecimal numbers.

Any text that isn't one of these keywords is a key, a named value, or the data for that item. Anything to the right of an equals sign is data to be placed in the registry. If the item to the left of the equals sign has the word val in front of it, then the data will be added to a named value; otherwise, it will be added as the default data for that key. The nested braces represent the levels of the keys in the registry. The %MODULE% keyword represents a replaceable parameter, rather like the ones you can use in DOS batch files. In this case, it represents the full pathname of our DLL.

There are a couple of important things to note:

❑ HKCR is HKEY_CLASSES_ROOT, so all the registry entries will be within that hive, as you would expect. Other strings you can use are HKCU (HKEY_CURRENT_USER), HKLM (HKEY_LOCAL_MACHINE), HKU (HKEY_USERS), HKPD (HKEY_PERFORMANCE_DATA), HKDD (HKEY_DYN_DATA) and HKCC (HKEY_CURRENT_CONFIG).

❑ The CLSID subkey has the NoRemove keyword applied. This is very important because the information in the RGS file is used to unregister the component, as well as to register it. When instructed to unregister the server, the Registrar can use the information in this file to find all the entries to remove. You can now see why NoRemove is important — if it weren't there, the entire CLSID key (and all its subkeys) would be wiped out when the server unregistered itself! RGS files can be *very* dangerous — be careful with them.

Changed Files

The file that has changed the most as a result of adding our coclass is the IDL file, which now looks like this (with the new lines shown highlighted):

```
import "oaidl.idl";
import "ocidl.idl";
    [
        object,
        uuid(A7E618A2-4283-11D3-922D-87C29F6BE648),
        dual,
        helpstring("ICalcEaster Interface"),
        pointer_default(unique)
    ]
    interface ICalcEaster : IDispatch
    {
    };

[
    uuid(8D152D61-4218-11D3-922D-C9790CAEC34F),
    version(1.0),
    helpstring("Simple 1.0 Type Library")
]
library SIMPLELib
{
    importlib("stdole32.tlb");
    importlib("stdole2.tlb");

    [
        uuid(A7E618A3-4283-11D3-922D-87C29F6BE648),
        helpstring("CalcEaster Class")
    ]
    coclass CalcEaster
    {
        [default] interface ICalcEaster;
    };
};
```

The IDL file now contains entries for the CalcEaster coclass and its interface ICalcEaster, which is derived from IDispatch (which in turn is derived from IUnknown). You can see that GUIDs have been automatically generated for the coclass and its interface, and that the CLSID in the IDL file matches the CLSID in the RGS file, as it should.

The only other significant change at this stage is to Simple.cpp, where we find a new header and an addition to the object map:

```
#include "stdafx.h"
#include "resource.h"
#include <initguid.h>
#include "Simple.h"

#include "Simple_i.c"
#include "CalcEaster.h"


CComModule _Module;

BEGIN_OBJECT_MAP(ObjectMap)
OBJECT_ENTRY(CLSID_CalcEaster, CCalcEaster)
END_OBJECT_MAP()
```

The object map is essentially a list of the coclasses in this server. We'll talk more about the details of this in the next chapter.

Adding Methods And Properties

We now have a server that we can build, but it doesn't do much except register itself, because we haven't added any methods that clients can call, or properties that they can manipulate. We need a simple task for the server to perform, and for this example we'll get it to calculate the date of Easter Day in any year.

Methods And Properties

A word is required about terminology at this point. Some programming languages have constructs that make things appear otherwise, but ultimately clients will always call the **methods** that form the implementation of a COM interface. However, it is also convenient for clients to think of servers as having **properties** (in other words, data items) that they can manipulate, so that instead of having to say something like:

```
myObj.SetYear(n)
```

one can write:

```
myObj.Year = n
```

Of course, we know that interfaces only expose methods, and that it isn't actually possible to access data within a COM object. This deception is managed through the IDL file, where properties are implemented in terms of 'get' and 'put' methods, as we'll see shortly. A language such as Visual Basic is then at liberty to let users write code in terms of variable-like properties, which it maps onto the appropriate 'get' and 'put' methods.

Since the main aim of this exercise is to demonstrate how to add methods and properties to an ATL component, we'll go about doing it in a fairly roundabout way, as follows:

❑   Add a property to set the desired year

❑   Add properties to return the day and month of Easter

❑   Add a method to do the actual calculation

In a real server, you probably wouldn't drag things out like this — you could merge the entire operation into one call. However, we want to see both properties and methods in use, so we'll split it up.

Adding Properties

To add a property, you should start by right clicking on the entry for the `ICalcEaster` interface in ClassView.

> `ICalcEaster` *appears twice in ClassView: once in its own right, and once as a member of the* `CCalcEaster` *class. You can click on either one.*

This will bring up a context menu that contains entries allowing you to add methods and properties. Select **Add Property...** to bring up the **Add Property to Interface** dialog, and enter a property called `Year`, of type `short`.

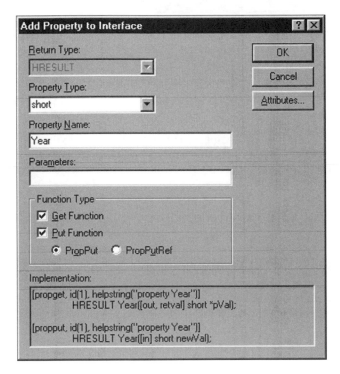

We can add a **Get** Function, a **Put** Function or both, depending on whether we want to be able to read or write the property. For the 'put' function, we can choose to make the function accept a copy of the property (**PropPut**), or a reference to it (**PropPutRef**). **PropPut** is the default, and you'd use this for most simple types.

The bottom pane in the dialog shows the entries that will be added to the IDL file. If you want to edit the attributes, such as the id() or the helpstring(), press the <u>A</u>ttributes... button:

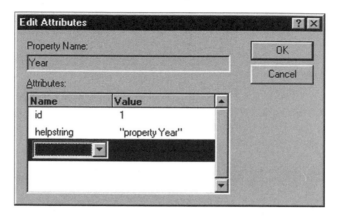

The id *here has nothing to do with the GUIDs we've been discovering throughout our examination of COM so far. This* id *is another artifact of Automation, which we'll be discussing in Chapter 5.*

Once you're happy with the property name, type and attributes, press the OK button to generate the code. Back in the project, several alterations are made to the project files. First, look at the IDL file, where you'll see additions for the property:

```
[
    object,
    uuid(B824074D-4995-11D3-88E4-00105A68BF5D),
    dual,
    helpstring("ICalcEaster Interface"),
    pointer_default(unique)
]
interface ICalcEaster : IDispatch
{
    [propget, id(1), helpstring("property Year")]
    HRESULT Year([out, retval] short *pVal);
    [propput, id(1), helpstring("property Year")]
    HRESULT Year([in] short newVal);
};
```

We've defined two new methods, which are used to implement the Year property. Both are called "Year" and have the same help string and ID, but they're distinguished by their attributes. The method that returns a value has the [propget] attribute. Since its parameter is used to return a value, the parameter has to have the [out] attribute, and as this is also the conceptual return value of the method, it has the [retval] attribute too.

> You know that the real return value of a COM method is always an **HRESULT**, but parameters marked with the **[retval]** attribute can serve a special purpose. Tools such as Visual Basic can 'hide' the **HRESULT** and make it look to the user as though a method returns the parameter marked **[retval]**. As you might expect, a method can have several parameters with **[out]** attributes, but only one with **[out, retval]**.

The method to *set* the value has the `[propput]` attribute, and its parameter is marked as an input parameter by the use of the `[in]` attribute.

Similar changes have been made to `CalcEaster.h`, where functions to `get_` and `put_` the property have been added to the class:

```
// CalcEaster.h : Declaration of the CCalcEaster

...

// ICalcEaster
public:
    STDMETHOD(get_Year)(/*[out, retval]*/ short *pVal);
    STDMETHOD(put_Year)(/*[in]*/ short newVal);
};
```

In `CalcEaster.cpp`, we have skeleton code for the two methods:

```
// CalcEaster.cpp : Implementation of CCalcEaster
#include "stdafx.h"
#include "Simple.h"
#include "CalcEaster.h"

/////////////////////////////////////////////////////////////////////////////
// CCalcEaster

STDMETHODIMP CCalcEaster::get_Year(short * pVal)
{
    // TODO: Add your implementation code here

    return S_OK;
}

STDMETHODIMP CCalcEaster::put_Year(short newVal)
{
    // TODO: Add your implementation code here

    return S_OK;
}
```

You can see that both functions use the STDMETHODIMP macro, which is similar in nature to the STDMETHOD macros we discussed back in Chapter 2; it translates to HRESULT __stdcall.

More Properties

You should add two other `short` properties to the interface, representing the month and the day. Since these are read-only, you can uncheck the <u>P</u>ut Function box when defining them. You should end up with an interface in your IDL file looking something like this:

```
[
    object,
    uuid(2D15E121-6CA4-11D1-A607-00A0C94BC9C3),
    dual,
    helpstring("ICalcEaster Interface"),
    pointer_default(unique)
]
interface ICalcEaster : IDispatch
{
    [propget, id(1), helpstring("property Year")]
     HRESULT Year([out, retval] short *pVal);
    [propput, id(1), helpstring("property Year")]
     HRESULT Year([in] short newVal);
    [propget, id(2), helpstring("property Month")]
     HRESULT Month([out, retval] short *pVal);
    [propget, id(3), helpstring("property Day")]
     HRESULT Day([out, retval] short *pVal);
};
```

Implementing The Properties

Notice that there are no data members in the `CCalcEaster` class to represent these properties yet — we've only dealt with the COM interface aspects, and not the C++ implementation details. We therefore need to add three variables of type `short` to the `CCalcEaster` class, and initialize them appropriately in the constructor:

```
class ATL_NO_VTABLE CCalcEaster :
    public CComObjectRootEx<CComSingleThreadModel>,
    public CComCoClass<CCalcEaster, &CLSID_CalcEaster>,
    public IDispatchImpl<ICalcEaster, &IID_ICalcEaster, &LIBID_SIMPLELib>
{
public:
    CCalcEaster() : m_Year(-1), m_Month(-1), m_Day(-1)
    {
    }

DECLARE_REGISTRY_RESOURCEID(IDR_CALCEASTER)

DECLARE_PROTECT_FINAL_CONSTRUCT()

BEGIN_COM_MAP(CCalcEaster)
    COM_INTERFACE_ENTRY(ICalcEaster)
    COM_INTERFACE_ENTRY(IDispatch)
END_COM_MAP()

private:
    short m_Year;
    short m_Month;
    short m_Day;
```

```
// ICalcEaster
public:
    STDMETHOD(get_Day)(/*[out, retval]*/ short *pVal);
    STDMETHOD(get_Month)(/*[out, retval]*/ short *pVal);
    STDMETHOD(get_Year)(/*[out, retval]*/ short *pVal);
    STDMETHOD(put_Year)(/*[in]*/ short newVal);
};
```

We can now edit the property put_ and get_ method skeletons to connect with these variables. Notice that this code doesn't use any proper error checking — we're just demonstrating the principles and keeping things simple.

```
STDMETHODIMP CCalcEaster::get_Year(short *pVal)
{
    // Retrieve the year value
    *pVal = m_Year;
    return S_OK;
}

STDMETHODIMP CCalcEaster::put_Year(short newVal)
{
    // Store the year value
    m_Year = newVal;
    return S_OK;
}

STDMETHODIMP CCalcEaster::get_Month(short *pVal)
{
    // Retrieve the month value
    *pVal = m_Month;
    return S_OK;
}

STDMETHODIMP CCalcEaster::get_Day(short *pVal)
{
    // Retrieve the day value
    *pVal = m_Day;
    return S_OK;
}
```

Adding Methods

Having added ways to get data in and out of the server, we now need to add the calculation method. Right-click on the `ICalcEaster` interface in ClassView again, but this time select **Add Method...** to bring up the **Add Method to Interface** dialog. Add a method called `CalculateEaster()` that takes no parameters, like this:

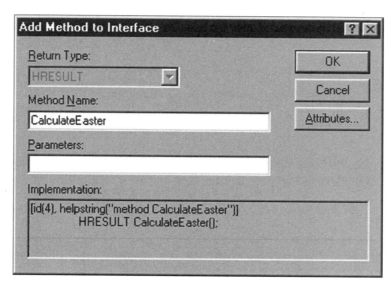

When you press **OK** and let the Wizard generate the code, you'll find another entry in the IDL file, and a skeleton function in the `CCalcEaster` class:

```
STDMETHODIMP CCalcEaster::CalculateEaster()
{
    // TODO: Add your implementation code here

    return S_OK;
}
```

All we need to do now is add the code to perform the calculation; we'll then be ready to test the server. In a real server, we'd probably pass the year as a parameter to this function rather than splitting it up as we have here, but that wouldn't have given us as much to demonstrate!

Calculating when Easter Sunday will fall is not trivial. There are several algorithms available, and the one you use will depend on factors such as what year you want, which part of the world you live in, and whether you're using the Julian or Gregorian calendar. We'll keep things simple, and use an algorithm suitable for calculating the Easter date for Europe and the US, for any date between 326AD and 4099AD. As you'll see, the algorithm is fairly complicated, and uses a lot of magic numbers! However, it does come up with the correct date.

```
STDMETHODIMP CCalcEaster::CalculateEaster()
{
    // First, check we have a year set, and that
    //  it is within the range for the calculation
    if(m_Year < 326 || m_Year > 4099)
        return E_FAIL;

    short first = m_Year / 100;       // First two digits
    short div19 = m_Year % 19;        // Remainder when divided by 19

    // Find the date of the PFM (Paschal Full Moon)
    short temp = (first - 15) / 2 + ((first > 26) ? -1 : 0) +
                ((first > 38) ? -1 : 0) + 202 - 11 * div19;

    if(first == 21 || first == 24 || first == 25 ||
                    first == 33 || first == 36 || first == 37)
        temp += -1;

    temp %= 30;

    short ta = temp + ((temp == 29) ? -1 : 0) +
                ((temp == 28 && div19 > 10) ? -1 : 0) + 21;

    // Find the next Sunday
    short tb = (ta - 19) % 7;
    temp = (40 - first) % 4;
    short tc = temp - ((temp > 1) ? -1 : 0) - ((temp == 3) ? -1 : 0);

    temp = m_Year % 100;
    short td = (temp + temp / 4) % 7;
    short te = ((20 - tb - tc - td) % 7) + 1;

    m_Day = ta + te;

    // Find the month
    if(m_Day > 61)
    {
        m_Day -= 61;
        m_Month = 5;
    }
    else if(m_Day > 31)
    {
        m_Day -= 31;
        m_Month = 4;
    }
    else
        m_Month = 3;

    return S_OK;
}
```

Once you've entered this code (or downloaded it from the Wrox Press web site), you'll be able to build the server, ready for testing. Notice that the server is automatically registered when you build the project.

Creating An ATL Test Client

Although ATL is primarily concerned with writing COM servers, it's possible to use it to write COM clients as well, so that's what we'll do next. As we build the client, you'll see:

❑   What an ATL executable looks like

❑   Some of ATL's window classes

❑   More of the ATL Wizards

Creating The Skeleton

Close your `Simple` project, and use the ATL COM AppWizard to create a new ATL project called `ATLClient`. All the Wizards will talk about servers, but ignore them — we're using ATL slightly out of context here to write a client!

ATL EXE servers are Win32 processes, and we'll use this section to talk about the code that the ATL Wizards generate for you. However, since we're writing a client process, we'll end up stripping out the server-specific code — after we've examined what it does, of course!

Put the project in a subdirectory of the `Simple` server's directory, so that we can use relative paths to the server's files. This time, make the project an executable, rather than a DLL or a service. As we said before, when you select the executable server type, you'll notice that executables don't have the option for supporting MFC, for merging the proxy-stub code, or for supporting MTS.

Once you've generated the project, a brief look will show that the list of files generated is broadly the same as for the DLL project. However, there are some important differences in content.

_tWinMain()

Most of `ATLClient.cpp` is taken up with the implementation of the `WinMain()` function, the standard entry point for Windows executables. This is actually specified as `_tWinMain()` so that it can be conditionally compiled for ANSI or for Unicode.

```
extern "C" int WINAPI _tWinMain(HINSTANCE hInstance,
    HINSTANCE /*hPrevInstance*/, LPTSTR lpCmdLine, int /*nShowCmd*/)
{
    lpCmdLine = GetCommandLine(); //this line necessary for _ATL_MIN_CRT

#if _WIN32_WINNT >= 0x0400 & defined(_ATL_FREE_THREADED)
    HRESULT hRes = CoInitializeEx(NULL, COINIT_MULTITHREADED);
#else
    HRESULT hRes = CoInitialize(NULL);
#endif
    _ASSERTE(SUCCEEDED(hRes));
    _Module.Init(ObjectMap, hInstance, &LIBID_ATLCLIENTLib);
    _Module.dwThreadID = GetCurrentThreadId();
    TCHAR szTokens[] = _T("-/");
```

```
        int nRet = 0;
        BOOL bRun = TRUE;
        LPCTSTR lpszToken = FindOneOf(lpCmdLine, szTokens);
        while (lpszToken != NULL)
        {
            if (lstrcmpi(lpszToken, _T("UnregServer"))==0)
            {
                _Module.UpdateRegistryFromResource(IDR_AtlClient, FALSE);
                nRet = _Module.UnregisterServer(TRUE);
                bRun = FALSE;
                break;
            }
            if (lstrcmpi(lpszToken, _T("RegServer"))==0)
            {
                _Module.UpdateRegistryFromResource(IDR_AtlClient, TRUE);
                nRet = _Module.RegisterServer(TRUE);
                bRun = FALSE;
                break;
            }
            lpszToken = FindOneOf(lpszToken, szTokens);
        }

        if (bRun)
        {
            _Module.StartMonitor();
#if _WIN32_WINNT >= 0x0400 & defined(_ATL_FREE_THREADED)
            hRes = _Module.RegisterClassObjects(CLSCTX_LOCAL_SERVER,
                REGCLS_MULTIPLEUSE | REGCLS_SUSPENDED);
            _ASSERTE(SUCCEEDED(hRes));
            hRes = CoResumeClassObjects();
#else
            hRes = _Module.RegisterClassObjects(CLSCTX_LOCAL_SERVER,
                REGCLS_MULTIPLEUSE);
#endif
            _ASSERTE(SUCCEEDED(hRes));

            MSG msg;
            while (GetMessage(&msg, 0, 0, 0))
                DispatchMessage(&msg);

            _Module.RevokeClassObjects();
            Sleep(dwPause); //wait for any threads to finish
        }

        _Module.Term();
        CoUninitialize();
        return nRet;
    }
```

If you've come to Windows programming through MFC or a similar class library that hides many of the details, it is possible that you've never seen a `WinMain()` function before. In the same way that a C or C++ program has to have a `main()` function, which is where execution commences, a Windows program must have a function called `WinMain()`. In many class libraries, it is buried deep in the library code.

Let's take a look at what _tWinMain() does.

```
extern "C" int WINAPI _tWinMain(HINSTANCE hInstance,
    HINSTANCE /*hPrevInstance*/, LPTSTR lpCmdLine, int /*nShowCmd*/)
{
    lpCmdLine = GetCommandLine(); //this line necessary for _ATL_MIN_CRT
```

This standard set of arguments will be familiar to anyone who has written a bare-bones Windows program:

❑ `hInstance` gives the instance handle of this task.

❑ `hPrevInstance` is a legacy from 16-bit days and is always `NULL` under Win32.

❑ `lpCmdLine` is used to pass in the command line string (but see below).

❑ `nShowCmd` says how the executable ought to display on startup — full-screen, as an icon, hidden, or normal. This parameter isn't used here.

_ATL_MIN_CRT

In the first line of code, we get the command line by means of a call to `GetCommandLine()`. You may be used to getting the command line from the `lpCmdLine` parameter, but that is not possible if you have the `_ATL_MIN_CRT` macro defined. This macro is defined for you automatically in release builds of ATL projects.

Again, we can see evidence of the care taken to ensure the efficiency of ATL-generated code. By default, the Visual C++ compiler links to the C run-time library (CRT), giving you access to the functions contained within that library. However, linking to the CRT means that startup code is automatically compiled in to your project, increasing the size of the executable image. This occurs even if you don't make any use of the CRT functions in your own code, due to the need to define static buffers for things like ANSI to Unicode conversion, `gmtime()`, and so on.

When `_ATL_MIN_CRT` is defined, ATL comes to the rescue by defining its own entry points for EXEs and DLLs, independent of the CRT's. This avoids incurring the overhead of the CRT startup code. However, there are cases when you *need* to make use of the CRT functions, and to do this you'll need to remove the `_ATL_MIN_CRT` macro from the settings of your project. There are a few CRT functions that you can use without requiring the startup code (such as the memory functions), but if you hit one that does require it, you will be able to tell because you'll receive a link error complaining about `_main` being missing:

```
error LNK2001:'unresolved external symbol _main
```

This error can appear when you build using one of the release configurations, not under a debug build. You can remove the _ATL_MIN_CRT macro by deleting it from the preprocessor definitions listed on the C/C++ tab of the Project Settings for each of the release configurations.

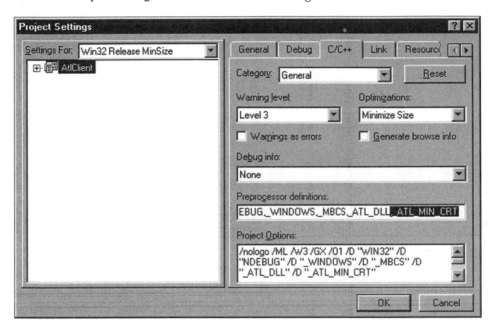

CoInitialize()

The second line of code makes sure that the COM libraries are loaded and ready to go, by calling CoInitialize().

```
#if _WIN32_WINNT >= 0x0400 & defined(_ATL_FREE_THREADED)
    HRESULT hRes = CoInitializeEx(NULL, COINIT_MULTITHREADED);
#else
    HRESULT hRes = CoInitialize(NULL);
#endif
    _ASSERTE(SUCCEEDED(hRes));
```

If our code is to run under NT 4.0 (or Windows 95 with DCOM installed), we have the option of making the main thread of the executable run in a multithreaded apartment by replacing the call to CoInitialize() with one to CoInitializeEx(). You will find that stdafx.h defines _ATL_APARTMENT_THREADED so that the second part of this conditional compilation is used. The call to CoInitialize() simply calls CoInitializeEx() with the COINIT_APARTMENTTHREADED option, to create an apartment-threaded executable. COM threading models are discussed in detail in Chapter 6.

Init()

If the COM initialization worked, the code then initializes the module object, and stores the current thread ID in its dwThreadID member. This thread will be the one implementing the message pump for the server, and storing its ID is necessary so that _Module knows where to send a WM_QUIT message when it is time for the server to shut down.

```
_Module.Init(ObjectMap, hInstance, &LIBID_ATLCLIENTLib);
_Module.dwThreadID = GetCurrentThreadId();
```

The LIBID of the type library is passed to Init() so that it can be stored in a static data member that will be used as the default type library for the implementation of dual interfaces.

All ATL classes have a static member called ObjectMain(). This is normally empty, but you can use it to perform once-only initialization when the EXE server starts, and cleanup when the EXE server shuts down. Init() will go through the object map and call ObjectMain(true) for every coclass that can be instantiated by COM. You can use this feature for creating static resources that will be used by objects created from the coclass.

Checking The Command Line

In the next section, the code parses the command line to determine whether the server should register or unregister itself:

```
TCHAR szTokens[] = _T("-/");

int nRet = 0;
BOOL bRun = TRUE;
LPCTSTR lpszToken = FindOneOf(lpCmdLine, szTokens);
while (lpszToken != NULL)
{
    if (lstrcmpi(lpszToken, _T("UnregServer"))==0)
    {
        _Module.UpdateRegistryFromResource(IDR_AtlClient, FALSE);
        nRet = _Module.UnregisterServer(TRUE);
        bRun = FALSE;
        break;
    }
    if (lstrcmpi(lpszToken, _T("RegServer"))==0)
    {
        _Module.UpdateRegistryFromResource(IDR_AtlClient, TRUE);
        nRet = _Module.RegisterServer(TRUE);
        bRun = FALSE;
        break;
    }
    lpszToken = FindOneOf(lpszToken, szTokens);
}
```

The code uses the helper function FindOneOf() to find the start of a command line parameter, and then compares it with "UnregServer" and "RegServer" to determine what action to take. If we're registering the server, the call to UpdateRegistryFromResource() adds the entries from the server's RGS file to the registry. The RGS file for an EXE server does two things: it adds the ProgIDs for all of the components in the server to registry, but it adds an AppID key as well. COM uses AppIDs to hold security information about EXE servers on Windows NT, including the account that the EXE server will run under, and the accounts that can launch the server and access any components created by it.

After this, `RegisterServer()` calls each of the classes listed in the object map, telling them to register themselves, and (as the parameter it receives is TRUE) also registers the type library. If we're unregistering, the call to `UpdateRegistryFromResource()` *removes* the entries indicated by the RGS file (and unregisters the type library), and then the server tells each of the classes to unregister themselves.

The Running Server

Registration is a standalone process, so if either of the registration flags was found, bRun is set to FALSE and the application exits. If the server *wasn't* started in order to register or unregister itself, it needs to register its class objects and go into a message loop.

```
    if (bRun)
    {
        _Module.StartMonitor();
#if _WIN32_WINNT >= 0x0400 & defined(_ATL_FREE_THREADED)
        hRes = _Module.RegisterClassObjects(CLSCTX_LOCAL_SERVER,
            REGCLS_MULTIPLEUSE | REGCLS_SUSPENDED);
        _ASSERTE(SUCCEEDED(hRes));
        hRes = CoResumeClassObjects();
#else
        hRes = _Module.RegisterClassObjects(CLSCTX_LOCAL_SERVER,
            REGCLS_MULTIPLEUSE);
#endif
        _ASSERTE(SUCCEEDED(hRes));

        MSG msg;
        while (GetMessage(&msg, 0, 0, 0))
            DispatchMessage(&msg);

        _Module.RevokeClassObjects();
        Sleep(dwPause); //wait for any threads to finish
    }
```

First, let's take a look at the calls to `RegisterClassObjects()` and `RevokeClassObjects()`. In Chapter 2, we said that when an EXE server starts, it must create the class objects for all of the components that it serves and register them with the system. We also said that just before the server shuts down, it must tell the system that these class objects are no longer available by revoking them. `_Module.RegisterClassObjects()` consults the object map and then creates and registers a class object for each creatable component; `_Module.RevokeClassObjects()` simply reverses the process.

There are two options here. If the server is free-threaded (that is, it can use more than one thread), COM will create threads for the server as they are needed, but there is a potential problem: if all of the class objects are registered together, you could get into a situation where a client requests an object before all of the class objects have been registered. If the requested object depends on a component created by a class object that has not yet been registered, object creation will fail.

The first conditional compilation code registers the class objects with the `REGCLS_SUSPENDED` flag, telling COM to 'remember' the class objects but not to allow anyone to call them until `CoResumeClassObjects()` is called. This is not a problem with apartment-threaded servers because there will only be one thread at this point in the initialization process, and that will be busy registering the class objects rather than accepting object creation requests.

After the conditional compilation code comes a message loop that has two purposes. A thread that's in a single-threaded apartment must have a message loop, because this type of apartment uses Windows messages to pass object creation and method calls. Multithreaded apartments (used by free-threaded EXE servers) do not need a message loop. However, both apartment-threaded *and* free-threaded servers use the message loop for another purpose. When _tWinMain() returns, the process will end, so there must be some code that prevents the end of the function from being reached before all the objects created by this server have been released.

When the message loop receives a WM_QUIT message, GetMessage() will return 0, the message loop will end and the class objects will be revoked ready for shutdown. When the server revokes the class objects, it must make sure that they are all released in one go, just as they all had to be registered in one go. This is the purpose of the monitor thread that was started with the call to _Module.StartMonitor(), and which we'll look at in a moment.

Term()

After the message loop has finished, the _Module.Term() method is called:

```
_Module.Term();
```

This does three things. First, it iterates through the object map and calls ObjectMain(false) for every coclass that can be instantiated by COM (compare this with Init(), which calls ObjectMain(true)). This allows you to perform cleanup for each class.

Next, it calls all of the registered **termination functions**. If your objects implement dual interfaces, ATL will cache the type information that describes each interface, and a map of the names of the methods on that interface. This is performed as an optimization, and these caches must be cleared before the server shuts down. To do this, ATL registers a termination function for every dual interface implemented by every component in the server.

Finally, if you define the _ATL_DEBUG_INTERFACES symbol in stdafx.h, ATL will track all reference counts made on an object. The Term() function checks these reference counts to make sure that they are zero — if they're not, a reference count leak has occurred and Term() will write a warning message to the output debug stream (the Output window when you run a server under the Visual C++ debugger).

CoUninitialize()

The final step is to call CoUninitialize(), to tell COM that the application is exiting. Every time we use CoInitialize() or CoInitializeEx() to initialize COM, we must also call CoUninitialize() on the same thread when we have finished using COM.

```
    CoUninitialize();
    return nRet;
}
```

CExeModule And The Monitor Thread

EXE servers do not use CComModule. Instead, a new class called CExeModule that derives from CComModule is defined in Stdafx.h:

```
class CExeModule : public CComModule
{
public:
    LONG Unlock();
    DWORD dwThreadID;
    HANDLE hEventShutdown;
    void MonitorShutdown();
    bool StartMonitor();
    bool bActivity;
};
extern CExeModule _Module;
```

As well as dwThreadID (which we've already met), this class has data members called hEventShutdown and bActivity, and methods that manipulate or will be used by the monitor thread. The monitor thread is created when _tWinMain() calls StartMonitor():

```
bool CExeModule::StartMonitor()
{
    hEventShutdown = CreateEvent(NULL, false, false, NULL);
    if (hEventShutdown == NULL)
        return false;
    DWORD dwThreadID;
    HANDLE h = CreateThread(NULL, 0, MonitorProc, this, 0, &dwThreadID);
    return (h != NULL);
}
```

This creates the hEventShutdown event object and indicates that the thread function should be MonitorProc(), which simply calls the MonitorShutdown() method in CExeModule:

```
static DWORD WINAPI MonitorProc(void* pv)
{
    CExeModule* p = (CExeModule*)pv;
    p->MonitorShutdown();
    return 0;
}
```

This method waits on the event object. In effect, this means that it sleeps until the event object is signaled. This occurs in Unlock() when the module lock count falls to zero, indicating that no more objects are alive.

```
LONG CExeModule::Unlock()
{
    LONG l = CComModule::Unlock();
    if(l == 0)
    {
        bActivity = true;
        SetEvent(hEventShutdown); // tell monitor that we transitioned to zero
    }
    return l;
}
```

At this point, all of the class objects must be revoked in such a way that no more client requests can be made:

```
//Monitors the shutdown event
void CExeModule::MonitorShutdown()
{
    while (1)
    {
        WaitForSingleObject(hEventShutdown, INFINITE);
        DWORD dwWait=0;
        do
        {
            bActivity = false;
            dwWait = WaitForSingleObject(hEventShutdown, dwTimeOut);
        } while (dwWait == WAIT_OBJECT_0);
        // timed out
        if (!bActivity && m_nLockCnt == 0) // if no activity let's really bail
        {
#if _WIN32_WINNT >= 0x0400 & defined(_ATL_FREE_THREADED)
            CoSuspendClassObjects();
            if (!bActivity && m_nLockCnt == 0)
#endif
                break;
        }
    }
    CloseHandle(hEventShutdown);
    PostThreadMessage(dwThreadID, WM_QUIT, 0, 0);
}
```

The first call to `WaitForSingleObject()` suspends the monitor thread until `Unlock()` wakes it up. The second call waits for a default timeout of 5 seconds to ensure that the server is not being used. If this is the case, and the server is free threaded, then `CoSuspendClassObjects()` is called to tell COM to suspend the class objects to disallow any more requests to activate objects. Finally, the event object is released and `PostThreadMessage()` is called to post `WM_QUIT` to the message loop in `_tWinMain()`, and hence initiate the shutdown of the process.

Adding A Dialog

Well, we've talked about a lot of things, but we still have an application that doesn't do anything. The next step, then, is to add a dialog, which we'll use to start up the server and test it. Use the Insert | New ATL Object... menu item to bring up the ATL Object Wizard dialog, and select the Miscellaneous tab:

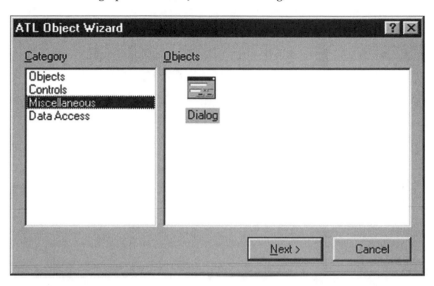

Since Dialog is the only choice, click on Next to bring up the Properties dialog:

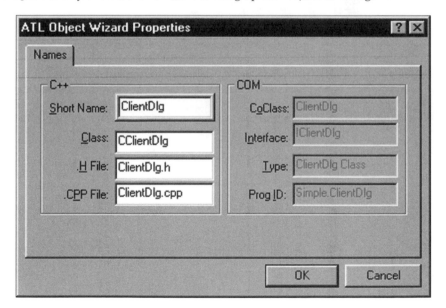

Give the dialog a suitable Ｓhort Name, such as ClientDlg, and press OK. The Wizard will add two files to the project, representing the dialog header and implementation. The header file (ClientDlg.h) shows that we have a dialog class derived from CAxDialogImpl<>:

```cpp
// ClientDlg.h : Declaration of the CClientDlg

#ifndef __CLIENTDLG_H_
#define __CLIENTDLG_H_

#include "resource.h"        // main symbols
#include <atlhost.h>

/////////////////////////////////////////////////////////////////////////////
// CClientDlg
class CClientDlg :
   public CAxDialogImpl<CClientDlg>
{
public:
   CClientDlg()
   {
   }

   ~CClientDlg()
   {
   }

   enum { IDD = IDD_CLIENTDLG };

BEGIN_MSG_MAP(CClientDlg)
   MESSAGE_HANDLER(WM_INITDIALOG, OnInitDialog)
   COMMAND_ID_HANDLER(IDOK, OnOK)
   COMMAND_ID_HANDLER(IDCANCEL, OnCancel)
END_MSG_MAP()
// Handler prototypes:
//   LRESULT MessageHandler(UINT uMsg, WPARAM wParam,
                            LPARAM lParam, BOOL& bHandled);
//   LRESULT CommandHandler(WORD wNotifyCode, WORD wID,
                            HWND hWndCtl, BOOL& bHandled);
//   LRESULT NotifyHandler(int idCtrl, LPNMHDR pnmh, BOOL& bHandled);

   LRESULT OnInitDialog(UINT uMsg, WPARAM wParam, LPARAM lParam, BOOL& bHandled)
   {
      return 1;  // Let the system set the focus
   }

   LRESULT OnOK(WORD wNotifyCode, WORD wID, HWND hWndCtl, BOOL& bHandled)
   {
      EndDialog(wID);
      return 0;
   }

   LRESULT OnCancel(WORD wNotifyCode, WORD wID, HWND hWndCtl, BOOL& bHandled)
   {
      EndDialog(wID);
      return 0;
   }
};

#endif //__CLIENTDLG_H_
```

Notice that CAxDialogImpl<>, the class that contains the implementation of the dialog box, takes our class as a template parameter. In effect, we're using the template to customize the base class to work with our derived dialog class. The ATL dialog implementation class knows how to create and use dialogs, but it knows nothing about what our particular dialog wants to do. Using a template is a convenient way to add our custom dialog behavior to the standard template class. This is a common idiom in ATL; we'll see precisely how it's used when we take a closer look at some of the classes that ATL provides, in the next chapter.

Although this code doesn't use MFC, we can see some similarities with the way MFC handles dialogs. Just like MFC dialogs, the ATL dialog is linked to a dialog resource (IDD_CLIENTDLG), and it uses a message map to implement message handlers. We'll see more about *exactly* how it does this in Chapter 9, but it's fairly clear from the code that by default we get message handlers for WM_INITDIALOG, and the OK and Cancel buttons. As you can see from their implementations, they don't do very much right now, and they've been placed inline for efficiency. When you come to implement them for yourself, you may wish to move the code into the .cpp file.

Displaying The Dialog

We want to structure our application so that it displays the dialog automatically on startup, and so that dismissing the dialog will terminate the application. We'll start by adding code to the _tWinMain() function to display the dialog, but you must first #include "ClientDlg.h" near the top of ATLClient.cpp.

Tidying Up The Code

Before we start, though, we can do a little weeding of the code skeleton. We've generated ourselves an ATL *server* executable, and we've been looking at what's in the skeleton code. However, you know that we're actually implementing a *client* program here, so we're not acting as a server for any COM objects. Some of the source code in the ATLClient.cpp file is therefore surplus to our requirements, and we can safely remove it.

The first thing to trim is stdafx.h. The code implemented by CExeModule was there to prevent the server shutting down before all its objects are released. Since we have no objects, we can just remove it, can't we? Well, not quite. The windowing classes used by the dialog class use _Module, so we must still define that global object. However, it can be created from the simpler CComModule, so edit the relevant code in stdafx.h to look like this:

```
#include <atlbase.h>
extern CComModule _Module;
#include <atlcom.h>
#include <atlwin.h>
```

Notice that adding a dialog to the project adds a #include for atlwin.h to this header file automatically.

Since we have no COM objects, we don't need the object map, and since we aren't going to check the command line for registration options, all that code (and the `FindOneOf()` function) can disappear too. The methods to delete from `ATLClient.cpp` are `MonitorProc()`, `Unlock()`, `MonitorShutdown()`, `StartMonitor()` and `FindOneOf()`.

Furthermore, you don't need the headers for COM objects served by the process (because it doesn't serve any) or the `dwTimeOut` or `dwPause` variables. Finally, you need to change the declaration of `_Module` to be an instance of `CComModule`, and remove all the code from `_tWinMain()` that registers and unregisters the server and revokes the class factory objects. When you've done all this, `ATLClient.cpp` should look like this:

```cpp
#include "stdafx.h"
#include "resource.h"
#include "ClientDlg.h"

CComModule _Module;

/////////////////////////////////////////////////////////////////////////////
//
extern "C" int WINAPI _tWinMain(HINSTANCE hInstance,
    HINSTANCE /*hPrevInstance*/, LPSTR lpCmdLine, int /*nShowCmd*/)
{
    HRESULT hRes = CoInitialize(NULL);
    _ASSERTE(SUCCEEDED(hRes));
    _Module.Init(NULL, hInstance);

    MSG msg;
    while (GetMessage(&msg, 0, 0, 0))
        DispatchMessage(&msg);

    CoUninitialize();
    return 0;
}
```

Notice that we're using `CoInitialize()` so that a single threaded apartment is created; this is required because we want to create a COM object in the dialog. The message loop remains because the dialog will be modeless, and your code must dispatch messages to it.

Clearing Up The Resources

The project has an IDL file, but as you know, this describes interfaces and type information to be used in the type library. Our project uses neither, so you can remove the IDL from the build — just select it in FileView and press the *Delete* button on your keyboard.

In a normal ATL EXE server, ATL will bind the type library created by the MIDL compiler to the EXE. This is because it is usually required for marshaling, and providing it as a resource means that wherever the EXE goes, the type library will follow. However, we don't need this facility — we neither have nor need an IDL file from which to generate a type library. So, select the View | Resource Includes... menu item to get the following dialog:

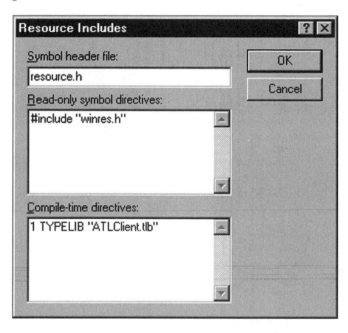

The line in the Compile-time directives box binds the type library, so remove it. Visual Studio will respond with a dialog asking if you really do want to do this, but you can just click OK.

Creating The Dialog

Now we can add the code to create and display the dialog. To do this, add the following code to the _tWinMain() function:

```
// Create and show a dialog
CClientDlg dlg;
dlg.Create(NULL);
dlg.ShowWindow(SW_SHOWNORMAL);

MSG msg;
while (GetMessage(&msg, 0, 0, 0))
{
    TranslateMessage(&msg);
    DispatchMessage(&msg);
}
```

You can see that we have declared an object (dlg) of class CClientDlg, called its Create() member to create the window for the class (the parameter is for the handle to the dialog's parent — it doesn't have one), and then called ShowWindow() to make the window show itself. ATL's dialog class is derived from a generic window class, CWindow, which provides thin wrappers for the Win32 APIs related to windows, much as MFC's CWnd class does. You'll see a lot more of CWindow in Chapter 7.

Note that we have also changed the message loop itself. The added call to TranslateMessage() ensures that virtual key messages are translated into character messages (WM_KEYDOWN and WM_KEYUP combinations produce a WM_CHAR, for example).

OnCancel()

Now we need to change the code in CClientDlg::OnCancel() to close the dialog and dismiss the server by sending a WM_QUIT message to the application. The Wizard-generated dialog class code assumes that it will run as a modal dialog, so we need to replace the call to EndDialog() with one to DestroyWindow():

```
LRESULT CClientDlg::OnCancel(WORD wNotifyCode, WORD wID,
                             HWND hWndCtl, BOOL& bHandled)
{
    DestroyWindow();
    PostQuitMessage(0);
    return 0;
}
```

At this stage, you can run the application and dismiss the dialog by pressing the close icon or the Cancel button.

> *Don't try to close the dialog with the OK button — the default implementation of OnOK() uses EndDialog(), which is only suitable for use when you display the dialog with DoModal() — and we've used ShowWindow() here. When we add code to the handler for this button, we'll need to add a call to PostQuitMessage(); without it, you'll get an assertion failure in debug builds, and running-but-invisible tasks in release builds.*

Editing The Dialog Resource

The next step is to edit the dialog resource so that it allows us to enter the year for which we want to calculate the date of Easter. Go to ResourceView and double-click the IDD_CLIENTDLG icon to open the dialog resource in Visual C++'s resource editor.

Change the caption of the OK button to read Calculate. We'll add code that will respond to this button to calculate the date of Easter for any year.

Now add an edit box to the dialog, and change its ID to IDC_YEAR. On the Styles page, check the Number check box, so that users of the dialog can only enter numbers into the edit box.

Add a static text control just to the left of the dialog, bring up its properties window, and set its caption to Enter Year:.

Finally, bring up the **Properties** window for the dialog itself. On the **More Styles** page, check the **Center** box. This will make the dialog appear in the center of the screen automatically when it's displayed. Your dialog resource should now look something like this:

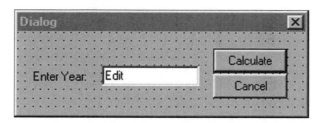

Now we're ready to change the code in `CClientDlg::OnOK()` to test our server. First, we need to get information about the server into our client. We'll do this in two ways, so that you can compare the methods. First, we'll use the MIDL compiler-generated header, as you've seen in earlier chapters. Then, we'll use the type library and the Visual C++ compiler's preprocessor directive, `#import`.

Using MIDL Compiler-Generated Files

Add the following line just below the existing `#include` directives at the top of `ClientDlg.cpp`:

```
#include "stdafx.h"
#include "ClientDlg.h"
#include "..\Simple.h"
```

This brings the header file that contains the server's interface and GUID definitions into the project, so that we can use them from code in the client dialog. Next, move the implementation of `CClientDlg::OnOK()` from the header into the `.cpp` file and replace it with the code shown below:

```
LRESULT CClientDlg::OnOK(WORD wNotifyCode, WORD wID, HWND hWndCtl, BOOL& bHandled)
{
    ICalcEaster* p = NULL;
    HRESULT hr = CoCreateInstance(__uuidof(CalcEaster), NULL, CLSCTX_ALL,
                                  __uuidof(ICalcEaster),
                                  reinterpret_cast<void**>(&p));
    if(SUCCEEDED(hr))
    {
        int Year = GetDlgItemInt(IDC_YEAR);
        p->put_Year(Year);
        p->CalculateEaster();

        short Day = -1;
        short Month = -1;

        // We should really check the return values of the next two method calls
        //  but the logic would get quite messy
        hr = p->get_Day(&Day);
        hr = p->get_Month(&Month);
```

```
        // Create a string containing the date of Easter Day in mm/dd format
        TCHAR buff[255] = {0};
        wsprintf(buff, _T("Easter: %d/%d in %d"), Month, Day, Year);
        MessageBox(buff, _T("Calculation"));

        p->Release();
    }
    else
    {
        // Don't Release() the pointer if CoCreateInstance() failed
        TCHAR buff[255] = {0};
        wsprintf(buff, _T("Error: 0x%x "), hr);
        MessageBox(buff, _T("Error"));
    }
    return 0;
}
```

The first part of the code declares an `ICalcEaster` pointer, then calls `CoCreateInstance()` to create an instance of our `CalcEaster` coclass, asking for a pointer to that interface.

```
ICalcEaster* p = NULL;
HRESULT hr = CoCreateInstance(__uuidof(CalcEaster), NULL, CLSCTX_ALL,
                             __uuidof(ICalcEaster),
                             reinterpret_cast<void**>(&p));
```

Next, we check the return value of `CoCreateInstance()` to determine whether we successfully created the object. If not, we display a simple message and leave the function. Note that we don't call `Release()` on the pointer unless `CoCreateInstance()` succeeded.

If `CoCreateInstance()` *did* succeed, we can set the year, call the `CalculateEaster()` method, and get back the day and month.

The year that we pass to the `put_Year()` method is obtained by calling the `CWindow::GetDlgItemInt()` method. This is a thin wrapper around the Win32 `GetDlgItemInt()` function, which returns an integer version of the text in a control. In this case, we're getting the value of the year entered by the user in our `IDC_YEAR` edit box.

> *You can see that the requirement for COM methods to return HRESULTs can lead to some ugly code. We have to declare some storage (the shorts Month and Day) and pass pointers to the get_() methods, and we should be checking the return values of each of the method calls to check whether they succeeded.*

Finally, we display a message box with the results of the calculation, and then call `Release()` on the interface pointer to release the object. Once again, we are using a thin wrapper for the Win32 API provided by ATL's `CWindow` class to display the message box.

When you build and run the project, you should see something like this:

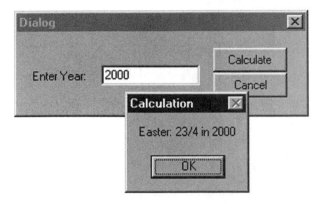

Using The Type Library: The #import Statement

The second way that we're going to test the server is by importing the type library using Visual C++ compiler COM support. Remove the #include directive for Simple.h from the top of ClientDlg.cpp, and replace it with the line shown highlighted below:

```
#include "stdafx.h"
#include "ClientDlg.h"
#import "..\Simple.tlb"
```

#import is a preprocessor directive that instructs Visual C++ to use the information in the specified type library to generate wrapper classes for the interfaces in that type library. These wrapper classes have a number of advantages over the header files that the MIDL compiler generates:

- ❑ The wrapper class functions can return values specified as [retval] directly

- ❑ The wrappers can throw errors instead of returning HRESULTs

- ❑ The wrappers hide the details of reference counting

- ❑ The wrappers replace certain types (VARIANTs and BSTRs) with classes (_variant_t, _bstr_t)

- ❑ The wrappers allow property methods to be accessed like data members

When processed, the #import directive produces the header for the wrapper classes in a file called Simple.tlh, and the implementation for these classes in a file called Simple.tli. These files will appear in the *output* directory for the current configuration. If you compile ClientDlg.cpp now, you can see these files being produced, but you'll get several compiler errors. This is because #import generates some C++ classes to wrap our server, and you'll need to change the implementation to use them. We'll come to those changes in good time; for now, let's look at the files that were generated.

If you examine them closely, you'll find that there's a big difference between the MIDL compiler-generated interface classes and those generated by #import. The former have no implementation at all — they're abstract classes designed purely to translate a vtable layout into C++ terms. The #import-generated classes, on the other hand, have an implementation for the wrapper methods that will be compiled into your application.

Let's open the files generated by #import to see what they contain. First, Simple.tlh (slightly edited for length):

```
#include <comdef.h>

namespace SIMPLELib {

// Forward references and typedefs
struct /* coclass */ CalcEaster;
struct __declspec(uuid("b824074d-4995-11d3-88e4-00105a68bf5d"))
/* dual interface */ ICalcEaster;

// Smart pointer typedef declarations
_COM_SMARTPTR_TYPEDEF(ICalcEaster, __uuidof(ICalcEaster));

// Type library items
struct __declspec(uuid("5dc86882-58f2-11d1-a159-04dcf8c00000"))
CalcEaster;
    // [ default ] interface ICalcEaster

struct __declspec(uuid("b824074d-4995-11d3-88e4-00105a68bf5d"))
ICalcEaster : IDispatch
{
    // Property data
    __declspec(property(get=GetYear,put=PutYear))
    short Year;
    __declspec(property(get=GetMonth))
    short Month;
    __declspec(property(get=GetDay))
    short Day;

    // Wrapper methods for error-handling
    short GetYear ( );
    void PutYear (
        short pVal );
    short GetMonth ( );
    short GetDay ( );
    HRESULT CalculateEaster ( );

    // Raw methods provided by interface
    virtual HRESULT __stdcall get_Year (
        short * pVal ) = 0;
    virtual HRESULT __stdcall put_Year (
        short pVal ) = 0;
    virtual HRESULT __stdcall get_Month (
        short * pVal ) = 0;
    virtual HRESULT __stdcall get_Day (
        short * pVal ) = 0;
    virtual HRESULT __stdcall raw_CalculateEaster ( ) = 0;
};

// Wrapper method implementations
#include "c:\windows\desktop\simple\atlclient\debug\Simple.tli"

} // namespace SIMPLELib
```

The first thing that you can see is the `#include` for `comdef.h`. This header file contains the definitions for the classes that are used in the generated wrappers (`_com_ptr_t<>`, `_bstr_t`, `_variant_t` and `_com_error`). If you ever want to use any of these classes in your own code without `#import`ing a type library, you can just `#include <comdef.h>` directly.

Next, you can see the start of a namespace called `SIMPLELib`. By default, all the code produced by `#import` will be wrapped in a namespace with the same name as the type library (its internal name as specified in IDL, *not* its filename). This not only helps to avoid naming collisions, but can also help the readability of your code. If you find that the namespace is not to your liking, you could change the directive in `ClientDlg.cpp` and rename it by using the `rename_namespace` attribute, or remove it completely by using `no_namespace`:

```
// This line would rename the namespace to 'Wrox'
#import "..\Simple.tlb" rename_namespace("Wrox")

// This line would generate the wrappers without a namespace
#import "..\Simple.tlb" no_namespace
```

Smart Pointers

Within the `namespace` block, you can see several items of interest. The first item (ignoring the forward references) is the "smart pointer typedef declaration" for the `ICalcEaster` interface:

```
// Smart pointer typedef declarations
_COM_SMARTPTR_TYPEDEF(ICalcEaster, __uuidof(ICalcEaster));
```

This uses the `_COM_SMARTPTR_TYPEDEF()` macro to declare a template specialization of a class called `_com_ptr_t<>`. This class takes two template parameters: the name of an interface and its IID. The `_COM_SMARTPTR_TYPEDEF()` macro takes the same parameters as `_com_ptr_t<>`, and declares a `typedef`'d specialization of that class with the name of the interface plus a suffix of `Ptr`. Thus, the line shown above declares `ICalcEasterPtr` to be a smart pointer class for our server's `ICalcEaster` interface. The IID is obtained from the `ICalcEaster` interface using the `__uuidof()` operator.

`_com_ptr_t<>` specializations are called "smart pointers" because they are used like pointers (we use the indirect member selection operator `->` to access most of their functionality), but take responsibility for allocating and freeing the memory that the pointer represents when it's no longer in use. The COM smart pointers that we're discussing here take responsibility for freeing interface pointers (they call `Release()` on them). You may come across other classes that are also referred to as smart pointers, but which have different capabilities and uses.

Type Library Items

Following the smart pointer `typedef`s, we have the "type library items". The first item is a `struct` for the coclass, `CalcEaster`. All that the `struct` does here is associate a CLSID with `CalcEaster` so that we can use the expression `__uuidof(CalcEaster)` in our code. This is similar to what the MIDL compiler does in a header file by using `DECLSPEC_UUID()`.

```
struct __declspec(uuid("5dc86882-58f2-11d1-a159-04dcf8c00000"))
CalcEaster;
    // [ default ] interface ICalcEaster
```

111

The only other item in the type library section is the `ICalcEaster` interface itself. You can see the use of `__declspec(uuid())` to associate the IID with the interface, so that it can be retrieved with `__uuidof()`. You can also see a selection of methods in the body of the `struct`, which is split into three main sections.

Property Data

The first section is entitled "property data", and it uses another extension to the Microsoft C++ compiler that allows COM properties to be called as if they were public data members.

```
// Property data
__declspec(property(get=GetYear,put=PutYear))
short Year;
__declspec(property(get=GetMonth))
short Month;
__declspec(property(get=GetDay))
short Day;
```

The `property()` attribute creates what Microsoft terms a **virtual data member** of a class. That is, although it looks like the class should contain a `Year` data member of type `short`, and you can write code that manipulates `Year` as if it were a data member of the class, it doesn't actually exist as a data member!

Instead, the compiler converts any code that manipulates `Year` into the appropriate function calls using the information provided in the `get` and `put` statements, depending on whether `Year` is being used as an rvalue or an lvalue. The same is true of the `Month` and `Day` properties, except they are read-only, since there's no `put` in the property specification. This means that `Month` and `Day` can only be used as rvalues — you'll get compiler errors if you try to use either of them on the left side of an assignment.

```
// These two statements are equivalent
p->Year = 1984;
p->PutYear(1984);

// This will cause the compiler to emit an error
// Day is a read-only property
p->Day = 21;
```

Note that the functions specified in the get and put statements need to be independently defined elsewhere in the class. We'll see that they are in the next section.

Wrapper Methods

The second section holds the wrapper methods. There is a wrapper method for each method in the original interface.

```
// Wrapper methods for error-handling
short GetYear ( );
void PutYear (
    short pVal );
short GetMonth ( );
short GetDay ( );
HRESULT CalculateEaster ( );
```

These wrapper methods do three things:

❑ They return [retval] parameters directly

❑ They throw errors if there is a failure in the method call

❑ They use _bstr_t and _variant_t types in place of standard VARIANTs and BSTRs (not shown here, because our example doesn't use these types)

These wrappers need implementations, which can be found in Simple.tli:

```
inline short ICalcEaster::GetYear ( ) {
    short _result;
    HRESULT _hr = get_Year(&_result);
    if (FAILED(_hr)) _com_issue_errorex(_hr, this, __uuidof(this));
    return _result;
}

inline void ICalcEaster::PutYear ( short pVal ) {
    HRESULT _hr = put_Year(pVal);
    if (FAILED(_hr)) _com_issue_errorex(_hr, this, __uuidof(this));
}

inline short ICalcEaster::GetMonth ( ) {
    short _result;
    HRESULT _hr = get_Month(&_result);
    if (FAILED(_hr)) _com_issue_errorex(_hr, this, __uuidof(this));
    return _result;
}

inline short ICalcEaster::GetDay ( ) {
    short _result;
    HRESULT _hr = get_Day(&_result);
    if (FAILED(_hr)) _com_issue_errorex(_hr, this, __uuidof(this));
    return _result;
}

inline HRESULT ICalcEaster::CalculateEaster ( ) {
    HRESULT _hr = raw_CalculateEaster();
    if (FAILED(_hr)) _com_issue_errorex(_hr, this, __uuidof(this));
    return _hr;
}
```

These simple inline functions simply call the raw versions of the methods, check the HRESULTs for failure, and throw a C++ error via the _com_issue_errorex() function if the method call failed.

Raw Interface Methods

The raw interface methods are declared in the third section of the struct. You can see that the properties are prefixed with get_ or put_, as appropriate, and the methods are prefixed with raw_:

```
// Raw methods provided by interface
virtual HRESULT __stdcall get_Year (
    short * pVal ) = 0;
virtual HRESULT __stdcall put_Year (
    short pVal ) = 0;
virtual HRESULT __stdcall get_Month (
    short * pVal ) = 0;
virtual HRESULT __stdcall get_Day (
    short * pVal ) = 0;
virtual HRESULT __stdcall raw_CalculateEaster ( ) = 0;
```

These method declarations are here to match the vtable of this `struct` with the vtable of the `ICalcEaster` interface, which is pretty important since the use of vtables depends on their layout, and not on method or property names. These method declarations are entirely equivalent to the ones generated by the MIDL compiler that we used earlier. Remember how we saw in Chapter 2 that the names of the methods don't affect the layout of the vtable.

Using The Wrappers

Now that we've seen the form that the wrappers take, it's time to put them to use. Replace the code in `CClientDlg::OnOK()` with the implementation shown below:

```
LRESULT CClientDlg::OnOK(WORD wNotifyCode, WORD wID, HWND hWndCtl, BOOL& bHandled)
{
    try
    {
        SIMPLELib::ICalcEasterPtr p(__uuidof(SIMPLELib::CalcEaster));

        p->Year = GetDlgItemInt(IDC_YEAR);
        p->CalculateEaster();

        // Create a string containing the date of Easter Day in mm/dd format
        TCHAR buff[255] = {0};
        wsprintf(buff, _T("Easter: %d/%d in %d"), p->Month, p->Day, p->Year);
        MessageBox(buff, _T("Calculation"));
    }
    catch(const _com_error& Err)
    {
        TCHAR buff[255] = {0};
        wsprintf(buff, _T("Error: 0x%x "), Err.Error());
        MessageBox(buff, _T("Error"));
    }
    return 0;
}
```

You should be able to see that the essential structure of this code is the same as the previous example:

❏ Create an instance of the `CalcEaster` coclass

❏ Set the year

❏ Tell the component to calculate Easter

❏ Display a message box with the results

The differences are important, however:

❏ We don't call `CoCreateInstance()` because we make use of one of the `_com_ptr_t<>` constructors:

```
SIMPLELib::ICalcEasterPtr p(__uuidof(SIMPLELib::CalcEaster));
```

This constructor takes the CLSID of a component, creates an instance of it, and queries for the appropriate interface (in this case, `ICalcEaster`), storing this in the smart pointer. If the underlying call to `CoCreateInstance()` fails, the constructor throws an error.

❑   We have complete error handling on *all* method calls thanks to the `try-catch` block, and the logic is cleaner because of it.

❑   We set and get the properties directly, as if they were data members.

❑   We don't call `Release()` because the smart pointer will handle that for us. This also has the benefit of further simplifying the error-handling logic.

Enabling Exception Handling

When you compile this code, you will get a warning that exception handling hasn't been enabled:

warning C4530: C++ exception handler used, but unwind semantics are not enabled. Specify -GX

What does this mean in practice? If you don't have exception handling enabled and an exception occurs, then any objects with automatic storage (that is, local objects) in the stack frame between the function doing the `throw` and the function `catch`ing the exception won't be properly destroyed.

You will need to enable exception handling for all the configurations in the project to ensure that everything works as it should in all circumstances. You can enable exception handling by using the Project | Settings... menu item to display the Project Settings dialog. Change the Settings For at the top-left of the dialog to say All Configurations, go to the C/C++ tab and select C++ Language from the Category list, then check the box labeled Enable exception handling.

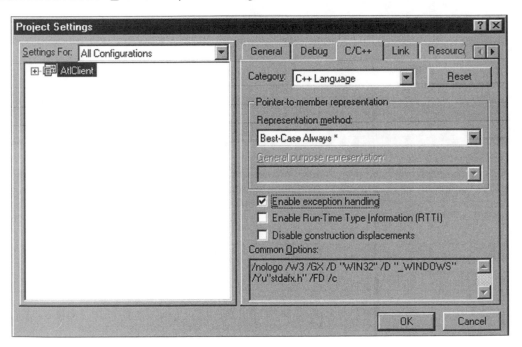

The reason why you have to change the settings is that by default, all ATL projects have no facility for exception handling. This is another optimization measure designed to keep the size of the code down. If you want to make use of exception handling within an ATL project, you'll need to make sure that you have explicitly enabled it.

In most cases, you can avoid using code that will throw exceptions in your ATL project. ATL code itself doesn't throw C++ exceptions, for example, and neither does any raw Win32 or COM code that you use. If you do need to use code that will throw or handle exceptions, you may still be able to get away without enabling exception handling in your project, but you should only do this after carefully analyzing the code you're using and if module size is an issue. In general, if you see the warning, enable exception handling. If you don't, don't.

Now you can run the project and see that it still works.

Testing The Server From Visual Basic

If you have access to Visual Basic, it is very easy to write the equivalent test application for our server:

❑ Create a **Standard EXE** project

❑ Add a reference to the server's type library (Simple 1.0 Type Library) using **P**roject | **R**eferences...

❑ Add a command button and text box to the form

❑ Add the following code to the button's `Click` handler:

```
Private Sub cmdCalculate_Click()
On Error GoTo err_Generic
    Dim itf As SIMPLELib.ICalcEaster
    Set itf = New SIMPLELib.CalcEaster

    itf.Year = CInt(txtYear)
    itf.CalculateEaster

    ' Output the date of Easter Day in mm/dd format
    MsgBox "Easter: " & itf.Month & "/" & itf.Day & " in " & itf.Year
    Exit Sub

err_Generic:
    MsgBox "Error: " & Err.Number & vbCrLf & Err.Description
End Sub
```

The code shows that the server can be controlled from Visual Basic as well as from a Visual C++ client.

Perhaps the most interesting thing about this code is that it shows how to declare interface references in Visual Basic. The variable `itf` *is declared as being of type* `SIMPLELib.ICalcEaster` — *in other words,* `itf` *is a reference to an* `ICalcEaster` *interface. The following line of code creates an instance of the* `CalcEaster` *coclass and* `QueryInterface()`*s for the* `ICalcEaster` *interface:*

```
Set itf = New SIMPLELib.CalcEaster
```

You may be more used to seeing object references used in Visual Basic, such as the following line of code:

```
Dim obj As SIMPLELib.CalcEaster
```

For COM objects, an object reference is equivalent to an interface reference to the `[default]` *interface on a coclass.*

Summary

We've covered a lot of ground in our first look at ATL. For a start, we looked at the facilities and Wizards that Visual C++ provides to make ATL programming easier. You saw that:

❑ The ATL COM AppWizard can create components packaged as DLLs, EXEs or NT services

❑ The ATL Wizards manage the content and compilation of the IDL file on our behalf

❑ The ATL Object Wizard can add skeleton implementations of many different kinds of component to your servers

❑ There are further Wizards for adding methods and properties to COM interfaces that can be accessed from ClassView

❑ Visual C++ ATL projects deal with the process of registering your components, through the use of RGS files that are kept up-to-date as your servers evolve

We also began to examine some of the characteristics of the code that the Wizards produce for us, and discovered that:

❑ ATL uses multiple inheritance to provide the default functionality your components require

❑ All ATL servers have a global object called `_Module` that provides basic services for the COM objects they contain

❑ Wizard-generated DLL servers come with default implementations of the five functions that all COM DLLs require

❑ Wizard-generated EXE servers come with a default implementation of `WinMain()`, the standard entry point for Windows executables

❑ EXE servers register all their class objects with the system on startup, and revoke them on shutdown

❑ The COM map is used in ATL's implementation of QueryInterface()

❑ The object map is a list of the objects in the server that contains it

❑ ProgIDs are text-based alternatives to GUIDs that can be used to identify components

❑ ATL uses a template class called CAxDialogImpl<> to implement a dialog

❑ The #import directive can process a type library and produce wrapper classes that make many aspects of COM programming easier

In the next chapter, we'll take a deeper look at the structure of ATL, we'll move beyond the Wizards, and we'll see how ATL provides the COM foundation of class objects and reference counting that we had to build for ourselves in the last chapter.

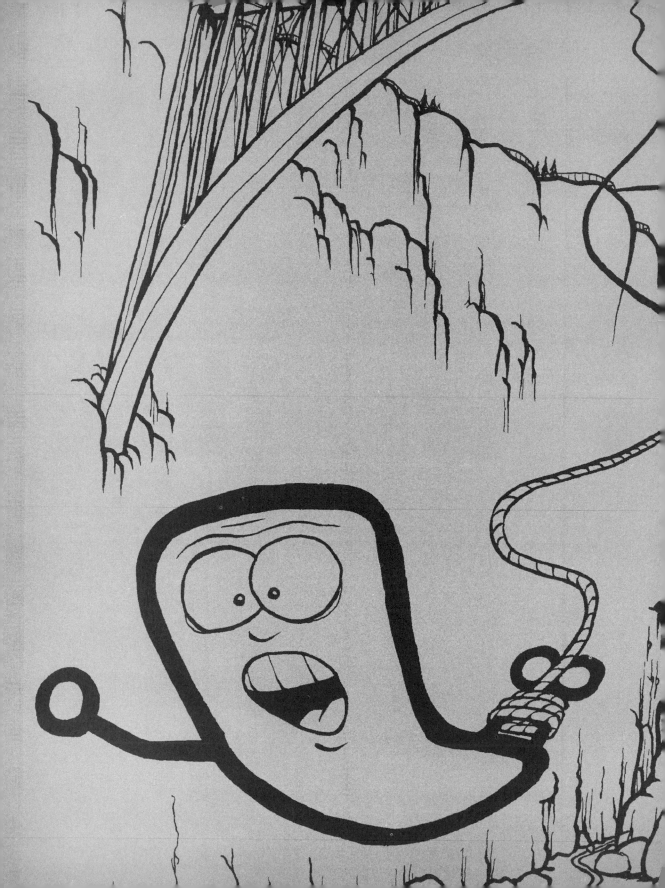

ATL Architecture

In the first two chapters of this book, you saw how COM works, and what COM requires from the coclasses that you write and the modules that serve them.

In Chapter 3, you saw how to use the ATL COM AppWizard to create an ATL project, how to use the ATL Object Wizard to add coclasses to your project, and how to use the dialogs provided by ClassView to add methods and properties to your coclasses. We also started to take a look at how ATL provides the infrastructure necessary for your COM servers.

In this chapter we'll take a closer look at ATL, and particularly at the way it provides class objects and the IUnknown methods for your coclasses. As we progress through the chapter, you'll build up an understanding of the relationship between the classes you create, their base classes, and their derived classes.

We'll start by taking a high-level look at the structure of ATL, before getting a little deeper into the macros that make it all work.

The Structure Of An ATL Class

All COM classes generated with ATL follow a similar pattern:

```
class ATL_NO_VTABLE CYourClass :
    public CComObjectRootEx<CComxxxThreadModel>,
    public CComCoClass<CYourClass, &CLSID_YourClass>,
    public ISomeInterface1,
    public ISomeInterface2,
    ... // List of interfaces
{
    ... // Construction

DECLARE_REGISTRY_RESOURCEID(IDR_YOURCLASS)

DECLARE_PROTECT_FINAL_CONSTRUCT()

BEGIN_COM_MAP(CYourClass)
    COM_INTERFACE_ENTRY(ISomeInterface1)
    COM_INTERFACE_ENTRY(ISomeInterface2)
    ... // List of interface entry macros
END_COM_MAP()

    ... // Method implementations
};
```

CComObjectRootEx<> and its base class CComObjectRootBase are responsible for handling the implementation of the IUnknown methods for your class. Although they don't actually provide the IUnknown methods themselves, these classes provide much of the code used in their implementation.

CComCoClass<> defines how COM objects should be created from your class, so it's used as a base class for all externally creatable classes. CComCoClass<> provides a couple of typedefs that determine what sort of class object is responsible for creating your objects, and how (or whether) your class supports aggregation. By default, objects will be created by ATL's class object implementation (CComClassFactory), and the objects *will* support aggregation.

> *All* ATL COM classes derive from **CComObjectRootEx<>**. Externally creatable classes (those that can be created with **CoCreateInstance()** or via a class object returned via **CoGetClassObject()**) also derive from **CComCoClass<>**.

Your class also derives from the interfaces that it implements. In general, these interface classes just provide the vtable layout. However, ATL does provide some classes that provide default implementations of various interfaces, which you may also use as base classes. We'll meet some of these implementation classes later in the book.

Except for IUnknown, all the interfaces exposed by the coclass have entries in the COM map, which provides the information that's used by ATL's QueryInterface() implementation.

> Your class derives from the interfaces that it implements. Each interface has an entry in the COM map.

The DECLARE_REGISTRY_RESOURCEID() macro links the registry script identified by the resource ID to your class, so that it can be automatically registered. This macro is present in all the Wizard-generated ATL COM classes, although registration is only *necessary* for externally creatable classes. Finally, as we saw in the last chapter, DECLARE_PROTECT_FINAL_CONSTRUCT() deals with a potentially tricky problem with reference counting.

The Object Map

Each coclass in the project has an entry in the object map (which lives in the project's main source file). For externally creatable objects, the object map has the following layout:

```
BEGIN_OBJECT_MAP(ObjectMap)
    OBJECT_ENTRY(CLSID_YourClass, CYourClass)
    OBJECT_ENTRY(CLSID_YourClass2, CYourClass2)
    ...
END_OBJECT_MAP()
```

Each `OBJECT_ENTRY()` hooks up your class to a class object. If your class doesn't have an entry like this in the map, clients won't be able to create objects of that type, and your class won't even register itself. Classes that *do* appear in the object map should derive from `CComCoClass<>`, as mentioned previously.

Objects that aren't externally creatable (that is, those that are only created within your server, rather than by a class object) can be placed in the object map using the `OBJECT_ENTRY_NON_CREATEABLE()` macro, for reasons that we will see later. Such objects need no CLSID, so this macro only takes one parameter: the C++ class name. For example:

```
BEGIN_OBJECT_MAP(ObjectMap)
    OBJECT_ENTRY(CLSID_YourClass, CYourClass)
    OBJECT_ENTRY(CLSID_YourClass2, CYourClass2)
    OBJECT_ENTRY_NON_CREATEABLE(CYourClass3)
    . . .
END_OBJECT_MAP()
```

CComObject<>

The important thing to realize is that your class is never instantiated directly; it always acts as a base class. There's at least one important clue to this in the definition of the class itself: the `ATL_NO_VTABLE` macro. In the last chapter, we explained how this macro provides an optimization that eliminates the initialization of the vtable from your class's constructor. We also explained that it couldn't be used in classes at the end of the inheritance chain. Clearly, there must be a class beneath the class that we define.

In simple terms, that class is `CComObject<>`, or more accurately `CComObject<CYourClass>`. `CComObject<>` provides the actual implementation of the `IUnknown` functions (which ultimately delegate to methods in `CComObjectRootEx<>`). It also provides the code for locking the module while the object is alive.

Here you can see the class hierarchy of COM objects based on your class.

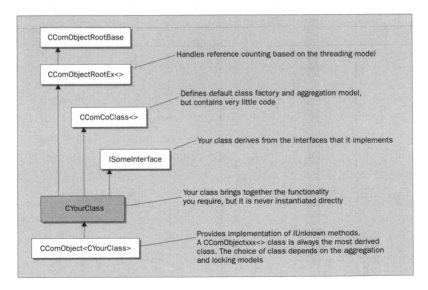

CComObject*xxx*<> Classes

Why *does* ATL use your class as a base class, rather than instantiating it directly? The simple reason is that the behavior provided by the class at the bottom of the hierarchy can be changed depending on its circumstances. This change can be accomplished without changing the class that you create, which wouldn't be possible if all the behavior was provided by base classes of your class.

ATL provides a number of classes (which we'll refer to as the CComObject*xxx*<> classes) to fulfill the role of most-derived class in this hierarchy. The CComObject*xxx*<> classes are responsible for three key areas:

- ❑ Aggregation
- ❑ Locking
- ❑ Destruction

We'll discuss **aggregation** later in the chapter; **locking** refers to the way in which the COM object interacts with the lock count of the module; and **destruction** refers to the mechanism used (if any) to destroy the object when the final reference count on it is released. None of these issues is part of the functionality of a specific coclass; they are generic features that can be switched around as the need arises. Some classes may support aggregation, others may not; some objects may need to keep the module locked while they're active and others may not; some objects may need to be created on the heap and others on the stack.

Through correct use of the CComObject*xxx*<> classes, all of these requirements can be accommodated without the need for any changes to the classes that you create.

The Maps

In the sections that follow, we'll explore the macros that provide a good deal of ATL's COM support. Specifically, we'll take a close look at the COM map and object map macros. Although you can do quite a lot with the knowledge you've gained already, the following sections will form a solid foundation that can inform all your future use of ATL.

We're going to examine the COM map and object map *in detail*. If you find that you're getting bogged down, skip through the text until you get to the summary at the end of each section. Use the examples to get a better "feel" for ATL, then come back to this part of the chapter as your comfort level and experience with ATL grows.

You can use the knowledge that you glean from the following sections to give you a starting point for debugging any problems that you might encounter. By the end, you'll be in a position where you understand what's possible and what's not, you won't start writing code that ATL already provides for you, and you'll be able to decide whether to use the code provided by the Wizards or some alternatives provided by ATL.

The COM Map

We'll start by examining the **COM map**, the macro-wrapped structure that ATL uses to keep track of the interfaces exposed by your classes. In the last chapter, we had a class called CCalcEaster, with a COM map (in CalcEaster.h) that looked like this:

```
BEGIN_COM_MAP(CCalcEaster)
    COM_INTERFACE_ENTRY(ICalcEaster)
    COM_INTERFACE_ENTRY(IDispatch)
END_COM_MAP()
```

Each interface implemented by the CCalcEaster class and exposed by QueryInterface() has an entry in the COM map (except for IUnknown).

BEGIN_COM_MAP()

BEGIN_COM_MAP() is a macro defined in the file Atlcom.h:

```
#define BEGIN_COM_MAP(x) public: \
    typedef x _ComMapClass; \
    static HRESULT WINAPI _Cache(void* pv, REFIID iid,\
                                 void** ppvObject, DWORD dw)\
    {\
        _ComMapClass* p = (_ComMapClass*)pv;\
        p->Lock();\
        HRESULT hRes = CComObjectRootBase::_Cache(pv, iid, ppvObject, dw);\
        p->Unlock();\
        return hRes;\
    }\
    IUnknown* _GetRawUnknown() \
    { ATLASSERT(_GetEntries()[0].pFunc == _ATL_SIMPLEMAPENTRY); \
      return (IUnknown*)((int)this+_GetEntries()->dw); } \
    _ATL_DECLARE_GET_UNKNOWN(x)\
    HRESULT _InternalQueryInterface(REFIID iid, void** ppvObject) \
    { return InternalQueryInterface(this, _GetEntries(), iid, ppvObject); } \
    const static _ATL_INTMAP_ENTRY* WINAPI _GetEntries() { \
    static const _ATL_INTMAP_ENTRY _entries[] = { DEBUG_QI_ENTRY(x)
```

Although it looks pretty confusing at first glance, we can soon see the important elements of the macro.

If you're not used to looking at complicated macros, remember that each line of a multi-line macro must end with a backslash, which acts as a line continuation character.

_ComMapClass

First, we have a typedef for _ComMapClass that evaluates to the class used as the macro argument. In other words, _ComMapClass is *our* class — the one that we have control over, and the one that contains the COM map itself. In this example, that's CCalcEaster.

```
#define BEGIN_COM_MAP(x) public: \
    typedef x _ComMapClass; \
```

This typedef is used in the definition of the _Cache() method and in many of the ATL macros associated with the COM map, including COM_INTERFACE_ENTRY(). (You'll get to see these other macros shortly.) The typedef is a great way of simplifying the code associated with the COM map macros.

_Cache()

_Cache() is a static function used for returning cached interface pointers. It is typically used for advanced features like auto-aggregation and tear-off interfaces. If you're interested, take a look at the documentation supplied with Visual C++, or try *Professional ATL COM Programming* (1-861001-40-1) — they are beyond the scope of this book.

_GetRawUnknown()

_GetRawUnknown() is a function that simply returns a pointer to IUnknown for the object:

```
IUnknown* _GetRawUnknown() \
{ ATLASSERT(_GetEntries()[0].pFunc == _ATL_SIMPLEMAPENTRY); \
    return (IUnknown*)((int)this+_GetEntries()->dw); } \
```

You should not call this method yourself; instead, you should call GetUnknown(), which is defined through the _ATL_DECLARE_GET_UNKNOWN() macro:

```
#ifdef _ATL_DEBUG_INTERFACES
#define _ATL_DECLARE_GET_UNKNOWN(x) \
    IUnknown* GetUnknown() \
    { \
        IUnknown* p; \
        _Module.AddNonAddRefThunk(_GetRawUnknown(), _T(#x), &p); \
        return p; \
    }
#else
#define _ATL_DECLARE_GET_UNKNOWN(x) \
    IUnknown* GetUnknown() {return _GetRawUnknown();}
#endif
```

Usually, GetUnknown() just calls _GetRawUnknown(). If you ever need to get an IUnknown* for your object from within one of its methods, GetUnknown() is the way to do it.

> _ATL_DEBUG_INTERFACES *is a debugging symbol, used to tell the compiler to generate reference count tracking code (which you should* never *do in production code). It ensures that all accesses made through the* IUnknown* *returned by* GetUnknown() *are reference count-checked. This is not a subject we'll be pursuing further in this book.*

_GetRawUnknown() uses the _GetEntries() function that's partially defined at the end of the BEGIN_COM_MAP() macro to get the **pointer offset** to IUnknown. It adds this value to the object's this pointer, then casts to IUnknown* to get the appropriate pointer. We'll discuss the _GetEntries() function and pointer offsets shortly.

_InternalQueryInterface()

`_InternalQueryInterface()` is the function responsible for returning the interface pointers supported by this object, but it's not the `QueryInterface()` function itself (note that it's not virtual, for example).

```
HRESULT _InternalQueryInterface(REFIID iid, void** ppvObject) \
{ return InternalQueryInterface(this, _GetEntries(), iid, ppvObject); } \
```

`_InternalQueryInterface()` delegates to `CComObjectRootBase::InternalQueryInterface()`, which in turn delegates to `AtlInternalQueryInterface()`. This latter is the function that actually contains the code to handle the `QI()` functionality.

This rather convoluted sequence of function calls is actually incredibly efficient. The code in `CComObjectRootBase::InternalQueryInterface()` provides some useful asserts and debugging aids, but in release builds it disappears, leaving only the call to `AtlInternalQueryInterface()`. Keeping all the code in this global function, rather than duplicating it among all the different classes that you might define in a project, keeps the size of the compiled code as tight as possible.

_GetEntries()

`_GetEntries()` returns an array of `_ATL_INTMAP_ENTRY` structures:

```
const static _ATL_INTMAP_ENTRY* WINAPI _GetEntries() { \
static const _ATL_INTMAP_ENTRY _entries[] = { DEBUG_QI_ENTRY(x)
```

The array that it returns is a `static` constant called `_entries` that's defined within the function. Each `_ATL_INTMAP_ENTRY` structure relates an interface identifier with a way of getting the interface pointer related to that IID. You can see the definition of this structure in `Atlbase.h`:

```
struct _ATL_INTMAP_ENTRY
{
    const IID* piid;          // the interface id (IID)
    DWORD dw;
    _ATL_CREATORARGFUNC* pFunc; //NULL:end, 1:offset, n:ptr
};
```

A pointer to the IID is held in the `piid` member. The meaning of the DWORD value, `dw`, depends on the contents of `pFunc`:

❑ If `pFunc` is NULL, `dw` has no meaning and both `dw` and `piid` should also be NULL (with one exception; see below). A NULL `_ATL_INTMAP_ENTRY` is used to signify the end of the array.

❑ If `pFunc` is 1 (or `_ATL_SIMPLEMAPENTRY`, which is defined as 1), `dw` is the offset to use to get from a pointer to the `_ComMapClass` to a pointer to the desired interface. As you'll see, this is the most common type of entry.

❑ If `pFunc` is anything other than NULL or 1, `pFunc` is a pointer to a function to call to get the desired interface pointer, and `dw` is passed as an argument to the function. ATL uses `pFunc` in this form to deal with auto-aggregation and tear-off interfaces. Since these are advanced topics, we won't concern ourselves with them.

The first item in the _entries array is DEBUG_QI_ENTRY(x), where x is the parameter passed to BEGIN_COM_MAP() — that is, the class name. *This* macro is defined as:

```
#ifdef _ATL_DEBUG
#define DEBUG_QI_ENTRY(x) \
    {NULL, \
    (DWORD)_T(#x), \
    (_ATL_CREATORARGFUNC*)0},
#else
#define DEBUG_QI_ENTRY(x)
#endif //_ATL_DEBUG
```

In other words, it does nothing in most builds, but if _ATL_DEBUG is defined it adds a dummy entry to the map that has a pointer to the class name as the dw field, and zero for the others. This class name is used by interface reference count tracking code in AtlInternalQueryInterface() to identify which class has been asked for an interface. It may seem odd that this is used as the first item, but as you'll see later in END_COM_MAP(), an adjustment is made to take it into account.

> The _ATL_DEBUG *symbol is used for backward compatibility with previous versions of ATL, and is defined if* _ATL_DEBUG_INTERFACES *is defined.*

COM_INTERFACE_ENTRY()

The other elements of the _entries array are defined using the COM_INTERFACE_*xxx*() macros, of which there are a number defined in Atlcom.h. The most important of them is the COM_INTERFACE_ENTRY() macro, which we used to expose the ICalcEaster and IDispatch interfaces in our example in the previous chapter:

```
#define COM_INTERFACE_ENTRY(x)\
    {&_ATL_IIDOF(x), \
    offsetofclass(x, _ComMapClass), \
    _ATL_SIMPLEMAPENTRY},
```

Whenever we use COM_INTERFACE_ENTRY(), we're just adding another _ATL_INTMAP_ENTRY structure to the _entries array. The interface ID pointer is generated using the _ATL_IIDOF() macro, which simply expands to the __uuidof() operator we first saw in Chapter 1.

offsetofclass() is defined in Atldef.h, and it just determines the offset of a base class from an inheriting class. In the context of COM_INTERFACE_ENTRY(), the offsetofclass() macro is used to determine the offset of the interface class from the class that derives from it.

```
#define offsetofclass(base, derived) \
    ((DWORD)(static_cast<base*>((derived*)_ATL_PACKING))-_ATL_PACKING)
```

The offsetofclass() *macro works like this:*

> *Take a value (*_ATL_PACKING *is actually a* #define *for 8!)*

> *Tell the compiler that it's a pointer to the derived class (by using a C-style cast)*

> *Cast the value to a pointer to the base class (using* static_cast<>*)*

> *To determine the offset, subtract the original value from the value returned by the cast*

> *Cast the result to a* DWORD.

The number 8 is not significant in this macro. All that really matters is that it's a non-zero value — zero is the same as NULL, *and the C++ language says that casting a null pointer will always result in a null pointer.*

Other important COM_INTERFACE_ENTRY_*xxx*() macros are:

❑ COM_INTERFACE_ENTRY_IID(), which allows you to pass the name of the IID directly; this is important for the few interfaces that are not defined in a header file with MIDL_INTERFACE().

```
#define COM_INTERFACE_ENTRY_IID(iid, x)\
    {&iid,\
    offsetofclass(x, _ComMapClass),\
    _ATL_SIMPLEMAPENTRY},
```

❑ COM_INTERFACE_ENTRY2(), which is used when you want to expose an interface that is a base class to two or more of your class's base classes. You'll see this macro in use later in the book; notice that the magical non-zero number 8 is being used again!

```
#define COM_INTERFACE_ENTRY2(x, x2)\
    {&_ATL_IIDOF(x),\
    (DWORD)((x*)(x2*)((_ComMapClass*)8))-8,\
    _ATL_SIMPLEMAPENTRY},
```

END_COM_MAP()

Finally, the COM map is closed with the END_COM_MAP() macro, the definition of which you can again find in Atlcom.h:

```
#ifdef _ATL_DEBUG
#define END_COM_MAP() {NULL, 0, 0}}; return &_entries[1];} \
    virtual ULONG STDMETHODCALLTYPE AddRef( void) = 0; \
    virtual ULONG STDMETHODCALLTYPE Release( void) = 0; \
    STDMETHOD(QueryInterface)(REFIID, void**) = 0;
#else
#define END_COM_MAP() {NULL, 0, 0}}; return _entries;} \
    virtual ULONG STDMETHODCALLTYPE AddRef( void) = 0; \
    virtual ULONG STDMETHODCALLTYPE Release( void) = 0; \
    STDMETHOD(QueryInterface)(REFIID, void**) = 0;
#endif // _ATL_DEBUG
```

The most obvious thing to notice is that the macro defines some pure virtual functions with __stdcall calling convention. These functions should be familiar to you as the IUnknown methods, and their presence here means that your class does *support* IUnknown, but does not *implement* it.

Now take a look at the first line of the macro, of which there are different versions depending on whether _ATL_DEBUG is defined. A null entry is added to the array in both cases, just to indicate that this is the last value. Next, if _ATL_DEBUG is *not* defined, the address of the first entry of the array is returned (_entries is the same as &_entries[0]). However, when reference count tracking is used (that is, when _ATL_DEBUG *is* defined), the first entry in the array is a dummy that gives access to the class name. Any code that wants to get interface information should get the *second* entry, which is why &_entries[1] is returned. This ensures that in all cases, _GetEntries() returns the address of the first interface entry in the array.

COM Map Summary

The COM map defines a few important functions in your class. The most important of these is _GetEntries(), which gives access to the array of _ATL_INTMAP_ENTRY structures. This array is vital to the correct operation of ATL's mechanism for handling QueryInterface(). You can add to the array by adding COM_INTERFACE_ENTRY_*xxx*() entries within the COM map.

Note that you don't need an entry for IUnknown, which is handled by the first entry in the COM map. Also be aware that the order in which the entries appear is the order in which the entries are searched. For maximum performance, place the interfaces that are queried for most frequently at the top of the map.

The COM map also defines an _InternalQueryInterface() function that delegates to CComObjectRootBase::InternalQueryInterface(), and ultimately to AtlInternalQueryInterface().

The Object Map

Another important group of macros in the world of ATL is the **object map**. The object map is present in all ATL projects, and lives in the main .cpp file. The object map controls the class objects and registration for the coclasses in your project. Each class that you want to be independently creatable — in other words, creatable by a call to CoCreateInstance() or a similar function — must have an OBJECT_ENTRY() entry in the object map. Classes that are *not* externally creatable (instances will be created by code in your class rather than through a class object) should also be added to the object map if they will need once-only class initialization with ObjectMain(). To do this, you can use the OBJECT_ENTRY_NON_CREATEABLE() macro.

In the example from the previous chapter, the object map looked like this:

```
BEGIN_OBJECT_MAP(ObjectMap)
OBJECT_ENTRY(CLSID_CalcEaster, CCalcEaster)
END_OBJECT_MAP()
```

Let's break open these macros to see how it all works.

BEGIN_OBJECT_MAP() and END_OBJECT_MAP()

The BEGIN_OBJECT_MAP() and END_OBJECT_MAP() macros are extremely simple. You can find them defined in Atlcom.h:

```
#define BEGIN_OBJECT_MAP(x) static _ATL_OBJMAP_ENTRY x[] = {
#define END_OBJECT_MAP()    {NULL, NULL, NULL, NULL, NULL, NULL, NULL, NULL}};
```

You can see that the object map is a straightforward, null-terminated array of _ATL_OBJMAP_ENTRY structures. The BEGIN_OBJECT_MAP() and END_OBJECT_MAP() macros define the start and end of the array, and each OBJECT_ENTRY() is a new element in the array.

Oddly, the END_OBJECT_MAP() macro sets eight NULL entries, but _ATL_OBJMAP_ENTRY has nine members. Happily, this is not a problem because the ATL code that iterates through the object map only checks to see if the first entry is NULL to indicate the end of the map, and in this case never reads the other members.

_ATL_OBJMAP_ENTRY

Unfortunately, the _ATL_OBJMAP_ENTRY structure isn't quite as straightforward. You can see this for yourself by examining its definition, taken from Atlbase.h:

```
struct _ATL_OBJMAP_ENTRY
{
    const CLSID* pclsid;
    HRESULT (WINAPI *pfnUpdateRegistry)(BOOL bRegister);
    _ATL_CREATORFUNC* pfnGetClassObject;
    _ATL_CREATORFUNC* pfnCreateInstance;
    IUnknown* pCF;
    DWORD dwRegister;
    _ATL_DESCRIPTIONFUNC* pfnGetObjectDescription;
    _ATL_CATMAPFUNC* pfnGetCategoryMap;
    HRESULT WINAPI RevokeClassObject()
    {
        return CoRevokeClassObject(dwRegister);
    }
    HRESULT WINAPI RegisterClassObject(DWORD dwClsContext, DWORD dwFlags)
    {
        IUnknown* p = NULL;
        if (pfnGetClassObject == NULL)
            return S_OK;
        HRESULT hRes = pfnGetClassObject(pfnCreateInstance,
                                IID_IUnknown, (LPVOID*) &p);
        if (SUCCEEDED(hRes))
            hRes = CoRegisterClassObject(*pclsid, p,
                                    dwClsContext, dwFlags, &dwRegister);
        if (p != NULL)
            p->Release();
        return hRes;
    }
// Added in ATL 3.0
    void (WINAPI *pfnObjectMain)(bool bStarting);
};
```

The structure holds a number of pointers and defines a couple of methods, all of which are related to the creation or registration of a particular class. The methods `RegisterClassObject()` and `RevokeClassObject()` just register and unregister the class object with the system (as described in Chapter 2). The data members are more interesting:

Data Member	Description
pclsid	Pointer to the CLSID.
pfnUpdateRegistry	Pointer to the function used to update the registry with information about the class.
pfnGetClassObject	Pointer to the function used to create a class object and return a pointer to one of its interfaces.
pfnCreateInstance	Pointer to the function used to create an instance of the class specified by `pclsid`.

Data Member	Description
pCF	Pointer to the class object's `IUnknown` interface.
dwRegister	A `DWORD` used to store the cookie returned from `CoRegisterClassObject()`. (`CoRegisterClassObject()` returns a cookie to the caller that it can pass back via `CoRevokeClassObject()` when the class object needs to be unregistered.)
pfnGetObjectDescription	Pointer to the function used to return a text description for the class. Note carefully the explanation of this member given below.
pfnGetCategoryMap	Pointer to the function that returns the category map. Categories provide a way of discovering an object's behavior without having to instantiate it.
pfnObjectMain	Pointer to the function responsible for once-only class initialization and termination.

OBJECT_ENTRY()

The `OBJECT_ENTRY()` macro provides values for all the structure's data members based on two pieces of information: the CLSID, and your class. `OBJECT_ENTRY()` is defined like this:

```
#define OBJECT_ENTRY(clsid, class) {&clsid, class::UpdateRegistry,\
    class::_ClassFactoryCreatorClass::CreateInstance,\
    class::_CreatorClass::CreateInstance, NULL, 0,\
    class::GetObjectDescription, class::GetCategoryMap, class::ObjectMain },
```

We'll look at where each of these entries comes from in turn.

pclsid = &clsid

`pclsid` is just set to the address of the CLSID passed as the first parameter to the macro. In the case of our simple example from the previous chapter, this CLSID constant is automatically generated by the MIDL compiler when it compiles the IDL file. If this member is NULL, then the entry marks the end of the map; if the class doesn't have a CLSID (it is not externally creatable), use &CLSID_NULL (which is not the same as NULL).

pfnUpdateRegistry = class::UpdateRegistry

`pfnUpdateRegistry` is the address of our class's `UpdateRegistry()` function. The `UpdateRegistry()` function is actually hidden behind a macro of its own in the definition of our class:

```
class ATL_NO_VTABLE CCalcEaster :
    public CComObjectRootEx<CComSingleThreadModel>,
    public CComCoClass<CCalcEaster, &CLSID_CalcEaster>,
    public IDispatchImpl<ICalcEaster, &IID_ICalcEaster, &LIBID_SIMPLELib>
{
public:
    CCalcEaster() : m_Year(-1), m_Month(-1), m_Day(-1)
    {
    }

    DECLARE_REGISTRY_RESOURCEID(IDR_CALCEASTER)
```

The DECLARE_REGISTRY_RESOURCEID() macro is defined in Atlcom.h, along with a number of other DECLARE_REGISTRY_*xxx*() macros that each define UpdateRegistry() in slightly different ways. All of them get their functionality from the _Module object:

```
#define DECLARE_NO_REGISTRY()\
    static HRESULT WINAPI UpdateRegistry(BOOL /*bRegister*/)\
    {return S_OK;}

#define DECLARE_REGISTRY(class, pid, vpid, nid, flags)\
    static HRESULT WINAPI UpdateRegistry(BOOL bRegister)\
    {\
        return _Module.UpdateRegistryClass(GetObjectCLSID(), pid, vpid, nid,\
            flags, bRegister);\
    }

#define DECLARE_REGISTRY_RESOURCE(x)\
    static HRESULT WINAPI UpdateRegistry(BOOL bRegister)\
    {\
    return _Module.UpdateRegistryFromResource(_T(#x), bRegister);\
    }

#define DECLARE_REGISTRY_RESOURCEID(x)\
    static HRESULT WINAPI UpdateRegistry(BOOL bRegister)\
    {\
    return _Module.UpdateRegistryFromResource(x, bRegister);\
    }
```

If you don't want to make any registry entries for your class, you can add the DECLARE_NO_REGISTRY() macro to your class definition. If you want to add registry entries based on a CLSID, ProgID, version-independent ProgID and a description string resource, you can use DECLARE_REGISTRY(). If you want to update the registry based on a resource created from an RGS file, use DECLARE_REGISTRY_RESOURCE() or DECLARE_REGISTRY_RESOURCEID().

You don't have to use any of these macros if you don't want to, but if you want to make use of the OBJECT_ENTRY() macro, you will need to provide an UpdateRegistry() method in your class.

pfnGetClassObject = class::_ClassFactoryCreatorClass::CreateInstance

OBJECT_ENTRY() sets the pfnGetClassObject member to be class::_ClassFactoryCreatorClass::CreateInstance(). This CreateInstance() function is used to create class objects. The _ClassFactoryCreatorClass is just a typedef scoped within your class; it's usually defined by one of the DECLARE_CLASSFACTORYxxx() macros that lurk in Atlcom.h.

By default, your class uses the typedef defined by the DECLARE_CLASSFACTORY() macro, because this macro is used in CComCoClass<>, from which your class derives.

```
#if defined(_WINDLL) | defined(_USRDLL)
#define DECLARE_CLASSFACTORY_EX(cf)\
    typedef CComCreator< CComObjectCached< cf > > _ClassFactoryCreatorClass;
#else
// don't let class factory refcount influence lock count
#define DECLARE_CLASSFACTORY_EX(cf)\
    typedef CComCreator< CComObjectNoLock< cf > > _ClassFactoryCreatorClass;
#endif
#define DECLARE_CLASSFACTORY() DECLARE_CLASSFACTORY_EX(CComClassFactory)
```

CComCreator<> is the class that exposes the CreateInstance() method to which we store a pointer in pfnGetClassObject. It creates instances of the class specified by its template parameter. When the project is a DLL, CreateInstance() will create objects of class CComObjectCached<CComClassFactory>; when the project is an EXE, it will create objects of class CComObjectNoLock<CComClassFactory>.

ATL's CComObjectxxx<> classes provide the implementation of the IUnknown methods. These classes not only handle the basics of reference counting for the object itself, but also interact appropriately with the module's (that is, the EXE's or the DLL's) lock count. There are a number of CComObjectxxx<> classes, each of which has slightly different behavior, but all the CComObjectxxx<> classes derive from the class specified as their template parameter, and delegate most of the functionality of QI() to the base class's _InternalQueryInterface() method.

Remember from Chapter 2 that a class object is a COM object, so it must expose IUnknown.

CComObjectCached<> is used when you want to cache COM objects. In other words, if you want to keep a COM object around even when there are no external clients with references to it, you should create it from CComObjectCached<>. CComObjectCached<> is aware that the first reference count on the object shouldn't also be used to hold the module in memory (or else it will never unload), so AddRef() and Release() are coded such that the module is only locked when the reference count rises to 2, and the module is unlocked when the reference count falls to 1. That means that you can create a CComObjectCached<> object as your module loads, so that it can be accessed swiftly. This is sensible behavior for class objects, and may also make sense if you decide to expose an Application object, for example.

CComObjectNoLock<> is used when you don't want the reference count of the object to affect the lock count of the module at all. We discussed the reason why the reference counts on the class objects of an executable can't also be used to keep that module in memory back in Chapter 2 (COM hangs on to the class objects). It therefore makes sense that the class objects for an ATL executable use CComObjectNoLock<> to provide the implementation of the IUnknown methods.

CComClassFactory is the class that implements the IClassFactory interface. The implementations of that interface's methods are extremely simple (as you can see if you take a look in Atlcom.h). The LockServer() method just calls _Module.Lock() or _Module.Unlock() depending on the value of its parameter. The CreateInstance() method does little more than call the CreateInstance() function that's passed to it as a pointer when the object is created by CComCreator<>. It turns out that this function pointer is the same as the pointer specified in the pfnCreateInstance member of the _ATL_OBJMAP_ENTRY structure.

Here you can see the class hierarchy for the class object used to generate ATL objects by default.

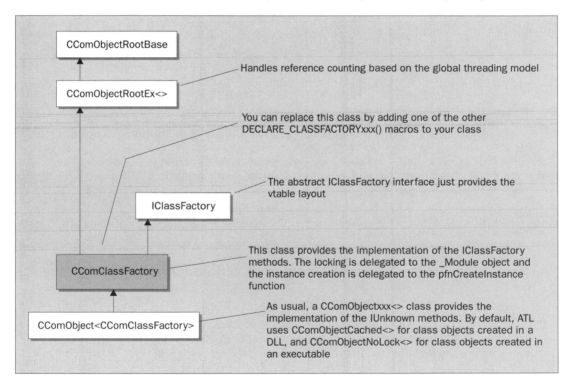

135

You can override the `typedef` defined in `CComCoClass<>` for the class object by setting up your own. The easiest way to do that is just to add one of the other `DECLARE_CLASSFACTORYxxx()` macros to the definition of your class. Typical alternatives are `DECLARE_CLASSFACTORY2()` if you want to support licensing, or `DECLARE_CLASSFACTORY_SINGLETON()` if you want all clients to connect to the same instance of an object.

```
#define DECLARE_CLASSFACTORY2(lic)\
    DECLARE_CLASSFACTORY_EX(CComClassFactory2<lic>)
#define DECLARE_CLASSFACTORY_SINGLETON(obj)\
    DECLARE_CLASSFACTORY_EX(CComClassFactorySingleton<obj>)
```

pfnCreateInstance = class::_CreatorClass::CreateInstance

`OBJECT_ENTRY()` sets the `pfnCreateInstance` member to be `class::_CreatorClass::CreateInstance`. *This* `CreateInstance()` function is used to create COM objects. Once again, `_CreatorClass` is just a `typedef` scoped within your class. This `typedef` is provided, by default, by the `DECLARE_AGGREGATABLE()` macro in the definition of `CComCoClass<>`. You can override this setting in your own class by using one of the other `DECLARE_xxxAGGREGATABLE()` macros.

We'll look at the `DECLARE_xxxAGGREGATABLE()` macros later in the chapter, when we examine aggregation in detail and look at an example. For now, we'll just take a closer look at the macro that's used by default:

```
#define DECLARE_AGGREGATABLE(x) public:\
    typedef CComCreator2< CComCreator< CComObject< x > >,\
                          CComCreator< CComAggObject< x > > > _CreatorClass;
```

`CComCreator2<>` is a simple class that exposes a single `CreateInstance()` function. The implementation of that function checks whether an object is being aggregated. If it *isn't* being aggregated, the function delegates to the `CreateInstance()` method of the first template parameter (in this case, `CComCreator< CComObject< x > >`). If it *is* being aggregated, `CComCreator2<>::CreateInstance()` calls the `CreateInstance()` method of the second template parameter (`CComCreator< CComAggObject< x > >`).

> *Note that the* `CreateInstance()` *functions in both the* `_ClassFactoryCreatorClass` *and the* `_CreatorClass` *must be* `static` *because they're not called through an object.*

Here, you can see that the COM object that actually gets created by the class object is *not* an instance of the class that we defined (represented by x in the macro, and evaluating to `CCalcEaster` in our example). It is actually an instance of `CComObject< x >` (when it's not being aggregated). Remember that our class, `CCalcEaster`, is abstract: it doesn't implement the `IUnknown` methods, and it doesn't have an independently instantiable vtable, thanks to the `ATL_NO_VTABLE` optimization applied to it. The COM classes that we create are only ever used as base classes for objects created from one of the `CComObjectxxx<>` classes, which provide the implementation of the `IUnknown` methods.

pCF = NULL and dwRegister = 0

The OBJECT_ENTRY() macro sets the pCF and dwRegister members of the _ATL_OBJMAP_ENTRY structure to NULL and 0 respectively. These members are set with useful values once a class object has been created (in which case a pointer to its IUnknown interface is stored in the pCF member) and registered (the cookie returned by a call to CoRegisterClassObject() is stored in the dwRegister member).

pfnGetObjectDescription = class::GetObjectDescription

The pfnGetObjectDescription member is set to the address of the static GetObjectDescription() function that's provided by your class — or (more accurately) by CComCoClass<>, from which your class derives. The implementation of this function in CComCoClass<> just returns a null pointer.

You can override (mask) this function in your own class to return something other than NULL, but you should be aware that if you return a non-NULL result from GetObjectDescription(), ATL's standard registration code will *not* register your coclass. This is because GetObjectDescription() is designed for use with a component registrar object, which is one of the object types that you can add to your project using the ATL Object Wizard. However, although the MSDN documentation suggests that the component registrar object is used by MTS, there is no evidence of this with either MTS 2.0 or COM+. It appears to be a nice idea that never quite made it into production.

> *If you provide a value for this member (by using the DECLARE_OBJECT_DESCRIPTION() macro), your component will not be registered, and so it won't be externally creatable. It is probably best to avoid using this macro.*

pfnGetCategoryMap = class::GetCategoryMap

pfnGetCategoryMap is set to the address of the static GetObjectDescription() function, which is provided by the **category map** macros used in your class — if such a map exists. This function returns a pointer to the category map, in the form of a pointer to a _ATL_CATMAP_ENTRY structure. If you aren't using a category map, the default function defined in CComCoClass<> is used, which simply returns NULL.

> *Category maps will be examined in detail in later on in the chapter.*

pfnObjectMain = class::ObjectMain

When a server is first loaded, it will iterate through all the entries in the object map, calling the ObjectMain() function of each with a parameter of true. When the server unloads, it calls this function for each object with a parameter of false. The default definition of this function is found in CComObjectRootBase and does nothing, but you can override it if you wish. pfnObjectMain is simply set to the address of this function.

OBJECT_ENTRY_NON_CREATEABLE()

The `OBJECT_ENTRY_NON_CREATEABLE()` is a new feature of ATL 3.0. It is used in object maps to represent objects that are contained in the module, but which are not externally creatable. Its definition is as follows:

```
#define OBJECT_ENTRY_NON_CREATEABLE(class) {&CLSID_NULL, class::UpdateRegistry, \
    NULL, NULL, NULL, 0, NULL, class::GetCategoryMap, class::ObjectMain },
```

You will immediately notice that the entries that usually refer to class objects or object creation methods are `NULL`. All the macro does is define the registration code and `ObjectMain()` for a class, although it is far from clear why you would want to register any details of a component that isn't externally creatable. Even if you do provide registration code, it will refer to the mythical coclass that has a GUID of `CLSID_NULL`. In other words, therefore, this part of the macro's operation is bugged.

Object Map Summary

The object map is a null-terminated array of `_ATL_OBJMAP_ENTRY` structures. Each element controls the registration and creation of one type of object.

Each element of the array is defined by using an `OBJECT_ENTRY()` or an `OBJECT_ENTRY_NON_CREATABLE()` macro. The Object Wizard usually adds object entries to the map automatically.

The class specified in the second macro parameter must implement the `UpdateRegistry()` and `GetObjectDescription()` functions, as well as providing `typedef`s for `_ClassFactoryCreatorClass` and `_CreatorClass`, each of which must implement a `CreateInstance()` function.

The `UpdateRegistry()` function is usually provided by one of the `DECLARE_REGISTRY_xxx()` macros. Typically, the `DECLARE_REGISTRY_RESOURCEID()` macro is added to your class when it's generated by the Object Wizard.

The `typedef` for `_ClassFactoryCreatorClass` is usually provided by one of the `DECLARE_CLASSFACTORYxxx()` macros. `CComCoClass<>` uses the `DECLARE_CLASSFACTORY()` macro by default. You can override this by adding a different macro to your class.

The `typedef` for `_CreatorClass` is usually provided by one of the `DECLARE_xxxAGGREGATABLE()` macros. `CComCoClass<>` uses the `DECLARE_AGGREGATABLE()` macro by default. You can override this by adding a different macro to your class.

ATL COM objects are instances of a template specialization of one of the `CComObjectxxx<>` classes. The `CComObjectxxx<>` class usually derives from the class that implements the COM methods. By default, objects are instances of a `CComObject<>` class when not being aggregated, or instances of a `CComAggObject<>` class when they are. The `CComObjectxxx<>` classes provide the implementation of the `IUnknown` methods and the code for locking the module if appropriate.

Here's the class hierarchy for the `CCalcEaster` class from the last chapter:

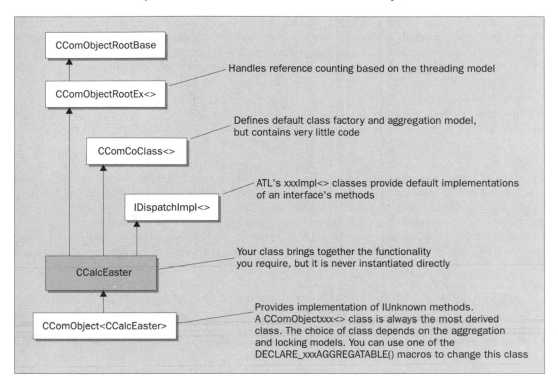

The Category Map

Category maps are a little different from the COM and object maps we've looked at so far, not least because they don't actually appear in Wizard-produced code. Nonetheless, they *are* an essential part of every COM component you create with ATL, and it's well worth understanding a little about how they work.

As we've said on a number of occasions now, interfaces represent the behavior of a component. If you want to find out what a component can do, you have to create an instance of the coclass and call `QueryInterface()` for the behavior that you are interested in. For example, when you open an object in `Oleview.exe`, it will show you all the interfaces the object supports. To determine this, however, the program has had to create an instance, read a list of all the interfaces for which your system has marshaling support (which it does by reading the `HKEY_CLASSES_ROOT\Interface` key in the registry), and then query the object for each interface in turn.

This is inefficient in two ways. First, creating an instance of a coclass can be expensive in terms of initialization time and memory usage. Second, if you want to ask the object to list *all* of its behavior, you resign yourself to that expensive task of querying for all possible interfaces.

Categories solve both of these problems. Using GUIDs, categories describe **behaviors**, which encapsulate the fact that a component implements one or more particular interfaces. For example, by declaring that it supports the `Control` category, a component can state unequivocally that it supports many different interfaces — in this case, those that are necessary for a component to be a control. The *really* neat thing about this is that you don't need to create an instance of the component to know what categories (and therefore what interfaces) it supports, because they are registered with the system.

If you want to determine whether a component supports a particular category, you simply create an instance of the **component categories manager***, passing it the CLSID of the component and a list of the category IDs that you're interested in. The component categories manager will determine the categories supported by the component, and tell you if they correspond to the ones you passed.*

So: categories are a registration issue, and the category map is only consulted during module registration and unregistration, but that still doesn't answer the question of why you can't see the map in your project. In fact, the `BEGIN_CATEGORY_MAP()` and `END_CATEGORY_MAP()` macros that are used to delimit the map define a `static` method called `GetCategoryMap()`, but a method of the same name is implemented by `CComCoClass<>` to return `NULL` — or in other words, to say that the map is empty. You don't actually *need* to use the macros until you want to, but when you do, they look something like this:

```
BEGIN_CATEGORY_MAP(CCatCtrl)
    IMPLEMENTED_CATEGORY(CATID_Insertable)
    IMPLEMENTED_CATEGORY(CATID_Control)
    REQUIRED_CATEGORY(CATID_DataSource)
END_CATEGORY_MAP()
```

Here you can see two types of categories: **implemented categories** that describe a component's behavior, and **required categories** that the component container (that is, the code that calls the component) should implement. This hypothetical category map indicates that the `CCatCtrl` class is an insertable control that can only be created by containers that are data sources (perhaps because the component needs to bind to data sources in the container).

For more information and examples of using category maps, take a look at the MSDN entry for the Component Categories Manager, and at Professional ATL COM Programming.

Other Maps

ATL uses a number of other maps, many of which we'll be covering elsewhere in the book. Here's a brief description of each:

Map	Description	Covered in
Connection Point Map	Indicates the interfaces on which a component can generate events	Chapter 8
Property Map	Indicates the Automation properties that a component supports, and also the property pages used to alter those properties	Chapter 9

Map	Description	Covered in
Message Map	Lists the methods used to handle the Windows messages sent to a control	Chapter 7
Services Map	Indicates the 'services' that a component or a collection of components supports	*Professional ATL COM Programming*
Sink Map	Indicates the methods that will handle events sent to a component	Chapter 10

Object Creation

Now that we've got a good understanding of the structure of ATL's COM map and object map, let's set that knowledge in stone by tracing through the creation of a COM object. We'll look at a typical example from the points of view of an EXE server and a DLL server. The differences really arise in the creation of the class objects; once the client has a pointer to an interface on a class object (usually IClassFactory), the code is identical for DLL and EXE.

If you want to see the code in action as we discuss it, you can put a breakpoint in the DllGetClassObject() function of the simple object and step through the code in the debugger.

Class Object Creation In A DLL

We'll start by looking at DllGetClassObject(), the global function that's called by COM when a client is requesting an interface on one of the class objects, and which is therefore a prelude to creating the object that the client's really after. At this stage, the DLL has been loaded and the _Module object has got hold of the object map.

```
STDAPI DllGetClassObject(REFCLSID rclsid, REFIID riid, LPVOID* ppv)
{
    return _Module.GetClassObject(rclsid, riid, ppv);
}
```

DllGetClassObject() just calls CComModule::GetClassObject(), which in turn calls the global function AtlModuleGetClassObject(). Once again, we can see an inline class method delegating to a global function to ensure that the compiled code is as tight as possible.

```
// Obtain a Class Factory (DLL only)
HRESULT GetClassObject(REFCLSID rclsid, REFIID riid, LPVOID* ppv)
{
    return AtlModuleGetClassObject(this, rclsid, riid, ppv);
}
```

AtlModuleGetClassObject()

`AtlModuleGetClassObject()` loops through the object map, comparing the `pclsid` member of each element of the array with the CLSID passed to `DllGetClassObject()`. When it finds a match, it checks the `pCF` member of the `_ATL_OBJMAP_ENTRY` against NULL.

If `pCF` is NULL, `AtlModuleGetClassObject()` knows that it needs to create the class object. It does this by calling the class object `CreateInstance()` function pointed to by `pfnGetClassObject`. It passes the COM object `CreateInstance()` function pointed to by `pfnCreateInstance` to initialize the class object as the first parameter. It also passes `IID_IUnknown` so that the function knows we want a pointer to the class object's `IUnknown` interface, and the address of the entry's `pCF` member so that the `IUnknown` pointer can be stored there.

If `pCF` isn't NULL, it must be a pointer to the `IUnknown` interface of a valid class object, so the code just calls `QueryInterface()` against it, using the IID and the indirect pointer passed to `DllGetClassObject()`, and its work is complete.

```
ATLINLINE ATLAPI AtlModuleGetClassObject(_ATL_MODULE* pM, REFCLSID rclsid,
                                         REFIID riid, LPVOID* ppv)
{
    ATLASSERT(pM != NULL);
    if (pM == NULL)
        return E_INVALIDARG;
    ATLASSERT(pM->m_pObjMap != NULL);
    _ATL_OBJMAP_ENTRY* pEntry = pM->m_pObjMap;
    HRESULT hRes = S_OK;
    if (ppv == NULL)
        return E_POINTER;
    *ppv = NULL;
    while (pEntry->pclsid != NULL)
    {
        if ((pEntry->pfnGetClassObject != NULL) &&
                    InlineIsEqualGUID(rclsid, *pEntry->pclsid))
        {
            if (pEntry->pCF == NULL)
            {
                EnterCriticalSection(&pM->m_csObjMap);
                if (pEntry->pCF == NULL)
                    hRes = pEntry->pfnGetClassObject(pEntry->pfnCreateInstance,
                                                     IID_IUnknown,
                                                     (LPVOID*)&pEntry->pCF);
                LeaveCriticalSection(&pM->m_csObjMap);
            }
            if (pEntry->pCF != NULL)
                hRes = pEntry->pCF->QueryInterface(riid, ppv);
            break;
        }
        pEntry = _NextObjectMapEntry(pM, pEntry);
    }
    if (*ppv == NULL && hRes == S_OK)
        hRes = CLASS_E_CLASSNOTAVAILABLE;
    return hRes;
}
```

Class Object Creation In An EXE

An executable doesn't wait for a client to request its class objects before creating them; instead, it creates them as it starts up and registers them with the system. This process begins with a call to `CComModule::RegisterClassObjects()`, which you can find in the Wizard-generated `_tWinMain()` function of an ATL executable:

```
    if (bRun)
    {
        _Module.StartMonitor();
#if _WIN32_WINNT >= 0x0400 & defined(_ATL_FREE_THREADED)
        hRes = _Module.RegisterClassObjects(CLSCTX_LOCAL_SERVER,
                                REGCLS_MULTIPLEUSE | REGCLS_SUSPENDED);
        _ASSERTE(SUCCEEDED(hRes));
        hRes = CoResumeClassObjects();
#else
        hRes = _Module.RegisterClassObjects(CLSCTX_LOCAL_SERVER,
                                REGCLS_MULTIPLEUSE);
#endif
```

Just as `CComModule::GetClassObject()` calls `AtlModuleGetClassObject()`, so `CComModule::RegisterClassObjects()` calls `AtlModuleRegisterClassObjects()`.

```
// Register/Revoke All Class Factories with the OS (EXE only)
HRESULT RegisterClassObjects(DWORD dwClsContext, DWORD dwFlags)
{
    return AtlModuleRegisterClassObjects(this, dwClsContext, dwFlags);
}
```

AtlModuleRegisterClassObjects()

`AtlModuleRegisterClassObjects()` just loops through the object map, calling `RegisterClassObject()` on each entry.

```
ATLINLINE ATLAPI AtlModuleRegisterClassObjects(_ATL_MODULE* pM,
                                    DWORD dwClsContext, DWORD dwFlags)
{
    ATLASSERT(pM != NULL);
    if (pM == NULL)
        return E_INVALIDARG;
    ATLASSERT(pM->m_pObjMap != NULL);
    _ATL_OBJMAP_ENTRY* pEntry = pM->m_pObjMap;
    HRESULT hRes = S_OK;
    while (pEntry->pclsid != NULL && hRes == S_OK)
    {
        hRes = pEntry->RegisterClassObject(dwClsContext, dwFlags);
        pEntry = _NextObjectMapEntry(pM, pEntry);
    }
    return hRes;
}
```

We saw `RegisterClassObject()` earlier in the chapter when we looked at the `_ATL_OBJMAP_ENTRY` structure; it calls `pfnGetClassObject()` followed by `CoRegisterClassObject()`. Note that unlike `AtlModuleGetClassObject()`, `_ATL_OBJMAP_ENTRY::RegisterClassObject()` doesn't store the class object pointer in the `pCF` member of the structure — once the class objects are registered, clients retrieve the class object directly from the system without intervention from the executable. EXE servers don't expose any entry points.

Object Creation In DLLs And EXEs

Once the client has a pointer to the requested interface on the class object, whether it's been created by a DLL or an EXE, it can use it to create an instance of the required object. In our example from the previous chapter, that means the client has a pointer to the IClassFactory interface. Calling CreateInstance() through this interface pointer results in a call to CComClassFactory::CreateInstance(), which uses the pfnCreateInstance member of the _ATL_OBJMAP_ENTRY to create the object. In our example, pfnCreateInstance is the address of the CComCreator2<T1, T2>::CreateInstance() function, where T1 is CComCreator< CComObject< CCalcEaster > > and T2 is CComCreator< CComAggObject< CCalcEaster > >.

```
template <class T1, class T2>
class CComCreator2
{
public:
    static HRESULT WINAPI CreateInstance(void* pv, REFIID riid, LPVOID* ppv)
    {
        ATLASSERT(*ppv == NULL);
        return (pv == NULL) ?
            T1::CreateInstance(NULL, riid, ppv) :
            T2::CreateInstance(pv, riid, ppv);
    }
};
```

This means that ultimately, CComCreator<>::CreateInstance() is called to construct either a CComObject<> or a CComAggObject<> object.

```
template <class T1>
class CComCreator
{
public:
    static HRESULT WINAPI CreateInstance(void* pv, REFIID riid, LPVOID* ppv)
    {
        ATLASSERT(*ppv == NULL);
        HRESULT hRes = E_OUTOFMEMORY;
        T1* p = NULL;
        ATLTRY(p = new T1(pv))
        if (p != NULL)
        {
            p->SetVoid(pv);
            p->InternalFinalConstructAddRef();
            hRes = p->FinalConstruct();
            p->InternalFinalConstructRelease();
            if (hRes == S_OK)
                hRes = p->QueryInterface(riid, ppv);
            if (hRes != S_OK)
                delete p;
        }
        return hRes;
    }
};
```

ATLTRY() is a macro used to prevent exceptions from propagating. If exception handling isn't enabled, the macro just resolves to its argument (that is, it does nothing). If exception handling is enabled, it wraps its argument in a try block and provides an empty 'catch all' block (catch(...)) to stop the exception propagating out of the current function.

Although the essence of the function is to create a new object on the heap (using new) and call QueryInterface() on it to return the pointer requested by the riid argument, there's a bit more going on here than that.

First, note that the function's first argument, pv, is passed to the constructor of the object *and* to the object itself, via the call to the SetVoid() method. When *objects* are being created, pv is NULL unless the object is being aggregated. In this situation, the value is of interest to the CComObject*xxx*<> class (because it affects the implementation of the IUnknown methods), which receives it via the constructor argument. The call to SetVoid() isn't used in that case (SetVoid() has an empty implementation).

When a *class object* is being created, pv represents the pfnCreateInstance member of the _ATL_OBJMAP_ENTRY structure. In other words, pv is the pointer to the function used by the class object to create its objects. In this case, the constructor ignores the argument (because the CComObject*xxx*<> classes used for class objects don't care about aggregation), and it's the call to SetVoid() that is used to pass the pointer to the CComClassFactory class.

The reason that there are two ways of passing the pv pointer to the object is that the constructor is always defined by the *most-derived* class, which is usually a CComObject*xxx*<> class that won't pass on the pointer to its base classes. SetVoid() gives the base class a chance to get hold of the pointer. CComObjectRootBase defines an implementation of SetVoid() that does absolutely nothing, just to ensure that this function is always defined.

Also note the call to FinalConstruct(). This call is present to allow you to have code that will be executed as the final step of constructing your object. FinalConstruct() is defined in CComObjectRootBase simply to return S_OK, but you can add a FinalConstruct() member to your own class to provide a different implementation. If you return *any* code other than S_OK (including other success codes) from FinalConstruct(), your object will be destroyed and that code returned to the client. Only ever return S_OK if you want to indicate success and continue with the creation of your object.

You should use FinalConstruct() in preference to adding code to your class's constructor for two reasons. First, FinalConstruct() gives you the opportunity to return errors and abort creation if something goes wrong. Second, the ATL_NO_VTABLE optimization limits the calls that you can make from the constructor — you can't make calls to virtual functions, because the vtable isn't properly initialized at that point.

The call to `FinalConstruct()` is wrapped in a pair of strange-looking calls to `InternalFinalConstructAddRef()` and `InternalFinalConstructRelease()`. These functions are implemented by `CComObjectRootBase` to do nothing in the release build. (There's an `ASSERT` in the debug build). These functions only need to be replaced with some real code to increment and decrement the reference count if the code that you add to your `FinalConstruct()` functions results in a pair of `AddRef()` and `Release()` calls on your object. This can cause your object to delete itself prematurely, and might happen if you pass out a pointer to your object for some reason. The `ASSERT` in the debug build is designed to let you know when you need this code.

You can see how the object might delete itself in these circumstances when you realize that `FinalConstruct()` is called as an object is being created, but *before* the reference count has been incremented for the first time. Any code from within `FinalConstruct()` that results in a pair of `AddRef()` (or `QueryInterface()`) and `Release()` calls on your object can cause your object's reference count to reach zero. At this point the object will delete itself, even though code in the object still needs to be executed to satisfy the creation of the object.

The easiest way to add the code to combat this problem is to add the `DECLARE_PROTECT_FINAL_CONSTRUCT()` macro to a class definition. By default, the Object Wizard will do this for you. This macro provides code to bump up the reference count for long enough to avoid premature deletion.

```
#define DECLARE_PROTECT_FINAL_CONSTRUCT()\
    void InternalFinalConstructAddRef() {InternalAddRef();}\
    void InternalFinalConstructRelease() {InternalRelease();}
```

`InternalAddRef()` and `InternalRelease()` are inherited from `CComObjectRootEx<>`.

> `CComObjectRootBase` *also defines a* `FinalRelease()` *function that can be overridden (masked) in your class to provide code that should be executed when the last reference to your object has been released.*

Creation Summary

Class objects are created in different ways, depending on whether the module is an EXE or a DLL.

In a DLL, class objects are created by the first request made for that object to `DllGetClassObject()`. The `IUnknown` pointer for a class object is stored in the `pCF` member of the corresponding `_ATL_OBJMAP_ENTRY` structure, ready for subsequent requests.

In an EXE, all class objects are created as soon as the application loads. The `IUnknown` pointer for each class object is stored in the system by a call to `CoRegisterClassObject()`.

Once a client has a pointer to an interface on a class object, DLL or EXE packaging makes no difference to the ATL code.

During creation, ATL calls the `FinalConstruct()` member of your class to give you a chance to initialize your class once the vtable is fully initialized, and a way of returning errors if something goes wrong. Add code to `FinalConstruct()` in preference to your class's constructor.

An Example of Object Creation

We've now seen how ATL provides class objects and the `IUnknown` methods for us, so it's about time we had another quick example. This time, we're going to create a project that contains *two* coclasses, only one of which will be externally creatable — clients will only be able to create instances of the second class by calling methods on the first. If you look at any reasonably complex COM server (like Microsoft Word, for example), you will see that it is built up of a hierarchy of objects, with many of the objects in the hierarchy only accessible through methods of the classes higher up.

First, create a new ATL COM AppWizard project called `ReturningAnObject`. Make this project a DLL server. Now use the ATL Object Wizard to create a new simple object. Give it the short name `MainObject`, and leave the rest of the dialog with its default settings. The generated class will act as the main (externally creatable) class for the server.

Start the ATL Object Wizard again. This time, generate a class with the short name `SeparateObject`, and once again leave the rest of the dialog with its default settings. This class will only be creatable via a call to one of the methods on the main object's interface.

To prevent clients from being able to create `SeparateObject`s, we need to replace the appropriate entry in object map with an `OBJECT_ENTRY_NON_CREATEABLE()` macro. Open `ReturningAnObject.cpp` and modify the entry for the separate object. The map should now look like this:

```
BEGIN_OBJECT_MAP(ObjectMap)
OBJECT_ENTRY(CLSID_MainObject, CMainObject)
OBJECT_ENTRY_NON_CREATEABLE(CSeparateObject)
END_OBJECT_MAP()
```

That seems simple enough, but you should bear in mind the warnings earlier in the chapter about the registration of objects that aren't externally creatable. (ATL is broken, and it will register the object under `CLSID_NULL`.) To prevent these problems, change the registration details of the `CSeparateObject` class:

```
CSeparateObject()
{
}

DECLARE_NO_REGISTRY()

DECLARE_PROTECT_FINAL_CONSTRUCT()
```

In this example, the object that can't be externally created doesn't have an `ObjectMain()` function, so the entry in the object map is not strictly necessary. However, it's useful to have it there as a visual reminder of what's going on.

Once the `OBJECT_ENTRY()` macro has been replaced, the class object that creates `SeparateObjects` will no longer be compiled into our DLL, and clients won't be able to create objects of that type. We can further slim down the size of our module by removing `CComCoClass<>` from the list of base classes, since it is only used by externally creatable classes. The RGS file for the class is no longer needed either, so you can go to ResourceView, expand the `"REGISTRY"` folder, select `IDR_SEPARATEOBJECT`, and hit the *Delete* key. (If you want to delete the actual RGS file, you need to do this manually from Explorer.)

Next, mark the definition of the `SeparateObject` coclass in the IDL file with the `[noncreatable]` attribute:

```
[
    uuid(04E053D6-5627-11D3-A074-00902707906A),
    helpstring("SeparateObject Class"),
    noncreatable
]
coclass SeparateObject
{
    [default] interface ISeparateObject;
};
```

The reason for using this attribute (rather than just deleting the coclass) is to give clients access to the type information of the class, even though they cannot create instances of it directly. They may still get access to objects of this class by indirect means.

> *Notice the inconsistent spelling here: the IDL attribute is* `[noncreatable]`, *while the object map entry macro is* `OBJECT_ENTRY_NON_CREATEABLE()`.

Finally, since we can no longer use the implementation of `GetCategoryMap()` supplied by `CComCoClass<>`, we need to add an empty category map to the class definition, right after the COM map:

```
BEGIN_CATEGORY_MAP(CSeparateObject)
END_CATEGORY_MAP()
```

We can now add one simple method to each of the `ISeparateObject` and `IMainObject` interfaces. We'll use these methods to display simple dialog boxes, so we know that everything is working as it should. Right-click on the `ISeparateObject` interface name in ClassView and select **Add Method...** from the context menu. Call the method `Display` and click **OK**. Repeat the process for the `IMainObject` interface.

Now add the following code to `CMainObject::Display()`:

```
STDMETHODIMP CMainObject::Display()
{
    MessageBox(NULL, _T("IMainObject::Display()"),
                     _T("IMainObject::Display()"), MB_OK);
    return S_OK;
}
```

And add this code to `CSeparateObject::Display()`:

```
STDMETHODIMP CSeparateObject::Display()
{
    MessageBox(NULL, _T("ISeparateObject::Display()"),
                     _T("ISeparateObject::Display()"), MB_OK);
    return S_OK;
}
```

Next up, we can add a method to `IMainObject` to return an interface pointer to a newly created `SeparateObject`. Use ClassView's **Add Method to Interface** dialog to add a new method called `CreateSeparateObject()`, like so:

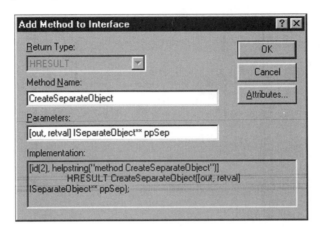

Implement the method as shown below, and add a `#include` for `SeparateObject.h` to the top of the file:

```
STDMETHODIMP CMainObject::CreateSeparateObject(ISeparateObject **ppSep)
{
    *ppSep = NULL;
    return CComCreator< CComObject<CSeparateObject> >::CreateInstance(
        NULL, IID_ISeparateObject, reinterpret_cast<void**>(ppSep));
}
```

The first line of the method simply ensures that the pointer returned to the client is `NULL` in case of failure (and avoids an assert from the ATL code). The `return` statement is the line that does all the hard work.

In this case, we're not interested in doing anything except creating the object and returning an interface to the client, so we can use the same mechanism that the ATL class object would use to create an object of this type. We've called the static function `CComCreator<>::CreateInstance()`, passing in `NULL` for the first parameter (which is usually used for aggregation), `IID_ISeparateObject` as the second parameter (the interface that we wish to receive a pointer to), and `ppSep` as the third parameter (the storage for the returned interface pointer).

`CComCreator<>` takes the type of object to create as its template parameter. In this case, we're creating objects of type `CComObject<CSeparateObject>`. Remember that `CComObject<>` is usually used to provide the `IUnknown` method implementations for your class, and that you can't instantiate your class directly.

149

You can have a look back to our discussion of `CComCreator<>::CreateInstance()` earlier in the chapter to see precisely what it's doing for you, but you can be assured that it constructs your objects fully, calling `FinalConstruct()` and handling errors as necessary. `CComCreator<>::CreateInstance()` is a nice bit of code; it makes sense to reuse it.

Be aware that the `CreateSeparateObject()` function has introduced an order dependency into your IDL file, since the parameter requires the MIDL compiler to know about the `ISeparateObject` interface in order to compile it. The solution for this kind of problem in IDL is the same as the one you'd use in C++: you can forward declare the interface at the top of the file. In fact, by adding partial definitions for *all* the interfaces defined in the file, you can rid yourself completely of the blight of order dependency:

```
import "oaidl.idl";
import "ocidl.idl";

interface IMainObject;
interface ISeparateObject;
```

At this stage, you can build the project so that it's ready to be tested.

The Client

Now we can create a simple client to test the server. Create a new, empty Win32 Console Application and give it the name `ConsoleClient`. Save this project in a subdirectory of `ReturningAnObject` so that we can use a relative path to get to the server's type library.

Add a new source file to the project and add the following code to it:

```
#import "..\ReturningAnObject.tlb"
using namespace RETURNINGANOBJECTLib;
#include <iostream>
using namespace std;

int main()
{
    CoInitialize(NULL);
    try
    {
        IMainObjectPtr pMain(__uuidof(MainObject));
        pMain->Display();

        // Uncomment the following line to trigger a runtime error
        // ISeparateObjectPtr pCantCreateSep(__uuidof(SeparateObject));
        ISeparateObjectPtr pSep = pMain->CreateSeparateObject();
        pSep->Display();
    }
    catch(const _com_error& Err)
    {
        cout << Err.ErrorMessage() << hex << " 0x" << Err.Error() << '\n';
    }

    CoUninitialize();
    return 0;
}
```

The code simply initializes COM, creates an instance of the main object class, calls `Display()` to show that the main object's working, calls `CreateSeparateObject()` to create a new separate object, and then calls `Display()` on the separate object to show that's working too. When you build the project and run this code, you'll see two message boxes in succession, telling you when each of the `Display()` methods is called.

If you uncomment the line indicated, you'll get an error at runtime complaining that the object isn't registered. This is because the server cannot find the class object for the component — and since you changed the `OBJECT_ENTRY()` macro for this class, that's exactly what you'd expect.

Initializing Objects

One reason that you might want to allow the creation of objects only through a method call on another object's interface is so that you can perform some initialization of the object before returning it to the client (you may not be able to add all your initialization code to `FinalConstruct()`). Our existing method for creating separate objects doesn't provide any initialization of the object, so we'll add a new method to the `IMainObject` interface to return *initialized* objects to the client.

Before we do that, we need to add a little bit of code to `CSeparateObject` to demonstrate whether it's been initialized. For this simple example, we'll just add a public member to the class to act as an initialization flag, and we'll change the `Display()` code to show whether this flag has been set or not.

First, add a public Boolean member called `m_bInitialized` to `CSeparateObject`:

```
public:
    STDMETHOD(Display)();
    bool m_bInitialized;
```

It is important that this data member is public, because it will be accessed from outside the object. Initialize it to `false` in the constructor:

```
public:
    CSeparateObject() : m_bInitialized(false)
    {
    }
```

Alter the code in `CSeparateObject::Display()` so that we can tell whether the object has been initialized:

```
STDMETHODIMP CSeparateObject::Display()
{
    if(!m_bInitialized)
        MessageBox(NULL, _T("ISeparateObject::Display()"),
                         _T("ISeparateObject::Display()"), MB_OK);
    else
        MessageBox(NULL, _T("ISeparateObject::Display() - Initialized"),
                         _T("ISeparateObject::Display() - Initialized"), MB_OK);
    return S_OK;
}
```

Now add a new method to the `IMainObject` interface to return an initialized, separate object. Use the ClassView dialog as usual, and name the method `CreateAndInitializeSeparateObject()`:

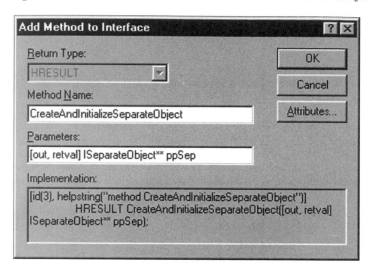

The code to implement this new method is shown below:

```
STDMETHODIMP CMainObject::CreateAndInitializeSeparateObject(
                                                ISeparateObject **ppSep)
{
    *ppSep = NULL;

    // Declare a CComObject<> pointer using your class as the template parameter
    CComObject<CSeparateObject>* pSub;

    // Call the static CComObject<>::CreateInstance() member,
    // passing a pointer to your pointer. This creates an instance of your
    // CComObject<> class, without any references counted on it.
    HRESULT hr = CComObject<CSeparateObject>::CreateInstance(&pSub);

    // Check the return result, and pass it back to the client on failure
    if(FAILED(hr))
        return hr;

    // Initialize the object according to your own rules
    pSub->m_bInitialized = true;

    // Call QI() to get the interface pointer to pass back to the client
    hr = pSub->QueryInterface(ppSep);

    // If the QueryInterface() failed, delete the object
    if(FAILED(hr))
        delete pSub;

    // Return the HRESULT
    return hr;
}
```

Once again, we set *ppSep to NULL right at the start, but this time the rest of the code is more involved because we can't let CComCreator<> do all the work.

First, we declare a CComObject<CSeparateObject>* that will hold the pointer to our newly created object, once it's been created. Next, we pass the address of this pointer to CComObject<>::CreateInstance(). This method creates an instance of its own class and stores a pointer to it in the parameter passed to the function. CreateInstance() ensures that our object is fully created (it calls FinalConstruct(), for example) before returning the pointer. It creates an object without any references counted on it (since references are counted on interfaces, and we haven't actually got a pointer to an interface on the object yet).

Assuming that the object is successfully created, we initialize it. In our case, this is a simple matter of setting a Boolean member to true, but in a real server this code would be much more complicated and would depend on your particular circumstances.

Once initialized, we query for the ISeparateObject interface, using the ppSep parameter that was passed to our method to store the interface pointer. If successful, the client will receive the interface pointer and can Release() it when it's done. The only thing to watch out for is that if the call to QueryInterface() is *not* successful, we need to make sure that the object gets deleted ourselves.

Type Safe QueryInterface()

You will surely have noticed the rather unusual-looking call to QueryInterface() that we used in the above code. At the risk of being repetitious, it went like this:

```
// Call QI() to get the interface pointer to pass back to the client
hr = pSub->QueryInterface(ppSep);
```

What's happened to the other argument, and where has the inevitable reinterpret_cast<>() gone? Well, one of the problems with the 'classic' QueryInterface() method is that the interface and type are passed as two separate parameters, which means that you can write erroneous code like this:

```
IInterfaceOne* pOne = NULL;
// This code is bad!
hr = pTwo->QueryInterface(__uuidof(IInterfaceTwo),
                          reinterpret_cast<void**>(&pOne));
```

However, the authors who wrote IUnknwn.h (the include file that contains standard implementations of the IUnknown methods), have provided the following as part of the IUnknown interface implementation:

```
#if (_MSC_VER >= 1200) // VC6 or greater
    template <class Q>
    HRESULT STDMETHODCALLTYPE QueryInterface(Q** pp)
    {
        return QueryInterface(__uuidof(Q), (void**)pp);
    }
#endif
```

This is a template function that allows you to call `QueryInterface()` in a type safe way. You have neither to cast the parameter to `void**` (because the template function does that for you), nor to specify the interface's IID. Because it uses `__uuidof()`, this will only work with interfaces defined with `MIDL_INTERFACE()`, but that's no problem here.

Updating The Client

Now you can build the server project again, ready to be tested. The changes that need to be made to the client are extremely simple, and they're shown below:

```
#import "..\ReturningAnObject.tlb"
using namespace RETURNINGANOBJECTLib;
#include <iostream>
using namespace std;

int main()
{
   CoInitialize(NULL);
   try
   {
       IMainObjectPtr pMain(__uuidof(MainObject));
       pMain->Display();

       // Uncomment the following line to trigger a runtime error
       // ISeparateObjectPtr pCantCreateSep(__uuidof(SeparateObject));
       ISeparateObjectPtr pSep = pMain->CreateSeparateObject();
       pSep->Display();

       ISeparateObjectPtr pSepInit = pMain->CreateAndInitializeSeparateObject();
       pSepInit->Display();
   }
   catch(const _com_error& Err)
   {
       cout << Err.ErrorMessage() << hex << " 0x" << Err.Error() << '\n';
   }

   CoUninitialize();
   return 0;
}
```

We just create a new smart pointer called `pSepInit` and fill it with the interface pointer returned from `CreateAndInitializeSeparateObject()`. The call to `pSepInit->Display()` results in a new message box that proves that the object was initialized.

Example Summary

Here's a quick summary of the lessons we've learned from this example:

❏ You can prevent Wizard-generated coclasses from being externally creatable by changing their object map entry to OBJECT_ENTRY_NON_CREATEABLE().

❏ You should make the following changes to classes that aren't externally creatable:

The registry script resource can be removed
The DECLARE_REGISTRY_RESOURCEID() macro should be replaced with DECLARE_NO_REGISTRY()
The CComCoClass<> base class can be removed
A blank category map should be added
The coclass definition in the IDL file should be marked with the noncreatable attribute.

❏ If you want to create an instance of a coclass and pass an interface pointer directly to a client, the easiest way is CComCreator< CComObject<CYourClass> >::CreateInstance().

❏ If you want to do some initialization of an object before returning an interface pointer to the client, use CComObject<CYourClass>::CreateInstance() to create the object.

❏ If you use CComObject<CYourClass>::CreateInstance(), don't forget to delete the object if the call to QueryInterface() fails.

Reusability

COM is a great way of reusing code by packaging it as programmable objects, but so far we've only looked at *clients* using COM objects. What happens when we want to reuse a component from within another component? How can we take advantage of the features of a commercial component, and how can we add to the functionality of a component once it's been compiled?

In COM, there are two primary mechanisms for reusing one component within another: **containment** and **aggregation**.

Containment

Containment is the equivalent of having one component as a member variable of another. The outer (controlling, containing) component makes use of the inner (contained) component, but does not directly expose the contained component to its clients.

The outer component can choose to use the inner component to implement some of its functionality. If the outer component decides to implement one or more of the interfaces of the inner component, as shown in the following figure, it must provide a wrapper for every method on the exposed interfaces. The method wrappers can simply call the inner component's methods directly, or they can perform additional tasks such as validating parameters, recording usage, or otherwise extending the inner component's interface.

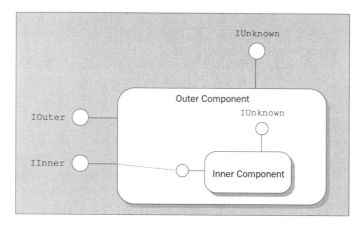

The outer component manages the lifetime of the inner component. It typically creates the inner component with `CoCreateInstance()` when it initializes itself (`FinalConstruct()`), and releases the inner component's interface pointer when it uninitializes itself (`FinalRelease()`). In containment, the outer component isn't doing anything very different from what a standard client would do.

Aggregation

Sometimes, it's more convenient to expose the interfaces of the inner object directly, without writing a collection of wrappers. This is aggregation. A client creates the outer object, and when it asks `QueryInterface()` for an interface supported by the inner object, it gets passed a pointer to the inner object's interface.

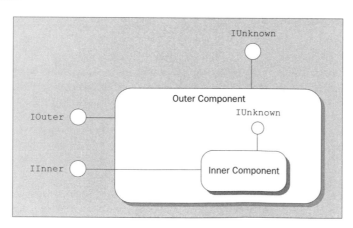

To a client, an aggregation (like containment) looks like one seamless object; the client does not know that there are actually two separate components acting in unison. (In fact, there could be more than two. There's no reason why the outer component cannot aggregate several different components, or why the inner component cannot aggregate another component into itself, like one of those Russian dolls that opens up to reveal another, smaller doll inside.)

One advantage of aggregation over containment is that it requires much less knowledge of the inner component on the part of the person implementing the outer component. Another is that bypassing the wrapper layer makes the component that bit more efficient.

The disadvantages of aggregation are that the inner (aggregated) object must be specially written so that it can be aggregated, and that the inner object can only be implemented in a DLL that is loaded directly into the same apartment as the outer object. There is no cross-apartment, cross-process or cross-machine aggregation.

To see why aggregation requires the knowledge and cooperation of the inner component, consider the diagram above. Suppose the client creates the aggregated object and asks for an IOuter interface pointer. Later, the client QI()s for and receives an IInner pointer. What happens when the client does a pIInner->QueryInterface(IID_IOuter)? If the inner component doesn't know that it has been aggregated, it's not going to be able to return an IOuter pointer. In Chapter 2, you saw that QueryInterface() must be both symmetric and transitive, so the inner component has somehow to return an IOuter interface pointer.

Identity and lifetime considerations also force the inner object to know that it is being aggregated. Clients know nothing of the aggregation, and see a single object. They expect AddRef() and Release() to control the lifetime of this object, no matter which interface pointer is being used. Thus, an AddRef() on the IInner interface should be sufficient to keep both the outer and inner objects alive, just as an AddRef() on the IOuter interface should.

An object knows when it's being aggregated because the aggregator calls IClassFactory::CreateInstance() (or CoCreateInstance()) with the punkOuter parameter set to the **outer unknown** of the aggregating component, and asks for a pointer to the IUnknown interface. The outer unknown of a component is its own IUnknown interface if it's not being aggregated, or the outer unknown that was passed to it through IClassFactory::CreateInstance() if it is. Thus, if there are many levels of aggregation, all the aggregated objects have a pointer to the same outer unknown that controls the lifetime and QueryInterface() functionality for the whole object.

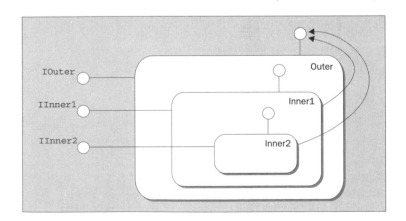

To be aggregatable, the inner component must have *two* distinct implementations of the three `IUnknown` methods, `QueryInterface()`, `AddRef()` and `Release()`. One of these implementations is for all the interfaces except `IUnknown`; in it, the three methods must delegate all calls to the outer unknown, because a client can get a pointer to any of these interfaces, and so call these methods directly.

The other implementation of these methods is used for `IUnknown` only. This implementation is known as the **explicit `IUnknown` implementation**. These methods do not delegate; they provide a traditional implementation of `IUnknown` and manage the lifetime and `QueryInterface()` functionality of the inner object. These methods do not delegate because the inner component still needs some way of managing its own lifetime and exposing its own interfaces, even when aggregated. A *client* can never get a pointer to this `IUnknown` when a component is being aggregated; only the outer object has a pointer to it. The outer component must ask for a pointer to `IUnknown` when creating the inner object so that it can call `QueryInterface()`, `AddRef()` and `Release()` on the non-delegating implementation.

The outer component is required to follow a handful of rules when dealing with the inner component:

❏ When creating the inner component, it must ask for `IUnknown` (the inner component should fail if any other interface is asked for when it's created as part of an aggregate).

❏ After obtaining any interface pointer on the inner object other than `IUnknown`, the outer object must `Release()` its own outer unknown pointer (which resolves to either its explicit unknown or the outermost outer unknown). This counteracts the implicit `AddRef()` delegated to the outer unknown by the inner object in its implementation of `QueryInterface()`.

❏ Conversely, before releasing an interface pointer on the inner object, the outer object must `AddRef()` its outer unknown.

❏ When the outer object shuts down, it must release the inner object. This means that it must `AddRef()` its outer unknown, then call `Release()` on the inner object. The call to `Release()` may, in turn, cause the inner object to call `Release()` on the outer object's interface. Without artificially bumping the reference count, we'd end up with problems. You can see this by looking at the sequence of events below:

Event	Outer Object's Reference Count
1. Client has reference to object	1
2. Client calls `Release()`	0
3. Outer object calls `AddRef()` on itself	1
4. Outer object releases inner object	1
5. Inner object releases outer object (back to Step 3)	0

❑   Generally, the outer object should not blindly delegate `QI()`s for unrecognized interfaces to the inner object. An inner object could support more interfaces than the outer object knows about.

Because of this combination of features, aggregation can be used to perform two tasks: 'black box' reuse of code, and some 'identity tricks'. You can view 'black box' reuse from two perspectives: either the outer object is adding functionality to the inner object, or else it's purposely creating the inner object to implement one or more interfaces. In both cases, the identity of the composite object *is* the outer object; the outer object can aggregate many different objects, each with their own identities, but they will be combined into one single object with one identity.

It can be useful to write your object deliberately so that it can be aggregated. Doing so has no effect at all on the object's intrinsic usefulness, but it enables some other code (the COM runtime, for example) to aggregate it. By this means, the aggregator can provide the identity of the object and use it to perform functions like tracking the object and its use. For example, the proxy object used in marshaling (see Chapter 1) is provided by standard marshaling code that's implemented by the COM runtime. As the client queries for interfaces, the appropriate interface proxies are aggregated into the proxy object.

The Inner Object In ATL

Thankfully, ATL handles the hard parts of aggregation for you. The `DECLARE_AGGREGATABLE()` macro, which is provided by default for your COM classes, means that when an object is being aggregated, it's created as a `CComAggObject<>`; when an object is being created independently, it's created as a `CComObject<>`.

`CComAggObject<>` provides the implementations of the explicit unknown methods, so it implements `AddRef()`, `Release()` and `QueryInterface()`. `QueryInterface()` returns a pointer to the `CComAggObject<>`'s `IUnknown` interface if there is a request for `IID_IUnknown`; otherwise it delegates to the `_InternalQueryInterface()` function of its `m_contained` member.

Unlike `CComObject<>`, `CComAggObject<>` doesn't derive from your class (for example, `CYourClass`). Instead, its `m_contained` member is an object of type `CComContainedObject<CYourClass>`, which *does* derive from `CYourClass`. This means that `m_contained`'s `_InternalQueryInterface()` function is the one provided by the `BEGIN_COM_MAP()` macro in your class.

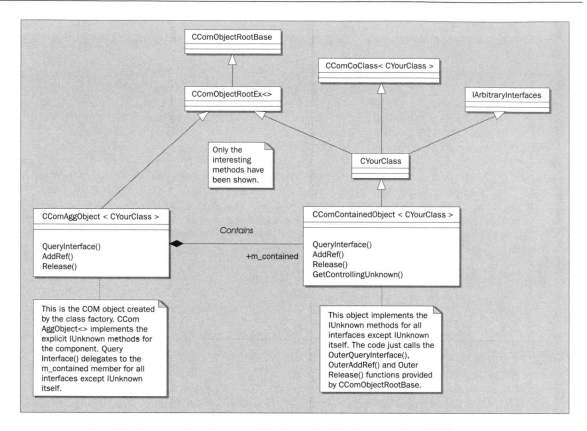

CComContainedObject<> therefore provides the other implementation of the AddRef(), Release() and QueryInterface() methods. This implementation delegates to the OuterAddRef(), OuterRelease() and OuterQueryInterface() functions provided by CComObjectRootBase. These implementations are just simple inline functions that call AddRef(), Release(), and QueryInterface() through the outer unknown pointer. They don't require any information about the interfaces provided by your class.

GetControllingUnknown()

CComContainedObject<> also provides a function called GetControllingUnknown(), which returns a pointer to the controlling unknown. If there's a chance that your object might be aggregated, and you need to get a pointer to the IUnknown interface for your object, have a think about whether you really want the explicit IUnknown of the component, or the controlling unknown.

There's just one problem with calling GetControllingUnknown() from our class: it's defined by a class lower down the inheritance tree. We can't call a function in our class if it's not defined!

The solution is simply to add the DECLARE_GET_CONTROLLING_UNKNOWN() macro to the definition of your class. This defines GetControllingUnknown() as a virtual function in your class. It's always safe to use this macro and call the function (even if the object is never aggregated) because it's implemented as a call to GetUnknown(). If the function isn't overridden by CComContainedObject<>::GetControllingUnknown(), then things will still work as expected.

```
#define DECLARE_GET_CONTROLLING_UNKNOWN() public:\
    virtual IUnknown* GetControllingUnknown() {return GetUnknown();}
```

Changing The Aggregation Model

It's possible to change the aggregation model for your class by using one of the other DECLARE_xxxAGGREGATABLE() macros. These macros can be added to your class definition by the ATL Object Wizard when you generate a simple object, by choosing the appropriate option in the **Aggregation** frame on the **Attributes** tab. Alternatively, you can add these macros by hand after your class has been generated.

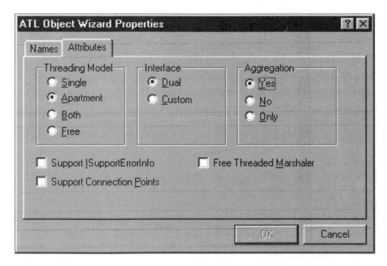

If you want to disallow aggregation, you can use the DECLARE_NOT_AGGREGATABLE() macro. Allowing aggregation increases the code size of an object, so you might want to do this for efficiency reasons. You can also add this macro to EXE-packaged classes when you generate them, because aggregation is *never* performed cross process. If, on the other hand, you want objects of your class to be created *only* as part of an aggregation, add the DECLARE_ONLY_AGGREGATABLE() macro to your class definition.

If you want to have your objects created from the same class whether they are being aggregated or not, add the DECLARE_POLY_AGGREGATABLE() macro to your class definition. The DECLARE_POLY_AGGREGATABLE() macro means that your COM objects will always be created as objects of type CComPolyObject<CYourClass>.

When you look at the documentation for CComPolyObject<>, you might be forgiven for thinking that it's a very different class from CComAggObject<>, but a look at the source code soon reveals that the differences are tiny. You can see them below:

```
// Constructor for CComAggObject<>
CComAggObject(void* pv) : m_contained(pv)
{
    _Module.Lock();
}
// FinalConstruct() for CComAggObject<>
HRESULT FinalConstruct()
{
    CComObjectRootEx<contained::_ThreadModel::ThreadModelNoCS>::FinalConstruct();
    return m_contained.FinalConstruct();
}

// Constructor for CComPolyObject<>
CComPolyObject(void* pv) : m_contained(pv ? pv : this)
{
    _Module.Lock();
}
// FinalConstruct() for CComPolyObject<>
HRESULT FinalConstruct()
{
    InternalAddRef();
    CComObjectRootEx<contained::_ThreadModel::ThreadModelNoCS>::FinalConstruct();
    HRESULT hr = m_contained.FinalConstruct();
    InternalRelease();
    return hr;
}
```

The variations between these two classes lie in the initializer lists of their constructors, and in the bumping up of the reference count around the call to the contained object's FinalConstruct() method.

The pv parameter of the constructor represents the outer unknown. In the case of CComAggObject<>, pv is passed untouched to the CComContainedObject<> constructor. In the case of CComPolyObject<>, pv is passed if it's not NULL, otherwise the CComPolyObject<>'s this pointer is passed as the outer unknown.

If you want your objects to be created both as part of an aggregation *and* independently, then switching over to CComPolyObject<> will almost certainly reduce the size of your compiled code, since you will no longer get the vtable and functions of CComObject<CYourClass> compiled into it. However, the CComObject<> class will be smaller at runtime than the CComPolyObject<> equivalent, so you may take a hit in your module's working set. ATL is designed to allow you maximum flexibility in optimizing your code for different circumstances.

The Outer Object In ATL

From the other side of things, how does ATL help us when we want to aggregate a component into one that we've written? We'll see just how easy it is to aggregate a component by aggregating the simple example from the previous chapter into a brand new object that we'll create here. This object will be fairly simple: given a date, it will return the corresponding weekday.

To begin then, create a new ATL DLL project called DatesSvr in the directory that contains the folder for the Simple project. Now use the ATL Object Wizard to add a simple object with the short name of WeekDay, and leave all the default settings on the **Attributes** page alone.

> *Note that choosing the default settings means that this component has a* ThreadingModel *of* Apartment. *It is important that any components to be aggregated into this component have a* ThreadingModel *of either* Apartment *or* Both, *to ensure that the aggregated object will be created in the same apartment. Aggregation does not work across apartment boundaries.*

This object will have a single method called GetWeekDay() that will return the name of the day, given the day, month and year. Use ClassView to add this method to the IWeekDay interface:

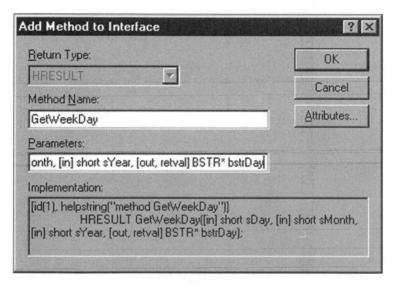

It's fairly simple to get the weekday by using functions of the CRT, but because ATL won't use the CRT by default, you will have to enable it to do so. Go into the **Project Settings** dialog and select **Multiple Configurations** from the <u>S</u>ettings For pull-down list. This will show a list of all the build configurations, from which you should select the four 'release' builds. Finally, go to the C/C++ tab, select **Preprocessor** from the **Category** pull-down list, and remove the _ATL_MIN_CRT symbol from the **Preprocessor** definitions edit box. This will allow you to use the CRT in all release builds (it is enabled by default in all debug builds).

```
// WeekDay.cpp : Implementation of CWeekDay
#include "stdafx.h"
#include "DatesSvr.h"
#include "WeekDay.h"
#include <time.h>

/////////////////////////////////////////////////////////////////////////////
// CWeekDay

// sMonth is indexed from 1 to 12, where January is 1
STDMETHODIMP CWeekDay::GetWeekDay(short sDay, short sMonth,
                                  short sYear, BSTR *bstrDay)
{
    struct tm tmTime;
    memset(&tmTime, 0, sizeof(tmTime));
    tmTime.tm_year = sYear - 1900;
    tmTime.tm_mon = sMonth - 1;
    tmTime.tm_mday = sDay;

    time_t tTime;
    tTime = mktime(&tmTime);

    // This is a static variable
    struct tm* ptmTime;
    ptmTime = gmtime(&tTime);

    CComBSTR bstrTime(50);
    wcsftime(bstrTime.m_str, bstrTime.Length(), L"%A", ptmTime);

    return bstrTime.CopyTo(bstrDay);
}
```

The first step is to initialize a `struct tm` with the date, and then convert it to a `time_t` with a call to `mktime()`. When this is converted back to a `struct tm` with a call to `gmtime()` the CRT will calculate the day of the week (it will be placed in `ptmTime->tm_wday`, indexed so that Sunday is 0). To get the name of the day, we call the CRT `wcsftime()` function.

This code uses an object of type `CComBSTR`, *which is a wrapper for a string type called* `BSTR` *that we will meet formally in the next chapter. The wrapper handles resource allocation for the string, and also provides utility methods like* `Length()` *that we've used above.* `wcsftime()` *is actually expecting a pointer to a* `wchar_t` *buffer in its first parameter, but our code is safe because a* `BSTR` *allocated by* `CComBSTR` *in this way will always be allocated as an array of wide characters.*

The size of the `BSTR` *returned from* `CComBSTR::Length()` *is the allocated size in characters, and not the number of characters in the buffer. Once the* `BSTR` *has been filled by the call to* `wcsftime()`, *it is returned to the caller by calling* `CopyTo()`. *Logically enough, this method creates a copy of the string, which is necessary because the destructor of* `CComBSTR` *will free the* `BSTR` *it contains, so a new copy must be made.*

The server can now be compiled, and we're in a position to be able to create a simple client to test it. Generate an empty console application in the `DatesSvr` folder and call it `DateClient`. Add a new source file to the project and fill it with the following simple code:

```
#import "..\DatesSvr.tlb"
#include <iostream>

int main(int argc, char* argv[])
{
    HRESULT hr = CoInitialize(NULL);

    try
    {
        DATESSVRLib::IWeekDayPtr p(__uuidof(DATESSVRLib::WeekDay));
        SYSTEMTIME st;
        GetLocalTime(&st);
        _bstr_t bstrDay;
        bstrDay = p->GetWeekDay(st.wDay, st.wMonth, st.wYear);
        std::cout << "Today is " << static_cast<LPCSTR>(bstrDay) << std::endl;
    }
    catch(const _com_error& Err)
    {
        std::cout << Err.ErrorMessage() << " 0x"
                  << std::hex << Err.Error() << '\n';
        hr = Err.Error();
    }

    CoUninitialize();
    return hr;
}
```

It's true that the weekday can be obtained through SYSTEMTIME::wDayOfWeek, *but that won't return a string. In any case, this quick test client aside, the point of the server is to demonstrate aggregation, which we will do next.*

Aggregating An Object

The steps you need to follow for aggregating an object are extremely simple:

❑ Add a member in the outer class to store an IUnknown pointer

❑ Create an instance of the object that we're aggregating (the inner object). Pass in a pointer to the outer class's outer unknown, and ask for the inner object's IUnknown interface when you do this. Store the resulting pointer in the member you added to the outer class.

❑ Add COM_INTERFACE_ENTRY_AGGREGATE() macros to the COM map for each interface on the inner object that you want to expose from your object. You do *not* have to add an entry for *every* interface exposed by the inner object, only those that you want clients to get hold of.

❑ Make sure that the inner object's IUnknown pointer is released when the outer object shuts down.

❑ Add the new interfaces to the coclass definition in the outer object's IDL file if appropriate.

First, we need to get the CLSID and IID definitions from the Simple project into the DatesSvr project, so open DatesSvr in Visual C++ and add a #include for Simple.h to the top of WeekDay.h. You should use the relative path from the DatesSvr directory to the Simple directory:

```
#include "resource.h"
#include "..\Simple\Simple.h"
```

Remember that `Simple.h` is the MIDL compiler-generated header containing the `extern` declarations of the `Simple` project's GUIDs.

We also need to add the non-`extern` definitions of the IDs into our project. The easiest way to do this is to add a `#include` for `Simple_i.c` to `DatesSvr.cpp`.

```
#include "DatesSvr.h"
#include "..\Simple\Simple_i.c"
```

It's a good idea to add this `#include` in the same file as the existing `#include` for `DatesSvr_i.c`, if only for consistency's sake.

Now we need to add a member to the `CWeekDay` class to hold the `IUnknown` pointer that we're going to get back from the aggregate when we create it. In this example, we're going to add a `CComPtr<>` member. Add the code shown to the `CWeekDay` class definition, just below the constructor:

```
CWeekDay()
{
}

CComPtr<IUnknown> m_pAgg;
```

`CComPtr<>` is a smart pointer class that handles reference counting automatically. It is similar to the `_com_ptr_t<>` class we met in Chapter 3, but it's an intrinsic part of ATL, so we don't need to add any extra headers when we use it, and we don't need to worry about it dragging huge amounts of code into our project. We'll use `CComPtr<>` simply so that we can forget about releasing the inner object's interface pointer when the outer component is released for the last time — `CComPtr<>` will do that for us without any intervention.

The next step is actually to create an instance of the inner object when the outer object (`CWeekDay`) first gets initialized. The place to do this is in `FinalConstruct()`, so add the following code right after the declaration of m_pAgg:

```
HRESULT FinalConstruct()
{
    // Create the inner object
    return CoCreateInstance(CLSID_CalcEaster,
                            GetControllingUnknown(),
                            CLSCTX_INPROC_SERVER,
                            IID_IUnknown,
                            reinterpret_cast<void**>(&m_pAgg));
}
```

You can see that we're using `CoCreateInstance()` to create an instance of the `CalcEaster` coclass. The second parameter to `CoCreateInstance()` is the outer unknown of the `CWeekDay` object. We do not know that the current instance of the `WeekDay` coclass is the controlling object, or whether it too has been aggregated. To take this into account, we use `GetControllingUnknown()`, which will either return the controlling outer `IUnknown` if it is aggregated, or its own `IUnknown` if it is not. In addition, you must use the following macro so that `GetControllingUnknown()` will work:

```
DECLARE_REGISTRY_RESOURCEID(IDR_WEEKDAY)
DECLARE_GET_CONTROLLING_UNKNOWN()
DECLARE_PROTECT_FINAL_CONSTRUCT()
```

The third parameter to `CoCreateInstance()` specifies the execution context for the server we're creating. We know that aggregation only works with in-process objects, so we're quite happy to be as specific as possible and request an in-process server. The fourth parameter is the interface we're asking for, which must be `IUnknown` when we're creating an object as part of an aggregate.

The final parameter is the address of the pointer that will store the `IUnknown` pointer for which we're asking. The `CComPtr<>` class implements an `operator&()` function that returns the address of the member that it uses to store its interface pointer — we're not actually taking the address of the `CComPtr<>` object itself.

Now we need to add a `COM_INTERFACE_ENTRY_AGGREGATE()` macro for the `ICalcEaster` interface to the COM map.

```
BEGIN_COM_MAP(CWeekDay)
    COM_INTERFACE_ENTRY(IWeekDay)
    COM_INTERFACE_ENTRY(IDispatch)
    COM_INTERFACE_ENTRY_AGGREGATE(IID_ICalcEaster, m_pAgg.p)
END_COM_MAP()
```

The `COM_INTERFACE_ENTRY_AGGREGATE()` macro takes an interface identifier for the interface that we're exposing, and an `IUnknown*` for the inner object that implements the interface. The macro itself hides the details that handle the implementation of `QueryInterface()`.

At this stage, we could compile and test the project and everything would work, but we'll just make the finishing touches by adding the new interface to the coclass definition in the type library. Add the code shown highlighted below to the `library` section of `DatesSvr.idl`:

```
library DATESSVRLib
{
    importlib("stdole32.tlb");
    importlib("stdole2.tlb");
    importlib("..\simple\simple.tlb");

    [
        uuid(7A2D3EA0-5945-11D3-89CD-00104BDC35E0),
        helpstring("WeekDay class")
    ]
    coclass WeekDay
    {
        [default] interface WeekDay;
        interface ICalcEaster;
    };
};
```

You can see that we've used the `importlib` statement to introduce the types from the `Simple` type library into the `DatesSvr` type library. This means that we can use the types and interfaces from `Simple.tlb` in the current library, without the types actually being duplicated in the library.

The `coclass` block just includes an extra line for the new interface exposed by `WeekDay`.

Client Changes

Once you've successfully recompiled the server project, you can turn your attention to the client. In order to be able to use the new interface, you must add its definition to the client code. This can be achieved simply by importing the `Simple.tlb` type library:

```
#import "..\DatesSvr.tlb"
#import "..\..\Simple\Simple.tlb"
#include <iostream>
```

Now you can create a `WeekDay` object, but access the `ICalcEaster` interface:

```
int main(int argc, char* argv[])
{
    HRESULT hr = CoInitialize(NULL);

    try
    {
        SIMPLELib::ICalcEasterPtr pEaster(__uuidof(DATESSVRLib::WeekDay));
        pEaster->Year = 2000;
        pEaster->CalculateEaster();
        _bstr_t bstrDay;

        DATESSVRLib::IWeekDayPtr pDay(pEaster);
        bstrDay = pDay->GetWeekDay(pEaster->Day, pEaster->Month, pEaster->Year);
        std::cout << "Easter day is on a " << static_cast<LPCSTR>(bstrDay);
        std::cout << " in " << pEaster->Year << std::endl;
    }
    catch(const _com_error& Err)
    {
        std::cout << Err.ErrorMessage() << " 0x"
                  << std::hex << Err.Error() << '\n';
        hr = Err.Error();
    }

    CoUninitialize();
    return hr;
}
```

This example is a little contrived — let's face it, Easter day is *always* a Sunday! However, you can see by examining this code that there is only *one* object being created. This takes place in the first new line, where an instance of `WeekDay` is created and the `ICalcEaster` interface is returned. You don't need to create an instance of `CalcEaster` because this is created by (and aggregated into) the `WeekDay` object.

You can see quite clearly that the object is an aggregate, because after calculating the date of Easter day for the year 2000, the object is queried for the `IWeekDay` interface in the following line:

```
DATESSVRLib::IWeekDayPtr pDay(pEaster);
```

The code then asks for the day of the week and prints it out. Cross your fingers and hope that it never returns anything other than Sunday!

Aggregation Summary

- ❑ Aggregation is a technique for reusing COM objects
- ❑ Aggregation requires the inner object to be implemented in a DLL
- ❑ Aggregation requires the inner object to be written with the possibility of aggregation in mind
- ❑ When the outer object creates the inner object as part of an aggregation, it *must* pass in its outer unknown pointer, and it *must* ask for the inner object's IUnknown interface
- ❑ ATL provides macro support for creating aggregatable objects and for exposing interfaces from objects that have been aggregated

Summary

This chapter has been heavy on detail, and to reflect that fact we've been providing detailed summaries at the end of each major section, rather than waiting until the end of the chapter to do it. Over four dozen pages, we've taken a very close look at how ATL provides core COM functionality to your classes.

Along the way, you've seen how the object map and COM map hide a lot of code that you can make use of use in your ATL projects, and you've seen techniques for customizing your objects using the various macros that ATL provides. With this essential knowledge under our belts, we can turn our attention to the next chapter, where we'll look at creating COM objects that are suitable for use from scripting clients.

Automation And Error Handling

Over the course of the last two chapters, the word 'Automation' has appeared with increasing regularity, and it's time we started to examine what it means and what implications it has. Broadly speaking, there are two types of interface in COM, categorized according to how the methods in the interfaces are accessed — static or dynamic invocation. **Static invocation** is the mechanism used by custom interfaces, and the way we have been doing things so far. **Dynamic invocation**, on the other hand, is the means by which Automation interfaces go about their business.

Static invocation is a contract between the client and a server object. The client knows *exactly* the number of methods in an interface, and the signatures of those methods. The object, for its side of the contract, *must* implement the methods described by the interface; if it does not, the two will not be able to communicate.

With custom interfaces, the only negotiation involved is the client querying for an interface with `QueryInterface()`, and therefore the client can only ask a server for interfaces that it already knows about. There is no other negotiation possible — the client cannot ask the object to list the interfaces it supports, nor can it ask the object to tell it about the methods on those interfaces. Furthermore, if the object only supports interfaces that the client does not know about, the client cannot access the object.

Automation interfaces use dynamic invocation. We'll see exactly how this works later on, but basically, Automation allows the client to ask an object to return information about the interfaces that it supports. Through **type information**, the object can list all the interfaces it supports and, when queried, it can return information about the methods on a specified interface. Using this information, the client can invoke a method *dynamically* — in other words, the client can package the parameters in a generic way, and then tell the object to call a particular method with those parameters. This invocation is done on the fly, and can be performed with no prior knowledge of the object.

Terminology

During this chapter, you'll see a number of different terms used to describe the interfaces supported by an Automation object. This is largely for historical reasons. The term 'Automation' was first coined in the phrase 'OLE Automation' when COM was first developed. The philosophy then was that a programmer could write several Automation objects — some with user interfaces and others without — and then 'glue' them together to create an application with a language like Visual Basic 3. Visual Basic would 'automate' these objects — that is, it would create them and then tell them what to do.

Over time, Automation (the 'OLE' has been dropped) has become a wider-ranging technology. Visual Basic is still important, of course, but now there is Visual Basic for Applications (VBA, which is present as a macro language in many applications), JScript and VBScript. All of these languages can talk to Automation objects.

Automation objects use a standard interface called IDispatch, which we first came across in Chapter 3 when the Wizards added support for it to our projects. You can tell whether an object can be 'automated' by querying for this interface. However, unlike those early OLE Automation objects that typically *only* exposed IDispatch, these days the interface is often just one way to get access to an object.

Server objects implement Automation by allowing clients to use a method on the IDispatch interface to call other methods. The collection of methods it makes available in this way is called a **dispinterface** (short for 'dispatch interface'). IDispatch allows an object to indicate what dispinterface methods it supports in two different ways. It can be done at runtime, through other IDispatch methods; or else the object can be a little more expressive and maintain information about its dispinterfaces that a client can use at compile time. The client can still ask the object for information about its dispinterfaces, and can call those interface methods dynamically.

The information that the object provides must include details of all the dispinterfaces it supports, all the methods on those dispinterfaces, and all the parameters of those methods. For an object to be an Automation object, a client must be able to get access to this information, which the object can choose to supply either directly or (more typically) through the **type library** files that we have seen generated by our projects in earlier chapters. Previously, we have used the type library along with the #import directive to take advantage of the compiler support for COM offered by Visual C++, but they are more versatile than that. Here, they are being usefully employed as suppliers of the **type information** that's used by Automation clients.

> A type library is effectively a tokenized version of the IDL file, and it describes all the interfaces supported by the object, all the methods, and the parameters of those methods. Since a type library describes *exactly* what an interface can do, it can be used to marshal data between processes.

The Need For Automation

There are several reasons why you would want to use Automation rather than custom interfaces, the most important of which arises when you're programming for clients that *only* support Automation interfaces. Such clients include those that use VBA and VBScript, but *not* clients programmed in Visual Basic 5 and above, which can use both Automation and custom interfaces.

When a web developer writes VBScript code, the code is not compiled, and so there is no checking on the methods that are called or on the data types of the parameters that are passed. Since a VBScript client passes parameters without knowing beforehand what the types of those parameters are, this check must be done at runtime by the object, using type information. If the object does not support a particular method, then the call will fail. If the data passed from the client is of the wrong type, the object can attempt to coerce the data to the required type.

Another situation in which you may want to use Automation interfaces is when you want to add functionality dynamically, at runtime. Indeed, using the derived interface IDispatchEx (an interface used by IE4 and later), client code can add and remove methods to a dispinterface. We won't cover that interface here (more details can be found in *COM IDL & Interface Design* (1-861002-25-4)), but it offers quite a lot of features, even to scripting clients.

Automation offers a great deal, and COM carries out much of the functionality. Before looking at some of these features of Automation, however, let's take a proper look at how it actually works.

Automation Interfaces

IDispatch is the COM interface behind Automation. Every machine that supports COM has the proxies and stubs for IDispatch. Once a client obtains this interface on an object, it can use the interface's methods to do two things:

❑ Find out about the Automation methods and properties that are supported by the object

❑ Invoke those methods, or access those properties

Combined, these abilities allow a client to have no prior knowledge about an object, and yet still be able to access it. In the following sections, we will outline what the IDispatch methods do. Even at this early stage, though, we should point out that our aim is to familiarize you with Automation. You won't have to implement these methods yourself, and in most cases you won't even need to access them, because ATL does all this work for you.

Accessing Methods And Properties

Automation objects can have both methods and properties (public functions and data members) that are available through Automation methods. For example, the Microsoft Word 9.0 Object Library ('object library' is just another name for a type library) defines the methods and properties of the Automation objects exported by Word 2000. The following Visual Basic code starts Word, loads a document and makes it visible:

```
Dim wordapp As New Word.Application
wordapp.Documents.Open "c:\my documents\test.doc"
wordapp.Visible = True
```

Here, the first line creates the Application Automation object, and the second line invokes the Open() method on the Word.Application.Documents sub-object. The syntax of Visual Basic dictates that the parentheses are missed out when a method returns no result. Open() is used to load a document, and it takes *ten* arguments. In this Visual Basic code, however, only *one* argument is passed: the name of the file that holds the document. The object must be able to handle this situation, determining which argument has been passed, and using default values for the rest. The last line sets the Visible property to True and makes Word 2000 visible, displaying the document.

> Accessing methods and properties like this is an artifact of using Visual Basic. If you
> used C++ to access the **Word.Application** object, then both calls would be made
> through the methods of a dispinterface.

Notice that here the property is called `Visible`: it is in English. If Visual Basic had to pass this name to the object, it would make the Automation interface useful only to English speakers. In fact, Visual Basic does not pass this string. Instead, it passes an identifier called a **DISPID** (or dispatch ID) that identifies the property. Methods and their parameters have DISPIDs, too.

Since a Visual Basic programmer will use textual names for properties and methods, Visual Basic must have some mechanism to get hold of the appropriate DISPIDs. In fact, it will use one of two mechanisms, depending on how the code is written. In the above code, the type checking is actually done at compile time, through the object's type library. The Visual Basic compiler looks at the code, sees that the `Open()` method and the `Visible` property will be used, and then uses the type library to find the DISPIDs. These are then placed in the compiled code so that when the object is accessed at runtime, the application can call the method (and access the property) directly. Notice that since DISPIDs are locale-independent, this compiled code will work in all locales.

If Visual Basic doesn't have access to the type library at compile time, the code can be written so that type checking is performed at runtime:

```
Dim wordapp As Object
Set wordapp = CreateObject("Word.Application")
wordapp.Documents.Open "c:\my documents\test.doc"
wordapp.Visible = True
```

This has exactly the same outcome as the earlier code, but whereas the former accessed the Automation object through a typed variable (of type `Word.Application`), this code uses an untyped variable (`Object`). You can think of this as being a bit like accessing a C++ object through a `void*` pointer. The `CreateObject()` line checks the local system to see if there is a `Word.Application` object type, and if so the object is created. In the next line, Visual Basic asks the object whether it has a method with the name `Open`, and if so the object will return the DISPID for this method. Visual Basic then uses the DISPID to invoke the method with the string parameter. This is in contrast to the previous code where Visual Basic *knew* that the object supported `Open()` because the variable was typed.

For this second example to work, the Automation interface must implement a method to return the DISPIDs for named methods, parameters and properties for locale, so that the Visual Basic application can ask the object what the DISPIDs for `Open` and `Visible` are. When this code is compiled, the strings "Open" and "Visible" are put into the compiled code. If this code is run on a machine in a non-English locale, the machine *must* still have the English type library to be able to get the right DISPIDs. This is clearly an administrative nightmare, and means that scripting languages that can only access Automation interfaces in this way are extremely locale-specific.

IDispatch

Now the scene has been set, let's look at the IDispatch interface itself. Automation interfaces use dynamic invocation, but since the client must use *some* interface to call the object, the invocation cannot be completely dynamic. In particular, Automation objects must implement IUnknown (as required by the COM specification) to define their identity and to manage their lifetime. In addition to this, Automation objects must provide a generic interface through which a client can talk to the object and ask the object what it can do. This is the IDispatch interface.

Here is the definition of IDispatch, as given in Oaidl.idl (and edited a little for clarity):

```
[
    object,
    uuid(00020400-0000-0000-C000-000000000046),
    pointer_default(unique)
]
interface IDispatch : IUnknown
{
    HRESULT GetTypeInfoCount(
        [out] UINT * pctinfo);

    HRESULT GetTypeInfo(
        [in] UINT iTInfo,
        [in] LCID lcid,
        [out] ITypeInfo ** ppTInfo);

    HRESULT GetIDsOfNames(
        [in] REFIID riid,
        [in, size_is(cNames)] LPOLESTR * rgszNames,
        [in] UINT cNames,
        [in] LCID lcid,
        [out, size_is(cNames)] DISPID * rgDispId);

    HRESULT Invoke(
        [in] DISPID dispIdMember,
        [in] REFIID riid,
        [in] LCID lcid,
        [in] WORD wFlags,
        [in, out] DISPPARAMS * pDispParams,
        [out] VARIANT * pVarResult,
        [out] EXCEPINFO * pExcepInfo,
        [out] UINT * puArgErr);
}
```

All Automation objects must implement IDispatch, and servers can implement methods and properties through it. The methods of IDispatch allow a client to ask an object about the methods and properties it supports, and also to invoke those methods and access those properties.

IDispatch looks wonderfully flexible. A client can ask the object, "Do you support a method called *MethodX*?" and the object can reply, "Yes, and it has a DISPID of *x*". The client can then ask the object, "So, what are the parameters of the method with DISPID *x*?" and the object can respond, "The parameters have DISPIDs of *0, 1, 2* and *3*. Oh, and by the way, they have names and types, and some of them have default values so they're optional." The client can now ask... well, you get the idea.

This is indeed wonderfully flexible, but terribly anarchic. If this conversation had to take place every time a client wanted to access an object, it would require a great many calls to the object. Since the object could quite easily be on another machine, the client could be in for a long wait.

Dispinterfaces

A dispinterface is not a new type of COM interface. Basically, it is an interface that supports a collection of methods and properties that can be called through `IDispatch::Invoke()`. The description of this interface is passed back to the client through the `IDispatch` type information methods, or through the object's type library.

Dispinterfaces are essentially a specialization of `IDispatch` — that is they implement the `IDispatch` methods. When the client calls these methods (or access the dispinterface properties) then `IDispatch::Invoke()` will be called, using the appropriate DISPID.

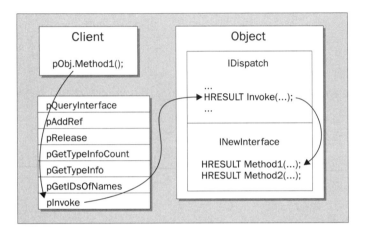

In the above diagram, a client obtains an interface pointer on an object that implements `INewInterface`; this interface is a dispinterface, and so derives from `IDispatch`. The interface pointer the client obtains is to `IDispatch` (shown on the left); notice that the `INewInterface` methods do not appear in the vtable. The client calls `Method1()` by calling `Invoke()` with the DISPID for `Method1()`. `Invoke()` then calls (or *dispatches* the request to) `Method1()`. Contrast this with calling a method on a derived non-dispinterface (a custom interface), where the client calls the derived interface method directly:

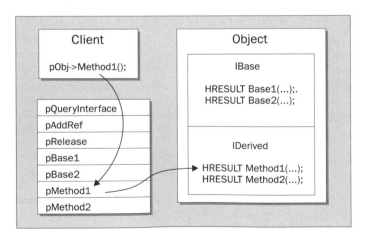

This time, the client obtains the `IDerived` interface, which derives from `IBase` and therefore has the methods of `IBase` *and* the additional methods of the new interface. Since the interface is not a dispinterface, the methods *are* available through the vtable, and the client can call `Method1()` through its function pointer.

The term 'dispinterface' was originally used when describing interfaces with ODL (Object Description Language), but IDL has been extended to use the `dispinterface` statement, so that ODL is now regarded as largely obsolete. The only place where you would see ODL is if you were to create Automation objects with MFC — but then we're not using MFC, we're using ATL!

When you develop objects using the ATL Wizards, you don't have to worry about writing IDL, because the Wizard will do it for you. When you create an ATL component, you specify through the Object Wizard whether you want to implement a Custom interface (where the methods of the object's interfaces are accessed directly through a vtable), or a Dual interface (in which methods can be called both directly *and* using DISPIDs. However, it does not give you the option of implementing a dispinterface (in which the methods are called *only* through `IDispatch`). We'll look at **dual interfaces** in more detail shortly.

IDispatch Methods

Let's take a look at the methods of `IDispatch`. Remember that when you implement a dual interface with the ATL Wizards, these methods will be provided for you. When a client application accesses your object, it will not normally need to access these methods directly (although the example will show you how to do this if necessary).

Invoke()

Let's start with the last method, `Invoke()`. This is the workhorse of `IDispatch`, and as its name suggests, it passes to the server an identifier indicating the method it wants invoked, and an array with the parameters it wants to pass to that method. The object can then take these parameters and *dispatch* the call to the appropriate method. Here's the definition of `Invoke()` again, along with an explanation of its parameters:

```
HRESULT Invoke(
    [in] DISPID dispIdMember,
    [in] REFIID riid,
    [in] LCID lcid,
    [in] WORD wFlags,
    [in, out] DISPPARAMS* pDispParams,
    [out] VARIANT* pVarResult,
    [out] EXCEPINFO* pExcepInfo,
    [out] UINT* puArgErr);
```

Parameter	Type	Description
dispIdMember	DISPID	A unique number identifying the method to invoke
riid	REFIID	Reserved
lcid	LCID	A locale ID
wFlags	WORD	A flag indicating the context of the method to invoke
pDispParams	DISPPARAMS*	A structure with the parameters to pass to the method

Table Continued on Following Page

177

Parameter	Type	Description
pVarResult	VARIANT*	The result from calling the method
pExcepInfo	EXCEPINFO*	Returned exception information
puArgErr	UINT*	An index indicating the first argument that is in error

Once a client knows about the methods and properties that an object supports (and you'll see how it does that in a moment), it uses `Invoke()` to tell the object to invoke a method. The first parameter is the DISPID of the method to invoke. Scripting languages will use a locale-dependent name for the method, but ultimately this must be converted to the unique ID of that method. The translation of name to DISPID is carried out by `GetIDsOfNames()`, which is called by the VBScript engine, for example. The `riid` parameter is not used and should always have a value of `IID_NULL`.

An Automation method may process some text or return a text value. If an error occurs in the method, information should be passed back to the client. This text will be locale-dependent — if the locale is France, then French will be used. Locales can be more specific than language; they can be dialect-based too: a locale could be French-speaking Canada, which is distinct from French-speaking France. The client must tell the object what locale it is in so that the object can handle text (as well as other things like date format and decimal separators) accordingly. This is the reason for the `lcid` parameter.

The `wFlags` parameter takes one of the following values that define the action to which the DISPID refers:

Value	Description
DISPATCH_METHOD	An object method
DISPATCH_PROPERTYGET	Retrieving the value of a property
DISPATCH_PROPERTYPUT	Setting the value of a property
DISPATCH_PROPERTYPUTREF	The property is set by reference

These give the implementation of `Invoke()` in the object a hint as to what the client wants to be done. However, retrieving a property value is conceptually no different from invoking a method that takes no parameters but returns a value, and so some objects do not distinguish between `DISPATCH_METHOD` and `DISPATCH_PROPERTYGET`. The oddball here is `DISPATCH_PROPERTYPUTREF`, which means that the parameter being passed in `pDispParams` is a reference to an object that is used to initialize the property referred to by the `dispIDMember`. Since a reference is used, this is equivalent to the following C++ code:

```
pObj1 = pObj2;
```

where pObj1 and pObj2 are pointers to objects of the same class (and it is assumed that there is no overloaded `operator=()`). Any changes to the object's properties will affect the referenced object; conversely, if the object passed to `Invoke()` through pDispParams changes, then so does the property in the Automation object. Compare this to `DISPATCH_PROPERTYPUT`, which means that the property's *value* should be set to the *value* of the object passed. This is equivalent to the following C++ code:

```
*pObj1 = *pObj2;
```

pDispParams

In the above discussion, we talked about pDispParams containing a reference to an object, but the issue of exactly how that is arranged, and how in the general case this parameter can be used to pass many arguments to the method being invoked, is not yet clear. In fact, pDispParams points to a structure containing an array of IDs for the parameters, and an array of the values that those parameters should take. As you have seen, however, Automation allows scripting clients to miss out parameters, to use default values, and even to pass parameters in a different order to the one defined in IDL. Even this solution, then, cannot be the whole truth.

The resolution of this problem is that the pDispParams parameter must always contain the total number of possible arguments, but if a method parameter is optional and the client doesn't specify it, a special 'empty' value can be used in its place. If the client chooses to pass the method parameters out of order, it must pass them as **named parameters** so that the object knows which parameter is which. You'll see how this works later on in the chapter.

Once pDispParams and the other parameters have been passed to Invoke(), the implementation of this function can parse through the arguments destined for the server method and check their data types. If the type of an argument is different from the type expected, the server object can try to coerce (convert) the data to the required type. If this is not possible, or the parameter is invalid, the object can return an error and indicate in puArgErr the argument in the pDispParams that caused the problem.

If the client is asking for a method invocation, the object can then find the method (this may be as simple as implementing a switch using the DISPID, or it may involve some other, more complicated, mechanism). If that method fails for some reason, it can pass back an HRESULT, but for a more detailed explanation of the problem it can pass back information in the pExcepInfo parameter.

The EXCEPINFO structure is quite interesting. It passes back to the client an error code and strings giving information about the source, a description of the error, a help context and a help file to find more information about the error. In addition to this, it can also pass back a function pointer that allows the server to ignore the other members, and only to return the values when the client calls this callback function. This deferment saves the object from incurring the cost of filling the other values when the client may well ignore them.

> We should point out that using EXCEPINFO is a legacy method of getting error information. The more up-to-date method uses an **error object** that's based on the information in the EXCEPINFO structure. This will be explained in more detail later in the chapter.

Finally, a method (or a property get) will return a value, and this is returned in the pVarResult parameter. The VARIANT type you can see being returned is a discriminated union that's used for passing data to and from the Invoke() function. VARIANTs can contain primitive data types like integers and floats, and also more complex types like strings and interface pointers. Furthermore, they can contain pointers to and arrays of any of these types. VARIANTs and other Automation types will be covered in detail later in the chapter.

DISPIDs

As we've already mentioned, the methods, properties and parameters of an Automation method all have identifiers called DISPIDs. Scripting languages do not work with DISPIDs; instead they use textual names that are locale-specific. The scripting language engine must convert the textual name into a DISPID, and to do this it can call `GetIDsOfNames()` on the object's Automation interface. The caller passes in an array containing the name of a function and any named parameters, an array to accept the DISPIDs, and the locale identifier. The method should return the DISPIDs corresponding to the names. If the object does not recognize a name, then it will return `DISPID_UNKNOWN` in the appropriate element.

When you write the IDL for an Automation interface, you need to supply the DISPIDs for the methods and properties. The DISPID for a parameter of a method is allocated according to the position of the parameter in the method's argument list by the MIDL compiler when it creates the type library.

Properties' and methods' DISPIDs are specified in IDL code by using the `[id()]` attribute. Here's the IDL file from the `Simple` project in Chapter 2:

```
[
    object,
    uuid(B824074D-4995-11D3-88E4-00105A68BF5D),
    dual,
    helpstring("ICalcEaster Interface"),
    pointer_default(unique)
]
interface ICalcEaster : IDispatch
{
    [propget, id(1)] HRESULT Year([out, retval] short *pVal);
    [propput, id(1)] HRESULT Year([in] short newVal);
    [propget, id(2)] HRESULT Month([out, retval] short *pVal);
    [propget, id(3)] HRESULT Day([out, retval] short *pVal);
    [id(4)] HRESULT CalculateEaster();
};
```

Here, the `ICalcEaster` interface has properties called `Year`, `Month` and `Day` with DISPIDs 1, 2 and 3 respectively, and a method called `CalculateEaster()` with a DISPID of 4. When you compile this IDL code, all the information about the interface, including the DISPIDs of the methods and properties, is put into the object's type library.

Standard DISPIDs

The last section showed how you could specify the DISPIDs for members of an Automation interface. If you have more than one Automation interface on an object, the same DISPID can be used in both interfaces. However, these DISPIDs are not generally polymorphic, and using the same DISPID on different Automation interfaces will not have the same effect. However, Microsoft has defined a few standard DISPIDs, which always have negative values.

> If you have more than one Automation interface on an object, the only one that you will be able to access through **IDispatch** will be the default interface — the one marked with the **[default]** attribute in the object's coclass definition. This does not preclude you from accessing dual interfaces through their vtables.

The DISPIDs pertinent to control properties are listed in Chapter 9; other values are given in the following table:

Symbol	Value	Description
DISPID_VALUE	0	The default member of the dispinterface
DISPID_UNKNOWN	-1	The value returned by GetIDsOfNames() if a name is not recognized
DISPID_PROPERTYPUT	-3	The DISPID to use when writing a property
DISPID_NEWENUM	-4	The _NewEnum() member of a collection (see Chapter 9)
DISPID_EVALUATE	-5	The Evaluate() member of an object
DISPID_CONSTRUCTOR	-6	Reserved
DISPID_DESTRUCTOR	-7	Reserved

These DISPIDs can be used in your properties and methods, and they are particularly useful for objects that are used by scripting languages. For example, DISPID_VALUE is used to indicate that this item is the default member of the dispinterface, so if a script uses the object without a method or property name, DISPID_VALUE will be used for the DISPID. However, this is of little use to C++ clients. More useful from everyone's point of view is DISPID_UNKNOWN that we have already seen — it is returned from GetIDsOfNames() when the object does not recognize the name.

DISPID_PROPERTYPUT (not to be confused with DISPATCH_PROPERTYPUT) is worthy of a little more explanation. It is used when a client is writing a value to a property. When you do this, you are *actually* calling a method that has a single parameter but no return value (put_Year() from the CalcEaster example, for instance) and so two DISPIDs are sent via Invoke(): the first is in dispIdMember to indicate the method (put_Year()) to call, and the second is used within the pDispParams structure to identify the parameter that is passed. However, properties don't have the concept of a 'parameter', so instead of passing the 'index' of the 'parameter' in the method, you must use DISPID_PROPERTYPUT, which Automation understands to be the default DISPID for data sent to assign a value to a property.

GetIDsOfNames()

The GetIDsOfNames() method sends an array of names to the object, and returns an array of DISPIDs for those names. Let's take a look at its parameters:

```
HRESULT GetIDsOfNames(
    [in] REFIID riid,
    [in, size_is(cNames)] LPOLESTR* rgszNames,
    [in] UINT cNames,
    [in] LCID lcid,
    [out, size_is(cNames)] DISPID* rgDispId);
```

Parameter	Type	Description
riid	REFIID	Reserved
rgszNames	LPOLESTR*	Array of names
cNames	UINT	Total number of names
lcid	LCID	A locale ID
rgDispId	DISPID*	Returned array of DISPIDs

It is the client's responsibility to allocate the name and DISPID arrays. To see GetIDsOfNames() in action, create an empty console application in a subdirectory of the Simple project, and enter the following program:

```
#include <stdio.h>
#include <tchar.h>
#include "..\simple.h"

int main()
{
    CoInitialize(NULL);

    IDispatch* pDisp = NULL;
    HRESULT hr = CoCreateInstance(__uuidof(CalcEaster),
                            NULL,
                            CLSCTX_ALL,
                            __uuidof(IDispatch),
                            reinterpret_cast<void**>(&pDisp));

    LPOLESTR pNames = L"CalculateEaster";

    // We only want a single value
    DISPID pDispID;
    hr = pDisp->GetIDsOfNames(IID_NULL,
                            &pNames, 1,
                            LOCALE_SYSTEM_DEFAULT,
                            &pDispID);

    if(pDispID == DISPID_UNKNOWN)
        _tprintf(_T("%ls is not recognized\n"), pNames);
    else
        _tprintf(_T("%ls has a DISPID of %ld\n"), pNames, pDispID);

    pDisp->Release();

    CoUninitialize();
    return 0;
}
```

This code demonstrates the use of GetIDsOfNames() on our ICalcEaster interface. Notice that the first parameter is IID_NULL. This parameter is not used, but a value of IID_NULL must be passed, or an error code will be returned. The third parameter is the number of names in the array, and also the size of the array that's passed in as the final parameter. The fourth parameter is the locale; we have used LOCALE_SYSTEM_DEFAULT, which is the locale of the client machine, but you can pass a particular locale if you choose.

Locale identifiers (**LCIDs**) *are made up from a combination of language IDs and sub-language IDs, so (for example) UK English is:*

```
LCID lcidUK = MAKELCID(LANG_ENGLISH, SUBLANG_ENGLISH_UK);
```

You can find these constants in OleNls.h.

GetTypeInfoCount() And GetTypeInfo()

The type information that describes Automation interfaces is held in one of two ways: either statically (as a type library resource, where the type library can live in a separate file or be bound to the EXE or DLL), or dynamically (through the type library interfaces ITypeLib and ITypeInfo). GetTypeInfoCount() and GetTypeInfo() allow a user to get access to these type library interfaces. Note that in practice, most Automation objects do not implement the type library interfaces, but instead load a type library resource (or file) with LoadTypeLibEx() and get COM to return system-generated interfaces.

```
HRESULT GetTypeInfoCount(
    [out] UINT* pctinfo);
```

The GetTypeInfoCount() method might just as well be called SuppliesTypeInfo(), because it will only return one of two values: 0 if the object does not supply type information, or 1 if it does. The reason why it has this name is for compatibility with its namesake in ITypeLib, which is used to get information for an Automation interface from a type library (which can describe many Automation interfaces). If an object doesn't supply type information, it does not mean that the object doesn't support Automation — it's just that the client must use some other source of type information to find out about the object.

The ITypeLib interface is implemented by the system to give access to entire type libraries (that may contain large amounts of type information) that are accessed through individual ITypeInfo pointers. Remember, type libraries are binary files and their content is not documented, so if you have a type library the only way to get access to type information in it is to ask the system to give you a ITypeLib interface pointer.

```
HRESULT GetTypeInfo(
    [in] UINT iTInfo,
    [in] LCID lcid,
    [out] ITypeInfo** ppTInfo);
```

The GetTypeInfo() function returns the ITypeInfo interface for the object's type information. The first parameter identifies the type information to return and should always be 0; again, the reason is for compatibility with ITypeLib. The second parameter is a locale ID, so that the type information returned can be specific to a locale, and finally the last parameter is an [out] parameter that returns a pointer to the type information for the interface through the double pointer you pass in.

The ITypeInfo interface has many methods that you can use to query for information about the Automation interfaces, methods and properties that an object supports. In addition to these information-gathering methods, there are two others of interest: CreateInstance() and Invoke(). The first will create an instance of the coclass described by the type library. Once you have an instance, you can then call ITypeInfo::Invoke(), passing a pointer to this instance, to invoke a method or access a property. This version of Invoke() can be used to implement IDispatch::Invoke(), which means that you can load a type library from a resource or disk file and use it to create an instance of the object that will provide most of the functionality of IDispatch. As you'll see later, this is how ATL implements IDispatch through the CComTypeInfoHolder class.

Dual Interfaces

We have described `IDispatch`, which allows clients to query an object for the Automation methods and properties that it supports. Those methods and properties are grouped together as dispinterfaces, but they must be called through `IDispatch::Invoke()`. This adds, at the very least, an extra layer of indirection, since `Invoke()` needs to call a dispinterface method. If the client has to go through `GetIDsOfNames()` as well, then access slows to a snail's pace while the client asks the object to resolve method and property names.

At the other end of the spectrum, custom interfaces are very efficient. Strictly speaking, a *custom* interface is a non-standard COM interface; interfaces like `IUnknown` and `ISupportErrorInfo` are *standard* COM interfaces, and are therefore not custom. However, the term is generally taken to mean a non `IDispatch`-derived interface, which is certainly true when you consider implementing your own interfaces. This is also the definition that Object Wizard uses when it asks you for the type of interface that your component will implement.

The rules of COM allow an Automation object to expose its interfaces both through `IDispatch` *and* through the vtable of a custom interface. Such an interface is called a **dual interface**, and is marked as such by using the `[dual]` attribute in its IDL. Methods on dual interfaces can be called *either* by using the type library at compile time, *or* by obtaining type information at runtime using the `IDispatch` type information methods. At most, this involves registering the object's type library on the client.

The interface can also be called using the vtable, and you know that for calls to go across apartment (and process, and machine) boundaries, a proxy object has normally to be registered on the client. However, if a registered type library that completely describes the interface is available, and the interface methods only use Automation compatible parameters, the **Universal Marshaler** can use the information contained in the type library to marshal the interface without the need for separate proxies and stubs. This type of marshaling is called **type library marshaling**.

The Universal Marshaler is a system-supplied object that is guaranteed to be present on all machines that support COM. It will cross our path on several occasions in the chapters to come.

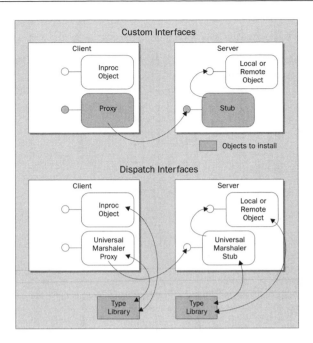

There is one final issue that must be aired here. COM objects allow you to expose *multiple* interfaces, each of which have the same access to the object, but provide different functionality. How is this handled with dual interfaces? In the discussion above, I have said that a dual interface is exposed both through IDispatch and its vtable, but if there is more than one dual interface, doesn't it mean that there will be more than one implementation of IDispatch?

This could indeed be true, and so it must be avoided. You will see exactly how this is handled by ATL later on, but basically the solution is to allow each of the object's dual interfaces to *implement* IDispatch, but only one of the interfaces to *expose* it. Each implementation of IDispatch provides type information through the *object's* type library and thus has information about the entire object, allowing access to the dispinterface parts of the other dual interfaces.

It must be pointed out that since scripting languages like VBScript are untyped, these languages can only access the default interface of the object (the one marked with [default] in the type library), and so any additional dual interfaces will be inaccessible. There is no 'clean' way to get round this problem: the solutions involve using a meta-object, or providing a custom implementation of Invoke(). It is usually acceptable either to pack all of your object's functionality into a single dual interface, or to factor out the functionality into several separate components.

Type Libraries

Type libraries are effectively a tokenized, binary form of IDL. Your code can read a type library by loading it with `LoadTypeLibEx()` to get the system to return a `ITypeLib` interface. You can then call `ITypeLib::GetTypeInfo()` to obtain the `ITypeInfo` interface in order to access the type information.

Type libraries can come as separate files, with an extension of `.tlb` or `.olb`, or they can be bound into a module as a resource. Here are some examples from `%systemroot%\system32`:

File	Description
mdisp32.tlb	Type library for OLE Messaging
vbaen32.olb	English type library defining the methods in `Vba32.dll`
comctl32.ocx	In-process server for the Windows common controls that contains a type library as a resource
shdocvw.dll	In-process server for the Internet Explorer web browser controls that contains a type library as a resource

An Automation object that wants to use the Universal Marshaler must register the type library to be used for the object. This screenshot shows the registry entry for the Excel 2000 `Sheets` interface. The `TypeLib` key gives the type library that the Universal Marshaler uses to determine how to marshal the interface. As we said earlier, any interface that can be described by a type library can use the Universal Marshaler.

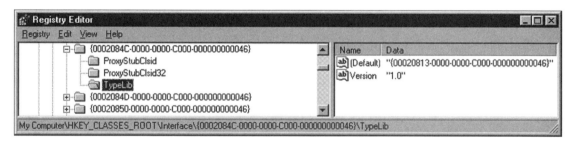

To view a type library, you should use the OLE/COM Object Viewer. This allows you either to specify a file that has type information, or to load a registered type library. Furthermore, if an object has an `IDispatch` interface, you can use `Oleview.exe` to call `GetTypeInfo()` on that interface and then display the type information. (Remember to make sure that **Expert Mode** is selected in the **View** menu.)

When you select View TypeLib... from the File menu, you can use the file browser dialog to open a file containing type information. Here is the result of loading `shdocvw.dll`:

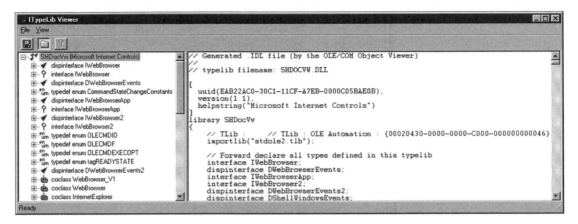

This next screenshot shows the branch in `Oleview.exe` that shows all the registered type libraries. Double clicking on the highlighted entry would open the **ITypeLib Viewer** window for this type library.

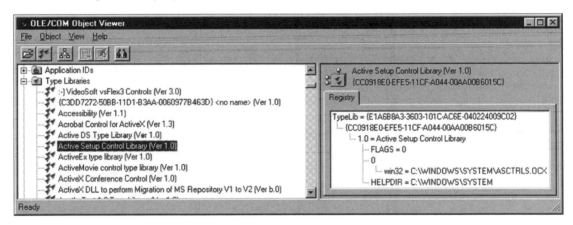

The final screenshot was obtained by clicking on the **Microsoft Excel Application** entry in the **All Objects** tree, and then double clicking on the `IDispatch` entry. Clicking on <u>V</u>iew **TypeInfo...** will produce the **ITypeLib Viewer** window for this type library (which is one of several interface viewers provided by `Oleview.exe` — you can even write your own!).

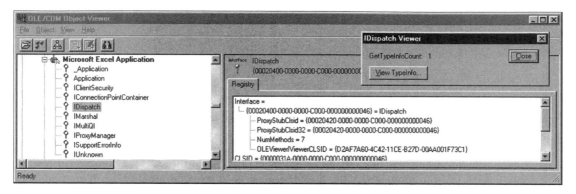

The ATL Wizards add the type library generated from the IDL file into the project as a resource. This type library is then used by the module to implement the registration (and unregistration) of the object in response to calls to `DllRegisterServer()` and `DllUnregisterServer()` (or to the command line switches `/RegServer` and `/UnregServer`). ATL also uses the type library to implement the default behavior of the `IDispatch` interface.

The type library need not be bound as a resource, however. Registration is carried out through a function called `AtlModuleRegisterServer()`, which will register the type library (and hence all the interfaces described therein) as well as run the RGS script for the server. It does this by calling `AtlModuleRegisterTypeLib()`, which obtains the server's module name (DLL or EXE) and attempts to load the type library as a resource. If that fails, then it will attempt to load the type library from a file with the same name (but with the `.tlb` extension) and in the same directory as the module.

`IDispatchImpl<>`, the ATL class that provides a default implementation of `IDispatch`, loads the type library using `LoadRegTypeLib()`, which uses the type library registration information to locate the type library. This will be correct, since `AtlModuleRegisterTypeLib()` will already have determined whether the type library is a bound resource or a separate type library.

Automation Data Types

Something we've mentioned several times but not yet explained is how you can pass data of different types as parameters to a method to be invoked through `IDispatch::Invoke()`. Consider this interface:

```
interface IWeird : IDispatch
{
    HRESULT SetLong([in] long l);
    HRESULT SetBSTR([in] BSTR bstr);
    HRESULT SetObject([in] IDispatch* pv);
    HRESULT SetFloat([in] float f);
};
```

If the interface has been defined with the `[dual]` attribute, these methods can be called through `Invoke()`, and so when creating the `pDispParams`, you must be able to send a `long`, a `BSTR`, an `IDispatch` pointer, and a `float`. How is this done? Well, the `pDispParams` parameter to `Invoke()` is a pointer to a `DISPPARAMS` structure:

```
typedef struct tagDISPPARAMS {
    VARIANTARG * rgvarg;
    DISPID * rgdispidNamedArgs;
    UINT cArgs;
    UINT cNamedArgs;
} DISPPARAMS;
```

The `cArgs` member specifies the number of arguments passed, and is the size of the (user allocated) `rgvarg` array. The `cNamedArgs` give the number of parameters that are named, and the DISPIDs of these are passed in the (user allocated) `rgdispidNamedArgs` array.

Named Parameters

What are named parameters? Well, when you write the IDL for an interface, you give the parameters names. Scripting languages like VBA can call the interface methods passing the parameters either by position or by name. For example, `Word.Application.9` has a method called `Move()` that's defined in IDL as:

```
HRESULT Move([in] long Left, [in] long Top);
```

This will move the application window by the specified number of pixels. In Visual Basic, you can move a Word 2000 window 200 pixels to the right and 100 pixels down with:

```
Word.Move 200, 100
```

However, Visual Basic also allows you to write the parameters in any order (and to miss out optional parameters) as long as the passed parameters are named. So the following line has the same effect as the previous one:

```
Word.Move Top:=100, Left:=200
```

The script interpreter will have to call `GetIdsOfNames()` on the named parameters to get the DISPIDs, and then place these in the `rgdispidNamedArgs` array. Thus, `rgdispidNamedArgs[0]` is the DISPID of the intended parameter of the value passed in `rgvarg[0]`. (If the client does not use named parameters, then `cNamedArgs` is zero and so `rgdispidNamedArgs` is NULL.)

The script does not have to use names for all the parameters, but parameters that are not named must be positional, so for:

```
HRESULT Method1([in] long param1, [in] long param2,
                [in] long param3, [in] long param4);
```

The following are legal Visual Basic statements:

```
Obj.Method1 1, 2, param4:=4, param3:=3
Obj.Method1 param4:=4, param1:=1, param2:=2, param3:=3
```

189

The named parameters are always the last parameters in the argument list. Incidentally, this method call in C++ would be:

```
pObj->Method1(1, 2, 3, 4);
```

Since named parameters are always optional, and because when you do use them they must come at the end of the parameter list, this means that the values in the rgvarg array are in the *reverse* order to their positions, so that the named parameters are always *first* in the array.

IDL can be used to mark some parameters as [optional]. If this is the case, the scripting language need not supply a value for that parameter (remember the example with Open() on Word.Application that you saw earlier?). However, the *interpreter* must pass values for all parameters, including the ones that have not been given a value in the script. If the interpreter does not have a value for a parameter, it indicates the fact by giving the parameter a type of VT_ERROR. The object detects this type and uses a default value for the parameter.

VARIANT

The client must be able to pass many different data types in the rgvarg array. To do this, the data type of the array is a discriminated union called a VARIANTARG, which is typedef'd to a VARIANT type. The discriminator is called vt, and must be set so that the marshaler knows how to marshal the data. The union itself contains one of the following types:

Type	Discriminator	By Ref	Description
BYTE	VT_UI1	✓	Unsigned char
USHORT	VT_UI2	✓	Unsigned short
UINT	VT_UINT	✓	Unsigned integer (size is system-dependent)
ULONG	VT_UI4	✓	Unsigned long
CHAR	VT_I1	✓	Signed char
SHORT	VT_I2	✓	Signed short
INT	VT_INT	✓	Signed integer (size is system-dependent)
LONG	VT_I4	✓	Signed long
FLOAT	VT_R4	✓	4 byte floating point number
DOUBLE	VT_R8	✓	8 byte floating point number
VARIANT_BOOL	VT_BOOL	✓	A Boolean (transmitted as a signed short)
SCODE	VT_ERROR	✓	Status code (HRESULT)
CY	VT_CY	✓	Currency

Table Continued on Following Page

Type	Discriminator	By Ref	Description
DATE	VT_DATE	✓	Date (transmitted as a double)
BSTR	VT_BSTR	✓	String
IUnknown*	VT_UNKNOWN	✓	Interface pointer
IDispatch*	VT_DISPATCH	✓	IDispatch interface pointer
SAFEARRAY*	VT_ARRAY	✓	Array type
VARIANT*	VT_VARIANT		Pointer to a VARIANT
DECIMAL*	VT_DECIMAL		Large decimal type
_tagBRECORD	VT_RECORD		Automation 'struct'

The table has a column called 'By Ref' that's used to indicate that the union has a member that allows a *pointer* to this data type to be put in the VARIANT. When data is passed by reference, the discriminator is OR-ed with the value VT_BYREF; this indicates to the marshaler that it should treat the data held in the VARIANT as a pointer and therefore marshal the data that it points to, rather than the pointer itself. These members are used when a method returns an [out] parameter (what Visual Basic calls ByRef). You'll remember from Chapter 2 that the *caller* must free any resources returned by reference.

Two of these types, BSTR and SAFEARRAY, will be described in the following sections, but there are other types with which you may not be familiar. CY is a currency type and is held in 64 bits. DATE holds a date and time, and DECIMAL holds a large decimal type that has 64 bits for the mantissa and 8 bits for the exponent — truly a large decimal!

> _tagBRECORD *is a new type in Windows 98, Windows 95 with DCOM95 1.2, and Windows NT 4.0 with Service Pack 4. It allows Visual Basic to pass parameters that are UDTs (or User Defined Types). UDTs are essentially structures, which is why we've called them "Automation 'structs'" in the table. The* _tagBRECORD *contains a pointer to an* IRecordInfo *interface that describes the UDT, and a pointer to a buffer that contains the actual data. We won't cover* _tagBRECORD *in this book.*

In the last section, we mentioned that even if a parameter is optional, there must still be a value in the pDispParams parameter of Invoke(). This member must have a type of VT_ERROR (== vt), and it should set the union member to an SCODE of DISP_E_PARAMNOTFOUND.

Maintaining Data

Before you use a VARIANT, you should use the VariantInit() function, which sets vt to VT_EMPTY, indicating that the VARIANT has no value. Some of the data types in a VARIANT have to be allocated (BSTRs and interface pointers, for example), and these need to be released before a VARIANT can be released. COM provides a function called VariantClear() that will use the discriminator to determine whether the resource should be released. Whenever you finish using a VARIANT, you should call this function.

As you can see, allocating VARIANTs, putting data into them, and then ensuring that the resources are properly released is quite a responsibility for a developer. To ease this responsibility, ATL provides a wrapper class called CComVariant that *ensures* the VARIANT is initialized with VariantInit() before it is used, and cleared with VariantClear() when it is finally released. To make life easier still, the class also provides overloaded assignment operators and constructors for the most popular data types that a VARIANT can take.

In the following code snippet, two methods are defined: one takes a VARIANT and the other takes a pointer to a VARIANT.

```
HRESULT GetNumberOfMessages(LPVARIANT varNum);
HRESULT LogMessage(VARIANT varMess);

CComVariant varData;
varData = _T("Hello");
LogMessage(varData);

varData = 0L;
GetNumberOfMessages(&varData);

_tprintf(_T("There are %ld messages\n"), varData.lVal);
```

This code begins by assigning a string to the VARIANT. It doesn't matter whether the string is ANSI or Unicode, as there is an assignment operator for both (in fact, the operator for wide characters is the same as for BSTR); both operators create a BSTR from the string. The VARIANT is then passed to the LogMessage() function. The next line assigns the VARIANT with a value of 0, ready for the next method call. The assignment operator of CComVariant calls VariantClear(), releasing the BSTR before reusing the variable.

CComVariant is derived from VARIANT, so passing a pointer to a CComVariant is effectively the same as passing an LPVARIANT. GetNumberOfMessages() returns a LONG in the VARIANT. Note that CComVariant's destructor also ensures that VariantClear() is called in order to release any resources that are held in the VARIANT. Thus, when a CComVariant goes out of scope, all the data in it will be released.

BSTR

Passing strings between processes is a problem. The reason for this is that unlike most other data types, there is no predetermined size for strings. "Hello" is smaller than "Goodbye", but the marshaling layer needs to know *exactly* how much data to send. Furthermore, once a process has determined how much data to transmit and then sent it, the marshaler at the other end will need to create a buffer for the data and pass that buffer to the server. The COM rules state that [out] parameters are released by the caller, so such a caller will need to have access to the same allocator that created the buffer.

Thinking over the first issue, you will come to two possible solutions. Either you can make sure that the marshaling layer checks the length of a string before transmitting it (by doing strlen() or wcslen() on the string), or else the string itself could be some kind of structure that always knows its own length. Automation takes the second option, which has the handy side effect of allowing BSTRs to contain embedded NUL characters, and hence to be used to pass binary data if required.

As to the second issue, a process receiving a BSTR from another process as an [out] parameter must release that data when it has finished with it. COM cannot use new (because it must be language neutral), and so instead it uses its own memory allocator.

BSTRs are created with SysAllocString() and released with SysFreeString(). SysAllocString() takes a wide character string, and it will do a wcslen() on this string and create a buffer for it. The function also keeps the size of the buffer alongside the buffer itself in memory. The pointer that you get back from SysAllocString() is a BSTR, which is just a wide character (LPWSTR) pointer.

For example, if you call this:

```
BSTR bstr = SysAllocString(L"Hello");
```

and then use the Visual C++ debugging tools to examine the pointer returned, you'll see something like this:

```
0013369C                      0A 00 00 00    ........
001336A4    48 00 65 00 6C 00 6C 00    H.e.l.l.
001336AC    6F 00 00 00               o...
```

The data is saved as a Unicode string, so there are two bytes per character. The ULONG before the buffer contains the number of bytes taken up by the buffer, not including the final NUL (in this case, "Hello" has five characters, so this will require ten bytes — or 0A in hexadecimal). To get the length of a BSTR, you should pass it to SysStringLen(). Once you have created a BSTR, you can change it using SysReAllocString(). This function takes a pointer to your BSTR and the new string, and will return a new pointer to the BSTR in your BSTR argument.

The BSTR type is actually a typedef for LPWSTR, but you should treat it as LPCWSTR (that is, a constant) so that you don't inadvertently write beyond the end of the allocated buffer. There are no functions to allow you to manipulate sub-strings within a BSTR; instead, you should convert it to a convenient data type (like an MFC CString or an STL basic_string<>) and then use SysReAllocString() when you have finished your manipulations. Finally, when you've finished using a BSTR, you must free it with SysFreeString(). This will free the string, returning the memory back to the BSTR cache.

Just as with VARIANT, there is a lot of maintenance required here, and thankfully ATL helps once again by providing the CComBSTR class. There are several constructors that you can use:

```
CComBSTR();
CComBSTR(int nSize);
CComBSTR(int nSize, LPCOLESTR sz);
CComBSTR(LPCOLESTR pSrc);
CComBSTR(const CComBSTR& src);
CComBSTR(REFGUID src);
```

You saw the second of these in the last chapter — it allocates an empty buffer for nSize characters. The third constructor allocates and initializes a buffer with a string. The fourth constructor does this as well, but determines the size of the required buffer by counting the characters up to the termination character. The final constructor will take a GUID and convert it to a string before placing it in the BSTR.

If you create a buffer with these constructors, the contained BSTR can be accessed through a public member called m_str, which can be used either directly or via the BSTR conversion operator (operator BSTR()). The class also defines various overloaded versions of Append() and an operator+=(). These allow you to add strings together, rather like using strcat():

```
CComBSTR bstrGreeting(_T("Hello "));
bstrGreeting.Append(_T("there!"));
_tprintf(_T("%ls"), bstrGreeting.m_str);   // Gives "Hello there!"
```

Notice that Append() allocates the resulting BSTR and assigns it to the m_str data member.

> *The other interesting thing about CComBSTR is that it allows data to be written to or read from an OLE stream (IStream). This would be used when a control initializes itself from, or saves itself to, persistent storage, and you'll see an example of this in Chapter 10.*

SAFEARRAY

Passing *arrays* of data between processes requires special handling. The reason for this is that while languages like C and C++ get access through pointers, other languages like Visual Basic and Java, which do not have pointers, must still be able to access the same COM arrays. Before I explain about SAFEARRAYs, I should point out that in sharp contrast to MFC, which provides the COleSafeArray class, ATL does not have a wrapper class for SAFEARRAY. If you want to use SAFEARRAYs in your ATL object code, you must either use MFC (and suffer the necessary overhead entailed), or access the SAFEARRAY functions directly.

Here is the SAFEARRAY structure:

```
typedef struct tagSAFEARRAY {
    USHORT  cDims;
    USHORT  fFeatures;
    ULONG   cbElements;
    ULONG   cLocks;
    PVOID   pvData;
    SAFEARRAYBOUND rgsabound[];
} SAFEARRAY;
```

The first, third and last members describe the structure of the array: how many dimensions it has, the size of a single element in the array, and information about the number of elements in each dimension. The actual data is pointed to by the pvData member, which can only be accessed if the SAFEARRAY has been locked using the SafeArrayLock() function. cLocks is a count of how many times the SAFEARRAY has been 'locked', and it can be unlocked by using the SafeArrayUnlock() function. Happily, locking is carried out automatically by most of the access functions you'll use, so you won't normally have to do it yourself.

The SAFEARRAYBOUND structure is declared as:

```
typedef struct tagSAFEARRAYBOUND {
    ULONG  cElements;
    LONG   lLbound;
} SAFEARRAYBOUND, *LPSAFEARRAYBOUND;
```

Here, `cElements` is the number of elements in an array, and `lLbound` is the lower bound index. For arrays that will only be accessed through C++, you should use a value of 0, since C++ arrays are accessed with a base index of 0. Visual Basic arrays, however, can be accessed with a different base index. For example, consider this 11 x 11 array:

```
Dim Values(-5 To 5, 5 To 15) As Integer
```

The corresponding `SAFEARRAY` has `cDims` of 2, `cbElements` of 4 and an `rgsabound` with two elements, `{{11, -5}, {11, 5}}`.

You do not create `SAFEARRAY`s yourself. Instead, you should call the `SafeArrayCreate()` function to do the work:

```
SAFEARRAY* SafeArrayCreate(VARTYPE          vt,
                           UINT             cDims,
                           SAFEARRAYBOUND*  rgsabound);
```

The first parameter determines the type of each element; this is followed by the number of dimensions in the array, and then a pointer to a `SAFEARRAYBOUND` that you use to give information about the dimensions. The previous 11 x 11 array would therefore be created with:

```
SAFEARRAYBOUND rgb[] = {{11, -5}, {11, 5}};
SAFEARRAY* psa = NULL;
psa = SafeArrayCreate(VT_I4, 2, rgb);
```

Although superficially similar to the discriminator of a `VARIANT`, the first parameter is restricted to a subset of the types a `VARIANT` may have. It can be one of:

VARTYPE	Description
VT_UI1	Unsigned char
VT_I2	Signed short
VT_I4	Signed long
VT_R4	Float
VT_R8	Double
VT_CY	Currency
VT_DATE	Date
VT_BSTR	String
VT_ERROR	Status code
VT_BOOL	Boolean
VT_VARIANT	VARIANT pointer
VT_UNKNOWN	IUnknown pointer
VT_DISPATCH	IDispatch pointer
VT_DECIMAL	DECIMAL pointer

Thus, if you want to pass binary data to another process, you can do it with a SAFEARRAY of type VT_UI1.

When SafeArrayCreate() (or a method on an interface) returns a SAFEARRAY, you cannot access the buffer that's been created for you immediately. First, you must call SafeArrayAccessData(), which returns the pvData pointer. When you have finished, you must call SafeArrayUnAccessData(). The reason for these two function calls is to lock the SAFEARRAY to access by other threads, so you don't need to call SafeArrayLock() or SafeArrayUnlock() yourself.

The pointer returned to you by SafeArrayAccessData() is a void* that you need to cast to the appropriate type, and if the array has more than one dimension, *you* must perform the calculation to access parameters according to the lower bound and dimension size. There are functions called SafeArrayGetElement() and SafeArrayPutElement() that will get and set a single element from a SAFEARRAY and do these calculations for you.

Once you've finished using a SAFEARRAY, both it and the data it holds must be released. This is carried out by the single function called SafeArrayDestroy() that mirrors SafeArrayCreate().

> *Note that one of the types that can be put in a* SAFEARRAY *is* LPVARIANT. *This means that a* SAFEARRAY *can contain data of various types by wrapping these values in* VARIANTs. *You are most likely to use this when you want to pass the equivalent of a C-style* struct *to a method as a single parameter rather than as multiple parameters on operating systems that cannot marshal UDTs using* IRecordInfo. *Of course, this means that the client and server must agree on the order of the elements in the* SAFEARRAY.

Before we move on to a quick example of using SAFEARRAYs, there is one final issue that needs to be addressed: how do you describe a SAFEARRAY in IDL? The answer is that the MIDL compiler supports the data type SAFEARRAY(type), where type is one of the types given in the previous table (the type, not the VT_ value). So, an interface method that returns a SAFEARRAY of BSTRs would be defined as:

```
HRESULT ArrayOfNames([out, retval] SAFEARRAY(BSTR)* pNames);
```

Specifying the type of the elements in the SAFEARRAY is important because the interface may be marshaled cross-process (or cross-machine), and the marshaler will need to know what the types in the untyped pvData buffer really are.

An Example

Let's look at an example that demonstrates how to expose a SAFEARRAY as a property. We'll start by creating a simple object that exposes an array of strings, and then we'll see how to access this property both from Visual C++ (using compiler COM support) and from Visual Basic.

Create a new project with the ATL COM AppWizard and call it Colors (the array that we expose will be a selection of color names). Accept all the default settings. Then add a new **Simple** object with the short name of ColorObject. We want to add a SAFEARRAY property to the class, so use ClassView to add a property of type VARIANT with the name Colors.

We've chosen to use VARIANT *here because the dialog doesn't allow us to select a* SAFEARRAY.

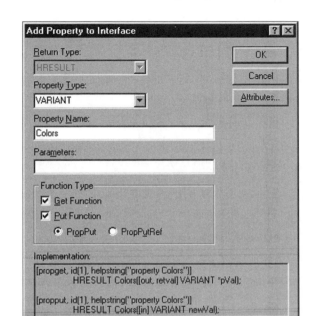

For this example, we'll use the C++ standard library's vector<> template to hold the names of the colors, so open ColorObject.h and add the following #include near the top:

```
#include "resource.h"        // main symbols
#include <vector>            // use the standard library's vector class
```

We can add a vector<> member called m_vecColors to our class to hold a list of CComBSTRs. We'll also add a prototype for FinalConstruct(), which we can use to initialize the data, as we discussed in the previous chapter. Add the code shown below to the class definition of CColorObject.

```
// IColorObject
public:
    STDMETHOD(get_Colors)(/*[out, retval]*/ VARIANT *pVal);
    STDMETHOD(put_Colors)(/*[in]*/ VARIANT newVal);

    HRESULT FinalConstruct();

private:
    std::vector<CComBSTR> m_vecColors;
};
```

Add the implementation of the `FinalConstruct()` function to `ColorObject.cpp`. We'll just initialize the array to hold the seven colors of the visible spectrum:

```
HRESULT CColorObject::FinalConstruct()
{
    m_vecColors.push_back(CComBSTR(L"Red"));
    m_vecColors.push_back(CComBSTR(L"Orange"));
    m_vecColors.push_back(CComBSTR(L"Yellow"));
    m_vecColors.push_back(CComBSTR(L"Green"));
    m_vecColors.push_back(CComBSTR(L"Blue"));
    m_vecColors.push_back(CComBSTR(L"Indigo"));
    m_vecColors.push_back(CComBSTR(L"Violet"));
    return S_OK;
}
```

Now we need to add the code to return the array to callers of `get_Colors()`. Add the following code to the handler for accessing the array:

```
STDMETHODIMP CColorObject::get_Colors(VARIANT * pVal)
{
    VariantInit(pVal);
    pVal->vt = VT_ARRAY | VT_BSTR;
    SAFEARRAY* psa;
    SAFEARRAYBOUND bounds = {m_vecColors.size(), 0};
    psa = SafeArrayCreate(VT_BSTR, 1, &bounds);

    BSTR* bstrArray;
    SafeArrayAccessData(psa, reinterpret_cast<void**>(&bstrArray));
    std::vector<CComBSTR>::iterator it;
    int i = 0;
    for(it = m_vecColors.begin(); it != m_vecColors.end(); it++, i++)
    {
        bstrArray[i] = SysAllocString((*it).m_str);
    }
    SafeArrayUnaccessData(psa);
    pVal->parray = psa;
    return S_OK;
}
```

First, we've called `VariantInit()` to initialize the VARIANT, then set the type of the VARIANT parameter to show that we're using it to hold an array of BSTRs. It is important to specify the type of the elements in the array like this, because when the data is marshaled across machine boundaries, the marshaler will need to know how to treat the data held in the SAFEARRAY.

After that, a SAFEARRAYBOUND is created and initialized to hold the number of colors in the vector, and to indicate that the lower bound is zero (Those C/C++ habits die hard!). `SafeArrayCreate()` is used to create a one-dimensional array that contains BSTRs. This will allocate memory for the array of pointers (don't forget that a BSTR is a pointer).

The buffer is accessed with the call to `SafeArrayAccessData()`, and then we use the vector's iterator to access the data in the vector and insert a new BSTR into the array. After relinquishing access to the array data, we set the `parray` member of the VARIANT to the newly created SAFEARRAY. The VARIANTs in the SAFEARRAY own the BSTRs, and when (at a later stage) the SAFEARRAY is freed, it will call `VariantClear()` on each member to free the BSTR.

The next step is to add the following code to the handler for setting the array:

```
STDMETHODIMP CColorObject::put_Colors(VARIANT newVal)
{
    if((newVal.vt & VT_ARRAY) == 0)
        return E_INVALIDARG; // Not an array

    if((newVal.vt & VT_BSTR) == 0)
        return E_INVALIDARG; // Not an array of BSTRs

    m_vecColors.clear();
    SAFEARRAY* psa = newVal.parray;
    BSTR* bstrArray;
    SafeArrayAccessData(psa, reinterpret_cast<void**>(&bstrArray));

    // Assume just one dimension
    for(int i = 0; i < psa->rgsabound->cElements; i++)
    {
        m_vecColors.push_back(CComBSTR(bstrArray[i]));
    }

    SafeArrayUnaccessData(psa);
    return S_OK;
}
```

First, we check the type of the VARIANT to ensure that the data passed in is a SAFEARRAY of BSTRs. If it is, we clear the vector and then add the new data to the array, using the vector's push_back() method.

We could compile the code at this point, ready to start creating the clients, but before we do, we'll add a small amount of debugging code. We'll create a simple method called DumpVector() that we can use to send the elements of the vector member of our class to the Output window. Add the declaration to the class definition:

```
private:
    std::vector<CComBSTR> m_vecColors;
    void DumpVector();
};
```

And add the implementation to the ColorObject.cpp file:

```
void CColorObject::DumpVector()
{
#ifdef _DEBUG
    std::vector<CComBSTR>::iterator it;

    ATLTRACE(_T("[\n"));
    for(it = m_vecColors.begin(); it != m_vecColors.end(); it++)
    {
        ATLTRACE(_T("\t%ls,\n"), (*it).m_str);
    }
    ATLTRACE(_T("]\n"));
#endif
}
```

Here, you can see that we are making use of the ATLTRACE() macro. In release builds, this compiles to (void)0 (in other words, it does nothing). In debug builds, the macro passes its arguments to the AtlTrace() function. AtlTrace() takes a variable-length argument list and outputs a _vstprintf()-formatted string to the debug window. We've wrapped the implementation in #ifdef _DEBUG so that the code isn't executed during release builds.

Finally, add the following code that uses our new function to the end of the get_Colors() and put_Colors() methods:

```
STDMETHODIMP CColorObject::get_Colors(VARIANT * pVal)
{
    ...

    ATLTRACE(_T("Returning SafeArray which has these members:\n"));
    DumpVector();
    return S_OK;
}

STDMETHODIMP CColorObject::put_Colors(VARIANT newVal)
{
    ...

    ATLTRACE(_T("Changing SafeArray to have these members:\n"));
    DumpVector();
    return S_OK;
}
```

Now you can compile the project. You will find that the compiler complains that the vector header file uses C++ exceptions and that unwind semantics are not enabled. This is because, by default, the ATL AppWizard turns off C++ exceptions to try and make the code as tight as possible. Still, it *is* only a warning, and problems will only arise when exceptions occur in the STL allocator. Since these truly are exceptional, you may decide to ignore the warning.

> *To prevent the warning, you can enable C++ exceptions by going to the project settings (*Project | Settings...*), selecting* C++ Language *from the* Category *box on the* C/C++ *tab, and checking the* Enable exception handling *box. If you compile again, the warnings should disappear.*

A C++ Client

Let's create a simple C++ client for the object. Create an empty Win32 Console Application called ColorClient, and place it in the Colors project directory. Add a single source code file called ColorClient.cpp to the project, and enter the following code:

```
// ColorClient.cpp
#include <windows.h>
#include <stdio.h>
#include <tchar.h>

#import "..\Colors.tlb"

using namespace COLORSLib;

void _tmain()
{
    CoInitialize(NULL);

    try
    {
        IColorObjectPtr pSA(__uuidof(ColorObject));
        _variant_t var = pSA->Colors;
        SAFEARRAY* psa = var.parray;
        BSTR* bstrArray;
        SafeArrayAccessData(psa, reinterpret_cast<void**>(&bstrArray));
```

```
        for(UINT i = 0; i < psa->rgsabound->cElements; i++)
            _tprintf(_T("%ls\n"), bstrArray[i]);

        SafeArrayUnaccessData(psa);
    }
    catch(_com_error e)
    {
        _tprintf(_T("Error: 0x%08x %ls\n"), e.Error(), e.ErrorMessage());
    }

    CoUninitialize();
}
```

Once again, we #import the type library from the server, and create a ColorObject using the smart pointer's constructor. We get the VARIANT returned by the Colors property and put it into a _variant_t. Like CComVariant, the _variant_t class takes responsibility for freeing the VARIANT and its contents in its destructor, so we don't need to worry about explicitly freeing anything. Next, we call SafeArrayAccessData() so that we can start looping through the BSTR array, and SafeArrayUnaccessData() when we've finished.

Here are the results in a console window:

The code isn't too complicated, but it isn't exactly intuitive, either. However, SAFEARRAYs are *really* designed for use with Visual Basic, so let's see how to use our object in a Visual Basic 6 application.

A Visual Basic 6 Client

Start Visual Basic 6 and select **Standard EXE** in the **New Project** dialog. Add the following controls to the project's form; you can see the names to use in the diagram below:

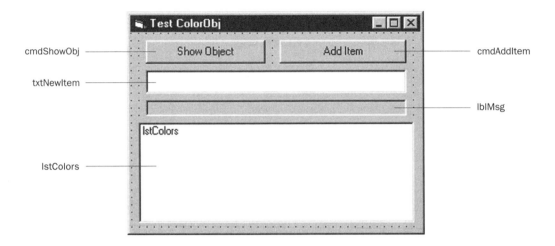

Now add support for the `ColorObject` object by opening the **References** dialog (**P**roject | Refere**n**ces...) and selecting the Colors 1.0 Type Library:

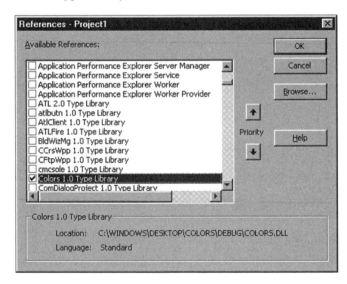

As for the code, you can begin by declaring a variable for the `IColorObject` interface at module scope:

```
Option Explicit
Private itf As IColorObject
```

Now create the `ColorObject` and initialize the variable in the form's `Load` event:

```
Private Sub Form_Load()
    Set itf = New ColorObject
End Sub
```

Double click on the `cmdShowObj` button and add this code:

```
Private Sub cmdShowObj_Click()
    Dim Size As Long
    Dim ColorArray As Variant
    ColorArray = itf.Colors
    lstColors.Clear
    Size = UBound(ColorArray) - LBound(ColorArray) + 1
    lblMsg.Caption = "There are " & Str$(Size) & _
                     " elements in " & TypeName(ColorArray)
    Dim x As Integer
    For x = LBound(ColorArray) To UBound(ColorArray)
        lstColors.AddItem ColorArray(x)
    Next
End Sub
```

When the client is executing, clicking on the `cmdShowObj` button will cause the number of items to be calculated and this, together with information about the type of the array, is put into the `lblMsg` label. Then the code loops through the items in the array and adds them to the list box.

Notice that a copy of the `Colors` property is made by assigning it to the `ColorArray`. This may look unnecessary, but consider this hypothetical code:

```
For x = LBound(itf.Colors) To UBound(itf.Colors)
    lstColors.AddItem itf.Colors(x)
Next
```

This results in a call to the `CColorObject::get_Colors()` method, and hence a copy of the array being made, for every iteration of the loop. Indeed, *wherever* a reference to `itf.Colors` is made, there will be a call to `CColorObject::get_Colors()`. This would be even more of a problem if the object were out-of-process — the number of method calls (property accesses) should be kept to a minimum. By acting on your own copy of a property, you can avoid the overhead of frequent method calls.

Add the following code to the `Click` event of the `cmdAddItem` button:

```
Private Sub cmdAddItem_Click()
    If txtNewItem.Text = "" Then
        Exit Sub
    End If

    ' Read data into an array
    ReDim ColorArray(lstColors.ListCount) As String
    Dim x As Integer
    For x = 0 To lstColors.ListCount - 1
        ColorArray(x) = lstColors.List(x)
    Next
    ColorArray(lstColors.ListCount) = txtNewItem.Text
    itf.Colors = ColorArray
    cmdShowObj_Click
End Sub
```

203

The `cmdAddItem` button is used to add a new item to the array. It does this by creating a `String` array (using `ReDim` so that the size is given at runtime), and then copying all the items from the list box. It then reads the string in the `txtNewItem` edit box and adds this to the end of the array. The object's array property is then set in the single line of code:

```
itf.Colors = ColorArray
```

To test this, run it (either from the Visual Basic IDE, or by compiling it first and then running the EXE) and click on the **Show Object** button.

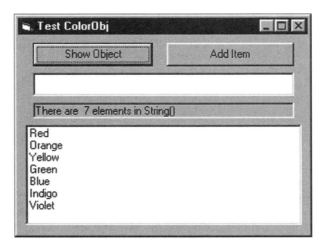

These are the default colors in the array. To add a new color, type the name into the edit box and click on **Add Item**:

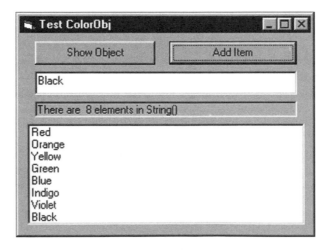

As you can see, SAFEARRAY access in Visual Basic is simple and natural.

A Final Note About ATL And STL

In the `Colors` object, we've used `std::vector<>`, which is one of STL's container types. It was chosen because we were able to use `CComBSTR` as a parameter to the template, but there are several other container types you can use, depending on how the data is indexed and how it is accessed. For example, if you will only ever access the data serially, from the beginning of the array, then a `std::list<>` will be more efficient than a `std::vector<>`. However, if you try to do this:

```
std::list<CComBSTR> m_listColors;
```

You will get a rather cryptic error:

error C2664: 'destroy' : cannot convert parameter 1 from 'unsigned short ** ' to 'class ATL::CComBSTR *'

The problem is that `list<>::destroy()` will attempt to get the address of a `CComBSTR` item and expect a `CComBSTR*` pointer. However, `CComBSTR` defines an `operator&()` that returns a `BSTR*` (which the compiler interprets as a `unsigned short**`). To get round this problem, you can use the `CAdapt<>` class as the type to be used in the list instead. This does not define an address operator for `CAdapt<>`, but it *does* define one for its template parameter. `std::list<>` will then be happy, because `destroy()` will want the address of a `CAdapt<CComBSTR>`, which will be returned.

Basically, if you want to use either `CComBSTR` or `CComPtr<>` in a `std::list<>` or a `std::set<>`, you should use `CAdapt<>`.

Accessing Automation Objects

Following our little departure into `SAFEARRAY`s, and before moving on to the intricacies of creating Automation interfaces in ATL, we'll look briefly at how to *access* Automation interfaces in different languages, without assistance.

C++

If the Automation interface is a dual interface, then it can be accessed just like any custom interface. The client must have the MIDL compiler-generated interface definition, so that it can cast the interface pointer returned from `QueryInterface()`. If the object is in a different apartment from the client, or in a different process, then a proxy must be used. In the following examples, we'll use the `CalcEaster` object from the `Simple` project you created in Chapter 3.

Dual Interface Access

Create a new, empty Win32 Console Application and place it in a subdirectory of the `Simple` project — the one we'll use is called `ConsoleClient`. Add a new source code file to the project, and enter the following code:

```
#include <stdio.h>
#include <tchar.h>

// Bring in the interface and GUID definitions
#include "..\simple.h"
```

```
int main()
{
   CoInitialize(NULL);
   ICalcEaster* pCalc = NULL;
   HRESULT hr = CoCreateInstance(__uuidof(CalcEaster),
                                 NULL,
                                 CLSCTX_ALL,
                                 __uuidof(ICalcEaster),
                                 reinterpret_cast<void**>(&pCalc));
   if(SUCCEEDED(hr))
   {
      short sYear = 1998, sMonth, sDay;
      pCalc->put_Year(sYear);
      pCalc->CalculateEaster();
      pCalc->get_Month(&sMonth);
      pCalc->get_Day(&sDay);
      _tprintf(_T("Easter day was %d/%d in %d\n"), sMonth, sDay, sYear);
      pCalc->Release();
   }

   CoUninitialize();
   return 0;
}
```

The client gets access to methods in the vtable using an interface pointer, by a process that's sometimes called **vtable binding**. This is exactly the same as what goes on when you're using a non-dispinterface, and we shall dwell on it here no longer.

Access Through IDispatch

If the interface is derived from IDispatch (either a dispinterface or a dual), you *can* access it using the IDispatch interface, but things get a lot trickier. Consider this code, for example:

```
CoInitialize(NULL);
IDispatch* pObj = NULL;
HRESULT hr = CoCreateInstance(__uuidof(CalcEaster),
                              NULL,
                              CLSCTX_ALL,
                              __uuidof(IDispatch),
                              reinterpret_cast<void**>(&pObj));
short sYear = 1998;

VARIANTARG* pvars = new VARIANTARG[1];
VariantInit(&pvars[0]);
pvars[0].vt = VT_I2;
pvars[0].iVal = sYear;
DISPID dispid = DISPID_PROPERTYPUT;
DISPPARAMS disp = { pvars, &dispid, 1, 1 };

VARIANT varResult;
VariantInit(&varResult);
pObj->Invoke(0x1, IID_NULL,
             LOCALE_USER_DEFAULT,
             DISPATCH_PROPERTYPUT,
             &disp,
             &varResult, NULL, NULL);

delete [] pvars;

// Do other things with the object

pObj->Release();
CoUninitialize();
```

Complicated, huh? First we create the object, and specify that we need the IDispatch interface. Then a VARIANTARG array with a single member is declared; this member is initialized with a call to VariantInit() and then given a value. Remember that VARIANTs (and therefore VARIANTARGs) are discriminated unions, so the first task is to set the type of the value it's going to hold (VT_I2) in the discriminator, and then the appropriate part of the union is assigned with the value we wish to pass.

The actual data needs to be passed to Invoke() in a DISPPARAMS structure that has pointers to the array of arguments and the array of parameter DISPIDs as the first two parameters. Notice here that since this is passing a property value to the object, the special value DISPID_PROPERTYPUT is used. The call should not return a value, but we still need to pass in a VARIANT to Invoke(), and this too needs to be initialized. Finally, Invoke() is called. The DISPID passed is 0x1 — we know that this is the DISPID of Year, and because we do not have to ask the object for it, this method of accessing the property is called **early binding**.

This code is passing a value to a property, so there is only one parameter to pass — if it was a method call with more parameters, then there would be even more code to construct the DISPPARAMS parameter passed to Invoke(). Furthermore, you'll surely have realized that this code has only a quarter of the functionality of our custom interface example. We'd have to go through this rigmarole three more times to retrieve the day and month of Easter 1998!

The situation gets worse still when you consider **late binding**. Here, the client asks the object for information about the method, which involves calling GetIDsOfNames():

```
// Do other things with the object
LPOLESTR pszName = L"CalculateEaster";
pObj->GetIDsOfNames(IID_NULL, &pszName, 1, LOCALE_USER_DEFAULT, &dispid);
```

This obtains the DISPID for the method to pass to Invoke(). If you don't know about the parameters that the method takes, you also need to obtain the type information using GetTypeInfo(), and then query that:

```
ITypeInfo* pType = NULL;
pObj->GetTypeInfo(0, LOCALE_USER_DEFAULT, &pType);

TYPEATTR* pTypeAttr = NULL;
hr = pType->GetTypeAttr(&pTypeAttr);

if(SUCCEEDED(hr))
{
    for(short i = 0; i < pTypeAttr->cFuncs; i++)
    {
        FUNCDESC* pFuncDesc = NULL;
        hr = pType->GetFuncDesc(i, &pFuncDesc);
        if(SUCCEEDED(hr))
        {
            if(pFuncDesc->memid == dispid)
            {
                _tprintf(_T("returns %ld\n"), pFuncDesc->elemdescFunc.tdesc.vt);
                for(short n = 0; n<pFuncDesc->cParams; n++)
                {
                    _tprintf(_T("param %ld is type %ld\n"), n,
                        pFuncDesc->lprgelemdescParam[n].tdesc.vt);
                }
```

```
            }
        pType->ReleaseFuncDesc(pFuncDesc);
      }
    }
    pType->ReleaseTypeAttr(pTypeAttr);
}

pType->Release();
pObj->Release();
```

We won't go into this code in detail (we'll certainly never have to do anything as long-winded as this using ATL), but it does show how to get information about a method's parameters, and give an idea of just how much help ATL provides for us. Incidentally, if you compile and run this code, the answer you'll get is 24, which is the value of VT_VOID in the enumeration that defines the possible values for the VARIANT discriminator. This is just what we'd expect: the CalculateEaster() method does not return a value.

Visual Basic

Visual Basic 6 programs can access any interface, through IDispatch or through a vtable, provided that the interface is described by a type library. If a type library is not used, Visual Basic can only use late binding, which means that it can only access an Automation interface. In this case, it must ask the object to convert textual method names and parameters to DISPIDs, as we saw earlier on in this chapter with IDispatch::GetIDsOfNames(). This is clearly inefficient, because many extra calls have to be made to the object before the actual method can be called.

Late Binding

Late binding is characterized by the use of a variable of type Object. This is equivalent to using IDispatch pointers in C++. To obtain an object, the client uses CreateObject():

```
Dim obj as Object
Set obj = CreateObject("Simple.CalcEaster.1")
obj.Year = CInt(txtYear)
obj.CalculateEaster
MsgBox "Easter: " & obj.Month & "/" & obj.Day & " in " & obj.Year
```

The call to CreateObject() obtains the IDispatch pointer, while the call to CalculateEaster() does the necessary querying of the object for the DISPID of the method and checks that the method takes no other parameters. This is considerably easier than late binding in C++!

Note that the type library does *not* need to be on the client machine. This Visual Basic application obtains type information via GetTypeInfo(), similar to the C++ code given above.

Early And Vtable Binding

For early and vtable binding, the Visual Basic IDE is told about the object type information at compile time by using the Project | References... menu item. As the IDE then knows about the types, we are free to use them explicitly, instead of resorting to the Object type:

```
Dim obj As New SIMPLELib.CalcEaster
obj.Year = CInt(txtYear)
obj.CalculateEaster
MsgBox "Easter: " & obj.Month & "/" & obj.Day & " in " & obj.Year
```

In this code, `SIMPLELib.CalcEaster` is the ProgID of the coclass, `New` creates an object, and the variable `obj` is assigned to the default interface of the object, in this case `ICalcEaster`. If `ICalcEaster` is not the default interface, then the following code can be used:

```
Dim obj As New SIMPLELib.CalcEaster
Dim itf As SIMPLELib.ICalcEaster
Set itf = obj
itf.Year = CInt(txtYear)
itf.CalculateEaster
MsgBox "Easter: " & itf.Month & "/" & itf.Day & " in " & itf.Year
```

This time, the first line creates the object and returns the default interface. The third line does a `QueryInterface()` for the `ICalcEaster` interface, enabling `CalculateEaster` to be called.

> **The choice of whether to use vtable or early binding is made for you by Visual Basic. If the default interface is a dual, then vtable binding will be used. If it's a plain dispinterface — that is, if it has no custom component — then early binding will be used, with its associated performance hit. Note that plain dispinterfaces can't be created in ATL, so Visual Basic will access your ATL objects using vtable binding if the type library is referenced.**

Java

The Java SDK is Microsoft's extension of the Java language. Specifically, it provides extensions to the Java language and classes that allow programmers to get access to the Microsoft Java Virtual Machine (JVM) COM facilities.

Version 2 of the SDK provides a tool called `JActiveX` that takes a type library and creates Java classes for the Automation object's coclass, and Java interfaces for the object's interfaces. These classes and interfaces derive from the Java SDK classes used to access the object, and also have special comments that specify the GUIDs of the coclass and interfaces. The command

```
>JActiveX simple.tlb
```

will create an interface for the `ICalcEaster` COM interface, and a class for the `CalcEaster` coclass, putting the Java code in the `simple` directory under `Java\Trustlib`. The Java code to access this object is incredibly straightforward:

```java
import simple.*;
class Test
{
    public static void main(String[] args)
    {
        CalcEaster Obj = new CalcEaster();
        ICalcEaster ICalc = Obj;
        ICalc.setYear((short)1998);
        ICalc.CalculateEaster();
        System.out.println("Easter day is: " + ICalc.getDay() +
            "/" + ICalc.getMonth() + "/" + ICalc.getYear());
    }
}
```

Notice how the JActiveX tool generates accessor functions for the properties. The read-only properties Day and Month have only a 'get' method, whereas Year has both a 'get' and a 'set' method. This simple code shows how easy COM programming with MS Java is: there is no CoCreateInstance() (you just create a new object with new), there is no QueryInterface() (you just cast to the appropriate interface), and there is no call to Release() (the Java garbage collector does that).

If you look in the ICalcEaster.java file generated by JActiveX, you will find an interface interspersed with comments:

```
// Dual interface ICalcEaster
/** @com.interface(iid=5DC86881-58F2-11D1-A159-04DCF8C00000,
                   thread=AUTO, type=DUAL) */
public interface ICalcEaster extends IUnknown
{
    /** @com.method(vtoffset=4, dispid=1, type=PROPGET, name="Year",
           addFlagsVtable=4)
       @com.parameters([type=I2] return) */
    public short getYear();

    /** @com.method(vtoffset=5, dispid=1, type=PROPPUT, name="Year",
           addFlagsVtable=4)
       @com.parameters([in,type=I2] pVal) */
    public void setYear(short pVal);

    /** @com.method(vtoffset=6, dispid=2, type=PROPGET, name="Month",
           addFlagsVtable=4)
       @com.parameters([type=I2] return) */
    public short getMonth();

    /** @com.method(vtoffset=7, dispid=3, type=PROPGET, name="Day",
           addFlagsVtable=4)
       @com.parameters([type=I2] return) */
    public short getDay();

    /** @com.method(vtoffset=8, dispid=4, type=METHOD,
           name="CalculateEaster", addFlagsVtable=4)
       @com.parameters() */
    public void CalculateEaster();

    public static final com.ms.com._Guid iid
       = new com.ms.com._Guid((int)0x5dc86881, (short)0x58f2, (short)0x11d1,
                              (byte)0xa1, (byte)0x59, (byte)0x4, (byte)0xdc,
                              (byte)0xf8, (byte)0xc0, (byte)0x0, (byte)0x0);
}
```

The comments show that MS Java uses **attribute-based programming**. The interface is marked with the iid, thread and type attributes, while the methods in the interface are marked with attributes that give the offset of the method within the vtable, the DISPID, and the wFlags value (the type of method access) used in calls to Invoke(). Although this is the only current Microsoft tool that uses attribute-based programming in its treatment of COM, it is worth paying attention to, since this is the direction in which COM programming is going.

The Java attributes are used to indicate the code that should be generated by virtual machine at runtime, when the actual COM object is being created. These attributes indicate the threading model of the component, the interface type and all of its methods, allowing the JVM to generate the correct COM code even though the Java code for the object knows nothing about COM.

At this point, Java purists might start to feel nervous — after all, a Java compiler should create byte code in a `.class` file that can be run on *any* Java virtual machine. The previous discussion appears to indicate that Microsoft is generating non-standard byte code, but in fact this is not the case. The Java specification indicates that `.class` files should contain several tables of information, including tables of constants, Java interfaces implemented by the class, and tables of methods and fields. In addition, `.class` files will also contain **attribute tables** that have named 'attributes' applied to methods, fields and classes, for things like exceptions and debugging information.

A compiler vendor can add extra 'attributes' to these tables for private use. A `.class` reader (like a virtual machine) must ignore any attributes that it does not understand, and this allows Java code to run on different virtual machines. Microsoft has merely added attribute tables (with names that start with 'COM') to hold COM-relevant information. The byte code is still pure Java, but if it is run under a virtual machine that understands the COM attribute tables, the Java object can be exposed as a COM component.

If this has whetted your appetite for Java attribute tables, take a look at the `ClassDecoder` *sample in the Microsoft Java SDK for more details.*

Automation With ATL

So, how do you create Automation interfaces using ATL?

The first thing you must be aware of is that the Object Wizard will only give you the option of creating custom or dual interfaces — it does not give you the choice of a non-dual Automation interface. If you decide that you want the interface to be non-dual (we'll see an example of when you might do this in Chapter 8), you can edit the IDL to comment out the `[dual]` attribute, or even to declare the interface as a dispinterface.

From the previous discussion, you will be aware that a dual interface needs an implementation of `IDispatch`. For the purpose of looking at how ATL handles dual interfaces, we'll create a simple project called `Automation`. This will be a *very* simple project; the purpose for now is to learn about what the Wizards do for you.

Crank up the ATL COM AppWizard, and create a DLL ATL project called `Automation`. Next, add a new simple object with a short name of `Auto`, ensure that **D**ual interface is selected on the **Attributes** tab, and that the **Support ISupportErrorInfo** check box is checked (you'll see why later).

Here is the header file produced by the Object Wizard as a result of this sequence of actions:

```
class ATL_NO_VTABLE CAuto :
    public CComObjectRootEx<CComSingleThreadModel>,
    public CComCoClass<CAuto, &CLSID_Auto>,
    public ISupportErrorInfo,
    public IDispatchImpl<IAuto, &IID_IAuto, &LIBID_AUTOMATIONLib>
{
public:
    CAuto()
    {
    }
```

```
DECLARE_REGISTRY_RESOURCEID(IDR_AUTO)

DECLARE_PROTECT_FINAL_CONSTRUCT()

BEGIN_COM_MAP(CAuto)
    COM_INTERFACE_ENTRY(IAuto)
    COM_INTERFACE_ENTRY(IDispatch)
    COM_INTERFACE_ENTRY(ISupportErrorInfo)
END_COM_MAP()

// ISupportsErrorInfo
    STDMETHOD(InterfaceSupportsErrorInfo)(REFIID riid);

// IAuto
public:
};
```

The significant lines are highlighted. Firstly, the class derives from the `IDispatchImpl<>` template class. If the object had implemented `IAuto` only as a custom interface, then the `CAuto` class would derive from the `IAuto` interface. The second line to notice is that the `IDispatch` interface has been added to the COM map in addition to the `IAuto` interface.

Over in the IDL file, the Wizard has defined the `IAuto` interface as the default interface of the coclass. It will be the interface that is accessed by (say) Visual Basic if the following code is used:

```
Dim obj As Object
Set obj = CreateObject("Automation.Auto")
obj.MethodName
```

If we were to add any other interfaces to the object, we would *not* be able to access them from Automation clients. However, as already pointed out, Visual Basic can access them through the vtable binding that it provides — if a type library is specified.

IDispatchImpl<>

Let's look at why the class is declared the way it is. For a start, somewhere in the class hierarchy there must be a declaration of the `IAuto` interface. This is achieved through the `IDispatchImpl<>` template class, which is declared in `Atlcom.h` like this:

```
template <class T,
          const IID* piid,
          const GUID* plibid = &CComModule::m_libid,
          WORD wMajor = 1,
          WORD wMinor = 0,
          class tihclass = CComTypeInfoHolder>
class ATL_NO_VTABLE IDispatchImpl : public T
{

...

};
```

Rather than deriving from `IAuto` directly, `CAuto` derives from the interface via the first template parameter of `IDispatchImpl<>`.

Notice that the last four template parameters all have default values. Implementation of IDispatch is performed using a type library that's passed in through plibid, and while Wizard-generated code will pass a pointer to the project's LIBID (for backward compatibility with other versions of ATL), doing so isn't strictly necessary. The default value refers to the value passed during the call to _Module.Init() that we saw in Chapter 3.

> **The wMajor and wMinor parameters give the version of the type library to be used in the implementation, but note that all Wizard-generated code will use the default values — that is, version 1.0. If you change your project and change the major version of the type library, the IDispatch implementation of your dual interfaces will no longer work. It is a good idea to edit the Wizard-generated code to mention the version of the type library to be used explicitly. It is a pity that ATL does not explicitly add the version of the type library to _Module along with the LIBID.**

The code that accesses the type library in order to implement IDispatch is in the tihclass template parameter. If you look at the declaration of the template, you can see all the IDispatch methods, and that each is implemented in terms of tihclass. For example, GetTypeInfo():

```
public:
    typedef tihclass _tihclass;
...

    STDMETHOD(GetTypeInfo)(UINT itinfo, LCID lcid, ITypeInfo** pptinfo)
    {
        return _tih.GetTypeInfo(itinfo, lcid, pptinfo);
    }
...

protected:
    static _tihclass _tih;
```

So, every class derived from IDispatchImpl<> delegates its IDispatch implementation through to the tihclass, which by default is implemented by CComTypeInfoHolder. The static member _tih is initialized from the parameters of IDispatchImpl<> in the following code:

```
template <class T, const IID* piid,
          const GUID* plibid, WORD wMajor, WORD wMinor, class tihclass>
IDispatchImpl<T, piid, plibid, wMajor, wMinor, tihclass>::_tihclass
IDispatchImpl<T, piid, plibid, wMajor, wMinor, tihclass>::_tih =
                              {piid, plibid, wMajor, wMinor, NULL, 0, NULL, 0};
```

CComTypeInfoHolder uses the plibid parameter to load the type library, and then obtains the system implementation of the IDispatch methods through the ITypeInfo* interface. If you decide that you want to implement these methods yourself, you can write your own version of CComTypeInfoHolder.

The following diagram illustrates this chain of command:

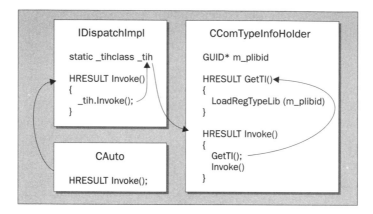

Multiple Dual Interfaces

As we've already pointed out, a COM object may only *expose* a single implementation of IDispatch. However, it is possible to have multiple interfaces that *derive* from IDispatch (that is, multiple dual interfaces) if certain steps are taken. Note, however, that clients that can't use vtable binding will only be able to access the interface that exposes its implementation of IDispatch.

With this in mind, let's add another dual interface to our object. There is no Wizard to do the work for you, so you'll have to get your hands dirty and edit the IDL file yourself. Along the way, you'll need to generate a new IID, which you can do by running Guidgen.exe, just as you did in Chapter 2. Select the fourth option (Registry Format), and then click on **C**opy. In Visual C++, open the Automation.idl file and add the following interface, pasting in the created GUID as the [uuid()] attribute (note that you will need to remove the braces):

```
import "oaidl.idl";
import "ocidl.idl";

[
    object,
    uuid(FE71E291-4FF3-11D3-88E4-00105A68BF5D),
    dual,
    helpstring("IAuto Interface"),
    pointer_default(unique)
]
interface IAuto : IDispatch
{
};

[
    object,
    uuid(9542BEB3-6FB8-11D1-A607-00A0C94BC9C3),
    dual,
    helpstring("IAuto2 Interface"),
    pointer_default(unique)
]
interface IAuto2 : IDispatch
{
};
```

```
[
    uuid(FE71E285-4FF3-11D3-88E4-00105A68BF5D),
    version(1.0),
    helpstring("Automation 1.0 Type Library")
]
library AUTOMATIONLib
{
    importlib("stdole32.tlb");
    importlib("stdole2.tlb");

    [
        uuid(FE71E292-4FF3-11D3-88E4-00105A68BF5D),
        helpstring("Auto Class")
    ]
    coclass Auto
    {
        [default] interface IAuto;
        interface IAuto2;
    };
};
```

The second insertion adds IAuto2 to the coclass, so you will also need to add the interface to the implementation in CAuto. To do this, open Auto.h and add the following lines:

```
class ATL_NO_VTABLE CAuto :
    public CComObjectRootEx<CComSingleThreadModel>,
    public CComCoClass<CAuto, &CLSID_Auto>,
    public ISupportErrorInfo,
    public IDispatchImpl<IAuto, &IID_IAuto, &LIBID_AUTOMATIONLib>,
    public IDispatchImpl<IAuto2, &IID_IAuto2, &LIBID_AUTOMATIONLib>
{
public:
    CAuto()
    {
    }

DECLARE_REGISTRY_RESOURCEID(IDR_AUTO)

DECLARE_PROTECT_FINAL_CONSTRUCT()

BEGIN_COM_MAP(CAuto)
    COM_INTERFACE_ENTRY(IAuto)
    COM_INTERFACE_ENTRY(IAuto2)
    COM_INTERFACE_ENTRY2(IDispatch, IAuto)
    COM_INTERFACE_ENTRY(ISupportErrorInfo)
END_COM_MAP()

// ISupportsErrorInfo
    STDMETHOD(InterfaceSupportsErrorInfo)(REFIID riid);

// IAuto
public:

// IAuto2
public:
};
```

The first addition is quite obvious: you want to expose the new interface from the object, so your object will need to implement the vtable somewhere. Equally understandable is the addition of the IAuto2 interface to the COM map, but what is the COM_INTERFACE_ENTRY2() macro, and why is it used? From our discussion, you will be aware that the object must export a *single* implementation of IDispatch, through the COM map. As you saw in Chapter 4, the COM map holds all the interfaces that the object will export. However, both IAuto and IAuto2 derive from IDispatch, and through the IDispatchImpl<> class, each will have an implementation of the IDispatch methods. If we have two implementations, which will be exposed? This problem is the reason why the _ENTRY2() macro is used instead of _ENTRY(). It specifies that the IDispatch implementation to be exposed should come from IAuto and not IAuto2.

Forgetting to use the COM_INTERFACE_ENTRY2() macro is one of the most common mistakes made by newcomers to ATL. If you do forget to do it, and the COM map looks like this:

```
BEGIN_COM_MAP(CAuto)
    COM_INTERFACE_ENTRY(IAuto)
    COM_INTERFACE_ENTRY(IAuto2)
    COM_INTERFACE_ENTRY(IDispatch)
    COM_INTERFACE_ENTRY(ISupportErrorInfo)
END_COM_MAP()
```

You will get the following error when you try to compile the project:

error C2594: 'static_cast' : ambiguous conversions from 'class CAuto *' to 'struct IDispatch *'

Remember this error well — it might just save you some debugging time when you come across it.

Handling Errors

Do you remember checking the Support ISupportErrorInfo box in the Object Wizard? Well, here's why you did it. If an error occurs when you're accessing an Automation method through IDispatch, the implementation can return error information through the EXCEPINFO parameter of Invoke(). This is the way error information was passed in the early days of OLE Automation.

Because the ability to get hold of rich error information is important, Microsoft improved its availability by introducing **error objects**. In fact, error objects are now the preferred method, to the extent that if a client chooses to use the EXCEPINFO parameter, it will be initialized from the values in an error object. Where possible, it is far better to access an error object directly, and the fact that our Auto component implements the ISupportErrorInfo interface indicates that it can pass back error information in error objects.

> *When you access the Err object in Visual Basic, you are accessing the error object for the current thread. However, error objects can be accessed by any client, and they can be generated by objects that do not implement IDispatch.*

To see how error objects work, though, we need first to go back to error handling with Invoke(). If a client wants to receive rich error information when it calls Invoke(), it can pass in a pointer to an EXCEPINFO structure as the 7th parameter. This structure has the following members:

```
typedef struct tagEXCEPINFO {
    WORD   wCode;
    WORD   wReserved;
    BSTR   bstrSource;
    BSTR   bstrDescription;
    BSTR   bstrHelpFile;
    DWORD  dwHelpContext;
    PVOID  pvReserved;
    HRESULT (*pfnDeferredFillIn)(struct tagEXCEPINFO*);
    SCODE  scode;
} EXCEPINFO, *LPEXCEPINFO;
```

The scode or wCode member (but not both) holds a code that determines what error occurred. There are two ways to return error codes because Visual Basic typically uses just the wCode, which can't be used to return HRESULTs (unsigned short is only 16-bit). Having the scode available as well gives you this option. The client that receives this structure should check both scode and wCode to see which is non-zero.

The pfnDeferredFillIn member can either point to a function that will fill an EXCEPINFO structure, or it can be NULL. If it has a non-NULL value, then the client can choose when to ask the object for error information, but note that the rest of the members in the structure will be empty. If deferred error information is not used (the member *is* NULL) then the other members of the structure *are* filled. The three BSTR members are strings that indicate the source (its ProgID), a description of the error, and the name of a help file that contains further information. The appropriate position in the help file is indicated by the dwHelpContext member.

A server can use this structure to provide rich error information to a client. Not only can the client process display a dialog with the name of the object that caused the problem and a description, but also it can start Winhelp.exe and load the appropriate file and context.

> *The dialog produced by the Visual Basic IDE when an error occurs contains a* **Help** *button. If you click on this button, Visual Basic will use the information in the* EXCEPINFO *structure to start up* Winhelp.exe. *Note that help information is* not *based on* hh.exe, *a newer help file viewer that uses compiled HTML.*

An error object is essentially a wrapper around the EXCEPINFO structure. Error objects implement two interfaces: ICreateErrorInfo to set values, and IErrorInfo to get them.

```
interface ICreateErrorInfo: IUnknown
{
    HRESULT SetGUID([in] REFGUID rguid);
    HRESULT SetSource([in] LPOLESTR szSource);
    HRESULT SetDescription([in] LPOLESTR szDescription);
    HRESULT SetHelpFile([in] LPOLESTR szHelpFile);
    HRESULT SetHelpContext([in] DWORD dwHelpContext);
}

interface IErrorInfo: IUnknown
{
    HRESULT GetGUID([out] GUID* pGUID);
    HRESULT GetSource([out] BSTR* pBstrSource);
    HRESULT GetDescription([out] BSTR* pBstrDescription);
    HRESULT GetHelpFile([out] BSTR* pBstrHelpFile);
    HRESULT GetHelpContext([out] DWORD* pdwHelpContext);
}
```

These methods get and set the appropriate members of the error object; the new item not present in EXCEPINFO is the GUID, which is used to hold the IID of the interface that the error object is associated with. There will often be more than one interface callable on a single thread, so the GUID indicates which interface generated the error. Note that each thread of execution has an associated error object — if this were not the case, then a client using an object on one thread could access the error object while another thread was setting it.

The ISupportErrorInfo interface itself has a single method:

```
interface ISupportErrorInfo: IUnknown
{
    HRESULT InterfaceSupportsErrorInfo([in] REFIID riid);
}
```

A client calls this method to determine whether the object supports rich error information for a particular interface. The client passes in the IID of the interface that it is interested in, and the method returns S_OK if the interface has an error object, or S_FALSE if it doesn't.

Your objects must keep a list of all the interfaces and the error objects that they support. If you look in the implementation file for the CAuto class, Auto.cpp, you will find that the Object Wizard has added the following method:

```
STDMETHODIMP CAuto::InterfaceSupportsErrorInfo(REFIID riid)
{
    static const IID* arr[] =
    {
        &IID_IAuto
    };
    for (int i=0; i < sizeof(arr) / sizeof(arr[0]); i++)
    {
        if (InlineIsEqualGUID(*arr[i],riid))
            return S_OK;
    }
    return S_FALSE;
}
```

Notice that because the Object Wizard did not know about the new interface IAuto2 when it generated this code, the array contains only the IAuto interface. To allow IAuto2 methods to return rich error information, you need to add its IID to the map:

```
static const IID* arr[] =
{
    &IID_IAuto,
    &IID_IAuto2
};
```

The code is pretty self-explanatory: it just goes through every item in the array and compares the IID with the parameter passed to the method.

Note that the Wizard has derived the CAuto class from ISupportErrorInfo, which is fine in our case, because we want to provide error objects for two interfaces. If the object had a single interface, you could derive the class from ISupportErrorInfoImpl<> instead. This template takes the IID of the interface that supports error objects, and provides an even more trivial implementation of the InterfaceSupportsErrorInfo() method.

How do you set one of these error objects, and how does a client use one? To see how they work, add a method to each of the interfaces on the Auto object. Right click on the IAuto interface in ClassView and select Add **M**ethod.... Add a method called Value() that takes a single [in] parameter of type LONG:

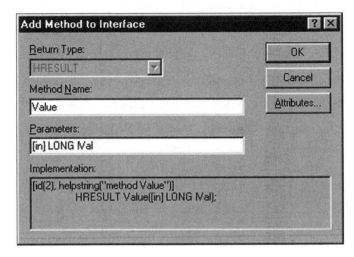

Do the same for the IAuto2 interface, but call the method Value2(). These methods will check the passed parameter and generate an error if the value is less than 0 (in the case of Value()) or if it is greater than 0 (in the case of Value2()).

> *You cannot give the name* Value() *to the method in* IAuto2 *because of the way that ATL uses multiple inheritance to implement interfaces (there would be two methods called* Value() *with the same parameters in the* CAuto *class, which would therefore not compile). This is one area where MFC is better than ATL: MFC uses nested classes to implement interfaces in a C++ class, and this would enable you to have two interfaces with the same method signatures.*

```
STDMETHODIMP CAuto::Value(LONG lVal)
{
    if(lVal < 0)
    {
        TCHAR str[256] = {0};
        wsprintf(str, _T("IAuto: %ld is too small, use a value > 0"), lVal);
        Error(str, IID_IAuto);
        return E_FAIL;
    }
    return S_OK;
}

STDMETHODIMP CAuto::Value2(LONG lVal)
{
    if(lVal > 0)
    {
        TCHAR str[256] = {0};
        wsprintf(str, _T("IAuto2: %ld is too big, use a value < 0"), lVal);
        Error(str, IID_IAuto2);
        return E_FAIL;
    }
    return S_OK;
}
```

These functions both call the inherited `CComCoClass<>` method, `Error()`. There are several overloaded versions of this method, depending on whether you want to pass the descriptive text as an `LPCSTR`, an `LPCOLESTR` or an ID to a string resource; and on whether you want to pass information about a help file and help context. These overloaded methods call various file-scope overloaded functions called `AtlReportError()`. Finally, these methods in turn call the single function `AtlSetErrorInfo()` that actually does the work. You can find this function in `AtlBase.h`, so take a look: the code is straightforward and creates an error object from the CLSID, IID and descriptive text.

Visual Basic Error Client

Once you've compiled the code, the easiest way to test it (using both `IDispatch` and vtable binding) is to use a Visual Basic client. So, start Visual Basic, and select **Standard EXE** in the **New Project** dialog. Add a textbox called `txtName` and a button to the form provided. To test the Automation error handling, simply add the following code to the button click handler:

```
Private Sub Command1_Click()
    Dim obj As Object
    Set obj = CreateObject("Automation.Auto")
    obj.Value Val(txtName)
End Sub
```

Note that we only have access to the `Value()` *method, supplied by the default* `IAuto` *interface.*

Alternatively, to use vtable binding, we need to add a reference to our generated type library. To do this, select **Project | References...**, check the Automation 1.0 Type Library, and click **OK**. This time we can access `Value2()` as well, since we can obtain a reference to `IAuto2`:

```
Private Sub Command1_Click()
    Dim obj As New Auto
    Dim itf As IAuto2
    Set itf = obj
    lblRet = ""
    obj.Value Val(txtName)
    itf.Value2 Val(txtName)
    Set obj = Nothing
    Set itf = Nothing
End Sub
```

Whichever way you access the instance of the `Auto` coclass, you will receive helpful error information. For example, if you take the example that uses vtable binding, enter a (positive) number in the text box, and click on the button, you will get the following dialog from the Visual Basic IDE:

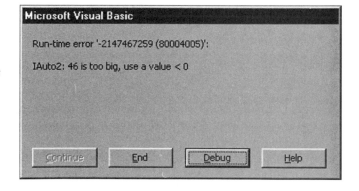

The `IDispatch` bound client will not display this window, as it has no access to `IAuto2`. You can, however, get a similar message by entering a negative number in the text box and clicking the button. Alternatively, if you compile the project and then run it, you'll get a dialog along the lines of this one:

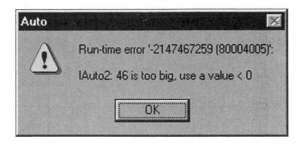

Notice that in both cases, the error number returned from the `Value()` (or `Value2()`) method is `E_FAIL`. Visual Basic also gives the string that you constructed in the method.

The problem with allowing Visual Basic to handle the error object is that when you dismiss the dialog, it will stop the application. So just to finish off this example, let's handle the error (shown here for the vtable-bound example, although it will work just as well for both pieces of code):

```
Private Sub Command1_Click()
On Error GoTo except
    Dim obj As New Auto
    Dim itf As IAuto2
    Set itf = obj
    lblRet = ""
    obj.Value Val(txtName)
    itf.Value2 Val(txtName)
    Set obj = Nothing
    Set itf = Nothing
    Exit Sub
except:
    Dim str As String
    str = "Error from " & Err.Source & Chr$(10) & Chr$(13)
    str = str & Err.Description & Chr$(10) & Chr$(13)
    str = str & "HRESULT: " & Hex$(Err.Number)
    MsgBox str
End Sub
```

The `On Error` line catches the error, and in the handler we use the Visual Basic `Err` object to extract information from the error object:

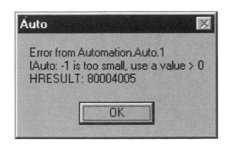

C++ *Error Client*

The Visual Basic client caught the error object generated when an error occurred, but Visual Basic hid the full details of what was going on. This next example will show you how to catch error objects in a C++ project.

To do this, the client should query the object for the ISupportErrorInfo interface. If a valid interface pointer is returned, it means that the object supports error objects. Next, the client must call the InterfaceSupportsErrorInfo() method, passing the IID of the interface it is interested in. If this method returns S_OK, the client can obtain the error object for the current (server) thread of execution for this Automation interface.

To obtain the error object itself, the client must call GetErrorInfo().This function is a little odd, because it is a *global* function, rather than a method on an interface implemented by the server object. You don't pass any sort of reference to an object to this method: it just *knows* that you want to get the current error object on the current object for the current thread of execution. In fact, the Microsoft documentation states that the function returns the most recently set error object in the current logical thread. If the current client thread has more than one Automation object (and each object may have more than one Automation interface), COM on the client side will only maintain the error object that was most recently set. You really don't need to worry about all this, because if you use the COM native support classes, they will do all the work for you.

Creating a client is straightforward. You could create a GUI project, but it is much easier to write a console application. Start up Visual C++ and create a new, empty Win32 Console Application in a subdirectory of the Automation project directory — the one you can download from the Wrox Press web site is called AutoClient. Add a source file to the project, and enter the following code:

```
#include <windows.h>
#include <stdio.h>
#include <tchar.h>

#import "..\automation.tlb"

using namespace AUTOMATIONLib;

int _tmain(int argc, _TCHAR** argv)
{
    CoInitialize(NULL);

    try
    {
        IAutoPtr pAuto(__uuidof(Auto));
        IAuto2Ptr pAuto2 = pAuto;

        // Get the user to pass values to the object
        TCHAR str[256] = {0};
        LONG lVal = 0;
        while(true)
        {
            _tprintf(_T("(enter 0 to stop)> "));
            _tscanf(_T("%s"), str);
            lVal = _ttol(str);
            if(lVal == 0)
                break;
            try
            {
                pAuto->Value(lVal);
                pAuto2->Value2(lVal);
            }
```

```
            catch(_com_error e)
            {
                _tprintf(_T("There is an error (%08x) in %s: \n\t\"%s\"\n"),
                        e.Error(), static_cast<LPCSTR>(e.Source()),
                        static_cast<LPCSTR>(e.Description())));
            }
        }
    }
    catch(_com_error e)
    {
        _tprintf(_T("There is an error (%08x): %s\n"),
                e.Error(), e.ErrorMessage());
    }

    CoUninitialize();
    return 0;
}
```

This code uses the Visual C++ compiler COM support smart pointers, so it needs to import the type library from the Automation project right at the top of the listing.

Type in and compile this code, and then look in the Debug (or the appropriate Release) directory for the two files automation.tlh and automation.tli that were generated from the type library by the #import directive. In the .tlh file, you will find the wrapper structures for the interfaces, among which will be one called IAuto. This declares the pure virtual method raw_Value(), which is the actual vtable method that the IDL file calls Value(); and also a wrapper Value() method that you call in the client code. Take a look in the .tli file, and you'll find:

```
inline HRESULT IAuto::Value ( long lVal ) {
    HRESULT _hr = raw_Value(lVal);
    if (FAILED(_hr)) _com_issue_errorex(_hr, this, __uuidof(this));
    return _hr;
}
```

When you call IAuto::Value() in the client code, the wrapper method actually calls the object vtable method raw_Value(). If this returns a non-success HRESULT, it goes on to call _com_issue_errorex(). This method creates a _com_error object and throws it as an exception.

The interesting thing from our point of view is that this function will do all the work of querying for ISupportErrorInfo and testing to see if the error supports rich error information for the interface that we discussed above. If everything's OK, then the _com_issue_errorex() function will get access to the error object for the logical thread and hold this in the _com_error object. When the exception is caught, you can use the exception object's convenient methods to access the error object's values. This is shown later in the code, but first let's look at how the object is created.

Within the outer try-catch block, we first initialize our smart pointers:

```
            IAutoPtr pAuto(__uuidof(Auto));
            IAuto2Ptr pAuto2 = pAuto;
```

Next, the code goes into a loop getting input from the user, which is broken if the user enters 0. The code converts the string to a number, and then passes this to the Value() and Value2() methods of the IAuto and IAuto2 interfaces via calls to the wrapper methods. The calls are wrapped in a try-catch block to catch any exceptions thrown by these wrapper methods.

The exception handler just prints out the data in the error object. Here are some test results:

```
AutoClient                                                    _ □ X
<enter 0 to stop>> 25
There is an error <80004005> in Automation.Auto.1:
        "IAuto2: 25 is too big, use a value < 0"
<enter 0 to stop>> -50
There is an error <80004005> in Automation.Auto.1:
        "IAuto: -50 is too small, use a value > 0"
<enter 0 to stop>> 0
Press any key to continue
```

As expected, when `IAuto2::Value2()` is called with a positive number, an exception is thrown. The
`HRESULT` is E_FAIL, which is just the return value from the `Value2()` method. The source of the error is
given as `Automation.Auto.1`, which is the ProgID of the object, and the description is "IAuto2: 25 is
too big, use a value < 0", indicating that it did indeed come from `IAuto2`.

When you enter a negative number, `IAuto::Value()` complains, saying that you should use a positive
number. Lastly, we can stop the process by entering a value of 0.

This is just as you would expect — the error object is being propagated from the `Auto` object to the client.
One thing that is not immediately obvious from this code, though, is that error objects can be propagated
across process and machine boundaries, and *still* be associated with their logical thread.

But what if the client accesses the object through `IDispatch`? Try this code. First, add an `IDispatch`
smart pointer:

```
IAutoPtr pAuto(__uuidof(Auto));
IAuto2Ptr pAuto2 = pAuto;
IDispatchPtr pDisp = pAuto;
```

And add the following code:

```
try
{
    pAuto->Value(lVal);
    pAuto2->Value2(lVal);
}
catch(_com_error e)
{
    _tprintf(_T("There is an error (%08x) in %s: \n\t\"%s\"\n"),
            e.Error(), static_cast<LPCSTR>(e.Source()),
            static_cast<LPCSTR>(e.Description()));
}

VARIANT varResult;
VariantInit(&varResult);

VARIANTARG vars;
VariantInit(&vars);
vars.vt = VT_I4;
vars.lVal = lVal;

DISPPARAMS disp = {&vars, NULL, 1, 0};
EXCEPINFO excepInfo;
HRESULT hr = pDisp->Invoke(0x1, IID_NULL, LOCALE_USER_DEFAULT,
                           DISPATCH_METHOD, &disp,
                           &varResult, &excepInfo, NULL);
```

```
if(hr == DISP_E_EXCEPTION)
{
    _tprintf(_T(
        "There is an error in Invoke() (%08x) in %ls: \n\t\"%ls\"\n"),
        excepInfo.scode, excepInfo.bstrSource, excepInfo.bstrDescription);
    SysFreeString(excepInfo.bstrSource);
    SysFreeString(excepInfo.bstrDescription);
    SysFreeString(excepInfo.bstrHelpFile);
}
```

Make sure that the call to Invoke() has the DISPID of Value() as given in the IDL; the code above uses 0x1. When IAuto::Value() is called, and when a negative number is passed, Invoke() will return DISP_E_EXCEPTION and you can then print out the rich error information. Notice that you haven't changed the object at all — the system-generated version of Invoke() will check for an error object and use the values therein. Here are some results:

This calls the Value() method on IAuto, but what about Value2() on IAuto2? Add some more code:

```
IDispatchPtr pDisp = pAuto;
IDispatchPtr pDisp2 = pAuto2;
```

And:

```
if(hr == DISP_E_EXCEPTION)
{
    _tprintf(_T(
        "There is an error in Invoke() (%08x) in %ls: \n\t\"%ls\"\n"),
        excepInfo.scode, excepInfo.bstrSource, excepInfo.bstrDescription);
    SysFreeString(excepInfo.bstrSource);
    SysFreeString(excepInfo.bstrDescription);
    SysFreeString(excepInfo.bstrHelpFile);
}

hr = pDisp2->Invoke(0x1, IID_NULL, LOCALE_USER_DEFAULT,
                    DISPATCH_METHOD, &disp,
                    &varResult, &excepInfo, NULL);

if(hr == DISP_E_EXCEPTION)
{
    _tprintf(_T(
        "There is an error in Invoke() (%08x) in %ls: \n\t\"%ls\"\n"),
        excepInfo.scode, excepInfo.bstrSource, excepInfo.bstrDescription);
    SysFreeString(excepInfo.bstrSource);
    SysFreeString(excepInfo.bstrDescription);
    SysFreeString(excepInfo.bstrHelpFile);
}
```

225

Here are the results:

```
AutoClient                                                    _ □ ✕
<enter 0 to stop>> 1
There is an error <80004005> in Automation.Auto.1:
        "IAuto2: 1 is too big, use a value < 0"
<enter 0 to stop>> -1
There is an error <80004005> in Automation.Auto.1:
        "IAuto: -1 is too small, use a value > 0"
There is an error in Invoke() <80004005> in Automation.Auto.1:
        "IAuto: -1 is too small, use a value > 0"
There is an error in Invoke() <80004005> in Automation.Auto.1:
        "IAuto: -1 is too small, use a value > 0"
<enter 0 to stop>> 0
Press any key to continue
```

This is clearly not what we want. In the first test (with a parameter of 1) you would expect an exception from `IAuto2::Value2()`. This is happening, but only for the call through the smart pointer. To work out what's happening, you have to look at the next text. This time the parameter is –1, so you would expect `IAuto::Value()` to throw an exception. It does so *three* times: once for the call through the smart pointer, a second time when a call is made through `pDisp->Invoke()` and a third time when there is a call through `pDisp2->Invoke()`.

The reason for this behavior stems from something we looked at right at the start of the chapter. As I said then, there is just one implementation of `IDispatch`, so `pDisp` and `pDisp2` point to the same interface! Since the same DISPID is passed to `Invoke()`, the same method will be called (`CAuto::Value()`).

You may think that the solution is to change the DISPID of `Value2()` to a different value (say, 4), but this won't work either, because the call to `pDisp2->Invoke(0x4, ...)` will return `DISP_E_MEMBERNOTFOUND` — in other words, a method with a DISPID of 0x4 cannot be found on `IAuto`. The reason for this return value is that the implementation of `GetIDsOfNames()` used internally only recognizes the DISPIDs of `IAuto`. There is no way to specify which Automation interface should be called through `IDispatch`, and the only solution would be to provide custom implementations of `Invoke()` and `GetIdsOfNames()`.

> The experiments we've conducted on the **Auto** component here should convince you that it is not a good idea to have multiple dual interfaces on a single component. Doing so restricts clients that only deal with **IDispatch** to using the default interface on the object, and any other interfaces will be hidden from them.
>
> In general, if you want an object to have multiple interfaces, only one of them should be a dual interface — the others should be custom. If the object will be used by scripting clients, the dual interface can be marked as **[default]**.

Summary

This chapter has said a little about rich error information, and a lot about Automation: how it works, why you'd want to use it, and how the components you write in ATL support it. Some of the points that you should take away from this chapter are:

- ❑ The methods in the COM interfaces we've been looking at prior to this chapter are called by static invocation. Automation allows dynamic invocation, in which objects can be queried for information about their interfaces at runtime.

- ❑ The collection of methods and properties available to clients that use Automation is called a dispinterface.

- ❑ Automation methods and properties have identifiers called DISPIDs, and they're accessed using the Invoke() method of the IDispatch COM interface.

- ❑ Information about Automation methods and properties is contained in type libraries, which are a tokenized, binary form of IDL. Type libraries can come as separate files, or they can be bound into a module as a resource.

- ❑ If type information is present, calls to methods can be set up at compile time, using vtable or early binding. If it isn't available, called to methods must be set up at runtime using IDispatch::GetIDsOfNames(). This is called late binding.

- ❑ Dual interfaces expose methods that can be called through IDispatch and through a vtable.

- ❑ VARIANTs allow data of many different types to be transmitted to Automation methods. The set of types that VARIANTs can contain are known as Automation-compatible types.

- ❑ ATL provides support for Automation through the IDispatchImpl<> template class, which accesses the information in the type library in order to implement IDisplatch::Invoke().

- ❑ COM objects indicate that they can pass rich error information back to their clients by implementing the ISupportErrorInfo interface.

In the next chapter, we'll finally address a couple of topics that have been dogging us for some time; indeed, they raised their heads again in this chapter. Marshaling and threading are subjects central to the way COM works, and understanding them can have a big impact on the efficiency and functionality of the components you write. What more incentive could you ask for?

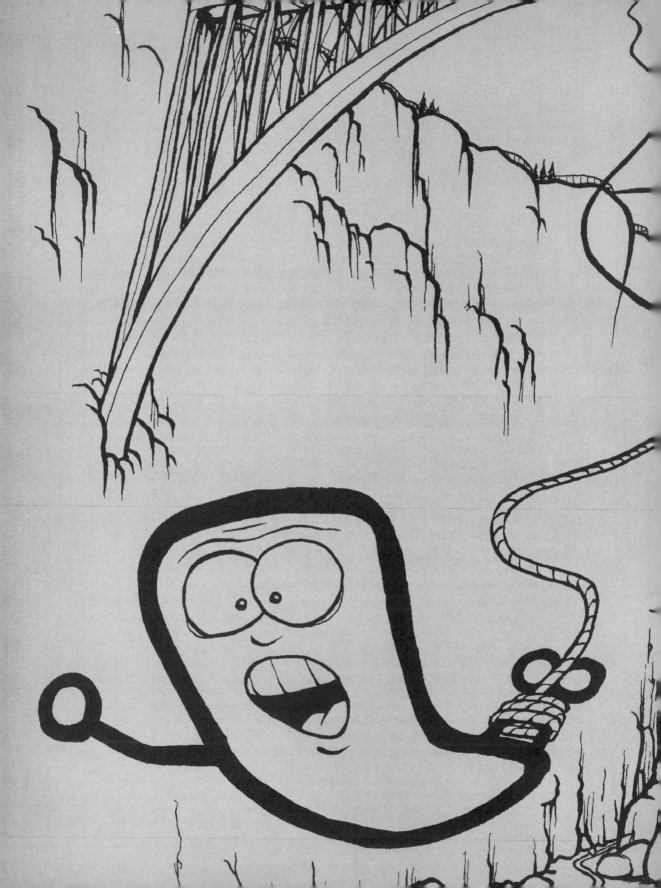

DCOM, Marshaling, And Threading

Although we've spoken about COM's much-vaunted location independence, the theory and examples we've looked at so far have shown only how to create simple in-process and local objects. Along the way, you've seen a little about how **marshaling**, provided by **proxies** and **stubs**, enables communication between components in different locations without requiring any changes to the client code. In all cases, the client code accesses methods on COM components via pointers to interfaces.

In this chapter, we're going to take a more detailed look at the different types of marshaling available. We'll discuss more carefully the pros and cons of packaging your components as DLLs and EXEs, and look at setting up your components to allow clients on a different machine to access them. Finally, we'll examine the past, present, and future development of COM threading.

DLL And EXE Servers

We'll start with a quick reminder of the two module types available to COM servers: DLLs and EXEs. As we've already seen, the module type is chosen when the ATL COM AppWizard generates the project. It is important to know which option you want at that stage, so let's look at the key differences.

DLLs

DLLs are dynamic-link libraries that are loaded into the process space of an application.

- ❑ The thread in the client that loads the DLL calls `CoInitialize()` or `CoInitializeEx()`. The DLL doesn't initialize COM for itself (nor must the DLL call `CoUninitialize()`).

- ❑ DLLs do not have any direct control over their own lifetime — they are loaded and unloaded by an external force: the client process.

- ❑ *But* COM shifts control over a DLL server's lifetime back to the DLL itself through the use of a protocol based around the `DllCanUnloadNow()` function, which all COM DLLs must export. Client processes must never unload DLLs without checking the `DllCanUnloadNow()` function. Typically, client processes can call `CoFreeUnusedLibraries()` to free unused DLLs. This function calls `DllCanUnloadNow()` internally.

- ❑ DLL servers can delay creating their class objects until `DllGetClassObject()` is called for that particular class object. Clients get pointers to the server's class objects from (indirect) calls to `DllGetClassObject()`.

❑ DLL servers are efficient in terms of clients accessing their interfaces' methods. In the best case, no proxy will be used to access the component's interfaces; compared with creating a C++ stack-based object, there is just one extra level of indirection to get to the component.

❑ DLL servers are risky. They are loaded into the memory space of the client, so they have complete access to the client's memory. A badly written server could write over the client's memory, causing the process to crash. A malicious server could wreak havoc.

❑ DLL servers run in the security context of the client process. This means that the components from the DLL have the same security clearance and identity as the client process. This is fine if you trust the component to use your identity responsibly, but if the component has been written by an unknown third party, you may feel a little reticent about this, preferring the component to be run under a less privileged account.

❑ If multiple client processes create components from the DLL, the in-process server is loaded into each process. Code from the DLL is shared between the processes, but data is not. This limits ATL singletons to being per-process.

EXEs

EXEs are executables. Each executable has/is/defines its own process.

❑ EXE servers call `CoInitialize()` or `CoInitializeEx()` (and, ultimately, `CoUninitialize()`) for themselves on each thread that will use COM.

❑ EXEs have control over their own lifetimes. An executable will unload when its code finishes running. In C++, that means it will unload whenever it returns from its `main()` or `WinMain()` function.

❑ EXE servers create their class objects when the process is first loaded, and register them with the system. Clients get pointers to interfaces on the class objects (indirectly) from the system.

❑ EXE servers are usually less efficient than DLL servers, because communication with an EXE always involves a proxy-stub.

❑ EXE servers offer more protection to the client application than DLLs — EXEs have their own memory address space, so they can't write across the client's memory.

❑ EXE servers have their own security context.

❑ Multiple clients can connect to the same instance of an EXE server (if the server will allow it).

Marshaling

Marshaling is the process of packaging and sending data across apartment, process, or machine boundaries. It is carried out by proxies and stubs, which are always implemented as in-process servers. Each proxy is loaded into the client process, and communicates with a corresponding stub in the server process. The proxy and stub are usually implemented in the same DLL. Each proxy object is responsible for marshaling the methods on a single interface, but each DLL can serve the proxy objects for a number of different interfaces.

The in-process nature of the proxy and stub allows the feature of COM known as **location transparency**. It means that the server programmer can write essentially the same code for their coclasses, regardless of the relative locations of the client and server at runtime. Logically, it also means that the client programmer can do the same. The basis of COM is that clients always call methods on pointers in their own address space. These pointers may be directly to a server's interfaces, or to a proxy's. COM handles the loading of proxies and stubs as necessary; it's up to the proxies and stubs themselves to handle the inter-process communication behind the scenes.

You don't really need to know a great deal about marshaling in order to use it successfully, but you do need a basic understanding of the different mechanisms and terms involved. There are three main types of marshaling, which we'll examine in the following sections:

❑ MIDL compiler-produced marshaling
❑ Type library marshaling
❑ Custom marshaling

MIDL Compiler-Produced Marshaling

Here's a statement of the obvious: MIDL compiler-produced marshaling is marshaling code that's produced by the MIDL compiler. In other words, it's what you get for free when you write an IDL file (or allow the Wizards to do it for you), and then run it through the MIDL compiler.

In ATL AppWizard-produced projects, the marshaling code is generated automatically from your project's IDL file whenever the project is built. Back in Chapter 3 we had a quick look at the files that the MIDL compiler generates for you. Let's recap and describe these files (we'll assume that the IDL file used to generate these files is called `Simple.idl`):

Filename	Description
Simple.h	The interface header file
Simple.tlb	The type library
Simple_i.c	Constant definitions
Simple_p.c	Proxy and stub code
dlldata.c	Start-up code for the proxy-stub DLL

In addition to these files, the AppWizard will generate the following files when your project is created:

Filename	Description
Simpleps.mk	Makefile to produce the proxy-stub DLL
Simpleps.def	Module definition file to export in-process server methods (`DllGetClassObject()`, etc.)

Although the MIDL compiler produces all the necessary source code files, it is up to you to build the proxy-stub DLL from the makefile. The makefile compiles all the C files in the project directory, but links together only the object files produced from the .c files listed above. You can build the proxy-stub DLL using the following command line (replacing Simpleps.mk with the name of your own makefile!):

```
>nmake Simpleps.mk
```

To enable command line builds, you should run the Vcvars32.bat file that's located in your installation's \bin directory to modify the PATH, LIB and INCLUDE environment variables.

To register the proxy-stub DLL as the handler for a particular interface, you can just pass the name of the DLL to regsvr32.exe, just as you would with any other DLL COM server:

```
>regsvr32 Simpleps.dll
```

The proxy-stub DLL is self-registering, adding the necessary entries to the registry to hook it up to a particular interface. This means that it adds a CLSID entry and, beneath that, an InprocServer32 entry to HKEY_CLASSES_ROOT\CLSID, just as any COM server would.

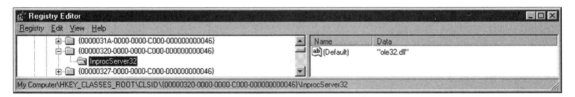

The screenshot shows the registry entry for Ole32.dll, which provides the proxy-stub implementation for many of the standard interfaces.

Registering the proxy-stub DLL also adds an entry for the IID in the HKEY_CLASSES_ROOT\Interface key, and beneath that a ProxyStubClsid32 key that relates the interface to the CLSID.

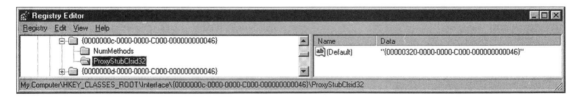

This screenshot shows the interface entry for IStream, one of the standard interfaces handled by Ole32.dll.

> **MIDL compiler-produced proxy-stub DLLs register themselves with the same CLSID as the IID of the first interface for which they provide the proxy.**

Remember that whenever an interface changes, so must the proxy-stub; you will need to rebuild the proxy-stub DLL and re-register it. Also remember that the proxy-stub DLL must be registered on *all* machines that use that interface, whether as client or server.

By default, the ATL AppWizard generated project files will compile your IDL file using the MIDL compiler's /Oicf command line switch (set by the Stubless Proxies box on the MIDL tab of the Project Settings dialog for IDL files). This produces proxy-stubs that are variously described as **stubless** (not a good description, as stub code is provided) or **codeless** (a better description). What this means is that very little code is actually generated — instead, the interface methods are described in tables of so-called **fast format strings**. The system provides the 'real' marshaler, which interprets these tables of strings to determine how to marshal methods.

If you choose to use the /Os switch (by unchecking the Stubless Proxies box), you will get code for the proxies and stubs that do not use this interpreter-marshaler, and although this will have better performance (and work on a wider range of operating systems), the resultant DLL will be bigger. Furthermore, components that are used in MTS (or COM+) must be either type library marshaled or marshaled with a proxy-stub generated with /Oicf.

Type Library Marshaling

As we've mentioned a few times now, COM provides a group of proxy-stubs collectively called the **Universal Marshaler**, which is implemented in Oleaut32.dll. This marshaler can be used to marshal *any* interface described in a type library.

> *Note that not all interfaces can be described in type libraries. The interfaces that can are those that only use a subset of the data types supported by the MIDL compiler. These are the Automation-compatible types that we described in the previous chapter.*

The only requirements for an interface to use the Universal Marshaler are that Oleaut32.dll must be registered as the proxy-stub for that interface (on client *and* server machines), and that the interface's type library must be registered. In practice, when you register the component on the server machine, these two criteria will be met. On the client machine, you will need to register the type library some other way.

> *The tools RegRgs32 and RegTlb32, available for download from the World of ATL web site (http://www.worldofatl.com), can be used to register the type library on the client.*

When the client accesses an object's interface, COM will read the interface's registry entry to see what proxy-stub to use. This entry will contain the CLSID of the Universal Marshaler, so COM will then look into the interface's registry entry for a TypeLib entry. This allows the Universal Marshaler to read the type library and hence determine the types of all the parameters of all the methods. When the client makes a method call, the Universal Marshaler can determine the types of the parameters on the stack, and construct an appropriate package to marshal to the server.

The Universal Marshaler still requires information to be registered on the client, and since you have to distribute a type library and register it, there is no particular gain over distributing and registering proxy-stub DLLs. However, the UM is particularly useful in one niche area: interoperability between 16-bit and 32-bit machines. 16-bit COM also has a Universal Marshaler (although it's somewhat restricted compared to the 32-bit version), and it can talk to the 32-bit Universal Marshaler using remote Automation. If you have a 16-bit COM application, you can write 32-bit code to talk to it over the network. Of course, if you have a 16-bit *and* a 32-bit proxy-stub registered for a 16-bit local server, this will allow you to use the component in a 32-bit process. However, you do need to make sure that you do not use 32-bit-only data types, because a 16-bit component will not know how to use them. This is another area where the Universal Marshaler adds value: it knows that BSTRs are char strings on 16-bit systems but wchar_t on 32-bit systems, and will do the necessary conversion for you.

To use type library marshaling, the type library must be registered, which is usually done with a call to the RegisterTypeLib() API function. In addition to adding an entry under the HKEY_CLASSES_ROOT\TypeLib key, RegisterTypeLib() adds registry entries for all the Automation-compatible interfaces in the library, hooking them up to the Universal Marshaler. This means that all dispinterfaces, dual interfaces, and interfaces with the [oleautomation] attribute will be registered along with the type library.

By default, ATL AppWizard-generated projects register the type library when the server is registered. The first parameter to CComModule::RegisterServer() is a BOOL value that indicates whether the type library should be registered at the same time as the server. If the value is TRUE, CComModule::RegisterServer() uses the RegisterTypeLib() API to register the type library. If you don't want the type library to be registered at this time, you should set the value to FALSE when the function is called. CComModule::RegisterServer() is called in the _tWinMain() function of an ATL EXE, and in the DllRegisterServer() function of an ATL DLL.

It is this behavior that has allowed us to avoid explicitly registering a proxy-stub DLL for the interfaces that we have created up to this point. All of our interfaces have been Automation-compatible, and registering the servers has automatically registered the type libraries and interfaces in them, so that they can be marshaled by Oleaut32.dll.

Choosing Your Marshaler

In which situations would you want to use type library marshaling, and when would you use MIDL compiler-produced marshaling? Well, if you want to use data types that aren't supported by the Universal Marshaler, you'll *have* to use MIDL compiler-produced marshaling code, because you simply can't use type library marshaling.

If you want to minimize the number of files distributed with your server, you'll probably prefer type library marshaling, since the type library can be compiled into your server as a resource. It is possible to combine the MIDL compiler-generated proxy-stub code into the module for a DLL server, but this is not possible for an EXE server (since the proxy-stub must be in-process).

If performance is an issue, you may choose MIDL compiler-generated marshaling code over type library marshaling. The Universal Marshaler appears to convert type library type information into fast format strings and then use the interpreter-marshaler. There is therefore an initial slight overhead due to the Universal Marshaler having to load and consult the type library.

> **MIDL compiler-produced marshaling and type library marshaling are both forms of standard marshaling.**

Custom Marshaling

Type library marshaling and MIDL compiler-produced marshaling are adequate for most needs, but occasionally you may seek better performance, or want to add value to the marshaling. **Custom marshaling** allows you to replace the existing marshaling mechanisms with one of your own.

Because it's an advanced optimization technique, we won't look at custom marshaling in detail, but we will explain enough that you won't be surprised by the behavior of your components, and so that you can choose to investigate further if you find custom marshaling of interest. ATL provides no special help for implementing custom marshaling.

Standard marshaling has to be generic, which means that the marshaling mechanism is not necessarily the most efficient for all circumstances. Typical situations in which you might want to implement custom marshaling are:

❑ You're marshaling a data type that standard marshaling doesn't handle well, or where some of the values you're transmitting are irrelevant in the other process. An example might be a node in a doubly-linked list, for which the process you're sending data to isn't interested in the pointer to the next node.

❑ You're marshaling a constant property across the network. With standard marshaling, the data would need to flow across the network each time the property is read by a client. By implementing custom marshaling, you can cache the state of the property on the client machine for speedier access.

❑ You want to optimize the marshaling according to the context of the server (in-process, local, or remote).

A component that uses custom marshaling must implement the IMarshal interface. When COM gets a request to create a component, and the class object has returned an instance of the class, COM QI()s the component for IMarshal. If the component returns an IMarshal interface pointer, COM knows that custom marshaling is being used (if E_NOINTERFACE is returned, COM will use standard marshaling instead). This extra call to QueryInterface() for the IMarshal interface is often a cause of confusion to people; now you know what it is if you see it when you're QI() debugging! IMarshal has an IID of 00000003-0000-0000-C000-000000000046.

In addition to supporting IMarshal on your component, you still need to implement a proxy object (you don't need a separate stub object, because the proxy object will talk directly to the component through whatever IPC mechanism you choose). This in-process component also needs to implement IMarshal, plus all the interfaces that the component supports. The IMarshal interface has some methods that are specific to the proxy and others that are specific to the component, but basically it's used to set up the connection between these two components.

Now, when the client calls methods on the interface, it will actually be calling methods on the proxy. These methods will use whatever scheme is appropriate for the interface to package up the method requests and parameters and send this data to the server. The server unpacks this data and dispatches the request to the appropriate handling routine, which can then return a reply back to the proxy, again in a packaged form. The proxy unpacks the data and returns it to the client.

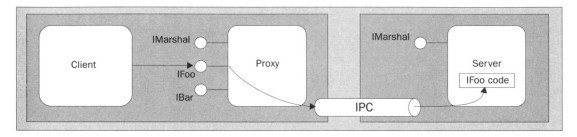

Note that in this mechanism, the component doesn't actually have to implement the interfaces that the client thinks it does — it is up to the proxy to decide how to dispatch the method requests. In the example shown in the diagram, the server only implements IMarshal, but the client's calls on the IFoo interface result in the proxy telling the server to perform an action via a non-COM call.

Remote Servers

Let's return now to the theme we had at the start of the chapter — location independence — and take the subject to its logical conclusion. **Remote servers** are simply servers running on a different machine from the client. The original COM specification always had interface remoting (that's what proxy-stubs are for), but prior to NT 4.0, the only way this could be used was in cross-process calls on a single machine. Although DCOM is often discussed separately from COM, DCOM *is* COM. It's simply an extension of Microsoft RPC that supports access to remote (networked) COM objects.

> *DCOM comes as standard with Windows NT 4.0 and Windows 2000. It is provided as an add-on*
> *for Windows 95 and Windows 98. You can obtain DCOM95 and DCOM98 from*
> http://www.microsoft.com/com/resources/downloads.asp.

RPC can use many different protocols, including named pipes, IP, SPX and IPX. On Windows 2000 (and on NT4 with the appropriate option pack applied), MSMQ can be used too. NT 4.0 *prefers* UDP/IP as the protocol, but if a request comes in on another protocol, it will lazily load the required drivers. Windows 2000 prefers TCP/IP as the protocol, and Windows 9x *only* uses TCP/IP. Note that if the client initially uses a protocol that's different from the one the server is expecting, there will be a delay while the server searches for and loads the drivers of other transports.

Surrogates

Both DLL and EXE servers can be accessed remotely, but a DLL needs the support of a surrogate process. As we mentioned earlier in the chapter, a DLL must be loaded into a process in order for it to run. When that process is designed to allow a DLL server to be accessed remotely (or to be accessed from another process on the same machine), it's known as a **surrogate**.

Surrogates were introduced in NT 4.0 service pack 2 and DCOM95. The system provides a standard surrogate called `DllHost.exe`, which can be used as the surrogate for any DLL server. Alternatively, you can write your own, which you may decide to do if you want to apply special security code. Writing a custom surrogate is beyond the scope of this book, but we'll look at an example of using the standard surrogate later in the chapter.

> *MTS for NT 4.0 and Windows 9x provides another surrogate called* `mtx.exe`, *but although this too is used to allow DLL servers to be run in a separate process (or machine) from the client, it uses a different registration process and so the following discussion does not apply to it. Windows 2000 has subsumed MTS into the operating system and confuses matters further by using* `DllHost.exe` *as its MTS surrogate and yet another different registration process.*

Surrogates are associated with DLLs via entries in the system registry. The server needs an AppID value beneath its CLSID key, which relates the coclass back to a key under `HKEY_CLASSES_ROOT\AppID`. This key holds information about the server, and if the DLL should be loaded into a surrogate, it will contain a named value called `DllSurrogate`. This value may have the path to the surrogate to use, or it may be blank, in which case the system surrogate is used. We'll look in detail at the registry entries required when we come to create an example later in the chapter.

When a client requests a component from a remote machine, COM will perform a lookup in the registry for the server for the requested class. If it finds that the class is in-process and has an AppID, it will check for the `DllSurrogate` value. If *that* is present then COM will start the appropriate surrogate process and pass it the CLSID of the in-process server. The surrogate then loads the DLL server, obtains the required class object, and registers it with the system. After this, COM will request the instantiation of a component, just as it would for a local server.

Accessing Remote Servers

There are two options for accessing remote servers. The first is to configure the registry on the client machine to create a component on another, specified, machine. The second is to pass a machine name to the `CoCreateInstanceEx()` function when you create a component.

The advantage of the first method is that your client code can continue to call `CoCreateInstance()`. It doesn't need to know anything about the machine that the component will be created on, and you can change the way in which the server is created without recompiling the client. The disadvantage of the registry method is that the settings affect all the clients on that machine, which may not be appropriate. For example, you may have several components on different machines across a network, and the client may want to access a particular component depending on some run-time criteria (for load balancing, perhaps).

The second method gives the client application fine control over the way in which the server is created, and allows it to make use of some optimizations provided by the `CoCreateInstanceEx()` function. We'll look at these two methods in turn, in sections that assume you're running a DCOM-enabled operating system.

Registering A Server For Remote Access

To register a server for remote access, it first requires an AppID value beneath its CLSID key. In this figure, you can see the AppID entry for the MSDEV.APPLICATION coclass. (This coclass represents the Visual C++ application — even your development environment is a COM server!)

The AppID value's data is a GUID that also appears as a sub-key under the HKEY_CLASSES_ROOT\ AppID key.

The AppID sub-key is used to control configuration options for a single executable. Since an executable can serve several different coclasses, the configurations applied to the AppID key will affect all of those coclasses.

ATL AppWizard-generated EXE projects will automatically add the AppID key and value to the project's coclasses. The registry entries come from the RGS files that we examined in Chapter 3. The (Default) named value of the AppID key is meant as a description of the application. Wizard-generated projects will use the name of the project for this value. Note that Wizard-generated *DLL* projects won't register any AppID information, so if you want to use a surrogate, you will have to edit this file yourself.

To get the application to be activated on another machine, you need to add a RemoteServerName string value under the AppID sub-key for your object server. However, you don't need to do this by hand, because Dcomcnfg.exe, a utility supplied with DCOM, enables you to set the required registry entry using a simple dialog. If you run Dcomcnfg.exe by typing its name into the Run dialog accessible from the Start menu, you'll see the dialog shown below. The first tab lists the applications registered on your system, as shown on the next page:

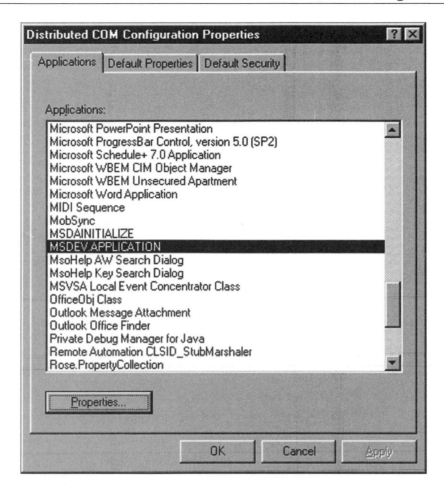

To reiterate, despite the impression that some of these entries give, the values that you change with Dcomcnfg.exe are for the entire server, and will apply to all coclasses in that server. If Dcomcnfg.exe gives the name of a coclass, it just means that it cannot find a descriptive name for the server.

If you double-click on one of the entries in the list (or select one and hit the Properties... button), you'll bring up a new dialog displaying the properties for that application. The Location tab allows you to set the location at which the server will run.

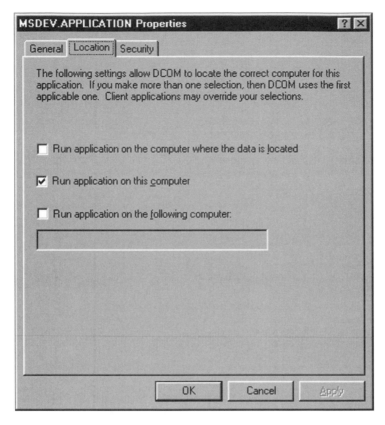

If you choose to run the application on another computer, the name that you use to specify it will depend on the network transport being used. However, UNC names like \\MyServer and MyServer, as well as DNS names like myserver.com and IP addresses like 194.222.147.74, are accepted.

Note that the options on the Location page are non-exclusive, so that you can allow a server to be launched locally *or* remotely depending on the context supplied to the creation function. COM will check the contexts specified by the client and then access the server according to the preferred order given below:

❑ If the CLSID has an InprocServer32 or InprocHandler32, the specified DLL is used.

❑ If the AppID has a LocalService value, COM checks to see if there is a class object registered with the system, and if not it starts an NT service on the local machine. (This step only applies to COM on Windows NT.)

❑ If the CLSID has a LocalServer32 value, COM checks to see if there is a registered class object, and if not it starts the specified process.

❑ If the AppID has a value called DllSurrogate, but the value is empty, Dllhost.exe is used.

❑ If DllSurrogate is present and gives a path to a server, the specified surrogate is used.

❑ If the AppID has a RemoteServerName then the request is forwarded to COM on the specified machine.

Note that if the component is launched on a remote machine, it will use the same search order *except* that it starts the search with the check on `LocalService`. If the remote machine tries to delegate the activation to yet another machine, it will fail because all activations require a security context (an access token) that cannot be passed from machine to machine under Windows NT 4.0.

To do otherwise would require a facility called **delegation** *that is possible under Kerberos on Windows 2000. However, it requires extra security administration because the account that is being delegated must trust not only the immediate server to use it responsibly, but also any other machines that the call may be delegated to.*

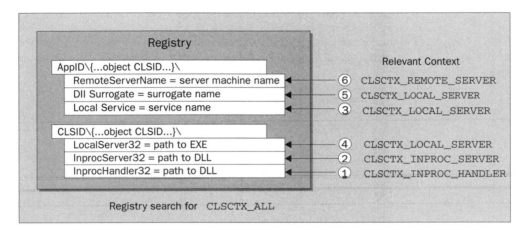

CoCreateInstanceEx()

The second way to access remote components is to use `CoCreateInstanceEx()` and its parameters to specify the name of the server machine.

```
HRESULT CoCreateInstanceEx(
    REFCLSID        rclsid,         // CLSID of the component to be created
    IUnknown*       punkOuter,      // If part of an aggregate, the controlling
                                    //   IUnknown
    DWORD           dwClsCtx,       // CLSCTX values
    COSERVERINFO*   pServerInfo,    // Machine on which the component is to be
                                    //   instantiated
    ULONG           cmq,            // Number of MULTI_QI structures in pResults
    MULTI_QI*       pResults        // Array of MULTI_QI structures
);
```

Like `CoCreateInstance()`, this function takes parameters for the CLSID of the component to be created and context values for the server. These context values can be a combination of flags from the `CLSCTX` enumeration we saw in Chapter 2. Note that it also has a parameter for the outer unknown in an aggregate, but since aggregation is only possible in-apartment, this is only applicable when `dwClsCtx` is `CLSCTX_INPROC_SERVER`.

Unlike `CoCreateInstance()`, `CoCreateInstanceEx()` takes a `COSERVERINFO*` parameter that's used to determine the security settings for connecting to the server, and the name of the server to connect to. It also takes an array of `MULTI_QI` structures (with a related `ULONG` parameter) that is used to request and return a number of interfaces from the newly created component. `COSERVERINFO` is a `struct` that looks like this:

```
typedef struct _COSERVERINFO
{
    DWORD dwReserved1;
    LPWSTR pwszName;
    COAUTHINFO* pAuthInfo;
    DWORD dwReserved2;
} COSERVERINFO;
```

The reserved parameters `dwReserved1` and `dwReserved2` must be set to 0. These parameters may be used in the future, but at the moment they do nothing. `pwszName` is a null-terminated Unicode character string that gives the name of the server machine. It follows the same conventions as the `RemoteServerName` registry entry we looked at earlier in the chapter.

`pAuthInfo` passes security information to the server. This is required because a remote server machine should not allow just anyone to launch or access a process. Instead, the server machine should be more careful. It should check that the client is who they say they are (known as **authentication**), and then that the client can do what it asks (**authorization**). The `COAUTHINFO*` parameter depends on the authentication authority that is used. You can use the default security authority (NTLM security for NT 4.0 and Kerberos for Windows 2000) by passing a `NULL` value for this parameter. This will be adequate for most needs.

For more details on DCOM security, take a look at Professional DCOM Programming *(1-861000-60-X).*

Note that if the `COSERVERINFO*` parameter passed to `CoCreateInstanceEx()` is `NULL`, COM will consult the value of the corresponding `RemoteServerName` in the registry. If that is empty, COM will create the component on the local machine.

The `MULTI_QI*` parameter allows you to request several interfaces in one go. `CoCreateInstance()` allows you to ask COM to create an instance of a COM component and return a single interface on that component. If you want more than one interface, you must make multiple calls to `QueryInterface()`, and if the component is remote, that means multiple calls across the network. Calls across a network are relatively slow, so it's more efficient to request a number of interfaces with a single call — and `CoCreateInstanceEx()` allows you to do just that. The `MULTI_QI` structure looks like this:

```
typedef struct tagMULTI_QI
{
    const IID* pIID;
    IUnknown*  pItf;
    HRESULT    hr;
} MULTI_QI;
```

You pass in the IID of the interface that you want in `pIID`, and `CoCreateInstanceEx()` will return the status code in `hr`. If the interface request was successful, the interface pointer will be in `pItf`.

Finally for `CoCreateInstanceEx()`, the `cmq` parameter must be set by the caller to the number of elements in the `pResults` array.

> *Note that the compiler COM support smart pointers don't provide a wrapper function for* `CoCreateInstanceEx()` *(although they do provide a* `CreateInstance()` *method that wraps* `CoCreateInstance()`*). However, you can still use smart pointers when creating remote servers, as you'll see in the example later in the chapter.*

Remote Components With ATL

Now that you've seen some theory of remote components, let's look at what it takes to get some ATL objects communicating with clients on another machine. In two examples, we'll create a DLL server and hook it up to the standard surrogate, and we'll create an EXE server. In each case, we'll show how the client can talk to a server on another machine via registry entries or a call to `CoCreateInstanceEx()`. You'll also see how to set up separate projects to share the definition and implementation of a coclass.

This example implements a simple component that exposes one method — `GetFreeDiskSpace()` — to return the amount of free disk space on the machine it's running on. The chances of two machines having the same amount of free disk space are very small, so it is a useful component to show that remote activation is working.

For our example, we want to create a DLL project and an EXE project that expose the same coclass with the same interface and implementation. Clearly, we don't want to duplicate code or interface definitions between the projects, so we'll set up the projects in such a way that they refer to the same files as much as possible. In this small example, the effort required to share the files is quite large in proportion to the size of the project, but the benefits of minimizing effort and increasing maintainability quickly grow along with the size of the project.

The first step is to create a new folder with the name `ServerInfo`. We'll use this folder to store all the files to be shared between the projects. That will include the IDL file (and the files that the MIDL compiler will produce from it), as well as the header and implementation files that will be common to both projects.

A DLL Server

The next step is to create the DLL version of the project. Fire up Visual C++ and create a new ATL COM AppWizard project called `ServerInfo`. Store it in a subdirectory of the `ServerInfo` directory you just created, and call this subdirectory `ServerInfoDll`. (Use the `...` button to select the `ServerInfo` directory, then type `ServerInfo` as the **Project** n̲ame and finally add `Dll` to the end of the text in Lo̲cation.) You can see the settings you need to make in the screenshot below:

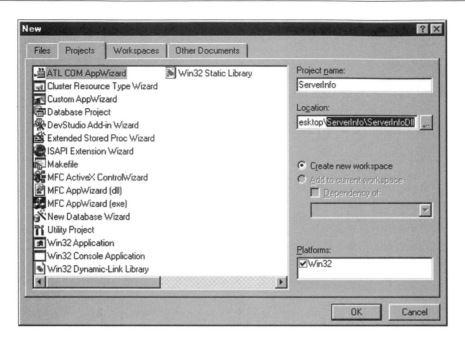

On **Step 1** of the AppWizard, choose <u>D</u>ynamic Link Library (DLL) as the server type and press <u>F</u>inish. Then click **OK** on the next dialog.

After that, add a new **Simple Object** to the project using the ATL Object Wizard. Use `DiskInfo` for the <u>S</u>hort Name, and the remainder of the fields can be left with their default values. On the **Attributes** tab, ensure that the <u>C</u>ustom interface radio button is selected, and click on **OK**:

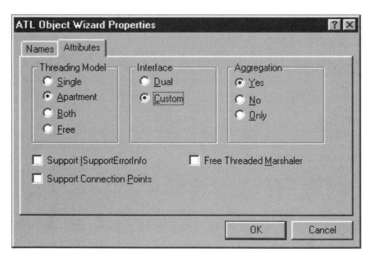

Using ClassView, add the following method to the `IDiskInfo` interface:

```
HRESULT GetFreeDiskSpace(/*[in, string]*/ const wchar_t* wszDrive,
                         /*[out]*/         hyper*         hypFreeBytes);
```

Here, `wszDrive` is the name of the drive on the machine on which the component is running, and it's an [in, string] parameter. Note the use of the [string] attribute here; `wchar_t*` could be treated by the marshaling code as a pointer to a *single* `wchar_t`, so this attribute tells the marshaler to call `wcslen()` on the parameter to find out exactly how many characters to marshal. The results are returned in the [out] parameter `hypFreebytes`. The 64-bit integer `hyper` is used here because the Win32 function that we will use returns this data type to accommodate very large disks. Because the method uses this data type, which is an IDL-specific data type and not one of the Automation-compatible types, you cannot implement the interface as a dual.

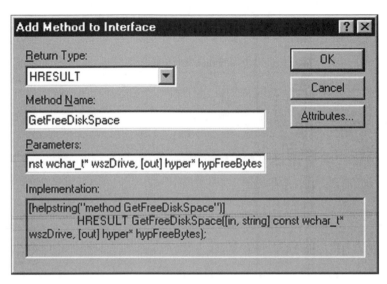

Next, open the `CDiskInfo` and then the `IDiskInfo` tree in ClassView, and then double-click on the `GetFreeDiskSpace()` method. Enter the following code:

```
STDMETHODIMP CDiskInfo::GetFreeDiskSpace(const wchar_t* wszDrive,
                                         hyper* hypFreeBytes)
{
    USES_CONVERSION;

    DWORD dwSectorsPerCluster;
    DWORD dwBytesPerSector;
    DWORD dwNumberOfFreeClusters;
    DWORD dwTotalNumberOfClusters;

    // GetDiskFreeSpaceEx() is not available
    // before Win95 OSR2, so we'll use GetDiskFreeSpace()
    if(!GetDiskFreeSpace(W2T(wszDrive), &dwSectorsPerCluster, &dwBytesPerSector,
                    &dwNumberOfFreeClusters, &dwTotalNumberOfClusters))
    {
        *hypFreeBytes = 0;
        return HRESULT_FROM_WIN32(GetLastError());
    }

    // The number of bytes per cluster should fit into a DWORD
    DWORD dwBytesPerCluster;
    dwBytesPerCluster = dwSectorsPerCluster * dwBytesPerSector;

    // But the number of bytes on the disk needs careful handling
    *hypFreeBytes =  UInt32x32To64(dwNumberOfFreeClusters, dwBytesPerCluster);

    return S_OK;
}
```

The W2T() *macro we use in the above code is one of a sizable group of macros that are defined in*
Atlconv.h *for converting text — this one converts a wide character string into a text string. To
do this, the macros create a temporary buffer by using the* _alloca() *CRT function to allocate
memory on the stack. Since the memory is allocated locally (in the function's stack frame), it is
automatically freed when the function returns.*

To be able to allocate memory, W2T() *needs to know how big the buffer should be. The macro could
define a code block (within braces) and a local variable, but this would restrict its use in a function's
parameter list, so instead a variable needs to be declared that's local to the entire code block where
the conversion macros will be used. This is done by the* USES_CONVERSION *macro.*

Finally, open DiskInfo.rgs and edit it to ensure that registry entries used by both the DLL and EXE
server have the NoRemove keyword applied. This means that the shared entries won't be removed when
one of the servers is unregistered. The registry script should now look like this:

```
HKCR
{
    NoRemove ServerInfo.DiskInfo.1 = s 'DiskInfo Class'
    {
        NoRemove CLSID = s '{7CBADAE0-5B94-11D3-89D0-00104BDC35E0}'
    }
    NoRemove ServerInfo.DiskInfo = s 'DiskInfo Class'
    {
        NoRemove CLSID = s '{7CBADAE0-5B94-11D3-89D0-00104BDC35E0}'
        NoRemove CurVer = s 'ServerInfo.DiskInfo.1'
    }
    NoRemove CLSID
    {
        NoRemove {7CBADAE0-5B94-11D3-89D0-00104BDC35E0} = s 'DiskInfo Class'
        {
            InprocServer32 = s '%MODULE%'
            {
                val ThreadingModel = s 'Apartment'
            }
            NoRemove ProgID = s 'ServerInfo.DiskInfo.1'
            NoRemove VersionIndependentProgID = s 'ServerInfo.DiskInfo'
        }
    }
}
```

You can see that the NoRemove keyword has been applied to every entry except InprocServer32 —
only the InprocServer32 entries will be removed when the DLL server is unregistered. Notice that the
ProgID and VersionIndependentProgID lines have been moved to the bottom of the registration
block. The reason for this is that the registrar uses a recursive routine to register keys, which detects when
NoRemove is used. After this, no other sub-key can be removed from that key. If the ProgID line was
above the InprocServer32 line, neither key would be removed (even though InprocServer32 has *not*
been marked NoRemove); the solution is to put all items that need to be removed before those that must
not be removed. The reference to the TypeLib has been removed, since we will not use it.

Because we're also going to be using this DLL server with a surrogate, we need an AppID value for it.
Although ATL EXE projects are automatically set up to register AppIDs, ATL DLL projects are not. To
rectify this, we need to generate a new GUID for the AppID using the GUID Generator, and then we can
add the AppID value to the DiskInfo.rgs file, just below the closing brace of the InprocServer32
entry. Once again, we use the NoRemove keyword because this entry will be shared with the EXE server.

```
                 val ThreadingModel = s 'Apartment'
            }
            NoRemove ProgID = s 'ServerInfo.DiskInfo.1'
            NoRemove VersionIndependentProgID = s 'ServerInfo.DiskInfo'
            NoRemove val AppID = s '{F51B0D13-5184-11D3-88E4-00105A68BF5D}'
        }
```

This registers the coclass with the AppID, but the AppID itself also needs some registry settings. In EXE projects, these are generated as a separate RGS file. We'll follow that convention in our DLL project.

Create a new text file and save it in the `ServerInfoDll` directory as `ServerInfo.rgs`. Add the following text to this file, and save it again:

```
HKCR
{
   NoRemove AppID
   {
      NoRemove {F51B0D13-5184-11D3-88E4-00105A68BF5D} = s 'ServerInfo'
      'ServerInfo.dll'
      {
         val AppID = s {F51B0D13-5184-11D3-88E4-00105A68BF5D}
      }
   }
}
```

The two GUIDs in this file are the same as the AppID we added to the `DiskInfo.rgs` file.

Now import this file as a "REGISTRY" resource. Go to ResourceView, right-click on the "REGISTRY" folder, and hit Import.... Set the Files of type list to show All Files (*.*), and the Open as list to show Custom, then select `ServerInfo.rgs`. Set the resource type to be "REGISTRY", and then hit OK. Once the resource has been imported, bring up its Properties dialog and set its ID to IDR_SERVERINFO.

Since we have an additional registry script in the project, you need to make sure that it gets run during registration and unregistration. Add these lines of code to `DllRegisterServer()` and `DllUnregisterServer()` in `ServerInfo.cpp`:

```
STDAPI DllRegisterServer(void)
{
    _Module.UpdateRegistryFromResource(IDR_SERVERINFO, TRUE);
    return _Module.RegisterServer(FALSE);
}

STDAPI DllUnregisterServer(void)
{
    _Module.UpdateRegistryFromResource(IDR_SERVERINFO, FALSE);
    return _Module.UnregisterServer(FALSE);
}
```

This code just registers the information in the new RGS file whenever the server is asked to register itself, and unregisters it when the server is asked to unregister itself. Notice also that the parameters to `_Module.RegisterServer()` and `UnregisterServer()` should be changed to `FALSE`. This will prevent the server from registering the type library.

Since the type library is now completely redundant in this example, you should remove it from the code module. The ATL AppWizard will add it as a resource, but you cannot remove it using the Resource View. Instead, select View | Resource Includes... and remove the line from the Compile-time directives box you can see here:

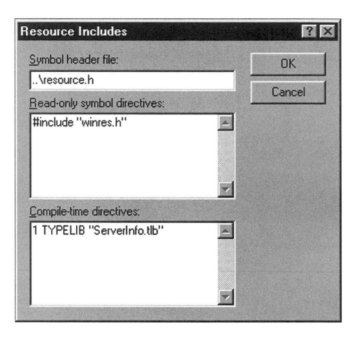

When you click OK, Visual C++ will warn you about the action that you're going to take, but you can safely ignore this and press the OK button on the message box.

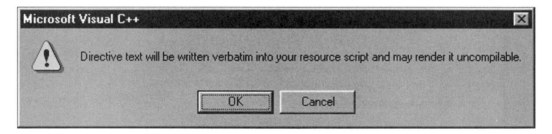

Moving The Files

At this stage, we have a fairly standard DLL server project (that also registers its own AppID). Before we compile the project, however, we need to move files that will be common to both the EXE server and the DLL server into the ServerInfo folder.

First, move the ServerInfops.def and ServerInfops.mk files, so that we can make the proxy-stub using files from the ServerInfo folder. The proxy-stub DLL will be used by both versions of the server.

Next *copy* the `ServerInfo.idl` file from the `ServerInfoDll` folder to its parent, `ServerInfo`. The reason that we're copying this file (rather than moving it) is that the ATL Wizards automatically add their interface definitions to the *ProjectName*.`idl` file. If we ever needed to run the Wizards again, we could do so. We'd then have to copy the Wizard-generated IDL from the file in the `ServerInfoDll` folder into the IDL file in the `ServerInfo` folder.

However, we don't want the original IDL file to be 'live', so we need to remove it from the project. The easiest way to do that is to go to FileView, select the IDL file and hit the *Delete* key. Once you've done this, the file will no longer appear in FileView, and it will no longer be run through the MIDL compiler when the project is built. You would only ever need to look at that file again if you ran a Wizard that changed it. We don't have to worry about that in this example.

Now we need to hook up the *new* IDL file to the project. The first step is to add the file by right clicking on the **Source Files** icon in FileView and selecting the **Add Files to Folder...** menu item. This will bring up the **Insert Files into Project** dialog. Set the Files of type to All Files (*.*), then navigate to the `ServerInfo` folder, select the IDL file, and hit **OK**.

Once the IDL file has been added to the project, we need to set up its output files. We want the MIDL compiler to produce the marshaling code, interface header and GUID definition files in the *ServerInfo* directory, since they will be shared by both of our server projects.

Right-click on the IDL file in FileView and select the **Settings...** menu item. Make sure that the **Settings For** list at the top-left of the **Project Settings** dialog displays **All Configurations**, then switch to the **General** tab and check the **Always use custom build step** box. The reason for doing this is that we want to specify the *exact* command line for the MIDL compiler, and unfortunately the MIDL tab isn't quite as flexible as it could be.

Now click on the new Custom Build tab and enter the following in the Commands box:

```
midl /out ..\ /Oicf /h ServerInfo.h /iid ServerInfo_i.c ..\ServerInfo.idl
```

To the Outputs box, add the following as individual entries on separate lines:

```
..\ServerInfo.h
..\ServerInfo_i.c
```

The dialog should now appear as shown below:

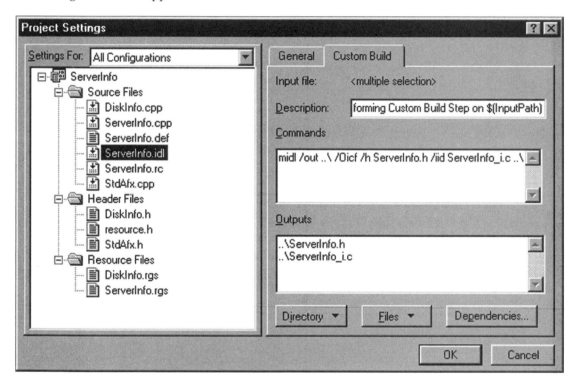

The result of this custom build step is that all the MIDL compiler-generated files will be produced in the parent directory of this project: the ServerInfo directory.

As a result of these changes, we need to make a few changes to the files in the project so that they refer to the new location of the MIDL compiler-generated files. In ServerInfo.cpp, we need to change the #includes for ServerInfo.h and ServerInfo_i.c so that they point to the project's parent directory where the files now live. We're eventually going to move the resource.h and DiskInfo.h files into the ServerInfo directory, so we might as well change the #includes for these now, too.

```
#include "stdafx.h"
#include "..\resource.h"
#include <initguid.h>
#include "..\ServerInfo.h"

#include "..\ServerInfo_i.c"
#include "..\DiskInfo.h"
```

Move the symbol header file (`resource.h`) to the `ServerInfo` directory, and remove this file from the project by clicking on its icon in FileView and hitting the *Delete* key. This file is used by the resource file `ServerInfo.rc`, so you need to change that file too. Once again, this is done through the <u>V</u>iew | Resource <u>I</u>ncludes... dialog; change the contents of the <u>S</u>ymbol header file box to `..\resource.h`.

The final step involved in moving the common files into the `ServerInfo` directory is to move the header and implementation of the `CDiskInfo` class. First, close all open files, then remove the `DiskInfo.h` and `DiskInfo.cpp` files from the project by clicking on their icons in FileView and hitting the *Delete* key. Now move the files from the `ServerInfoDll` directory to the `ServerInfo` directory. Add these files (and `Resource.h`) back into the project by using the <u>P</u>roject | <u>A</u>dd To Project | <u>F</u>iles... menu item.

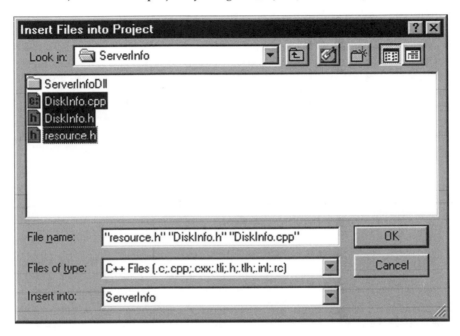

Compile the project now to see that everything is still working after all our changes. You may get a dialog suggesting that `resource.h` will be overwritten, but don't worry about this — it's just Visual C++ adding the resource ID for `IDR_SERVERINFO` to this file. Click on <u>Y</u>es to continue the build.

An EXE Server

The next step is to create the EXE version of our COM server. Create another new ATL COM AppWizard project called `ServerInfo`, but this time generate it in the `ServerInfo\ServerInfoExe` directory, and make sure that the server type is set to <u>E</u>xecutable (EXE).

Now go to FileView, select the IDL file, and hit the *Delete* key. Use the <u>P</u>roject | <u>A</u>dd To Project | <u>F</u>iles... menu item to add the `ServerInfo.idl`, `DiskInfo.cpp` and `DiskInfo.h` files from the `ServerInfo` directory into the project.

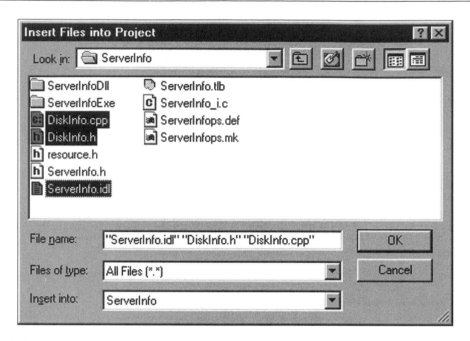

Right-click on the icon for the new IDL file in FileView and select the **Settings...** menu item. Give the IDL file the same settings as the IDL file we added to the DLL project (that is, check **Always use custom build step** on the **General** tab, and add the command line and output files on the **Custom Build** tab). Don't forget to set this for *all* the project's configurations!

In `ServerInfo.cpp`, we need to change the `#include` paths just as we did in the DLL server. Since we didn't use the Object Wizard to add the component to the project, you need to do the work that it would have done. So, add a `#include` for `..\DiskInfo.h`:

```
#include "stdafx.h"
#include "..\resource.h"
#include <initguid.h>
#include "..\ServerInfo.h"

#include "..\ServerInfo_i.c"
#include "..\DiskInfo.h"
```

And add an entry for the `CDiskInfo` class to the object map in the same file; in the DLL project, this entry was added automatically by the Wizard.

```
BEGIN_OBJECT_MAP(ObjectMap)
   OBJECT_ENTRY(CLSID_DiskInfo, CDiskInfo)
END_OBJECT_MAP()
```

Next, we need to add the component's resource script to the project. The registry entries are slightly different between the DLL and EXE projects, but similar enough that we can use the RGS file from the DLL project as a starting point. Copy `DiskInfo.rgs` from the `ServerInfoDll` directory into the `ServerInfoExe` directory, and replace the `InprocServer32` block with a `LocalServer32` entry, as shown:

```
         LocalServer32 = s '%MODULE%'
         NoRemove ProgID = s 'ServerInfo.DiskInfo.1'
```

We also need to edit the Wizard-generated `ServerInfo.rgs` file to ensure that the AppID is exactly the same as the AppID used for the DLL, and we'll apply the `NoRemove` keyword so that it won't be removed when the server unregisters itself:

```
HKCR
{
    NoRemove AppID
    {
        NoRemove {F51B0D13-5184-11D3-88E4-00105A68BF5D} = s 'ServerInfo'
        NoRemove 'ServerInfo.EXE'
        {
            val AppID = s {F51B0D13-5184-11D3-88E4-00105A68BF5D}
        }
    }
}
```

You will need to add the `DiskInfo.rgs` file to the project as you did for `ServerInfo.rgs` in the DLL project. So, go to ResourceView, right-click on the "REGISTRY" folder and hit **Import**.... Set the **Files of type** list to show **All Files (*.*)** and the **Open as** list to show **Custom**, then select `DiskInfo.rgs` from `ServerInfoExe`. Set the resource type to be `"REGISTRY"`, and then hit **OK**. Once the resource has been imported, bring up its **Properties** dialog and set its ID to `IDR_DISKINFO`. Now the resources should have the same IDs as in the DLL project.

Finally, we need to remove the type library from the project and ensure that it is not registered, as we did for the DLL project above, and we can do it in exactly the same way. Use the **View | Resource Includes**... menu item to bring up the **Resource Includes** dialog box, change the **Symbol header file** to refer to the new location of `resource.h` and delete the entry in the **Compile-time directives** box. You may get warnings, but once again you can safely ignore them. So that the dependencies are correctly set up, remove `Resource.h` from the FileView and add it back again from the `ServerInfo` directory.

Proxy-Stub DLL

Now that we've got our servers set up, we're almost ready to try them out with a client. Make sure that you've compiled the `ServerInfoDll` and `ServerInfoExe` projects. Next, build the proxy-stub DLL by opening a command prompt at the `ServerInfo` directory and using the following command line:

```
>nmake ServerInfops.mk
```

Register the DLL with:

```
>regsvr32 ServerInfops.dll
```

If you now run `Regedit.exe` and look at the CLSID for the class, you will find that the class has both an `InprocServer32` and a `LocalServer32` key, as well as having an `AppID` named value:

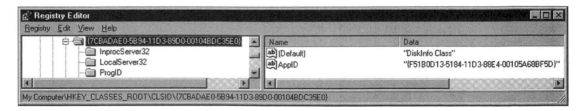

You can also see the entry for the IDiskInfo interface in the Interface section of the registry:

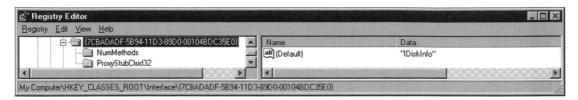

A Configurable Client

Now we'll create the client for these servers. Create a new, simple Win32 Console Application called GetDiskSpace and save it in a subdirectory of ServerInfo. Open stdafx.h and add:

```
// TODO: reference additional headers your program requires here
#include <atlbase.h>
#include <tchar.h>
#include <stdio.h>
```

Next add the following to GetDiskSpace.cpp:

```
#include "stdafx.h"
#include "..\ServerInfo.h"

int _tmain(int argc, _TCHAR** argv)
{
   if(argc < 1)
   {
      _tprintf(_T("USAGE: GetDiskSpace disc\n"));
      return 0;
   }

   HRESULT hr = CoInitialize(NULL);
   if(SUCCEEDED(hr))
   {
      USES_CONVERSION;
      CComPtr<IDiskInfo> pDiskInfo;
      hr = pDiskInfo.CoCreateInstance(__uuidof(DiskInfo));
      {
         hyper hypDiskSize;
         pDiskInfo->GetFreeDiskSpace(T2W(argv[1]), &hypDiskSize);
         _tprintf(_T("There are %I64d free bytes\n"), hypDiskSize);
      }
   }
   else
   {
      _tprintf(_T("There is an error (%08x)\n"), hr);
   }

   CoUninitialize();
   return 0;
}
```

We have used a relative path to the header file to get the interface definition and the GUIDs. In the body of the code, we use CComPtr<>::CoCreateInstance() to create an instance of the DiskInfo coclass:

```
HRESULT CoCreateInstance(REFCLSID  rclsid,
                         LPUNKNOWN pUnkOuter = NULL,
                         DWORD     dwClsContext = CLSCTX_ALL);
```

This version of the method makes a call to the `CoCreateInstance()` API using the third (optional) parameter as the context of the component to create. In this case, we're using `CLSCTX_ALL` because we haven't specified anything else, so COM will use the search order that we examined earlier in the chapter to decide how to activate our server. Our server has both a `LocalServer32` and an `InprocServer32` entry, so we'd end up using the in-process server if we compiled and ran the code at this point.

> *You can do exactly that to see that the code works as advertised: run the tool from the command line and give the path to a drive on your machine (e.g.* c:*), and it will print out the number of free bytes on that drive. Check this value with the value given by the* dir *command. (Note that if you are running low on conventional memory, running* GetDiskSpace *may result in the virtual memory swap file grabbing an extra chunk of disk space, which may make the two disk space sizes appear different.)*

With the client code as supplied, you could force the client to load the EXE server by unregistering the DLL. However, a more flexible client would be able to get the desired context from the command line and load the appropriate server. Let's change our client to do that. The changes to make are shown highlighted below:

```
int _tmain(int argc, _TCHAR** argv)
{
    if(argc < 1)
    {
        _tprintf(_T("USAGE: GetDiskSpace disc [L]\n"));
        return 0;
    }

    HRESULT hr = CoInitialize(NULL);
    if(SUCCEEDED(hr))
    {
        USES_CONVERSION;
        CComPtr<IDiskInfo> pDiskInfo;
        if(argc == 3 && argv[2][0] == _T('L'))
            hr = pDiskInfo.CoCreateInstance(__uuidof(DiskInfo), NULL,
                                                        CLSCTX_LOCAL_SERVER);
        else
        hr = pDiskInfo.CoCreateInstance(__uuidof(DiskInfo), NULL,
                                                    CLSCTX_INPROC_SERVER);
        if(SUCCEEDED(hr))
        {
            hyper hypDiskSize;
            pDiskInfo->GetFreeDiskSpace(T2W(argv[1]), &hypDiskSize);
            _tprintf(_T("There are %I64d free bytes\n"), hypDiskSize);
        }
        else
        {
            _tprintf(_T("There is an error (%08x)\n"), hr);
        }
    }
    else
    {
    _tprintf(_T("There is an error (%08x)\n"), hr);
    }
    CoUninitialize();
    return 0;
}
```

Now we're using `CComPtr<>::CoCreateInstance()` to create the component with a *specific* context. If our client is executed with a single command line parameter, then `argc` will be 2 (because the first argument that gets counted is the name of the client executable) and the parameter will be the disk name. In this case, the server will be loaded in-process. If there are two parameters, `argc` will be 3, and if the second parameter is the letter `L` (case sensitive) we create the local server.

You can now compile the project again. To convince yourself that the client can call either the in-process or the local server, run it under the debugger by typing `C:\` in the **Program arguments** box under the **General** category of the **Debug** tab in the **Project Settings** dialog. Place a breakpoint on the line that calls `GetFreeDiskSpace()`, then press *F5*. When the debugger stops, we know that the server component has been created and the module for it must be loaded. If you're running Windows 9x, bring up the Process Viewer (`Pview95.exe`); otherwise, use the NT Task Manager (right click on the Taskbar and select **Task Manager**) and look for `Serverinfo.exe` in the list of running processes. You won't see it, because in this case the command line does not have a second parameter and we're creating our component from the in-process server. Run the client to completion.

Next, go back to the project settings and add `Local` to the existing **Program arguments** (notice the capital 'L'). Now press *F5* to debug the process again. When the debugger stops this time, you can run the Process Viewer and you'll see that `Serverinfo.exe` is in the list of running processes, proving that we're creating our component from the EXE server. `Pview95.exe` will look something like this:

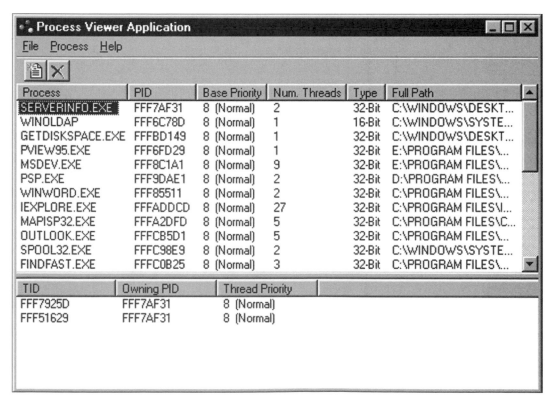

While the NT Task Manager will show:

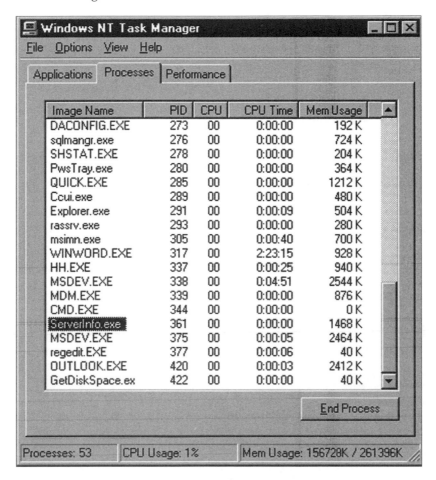

You will also notice that GetDiskSpace takes a little longer to run, since it has to load the component in a separate process.

Distributed COM

Now we have all the server code we need to run the component on a remote machine. In this section, we'll look at three ways to do this:

- ❑ How to use the existing client to communicate with the EXE server on another machine by changing some registry settings on the client machine
- ❑ How to create a new client to communicate with the EXE server on a machine specified by a command line argument
- ❑ How to use the new client to communicate with the DLL server on another machine by using a surrogate

RemoteServerName

First, we need to copy `ServerInfo.exe` and `ServerInfops.dll` to a local drive on the remote host machine of your choice (if you have a choice!). It's obvious why the EXE server needs to be on the host machine; it's also vital that the proxy-stub information be available so that the interfaces used by the server can be properly marshaled.

You can register the proxy-stub DLL straight away by using `regsvr32.exe`:

```
>regsvr32 ServerInfops.dll
```

You'll also need to register the EXE server. If you haven't built the EXE server with a MinDependency build, you'll need to ensure that `Atl.dll` (which contains ATL's registrar code) is available and registered on the host machine. `Atl.dll` should be in the `System` (on Windows 9x) or `System32` (on Windows NT) directory. If it isn't there, copy it to the correct location from your Visual C++ product CD and register it with:

```
>regsvr32 Atl.dll
```

> *Note that there are two versions of* `Atl.dll`. *For Windows NT, use the one in the* `OS\System` *directory on the Visual C++ product CD. This is a Unicode DLL, so it won't work on Windows 9x. For Windows 9x, use the version in the* `OS\System\Ansi` *directory.*

Once you're sure that `Atl.dll` is available if necessary, you can register the server by typing the following at a command prompt:

```
>ServerInfo.exe /regserver
```

Now you need to make sure that the client has permission to launch (NT) and access (NT and Windows 9x) the remote component. On the *host* machine, run `Dcomcnfg.exe`. Depending on your operating system, our application will appear in the **Applications** tab under the name **DiskInfo Class** or **ServerInfo**; in either case double-click on it and select **Use custom access permissions** from the **Security** tab. Next, click on the **Edit...** button, then the **Add...** button, and add **Everyone** to the list (if you're using Windows NT) or grant access to **The World** (if you're using Windows 9x).

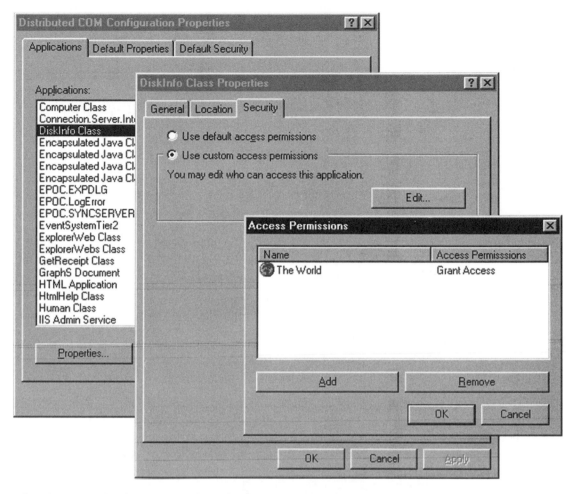

If you're using Windows NT, perform the same procedure for the launch permissions. If you're using Windows 9x, you won't be able to edit launch permissions, because Windows 9x doesn't allow servers to be launched remotely. If you want a COM server to be accessed remotely, it must be run by an already logged on user before a client tries to connect to it.

Exceptions apart, this will allow any user account to launch and then access a component. Typically, you would be more careful in choosing users or groups to whom you give permissions For this example, giving access to everyone will be safe enough, unless you're overcome with paranoia at the thought of letting the world know how much free disk space you have.

The final step on the host machine is to make sure that DCOM itself is enabled by ticking the checkbox labeled Enable Distributed COM on this computer on the Default Properties page of the main Dcomcnfg.exe dialog. On Windows 9x, you must make sure that remote connections are enabled by checking the Enable remote connection checkbox on the Default Security page. We can then turn our attention to the client machine.

First, make sure that `GetDiskSpace.exe` is available on the client machine, and that `ServerInfops.dll` is registered on that machine. Also ensure that `ServerInfo.exe` is registered on that machine — although we don't need the server EXE to be on the client machine (in fact, you can remove it as soon as it's been registered), we *do* need the `AppID` entry that its registration creates.

> **If this worries you (as well it might), you can create an RGS file that will register the AppID and the necessary CLSID entries for the client machine using the RegRgs tool from the World Of ATL web site. This will remove the need to register the server on the client machine. An RGS file that was generated in this way can be found in the sample code for this chapter.**

On the *client* machine, run `Dcomcnfg.exe`, double-click ServerInfo to bring up the ServerInfo Properties dialog, and select the Location tab. On this page, deselect Run application on this computer and select Run application on the following computer. In the edit box, add the name of the remote computer. (The screenshot shows that my remote computer is called ATHENA; you should use the name of the computer you set up as the server's host machine).

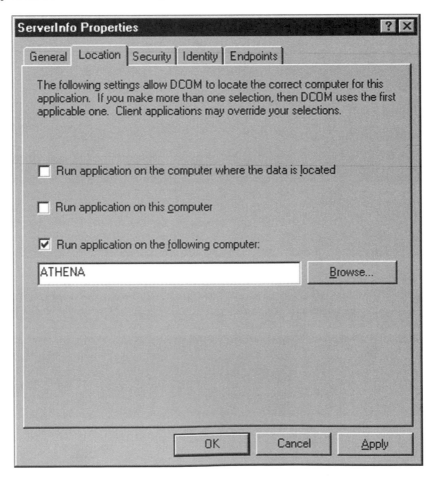

If you're using Windows NT as the server machine, that's all you need to do! Run the client application as if you want to use a local server:

```
>GetDiskSpace C:\ Local
```

One thing you will notice immediately is that the client now takes much longer to run. Part of this delay is due to the security checks that ensure you can launch and access the server, while the rest is attributable to the time it takes to transmit data across the network.

If you're using Windows 9x, you need to launch the server on its host machine manually (just double-click `ServerInfo.exe`) before running the client. Note that you will need to re-launch the server manually each time you want to run the client. When the client finishes and releases its reference to the `DiskInfo` component, the server will shut down and Windows 9x won't allow you to reactivate it remotely.

When you run the client as described, you'll now be able to see the free space on a specified drive of the remote machine. Because you have disabled the launching of the server on the client machine, COM searches for and finds the `RemoteServerName` entry for the remote host and asks that host to run the server.

```
C:\>GetDiskSpace C:\
There are 67403776 free bytes

C:\>GetDiskSpace C:\ Local
There are 290792448 free bytes

C:\>
```

This screenshot shows an example of what you should get. My client machine has 67Mb free, whereas the remote machine has 291Mb free.

Before we move on to the next test, undo the changes you made on the client with `Dcomcnfg.exe`. In other words, check Run application on this computer and uncheck Run application on the following computer.

CoCreateInstanceEx()

Now we're going to see how to pick the server host name programmatically. The first change to make is to `stdafx.h`:

```
#define _WIN32_DCOM
#include <atlbase.h>
#include <tchar.h>
#include <stdio.h>
```

Defining the `_WIN32_DCOM` symbol before `atlbase.h` will allow us to use the `CoCreateInstanceEx()` API function (`atlbase.h` includes `windows.h`, which will include `objbase.h`).

Next, open `GetDiskSpace.cpp` and make the following changes:

```
USES_CONVERSION;
CComPtr<IDiskInfo> pDiskInfo;
if(argc == 4 && argv[2][0] == _T('R'))
{
    COSERVERINFO csi = {0, T2W(argv[3]), NULL, 0};
    MULTI_QI qi = {&__uuidof(IDiskInfo), NULL, S_OK};
    hr = CoCreateInstanceEx(__uuidof(DiskInfo), NULL,
                            CLSCTX_REMOTE_SERVER, &csi, 1, &qi);
    if(SUCCEEDED(hr))
    {
        IDiskInfo* pInt = static_cast<IDiskInfo*>(qi.pItf);
        pDiskInfo.Attach(pInt);
    }
}
else if(argc == 3 && argv[2][0] == _T('L'))
    hr = pDiskInfo.CoCreateInstance(__uuidof(DiskInfo), NULL,
                                    CLSCTX_LOCAL_SERVER);
```

The new code checks for the presence of *three* command line parameters (the '4' value you see in the `if` statement includes the name of the EXE). The first of these parameters should be the drive to check (in the form `D:\`), the second one should be `Remote` (or any other word beginning with a capital 'R'), while the last parameter should be the name of the remote host.

Next, we initialize the `COSERVERINFO` and `MULTI_QI` structures to pass to `CoCreateInstanceEx()` with the name of the server and the interface to return. After the call to `CoCreateInstanceEx()` (in which we specify the context of the server to be remote), we extract the interface pointer from the `pItf` member of the `MULTI_QI` structure, and then attach it to the smart pointer.

Now you can build the new version of the client, and run it with the `Remote` command line argument and the name of the remote host, like this:

>**GetDiskSpace C:\ Remote Athena**

If you have Task Manager open on the remote host, you should see `ServerInfo.exe` appear briefly in the list of processes. Here's the result for my remote machine `Athena`:

```
C:\>GetDiskSpace C:\
There are 67403776 free bytes

C:\>GetDiskSpace C:\ Local
There are 67403776 free bytes

C:\>GetDiskSpace C:\ Remote Athena
There are 290792448 free bytes

C:\>
```

If you're running on Windows 9x, don't forget to pre-launch the server!

Using A Surrogate

The final test of our remote server is to show that we can talk to the DLL version of the server using the system-supplied surrogate process. We don't need to write any new code for this test.

First, install the *DLL* server, `ServerInfo.dll`, on a remote host. Copy it to the machine and run `regsvr32.exe` on it. Ideally, this should be a different machine from the one you were using for the previous remote component tests. If you cannot get access to another machine, make sure that you unregister `Serverinfo.exe` on that machine. To test that the server has been unregistered, you can go to the client machine and run `Getdiskspace.exe` for a *remote* component. This should fail with the error code 0x80040154 (REGDB_E_CLASSNOTREG):

```
C:\>GetDiskSpace C:\ Remote Athena
There is an error (80040154)

C:\>
```

If you are using a fresh host machine, make sure that you install `Serverinfops.dll` on it. The proxy-stub DLL must be registered on all machines that use the `IDiskInfo` interface, whether they are servers or clients.

Now run the OLE/COM Object Viewer (`Oleview.exe`) on the remote host. Make sure that **Expert Mode** is selected in the **View** menu. Open the **All Objects** tree and look for **DiskInfo Class**. Select the class in the tree view and then select the **Implementation** and **Inproc Server** tabs in the right hand pane.

> *Don't click on the + when you select* **DiskInfo Class**. *That will create an instance of the component. If you have done this, use* **Release** **Instance** *from the* **Object** *menu to release the component.*

You can now check the **Use Surrogate Process** box. This will hook the server up to the system-supplied surrogate, `Dllhost.exe`. To update the registry, click on an entry for another component.

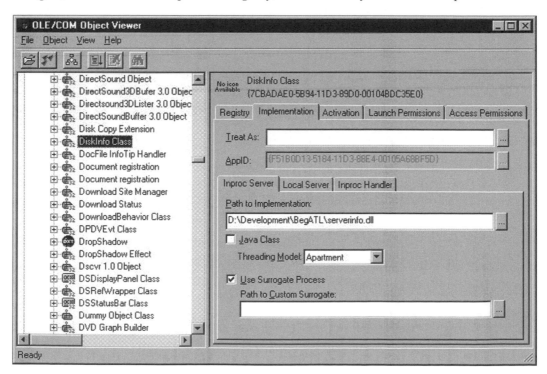

If the remote host is running Windows NT, start up Task Manager and move to the **Processes** tab. Now on the client machine, try running `Getdiskspace.exe` for the remote component. While you're doing this, check Task Manager on the remote host. You will find that the call will succeed, and that on the host you'll see `Dllhost.exe` appear in the Task Manager.

If you're running the component on Windows 9x, you need to start `Dllhost.exe` with the in-process server by passing the CLSID of the component as a command line parameter. Type the following command line into the **Run** box on the server machine:

```
DllHost {7CBADAE0-5B94-11D3-89D0-00104BDC35E0}
```

If this still doesn't convince you, you can use the Visual C++ debugger again. On the machine where you registered `ServerInfo.dll` to run under the surrogate, run Visual C++ and open the `GetDiskSpace` project. Place a breakpoint on the line that calls `GetFreeDiskSpace()`, just as you did earlier on in the chapter. Then, set the **Program arguments** to `Local`; this machine should not have `ServerInfo.exe` registered, so COM will check the server's AppID for either the `LocalService` (for an NT Service) or the `DllSurrogate` value.

Now when you run `GetDiskSpace` under the debugger, execution will stop at the call to `GetFreeDiskSpace()`, and switching to Process Viewer or the NT Task Manager should confirm that `Dllhost.exe` is running.

Security

In the example we've been experimenting with so far, we gave the whole world permission to launch and access our server. This is clearly not the best policy, and in the next few pages we'll examine some of the issues surrounding COM security, with a view to enabling you better to tailor the accessibility of your servers.

When a client calls `CoCreateInstanceEx()` to get access to a remote component, this may mean that another process (a local server or a surrogate) will be launched on another machine. Think about this for a moment. If you have a server on your machine, do you want just anyone to launch it whenever they like? More worrying still, if the component has access to your machine's resources (as in the case of the `DiskInfo` component), do you want the whole world to be able to use it? We suspect not.

Reassuringly, COM can apply security to the action of launching or accessing COM components. This applies to remote components *and* local components, because both are implemented in a different process from the client. However, COM security does *not* apply to in-process components, because they are created in (and take on) the security context of the client process.

You can apply security in two ways: **declaratively** or **programmatically**. In the first case, the security settings are held as part of the component server's registry values. These values are in the AppID for the component server, and thus do not allow for security on a fine-grained, per-coclass or per-object call basis. To do that, you need to apply security programmatically.

ATL effectively assumes that you will apply declarative security, in that there is currently no support for programmatic security. However, if you want to apply programmatic security, you are free to do so yourself. In this section, we will explain how to use `Dcomcnfg.exe` to apply declarative security to a component server.

Authentication And Authorization

Authentication is a mechanism whereby a security authority determines whether a user is who they say they are. Authentication typically involves asking for a password and then comparing it with the password for the user account. Windows NT and Windows 2000 do this using a challenge-response scheme where passwords are passed over the network in an encrypted form to prevent eavesdroppers from obtaining them.

> **Windows 9x does not have native security. With these operating systems, you have the choice of nominating a peer NT 4.0 (or Windows 2000) machine for authentication, or just running on an all-Windows 9x network where there is no security at all.**

Authentication can be carried out when a client first connects, when a method call is made, or on every packet of data passed from the client to the server machine. `Dcomcnfg.exe` allows you to determine the default authentication level for all servers on the Default Properties tab.

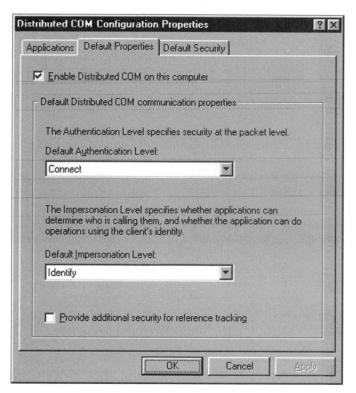

> **On Windows 2000, you will see another check box at the top of this dialog labeled Enable COM Internet Services on this computer. Checking this box will allow you to tunnel DCOM calls through firewalls by channeling them through TCP port 80. This only works if you have IIS running on the machine.**

You may decide to turn off authentication entirely, but this is obviously very risky. Note that the default authentication level is applied only when there is not a server-specific value; currently the only way to apply this on a per-server level is programmatically, or by editing the registry by hand. If the client and server use two different authentication levels, the higher of the two is used.

This screenshot also shows the default **impersonation** level used by servers on this machine. The impersonation level is only available on Windows NT. If enabled to a sufficient level, a component can get the identity of a connected client and use this identity (the server impersonates the client) to access server resources as if the component is running under that client's user account. The options are:

❑ **Anonymous**, where the client's identity is not available (not implemented).

❑ **Identify**, where the component can impersonate the client only for the purposes of obtaining its identity.

❑ **Impersonate**, where the component can impersonate the client in order to access secured components.

❑ **Delegate**, where the component can impersonate the client to call a remote component, and that component will get the security of the original client. This requires distributed security, so it's only available on Windows 2000, and only then when an account allows delegation.

Only the client's value for the impersonation level is used; if the server sets an impersonation level with a programmatic call, this will be ignored. (If the server generates events, then it will *also* be a COM 'client' — there are more details about this in Chapter 8.)

Authorization is the process by which a security authority checks that a user (who has been authenticated) is allowed to perform the task that they are attempting. COM applies authorization on two tasks: *launching* a server and *accessing* a server. Default authorization can be applied through the Default Security tab, and these values are used whenever a server does not have a list of authorized accounts. The default values are to disallow all users from launching a server, and allowing only the Administrators, the Interactive user and the System accounts to access a component in a running server.

> *The Interactive account is any account that is currently logged onto the local machine, and so does not apply to the remote access of components. The System account is a special account used by Windows NT that has complete access to the local machine but no access to remote resources. It is typically used by NT services.*

Server Authorization

The Applications tab of Dcomcnfg.exe lists all of the servers that have an entry in the AppID key. If it cannot find the descriptive name of a server, it will give the first coclass it can find that uses the AppID, but you shouldn't be fooled when this happens. The settings are applied to the AppID, and not to a coclass.

When you double-click on an entry, you'll get another dialog that allows you to change the security settings for that server. Let's look at the information it provides.

The General tab gives information about the server: the name of the server file, and details about whether an EXE, a service, or a surrogate will be used. You have already seen the Location tab, which is used to set the RemoteServerName value. The Security tab allows you to specify the user accounts that are authorized to launch and access the server. Finally, the Identity tab sets the account that a server will use (and is discussed in the next section).

The following figure shows the Security tab for Dcomcnfg.exe on Windows NT. Since you can't launch servers remotely to run on Windows 9x, its Security tab just has a button to allow you to edit the custom access permissions (effectively the top third of the NT tab).

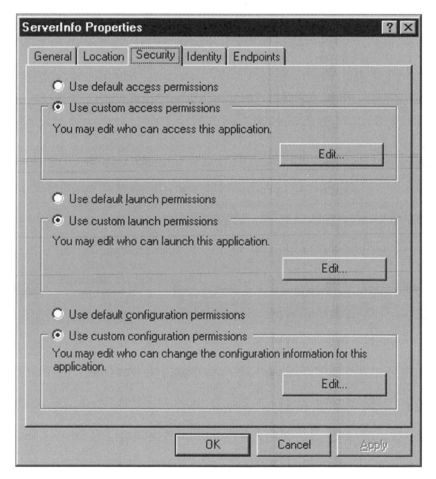

To specify who can launch a server, click on Use custom launch permissions and then on the Edit... button. This will bring up a standard NT dialog that contains the accounts and groups of accounts that can launch the server. You may edit these values to allow some users to launch the server, and to deny others that right. Accounts are added from lists of accounts obtained from the local NT machine and any domains that the machine may be a member of.

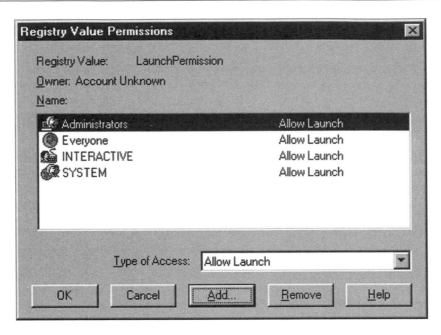

On Windows NT, giving *access* to a component is a very similar procedure. On Windows 9x, however, this is the only security that you can set, and you'll be presented with a list of accounts and groups from a specified security authority:

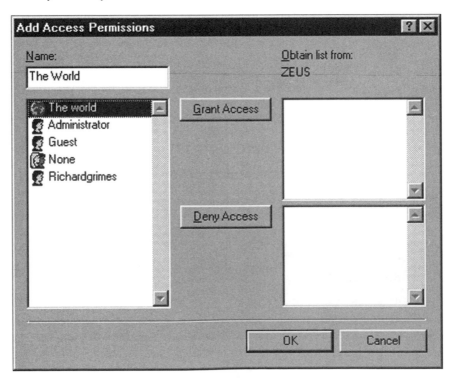

The previous screenshot shows the groups and users available on the NT machine ZEUS. You specify this security authority using the **Network** applet in the control panel:

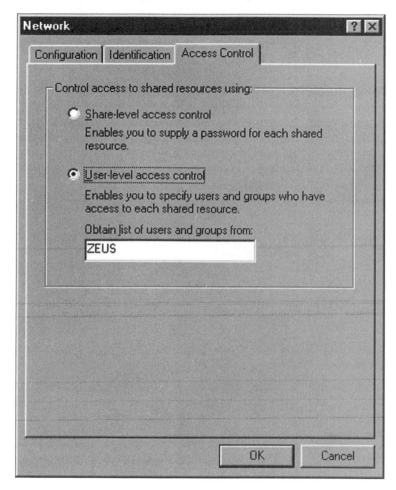

When you're developing a component, it's often convenient to give access to Everyone (NT) or The World (Windows 9x), but for final system testing, and in production code, you should use an appropriate account or group.

Identity

The next tab in the NT version of Dcomcnfg.exe (it's not available in the Windows 9x version) is the Identity tab, which is used to specify the account that will be used when the server is launched. There are four options here: The interactive user, The launching user, This user and The System Account. The final option is only available for COM servers implemented in a service.

When a user logs on to an NT machine (either locally or over a network), NT creates a secured component called a **WinStation**. This holds the desktop for that user, so if the user launches a process on the remote machine, and this process has a user interface, the UI will appear in the desktop of the WinStation of the user. Obviously, only the desktop of the interactive user is ever visible on the monitor, and this can cause a problem if the process creates a modal dialog. If the process is running in a desktop other than the interactive user's, the dialog will not be visible, and no one will be able to dismiss it, effectively blocking that particular thread of the process. (There are ways to get modal dialogs shown on the interactive desktop, but generally it is a bad idea to use them.) Let's look at how the identity helps this situation.

If you use Dcomcnfg.exe to specify that the server should run as the interactive user, this means that it will take on the security of the user who's currently logged on, and use the interactive WinStation. If any components created by the server need access to **secured objects** on the host machine, it will use the interactive user's security. Since the server will use the interactive WinStation, it means that any UI *will* be visible on the host machine's desktop.

The problem with this identity, however, is that there must be a user logged onto the host machine. This will not be the best choice in many situations, since it is clearly a security risk to leave a machine unattended with a user logged on — anyone with physical access to that machine will be able to use it.

If there is no logged-on user, you can still access a server if it uses the identity of the launching user. In this case, the host machine will create a WinStation for the user, and this WinStation will not have a visible desktop. Now the server will have the security of the client that launched it and this security will be used whenever the component attempts to access a secured NT object. However, WinStations are quite expensive in terms of system resources, so you will be restricted in the number of clients that can connect.

> *Secured NT objects are things like files (if you are using NTFS), registry keys, processes, threads and synchronization objects like events, semaphores and mutexes.*

Finally, we come to This user. This option allows you to specify a particular user that will be used whenever the server is launched. The advantage of this approach is that only one WinStation will be created, and thus resources are conserved. It also simplifies security administration, since if the component uses secured NT objects, you only need to allow access to these objects from this single account.

Endpoints

On machines running Windows NT 4.0 Service Pack 4 and later, the final tab on an application's Properties dialog in Dcomcnfg.exe is called Endpoints, and while this isn't a security issue, it makes for an interesting sidebar because it gives some insight into how COM works when it is used for cross machine calls.

> **In fact, although Dcomcnfg.exe on NT 4.0 SP4 has a tab called Endpoints, it turns out that using it can damage registry, so unless you are sure that your current service pack fixes this problem, it is best to avoid the tab on such a system.**

The idea of the tab is that it allows you to configure the protocol (UDP, TCP, etc.) that will be used when accessing a server, to which your first response is likely to be, "Why would I want to do that?" The answer is that if your network uses a protocol that's different from the default (if, for example, you have a Novell network), you will always get a delay while Windows 2000 listens on TCP, times out, and then loads the SPX driver to finally get the class activation request. In such a situation, it is better to make SPX the default transport.

The other situation in which you may want to change the transport properties is if you are using TCP. When DCOM is working over TCP, all activation requests come in on port 135, and after that COM will choose a different port (> 1024) to be used solely for this client-server connection. These ports are called **endpoints**. If you wish to allow connections to the server to go through a firewall, you must configure the firewall to allow all TCP traffic on port 135 and *all* the ports that will be used for connections to servers. Since you are unlikely to want to open all ports over 1024, it makes sense to restrict the ports that will be used by DCOM.

Threading

In the final section of this chapter, our aim is to provide you with a one-stop reference for the questions about **threading** that must have been forming in your mind during our discussions so far, culminating in the material about marshaling you saw earlier.

There are no two ways about it: threading is a complicated topic. In this section, we aim only to give you a quick overview of the issues related to COM threading. This is certainly not intended as an exhaustive treatment of the subject, but it should give you a feel for the concepts involved, and a good idea of where to start concentrating your efforts if you find that you do need to research the area further.

We'll start by examining one of the most important concepts of COM threading — **apartments** — before taking a quick look at the requirements placed upon the developer by different types of apartment.

Apartments

An apartment is a conceptual entity that contains one or more threads running in the same process. An apartment contains components with similar concurrency requirements. There are two types of apartment on Windows 9x and Windows NT 4.0: **single-threaded apartments** (**STAs**) and **multithreaded apartments** (**MTAs**). Windows 2000 defines a third type: the **thread-neutral apartment** (**TNA**).

As their name implies, single-threaded apartments only ever contain a single thread. That thread joins the STA by calling `CoInitialize(NULL)` or `CoInitializeEx(NULL, COINIT_APARTMENT_THREADED)`. (These calls are identical, since `CoInitialize()` just calls `CoInitializeEx()`.) There can be zero or more STAs in a single process.

> *STAs are useful for components that have **thread affinity** — in other words, that must run on a particular thread. This is the case for components that use **thread local storage** (**TLS**) or window handles.*

Multithreaded apartments can contain one or more threads. Each thread must join the MTA by calling `CoInitializeEx(NULL, COINIT_MULTITHREADED)`. There can be zero or one MTA in a single process.

You may see multithreaded apartments referred to as 'free-threaded apartments', but this term has largely fallen out of use.

On machines running operating systems earlier than Windows 2000 (in other words, machines that do not use COM+), COM calls that are made across apartment boundaries need marshaling, and interface pointers from one apartment won't work in a different apartment unless they are marshaled first. Conversely, calls from one component to another inside an MTA can always occur without marshaling.

As you'll see later, COM+ requires us to make some modifications to this statement, although we're still able to say something that's broadly similar, and equally definitive.

A COM object lives in only one apartment: the one in which its class object was created. An in-process component indicates what kind of apartment it should run in, and COM will check the activation apartment to see whether it is compatible. If it isn't, COM will create a new apartment for the component.

Context

Threads are initialized to run in a single apartment: they cannot leap around from one to another in order to access different objects, and of course this is the reason for proxy-stubs. In addition to the marshaling between apartments, however, there is another issue to contend with. Since threads are executable environments, it means that they have information that is thread-specific (like the stack, various processor registers, and thread local storage). This is called the **thread context**. When a call is made from a STA to an MTA, the processor must switch thread contexts, and this is expensive in performance terms.

The apartment type that a component is designed to run in is called its **threading model**. The threading model is one of the **attributes** that describe the **context** of a component. These two terms were first introduced with MTS, but they are applicable to non-MTS components on NT4 and Windows 9x as well. For these components, the threading model is the *only* context attribute available — in fact, to all intents and purposes, the context *is* the threading model.

For MTS components, the context includes the threading model, the transaction support it needs and the security that is required; Windows 2000 extends this further by including other attributes like whether the component will be accessed as a queued component (via MSMQ) or if it will be load balanced or pooled.

The context of a component defines the runtime environment that the component needs to run. If the calling code runs under a different context, COM will attempt to create a new context for the component. However, there is a problem: how does the client code call the component if the two are in different contexts? The answer is that COM creates a proxy in the client that allows the call to be made across the context boundary — and this call, of course, requires marshaling. Marshaling is designed to protect code that has been written for one context from being called by code that has been written for a different context.

ATL 3.0 was written before the release of Windows 2000, and knows nothing about context attributes other than **ThreadingModel**. In the following discussion, therefore, we will concentrate on marshaling in terms of cross-apartment calls. However, the same sentiments apply to cross-context calls in Windows 2000.

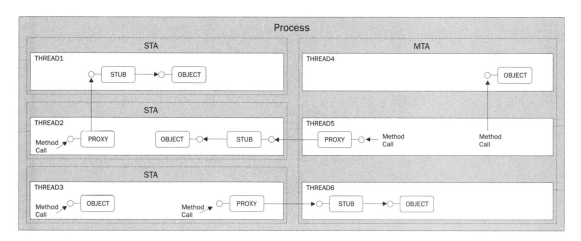

The diagram shows that when cross-apartment calls are made, a proxy-stub is used. If a component in one apartment calls a component in another apartment (you can see STA-to-STA, MTA-to-STA and STA-to-MTA), there is a context switch, so marshaling is used. Inside the MTA, and provided that the contexts match, calls can be made between threads without the need for marshaling.

STAs And Message Pumps

When a component is run in an STA, access from multiple threads must be synchronized to prevent corruption of the component's state. The developer can feel reassured that the component's state will be protected from multi-threaded access, because no other thread has direct access to the component. All other threads must communicate with the component through a proxy-stub. It's up to COM and the marshaling code to provide synchronization, which is done using the STA's Windows message queue. When a method request is made, a message is posted to the message queue. Since the messages are read and dispatched from the queue one at a time, this ensures that access to a component is from a single thread at any one time.

The corollary of this is that each STA must have a message pump:

MTAs And Thread Safety

When a component is running in an MTA (and assuming for now that the other context attributes match), any other thread in the MTA can access it directly. Because of this, any internal state of the component must be protected from concurrent access, and all methods must be reentrant. This protection must be provided by the creator of the component.

Writing thread-safe code is quite an intricate business, but at the very, very least, the reference count must be changed with `InterlockedIncrement()` and `InterlockedDecrement()`. This is because C++'s ++ and -- operators may be pre-empted by another thread before the operation has completed.

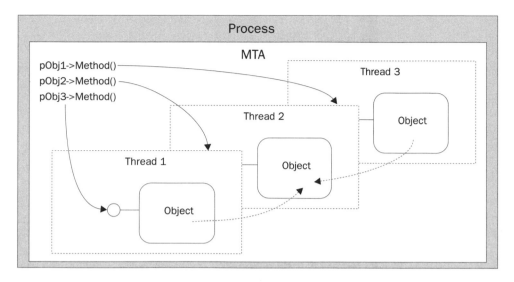

The advantage of this direct access is that well written, thread safe code running in an MTA should be faster than the equivalent code in an STA, since it gets round the potential bottleneck of the Windows message queue we're forced to use in the case of STAs. However, it does put the onus on the developer to make sure that component state access is thread safe, and that methods are reentrant.

Threading And In-Process Servers

In-process servers do not call CoInitializeEx(), because the COM libraries will already have been initialized before the server is loaded. There is obviously a potential conflict here: what if a client thread is part of an MTA, and it attempts to create an in-process component that is written to run in an STA? Without some extra mechanism, a non-thread safe component could be created in an MTA.

To avoid such problems, COM requires that in-process components register their preferred context. For pre-COM+ operating systems, this essentially means the threading model of the component. Both COM+ and 'classic' COM components register their threading model using the ThreadingModel value in the component's CLSID key.

Before COM activates a component, it compares the calling code's context and the component's context. If they are incompatible, COM will create a new context. In terms of threading, COM will check the ThreadingModel value of the component, and if the apartment of the calling code is incompatible with this value it will create a new apartment. On COM systems, ThreadingModel takes one of four values:

ThreadingModel	Apartment	ATL Threading Model
(absent)	Main STA	Single
Apartment	STA	Apartment
Free	MTA	Free
Both	STA or MTA	Both

In this table, the first column is the contents of the ThreadingModel *value of the component's CLSID key. The third column is the* **Threading Model** *offered on the* **Attributes** *page of the ATL Object Wizard.*

If the ThreadingModel is absent, the component should run in the **main STA** of the process. This means that the component knows nothing at all about threads, which is the case for COM components that were written before the new threading models were introduced. Every component that is 'single' threaded will run in the first STA that is created in the process — COM will create an STA if one has not already been created.

Apartment means that the component can run in *any* STA in a process (not just the main STA).

Both means that the component can run in either an STA or an MTA, implying that all methods are reentrant and component state is protected from concurrent access. Such a component is *designed* to run in an MTA, but will work fine in an STA. Although there will be more synchronization code than necessary when such a component runs in an STA (the message loop, and the component's own synchronization code), this won't degrade performance greatly. The STA synchronization will ensure that two threads can never access the component at one time, so the component's synchronization code will have little effect.

Free means that the component should *only* run in an MTA, and is used to indicate that the component will create and use worker threads. Doing this indicates to COM that efficient execution of the component will only happen if the component is created in an MTA. If the component is created in an STA (which would be possible were it marked as Both), then as the worker threads are created and enter an MTA (with a call to CoInitializeEx()), access to the component will be through a proxy loaded by COM, degrading performance. When a component is marked as Free, the client *must* create the component in an MTA, which ensures that the worker threads have direct access to the component. The client, on the other hand, may be in a different apartment and thus require access through a proxy.

Generally, a component that uses worker threads should be marked as Free to enable direct access between component and workers. However, if the client makes more calls to the component than the component makes to the worker threads (or the threads make to the component), it may be more efficient to mark the component as Both so that the client has direct access to the component.

If the client apartment is incompatible with the threading model of the component, COM will silently create a proxy to perform the cross-apartment access. In the following table, you can see the threading model of the component and the client apartment that called CoCreateInstance() to create the component. The values in the table indicate where the component will be created; if a proxy must be used, the cell is shown shaded.

		ThreadingModel			
		(absent)	**Apartment**	**Both**	**Free**
	Main STA	Main STA	Main STA	Main STA	MTA
Client Apartment	**STA**	Main STA	Client STA	Client STA	MTA
	MTA	Main STA	New STA	MTA	MTA

Threading And EXE Servers

EXE servers are responsible for creating apartments in which components will run. An EXE server that will serve STA-based components must create the threads that will be used and call `CoInitializeEx(NULL, COINIT_APARTMENTTHREADED)` in each thread. Each thread should then register the class objects for the components that will be created in that apartment. If the server wants to serve MTA-based components, it needs to create a single thread, call `CoInitializeEx(NULL, COINIT_MULTITHREADED)`, and create and register the class objects for the components that will be created in the MTA.

Note that there are no 'Both' components because the class object defines the apartment in which the component will run when it is created. EXE-based components do not need a `ThreadingModel` registry value. Also note that you only need to create a single thread for the MTA, because COM will maintain a dynamic pool of threads for the MTA. Indeed, you do not even need to create a thread to initialize the MTA if you make the main thread of the process (the one used to call `_tWinMain()`) join the MTA.

ATL And Threading Models

Let's look at the ways that threading interacts directly with ATL code. The first and most obvious way is the Threading Model frame of the **Attributes** tab provided by the Object Wizard. When you create a new coclass, you have the choice of setting the threading model to one of the values from the earlier table.

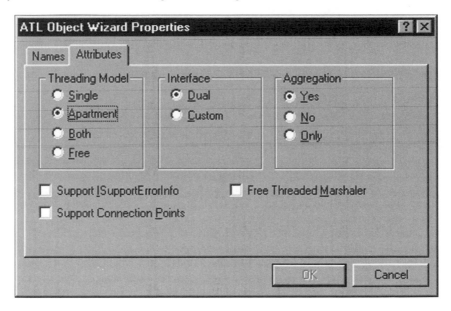

The value that you choose has two main effects: it sets the threading model class used as the template parameter to `CComObjectRootEx<>`, and (for DLL servers only) it sets the `ThreadingModel` registry entry in the RGS file.

As you know, `CComObjectRootEx<>` is the base class used to handle the `IUnknown` methods of your generated class and is therefore responsible for reference counting. If you pick **Single** or **Apartment**, `CComObjectRootEx<CComSingleThreadModel>` is used as the base class. If you pick **Both** or **Free**, `CComObjectRootEx<CComMultiThreadModel>` is used.

CComSingleThreadModel is used to implement AddRef() and Release() with the C++ increment and decrement operators. The CComMultiThreadModel class ensures that AddRef() and Release() are implemented using InterlockedIncrement() and InterlockedDecrement(), thus preventing concurrent access to the reference count when it is being changed.

For DLL servers, a ThreadingModel value is added to the component's CLSID key in the generated RGS file, with the appropriate data value (except in the case of Single, when the ThreadingModel entry is simply omitted).

For EXE servers, you still have to choose a threading model, because you will have made some choice as to the apartments that will be present in the EXE and which components will run in them. However, you do not have to worry about registration values, because none are made for the threading model of EXE-based components. This means that your choice should be made on the synchronization that you need: if the component is to run in the process's MTA then use either **Free** or **Both**; if the component will run in an STA then use either **Single** or **Apartment**.

> **The Object Wizard will never make an informed choice for you, even if you specify that you will only use one apartment type in your server (as explained in the next section). This means that when you write an EXE server, you must make a careful choice about what threading models your components will use.**

The Global Threading Model

The **global threading model** for an ATL project is defined in StdAfx.h by one of the following symbols:

- ❑ _ATL_SINGLE_THREADED
- ❑ _ATL_APARTMENT_THREADED
- ❑ _ATL_FREE_THREADED

The default setting is _ATL_APARTMENT_THREADED.

These symbols are used to typedef one of the threading model classes (CComSingleThreadModel or CComMultiThreadModel) to CComObjectThreadModel and CComGlobalsThreadModel, as you can see in this code taken from Atlbase.h.

```
#if defined(_ATL_SINGLE_THREADED)
   typedef CComSingleThreadModel CComObjectThreadModel;
   typedef CComSingleThreadModel CComGlobalsThreadModel;
#elif defined(_ATL_APARTMENT_THREADED)
   typedef CComSingleThreadModel CComObjectThreadModel;
   typedef CComMultiThreadModel CComGlobalsThreadModel;
#else
   typedef CComMultiThreadModel CComObjectThreadModel;
   typedef CComMultiThreadModel CComGlobalsThreadModel;
#endif
```

We can ignore CComObjectThreadModel, because this typedef is only used for compatibility with ATL 1.1 code, but CComGlobalsThreadModel is more important because it controls the increment and decrement method used for both the lock count and reference counts of the module and the class objects in your project. The default global threading model results in thread safe code, so you don't actually need to worry about this, but now you know precisely what that #define in StdAfx.h means.

Manual Marshaling

There are times when it is necessary to marshal interface pointers manually. Whenever you want to pass an interface pointer from one thread to another across an apartment boundary without doing it via a COM method call, you'll need to marshal that pointer yourself. For example, you may have two threads, each in a different STA, and each with an (already created) object. You'll need to manually marshal the interface pointers if one component is to get access to the other.

There are a couple of ways to marshal an interface pointer across apartments. One way requires the use of the `CoMarshalInterThreadInterfaceInStream()`, and `CoGetInterfaceAndReleaseStream()` functions, but this is pretty complicated. The second way is much simpler, and uses an object called the Global Interface Table (GIT), but this is only available on NT 4.0 with Service Pack 3 or later and Windows 9x with the appropriate DCOM add-on (Windows 2000 has this object as part of the operating system).

> *This kind of manual marshaling is beyond the scope of this book. You'll only need to find out about marshaling interfaces manually if you're using multithreaded techniques. For a fuller discussion of manual marshaling, take a look at* Professional ATL COM Programming *(1-861001-40-1).*

In general, you can lead a trouble-free life by sticking to the apartment threading options that ATL uses by default. Your code will be reasonably efficient, and you don't need to worry about making it thread-safe, because ATL and COM handle that for you.

A Look To The Future

Because a context is about more than just a threading model, context switching can occur when *intra*-apartment calls are made on Windows 2000 machines. This might happen if, for example, a queued component in an MTA is accessed by another MTA component that isn't queued. It would seem that your proxy-stubs are in for a lot of work.

Thankfully, Windows 2000 goes some way to relieving these potential performance problems with the introduction of the **thread neutral apartment** (**TNA**). A process can have at most one TNA, and as with other apartments, *components* that are marked to live in the TNA will only ever live in the TNA. However, unlike the other two apartment types, no *threads* live in the TNA at all. Instead, STA or MTA threads enter the TNA for the duration of a component method call. Because the same thread is used to initiate the call and to perform it, no thread context switch occurs. There is still an *apartment* switch, so some marshaling does happen, but Windows 2000 provides a lightweight form of marshaling to do this. The net effect is that under Windows 2000, TNA-based components are preferred.

Summary

This chapter has introduced you to local COM and remote DCOM components. It has demonstrated that remote components really are just local components on another machine, and that making them remote is either an administrative task performed with a tool like Dcomcnfg.exe or Oleview.exe, or a programmatic task that the client can perform with CoCreateInstanceEx().

The example we used was a simple component that gave a fairly banal piece of information about the machine on which it was activated. However, by building this as both a DLL-based and an EXE-based server, we showed you some of the benefits and pitfalls of in-process and local servers. With just a small amount of administration, we were able to run both servers on a remote machine. In the case of the DLL server, the system-provided surrogate DllHost.exe was used.

Running code on a remote machine meant that you had no option but to get familiar with security. As you have seen, this is a fairly simple task once you understand what the issues are and have access to Dcomcnfg.exe on the server.

The chapter concluded with a discussion about threading. DLL servers can implement components that run in one of the two types of apartments that COM provides (or three for COM+ configured components), and ATL provides you with all of the code required to register the component's threading model and to apply appropriate synchronization. EXE servers are a more complicated issue, but it is generally best to implement them so that as their components run in an MTA.

In the section about security, we talked about impersonation, and mentioned that this was an important issue for remote servers that generated events. What we didn't mention was why it is important, or how to generate events. Chapter 8 will cover these issues when it deals with **connectable objects**.

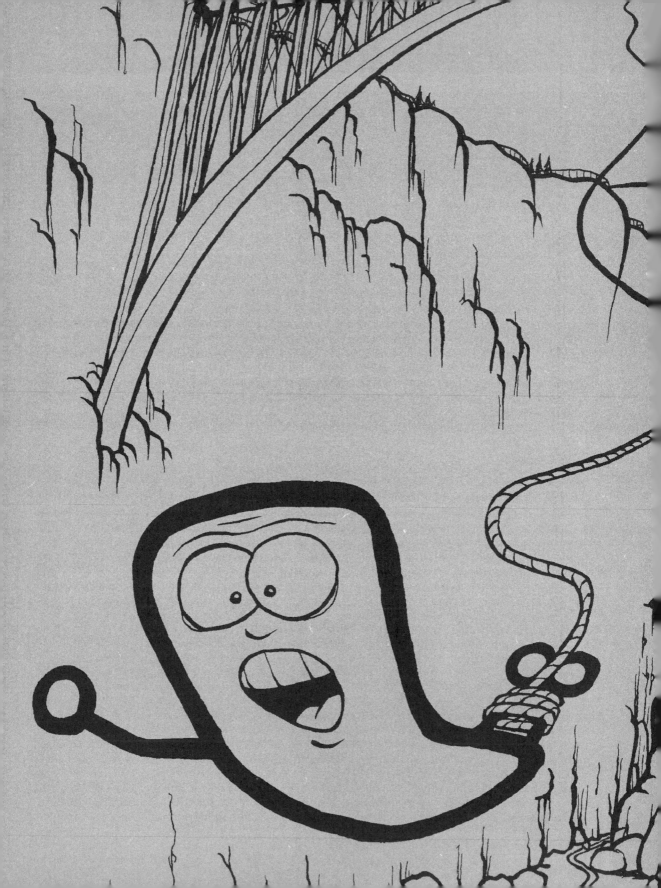

ATL Window Classes

So far, we've concentrated on using ATL to create COM components. The user interface code we have looked at has been relatively incidental, making use of little more than simple dialogs. This chapter concerns the **window classes** that were enhanced in ATL 3.0. Using these, it becomes easier to create rich user interfaces, both as part of the controls you may develop, and as full client applications.

We'll start by looking at the basic ATL window class, CWindow, and use it to create simple windows — 'dialog-like' pop-ups, and controls on an existing window. We'll take a brief look at how the methods of this class can be used to manipulate windows, and then we'll see how a handy collection of wrapper classes (which are supplied with one of the examples that ships with Visual C++) can make our life much easier by encapsulating the functionality of many popular visual controls.

In order to create more complex windows, or to customize the functionality of existing ones, you need to learn about **window procedures**. The next section of this chapter explains what they are and how to create them, discussing **message maps** along the way. Finally, we'll combine the techniques that have been used throughout the chapter to create an example window hosting a simple number-sorting game.

During the course of the chapter, you'll also see some examples of using ATL to create standalone Windows applications. The footprint of an application written using ATL is much smaller than an equivalent MFC application, and ATL is also more flexible — less of the functionality is hidden away from you. Why write applications with anything else?

Basic Window Techniques

The fundamental ATL class used to create windows is CWindow. In fact, you've already seen this class in use: it is one of the base classes of CAxDialogImpl<>, which we used as a base class of the dialog in Chapter 3. Perhaps surprisingly, though, CWindow doesn't actually *implement* a window; rather it provides access to the Win32 windowing functions through its methods, and manages a Windows HWND. This means that although the methods of CWindow have the same names as the corresponding Win32 functions, they don't take HWND parameters because the encapsulated HWND is used instead.

> *This chapter is not intended to give you a complete induction in Windows programming, but the techniques introduced should be enough to get you started. If you are interested in following up any of the Windows issues raised, there is a wealth of published material on the subject — for example* Programming Windows, The Definitive Guide to the Win32 API *(1-57231-995-X).*

CWindow

The CWindow class is defined in the header file Atlwin.h, but we're not going to examine all of its methods here — there are more than a hundred of them! In fact, most of the methods are *very* thin wrappers; they simply forward their parameters to the Win32 API, with reference to the HWND contained in the class. This HWND is contained in the member variable m_hWnd, which is public, allowing direct access if necessary. The handle can be set either by creating a new window using the Create() method, or by attaching to an existing window with Attach(). (There is also a Detach() method you can use to extract the HWND and set m_hWnd to NULL.)

> One of the most useful features of **CWindow** is its use of conversion operators to give access to **m_hWnd**. Put simply, you can substitute an instance of **CWindow** in any place where an **HWND** could be used. This makes for very readable code when **HWNDs** are required as function parameters.

As mentioned, you can create a simple window of a registered class using the Create() method of CWindow that can be called in either of the following ways (which differ only slightly, as detailed in the parameter list):

```
HWND Create(LPCTSTR lpstrWndClass,
            HWND     hWndParent,
            RECT&    rcPos,
            LPCTSTR  szWindowName = NULL,
            DWORD    dwStyle = 0,
            DWORD    dwExStyle = 0,
            UINT     nID = 0,
            LPVOID   lpCreateParam = NULL)

HWND Create(LPCTSTR lpstrWndClass,
            HWND     hWndParent,
            LPRECT   lpRect = NULL,
            LPCTSTR  szWindowName = NULL,
            DWORD    dwStyle = 0,
            DWORD    dwExStyle = 0,
            HMENU    hMenu = NULL,
            LPVOID   lpCreateParam = NULL)
```

Where the parameters are:

Parameter	Description
lpstrWndClass	The class of window to create. (A full list of these is given later in the chapter.)
hWndParent	If the window is to be a child window, this will contain the HWND of the parent window. If not, it will contain NULL.

Parameter	Description
rcPos, lpRect	A RECT structure (or a pointer to a RECT structure) defining the position and dimensions of the window. lpRect defaults to NULL, which Create() interprets by substituting a rectangle of dimensions {CW_USEDEFAULT, CW_USEDEFAULT, 0, 0}, where CW_USEDEFAULT is defined as ((int)0x80000000) in Winuser.h.
szWindowName	The name of the window, displayed in the title bar if the window has one.
dwStyle, dwExStyle	The style and extended style of the window (for a list of predefined styles, see the MSDN library).
hMenu	A handle to the menu of the window.
nID	This parameter is a handle to the window menu (it's passed to the relevant Win32 API as (HMENU)nID) or, if the window is a child, the identifier of the child window. The default value is 0.
lpCreateParam	A pointer to additional window-creation data that will usually be contained in a CREATESTRUCT structure. However, you can also use this parameter to pass other initialization data to a window, in whatever form that window expects.

Creating A Basic Window

Most of the parameters of the Create() method we just looked at have default values, so it can be used in a very minimal form if you desire. Let's take a look at Create() in action.

In Chapter 3, you saw how to create an ATL client application by starting with an ATL COM AppWizard-generated EXE project and removing surplus code. Here, we'll take a different route: we'll start with a Win32 Application and *add* the ATL support we require. Start Visual C++ and create a new project of this type called ATLWindows. On the Wizard's single step, choose A simple Win32 application and click Finish.

We'll be using this project for several examples throughout this chapter, adding and removing functionality as necessary to illustrate principles as we go.

Once all the files have been generated, the first thing you should do is replace this line in stdafx.h:

```
#include <windows.h>
```

With the code required for ATL support:

```
#include <atlbase.h>
extern CComModule _Module;
#include <atlwin.h>
#include <atlcom.h>
```

If you compare this with the code in Chapter 3, you'll see that we're already converging on a similar application. There we replaced CExeModule *with* CComModule, *to reduce our code size and do away with the extra features we didn't need.*

Also, add the declaration of _Module that's required by atlwin.h and atlcom.h to ATLWindows.cpp:

```
#include "stdafx.h"

CComModule _Module;
```

Then, modify WinMain() to initialize _Module and create our window:

```
int APIENTRY WinMain(HINSTANCE hInstance,
                     HINSTANCE hPrevInstance,
                     LPSTR     lpCmdLine,
                     int       nCmdShow)
{
    _Module.Init(NULL, hInstance);
    CWindow TestWin;
    TestWin.Create(_T("EDIT"), NULL);
    TestWin.ShowWindow(SW_SHOW);

    MSG msg;
    while(GetMessage(&msg, 0, 0, 0))
    {
        TranslateMessage(&msg);
        DispatchMessage(&msg);
    }

    return 0;
}
```

The call to ShowWindow() makes our window visible (Create() doesn't do that for us by default), and the while loop forwards messages to its window procedure (more details on this later). Message forwarding is necessary in order to do *anything* with the window, such as moving it around the screen by dragging the title bar. You can try this for yourself: if you replace the loop with while(true) {}, you won't be able to manipulate the window in any way.

Unfortunately, this simple window has very little functionality. In fact, it can't even shut itself down — if you build and run this code, you'll have to terminate it manually using the task manager (or by stopping the debugger if it's a debug build). The windows we create later on will behave rather better than this!

You can also use CWindow to add child windows to an existing window by employing the hWndParent parameter of the Create() method. Add the following code to ATLWindows.cpp:

```
    _Module.Init(NULL, hInstance);
    CWindow TestWin;
    TestWin.Create(_T("EDIT"), NULL);
    TestWin.ShowWindow(SW_SHOW);

    CWindow AddedButton;
    RECT rPos = {10, 10, 100, 50};
    AddedButton.Create(_T("BUTTON"), TestWin, rPos, _T("Click me"), WS_CHILD);
    AddedButton.ShowWindow(SW_SHOW);
```

The new call to Create() will create a simple button labeled Click me, with dimensions as specified by rPos. Passing TestWin as the hWndParent parameter tells Create() that the new button will be a child of the edit window we've already created. However, as you'll see if you execute this code, this button does very little. Later on, when we've looked at window procedures, we'll be able to do much more interesting things.

Manipulating CWindow Objects

Once a window is 'held' in a CWindow object, it can be manipulated using the methods of CWindow. For example, to append text to the contents of an edit box, you could use the GetWindowText() and SetWindowText() methods:

```
USES_CONVERSION;        // Required for string conversion macros
CComBSTR bstr;
TestWin.GetWindowText(bstr.m_str);
bstr += L" And the barman said, 'So that's what happened to my keys!'";
TestWin.SetWindowText(W2T(bstr));
```

If you need to perform an operation that isn't covered by the CWindow methods (usually an operation that's specific to a particular type of window), it's possible to send messages to the window. For example, to get the starting and ending character positions of the selection in a text box, you could use:

```
int iStart, iEnd;
TestWin.SendMessage(EM_GETSEL, (WPARAM)&iStart, (LPARAM)&iEnd);
```

This works fine, but it hardly seems elegant, and it can be confusing. In the next section, you'll find out how to manipulate ATL windows with less effort and considerably more style.

CWindow Wrappers: Atlcontrols.h

To avoid this clumsy form of message sending, it would seem like a good idea to define some classes that wrap the functionality of individual window classes, rather like the wrapper around dialog boxes we used earlier in this book, or the various MFC classes you may have used before. In fact, this has already been done for you! Visual C++ comes with an example called AtlCon whose ostensible purpose is to demonstrate how to implement a simple OLE container, but which also includes a header file called Atlcontrols.h. This file contains wrappers for *all* of the Win32 and common controls.

Although it's officially unsupported and not a part of the core ATL library, this file is very useful indeed, to the point that it would be foolish not to make use of it. In fact, if you're going to use it a lot, you might just as well copy it into your VC98\ATL\Include directory — it's that good.

By way of an example, one of the classes in Atlcontrols.h is a wrapper around an edit control, conveniently called CEdit. We can create edit windows using this class like so:

```
#include "stdafx.h"
#include "atlcontrols.h"

    ...

    _Module.Init(NULL, hInstance);
    ATLControls::CEdit TestWin;
    TestWin.Create(NULL);
    TestWin.ShowWindow(SW_SHOW);
```

It is no longer necessary to specify EDIT as the type of class to create as the first parameter of the Create() method — the type is now wrapped up in CEdit.

> Note that **CEdit** is accessed through the **ATLControls** namespace. If you want to avoid that, simply add this line to your file:
>
>   using namespace ATLControls;
>
> You can then replace code such as this:
>
>   ATLControls::CEdit TestWin;
>
> With code like this:
>
>   CEdit TestWin;

The purpose of these wrappers is to provide you with a more useful, more complete set of methods for the type of window you're using. For example, text can be appended to the contents of the edit box simply by using the AppendText() method. Also, instead of having to use the EM_GETSEL message to find the current selection, the following code can be used:

```
int iStart;
int iEnd;
TestWin.GetSel(iStart, iEnd)
```

This sort of method is typical of the Atlcontrols.h wrapper classes. In other cases, the wrappers simplify what can be a complicated series of messages containing structures that are often large and arcane in nature. The complete set of classes contained in Atlcontrols.h is shown in the table below:

Class	Win32 class name	Description
CStatic	STATIC	A Win32 label
CButton	BUTTON	A command button
CListBox	LISTBOX	A list box
CDragListBox	LISTBOX	A list box with support for dragging items
CComboBox	COMBOBOX	A combo box
CEdit	EDIT	A text box
CScrollBar	SCROLLBAR	A scrollbar
CRichEditCtrl	RICHEDIT	A rich edit control

Class	Win32 class name	Description
CListViewCtrl	SysListView32	A list view, like the right hand pane of Explorer
CTreeViewCtrl	SysTreeView32	A tree view, like the left hand pane of Explorer
CTreeViewCtrlEx	SysTreeView32	Uses CTreeItem (see below) rather than the raw HTREEITEM
CHeaderCtrl	SysHeader32	A header control with resizable columns
CToolBarCtrl	ToolbarWindow32	A toolbar positioned below a menu bar
CStatusBarCtrl	msctls_statusbar32	A status bar positioned at the bottom of a window
CTabCtrl	SysTabControl32	Tabs, like those used in a tabbed dialog
CToolTipCtrl	tooltips_class32	A tooltip
CTrackBarCtrl	msctls_trackbar32	A slider control, used to set a value
CUpDownCtrl	msctls_updown32	A control used to increment and decrement values
CProgressBarCtrl	msctls_progress32	A visual progress indicator
CHotKeyCtrl	msctls_hotkey32	Used to specify that a key combination will perform some action
CAnimateCtrl	SysAnimate32	A control used to play an AVI file
CReBarCtrl	ReBarWindow32	A rebar, as used by MS Internet Explorer 4+
CComboBoxEx	ComboBoxEx32	A combo box that can have images for the items
CDateTimePickerCtrl	SysDateTimePick32	An edit box-like control through which you can pick a date or time
CMonthCalendarCtrl	SysMonthCal32	A control that shows a month's dates
CIPAddressCtrl	SysIPAddress32	An edit box-like control with 4 fields separated by dots
CPagerCtrl	SysPager	A control that allows you to 'scroll' another window

The easiest way to check the methods of these classes is to examine `Atlcontrols.h`, comparing them with Win32 control messages where necessary. Often, you'll find that they operate in a very similar way to their MFC brethren. It can therefore be useful to consult the MFC documentation in order to work out how to use these ATL classes, however unusual that may seem.

The header file also contains a few utility classes that you may find useful:

Class	Description
CImageList	Wraps an HIMAGELIST, for use with list views and tree views
CTreeItem	Wraps an HTREEITEM, used with CTreeViewCtrlEx
CToolInfo	Wraps a TOOLINFO, used with CToolTipCtrl
CDragListNotifyImpl	Class used to handle notifications from a drag list box
CFlatScrollBar	Changes a window to use flat control bars
CCustomDraw	Class used to add custom draw support

We'll be using these classes for the rest of this chapter (and liberally throughout the remainder of the book), so you'll get to see a fair number of them in action.

Window Procedures

Let's recap what we have so far. You've seen how to implement some extremely simple windows, but we haven't really done anything interesting with them. Similarly, we haven't really explored the functionality of the few classes we've used. Basically, we haven't yet entered the realm of the **window procedure**.

The window procedure contains code that is central to the operation of a window. It is the part of the window that deals with messages (responding to events such as mouse clicks) and includes the underlying control logic for the window. In order to extend the functionality of a window beyond the default handling provided by Windows, you need to implement your own window procedure and register it — either by creating a new window class, or by **subclassing** or **superclassing** an existing one.

> *Subclassing means intercepting messages destined for an existing window and handling them with a window procedure of your own (you can choose to pass them on to their original destination if you wish). Superclassing is where your window is based on an existing window class, but uses its own window procedure. We won't cover either of these subjects in great depth in this chapter.*

In ATL, you can get a window procedure for your window classes by using a combination of the `CWindowImpl<>` template (or another more specialized template, such as `CAxDialogImpl<>`) and message maps. As you will see shortly, a **message map** is a means of associating window messages with handler functions in your class.

A Window Of Your Own

The first step to creating your own window class is to add a new header file to your project. We will modify the ATLWindows project we created earlier, although you could just as easily create a new Win32 Application, adding the required ATL support in the same way as before.

Create a new header file called ATLWindow.h, add it to your project, and supply it with the following code:

```
// ATLWindow.h : Declaration of CATLWindow

//////////////////////////////////////////////////////////////////////////////////
// CATLWindow

class CATLWindow :
    public CWindowImpl<CATLWindow>
{
public:
    CATLWindow()
    {
    }

    ~CATLWindow()
    {
    }

    BEGIN_MSG_MAP(CATLWindow)
    END_MSG_MAP()
};
```

Let's break this down piece by piece. For a start, our class is derived the CWindowImpl<> template class that, in traditional ATL style, takes our class as its first template parameter. We'll examine why it does this in a moment, but first you should know that it has two more parameters. Its complete syntax is:

```
template <class T,
          class TBase = CWindow,
          class TWinTraits = CControlWinTraits> class CWindowImpl;
```

Where:

Parameter	Description
T	Your class; the one derived from CWindowImpl<>.
TBase	The base class of the class you're writing; the class for which we're providing a window procedure. Defaulting to CWindow, this class must provide (at least) basic Win32 functionality.
TWinTraits	The default style of the window. This class must be a specialization of CWinTraits<>, which takes parameters that define the style and extended style of the window.

CWindowImpl<> provides message handling for the class passed as its second template parameter by calling a method called ProcessWindowMessage() that's declared in one of its base classes — an ATL class called CMessageMap. The *implementation* of this function, however, is provided as part of the BEGIN_MSG_MAP() macro that you write in your class, which is why CWindowImpl<> has it as a template parameter. If it didn't, it would have no way of getting to the implementation.

Here's a simplified diagram of `CWindowImpl<>`'s default inheritance tree, in which you can see some of the classes we've been looking at so far:

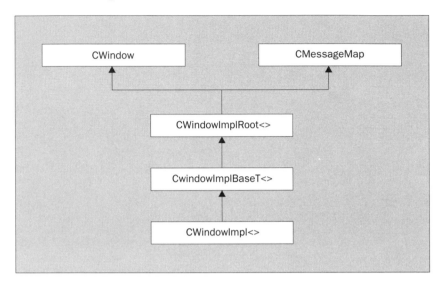

If you wish, you can specify a different base class as the second template parameter, to be used instead of the default `CWindow`. You might want to do this in order to implement a window procedure for a class contained in `Atlcontrols.h`, for example:

```
class CMySoupedUpEditBox : public CWindowImpl<CMySoupedUpEditBox,
                                              ATLControls::CEdit>
{
  ...
}
```

Getting back to our `CATLWindow` class, and before we move on to looking at the message map itself, we can change the declaration to define a style for our new window:

```
class CATLWindow :
    public CWindowImpl<CATLWindow, CWindow,
            CWinTraits<WS_SIZEBOX | WS_CAPTION | WS_POPUPWINDOW | WS_VISIBLE, 0> >
```

Next, we can fill in the constructor and the destructor. The constructor will be blank in our case, as we'll initialize the window manually. The destructor will check to see if the window still exists (that is, it has a non-NULL HWND) and destroy it if it does. This is necessary because, as we've already mentioned, the m_hWnd variable is public and may have been set to NULL manually.

```
~CATLWindow()
{
    if(::IsWindow(m_hWnd))
        DestroyWindow();
}
```

Now we can start to add entries in the message map for the messages we're interested in receiving, and write handler functions that perform actions when messages are received. Our first such handler will terminate the application when the window is closed, and for that we will need to act on the WM_CLOSE message being sent by the window.

The **Add Windows Message Handler** Wizard makes this task trivial, so right click on `CATLWindow` in the ClassView and select this option. Then, simply double click on `WM_CLOSE` and hit **OK**. The message map will be updated to include our new handler function, for which a prototype is also added:

```
BEGIN_MSG_MAP(CATLWindow)
    MESSAGE_HANDLER(WM_CLOSE, OnClose)
END_MSG_MAP()

LRESULT OnClose(UINT uMsg, WPARAM wParam, LPARAM lParam, BOOL& bHandled)
{
    // TODO : Add Code for message handler. Call DefWindowProc if necessary.
    return 0;
}
```

We'll just send a message to quit the application, in the same way as the dialog box back in Chapter 3:

```
LRESULT OnClose(UINT uMsg, WPARAM wParam, LPARAM lParam, BOOL& bHandled)
{
    PostQuitMessage(0);
    return 0;
}
```

We can now create and use this window in `ATLWindows.cpp` with the following code:

```
#include "stdafx.h"
#include "ATLWindow.h"

CComModule _Module;

int APIENTRY WinMain(HINSTANCE hInstance,
                     HINSTANCE hPrevInstance,
                     LPSTR     lpCmdLine,
                     int       nCmdShow)
{
    _Module.Init(NULL, hInstance);
    CATLWindow TestWin;
    RECT rcPos = {0, 0, 400, 200};
    TestWin.Create(NULL, rcPos, _T("Your Very Own Window!"));
    TestWin.ShowWindow(SW_SHOW);

    MSG msg;
    while(GetMessage(&msg, 0, 0, 0))
    {
        TranslateMessage(&msg);
        DispatchMessage(&msg);
    }

    return 0;
}
```

If you build and execute the project, you should see something like this:

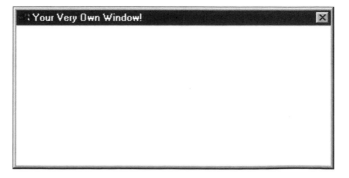

This window can be resized at will, and closing it will quit our application. At first glance, it may not seem that we've achieved much more than we did when we instantiated a simple edit window, but this code allows us a lot more flexibility. We can customize this window far beyond what was possible before; we can add contained windows; we can intercept whatever window messages we want. Before we set about doing that, however, we should examine message maps a little more closely.

Message Maps

Our first attempt at using message maps has been a success, but to create more interesting applications, we'll need to know rather more about them. After all, messages are absolutely central to the working of Windows.

If you have any experience with MFC, you've probably noticed that ATL's message maps look very similar to the maps provided by the former. Each handler entry in the message map associates a message (or a range of messages) with a function. (In fact, each entry adds an if statement that tests whether the message passed to the function should be handled by that entry. If so, the code calls the function specified, passing the arguments in a form appropriate to that message type.)

The macro you'll use to handle messages most of the time is MESSAGE_HANDLER(), but there are others, as shown in the following table:

Macro	Parameters
MESSAGE_HANDLER()	msg, func
MESSAGE_RANGE_HANDLER()	msgFirst, msgLast, func
COMMAND_HANDLER()	id, code, func
COMMAND_ID_HANDLER()	id, func
COMMAND_CODE_HANDLER()	code, func
COMMAND_RANGE_HANDLER()	idFirst, idLast, func
NOTIFY_HANDLER()	id, code, func
NOTIFY_ID_HANDLER()	id, func
NOTIFY_CODE_HANDLER()	code, func
NOTIFY_RANGE_HANDLER()	idFirst, idLast, func

Where:

Parameter	Description
msg	The message to handle.
func	The handler function.
msgFirst, msgLast	A range of messages to handle. (For example, using WM_MOUSEFIRST and WM_MOUSELAST will set up a handler for the full range of mouse messages.)
id	The identifier of the menu item, control, or accelerator.
code	The notification code.
idFirst, idLast	A range of identifiers of message sources whose messages you want to handle.

The different handler types (MESSAGE, COMMAND, and NOTIFY) require different signatures for the handler functions. These are shown in the table below:

Handler Type	Function Signature
MESSAGE	LRESULT MessageHandler(UINT uMsg, WPARAM wParam, LPARAM lParam, BOOL& bHandled);
COMMAND	LRESULT CommandHandler(WORD wNotifyCode, WORD wID, HWND hWndCtl, BOOL& bHandled);
NOTIFY	LRESULT NotifyHandler(int idCtrl, LPNMHDR pnmh, BOOL& bHandled);

As an example, here is the message map provided by ATL when an ATL dialog is added to a project:

```
BEGIN_MSG_MAP(CSimpleDlg)
    MESSAGE_HANDLER(WM_INITDIALOG, OnInitDialog)
    COMMAND_ID_HANDLER(IDOK, OnOK)
    COMMAND_ID_HANDLER(IDCANCEL, OnCancel)
END_MSG_MAP()
```

This provides support for the WM_INITDIALOG message (which is sent by Windows on creating an instance of this class), and handler functions that are called when the default OK and Cancel buttons are pressed. Of course, the window is capable of acting on many more messages than these (those sent when the window is moved or resized, for example), so how does this work?

All three types of handler function take a reference to a BOOL as the final parameter, which is set to TRUE when ATL calls the handler function. You should set this parameter to FALSE if the handler does not handle the message, or it wants other handlers to see the message as well — it will be passed on to the other entries in the message map to see if it matches the messages that they handle. Ultimately, if a message is not handled after all the message map entries have been checked, it will be sent to a default message handler. This is standard practice in Windows programming, and explains the brevity of the map shown above.

The return value of the handler depends on the message being handled, and you'll need to look into the Win32 SDK documentation for the message to see what this return value should be. For most messages, the return value is 0 for a successfully handled message.

The macros starting with MESSAGE_ handle Windows messages — either a single message or a range of messages. The function that handles the message is passed the message ID, so if you want to handle a range of messages with a single function, you can determine which message was sent. The command and notify handlers are specifically for WM_COMMAND and WM_NOTIFY messages, which *could* be handled using a MESSAGE_ macro, but contain a lot of information that is best split out using the macros designed specifically for the task. Command and notify messages are invariably sent from child windows to their parents.

That completes 'phase one' of our tour of message maps, but there are a few subtleties we have yet to cover. For example, it is apparent from our earlier examples that windows can contain other windows, in a parent-child relationship. The example message map above showed how we could detect when a user clicked on one of two buttons on a dialog. This begs the question, "How can we distinguish between messages sent to child windows and those sent to parent windows?"

Alternate Message Maps

ATL provides three ways of handling messages sent by different windows in a single message map: **alternate message maps**, **chained message maps**, and **reflecting messages**. We'll consider alternate message maps first, as that's the technique we'll be using in this chapter, and look briefly at chaining messages after that.

The idea behind alternate message maps is that they allow you to handle in one class a message that originates from another class. That could mean, for example, a child window being configured to send all its messages to a particular message map in its parent. That message map can be split up, so that messages from one source are treated differently from the messages from another.

Typically, this behavior will be used by a main window class (such as one that represents a dialog) that contains other Windows controls. The main window class subdivides its message map (using numeric IDs) so that it can have handlers for both for its own messages and the messages sent by the contained windows — to differentiate between mouse clicks in its own space and in its contained windows, for example.

Here is a message map from a main window, with an alternate map shown highlighted:

```
BEGIN_MSG_MAP(CMainCtrl)
    MESSAGE_HANDLER(WM_PAINT, OnPaint)
    MESSAGE_HANDLER(WM_SETFOCUS, OnSetFocus)
    MESSAGE_HANDLER(WM_KILLFOCUS, OnKillFocus)
    MESSAGE_HANDLER(WM_CREATE, OnCreate)
ALT_MSG_MAP(1)
    MESSAGE_HANDLER(WM_LBUTTONDBLCLK, OnLButtonDblClk)
END_MSG_MAP()
```

As we mentioned earlier, `BEGIN_MSG_MAP()` defines the `ProcessWindowMessage()` function. This function has a parameter called `dwMsgMapID` that specifies the message map to use, the default value of which is 0. After the function declaration, `BEGIN_MSG_MAP()` initiates a `switch` construct, starting with `case 0:`, that results in the handlers appearing immediately after `BEGIN_MSG_MAP()` being in message map 0. The `ALT_MSG_MAP()` macro then inserts a `case` statement with the identifier specified by the macro parameter, so the alternate message map declared above expands to `case 1:`. After all the alternate message maps have been defined, the `END_MSG_MAP()` macro terminates the `switch`, forwarding any unhandled messages to default handlers.

This structure is illustrated in the figure below:

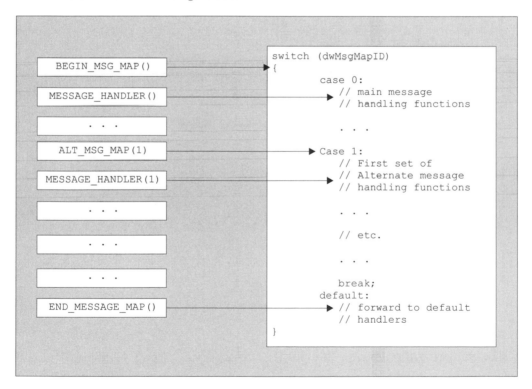

Contained windows are usually created as members of type `CContainedWindow` (or specializations of `CContainedWindowT<>`, as we shall see later). When they are initialized in the constructor of their parent, they can be passed a pointer to a class containing a message map and an alternate message map ID to use. For example, we could initialize a contained window in the following way:

```
CMainCtrl() : m_ContainedWindow(this, 1)
{
}
```

Here, we are using the `this` pointer of the parent class to give access to its message map, and instructions to use alternate message map number 1. (The alternate message map ID can be omitted if we wish to use the default message map, which has ID 0.)

When contained windows receive a message, they call `ProcessWindowMessage()` in their parent, passing all the information for the message itself *and* the message map ID that the contained window was initialized with in its constructor. In the above example, messages received from `m_ContainedWindow` will be routed to `ALT_MSG_MAP(1)`.

The main window can use as many `ALT_MSG_MAP()` macros as it needs, and it can initialize the contained window members to use whichever of the alternate message maps is most appropriate. Multiple contained windows can use the same alternate message map in their parent if they need to; it is possible to differentiate between them by looking at their child window ID.

Chaining Message Maps

ATL also provides a mechanism for **chaining** message maps, which is the term given to routing a message through to a message map in another class or object. If a handler in that class handles the message, no other handler will get a chance; otherwise the rest of the original message map is checked for a handler.

There are three types of `CHAIN_MSG_MAPxxx()` macro (with two variants of each of the first two, bringing the total to five):

Macro	Parameters	Description
CHAIN_MSG_MAP()	theChainClass	Routes the message to the default message map in a base class
CHAIN_MSG_MAP_ALT()	theChainClass, msgMapID	Routes the message to an alternate message map of a base class
CHAIN_MSG_MAP_MEMBER()	theChainMember	Routes the message to the default message map in a data member
CHAIN_MSG_MAP_ALT_MEMBER()	theChainMember, msgMapID	Routes the message to an alternate message map of a data member
CHAIN_MSG_MAP_DYNAMIC()	dynaChainID	Routes the message to the default message map of a member that is determined at runtime

Where:

Parameter	Description
theChainClass	Base class containing the message map
msgMapID	Alternate message map identifier
theChainMember	A data member that has a message map
dynaChainID	Identifies an object with a message map

The first four macros are fairly straightforward; you might use CHAIN_MSG_MAP() to route messages to a base class of your window class. Earlier on, for example, we defined a window class called CMySoupedUpEditBox. If we based a new class on this class, like so:

```
class CMyEvenBetterEditBox : public CMySoupedUpEditBox
{
    ...
};
```

We could instruct this class to use the message map in CMySoupedUpEditBox like this.

```
BEGIN_MSG_MAP(CMyEvenBetterEditBox)
    MESSAGE_HANDLER(WM_PAINT, OnPaint)
    CHAIN_MSG_MAP(CMySoupedUpEditBox)
END_MSG_MAP()
```

Here, CMyEvenBetterEditBox deals with drawing itself when requested to do so by Windows, but passes off all other message handling to its base class.

The dynamic chaining macro allows you to build up routing at runtime; to use it, the class in whose message map the macro appears must derive from CDynamicChain. The single parameter to the CHAIN_MSG_MAP_DYNAMIC() macro is just a number that can be associated with an object containing a message map at runtime, with a call to CDynamicChain::SetChainEntry():

```
BOOL SetChainEntry(DWORD        dwChainID,
                   CMessageMap* pObject,
                   DWORD        dwMsgMapID = 0 );
```

Then, when the CHAIN_MSG_MAP_DYNAMIC() macro is encountered during the normal process of message handling, the message map contained in pObject will be asked to handle the message. You can add as many dynamic maps as you like, as long as each has a unique ID.

Reflected Messages

In message reflection, a parent will 'reflect' messages straight back to the child control that sent them, in order for the latter to deal with them. The reflected message consists of the original message plus the constant OCM_BASE. When the child control gets these messages, it can identify them as having been reflected from its container, and handle them appropriately.

The macros you can use to implement this functionality are:

Macro	Description
DEFAULT_REFLECTION_HANDLER()	A default handler for reflected messages that you can place in the message map of the child control.
REFLECT_NOTIFICATIONS()	When encountered in the message map of the parent, this macro will cause a message to be reflected back to the child control whose identifier is specified in the message.

We won't be using these macros in this book. For more information about them, and about message reflection in general, take a look at the MSDN library.

An Example Application

Now that you have a feel for message maps and how to handle contained windows, let's put this into practice by using some contained windows in an ATL dialog class. These dialogs, which you've seen in action already, use the CAxDialogImpl<> template to implement their window procedure. We now know enough about window procedures and message maps to customize what's provided for us by the ATL Object Wizard when we choose to add an ATL dialog class to our project.

We will go down this route (rather than starting from scratch or modifying the skeleton window we looked at earlier) because doing so makes it a lot easier to customize windows using the resource editor provided with Visual C++. An ATL dialog class comes with such a resource already in place when we create it.

This is where we run up against our first problem. Ideally, we'd like to add a dialog via the ATL Object Wizard (through the Insert | New ATL Object... menu item), but if you try this now you'll see the following error message:

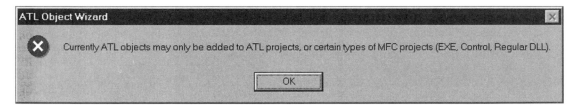

This makes sense when you consider what the ATL Wizard was designed for. Its primary purpose is to add ATL objects to ATL server projects, or to MFC projects that make use of ATL objects. We, on the other hand, want to make use of ATL code to create a small, efficient client application — involving no COM at all. This probably wasn't exactly what the architects of the ATL library had in mind, which is why the Wizard was designed this way.

Using The ATL Object Wizard In A Win32 Application

Fortunately, we can convince the ATL Object Wizard that adding an object really is what we want to do, and make it perform that task for us. This is possible through the addition of the features that the Wizard looks for when it starts up, which are:

❑ The project must contain a .cpp file with the same name as the project.

❑ An ATL object map must be present (although it can be empty).

❑ A .idl file must exist with the same name as the project.

❑ The .idl file must contain a library block (again, this can be empty)

The first of these conditions is already satisfied. The second can be solved by adding the following 2 lines to the top of ATLWindows.cpp:

```
BEGIN_OBJECT_MAP(ObjectMap)
END_OBJECT_MAP()
```

Next, we need to add an IDL file, the simplest means of doing which is to add a text file called ATLWindows.idl via File | New. This file needs to contain a library block, so add the following code:

```
library ATLWindows
{
};
```

We won't be using this file as part of our project (apart from the fact that we need to use the ATL Object Wizard), so right click on it in FileView and change its settings to exclude it from all builds, as shown below:

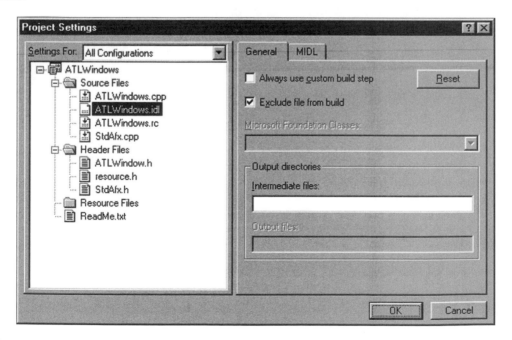

These are all the steps necessary to enable the addition of dialogs through the ATL Object Wizard.

Modifying A Dialog

We'll be creating a dialog that presents the user interface for a simple game, where the object is to sort the numbers from 0 to 9 into even and odd list boxes (assuming for simplicity's sake that 0 is even).

The Window Template

Add an ATL dialog object called GameWindow to the ATLWindows project (or to a new project equipped with ATL Wizard support if you prefer). Using the resource editor, remove the existing OK and Cancel buttons, and add components to the dialog window as follows:

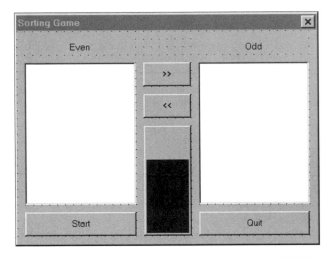

Control ID	Type	Notes
IDC_STATIC1	Static Text	Caption: Even
IDC_STATIC2	Static Text	Caption: Odd
IDC_LISTLEFT	List Box	Sorted
IDC_LISTRIGHT	List Box	Sorted
IDC_BUTTONSTART	Button	Caption: Start
IDC_BUTTONQUIT	Button	Caption: Quit
IDC_BUTTONLEFT	Button	Caption: <<
IDC_BUTTONRIGHT	Button	Caption: >>
IDC_TIMELEFT	Progress	Vertical, Smooth, Modal Frame

Before we start changing any of the code for the window, let's define exactly how it should behave. When the user clicks on the Start button, the two list boxes will be randomly populated with the numbers from 0 to 9, and the timer (progress bar) will start to go down. After 10 seconds, if the numbers are not sorted, a message box will appear to inform the user that they have lost. If the numbers are successfully sorted (by clicking first on a number and then on the appropriate transfer button, << or >>) before the timer runs out, a victory message box will be displayed. In either case, OK'ing the message box will reset the window to its original state. In addition, the Quit button can be used at any time to exit the application.

Basic Modifications

So, let's take our basic dialog class and set about modifying it. Note that the generated class has the following declaration in GameWindow.h:

```
class CGameWindow :
    public CAxDialogImpl<CGameWindow>
```

The CAxDialogImpl<> template allows us to host ActiveX controls. We won't be using any of these, so we can replace this straight away with the simpler CDialogImpl<> template:

```
class CGameWindow :
    public CDialogImpl<CGameWindow>
```

This removes our dependency on the atlhost.h header file, so we can remove this #include. While we're looking at the include files, add the atlcontrols.h header — we'll be using the wrapper classes we looked at earlier to make our life easier. The top of GameWindow.h should now look like this:

```
// GameWindow.h : Declaration of the CGameWindow

#ifndef __GAMEWINDOW_H_
#define __GAMEWINDOW_H_

#include "resource.h"       // main symbols
#include "atlcontrols.h"
```

The next thing to notice is that, although we've removed the OK and Cancel buttons, event handlers still exist for them. Remove the following two lines:

```
        COMMAND_ID_HANDLER(IDOK, OnOK)
        COMMAND_ID_HANDLER(IDCANCEL, OnCancel)
```

And the associated handler functions, OnOK() and OnCancel().

Adding And Initializing Contained Window Members

Next, we'll add member variables for our contained windows, whose types will all be specializations of CContainedWindowT<>:

```
    template < class TBase = CWindow, class TWinTraits = CControlWinTraits >
    class CContainedWindowT : public TBase
```

As you can see, the parameters to this template are similar to those to CWindowImpl<>. However, there is no need to specify a class containing a message map — it is simply assumed that one will be available in the class where objects of these types are defined. Add the following private members to CGameWindow:

```
private:
    CContainedWindowT<ATLControls::CButton>         m_btnRight;
    CContainedWindowT<ATLControls::CButton>         m_btnLeft;
    CContainedWindowT<ATLControls::CButton>         m_btnStart;
    CContainedWindowT<ATLControls::CButton>         m_btnQuit;
    CContainedWindowT<ATLControls::CListBox>        m_lstLeft;
    CContainedWindowT<ATLControls::CListBox>        m_lstRight;
    CContainedWindowT<ATLControls::CProgressBarCtrl> m_prgTimeLeft;
```

Once again, we've replaced the default CWindow parameter with classes from the Atlcontrols.h header file in order to make use of the extra functionality they provide. These contained windows need to be initialized in our constructor:

```
CGameWindow() : m_btnStart(this),
                m_btnQuit(this),
                m_btnRight(this),
                m_btnLeft(this),
                m_lstLeft(this),
                m_lstRight(this),
                m_prgTimeLeft(this)
    {
    }
```

Here, we are using the CContainedWindowT<> constructor, which takes the parent window as its first parameter (this in our case) and the alternate message map to use as its second. We won't use any alternate message maps for now, but you'll see how to modify the example to use them later on.

Once our contained windows are initialized, we need to set them to correspond to the controls we have placed in our dialog resource. We do this by using the Attach() method of CWindow, which is available through our CContainedWindowT<> member variables because all of the Atlcontrols.h classes derive from it. This method accepts window handles that we can obtain using the GetDlgItem() function, which makes use of the control IDs we assigned to the controls earlier.

We'll do all of this in the supplied OnInitDialog() function. While we're about it, we'll also set the seed for random number generation (using the current time, obtained using GetTickCount()) and disable the << and >> buttons, which serve no function when the game isn't running:

```
LRESULT OnInitDialog(UINT uMsg, WPARAM wParam, LPARAM lParam, BOOL& bHandled)
    {
    srand((unsigned)GetTickCount());
    m_btnRight.Attach(GetDlgItem(IDC_BUTTONRIGHT));
    m_btnLeft.Attach(GetDlgItem(IDC_BUTTONLEFT));
    m_btnStart.Attach(GetDlgItem(IDC_BUTTONSTART));
    m_btnQuit.Attach(GetDlgItem(IDC_BUTTONQUIT));
    m_lstLeft.Attach(GetDlgItem(IDC_LISTLEFT));
    m_lstRight.Attach(GetDlgItem(IDC_LISTRIGHT));
    m_prgTimeLeft.Attach(GetDlgItem(IDC_TIMELEFT));
    m_btnRight.EnableWindow(FALSE);
    m_btnLeft.EnableWindow(FALSE);
    return 1;  // Let the system set the focus
    }
```

Application Framework

Now we have our initialized, contained windows, we should think about how we want our application to work in a little more depth, mapping out the handler and utility functions we'll be needing along the way.

First of all, we have four buttons for which we need to implement message handlers. These are easily added using the **Add Windows Message Handler** Wizard, as we shall see later. These handlers will access the underlying logic of our application, which will be contained in private member functions.

The basic operations a user can perform are:

❑ Start a game
❑ Move a number
❑ Quit the application

In addition to this, our application will need to be able to:

❑ Initialize a game
❑ Determine whether victory conditions have been met
❑ Handle the time remaining control
❑ Terminate a game

Initialization will be performed by a function called `StartGame()`, which will be called when the user clicks on the **Start** button.

Moving numbers will be handled by `MoveItem()`, called when the << or >> button is pressed. `MoveItem()` will accept the source and destination list boxes as parameters, allowing us to reuse this code to handle both buttons.

Victory conditions will be checked by a function called `Victorious()`, which we will use whenever an item is moved. This function will return a `bool` value indicating whether the numbers are sorted correctly.

A timer will be created when the game is started, and we'll respond to `WM_TIMER` messages with a function called `UpdateTimeLeft()`. This function will also detect if time has run out.

When the game is over, whether the result is success or failure, a function called `EndGame()` will be called, which will return the window to its original state.

So, add the following `private` declarations to `GameWindow.h`:

```
private:
    void StartGame();
    void EndGame();
    void MoveItem(CContainedWindowT<ATLControls::CListBox>* lstSource,
                  CContainedWindowT<ATLControls::CListBox>* lstDest);
    void UpdateTimeLeft();
    bool Victorious();
```

We'll implement these functions shortly, but before we do that, we'll add our message handlers.

Message Handlers

Adding message handlers is simple: right click on the CGameWindow class in ClassView and select the **Add Windows Message Handler** Wizard.

First, we'll add our handler functions for clicking on each of the four buttons, starting (naturally enough) with the **Start** button. Select IDC_BUTTONSTART in the window labeled **Class or object to handle** and double click on BN_CLICKED in the left hand list box, accepting the default name for the function. When you click on **OK** and look at GameWindow.h, you will notice the following changes:

❑ A COMMAND_HANDLER() macro has been added to the message map

❑ A function called OnClickedButtonstart() has been added

> **Note that if you have already added `private` members, as we have here, the message handler function will also be private, as it is added to the end of your class definition. You will either have to move the function in front of the `private` declaration, or add a new `public:` section.**

Repeat this procedure to add handler functions for the other three buttons.

Next, we need to add a handler for the WM_TIMER event, so that we can update the time remaining indicator accordingly. This time, select CGameWindow in the **Class or object to handle** window, then double click on the WM_TIMER event.

As we've already defined the member functions we'll be using, we can add the code for all of these handlers straight away:

```
LRESULT OnClickedButtonquit(WORD wNotifyCode, WORD wID, HWND hWndCtl,
                            BOOL& bHandled)
{
    DestroyWindow();
    PostQuitMessage(0);
    return 0;
}

LRESULT OnClickedButtonstart(WORD wNotifyCode, WORD wID, HWND hWndCtl,
                             BOOL& bHandled)
{
    StartGame();
    return 0;
}

LRESULT OnClickedButtonleft(WORD wNotifyCode, WORD wID, HWND hWndCtl,
                            BOOL& bHandled)
{
    MoveItem(&m_lstRight, &m_lstLeft);
    return 0;
}

LRESULT OnClickedButtonright(WORD wNotifyCode, WORD wID, HWND hWndCtl,
                             BOOL& bHandled)
{
    MoveItem(&m_lstLeft, &m_lstRight);
    return 0;
}
```

```
LRESULT OnTimer(UINT uMsg, WPARAM wParam, LPARAM lParam, BOOL& bHandled)
{
    UpdateTimeLeft();
    return 0;
}
```

Member Function Implementation

The first member function we'll look at is `StartGame()`. We'll place this (and the other member functions) in GameWindow.cpp, so insert the following skeleton definition into that file:

```
void CGameWindow::StartGame()
{
}
```

This function is responsible for the following:

❑   Enabling/disabling buttons

❑   Populating the list boxes with the numbers from 0 to 9

❑   Initializing the timer

The first of these is the easiest. We'll simply disable the **Start** button and enable the **>>** and **<<** buttons with the following lines of code:

```
void CGameWindow::StartGame()
{
    m_btnRight.EnableWindow();
    m_btnLeft.EnableWindow();
    m_btnStart.EnableWindow(FALSE);
}
```

Next, we'll populate the list boxes. We've already set the seed for the random number generator; all we have to do is loop through the numbers from 0 to 9, randomly decide which window to place them in, and then use the `AddString()` method of `CListBox` to add them:

```
void CGameWindow::StartGame()
{

    ...

    TCHAR strItem[2];
    for(int iLoop = 0; iLoop <= 9; iLoop++)
    {
        wsprintf(strItem, _T("%d"), iLoop);
        if(rand()%2 == 0)
            m_lstLeft.AddString(strItem);
        else
            m_lstRight.AddString(strItem);
    }
}
```

`AddString()` expects a pointer to a null-terminated string, so a `TCHAR` array with two members is used here. The array is then set to the character representing the value of `iLoop` using `wsprintf()`.

Finally, we'll initialize the timer. This requires three operations:

❑ Setting the position of the progress bar
❑ Recording the current time
❑ Initializing a timer

The second and third of these will require two more member variables: one to record the starting time, the other to store the timer ID. Add the following lines to the constructor and private declaration sections of GameWindow.h:

```
public:
    CGameWindow()  : m_btnStart(this),
                     m_btnQuit(this),
                     m_btnRight(this),
                     m_btnLeft(this),
                     m_lstLeft(this),
                     m_lstRight(this),
                     m_prgTimeLeft(this),
                     m_tStartTime(0),
                     m_timTimer(0)
    {
    }

    ...

private:
    CContainedWindowT<ATLControls::CButton>            m_btnRight;
    CContainedWindowT<ATLControls::CButton>            m_btnLeft;
    CContainedWindowT<ATLControls::CButton>            m_btnStart;
    CContainedWindowT<ATLControls::CButton>            m_btnQuit;
    CContainedWindowT<ATLControls::CListBox>           m_lstLeft;
    CContainedWindowT<ATLControls::CListBox>           m_lstRight;
    CContainedWindowT<ATLControls::CProgressBarCtrl>   m_prgTimeLeft;
    DWORD                                              m_tStartTime;
    UINT                                               m_timTimer;
```

And then the following to StartGame():

```
void CGameWindow::StartGame()
{

    ...

    m_prgTimeLeft.SetPos(100);
    m_tStartTime = GetTickCount();
    m_timTimer = SetTimer(1, 100);
}
```

The first line of code simply uses the SetPos() method of CProgressBarCtrl. By default, objects of this class will have a range from 0 to 100, we'll use these default values here. Next we use GetTickCount() to get the current time, and initialize our timer. CWindow, which our Atlcontrols.h wrappers are based on, has two methods to do this: SetTimer() and KillTimer(). SetTimer() requires a non-zero first parameter and an interval in milliseconds as its second. It returns an ID, which we store away for later use. Every time this interval passes, a WM_TIMER message is sent to our window. We've already added our handler function for this, so let's look at the member function it uses: UpdateTimeLeft().

This function is very simple. It calculates the elapsed time from the stored start time and the current time, checks to see whether 10 seconds have elapsed, and updates the progress bar control:

```
void CGameWindow::UpdateTimeLeft()
{
    DWORD tElapsed;
    tElapsed = GetTickCount() - m_tStartTime;
    if(tElapsed >= 10000)
    {
        KillTimer(m_timTimer);
        MessageBox(_T("You Lost!"));
        EndGame();
    }
    else
    {
        m_prgTimeLeft.SetPos(100 - (tElapsed / 100));
    }
}
```

Notice that we call `KillTimer()` before displaying the message box indicating failure. If we don't do this, `WM_TIMER` messages will continue to be sent, resulting in multiple message boxes appearing as this function is recursively called.

Next, we'll look at what happens when the user clicks on the >> and << buttons. In this case, the message handler calls `MoveItem()`, passing pointers to the source and destination lists as parameters. The first thing that this function does is to check whether there is an item selected in the source list box; if there isn't, the function does nothing more. If there is an item selected, it is removed and added to the other list, via a temporary TCHAR array.

After this movement has occurred, the function checks to see whether the game has been won by using the `bool` result of the `Victorious()` function we'll look at next. If this function returns `true`, we kill the timer, display the appropriate message, and end the game. Here is the code to do all that:

```
void CGameWindow::MoveItem(CContainedWindowT<ATLControls::CListBox>* lstSource,
                           CContainedWindowT<ATLControls::CListBox>* lstDest)
{
    TCHAR strItem[2] = {0};
    int iSelected = lstSource->GetCurSel();
    if(iSelected >= 0)
    {
        lstSource->GetText(iSelected, strItem);
        lstSource->DeleteString(iSelected);
        lstDest->AddString(strItem);
        if(Victorious())
        {
            KillTimer(m_timTimer);
            MessageBox(_T("You Won!"));
            EndGame();
        }
    }
}
```

`Victorious()` iterates through the contents of each list box, returning `false` as soon as it discovers a number in the wrong place. Again, this function uses a temporary TCHAR array to store the number, this time using `_ttoi()` to convert the string into an integer.

```
bool CGameWindow::Victorious()
{
    int iLoop;
    TCHAR strItem[2] = {0};
    if(m_lstLeft.GetCount() > 0)
    {
        for(iLoop = 0; iLoop <= m_lstLeft.GetCount(); iLoop++)
        {
            m_lstLeft.GetText(iLoop, strItem);
            if(_ttoi(strItem)%2 != 0)
            {
                return false;
            }
        }
    }
    if(m_lstRight.GetCount() > 0)
    {
        for(iLoop = 0; iLoop <= m_lstRight.GetCount(); iLoop++)
        {
            m_lstRight.GetText(iLoop, strItem);
            if(_ttoi(strItem)%2 == 0)
            {
                return false;
            }
        }
    }
    return true;
}
```

Finally, let's look at `EndGame()`. This function has the responsibility of clearing the time remaining display, enabling and disabling buttons according to the 'no game in progress' state of the window, and clearing the contents of the list boxes using the `CListBox::ResetContent()` method. The code to do this is simple:

```
void CGameWindow::EndGame()
{
    m_prgTimeLeft.SetPos(0);
    m_btnRight.EnableWindow(FALSE);
    m_btnLeft.EnableWindow(FALSE);
    m_btnStart.EnableWindow(TRUE);
    m_lstLeft.ResetContent();
    m_lstRight.ResetContent();
}
```

This completes our discussion of the code for our window class. Now let's look at the code and project settings required to run our game.

Playing The Game

Most of the code to display our window is familiar: we can include the header file containing our class and call `Create()` and `ShowWindow()` to display it, as we have done before.

There are two more things we need to do. First, the project must be linked with `Comctl32.lib`, which contains the window classes for all the controls we've used in our window. We haven't needed this library until now because the controls we've been using are intrinsic Windows controls (like buttons and edit controls). When we use the common controls (such as the progress bar), we must link with and initialize the common control library.

To link the project with Comctl32.lib, select the Project | Settings menu item, choose the Link tab, and change the Settings For drop-down list box to read All Configurations. Then, simply add Comctl32.lib to the list of Object/library modules:

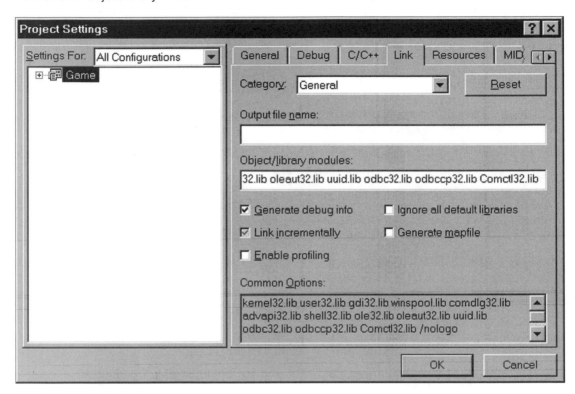

Second, we need to initialize the common controls in our code, in order to register their window procedures with the system. Initializing the controls simply requires a call to an API function called ::InitCommonControls(), and putting this together with what we've already seen, our code to run the window looks like this:

```
#include "stdafx.h"
#include "GameWindow.h"

BEGIN_OBJECT_MAP(ObjectMap)
END_OBJECT_MAP()

CComModule _Module;

int APIENTRY WinMain(HINSTANCE hInstance,
                     HINSTANCE hPrevInstance,
                     LPSTR     lpCmdLine,
                     int       nCmdShow)
{
    _Module.Init(NULL, hInstance);
    ::InitCommonControls();
    CGameWindow GameWindow;
    GameWindow.Create(NULL);
    GameWindow.ShowWindow(SW_SHOW);
```

```
MSG msg;
while (GetMessage(&msg, 0, 0, 0))
{
    TranslateMessage(&msg);
    DispatchMessage(&msg);
}

return 0;
}
```

And that's all you have to do. This will now run fine, so try it out — enjoy the game!

If you compile a release version of this application you may be surprised by its small size. On my computer, the full EXE file came to 37KB!

Using Alternate Message Maps

In this final section, we'll modify the window code we've been using so far to demonstrate the use of alternate message maps. Specifically, we'll intercept the WM_SETCURSOR message for the >> and << buttons, allowing us to change the mouse cursor when the mouse is over them.

First of all, let's add two new resources, representing the cursors we'll use when the mouse moves over the buttons. Select the Insert | Resource menu item, then select IDC_POINTER and hit New.

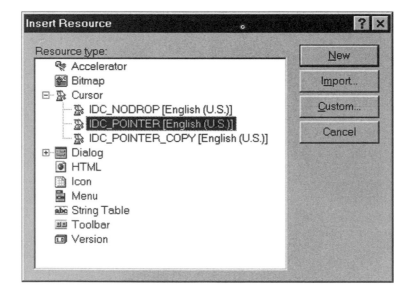

The new pointer is added to the resources for the module. Change its identifier to IDC_POINTERRIGHT and modify the bitmap to look something like this:

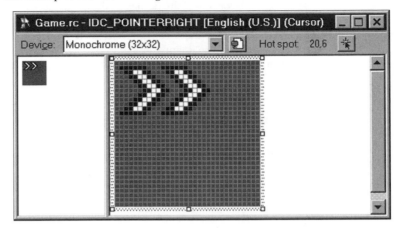

Note that the 'hot spot' of the cursor (the bit that does the clicking) is located at the rightmost point of the arrows.

Repeat this procedure for a second pointer, IDC_POINTERLEFT, drawing it like this:

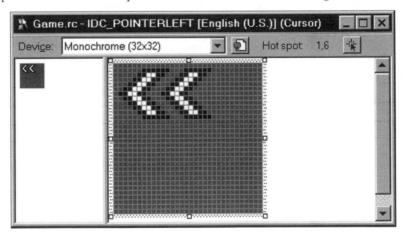

These cursors are now part of our application and can be accessed from our class, so we should now be able to do something about using them. First, we need to add our alternate message maps to the code in GameWindow.h:

```
BEGIN_MSG_MAP(CGameWindow)
    MESSAGE_HANDLER(WM_INITDIALOG, OnInitDialog)
    COMMAND_HANDLER(IDC_BUTTONLEFT, BN_CLICKED, OnClickedButtonleft)
    COMMAND_HANDLER(IDC_BUTTONRIGHT, BN_CLICKED, OnClickedButtonright)
    COMMAND_HANDLER(IDC_BUTTONQUIT, BN_CLICKED, OnClickedButtonquit)
    COMMAND_HANDLER(IDC_BUTTONSTART, BN_CLICKED, OnClickedButtonstart)
    MESSAGE_HANDLER(WM_TIMER, OnTimer)
ALT_MSG_MAP(1)
    MESSAGE_HANDLER(WM_SETCURSOR, OnMouseInRight)
ALT_MSG_MAP(2)
    MESSAGE_HANDLER(WM_SETCURSOR, OnMouseInLeft)
END_MSG_MAP()
```

We now have three separate ways of handling the WM_SETCURSOR message: we can use the default handler (which will simply result in the default mouse pointer), or one of our two new message handlers, OnMouseInRight() and OnMouseInLeft(). From the names of these functions, you'd be right to guess that OnMouseInRight() is used when the mouse enters the space of the >> button, and OnMouseInLeft() is used when the mouse is in the << button. We need to change the constructor of our window to specify that these buttons use the alternate message maps. As we said earlier, this is simply a matter of supplying the constructor of these buttons with a second parameter:

```
CGameWindow()  : m_btnStart(this),
                 m_btnQuit(this),
                 m_btnRight(this, 1),
                 m_btnLeft(this, 2),
                 m_lstLeft(this),
                 m_lstRight(this),
                 m_prgTimeLeft(this),
                 m_tStartTime(0),
                 m_timTimer(0)
{
}
```

All we need to do now is provide the handler functions themselves. We'll use a couple of system functions: SetCursor() to set the mouse cursor, and LoadCursor() to extract our cursor from the resources contained in our application module.

LoadCursor() takes two parameters: the HINSTANCE of the module containing the resource, and a pointer to the cursor resource required. It returns an HCURSOR that can be passed to SetCursor(). We can convert the identifiers we have assigned to our cursor resources into pointers by using the handy MAKEINTRESOURCE() macro. Here, then, is the code required for our handlers:

```
LRESULT OnMouseInRight(UINT uMsg, WPARAM wParam, LPARAM lParam,
                       BOOL& bHandled)
{
   ::SetCursor(::LoadCursor(_Module.GetModuleInstance(),
                         MAKEINTRESOURCE(IDC_POINTERRIGHT)));
   return 0;
}

LRESULT OnMouseInLeft(UINT uMsg, WPARAM wParam, LPARAM lParam,
                      BOOL& bHandled)
{
   ::SetCursor(::LoadCursor(_Module.GetModuleInstance(),
                         MAKEINTRESOURCE(IDC_POINTERLEFT)));
   return 0;
}
```

If you run this application now, you won't see any change in the mouse cursor because we've assigned windows to our contained window members using the Attach() method, which doesn't result in messages destined for those windows arriving in our class. If we want to intercept messages for these windows, we need to use the SubclassWindow() method instead, giving us an extra layer of control:

```
LRESULT OnInitDialog(UINT uMsg, WPARAM wParam, LPARAM lParam, BOOL& bHandled)
{
   srand((unsigned)GetTickCount());
   m_btnRight.SubclassWindow(GetDlgItem(IDC_BUTTONRIGHT));
   m_btnLeft.SubclassWindow(GetDlgItem(IDC_BUTTONLEFT));
   m_btnStart.Attach(GetDlgItem(IDC_BUTTONSTART));
   m_btnQuit.Attach(GetDlgItem(IDC_BUTTONQUIT));
   m_lstLeft.Attach(GetDlgItem(IDC_LISTLEFT));
   m_lstRight.Attach(GetDlgItem(IDC_LISTRIGHT));
   m_prgTimeLeft.Attach(GetDlgItem(IDC_TIMELEFT));
   m_btnRight.EnableWindow(FALSE);
   m_btnLeft.EnableWindow(FALSE);
   return 1;  // Let the system set the focus
}
```

Make these changes, and we're away. When you run the application, and when they are enabled, you'll see the mouse cursor change when it hovers over the >> and << buttons.

Summary

This chapter has shown you how to create UI-based applications using ATL. It introduced the basic CWindow class, and then explained how the wrapper classes found in Atlcontrols.h can be used to avoid having to send esoteric messages to manipulate our controls.

We also discussed how ATL uses message maps to implement the window procedures of the windows you create. You saw how the **Add Windows Message Handler** Wizard makes it extremely easy to add almost any functionality you desire to your windows.

In the second half of the chapter, we created a whole application that (thanks to ATL) was very compact. This application demonstrated how to use contained windows, and later how to use alternate message maps to give flexibility to our message handling.

Over the next three chapters, the things you've learned here will be used on numerous occasions as we build towards the implementation of a full ActiveX control with (inevitably) a visual user interface. Our immediate concerns in this area, though, are the issues surrounding connectability and connection points, and that's where we're headed next.

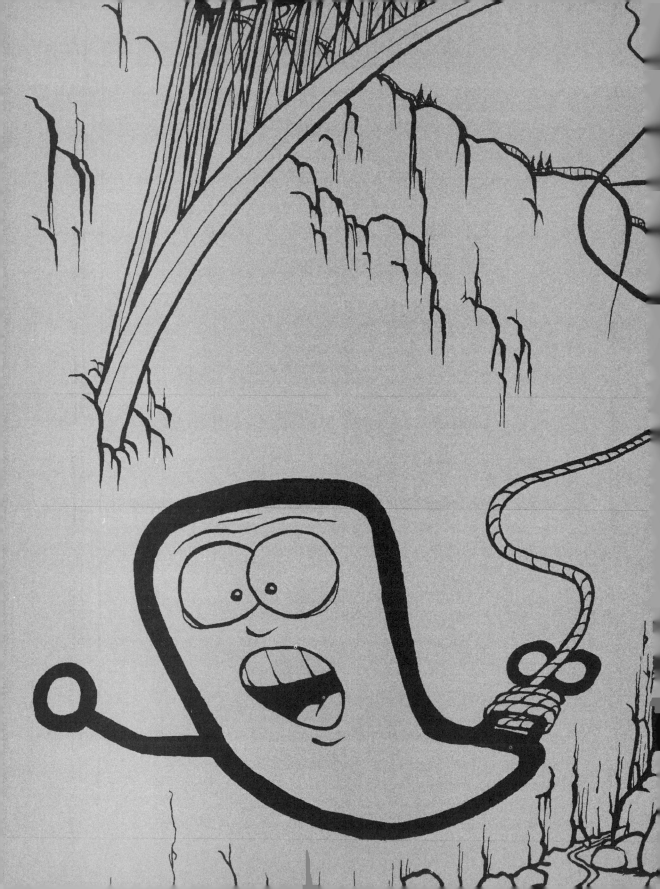

Connectable Components

ActiveX control is a term that gets bandied around a lot, but it *actually* means *any* COM component that has the IUnknown interface and is self-registering. A **full control**, on the other hand, implements many interfaces that enable it to interact with the user and the program in which it is contained. Full controls are in-process components, and as such they can only be created as part of another process. Such a process is called a **container**, and examples of them include Internet Explorer, Word 2000, and applications created with Visual Basic 6.0.

What makes a process a control container? Well, it must understand the standard interfaces that a full control implements, and it must also implement COM interfaces that allow a contained control to inform the container when some event occurs in the control (the control's data changes, or maybe a user clicks on the control). This implies that the communication between the control and the container is two-way. The control is **connected** to the container.

However, the process can be quite complicated, since the container may make several connections to a single control, or even to several controls, and so there must be a way to manage all these connections. This is the reason for connection points, and this chapter is the second in a series of four that will lead you to the goal of creating a full control yourself. In the last chapter, we examined ATL's facilities for dealing with user interfaces. In this one, we'll hook up that functionality to some COM components.

Connection Points And Connectable Components

At this point, you have learned how to create a COM component without a user interface that can be created in-process, in another process, or on another machine. You have also seen how to apply the IDispatch interface so that scripting languages like VBScript can access a COM component, and how to make complete client applications with user interfaces using pure ATL. However, one of the great things about COM is that you can combine these features, creating powerful components that have a user interface, allowing them to react to user interaction. These components are sometimes called **controls**.

A History Of Controls

Let's set the scene with a little history. 'Control' is a label that has been applied to a number of different things as technologies have changed, so having some kind of perspective is no bad thing. Windows has always had controls; most of the interaction you have with applications is through controls, particularly when you're using applications that employ dialogs or forms. The basic Windows controls like edit boxes, list boxes, and buttons are part of the operating system, whereas more complicated controls like the list, tree and animation controls are provided in a separate DLL that requires specific initialization; these are the so-called Common Controls that were first introduced in Windows 95.

Visible controls of the kind we were dealing with in the previous chapter are characterized by the fact that they have a window. They need to have a window because they have to react to user actions, and to provide notifications. When you click on a button, for example, the button changes its appearance to make it look as if it has been pressed — this is the control reacting to user input. However, the button must do more than just *look* as if it has been pushed; it must inform the application that the user has clicked it, and it does this with a notification, as you have seen.

These are controls at their most basic: if the parent window wants the control to do something, it has to send the control a message — there is no equivalent of a COM method call. If the control holds some data and the parent window wants to access that data, it has to send a message to tell the control to change the data or return it — without COM method calls, what else is there to do? As a developer, you have to manage all these messages and notifications. ATL helps you to post these messages with wrapper classes that provide methods for communicating with Windows controls, and in addition it provides the ATL message map to allow you to catch and handle control and notification messages.

Unfortunately, this model is not very extensible because there is no standard way that a parent window can ask a control what it can do — whether it is capable of sending notification messages like BN_CLICKED, for example. Also, since the notifications are handled through Windows messages, it means that the parent window developer must program in a language that provides access to the window procedure. A language that hides the window procedure prevents the handling of these notifications.

To get round these problems, Microsoft introduced **Visual Basic eXtension controls** (**VBXs**) in Visual Basic 3.0. VBXs were DLLs that could contain more than one control, and each of these could have properties and methods, just like you can have on a COM component today. Through a convoluted mechanism, Visual Basic hooked the VBX notifications into a Visual Basic form's window procedure and exposed the notifications as Visual Basic events. A VBX container (usually your Visual Basic 3.0 project) could read and write control properties, and call control methods. This was a great boon, because the Visual Basic programmer could write some code that would be called when, for example, a control was clicked. Because Visual Basic had its own notification mechanism, there was no need to worry about implementing a window procedure or handling Windows messages.

However, there were several problems with VBXs. First of all, they were firmly fixed to the 16-bit Windows architecture, and it was not possible to write 32-bit VBXs. Secondly, although VBX controls could implement methods, they could only be chosen from a range of *eight* standard methods, which was extremely restrictive. The only way to get round this was to define an Action property that would direct the control to perform a custom method — an ugly compromise. Thirdly, the model for generating events was inflexible.

Then came COM, which allowed controls to have properties and methods. Type libraries allowed a control to say what properties and methods it supported. A tool like Visual Basic can query a control to find out what it can do, and then present the developer with a list of the properties and methods that they can work with. However, properties and methods provide only one-way communication, from the container to the control. To achieve two-way communication, the control must also be able to talk to the container.

To standardize their burgeoning technologies, Microsoft produced the OCX specification. OCXs are in-process Automation components, and therefore have properties and methods that are described by a type library. In addition to the controls themselves, the specification also describes OCX containers. These too are COM components, which means that a control can call methods on a container. Typically, this happens when an event occurs in the control and it wants to inform the container about it.

If a control has properties (which could be simple data like the background color, or the font used to draw text), then implementing controls as Automation components makes it easy for a tool to change these properties at design time in response to actions from the Visual Basic developer. However, when the developer saves a form or compiles the application, Visual Basic must be able to save all these property values in one go. The specification indicated how this should be done, using **persistence interfaces** and **property sets**. Of course, if a member of a property set changes, the container will want to know about it. The specification defined a mechanism whereby the control could inform the container.

It's not hard to see that there's a lot of communication going on here, and since there may be more than a single channel of communication, this two-way conversation has to be managed. For example, there may be two or more places in the container that require notifications when a single property changes, or a control could provide notifications of many different types. To manage all these notifications, Microsoft provided **connection points**, the subject of this chapter.

Callbacks

Callbacks are a technique used extensively in 16- and 32-bit Windows. They improve on a message-based notification mechanism because they involve passing the address of a handler function to a function that provides notifications. This notifying function then 'calls back' through this handler function pointer when it needs to inform it of some event or change of data. The great advantage of using a function instead of a message is that it can take typed parameters, so the notifying function can pass data to the handler specific to the event that has occurred. Although you can do this with a Windows message, it is cumbersome because the parameters to Windows messages are typeless.

As a Windows programmer, you will be most familiar with using callbacks when registering a window class, where the address of the window procedure is passed (via the WNDCLASS structure) to RegisterClass(). When you've created a window of this class, Windows will call the window procedure any time you dispatch messages (obtained from the message queue) with DispatchMessage(). Another example of a callback is when you want to enumerate Windows objects — the windows on the desktop, for example. To do this, you call EnumWindows() passing the address of a callback function. Windows will then call this function for every window it can find.

These callbacks have two important characteristics. First, the callback address is the address of a single function; second, in 32-bit Windows, the function accepting the callback address must be implemented in-process (most likely in a DLL) — otherwise, the callback address will be invalid.

COM both extends and restricts this idea. You have already seen that COM marshaling allows an interface pointer in one process to be used in another process — this improves on Windows callbacks, because it means that callbacks can be made cross-process. However, marshaling also applies a restriction (albeit a small one): marshaling can only be done on an interface, and not just on a single method. Callbacks in COM require the process requiring a notification to implement an interface and then pass a pointer to it to the notifying component. This interface may have just a single method, or it could have many methods to handle many different events.

Incoming And Outgoing Interfaces

The COM terms for callback interfaces can be a little confusing, so we need to explain them carefully. An interface that's designed to be used as a callback is called a **sink interface**, because it *sinks* event notifications. Sink interfaces are one type of **incoming interface**; these are interfaces containing methods that are called by clients, and so the calls are 'coming in' to the server. All the interfaces you have come across so far have been incoming interfaces.

For a COM component to notify another component of an event, it must make calls on the other COM component's sink interfaces. To enable this, the client wanting the notifications must pass its sink interface pointer to the component generating the events. This leaves the client in a bit of a dilemma: does the server know about its sink interface? Because of the way that connection points are designed, the interface pointer the client will pass will be an IUnknown pointer, so how can a client be sure that a component will know about the particular sink interface it should QI() for?

The server component supports connections to sink interfaces by implementing **connection points**, and it indicates the connection points it has by exposing the IConnectionPointContainer interface. The client can QI() for this interface to see if the component supports connection points, and then call a method on this interface to determine if a connection point exists for the specific sink interface. In addition to this, the server component designer lists the sink interfaces that it will call through the connection point mechanism as **outgoing interfaces** in the component's IDL. This is done by using the [source] attribute: the server component is indicating that the interface is a *source* of events, and that another component can implement the interface to *sink* the notifications.

This picture explains the terminology:

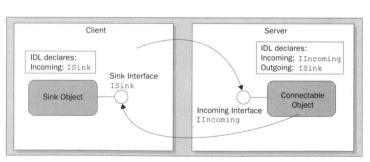

In this picture, the 'connectable component' uses connection points to manage connections between the server and client. The client implements a sink component, QI()s for IConnectionPointContainer, and then asks for the connection point object for the particular sink interface. The client passes the sink interface pointer to the connection point object to make the connection; it can then continue to call methods on the component's incoming interface.

However, at some point the connectable component will need to callback on the client, which it does by looking up the right connection point object and accessing it for the client's sink interface pointer. At some later stage, the client may decide that it no longer needs notifications, and so it can get access to the connection point object again, this time to tell it to stop providing notifications.

Connection Topologies

All the details of how the client obtains connection point objects and tells the component that it wants (or doesn't want) notifications are given in the next section, but first let's look at the different ways of connecting clients and components through connection points.

The example above demonstrated a one-to-one relationship — a single client connection to a single component — but this may not be the model that the designer requires. For example, there may be many clients (or many places in a single client's code) that will want to be informed by a single connectable component when an event occurs (many-to-one); or a single client could pass its sink interface to get notifications from many connectable components (one-to-many).

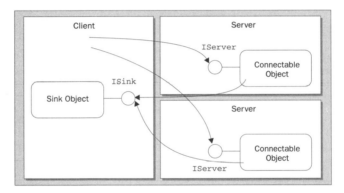

The above diagram shows the one-to-many case: the client has a single sink component, and it passes the sink interface pointer to two connectable components, so that notifications from both components are handled by the same client code. An example of this is a client that has two buttons on a form: the client sink component is used to handle click events, so when the user clicks on either button, it is handled by the same method in the client.

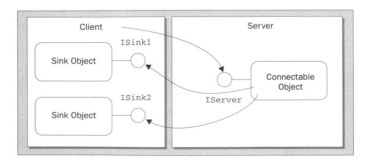

The second picture on the previous page shows the many-to-one case. Here, a single component may support callbacks to many different sink interfaces. The client in the picture has created two different sink objects, each with a different sink interface. An example of this would be a control that informs the client on one outgoing interface when the control is clicked, and on another when its internal state changes. To support this, the connectable component will have to support (at least) two different outgoing interfaces.

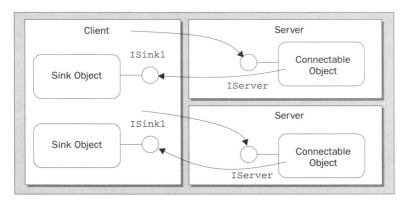

This third topology is a combination of the first two, and shows the client creating more than one sink component, with each implementing the *same* sink interface. The client passes these to different connectable components, and so the notifications from the components will be handled differently by the client.

As you can see, there is plenty of flexibility in how clients and components can connect. These different topologies are difficult to maintain, and the mechanism is rationalized using connection point objects.

Connection Points

For each outgoing interface that the connectable component supports, the component should implement a **connection point object**. This object is used to maintain an array of the client sink interfaces for the clients that are connected. So, if the connectable component can call back to (say) the `ISink` interface, then it will have a connection point object specifically for this outgoing interface. Whenever a client that has a sink component that supports the `ISink` interface makes a connection to the connectable component, it does so by registering itself with the appropriate connection point object. Now, when the connectable component generates an event that is handled by the `ISink` interface, it can use the connection point object to get access to all of the connected clients, and then fire the event.

Connection point objects expose the `IConnectionPoint` interface. Of its five methods, three are of particular interest to us here. The `Advise()` and `Unadvise()` methods are used by clients to register their sink interfaces with the connectable component: when a client calls `Advise()`, the connection point object will add the sink interface pointer to its list of interface pointers. When the connectable component needs to notify the connected clients, it should obtain the appropriate connection point object and then use its `EnumConnections()` method to get an **enumeration object** through which it can access all these client sink interfaces. The connectable component should then iterate through these interfaces and call the appropriate method.

The EnumConnections() method returns a pointer to an IEnumConnections interface. This interface enumerates the current connections for a connectable component in CONNECTDATA structures — you can call the Next() method to get back an array of CONNECTDATA structures. CONNECTDATA looks like this:

```
typedef struct tagCONNECTDATA
{
    IUnknown*   pUnk;
    DWORD       dwCookie;
} CONNECTDATA;
```

The pUnk is the client sink interface, and dwCookie is a unique identifier for this interface pointer. When the client calls Advise() on the connection point object, the latter should create a new CONNECTDATA structure filled with the sink interface pointer, and add it to its internal array of sink interfaces. The connection point object should then return the dwCookie back to the client through the [out] parameter of Advise() with the same name. The client should hold on to this cookie so that it can identify the interface when it decides it no longer wants to receive notifications and calls Unadvise().

Notice how the connection point object receives a sink interface pointer (for example ISink), but saves it internally as an IUnknown pointer. It needs to do this so that it can implement the enumerator component (which we shall cover in the next chapter). When the connection point object saves the sink interface, it up-casts to get the IUnknown pointer. This means that the pointer still points to the sink interface, but that only the IUnknown methods can be called through it.

When the component wants to notify the client and obtains a CONNECTDATA structure for it, it will need to downcast the pUnk back to the sink interface, so that it can call the appropriate method. This is perfectly fine, even for sink interfaces on clients that are out of process, since up-casting does not change the pointer: it merely slices off the methods not described by the up-cast interface. The downcast restores access to those methods.

Interface pointers in CONNECTDATA are held typeless, but connection point objects *are* typed — that is, they are specific to a particular outgoing interface. The IID of the connection point's outgoing interface can be obtained by calling IConnectionPoint::GetConnectionInterface().

Connection Point Containers

As we've already discussed, a connectable component can fire events to more than one outgoing interface. Each outgoing interface is handled by a connection point object, and to maintain all these connection point objects, the connectable component has a single **connection point container**. Connection point container objects expose the IConnectionPointContainer interface, which has two methods. The first, FindConnectionPoint(), allows a client to ask the connectable component for a particular outgoing interface: the method takes a parameter that is the IID of the client's sink interface. The other method is called EnumConnectionPoints(), and this returns an interface pointer to an enumeration object that a client can use to iterate through all the connection point objects that exist in the container.

The following diagram shows the relationship between the connectable component, the connection point container and the connection point objects:

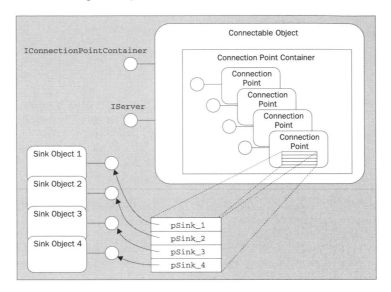

If a client wants to determine whether an component supports connections, it should first `QueryInterface()` for the `IConnectionPointContainer` interface. If a valid pointer is returned, the client knows that the component is connectable.

To determine whether the connectable component supports connections to a *particular* outgoing interface, the client has two choices. The first option is to iterate though all the connection point objects using the enumerator component obtained by calling `EnumConnectionPoints()` on the container, and then on each connection point object it can call `GetConnectionInterface()` to get the IID of the outgoing interface. The second option is to call `FindConnectionPoint()` on the container, passing the IID of the sink interface to see if there is a connection point for this as an outgoing interface.

ATL And Connection Points

The last diagram showed that the connection point container object and the server component are one and the same thing, in which case it's the server component that needs to implement the `IConnectionPointContainer` interface. ATL provides a default implementation of this interface with the `IConnectionPointContainerImpl<>` template. The single parameter of the template is the ATL class for the connectable component. For your ATL component to implement this interface, it must derive from this template (and the `IConnectionPointContainer` interface must be added to the COM map, of course).

A connection point container object must have access to the connection point objects that it supports, and ATL does this through a **connection point map**. This map is declared in your ATL class, and is the reason why your class is a parameter of the container template — normally in C++, a base class can only have access to a member in a derived class if the member is declared in the base class. However, for data members this would mean that every instance of the derived class would have a copy of this data. This is unnecessary for the connection point map, because a single connection point object should handle *all* connections to a particular outgoing interface. The map should be static — in other words, there should be just one copy for all instances of the derived class. Passing the derived class as a parameter of the template gives the `IConnectionPointContainerImpl<>` template access to this static member.

The connection point map is declared using these macros:

```
BEGIN_CONNECTION_POINT_MAP(class)
END_CONNECTION_POINT_MAP()
```

The first macro takes the ATL class as its only parameter. Connection point objects are added to the map using the `CONNECTION_POINT_ENTRY()` macro, which takes the IID of the outgoing interface that the connection point object supports.

If, for example, the `CEvents` class supports connections to the outgoing `IEventSink` interface, it must derive from `IConnectionPointContainerImpl<CEvents>`, and implement its connection point map like this:

```
BEGIN_CONNECTION_POINT_MAP(CEvents)
    CONNECTION_POINT_ENTRY(IID_IEventSink)
END_CONNECTION_POINT_MAP()
```

Before we move on to the main example in this chapter, let's create a lightweight application that consolidates what we've seen so far. In Visual C++, create a new ATL COM AppWizard project called `Clicker`. Because we are going to write a simple control, this should be a DLL project.

Next, start the Object Wizard, but instead of using the default **Objects** category, select **Controls**, and then choose **Full Control**. Give the component the short name of `ClickIt`, and remember the name of the interface on this component: `IClickIt`. (We will have more to say about the component's interfaces later on.) On the **Attributes** tab, make sure that **Support Connection Points** is checked. This will ensure that the component will derive from `IConnectionPointContainerImpl<>` and will have a connection point map. While you are on the **Attributes** tab, notice that the only available threading options are **Single** and **Apartment**, indicating that controls can only be run in an STA.

Our control will respond to mouse clicks by firing an event in its container. As you know from the last chapter, this can be achieved by adding a handler for the `WM_LBUTTONDOWN` message. To do this, right-click on `CClickIt` in ClassView, select **Add Windows Message Handler...**, and choose the `WM_LBUTTONDOWN` message from the left hand list box. Finally, click on **Add and Edit**.

Add the following simple implementation to the handler skeleton that has been generated for you:

```
LRESULT OnLButtonDown(UINT uMsg, WPARAM wParam, LPARAM lParam, BOOL& bHandled)
{
    ::MessageBox(NULL, _T("Handled in control"), _T("ClickIt"), MB_OK);
    return 0;
}
```

This just responds to the user clicking on the control by producing a message box. You can now compile the control.

The next thing to do is create a simple Visual Basic project to test the control. Start Visual Basic and create a Standard EXE project; then choose Components... from the Project menu and check Clicker 1.0 Type Library. This will add an "ATL" icon to the toolbox, so double click on it to add the ClickIt control to the form. You will see something like this (remember, you have added no drawing code, so the image you see is the default provide by the Object Wizard):

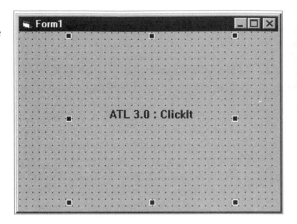

Now run the project and click in the middle of the form. You will get the following dialog:

As the text suggests, the click event has been caught and handled in the control. You didn't add any code to the Visual Basic form to handle the event. To illustrate our discussion, we need to change the control to generate events. The ATL Object Wizard has already done most of the work necessary, so let's close down Visual Basic and take a look at what it has done.

The Outgoing Interface

Move back to Visual C++ and take another look at the ClassView. You will see something like this:

What should be immediately obvious to you is that there are *two* interfaces: the IClickIt interface, and _IClickItEvents. Double click on the latter to bring up the IDL file:

```
[
    uuid(355602DF-5D4A-11D3-89D1-00104BDC35E0),
    helpstring("_IClickItEvents Interface")
]
dispinterface _IClickItEvents
{
    properties:
    methods:
};
```

This is a dispinterface, like the ones we examined in Chapter 5. Because it is a dispinterface, it does not need marshaling code, and so it is declared in the `library` block. This means that the interface will be described in the type library.

What component implements this interface? It's not the `ClickIt` component. Scroll down to the definition of the `coclass`, and you'll see something like this:

```
    [
        uuid(355602DE-5D4A-11D3-89D1-00104BDC35E0),
        helpstring("ClickIt Class")
    ]
    coclass ClickIt
    {
        [default] interface IClickIt;
        [default, source] dispinterface _IClickItEvents;
    };
```

The `_IClickItEvents` interface is declared as the `[default, source]` interface of the control — that is, it's an outgoing interface. As the name suggests, the control generates events on this interface, and a client that wants to sink these events should implement it.

A dispinterface is used for the events interface in order to make the range of clients that can sink its events as broad as possible. We will use Visual Basic for the client, which *isn't* restricted to catching events on a dispinterface — as long as the interface is described in a type library, the outgoing interface can be a custom interface. However, scripting languages like VBScript are also capable of catching events, and these languages don't understand custom interfaces.

The reason why this interface has a leading underscore is that ATL wants to hide it from Visual Basic programmers. (An interface whose name begins with an underscore will not appear in the Visual Basic Object Browser.) Hiding it is a good idea because Visual Basic programs should implement this interface, not call it. As you'll see in a moment, the Visual Basic IDE will do all the work of implementing a sink interface.

Next, open `ClickIt.h` to look at the control code. Because you selected a full control, you will get support for many interfaces, full descriptions of which will be left until Chapter 10. Here are just a few of the base classes:

```
    public IConnectionPointContainerImpl<CClickIt>,
    public IPersistStorageImpl<CClickIt>,
    public ISpecifyPropertyPagesImpl<CClickIt>,
    public IQuickActivateImpl<CClickIt>,
    public IDataObjectImpl<CClickIt>,
    public IProvideClassInfo2Impl<&CLSID_ClickIt, &DIID__IClickItEvents,
                                  &LIBID_CLICKERLib>,
    public IPropertyNotifySinkCP<CClickIt>,
    public CComCoClass<CClickIt, &CLSID_ClickIt>
{
```

The first line of this snippet shows that the class derives from `IConnectionPointContainerImpl<>`, which means that we have basic connection point container support. Further on down, you can see that the Object Wizard has added `IProvideClassInfo2Impl<>` to the class. `IProvideClassInfo2` is called by COM for two reasons:

❑   To obtain the component type information

❑   To obtain the IID of the component's default outgoing interface

The template parameters of `IProvideClassInfo2Impl<>` are used to pass this information to the `Impl` class. Do you remember the warning we gave in Chapter 5 about the type library version parameters to `IDispatchImpl<>`? Well, `IProvideClassInfo2Impl<>` has the same problems. The actual class looks like this:

```
template <const CLSID* pcoclsid, const IID* psrcid,
          const GUID* plibid = &CComModule::m_libid,
          WORD wMajor = 1, WORD wMinor = 0,
          class tihclass = CComTypeInfoHolder>
class ATL_NO_VTABLE IProvideClassInfo2Impl : public IProvideClassInfo2
```

The default parameters assume a type library version of `1.0`. This is *often* the case, but it's not *always* the case. It's far safer to amend the Wizard-generated code to mention the version you are using explicitly. This way, if the type library version changes, you can see where you have to change the code:

```
public IProvideClassInfo2Impl<&CLSID_ClickIt, &DIID__IClickItEvents,
                              &LIBID_CLICKERLib, 1, 0>,
```

The constant for the _IClickItEvents identifier is prefixed with D because the MIDL compiler has noticed that the interface is a dispinterface.

There are therefore two ways for a client to determine the control's default source interface. The first is to obtain the type library for the control, query that for the type information, and then look for the default source interface. This is suitable when a control is not running, because it doesn't require a running instance. The other way is to query the control for `IProvideClassInfo2` and call `GetGuid(GUIDKIND_DEFAULT_SOURCE_DISP_IID, &iid)`, where the IID will be returned in the `iid` parameter. This second method is clearly suitable for a running instance of a control.

Scroll down a bit further until you see the connection point map:

```
BEGIN_CONNECTION_POINT_MAP(CClickIt)
   CONNECTION_POINT_ENTRY(IID_IPropertyNotifySink)
END_CONNECTION_POINT_MAP()
```

The sole entry is for `IPropertyNotifySink`, which is why the class is derived from `IPropertyNotifySinkCP<>`. Events on this interface are generated when **bindable properties** are changed; containers will implement it as a sink interface so that they can express an opinion to the control about whether the property change is allowed. We will look at properties in the next chapter, but it's safe to say that since this control doesn't have any bindable properties, no such events will be generated. The "CP" in the name of `IPropertyNotifySinkCP<>` indicates that the base class implements the connection point objects for this source interface.

The connection point map does not have an entry for the _IClickItEvents interface. This is because there is no event firing code for this interface, which in turn is because there are no events to fire! Let's put that right by using ClassView to add a method called OnClick() to _IClickItEvents. When you open it, you'll find that the dialog is slightly different from the one you've been using to add methods to interfaces so far: it allows you to specify the return type of the method. The reason for this is that the method is not marshaled — it is called by the client calling IDispatch::Invoke(), passing the DISPID of OnClick(). It is Invoke() that gets marshaled, so any marshaling errors are returned in the return value of that method. Select void as the return type of OnClick(), and give it a BSTR parameter:

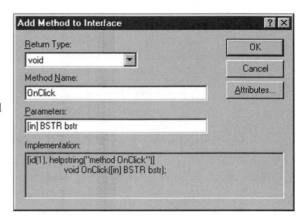

Now compile the project again to ensure that the type library is re-created with this method as part of the events interface. As you'll see in the next section, this is an important step.

Event Firing Code

This is the final step of this project, and in it we need to add code to the CClickIt class to do two things:

❏ Implement the connection point object
❏ Fire events

This code is generated for you, based on the type description of the event interface. Right click on the CClickIt class in ClassView and select **Implement Connection Point....** You will see the following dialog:

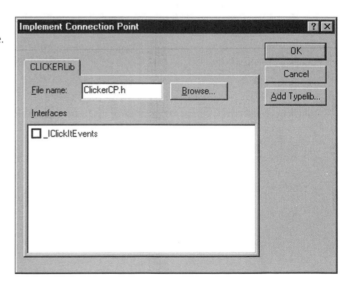

If you don't see the _IClickItEvents interface, or a dialog warns you that the type library does not exist, it means that you didn't compile the project after the last section. Stop to compile it now, and then repeat the last step.

Check the _IClickItEvents check box to specify that event-generating and connection point code should be generated for this interface and placed in ClickerCP.h. Click on OK, and then take another look at ClassView:

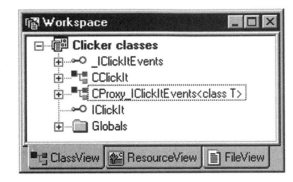

You have added a new class called CProxy_IClickItEvents<>, which despite its name has *nothing whatsoever* to do with the proxy objects used in marshaling. This is the class that will implement connection point objects and fire events; double click on it to take a look:

```cpp
#ifndef _CLICKERCP_H_
#define _CLICKERCP_H_

template <class T>
class CProxy_IClickItEvents :
    public IConnectionPointImpl<T, &DIID__IClickItEvents, CComDynamicUnkArray>
{
    //Warning this class may be recreated by the wizard.
public:
    VOID Fire_OnClick(BSTR bstr)
    {
        T* pT = static_cast<T*>(this);
        int nConnectionIndex;
        CComVariant* pvars = new CComVariant[1];
        int nConnections = m_vec.GetSize();

        for (nConnectionIndex = 0;
                nConnectionIndex < nConnections; nConnectionIndex++)
        {
            pT->Lock();
            CComPtr<IUnknown> sp = m_vec.GetAt(nConnectionIndex);
            pT->Unlock();
            IDispatch* pDispatch = reinterpret_cast<IDispatch*>(sp.p);
            if (pDispatch != NULL)
            {
                pvars[0] = bstr;
                DISPPARAMS disp = { pvars, NULL, 1, 0 };
                pDispatch->Invoke(0x1, IID_NULL, LOCALE_USER_DEFAULT,
                            DISPATCH_METHOD, &disp, NULL, NULL, NULL);
            }
        }
        delete[] pvars;

    }
};
#endif
```

The first thing to notice about this class is that it derives from IConnectionPointImpl<> — that is, it implements a connection point object. Edited a little for clarity, that class looks like this:

```
// From atlcom.h
template <class T, const IID* piid, class CDV = CComDynamicUnkArray >
class ATL_NO_VTABLE IConnectionPointImpl : public _ICPLocator<piid>
{
public:
    ~IConnectionPointImpl();
    STDMETHOD(_LocCPQueryInterface)(REFIID riid, void ** ppvObject);
    STDMETHOD(GetConnectionInterface)(IID* piid2);
    STDMETHOD(GetConnectionPointContainer)(IConnectionPointContainer** ppCPC);
    STDMETHOD(Advise)(IUnknown* pUnkSink, DWORD* pdwCookie);
    STDMETHOD(Unadvise)(DWORD dwCookie);
    STDMETHOD(EnumConnections)(IEnumConnections** ppEnum);
    CDV m_vec;
};
```

The reason for the methods in this class is that it is used to create *connection point objects*, which should have an identity separate from the connectable component. This is achieved by deriving the class from the abstract base class _ICPLocator<> that declares a vtable that looks like IUnknown, but has a method called LocCPQueryInterface() rather than QueryInterface(). If this class did not do this, the implementation of QueryInterface() of the connectable component (that is, CClickIt) would be used rather than IConnectionPointImpl<>'s and the two would have the same COM identity. LocCPQueryInterface() ensures that the connection point object only implements IConnectionPoint.

> *An understanding of how these identity tricks are performed and why they are necessary is not required to use this class. If you want more details, take a look in* Professional ATL COM Programming.

More interesting is the fact that this class has a data member called m_vec that by default is an instance of CComDynamicUnkArray. This is used to hold all the sink interface pointers of the connected clients. This array will grow and shrink as clients attach and detach, which is flexible, but involves calls to the CRT memory allocator (with calls to malloc() and free()). This has performance issues, and puts a dependency on the CRT.

If you know the maximum number of clients that will ever attach to the connectable component, you can use CComUnkArray<> instead, which will allocate a fixed sized array on the stack. This removes the CRT dependency and array allocation and deallocation; it is also the behavior that we need in this example, where we will only ever have one connected client. Change the class's base class to:

```
template <class T>
class CProxy_IClickItEvents :
    public IConnectionPointImpl<T, &DIID__IClickItEvents, CComUnkArray<1> >
{
```

Remember, if more than one client ever tries to attach, this control will die a horrible death. Your code must make sure this never happens.

Fire_OnClick()

When you use ClassView to implement a connection point, it will read the type information for the interface that you select, and generate event-firing code for every method in the interface. We saw an example of this a couple of pages ago, when we saw the code generated for `Fire_OnClick()`.

The first line does the downcasting that allows the code to access methods in CClickIt:

```
T* pT = static_cast<T*>(this);
```

Then the code accesses every entry in the array of sink interfaces. Remember that these interface pointers were up-cast to IUnknown* to save them in the array, so the firing code (knowing that the interface is a dispinterface) casts the pointer to IDispatch* before calling the event method.

The event method takes a single parameter, which is passed as the parameter to `Fire_OnClick()`. This is put into the pvars array that's used to initialize the DISPPARAMS parameter passed to Invoke(). Invoke() uses the DISPID of OnClick(), which is 0x1, to make the call.

Because we changed the type of m_vec from CComDynamicUnkArray to CComUnkArray<1>, we need to change this firing code. CComUnkArray<> doesn't implement GetSize() or GetAt(); instead, it implements the STL-like begin() and end(), so we need to change the loop to use them:

```
CComVariant* pvars = new CComVariant[1];
IUnknown** it = m_vec.begin();

while(it < m_vec.end())
{
    pT->Lock();
    CComPtr<IUnknown> sp = *it;
    pT->Unlock();
    IDispatch* pDispatch = reinterpret_cast<IDispatch*>(sp.p);
    if (pDispatch != NULL)
    {
        pvars[0] = bstr;
        DISPPARAMS disp = { pvars, NULL, 1, 0 };
        pDispatch->Invoke(0x1, IID_NULL, LOCALE_USER_DEFAULT,
                          DISPATCH_METHOD, &disp, NULL, NULL, NULL);
    }
    it++;
}
delete[] pvars;
```

Changes To CClickIt

So what did the Wizard do to CClickIt? Well, firstly, it derived it from the 'proxy' class and included ClickerCP.h in Clickit.h. This means that your code can call `Fire_OnClick()` whenever it needs to generate an event. The new base class also provides the code for the connection points for this event interface. If the class were to generate events on another interface, there would be a corresponding CProxy_ class for that interface too.

```
public CComCoClass<CClickIt, &CLSID_ClickIt>,
public CProxy_IClickItEvents< CClickIt >
{
```

Next, it added the following to the COM map:

```
COM_INTERFACE_ENTRY(IProvideClassInfo2)
COM_INTERFACE_ENTRY_IMPL(IConnectionPointContainer)
END_COM_MAP()
```

In fact, there is already an entry for `IConnectionPointContainer` that was added by the Object Wizard, so you can delete the new line if you wish. However, it is reassuring to know that if you forget to specify that the class will generate events in the Object Wizard, this Wizard will add that support for you.

Finally, it adds the event interface to the connection point map:

```
BEGIN_CONNECTION_POINT_MAP(CClickIt)
    CONNECTION_POINT_ENTRY(IID_IPropertyNotifySink)
    CONNECTION_POINT_ENTRY(DIID__IClickItEvents)
END_CONNECTION_POINT_MAP()
```

Firing The Event

To fire the event, you need to call `Fire_OnClick()`, so do this in `OnLButtonDown()`:

```
LRESULT OnLButtonDown (UINT uMsg, WPARAM wParam, LPARAM lParam, BOOL& bHandled)
{
    ::MessageBox(NULL, _T("Handled in control"), _T("ClickIt"), MB_OK);
    Fire_OnClick(CComBSTR("Fired from control"));
    return 0;
}
```

Now compile the project again, and then either reopen the Visual Basic client project you made earlier, or regenerate it. Open a code window for the form, and select the `ClickIt` control from the **Object** pull-down list box (it will probably be called `ClickIt1`). Look in the **Procedure** pull-down list box, and you will find that the `OnClick` event has been magically added to the list of events you can handle.

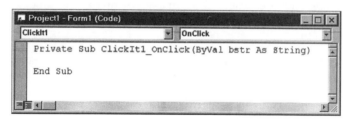

Since it is the default outgoing interface for the control, Visual Basic will add an event handler for you. Add the following code to it:

```
Private Sub ClickIt1_OnClick(ByVal bstr As String)
    MsgBox bstr + " and handled in VB"
End Sub
```

The theory goes that when the event is fired from the control, it is handled by the code in the Visual Basic application. This should take the string passed from the control and display it in a message box. To test out the code, run the application and click on the control. First of all, you'll get the message box we had earlier that said Handled in control. However, when you click on OK, you will get this message box:

This is the result of the code that you added to the Visual Basic application, proving that you caught the event that was fired from the control when you clicked on it.

Summary: Connection Point Example

In this example, you have seen:

- ❑ The changes made to the project file by Object Wizard to support connection points
- ❑ How to add event generation code to a component using the facilities of ClassView
- ❑ How this code generates events
- ❑ How Visual Basic implements sink interfaces

Sinking Events

The ClickIt example has demonstrated that Visual Basic can implement dispinterface sink interfaces that are the outgoing interfaces of a control, but that's by no means a unique ability. Internet Explorer, for example, can also implement dispinterface sink interfaces on controls, which means that DHTML code can catch events from controls that have been added to web pages.

However, Visual Basic is not restricted to dispinterfaces, and the connectable components don't have to be controls. A connectable component can have *custom* outgoing interfaces, and (as long as they are described by a type library) Visual Basic 5.0 and above will happily create a sink interface and make the connections to the component.

In the last example, you saw that because the connectable component was a control, its name was added to the Object pull-down list box when it was added to the form. However, if you were to create a COM object with code like this:

```
Dim o as MyObject
Set o = New MyObject
```

the component is not added to the Object pull-down list box, so you cannot select the events that it generates. The way to deal with this in Visual Basic 6 is to use the WithEvents keyword. When you add this to a global object declaration:

```
Private WithEvents o as MyObject
```

Visual Basic will read the component's type library to see what default outgoing interface it has, and then generate the code to handle events.

COM+ Events

Events are another of the areas in which COM+ makes some significant advances, and while there is no support for any of the features we'll discuss here in Visual C++ 6.0 or ATL 3.0, it's interesting to see how these ideas are being taken forward.

Problems With Connection Point Events

The spur for improving COM's event handling in COM+ was that there are several fairly obvious problems with connection point events. The first thing that you should consider is the issue of 'round-trips', which has been discussed at length in the computer press. This statement sums it up:

> *"It takes five round-trips to establish bidirectional communications using connection points, and four round-trips to tear it down."* (MSJ October 1998, "Effective COM Programming: Seven tips for building better COM-based applications", Tip 4.)

> **A 'round-trip' consists of one C++ call through a vtable to the component, and then another similar call back to the client.**

To quantify this, when a client makes the connection, it QI()s for IConnectionPointContainer (round-trip 1), calls FindConnectionPoint() (round-trip 2), and then calls Advise() on the connection point (round-trip 3), passing the IUnknown of the sink object. The connection point object then calls QI() to get the sink interface it requires to generate the event (round-trip 4), and then because the client no longer needs the connection point, it releases its reference count on it (round-trip 5).

When the connection is broken, the client needs to obtain the connection point object again (two round-trips) and then call Unadvise() with the cookie for the connection (round-trip 3) before releasing the connection point (round-trip 4).

However, when you actually *use* a connection point, the majority of the COM calls will be generating events, or calling the actual connectable component itself. Over the lifetime of the connectable component, the mere nine round-trips to make and break the connection will be insignificant compared with the other COM calls to (or from) the component.

If your application is not constantly making and breaking connections, the round-trips involved are not a problem, and if the component is a control then each round-trip is trivial. Look at the advantages:

- ❏ Many standard containers (Visual Basic, Internet Explorer, etc.) understand how to handle events and how to generate connection point events
- ❏ The protocol allows many useful topologies like many-to-one and one-to-many, and the same connection point code can be used for them all

More worrying is the fact that connection points are **tightly coupled**. Review the mechanism again: the client queries an instance of the connectable component for `IConnectionPointContainer` and then asks for the connection point for the sink interface. This implies that in order to accept events, a client *must* have access to the component that it wants to connect to, and it *must* keep this connection alive for as long as it wants to receive the events. This means that even if the client never makes any other COM calls to the connectable component, it must hold a reference on it.

Also, when the client has successfully advised the connectable component that it wishes to be sent events, the latter then holds a reference to the sink object in the client. This reference is held until the client explicitly breaks the connection, and even if the connectable component doesn't generate events during this time, it will still hold the reference.

Because COM events are actually COM method calls, they are made synchronously. So, if there are several clients connected to a component that generates an event, the calling thread that generates the event will be blocked while the client handles it. If a single thread is used to fire the event to all clients (as in the code generated by the ATL Wizard), the events will be generated *serially*: one client will only be sent the event when the previous client has handled it completely. You could create a pool of threads to generate the events — one thread per client — but this requires inter-thread marshaling and is not simple to generalize.

Publishers And Subscribers

Loosely coupled events (**LCE**) mean that the component that generates the event does not need to connect directly to the sink object that catches it. Instead, an intermediate object is used. Furthermore, the client does not have to call the component to indicate that it can catch events. Instead, a loosely coupled system will have some other mechanism to allow a client to indicate that it is interested in events generated by a component. The COM+ event system that is provided in Windows 2000 is one such LCE system.

A COM+ application that can generate events is called a **publisher**, and it indicates the events that it can generate by registering an **EventClass** with the COM+ catalog. This is a component that is *never* created by the COM+ system, and so its methods can have no implementation. The class is registered so that COM+ can read the interfaces and methods that are described in its type information. The COM+ events system can then create an instance of a component that implements these interfaces, which the publisher can then call to generate events. This component is entirely implemented by COM+, and it has code that tests to see which clients want events, ascertains the locations of those clients and generates the events. The class that the publisher registers is just a template (in the non-C++ sense of the word!).

In this system, clients that want to accept events do so by subscribing to them — predictably, they are known as **subscribers**. Clients will indicate that they want to accept events by making entries in the COM+ catalog called **subscriptions**, which detail a class implemented to handle the event. When an event is generated, the instance of the `EventClass` checks all the subscriptions, creates instances of the subscriber components, and calls the appropriate event method.

Both subscribers and publishers can have filters, allowing the subscriber to indicate that it will only accept an event when a certain condition is met. Similarly, a publisher can be told the list of current subscribers and make an informed choice about which of these can get the event.

This does not mean that the publisher and subscriber are coupled. The publisher creates an instance of the `EventClass` and calls it; it is the `EventClass` that calls the subscriber, and it can do this either directly or through MSMQ. The `EventClass` can create a pool of threads to generate the event, and the beauty of this is that COM+ does all the hard work! If the subscriber application is not running, COM+ can start up the subscriber and *then* generate the event. This means that the two applications don't need to be running at the same time.

As time goes on, expect COM+ events to replace the notifications that were previously performed by the system through connection points. This is why it is worth learning about them now. For example, MTS 2.0 generates events to indicate certain things that have happened (like component creation, or transaction abortion). Unsurprisingly, COM+ generates similar events, but it no longer uses connection points. The result of this is that the COM+ event system is used instead, making the MTS code redundant.

Example: EventWatcher

In the `ClickIt` example, Visual Basic was used to sink events. This time, let's try a beefier project: one that not only sinks events in a C++ control, but also involves *three* C++ projects (see if your virtual memory can handle that many instances of Visual C++ at a time!).

❑ Firstly, you need a server that implements the component to which you want to connect, and the connection point object that manages the connection.

❑ Secondly, you need a client, which in this case will be an ActiveX control. This does not have to be so, but an ActiveX control is used here as a convenient vehicle to get visual feedback when events occur.

❑ Finally, you need something to generate the event that will trigger the server component to notify the client.

These three projects will be called `EventWatcher`, `EventCtrl` and `SetEvent` respectively.

The example uses Win32 kernel event objects as the trigger for the server component. In case you haven't come across them before, a Win32 event object is used for synchronization, and it's particularly useful when used across processes.

You may have your own trigger to tell the server to notify the client (a clock tick, perhaps), but an event object is quite common. Win32 allows you to wait on a change to many parts of the operating system. For example, you can get notified when the NT event log changes by calling `NotifyChangeEventLog()`, or when some change is made to the system registry by calling `RegNotifyChangeKeyValue()`. Both of these functions take a handle to an event object that the system sets to the 'signaled' state when the event happens, and the process calling these functions waits on the event object to change state using the Win32 `WaitForSingleObject()` function.

Similarly, you can detect that a directory has changed by getting a *notification* handle with calls to `FindFirstChangeNotification()` and `FindNextChangeNotification()`. This handle can be used with the `WaitForSingleObject()` as well, just like waiting on an event object.

This example will show you how to wait on a Win32 event object, and how to use it to generate a control event. You can alter it according to the type of notification you want to receive.

The EventWatcher Server

This is the component that will wait on the Win32 kernel event object. An event object can be in one of two states — signaled and non-signaled — and you can set this state with the Win32 `SetEvent()` and `ResetEvent()` functions. In this example, we'll use a component called `EventChange` to notify the client when the event changes state from non-signaled to signaled (and vice versa). This example is a little contrived, since it checks for the state change in both directions — you would more likely check for the event object changing from non-signaled to signaled, indicating (say) that a file has been added to a directory.

The `EventChange` component will support the `IEventChange` interface:

```
interface IEventChange : IDispatch
{
    HRESULT WatchEvent([in] BSTR bstrEventName);
    HRESULT SetInterval([in] LONG lInterval);
};
```

The client control should establish a connection with the `EventChange` component. This component will check on the state of a named event object, and the client can start the process by calling `WatchEvent()`, passing the event object's name. The check will be carried out every 500ms, and to change this interval the client can call `SetInterval()`.

As we've mentioned already, to make the connection the client must get hold of the connection point container interface, ask it for the connection point object for the sink interface, and then call `Advise()`. The reverse process of telling the connectable component that the client no longer needs notifications is similar, except that it should call `Unadvise()`. All this is a lot of work, and ATL has simplified it with two functions: `AtlAdvise()` and `AtlUnadvise()`.

`ATLAdvise()` looks like this:

```
ATLAPI AtlAdvise(IUnknown*  pUnkCP,
                 IUnknown*  pUnk,
                 const IID& iid,
                 LPDWORD    pdw);
```

`ATLAPI` sets up the calling convention appropriately whether the function is linked statically or dynamically, and defines the function as returning a `HRESULT`. The first parameter is the `IUnknown` of the connectable component that the client wants to connect to, while the second parameter is the `IUnknown` on the sink component in the client. The third parameter is the IID of the sink interface, and the final parameter is the address of a `DWORD` that will take the cookie that uniquely identifies the connection.

When the client no longer wants to receive events, this cookie is used in a call to `AtlUnadvise()`:

```
ATLAPI AtlUnadvise(IUnknown*  pUnkCP,
                   const IID& iid,
                   DWORD      dw);
```

After making the connection, the client should call WatchEvent() on the IEventChange interface of the component, telling it to watch a particular event object. EventChange will create a new thread in the server and return immediately. The client can then continue doing its work.

This is an example of performing an asynchronous method call with COM. By nature, COM is synchronous — the calling thread is blocked while the callee is processing the call. By spinning a new thread, the EventChange component frees the client thread to continue its work. Using the connection point mechanism, the component can inform the client when an event has occurred.

The new server thread will go into a loop checking the state of the event object to see if it changes. When this happens, the thread should obtain the connection point for this outgoing interface, and then generate the appropriate event. After doing so, the server thread will continue to check the state of the event.

The process of obtaining the array of sink interface pointers and then going through each pointer and calling the appropriate method is tedious, so Visual C++ supplies a Wizard to write this code for you, as you saw earlier in the chapter.

Although calling Unadvise() will tell the component not to notify the client of the event object's state changes, it does not stop the worker thread. To kill this thread, the client should release the connectable component, and the FinalRelease() method on the component should tell the thread to die.

Before we go any further, there's one more choice to make. Our server needs to create a new thread, and we have two options. Either the server thread can be in an STA (so the client sink interface would have to be marshaled to the apartment that owns the worker thread), or the server and worker thread can be part of the same MTA (in which case marshaling is not required). For simplicity, let's go for the second option.

Creating The Project

Now that you have an idea of how this component will work, let's go through the steps of creating it. Start up the ATL COM AppWizard and create a new project called EventWatcher. On the dialog, select Executable (EXE) and click on Finish.

Next, you need to add a new component, so use Object Wizard to create a **Simple Object** and call it EventChange:

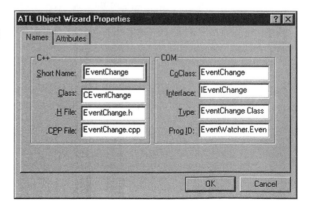

Click on the **Attributes** tab and select <u>F</u>ree for the Threading Model, and also select Support Connection <u>P</u>oints. Free threading is required because we want the connectable component to be part of an MTA. Remember: to an ATL component, 'free threading' means a multithreaded apartment.

Editing The Class

The next task is to edit the CEventChange class to make the component do something. In the project's ClassView, right-click on the IEventChange entry and add a new method called WatchEvent() with a single [in] BSTR bstrEventName parameter. Repeat this for the SetInterval() method (whose parameter is [in] LONG lInterval). ClassView should now look like this:

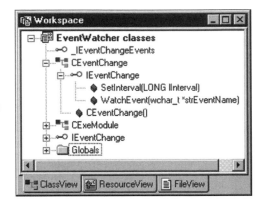

Our next responsibility is to add the code for these methods. The first task is to handle the interval that specifies how often our component should check the event. Open EventChange.h and add a new private data member called m_dwInterval, initializing it in the constructor:

```
class ATL_NO_VTABLE CEventChange :
    public CComObjectRootEx<CComMultiThreadModel>,
    public CComCoClass<CEventChange, &CLSID_EventChange>,
    public IConnectionPointContainerImpl<CEventChange>,
    public IDispatchImpl<IEventChange, &IID_IEventChange,
                         &LIBID_EVENTWATCHERLib, 1, 0>
{
public:
    CEventChange() : m_dwInterval(500)
    {
    }

DECLARE_REGISTRY_RESOURCEID(IDR_EVENTCHANGE)

DECLARE_PROTECT_FINAL_CONSTRUCT()

BEGIN_COM_MAP(CEventChange)
    COM_INTERFACE_ENTRY(IDispatch)
    COM_INTERFACE_ENTRY(IEventChange)
    COM_INTERFACE_ENTRY(IConnectionPointContainer)
END_COM_MAP()
BEGIN_CONNECTION_POINT_MAP(CEventChange)
END_CONNECTION_POINT_MAP()

// IEventChange
public:
    STDMETHOD(SetInterval)(/*[in]*/ LONG lInterval);
    STDMETHOD(WatchEvent)(/*[in]*/ BSTR bstrEventName);
private:
    DWORD m_dwInterval;
};
```

Note that the library version has also been added to the IDispatchImpl<> base class, as recommended in Chapter 5.

Because we chose to support connection points, the Object Wizard has derived the class from the IConnectionPointContainerImpl<> template, with our class as its parameter. The Object Wizard has also created a connection point map, which is empty at the moment.

Now open EventChange.cpp and add the code for SetInterval(), so that the client can change the interval between the occasions on which the server checks the event object:

```
STDMETHODIMP CEventChange::SetInterval(LONG lInterval)
{
    if(lInterval < 100)
        return E_FAIL;

    m_dwInterval = lInterval;
    return S_OK;
}
```

Notice that we've put a check in here: the interval is in milliseconds, so we're making sure that the component does not check the event more often than once every 100ms. If that happened, the component could take up too much CPU time. The default interval is 500ms, as set in the constructor's initializer list.

Creating The Worker Thread

When the client calls WatchEvent(), the server creates a new thread to watch for the specified event object to change state. This worker thread will watch the event tirelessly, only dying when it is told to, which happens when the EventChange component itself dies. However, since there are (at least) two threads trying to die, there must be some communication between them to make sure that they are destroyed in the correct order. The nature of threads is that they run independently of each other and so, in the few cases when one thread depends on what another is doing, the two must be able to indicate to each other what stage they are in.

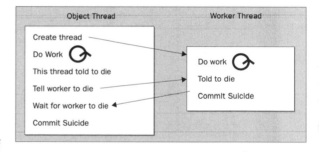

The two messages sent between the threads are:

- ❑ The component thread tells the worker thread to die
- ❑ The worker thread tells the component thread that it has died

This is handled using two more Win32 event objects. The component thread creates a non-signaled event object and passes it to the worker thread. The worker thread can check this event object periodically to see if it has been set. (Remember m_dwInterval? This is the interval between checks on this event object.) When the component thread is told to die (in other words, the EventChange component is being destroyed), it can set this event object to initiate the death of the worker thread. However, the component itself must not die at this point because the worker thread is still alive, and so there are resources that still need to be freed.

The component thread must wait until the worker thread has died, and it can do this by waiting on the worker thread handle. Once the thread has died, its handle becomes signaled (which means that it changes from the non-signaled to the signaled state), and the component thread can continue in its death throes.

Before we add the code, there is just a little more information about threads that you need to know. A thread is a unit of execution and, just like a process needs to have a main() function to operate, a thread needs a thread function. This function must have the signature:

```
unsigned __stdcall ThreadFunction(LPVOID);
```

The parameter is a void pointer that can be used to pass information to the thread when it is initialized. The return value is the handle of the thread, which can be used when waiting for a thread to die.

Our thread function should be a private method of the CEventChange class, since logically only the component can call it. However, to allow a method to access component data, C++ passes an implicit first parameter — the this pointer. If you did this, the thread function would not match the compulsory signature of a thread function. To prevent this from happening, you should make the function a class method, by declaring it as static. As a class method, however, it will not have access to any component's data (because it doesn't have a this pointer). To solve the problem, you should pass the this pointer via the LPVOID parameter of the method.

So, change the CEventChange class to add the thread function and associated data members:

```
private:
    DWORD m_dwInterval;
    static unsigned __stdcall Watch(LPVOID pThis);
    CComBSTR m_bstrEventName;
    HANDLE m_hThread;
    HANDLE m_hDie;
    HANDLE m_hEvent;
    BOOL m_bEventState;
};
```

Initialize these values in the constructor:

```
public:
    CEventChange()  : m_dwInterval(500),
                      m_hThread(NULL),
                      m_hDie(NULL),
                      m_hEvent(NULL),
                      m_bEventState(false)
    {
    }
```

m_bstrEventName is the name of the event for which the component should watch, and m_hEvent will hold the handle of the event that is being watched. Now we are ready to write the WatchEvent() method:

```
#include <process.h>

...

STDMETHODIMP CEventChange::WatchEvent(BSTR bstrEventName)
{
    // Check that the requested event actually exists
    USES_CONVERSION;

    HANDLE hEvent = OpenEvent(EVENT_ALL_ACCESS, false, W2T(bstrEventName));
    if(hEvent == NULL)
        return E_POINTER;

    m_bEventState = (WAIT_OBJECT_0 == WaitForSingleObject(hEvent, 0));

    if(m_hThread != NULL)
    {
        // Thread is already active, so suspend it and change the values
        SuspendThread(m_hThread);

        m_bstrEventName = bstrEventName;
        CloseHandle(m_hEvent);
        m_hEvent = hEvent;
        ResumeThread(m_hThread);

        return S_OK;
    }

    // Set up the values
    m_hEvent = hEvent;
    m_hDie = CreateEvent(NULL, true, false, NULL);
    m_bstrEventName = bstrEventName;

    // Start thread to watch this event
    unsigned threadID;
    m_hThread = (HANDLE)_beginthreadex(NULL, 0, Watch,
                                reinterpret_cast<void*>(this),
                                0, &threadID);
    return S_OK;
}
```

Let's go through this code line-by-line. First, we check to see if the named event exists — if it doesn't, there is no point in waiting for its state to change! The Win32 event object is created by another process, so we get access to it using OpenEvent(). If the named event does not exist, this function will return NULL and so the method should return immediately with an error.

The next section uses the WaitForSingleObject() function to test the state of the event. It does this by waiting with a timeout of 0ms, and testing to see if the return value is WAIT_OBJECT_0. If it is, the event is signaled.

Next, the code checks to see if the worker thread has already been created. If it has, then the code suspends it, clears up the previously set values, sets the new values and resumes the thread. There is a slight chance here that the worker thread could be suspended while it is using the m_bstrEventName or m_hEvent values. The code ignores this possibility, but you could use Win32 mutex objects to remove the risk completely.

If the thread has not already been created, this now needs to be done. Firstly, an event object is created that is used later in the program to indicate that the worker thread should die. Secondly, the name of the event object we are watching is cached, and finally the thread is created. The CRT method `_beginthreadex()` is used rather than Win32's `CreateThread()` because it ensures that the C runtime library is correctly initialized in the new thread. The address of the thread function is passed as a parameter, as well as the `this` pointer cast to a `void*`. The value returned from this function call is the handle of the thread.

Now that the worker thread has been created and started, the `WatchEvent()` method can return. As noted earlier, this is one way of writing an asynchronous COM method. Remember that COM calls are synchronous, so if `WatchEvent()` went into a loop checking for the state of an event object, it would block the client thread until `WatchEvent()` returned. A blocked client thread will freeze out its user interface, which is certainly not what we want.

You can now try to compile this file, but you will get the following error:

error C2065: '_beginthreadex' : undeclared identifier

The reason for this is that you've added a `#include` for the `process.h` header that declares `_beginthreadex()`, but this declaration is bracketed with the conditional compilation directive `#ifdef _MT`. To get the function declared, you need to define this symbol.

In order to do this, you'll have to change the CRT used by the project. Select Project | Settings... and then choose the C/C++ tab. From the **Category** box, select **Code Generation**, and finally in the **Use run-time library** select a multithreaded library appropriate to the build that is being performed. (One way is to select **All Configurations** from the **Settings For** box, and then select **Multithreaded** as the runtime library, then select **Multiple Configurations** with **Win32 Debug** and **Win32 Unicode Debug**, and in the runtime library select **Debug Multithreaded**.)

While you're editing the project settings, select all of the release builds and remove _ATL_MIN_CRT from the **Preprocessor definitions** section of the **Preprocessor** category dialog (also on the C++ tab). We are using the CRT in this example. You should be able to compile the project now, although it won't link, of course, because we haven't yet implemented the thread function.

The Worker Thread Function

The worker thread function should go into a loop to check for one of two events:

❏   The thread is told to die

❏   The requested event component changes state

Add this to `EventChange.cpp`:

```
unsigned __stdcall CEventChange::Watch(LPVOID pThis)
{
    CEventChange* pThisObject = static_cast<CEventChange*>(pThis);
    CoInitializeEx(NULL, COINIT_MULTITHREADED);

    while(true)
    {
        if(WAIT_OBJECT_0 == WaitForSingleObject(pThisObject->m_hDie, 0))
            break;

        if(WAIT_TIMEOUT == WaitForSingleObject(pThisObject->m_hEvent, 0))
        {
            // Event is not signaled
        }
        else
        {
            // Event is signaled
        }
        Sleep(pThisObject->m_dwInterval);
    }

    CoUninitialize();
    return 0;
}
```

The first thing to notice about this code is that the parameter passed to the thread function is cast to a `CEventChange` pointer, so that we can access the data members of the class. We have to do this because the `Watch()` method is `static`, so it has no `this` pointer and no direct access to a component's data.

Next, notice the calls to `CoInitializeEx()` and `CoUninitialize()`. This component is free-threaded, so it runs in a multithreaded apartment (MTA). Every thread in the MTA can access the COM component freely and concurrently, and it is the developer's responsibility to ensure that this will not cause a problem. To make a thread join an MTA, the thread must call `CoInitializeEx()` with the value `COINIT_MULTITHREADED`.

After that, there is the main loop. This checks to see if the thread should die by waiting on the `m_hDie` event object; again, a timeout of 0ms is used just to get the state of the event object. If this is signaled, then the loop is broken and the thread can clean up and die. If the thread should not die, then it needs to check for the state of the *named* event object and react according to the value returned. Between each iteration of the loop, the thread sleeps for the amount of time set by `SetInterval()`.

Since this server is going to be free threaded, you will need to change its initialization. By default, the server is initialized with a single-threaded apartment (STA) and all requests will come in via that STA. To make the object free-threaded, you will need to change the project so that the requests come in on a thread in the MTA. Open `stdafx.h` and change the definition of `_ATL_APARTMENT_THREADED` to define `_ATL_FREE_THREADED`:

```
#define _ATL_FREE_THREADED
```

```
#include <atlbase.h>
```

Killing The Worker Thread

The worker thread needs to be killed when the EventChange component is destroyed. The best way to do this is to give the CEventChange class a FinalRelease() method. This is effectively a destructor for the ATL component, and so the C++ component's state will still be valid.

In the declaration for CEventChange, add this line after the constructor:

```
CEventChange()  : m_dwInterval(500),
                  m_hThread(NULL),
                  m_hDie(NULL),
                  m_hEvent(NULL),
                  m_bEventState(false)
{
}

    void FinalRelease();
```

Now add the method itself to EventChange.cpp:

```
void CEventChange::FinalRelease()
{
    // Tell the thread to die
    SetEvent(m_hDie);

    // Wait for it to die
    WaitForSingleObject(m_hThread, INFINITE);

    CloseHandle(m_hDie);
    CloseHandle(m_hEvent);
    CloseHandle(m_hThread);
}
```

This method sets the m_hDie event object and then waits on the thread handle. This wait is infinite, so it won't time out. The WaitForSingleObject() function will return when the thread it is waiting on has died. At this point, the component can safely clean up the data members of the class. (Note that using CloseHandle() on a NULL parameter is perfectly safe.)

The next task is to define our outgoing interface. The Object Wizard has provided us with the _IEventChangeEvents dispinterface, so we may as well use that! Use ClassView to add the following methods:

```
[id(1)] void OnEventSet([in] BSTR bstrEventName);
[id(2)] void OnEventReset([in] BSTR bstrEventName);
```

These will be used by the EventChange component to inform the connected client that a particular Win32 event has changed its state, either from non-signaled to signaled (OnEventSet), or signaled to non-signaled (OnEventReset). The connected client can then perform some task based on this knowledge (if the event indicates that the NT event log has changed, for example, then the client can read the new event log record).

Now recompile the project so that the event methods are added to the type library. Then, right click on CEventChange and select Implement Connection Point... to bring up the proxy class generator again. Select _IEventChangeEvents and click on OK. We'll use the dynamic array implementation this time, so you don't need to change the CProxy_ class. The Wizard will derive CEventChange from the proxy class so that you can call the Fire_ methods in your component's code.

Before you do this, however, check the connection point map. Occasionally, the proxy generator will make a mistake and use the wrong interface IID:

```
BEGIN_CONNECTION_POINT_MAP(CEventChange)
    CONNECTION_POINT_ENTRY(IID__IEventChangeEvents)
END_CONNECTION_POINT_MAP()
```

The IID *should* be DIID__IEventChangeEvents (the D has been missed out). If this has happened, make the correction now. While you're looking at this header file, you can also remove the extra entry for the IConnectionPointContainer interface from the COM map if you wish:

```
BEGIN_COM_MAP(CEventChange)
    COM_INTERFACE_ENTRY(IEventChange)
    COM_INTERFACE_ENTRY(IDispatch)
    COM_INTERFACE_ENTRY(IConnectionPointContainer)
    COM_INTERFACE_ENTRY_IMPL(IConnectionPointContainer) // remove this line
END_COM_MAP()
```

Finally, you should fire events from the thread function:

```
unsigned __stdcall CEventChange::Watch(LPVOID pThis)
{
    CEventChange* pThisObject = static_cast<CEventChange*>(pThis);
    CoInitializeEx(NULL, COINIT_MULTITHREADED);

    while(true)
    {
        if(WAIT_OBJECT_0 == WaitForSingleObject(pThisObject->m_hDie, 0))
            break;

        if(WAIT_TIMEOUT == WaitForSingleObject(pThisObject->m_hEvent, 0))
        {
            // Event is not signaled
            if(pThisObject->m_bEventState)
            {
                // Previously signaled, state changed
                pThisObject->m_bEventState = false;
                pThisObject->Fire_OnEventReset(pThisObject->m_bstrEventName);
            }
        }
        else
        {
            // Event is signaled
            if(!pThisObject->m_bEventState)
            {
                // Previously not signaled, state changed
                pThisObject->m_bEventState = true;
                pThisObject->Fire_OnEventSet(pThisObject->m_bstrEventName);
            }
        }
        Sleep(pThisObject->m_dwInterval);
    }

    CoUninitialize();
    return 0;
}
```

The code checks the state of the Win32 event object against m_bEventState. If the state has changed, the appropriate event is generated. That's all the code you need to write for this component, so build the project, and we can move on.

EventCtrl Client

The client will contain an ActiveX control called EventControl. The component doesn't *have* to be an ActiveX control, but we'll need some visual feedback to demonstrate that events are being fired from EventChange. ATL does almost everything necessary to implement a control, so it makes the coding simple. You will see more about the details of controls in the remainder of this book.

Close the EventWatcher project and start a new one. Use the ATL COM AppWizard to create a DLL project with the name EventCtrl. We now need to perform two steps:

- ❑ Create the ActiveX control
- ❑ Create the sink interface

ActiveX Control

Insert a new Full Control using the Object Wizard, and give it a short name of EventControl. This control will catch events from the EventChange component, so it must implement the outgoing interface of EventChange. That means we have two options: we can either change our new control's interface to _IEventChangeEvents and use that to catch the event, or we can use an **event sink map**.

The outgoing interface of EventChange is a dispinterface, so the 'catcher' component must implement IDispatch and handle the DISPIDs of the methods on it. If you make sure that the methods in the control's dual interface have the same DISPIDs and signatures as the methods in the outgoing interface, then you can use that to implement the dispinterface. However, the connectable component will query the control for the dispinterface and not the control's interface, so you need to indicate that one is implemented by the other. If you were to go down this route, you would implement the COM map something like this:

```
BEGIN_COM_MAP(CEventControl)
    COM_INTERFACE_ENTRY(IEventControl)
    COM_INTERFACE_ENTRY(IDispatch)
    COM_INTERFACE_ENTRY_IID(DIID__IEventChangeEvents, IEventControl)
```

While this does work, there is a problem: it requires that the dual interface has the same methods as the dispinterface. The trouble is, dual interfaces are immutable, which means that once you have published it, you cannot change it. Dispinterfaces are not immutable, so once the event catcher component has been released, the event generator can add new methods to the dispinterface that won't be caught by the other component. To catch these new events, the new version of the catcher component will have to define a *new* dual interface (most likely deriving from the previous dual), a situation that can lead to a proliferation of interfaces. We won't implement the event catching code using dual interfaces, so don't make this change.

Event Sink Maps

ATL 3.0 introduced a new map called the **event sink map**, which allows a component to implement a generic IDispatch interface. It is used to map component methods to DISPIDs. The actual implementation of IDispatch is obtained by deriving from IDispEventImpl<> or IDispEventSimpleImpl<>, which provide for slightly different ways of doing things.

IDispEventSimpleImpl<> is so named because it requires static information about the event methods that it will handle, which is 'simpler' than the technique IDispEventImpl<> uses (it requires type information about the connectable component in order to determine the event method signatures at runtime). If you can get type information, this is often a good idea, because it makes the sink map simpler. However, providing static information within the sink component makes the catching code more efficient (because the type information lookup does not have to be performed). In this example, we will use IDispEventSimpleImpl<>.

> The event sink map is used by composite controls (in which a single 'parent' control is made up of several 'child' controls), where the parent needs to catch events from its children. When you're building a composite control, you can use the ClassWizard to add event handlers; in this example we will do the work by hand.

`IDispEventSimpleImpl<>` looks like this:

```
template <UINT nID, class T, const IID* pdiid>
class ATL_NO_VTABLE IDispEventSimpleImpl : public _IDispEventLocator<nID, pdiid>
```

The `nID` is a unique identifier for the source of the events. If the class were being used as part of a composite control, this would be the ID of a child control. (Composite controls are based on a dialog template, so in fact it would be the child window ID of the child control.) If our control were to sink events from many different connectable components, we would need a different ID for each source, which allows two things: we can use a different handler method for the same event generated by different sources, and we can provide a different identity for each sink object. (To do the latter we would need to derive from `IDispEventSimpleImpl<>` multiple times, once for each sink object.) The `nID` thus acts to create different classes from the template, so that we can derive from it multiply.

The `class T` is the control class, so that `IDispEventSimpleImpl<>` can access the sink map, and `pdiid` is the event dispinterface. `_IDispEventLocator<>` derives from a class called `_IDispEvent` that provides methods to make and break the connection to the connectable component.

Open `EventControl.h` and add the following:

```
#include "resource.h"        // main symbols
#include <atlctl.h>
#include "..\EventWatcher\EventWatcher.h"
#define EVENTCHANGE_ID 1
```

This gives us access to the sink interface's IID, and defines a symbol with a unique ID that can be used when deriving `CEventControl` from `IDispEventSimpleImpl<>`. While you're adding this derivation, add type library versions to `IDispatchImpl<>` and `IProvideClassInfo2<>`:

```
public CComObjectRootEx<CComSingleThreadModel>,
public IDispatchImpl<IEventControl, &IID_IEventControl,
                     &LIBID_EVENTCTRLLib, 1, 0>,
public CComControl<CEventControl>,

...

public IDataObjectImpl<CEventControl>,
public IProvideClassInfo2Impl<&CLSID_EventControl, NULL,
                     &LIBID_EVENTCTRLLib, 1, 0>,
public CComCoClass<CEventControl, &CLSID_EventControl>,
public IDispEventSimpleImpl<EVENTCHANGE_ID, CEventControl,
                     &__uuidof(_IEventChangeEvents)>
{
```

The parameters to `IDispEventSimpleImpl<>` are the unique ID, the control class and the address of the sink IID as obtained through `__uuidof()`. We can now add the sink map, just after the message map:

```
BEGIN_SINK_MAP(CEventControl)
    SINK_ENTRY_INFO(EVENTCHANGE_ID, __uuidof(_IEventChangeEvents), 1,
                    OnEventSet, &infoEventSet)
    SINK_ENTRY_INFO(EVENTCHANGE_ID, __uuidof(_IEventChangeEvents), 2,
                    OnEventReset, &infoEventReset)
END_SINK_MAP()
```

The entries contain the source ID and the dispinterface IID, which connects them to the `IDispEventSimpleImpl<>` base class. The next parameter is the DISPID of the event method that will be handled, and that's followed by the name of a method in the class that will be called when the event is generated. These handlers must have the same signature as the event method, and must use the `__stdcall` calling convention. Add these beneath the sink map:

```
    void __stdcall OnEventSet(BSTR bstrEventName);
    void __stdcall OnEventReset(BSTR bstrEventName);
```

`IDispEventSimpleImpl<>` implements `Invoke()`, which will use the sink map to dispatch calls based on their DISPIDs. The parameters of the event method will be passed to `IDispEventSimpleImpl<>::Invoke()` in a DISPPARAMS parameter. In order to call the control's handler method, this implementation of `Invoke()` uses an API method called `DispCallFunc()` that requires information about the method's calling convention, parameters and return type.

If you use `IDispEventImpl<>` to implement the sink interface, this data can be obtained from type information, but since we're using `IDispEventSimpleImpl<>`, we need to provide it ourselves. ATL uses a `struct` called `_ATL_FUNC_INFO`:

```
struct _ATL_FUNC_INFO
{
    CALLCONV cc;                        // The method calling convention
    VARTYPE vtReturn;                   // The return type
    SHORT nParams;                      // The number of parameters
    VARTYPE pVarTypes[_ATL_MAX_VARTYPES]; // Description of the parameters
};
```

The calling convention must always be `CC_STDCALL`. `vtReturn` gives the Automation type returned by the event method, so we can use `VT_EMPTY` to represent `void`. Similarly, `pVarTypes` gives the types of all the parameters. We can define two structures as global variables in `EventControl.h`:

```
#define EVENTCHANGE_ID 1
__declspec(selectany) _ATL_FUNC_INFO infoEventSet = {CC_STDCALL, VT_EMPTY, 1,
                                                     {VT_BSTR}};
__declspec(selectany) _ATL_FUNC_INFO infoEventReset = {CC_STDCALL, VT_EMPTY, 1,
                                                       {VT_BSTR}};
```

These could be defined in the `CEventsControl` class, but because the sink map defines a `static` array, it would mean that they too would have been `static`, introducing the pain of having to declare the storage in the CPP file. Declaring them as globals brings problems of its own, because every CPP file that includes this header will generate storage, and the linker will complain. The solution is to use `__declspec(selectany)`, which tells the linker to use just one of these and ignore the others.

Now let's look quickly at the code that will display the control. We won't go into great detail here because this kind of code will be covered in Chapter 10, but you should be able to understand what's going on. Go back to the `EventControl.h` file and add a private data member and two methods to the bottom of the class:

```
public:
    HRESULT FinalConstruct();
    void FinalRelease();

private:
    LPTSTR m_strEventStatus;
};
```

The variable will hold a textual description of the event object state — that is, whether the named event object that we will be checking is signaled or not. We need to initialize this, so the `FinalConstruct()` method is declared. The string must also be freed when the control is destroyed, so `FinalRelease()` is declared to do that. Finally, we need the control to tell us what the event object state is, which should be done by the `OnDraw()` method that the Object Wizard has added to the class; we need to change it to display the `m_strEventStatus` value.

We'll move `OnDraw()` into `EventControl.cpp`, so replace its code in `EventControl.h` with the simple declaration:

```
    HRESULT OnDraw(ATL_DRAWINFO& di);
```

And add the following to `EventControl.cpp` (the highlighted lines show the differences from the original code):

```
HRESULT CEventControl::OnDraw(ATL_DRAWINFO& di)
{
    RECT& rc = *(RECT*)di.prcBounds;
    Rectangle(di.hdcDraw, rc.left, rc.top, rc.right, rc.bottom);

    SetTextAlign(di.hdcDraw, TA_CENTER|TA_BASELINE);
    TextOut(di.hdcDraw,
            (rc.left + rc.right) / 2,
            (rc.top + rc.bottom) / 2,
            m_strEventStatus,
            lstrlen(m_strEventStatus));

    return S_OK;
}
```

The other two methods look like this:

```
HRESULT CEventControl::FinalConstruct()
{
    m_strEventStatus = new TCHAR[14 * sizeof(TCHAR)];
    lstrcpy(m_strEventStatus, _T("Uninitialized"));
    return S_OK;
}

void CEventControl::FinalRelease()
{
    delete [] m_strEventStatus;
}
```

We will change `m_strEventStatus` when the control discovers from `EventChange` that the named event object's state has changed.

Handler Methods

Next, we need to add code for the handler methods to change the status string when events are generated. In `EventControl.cpp`, add the definitions of the handler classes we declared earlier:

```
STDMETHODIMP_(void) CEventControl::OnEventSet(BSTR bstrEventName)
{
    USES_CONVERSION;
    LPTSTR strEvt = OLE2T(bstrEventName);
    delete [] m_strEventStatus;

    // Save space for name and message
    m_strEventStatus = new TCHAR[lstrlen(strEvt) + 8];
    wsprintf(m_strEventStatus, _T("%s is SET"), strEvt);
    FireViewChange();
}
```

```
STDMETHODIMP_(void) CEventControl::OnEventReset(BSTR bstrEventName)
{
    USES_CONVERSION;
    LPTSTR strEvt = OLE2T(bstrEventName);
    delete [] m_strEventStatus;

    // Save space for name and message
    m_strEventStatus = new TCHAR[lstrlen(strEvt) + 10];
    wsprintf(m_strEventStatus, _T("%s is RESET"), strEvt);
    FireViewChange();
}
```

The code copies the name of the event and the current state into the `m_strEventStatus` data member, and the `FireViewChange()` function is called to tell the control to redraw itself. Compile this code at this point to convince yourself that you have typed in everything correctly! The control now has all the code that it needs to update itself when the state of the event object changes.

Connecting The Two Together

Let's consider where we're up to:

❑ The server has a connection point to which the client can connect, and it will generate events

❑ The client has a sink interface and code to change the display of the control when the sink interface is called

Now we need to add code that actually makes the connection to the server.

Calling The Server

First, we need to create an `EventChange` object and hold an interface pointer to. Add the following private data member:

```
private:
    LPTSTR m_strEventStatus;
    CComPtr<IEventChange> m_ptr;
};
```

Now you need to create the `EventChange` object. `FinalConstruct()` is the best place to do it, so implement it like this:

```
HRESULT CEventControl::FinalConstruct()
{
    m_strEventStatus = new TCHAR[14 * sizeof(TCHAR)];
    lstrcpy(m_strEventStatus, _T("Uninitialized"));

    HRESULT hr = m_ptr.CoCreateInstance(__uuidof(EventChange));
    if(SUCCEEDED(hr))
    {
        if(m_dwEventCookie != 0xFEFEFEFE)
            DispEventUnadvise(m_ptr);

        // The event name
        CComBSTR bstrEventName = L"Test";

        // Make connection
        hr = DispEventAdvise(m_ptr);
        if(FAILED(hr))
            return hr;
        m_ptr->WatchEvent(bstrEventName);
    }
    return hr;
}
```

The smart pointer class `CComPtr<>` is used to create an instance of the connectable component with the `CoCreateInstance()` method. Next, the connection is made by calling `DispEventAdvise()`, which is inherited from the `_IDispEvent` class we mentioned earlier. If a connection has already been made to the component, the inherited `m_dwEventCookie` will contain a value other than the magic number `0xFEFEFEFE`, in which case the connection is broken before being remade.

The parameter to `DispEventAdvise()` is the `IUnknown` of the server component, which gets passed on to `AtlAdvise()`. The other parameters required by this method are provided by `IDispEventSimplImpl<>`. After that, the server is called and told to watch a particular event.

When the control is destroyed, the connection needs to be broken by calling `DispEventUnadvise()`. You may think that it should be called in `FinalRelease()`, but the latter is only called when the reference count falls to zero, and that won't happen because the `EventChange` component will still have a reference to the control's sink interface. We need to find a different solution.

Fortunately, the control implements the `IOleObject` interface, which has a method called `Close()` that's called when the control is being destroyed by the container. ATL implements this in `IOleObjectImpl<>`, which is a base class of our control, so you need override the method. In the header, add:

```
STDMETHOD(Close)(DWORD dwSaveOption);
```

And in the `.cpp` file:

```
STDMETHODIMP CEventControl::Close(DWORD dwSaveOption)
{
    HRESULT hr = IOleObjectImpl<CEventControl>::Close(dwSaveOption);
    if(m_dwEventCookie != 0xFEFEFEFE)
        DispEventUnadvise(m_ptr);

    return hr;
}
```

You now have a working version of the control that, barring any errors, you should be able to compile.

SetEvent

To be able to test this example, you need to be able to create (and change the state of) a Win32 kernel object. To do this, you need to create and compile the SetEvent project. This project will have a user interface, so we'll base it on an ATL dialog using the procedure we saw in the last chapter. First, create a new Win32 Application project called SetEvent, and on the Wizard's single step select A simple Win32 application.

Adding ATL Support

You've seen the steps required to add ATL support to a project before, but it will do no harm if we run through them quickly, to refresh your memory. The first step is to edit the stdafx.h file to support ATL, replacing the line that includes <windows.h> with:

```
#define WIN32_LEAN_AND_MEAN    // Exclude rarely-used stuff from Windows headers

#include <atlbase.h>
extern CComModule _Module;
#include <atlcom.h>
#include <atlwin.h>
```

Next, you need to add the following to SetEvent.cpp:

```
#include "stdafx.h"
CComModule _Module;

BEGIN_OBJECT_MAP(ObjectMap)
END_OBJECT_MAP()

int APIENTRY WinMain(HINSTANCE hInstance,
                     HINSTANCE hPrevInstance,
                     LPSTR     lpCmdLine,
                     int       nCmdShow)
{
    _Module.Init(NULL, hInstance);
    return 0;
}
```

You also need to add a file called SetEvent.idl to the project, containing simply:

```
library SetEvent
{
};
```

This IDL file shouldn't be compiled as part of the project, so exclude it via its Settings dialog.

Adding The Dialog Class

With the changes we've just made, we should be able to add a dialog using the ATL Object Wizard. Do this now, creating a dialog class with a short name of EventDialog.

Next, modify the dialog resource so that its caption is SetEvent. Delete the Cancel button and add the following controls (with the indicated IDs), resizing the dialog to accommodate them all:

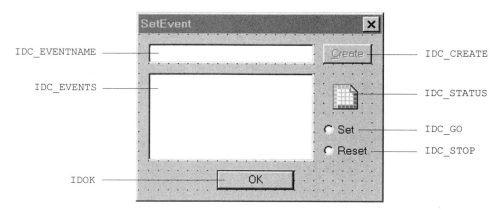

IDC_STATUS is a picture control of type Icon; IDC_EVENTS is a list box. You should arrange the controls so that the tab order is:

- ❑   IDC_EVENTNAME
- ❑   IDC_CREATE
- ❑   IDC_EVENTS
- ❑   IDC_STATUS
- ❑   IDC_GO
- ❑   IDC_STOP
- ❑   IDOK

Then, group the radio buttons by making sure that IDC_GO and IDOK (sic) have Group and Tab stop checked, and disable the Create button by selecting the Disabled check box in its properties.

The picture box holds icons that show the state of the selected event. To implement this, copy the 'traffic signals' icons from Visual Basic (they're in the common\graphics\icons\traffic folder of the first CD of the Enterprise Edition) into the project folder. Now move back to ResourceView, right-click on SetEvent resources folder, and select Import.... Once you have imported the three icons, use Explorer to remove their read-only attribute.

If you do not have the Visual Basic CDs to hand, create three icons: one that has a green circle, another with a yellow circle and the final one with a red circle.

Now rename the symbols by right clicking on them and selecting **Properties**. Here are the names to use:

File	Symbol
Trffc10a.ico	IDI_GO
Trffc10b.ico	IDI_READY
Trffc10c.ico	IDI_STOP

Now go back to the dialog and change the IDC_STATUS control to have the **Image** of IDI_READY.

Next, we need to make a few changes to the generated EventDialog.h header. We're not hosting any ActiveX controls, so we can derive our dialog from CDialogImpl<> instead of CAxDialogImpl<>. Because of this, we can also remove the #include for atlhost.h.

The other changes we can make are to remove the handler for IDCANCEL — we've removed the **Cancel** button — and include atlcontrols.h (we'll be using the wrapper classes it contains in this example).

The code for EventDialog.h should look like this (the lines that can be removed are shown highlighted and commented out for clarity):

```cpp
#include "resource.h"        // main symbols
// #include <atlhost.h>
#include "atlcontrols.h"

///////////////////////////////////////////////////////////////////////
// CEventDialog
class CEventDialog :
    public CDialogImpl<CEventDialog>
{
public:
    CEventDialog()
    {
    }

    ~CEventDialog()
    {
    }

    enum { IDD = IDD_EVENTDIALOG };

BEGIN_MSG_MAP(CEventDialog)
    MESSAGE_HANDLER(WM_INITDIALOG, OnInitDialog)
    COMMAND_ID_HANDLER(IDOK, OnOK)
    // COMMAND_ID_HANDLER(IDCANCEL, OnCancel)
END_MSG_MAP()

    LRESULT OnInitDialog(UINT uMsg, WPARAM wParam, LPARAM lParam, BOOL& bHandled)
    {
        return 1;  // Let the system set the focus
    }

    LRESULT OnOK(WORD wNotifyCode, WORD wID, HWND hWndCtl, BOOL& bHandled)
    {
        EndDialog(wID);
        return 0;
    }

    // LRESULT OnCancel(WORD wNotifyCode, WORD wID, HWND hWndCtl, BOOL& bHandled)
    // {
    //     EndDialog(wID);
    //     return 0;
    // }
};
```

Add an instance of this class to the main `.cpp` file (`SetEvent.cpp`) so that when the executable starts, the dialog is created. So that `WinMain()` does not return immediately, create the dialog as a modal dialog using `DoModal()`:

```
#include "stdafx.h"
#include "EventDialog.h"
CComModule _Module;

BEGIN_OBJECT_MAP(ObjectMap)
END_OBJECT_MAP()

int APIENTRY WinMain(HINSTANCE hInstance,
                     HINSTANCE hPrevInstance,
                     LPSTR     lpCmdLine,
                     int       nCmdShow)
{
    _Module.Init(NULL, hInstance);
    CEventDialog dlg;
    dlg.DoModal();
    return 0;
}
```

Handling Windows Events

The majority of the code in this project will be to handle various Windows events as the user navigates through the controls on the dialog. The user will use the dialog in this way:

❑ Create an event by typing a name in the top edit box and then clicking the **Create** button. This adds the event name to the list box.

❑ The user can then select the name of an event in the list box, and the state of the event will be shown using the radio buttons and the picture box.

❑ The user changes an event's state by clicking on the radio buttons.

The handles of the created kernel event objects will be held as data members of the list box, which simplifies the code so that you do not need to maintain a separate map. When the dialog is dismissed, the code will go through all these handles and release them.

The first event we need to handle is to enable the **Create** button if the edit box has a value. Right-click on `CEventDialog` in ClassView and select **Add Windows Message Handler...** to get the **New Windows Message and Event Handlers for class CEventDialog** dialog. From the **Class or object to handle** list box, select `IDC_EVENTNAME`, and from **New Windows messages/events** select the `EN_CHANGE` message. When you click on **Add and Edit** you will get a dialog asking you for a name; for now, accept the suggested `OnChangeEventname()`. In this method, you need to enable or disable the button depending on whether there is text in the edit box:

```
LRESULT OnChangeEventname(WORD wNotifyCode, WORD wID,
                          HWND hWndCtl, BOOL& bHandled)
{
    ATLControls::CButton btnCreate = GetDlgItem(IDC_CREATE);
    ATLControls::CEdit edEventName(hWndCtl);
    btnCreate.EnableWindow(edEventName.GetWindowTextLength() > 0);
    return 0;
}
```

This code simply initializes objects for the button and the edit box, then tests the number of characters in the edit box and passes this to `EnableWindow()` method of the button.

Next, we need to handle the user clicking on the **Create** button, and to do so we'll use another way to get to the message handler Wizard. Open the dialog from ResourceView, right click on it, and select **Events...** from the context menu. This will start the Wizard, and you can then select IDC_CREATE as the object to handle and BN_CLICKED as the message. Click on **Add and Edit** and accept the default name. Add the following code:

```
LRESULT OnClickedCreate(WORD wNotifyCode, WORD wID,
                        HWND hWndCtl, BOOL& bHandled)
{
    ATLControls::CListBox lstEvents = GetDlgItem(IDC_EVENTS);
    ATLControls::CEdit edEventName = GetDlgItem(IDC_EVENTNAME);

    LPTSTR strEvent;
    int len = edEventName.GetWindowTextLength() + 1;
    strEvent = new TCHAR[len];
    edEventName.GetWindowText(strEvent, len);

    if(lstEvents.FindString(-1, strEvent) == LB_ERR)
    {
        // Does not exist so we can add it
        HANDLE hEvent = CreateEvent(NULL, true, false, strEvent);
        if(hEvent)
        {
            int pos = lstEvents.AddString(strEvent);
            lstEvents.SetItemData(pos, reinterpret_cast<DWORD>(hEvent));
            lstEvents.SetCurSel(pos);
            OnSelchangeEvents(0, 0, 0, bHandled);
        }
    }
    delete [] strEvent;

    return 0;
}
```

This checks to see if the list box already has an entry for this event. If not, it creates an event kernel object and adds the event name into the list box. The handle for this event is added as the associated item data. Note that if the event object already exists, the handle for *that* event object is returned. The code then calls OnSelchangeEvents() to update the icon and radio buttons.

The next task is to add a handler for when the list box selection changes. Use the Wizard to add a handler for the LBN_SELCHANGE message of IDC_EVENTS and accept the method name of OnSelchangeEvents():

```
LRESULT OnSelchangeEvents(WORD wNotifyCode, WORD wID,
                          HWND hWndCtl, BOOL& bHandled)
{
    ATLControls::CListBox lstEvents = GetDlgItem(IDC_EVENTS);
    ATLControls::CStatic bmpIcon = GetDlgItem(IDC_STATUS);
    int pos = lstEvents.GetCurSel();

    HICON hIcon;
    HANDLE hEvent = reinterpret_cast<HANDLE>(lstEvents.GetItemData(pos));

    // Get the status of the event
    if(WAIT_OBJECT_0 == WaitForSingleObject(hEvent,0))
    {
        // Event is set
        hIcon = LoadIcon(_Module.GetResourceInstance(),
                         MAKEINTRESOURCE(IDI_GO));
        CheckDlgButton(IDC_GO, 1);
        CheckDlgButton(IDC_STOP, 0);
    }
```

```
      else
      {
         // Event is not set
         hIcon = LoadIcon(_Module.GetResourceInstance(),
                     MAKEINTRESOURCE(IDI_STOP));
         CheckDlgButton(IDC_STOP, 1);
         CheckDlgButton(IDC_GO, 0);
      }

      bmpIcon.SetIcon(hIcon);
      return 0;
   }
```

This gets the data associated with the selected list box item and casts it to an event handle. It then checks for the state of the event with `WaitForSingleObject()` and sets the radio buttons and the icon in the picture control.

The process can now add events and view their states. There are two more tasks to do: change the event state, and handle the shutdown of the process. The first is done by handling the 'click' events on the radio buttons, so in the Wizard add handlers for the `BN_CLICKED` messages, calling them `OnClickedGo()` and `OnClickedStop()`:

```
   LRESULT OnClickedGo(WORD wNotifyCode, WORD wID,
                     HWND hWndCtl, BOOL& bHandled)
   {
      ATLControls::CListBox lstEvents = GetDlgItem(IDC_EVENTS);
      ATLControls::CStatic bmpIcon = GetDlgItem(IDC_STATUS);

      int pos = lstEvents.GetCurSel();
      HANDLE hEvent = reinterpret_cast<HANDLE>(lstEvents.GetItemData(pos));
      SetEvent(hEvent);

      HICON hIcon = LoadIcon(_Module.GetResourceInstance(),
                     MAKEINTRESOURCE(IDI_GO));
      bmpIcon.SetIcon(hIcon);
      return 0;
   }

   LRESULT OnClickedStop(WORD wNotifyCode, WORD wID,
                     HWND hWndCtl, BOOL& bHandled)
   {
      ATLControls::CListBox lstEvents = GetDlgItem(IDC_EVENTS);
      ATLControls::CStatic bmpIcon = GetDlgItem(IDC_STATUS);

      int pos = lstEvents.GetCurSel();
      HANDLE hEvent = reinterpret_cast<HANDLE>(lstEvents.GetItemData(pos));
      ResetEvent(hEvent);

      HICON hIcon = LoadIcon(_Module.GetResourceInstance(),
                     MAKEINTRESOURCE(IDI_STOP));
      bmpIcon.SetIcon(hIcon);
      return 0;
   }
```

Finally, when the process closes, it needs to go through all the items in the list box and close all the handles held as item data. Note that if another process has opened one of these events, the event will not be destroyed. It is only when the last reference on an event handle has been closed with `CloseHandle()` that the object will be destroyed.

To do this, add a handler for WM_CLOSE. In the Wizard, select CEventDialog in the **Class** list box and WM_CLOSE in the **Messages** box. Then click on **Add and Edit** and enter the following:

```
LRESULT OnClose(UINT uMsg, WPARAM wParam, LPARAM lParam, BOOL& bHandled)
{
    // Release all the event objects
    ATLControls::CListBox lstEvents = GetDlgItem(IDC_EVENTS);

    int count = lstEvents.GetCount();
    count--;

    while(count >= 0)
    {
        HANDLE hEvent = reinterpret_cast<HANDLE>(lstEvents.GetItemData(count));
        CloseHandle(hEvent);
        count--;
    }
    EndDialog(0);
    return 0;
}
```

Now that you have a WM_CLOSE handler, change OnOK() so that the handles are released when the **OK** button is clicked:

```
LRESULT OnOK(WORD wNotifyCode, WORD wID, HWND hWndCtl, BOOL& bHandled)
{
    OnClose(0, 0, 0, bHandled);
    return 0;
}
```

Testing

At long last, you should be able to compile the project and test it out. The first test is to run the process and type a name in the edit box — the **Create** button should become enabled. Click on this to create a new event. You should be able to use the radio buttons to change the state, which should show up by the lights on the traffic lights changing. Try and add several events to check that they can have different states.

In the second test, run two instances of the process and use it to create the same named event in both instances. In one instance, change the state (say, from **Set** to **Reset**) and then tab to the other instance and select the event name from the list box. You should see the event state change to reflect the change caused in the other instance.

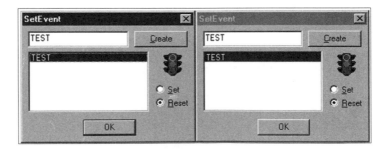

These checks should prove to you that the process is able to create and change the states of kernel event objects.

Testing The Whole Example

If there are problems when you test the example, you will need to debug the projects, and the three projects are debugged in different ways. The technique for SetEvent will be the most familiar to you: you should set breakpoints in the code and then run the project under the debugger. You can test how various Windows messages are handled by clicking on various controls on the dialog and checking that the code is handling them correctly.

For the EventWatcher project, you can still set breakpoints and run the server, but for any of the breakpoints to be reached, you will need to create an object using a client: the EventControl component. Since this is a DLL, you will need to use a container. The two options here are to use Internet Explorer (the ATL Wizard will have created an HTML file for you) or the ActiveX Control Test Container. The easier technique is to use the Test Container.

To specify that this should be used, select Project | Settings... and switch to the Debug tab. Then, click on the arrow button next to the Executable for debug session and choose ActiveX Control Test Container from the menu that appears. Now, when you press F5 to debug the component server, the Test Container will be started (ignore any warnings that it does not contain any debug information). From here, you can select Insert New Control... from the Edit menu and add the EventControl class.

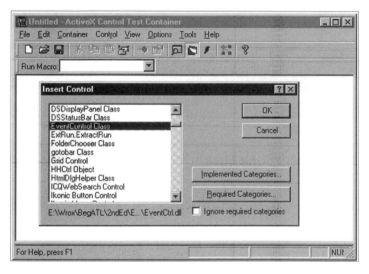

If the component is not created, the most likely reason for failure is security. COM on Windows NT 4 maintains a list of the user accounts (and groups) that can create and access a component. If you are logged on as a user other than one of those expressly allowed to launch and access the EventChange component, the EventControl control will not be able to create or access it. You should use Dcomcnfg.exe to add your user account to the list of accounts allowed to launch and access this class (Chapter 6 has details of how to do this). The EventChange component will need to callback on the EventControl control to fire an event, and so the account that the EventChange component is running under will need to have access to the EventControl.

At first, the control will not have had a callback from the server component, so you will get the Uninitialized caption:

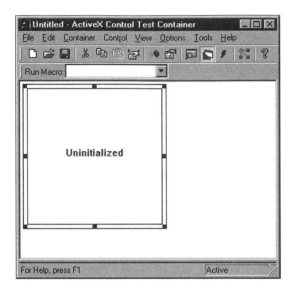

However, when you change the event state with SetEvent, the control will be updated with the value. Proof positive that your components are behaving as they should.

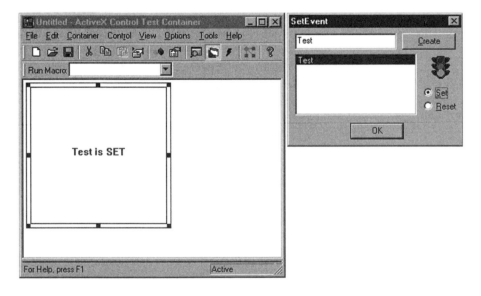

Summary

This chapter started by looking at controls, which are basically COM components with a user interface. In order to better communicate with other COM components in the Windows environment, we saw how these controls can utilize connection points. The advantage of this sort of communication is in its versatility; we saw several connection topologies that would be impossible otherwise.

After the general theory, this chapter has covered how ATL allows us to implement connection points, via templated implementations of the required interfaces, connection point maps, and sink maps. We also saw how the ATL Wizard for implementing connection points can make our life easier, illustrating all this with a simple event firing control.

Next, after a brief look into the future of COM+ events, a much larger example was presented. This example contained two connectable objects, one that monitored Win32 event objects, and the other (the client object) that was informed (via a connection with the monitoring object) when events occurred. A third project was created to manipulate Win32 events and trigger this process.

Along the way, we had the chance to experiment with some issues about events and threading, and to make use of some of the window classes introduced in the previous chapter.

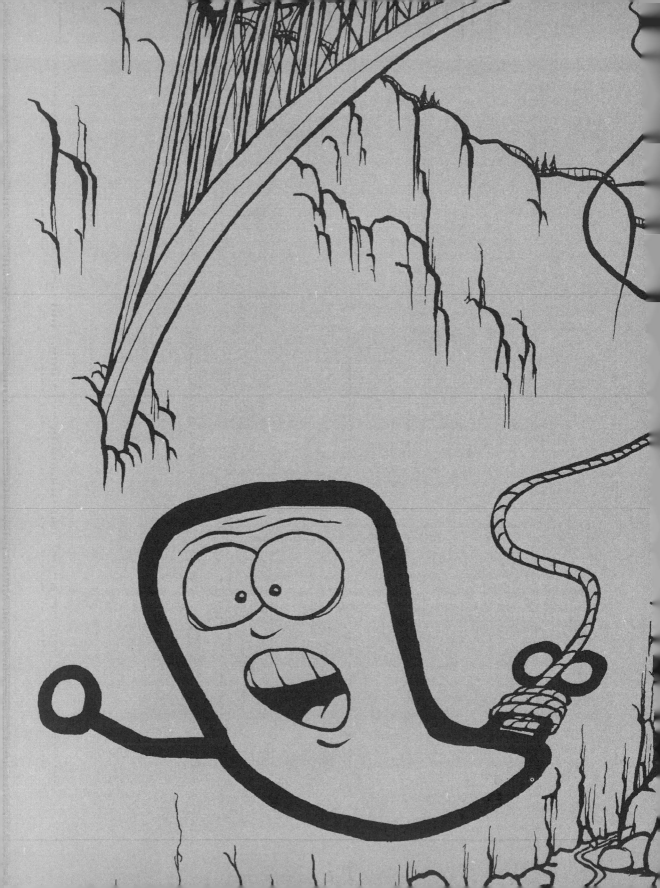

Properties, Persistence and Collections

An ActiveX control will usually hold some internal **state**, which in many cases will need to be initialized when the control is first created, and saved (made **persistent**) before the control is destroyed. Furthermore, if the control is part of a document (for example, a Word document, or an Excel spreadsheet), then when the document is made persistent, so should any objects within the document. To do this, the container should ask all its objects to save their state.

There are other situations where property persistence is important. When you put a control on a Visual Basic form, you use the Properties dialog to affect its display and behavior. When you save the Visual Basic project, these properties must be persisted to a file; when you compile a Visual Basic application, the properties must be persisted in way that can be saved in the compiled code. Also, if the control is used on a web page, the control's properties should be available on that web page to initialize it.

This chapter covers three main subject areas:

❏ **Properties** — the data items that controls expose
❏ **Persistence** — the general method of making a control persistent
❏ **Collections** — how to create and access collections of properties

Control Properties

An ActiveX control can have an internal state, and the object may expose this state using **properties**. Properties come in several forms. They can be simple, single items of data, or they can be arrays of data. As you have seen many times, although a property is viewed from the client as a data item, they are actually exposed from the object using methods: a readable property has a get_ method, and a writable property has a put_ method. Since properties are designed for use with scripting languages, the put_ method should have the [out] parameter marked as [retval], so that the scripting language treats it as the return value.

Single item properties can be exposed by single-parameter put_ and get_ methods, but array properties are rather more complicated. We looked at how to do this in Chapter 5: Automation defines an array type called a SAFEARRAY that describes the type, size and bounds of the array.

ActiveX controls that expose properties are intimately involved with Automation. Of course, you can expose properties without using Automation, but an object that does so will be excluded from use with containers that use late binding, and this means you will not be able to use the object with Internet Explorer or an Active Server Page. To make an ActiveX control useful for all common containers, it should be an Automation object, and so expose a dispinterface or a dual interface. When I talk about properties in this chapter, you can assume that I mean Automation properties.

Arrays are fine, but iterating through an array is tedious, and there are other ways of working with them. Arrays of data can be exposed as **enumerators** or **collections**. Enumerator objects expose an interface that has methods allowing you to read arrays of values. You saw an enumerator briefly in the last chapter when we looked at the connection point interfaces, but that is far from the extent of their usefulness. Enumerations are used extensively in COM.

A collection is an extended array of data that gives access to its members using a map-like syntax by using a keyword, or by using an array-like syntax with an index. Furthermore, iterating through collections really shines with VBA, because it has the `For Each` statement that allows iteration without requiring an index. Collections are not exposed from an object through a single method (like SAFEARRAYs) or a single interface (like enumerators), but instead are exposed through a number of methods.

The properties of an ActiveX control can be used to affect how a control displays itself. A control can implement two sorts of properties: **custom properties**, which are specific to a particular control and are described by its type library, and **stock properties**, which have standard DISPIDs and so are known to all control containers. Note that *containers* can also have **ambient properties**, which an ActiveX control can read and use to take on the look and feel of the container.

This first section will concentrate on single item properties. Array properties, enumerators and collections will be covered later in the chapter.

Custom Properties

Custom properties are simply properties on the control's interface, so adding to and maintaining properties on a control involves the same techniques as for the properties on any interface.

This is straightforward. When you want to add a property, you can either do it the hard way — editing the IDL by hand — or the easy way, by using ClassView. We will take the easy route. Usually, you can give the property a DISPID by allowing the Wizard to assign an `[id()]` attribute for you. However, if you want to, you can use ClassView to specify a value. Giving a property a specific DISPID is necessary when you want to expose the required properties of a collection (explained later), or a stock property.

Stock Properties

When you add a property to an interface, you give it a DISPID. However, a container does not normally know what a DISPID of (say) 2 means, since different interfaces will use it for different properties (if at all). On the other hand, controls of all types will have certain properties in common: background color, foreground color and text font, for example. It makes sense that these stock properties should have well known values, so that when a container sees that a control supports a property with a particular DISPID, it knows exactly what the property is. To distinguish between custom properties and system-defined stock properties, the DISPIDs of custom properties are positive and those of stock properties are negative.

The following table lists the standard stock properties:

Name	DISPID	Description
Appearance	DISPID_APPEARANCE	Appearance — 3D or flat, for example
AutoSize	DISPID_AUTOSIZE	Determines if a control can be resized
BackColor	DISPID_BACKCOLOR	The control's background color
BackStyle	DISPID_BACKSTYLE	Background style, usually opaque or transparent
BorderColor	DISPID_BORDERCOLOR	The color of the control's border
BorderStyle	DISPID_BORDERSTYLE	Determines how the border is drawn
BorderVisible	DISPID_BORDERVISIBLE	Determines if the control's border is visible
BorderWidth	DISPID_BORDERWIDTH	Width of the border
Caption	DISPID_CAPTION	Caption displayed on the control
DrawMode	DISPID_DRAWMODE	The paint style used to draw the control
DrawStyle	DISPID_DRAWSTYLE	Line style used to draw the control
DrawWidth	DISPID_DRAWWIDTH	Line width used to draw the control
Enabled	DISPID_ENABLED	Determines if the control is enabled
FillColor	DISPID_FILLCOLOR	The color used to fill the control
FillStyle	DISPID_FILLSTYLE	Determines how a control is filled in — solid or hatched, for example
Font	DISPID_FONT	The font used to draw text
ForeColor	DISPID_FORECOLOR	The color used for text in the control
HWND	DISPID_HWND	HWND of the control's window
MouseIcon	DISPID_MOUSEICON	The graphic to be used by the mouse pointer
MousePointer	DISPID_MOUSEPOINTER	The cursor to be used when over the control
Picture	DISPID_PICTURE	A graphic to be used as part of the control
ReadyState	DISPID_READYSTATE	Determines if the control is ready, or still loading
TabStop	DISPID_TABSTOP	Indicates if the control is a tab stop
Text	DISPID_TEXT	Text displayed by the control
Valid	DISPID_VALID	Determines if the control is valid

Clearly, you would not want to have all of these stock properties on your control. Some stock properties are only required when other properties are set, while others are mutually exclusive.

ATL makes adding a stock property to a control very easy: the Object Wizard allows you to specify which stock properties the control should support, and it will add a data member for this property in the generated C++ class. It will also derive your class from `CStockPropImpl<>`, which implements the `put` and `get` methods for the property that notify the container.

However, if you want to add a new property *after* you have created an object, life is a little harder. The **Attributes** tab of the **Add Property** dialog does not allow you to type in a negative number or a symbol, and the only workaround is to edit the IDL by hand. You will also need to edit the class header by hand to derive from `CStockPropImpl<>`, and trawl through the ATL header files to determine what class data members you should add. Clearly, it's a good idea to think carefully about the stock properties a control will support before you create it!

Ambient Properties

Ambient properties are not properties on your control; they are properties on the container that will house the control. However, your control will depend on the container's ambient properties, and so it is important to understand what they are used for, and how to access them.

Ambient properties are read-only properties like `Font` and `BackColor` that a control container exposes to a control. The control can read ambient properties and use them to set its own properties. This allows a control to blend in well with the container and the other controls it shows. If you can imagine how unprofessional a Visual Basic form would look if it had two buttons with captions written in completely different fonts, you can understand the need for ambient properties.

For ambient properties to be useful, the container must be able to inform the control when a property changes. It does this by passing the DISPID of the property to the control. However, so that the control knows what the DISPID means, it must have a value known to both the container and control. Unless your control container will only pass ambient properties to controls that you've written, ambient properties should have Microsoft-defined values (which are negative).

When a control is informed that a property has changed, it can handle this by obtaining the property value. The control specification (OCX '96) says that although ambient properties have names, the control should only access them using the standard DISPIDs assigned to them. (In other words, you should use early binding, where the DISPID is compiled into the control's code). The following table lists the standard ambient properties:

Name	DISPID	Description
BackColor	-701	The interior color of the control
DisplayName	-702	The name used in error messages
Font	-703	The font used by the control

Name	DISPID	Description
ForeColor	-704	The color used to display text and graphics
LocaleID	-705	The locale ID
MessageReflect	-706	Determines whether the container reflects window messages back to the control
ScaleUnits	-707	Specifies the coordinate unit name being used by the container
TextAlign	-708	Text alignment
UserMode	-709	Determines whether the control is in a design container or running in an application
UIDead	-710	If true, the control should not respond to the UI
ShowGrabHandles	-711	Determines whether grab handles should be displayed when the control is active
ShowHatching	-712	Determines whether the control should use UI active hatching feedback when UI active
DisplayAsDefaultButton	-713	Determines whether the button should display itself as the default button
SupportsMnemonics	-714	Determines whether the container supports mnemonics
AutoClip	-715	Determines whether the container will automatically clip the control

Controls that need to communicate with their container must implement the IOleControl interface, which has a method called OnAmbientPropertyChange() that gets called by the container when an ambient property has changed. The method is passed the DISPID of the changed property.

With the IOleControlImpl<> template, ATL does most of the work of implementing this interface for you, but the implementation for OnAmbientPropertyChange() does no more than return S_OK. If your control needs to react to changing ambient properties, it must override this method, obtain the value of the ambient property, and then use the value.

Adding Properties To A Control

As mentioned earlier, a control that is to support stock properties should have them added at creation time, using the Object Wizard. Handling stock properties requires adding a data member to the control class and managing the put and get methods for the property, as well as container notification.

To add properties later in the development process, you first have to edit the IDL by hand. To add the Caption property, for example, you would need to add these lines into your interface's IDL:

```
[propput, id(DISPID_CAPTION)]
    HRESULT Caption([in] BSTR strCaption);
[propget, id(DISPID_CAPTION)]
    HRESULT Caption([out, retval] BSTR* strCaption);
```

Next, you need to derive from your ATL class from `CStockPropImpl<>` (if it isn't already), using your ATL class, the interface and its IID, and the LIBID as parameters:

```
class ATL_NO_VTABLE CMyStockProp :
    public CComObjectRootEx<CComSingleThreadModel>,
    public CComCoClass<CMyStockProp, &CLSID_MyStockProp>,
    public CComControl<CMyStockProp>,
    public CStockPropImpl<CMyStockProp, IMyInterface,
                          &IID_IMyInterface, &LIBID_MYLib>,
```

Note that this template is passed a LIBID without a version number. This is required because `CStockPropImpl<>` derives from `IDispatchImpl<>` — in fact, Object Wizard uses the former rather than the latter as the implementation of the dual interface for your class. However, because it takes no version number, your component's stock properties can only be described in a version 1.x type library. The only way to get round this problem is to write your own version of `CStockPropImpl<>` that does take a version number — hardly a happy proposition.

This template provides `get` and `put` methods and notification for *all* stock properties. These stock properties are defined in `atlctrl.h`, and most have their `get` and `put` methods defined using one of `IMPLEMENT_STOCKPROP()`, `IMPLEMENT_BOOL_STOCKPROP()`, or `IMPLEMENT_BSTR_STOCKPROP()`. The other properties (`Font`, `HWND`, `MouseIcon` and `Picture`) have their `get` and `put` methods defined explicitly. However they are defined, the template class assumes the following data members in your ATL control class:

Name	ATL Class Data Member
Appearance	LONG m_nAppearance
AutoSize	BOOL bAutoSize
BackColor	OLE_COLOR m_clrBackColor
BackStyle	LONG m_nBackStyle
BorderColor	OLE_COLOR m_clrBorderColor
BorderStyle	LONG m_nBorderStyle
BorderVisible	BOOL m_bBorderVisible
BorderWidth	LONG m_nBorderWidth
Caption	CComBSTR m_bstrCaption
DrawMode	LONG m_nDrawMode
DrawStyle	LONG m_nDrawStyle
DrawWidth	LONG m_nDrawWidth
Enabled	BOOL m_bEnabled
FillColor	OLE_COLOR m_clrFillColor
FillStyle	LONG m_nFillStyle

Name	ATL Class Data Member
Font	CComPtr<IFontDisp> m_pFont
ForeColor	OLE_COLOR m_clrForeColor
MouseIcon	CComPtr<IPictureDisp> m_pMouseIcon
MousePointer	LONG m_nMousePointer
Picture	CComPtr<IPictureDisp> m_pPicture
ReadyState	LONG m_nReadyState
TabStop	BOOL m_bTabStop
Text	CComBSTR m_bstrText
Valid	BOOL m_bValid

Note that the DISPID_HWND stock property is not listed here because CStockPropImpl<> implements it using a property called Window (with the methods put_Window(), which will return E_FAIL, and get_Window()) that use the ATL class's m_hWnd data member. The Font, MouseIcon and Picture stock properties are objects, and hence are accessed through IDispatch-derived interfaces.

When you add a new stock property to your control, you need to add the appropriate data member from the table to your ATL class. So, what about all the other data members given in the table that you have *not* added to your ATL class? The stock property macros will still be used and will attempt to access these non-existent data members, so how does the code compile? The answer is that your control is derived from CComControl<>, and its base class, CComControlBase, has a union with members that have the names of these stock properties. If you do not specify a stock property in the Object Wizard, then the CStockPropImpl<> code accesses the member inherited from the union in CComControlBase.

Example: Adding Properties

To demonstrate how to use properties on a control, we will develop a simple example. This project will be reused later in the chapter to demonstrate how to make properties persistent, so to allow it to be used in a container like Word, we will create a full control. The difference between the various control types will be covered in the next chapter.

Create a new DLL ATL project called Properties, and then use the Object Wizard to add a full control to the project. Give it a Short Name of Prop, but rather than clicking on OK immediately as we usually do, switch to the Miscellaneous tab and select the Insertable check box. This will allow the control to appear in the Insert Object dialog, so that you can test it later with Microsoft Word. Now select the Stock Properties tab and add support for Background Color, Caption and Foreground Color by selecting them in the left-hand pane and clicking on >. This is illustrated on the next page.

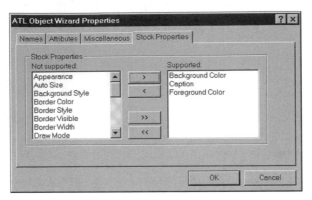

Now you can click on the OK button to add the control to the project. If you go to the ClassView, you can start to get a feel for the code that the Object Wizard has added for you:

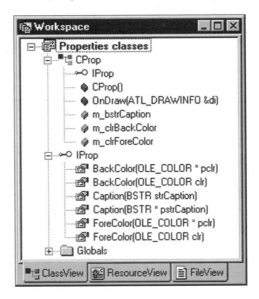

The Object Wizard will not provide default values for any of these properties. The constructor for the CComBSTR will initialize the Caption property to an empty string, but the color variables will not be initialized, so you should do this in the constructor:

```
public:
    CProp() : m_clrForeColor(0), m_clrBackColor(0xffffff)
    {
    }
```

If you look at the IDL file, you'll see that the IProp interface has get and put methods for each of the stock properties that you selected, but that these methods are not implemented as part of the CProp class. The reason for this is that they are implemented by the CStockPropImpl<> base class. Object Wizard has, however, added two OLE_COLORs and a BSTR member for these properties to the class, so you can manipulate them directly in your code (in the control initialization code, for example).

Next, we'll give our control some custom properties. To do this, use the Add Property... context menu from ClassView. Add the following two properties:

Name	Type
String	BSTR
Number	long

This time, the Wizard *will* add the get and put methods for you, but it *won't* add any data members. For this example you will need data members, so open the Prop.h header and add the following at the bottom of the class:

```
    OLE_COLOR m_clrBackColor;
    CComBSTR m_bstrCaption;
    OLE_COLOR m_clrForeColor;
    CComBSTR m_bstrString;
    long m_lNumber;
};
```

Initialize the m_lNumber variable in the constructor, near the top of the class declaration:

```
public:
    CProp() : m_clrForeColor(0), m_clrBackColor(0xffffff), m_lNumber(0)
    {
    }
```

You can now implement the get and put methods in Prop.cpp to use this storage:

```
STDMETHODIMP CProp::get_String(BSTR *pVal)
{
    ATLTRACE(_T("String returning: %ls\n"), m_bstrString);
    m_bstrString.CopyTo(pVal);
    return S_OK;
}

STDMETHODIMP CProp::put_String(BSTR newVal)
{
    ATLTRACE(_T("String assigned to: %ls\n"), newVal);
    m_bstrString = newVal;
    FireViewChange();
    return S_OK;
}
STDMETHODIMP CProp::get_Number(long *pVal)
{
    ATLTRACE(_T("Number returning: %ld\n"), m_lNumber);
    *pVal = m_lNumber;
    return S_OK;
}

STDMETHODIMP CProp::put_Number(long newVal)
{
    ATLTRACE(_T("Number assigned to: %ld\n"), m_lNumber);
    m_lNumber = newVal;
    FireViewChange();
    return S_OK;
}
```

Using a CComBSTR here ensures that the data member is initialized when the control is created, and that the enclosed BSTR is released when the control is destroyed. When making a copy of the string to return in get_String(), the CComBSTR::CopyTo() method is used.

Also, notice the use of the `FireViewChange()` function in the put_ methods. This ensures that whenever a property is changed, the visual representation also changes. This representation is drawn in the `OnDraw()` method, which you'll find in `Prop.h`. Add the following code and compile.

```cpp
HRESULT OnDraw(ATL_DRAWINFO& di)
{
    USES_CONVERSION;
    int iMode = SetMapMode(di.hdcDraw, MM_TEXT);
    RECT& rc = *(RECT*)di.prcBounds;

    COLORREF clrFront, clrBack;
    OleTranslateColor(m_clrBackColor, NULL, &clrBack);
    OleTranslateColor(m_clrForeColor, NULL, &clrFront);

    HBRUSH hBrush = CreateSolidBrush(clrBack);
    HBRUSH hOldBrush = (HBRUSH)SelectObject(di.hdcDraw, hBrush);
    HPEN hPen = CreatePen(PS_SOLID, 1, clrFront);
    HPEN hOldPen = (HPEN)SelectObject(di.hdcDraw, hPen);

    Rectangle(di.hdcDraw, rc.left, rc.top, rc.right, rc.bottom);

    SetTextColor(di.hdcDraw, clrFront);
    SetBkColor(di.hdcDraw, clrBack);

    CComBSTR bstrText = _T("Caption: ");
    bstrText += m_bstrCaption;
    ExtTextOut(di.hdcDraw, rc.left + 2, 2 + rc.top, ETO_CLIPPED, &rc,
            OLE2T(bstrText.m_str), bstrText.Length(), NULL);

    bstrText = _T("String: ");
    bstrText += m_bstrString;
    ExtTextOut(di.hdcDraw, rc.left + 2, 2 + rc.top + 25, ETO_CLIPPED, &rc,
            OLE2T(bstrText.m_str), bstrText.Length(), NULL);

    bstrText = _T("Number: ");
    TCHAR szNum[12];
    wsprintf(szNum, _T("%ld"), m_lNumber);
    bstrText += szNum;
    ExtTextOut(di.hdcDraw, rc.left + 2, 2 + rc.top + 50, ETO_CLIPPED, &rc,
            OLE2T(bstrText.m_str), bstrText.Length(), NULL);

    SelectObject(di.hdcDraw, hOldBrush);
    DeleteObject(hBrush);
    SelectObject(di.hdcDraw, hOldPen);
    DeleteObject(hPen);
    SetMapMode(di.hdcDraw, iMode);
    return S_OK;
}
```

Most of this is straightforward Win32 GDI code. The color properties are of the `OLE_COLOR` type, and so the `OleTranslateColor()` function is called to convert them to the `COLORREF` values used by GDI. Then we create a brush and a pen using the stock background and foreground colors, and select them into the device context before the call to `Rectangle()`.

Next, we draw the text on the screen. To do this, we need to put the values into a string; this code uses `CComBSTR`'s overloaded `+=()` operator to add strings together. It's probably not the most efficient code for doing this, but it is quite compact. The `ForeColor` stock property is then used to set the text foreground color, and the `BackColor` stock property to set the text background color, before drawing the text on the screen.

The actual drawing is done with the ExtTextOut() function. This is used because its output can be placed into a metafile, whereas that of DrawText() cannot. You will come across metafiles later in this chapter and in the next chapter, but basically they are recorded GDI commands. The name is something of a misnomer, because a metafile does not have to be a disk file — it can be an application resource, or an in-memory resource. Because of this feature, metafiles can be placed in OLE streams, as explained later.

Notice how careful we've been about using the bounding rectangle given in di.prcBounds. This is because you cannot assume that the top left corner will always be (0, 0) — the container may pass you a bounding rectangle that is part of another window. The full details of this aspect of control programming are investigated in the next chapter.

Testing The Control

The simplest way to test the control is to use the ActiveX Control Test Container, which you can run from the Tools menu in Visual C++. To test the control, select Insert New Control... from the Edit menu. From the resulting dialog, select Prop Class and click on OK. From the Control menu, select Invoke Methods... so that you can access the properties directly through their get and put methods:

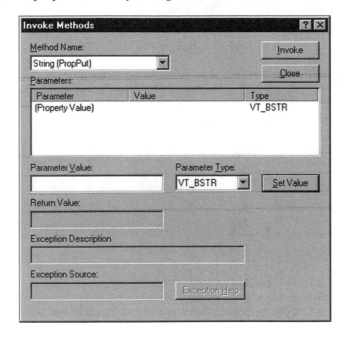

The methods are selectable from the Method Name drop down list box, and when you select a property the dialog will read its type information and fill the Parameters box. You can change the value of a property by selecting the appropriate put method and typing the value in the Parameter Value edit box. When you've done this, check that the Parameter Type is correct and then click on Set Value to add the value to the list box. When you click on Invoke, the value will be sent to the control.

Change the Caption property to The Caption and click on Invoke. You should find that the control is updated immediately. Try changing the String and Number properties as well.

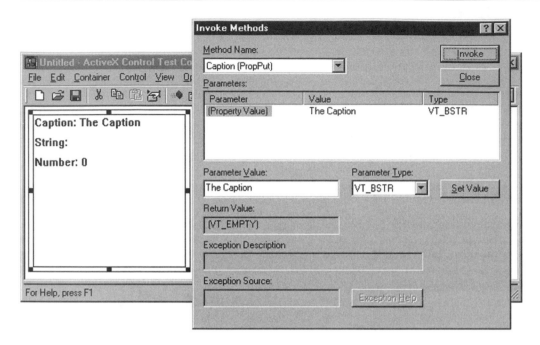

Next, close the Invoke Methods dialog and select Properties... from the Test Container's Edit menu instead. When you created the control, the Object Wizard added a **property page** for the BackColor and ForeColor stock properties that allows you to change them through a friendly user interface. (Property pages will be covered in detail in the next chapter.)

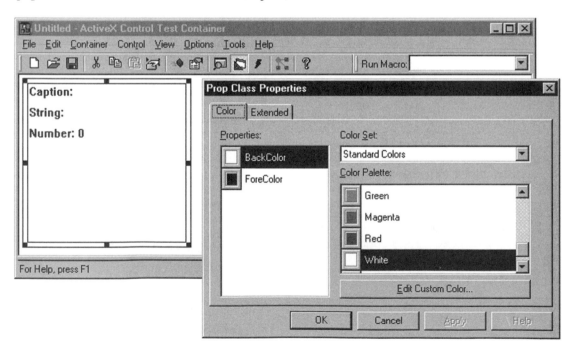

You can select colors from the <u>C</u>olor Palette and click on the <u>A</u>pply button to change the control's stock color properties.

Changing Properties From Script Code

The Object Wizard creates a minimal HTML file to demonstrate how to place the control on a web page — in this case, it's called `Prop.htm`. The properties that you have added can be accessed from script, as demonstrated by the following example (add the highlighted code):

```
<HTML>
<HEAD>
    <TITLE>ATL 3.0 test page for object Prop</TITLE>
</HEAD>
<BODY>
<OBJECT ID="Prop" CLASSID="CLSID:7B33B4FD-59B3-11D1-9A48-0060973044A8"></OBJECT>
    <P>
    <INPUT TYPE="BUTTON"
           NAME="bn"
           VALUE="Click me"
           LANGUAGE=VBS
           onclick="bnclick">
    <INPUT TYPE="TEXT"
           NAME="txtString"
           VALUE="">
    <SCRIPT LANGUAGE=VBS>
    Sub bnclick()
        Prop.Number = Prop.Number + 1
        Prop.String = txtString.Value
    End Sub
    </SCRIPT>
</BODY>
</HTML>
```

The HTML code gives the object a name and adds two HTML controls. The button click event is handled using the VBScript procedure called `bnclick()`, which merely increments the control's `Number` property and copies the data from the text box into the control's `String` property.

For this script to work in Internet Explorer, you may need to change its security settings. The reason for this is that the script code comes from a source external to the control, and to prevent the control from being accessed by a malicious script, Internet Explorer disables scripting by default. The next chapter will show you how to change your control so that it can tell Internet Explorer that the control allows scripting.

In this screenshot, I have clicked on the button a couple of times:

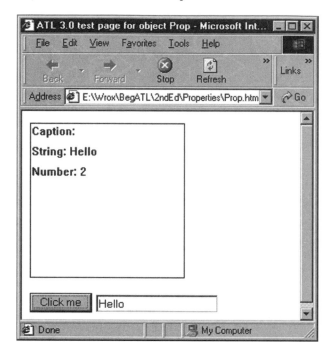

Persistence

Persistence involves initializing a control from some persistent values when it is created, and saving the control's state to some persistent store when the control stops running. ATL adds persistence for you automatically when your object class is derived from the correct class, as we'll discover later. The code that ATL provides for persistence steps through the properties supported by the control, loading or saving the values. This is adequate for most property types, but if you have a complex property (like a SAFEARRAY), or you want to make a value persistent that is not described by a property, you will need to write the persistence code yourself.

It will surely come as no surprise to you that this functionality is implemented using interfaces; what then are the interfaces required for persistence?

Persistence Interfaces

The COM interfaces for persistence all start with the name IPersist. If you peruse the documentation, the first such interface you will come across is IPersistFile. However, although it sounds a likely candidate, this interface is not used by controls. The reason for this is that controls are loaded into containers, and generally are one of many components that the container uses to maintain state. It is the responsibility of the container — not the control — to open a file and maintain the connection to the file object.

When writing to the file, the container asks its controls to serialize their states into a byte stream that can be written to the file. When reading from a file, the container obtains this byte stream and passes it to the control. Since the control created the byte stream, it should be able to read and interpret the data, and hence initialize itself. So how does this work?

COM defines two interfaces called IStream and IStorage that allow servers to implement **structured storage**. The IStream interface allows an object to read and write a byte stream. Simple data can be written to a stream, but more complicated data should be structured, and this is the reason for storages. The usual way of explaining storages and streams is to compare them with a file operating system; we will use that here too, but with a warning not to take the analogy too far: structured storage does not have to use a file.

Think of a storage as being a bit like a folder in Explorer. The folder has a name, and it can contain other folders, but it cannot hold raw data. To put data into a folder, you need to put the data into a file and then put the file into the folder. You should think of a stream as being like a file: it is there to hold raw data. A file cannot hold other files or have folders, and likewise a stream cannot have other streams or storages.

File Storage

Structured Storage

379

You can put storages and streams into a file called a **compound document**. Such a document can contain many storages, so to identify a particular storage (or a stream within a storage), storages and streams have names, just as folders and files do. One obvious application for storages is a container that has many controls: when it wants to save its state, it can create a storage for each control, and ask the controls to save their states to the storages. Within the storage assigned to it, the control is free to create as many storages and streams as it wants, because it has the responsibility of reading the data back from the storage in the future, when the control is initialized.

As we have said, the container has the responsibility of creating the structured storage file (also known, for historical reasons, as a **DocFile**). If a control can persist itself, then it should implement one of the persistence interfaces. When the container wants to persist its document, it will query each control for an appropriate persistence interface and, if the control supports it, call the persistence methods to let the control save its data. The appropriate interfaces for streams and storages are IPersistStreamInit and IPersistStorage.

Why both? Well, streams are where the actual data is saved, and are the leaves at the end of the storage tree — that is, streams cannot contain storages or other streams. Since a stream is a single object, it does not require any other objects to be created, and so it can be efficient for making simple data persistent. When using a stream to persist a control, the container will create the stream and then call IPersistStreamInit::Save(), passing this stream.

However, since the persisting object only has one stream to write to, it must handle structuring itself. If it has several data items, each must be serialized into a byte stream before they can all be written to same stream. For objects that contain complicated data, this can be a real inconvenience. If the control is passed a storage instead, it can structure the data accordingly, adding as many storages and streams as it needs. Since there are two ways to persist data, a container could use either, and so controls should support both. This does not necessarily mean that the persistence code is doubled, as demonstrated by the ATL code for IPersistStorageImpl<>: the Save() method creates a stream called "Contents" and passes this to the control's implementation of IPersistStreamInit::Save().

> *Incidentally, there is also an interface called simply* IPersistStream, *which has all the methods necessary to read data from and write data to a stream. However, what it does not do is provide a method to get the object to an initialized state — that is, a state not initialized from an external source.* IPersistStreamInit *has a method called* InitNew() *that the container can call when it creates a new object. This method should initialize the object's internal state to some default value (note that* IPersistStorage *has a method of the same name).*

All of the interfaces that have names of the form IPersist*xxx* derive from IPersist. This interface has just one method called GetClassID(), which returns the CLSID of the object that knows how to handle the persistent object. Usually this is the CLSID of the control, but it could be a proxy or a handler class. The container can call this method if it needs to save an ID in its persistence store, so that when it loads from the storage at a later stage, it can tell what type of object is persisted.

ATL provides default implementations of these two interfaces called IPersistStreamInitImpl<> and IPersistStorageImpl<>. These implementations use the same basic stream methods to save and load control state. The Load() and Save() methods of the stream interface call IPersistStreamInit_Load() and IPersistStreamInit_Save(). In turn, these call global methods called AtlIPersistStreamInit_Load() and AtlIPersistStreamInit_Save().

The storage implementation first creates a "Contents" stream (as explained above) to hold the data, and then QI()s itself for the IPersistStreamInit interface to actually save the data.

This is very basic handling of the IPersistStorage interface, and does not follow all the recommendations of the MSDN documentation. This explains that IPersistStorage should take part in a handshake protocol with the container, and pay particular attention to low memory conditions. If you intend to implement IPersistStorage on your controls, you are recommended to read the MSDN documentation and the relevant chapters in Inside OLE.

Property Maps

The Load() and Save() methods of the IPersistStreamInit interface need to know what data the control maintains, and the ATL class supplies this information through a **property map**. Property maps are multi-functional (as you'll see in the next chapter), but in this context they are used to list all of the control's persistable properties. Logically, this implies that only those properties that appear in the property maps are made persistent. If you need to persist other data that cannot be put into the property map, you will need to override the Load() and Save() methods of the persistence classes. An example of this is shown in the next chapter, where we will persist a SAFEARRAY.

Open the Prop.h file and look beneath the COM map. There you will find the property map:

```
BEGIN_PROP_MAP(CProp)
    PROP_DATA_ENTRY("_cx", m_sizeExtent.cx, VT_UI4)
    PROP_DATA_ENTRY("_cy", m_sizeExtent.cy, VT_UI4)
    PROP_ENTRY("BackColor", DISPID_BACKCOLOR, CLSID_StockColorPage)
    PROP_ENTRY("Caption", DISPID_CAPTION, CLSID_NULL)
    PROP_ENTRY("ForeColor", DISPID_FORECOLOR, CLSID_StockColorPage)
    // Example entries
    // PROP_ENTRY("Property Description", dispid, clsid)
    // PROP_PAGE(CLSID_StockColorPage)
END_PROP_MAP()
```

The Wizard has already added some entries for you: the first two are the size of the control, while the other three are the stock properties that you added. There are several macros that you can use in a property map, as explained in this table:

Macro	Description
PROP_ENTRY()	Gives the property name, its DISPID and (optionally) the CLSID of a property page that deals with it (see the color properties above)
PROP_ENTRY_EX()	In addition to the above, this allows you to specify the IID of an interface that implements the property
PROP_PAGE()	Gives the CLSID of a property page used to access one or more control properties
PROP_DATA_ENTRY()	Allows you to persist a property that is not part of an interface

The last entry here is interesting, because it means the properties that are persisted don't have to be described by type information. However, it isn't that great — if you want the data persisted to a property bag (see later in this chapter), the property must be an integer type. Although this is not technically a restriction if you are persisting to a stream or storage, it still means that you should only use integers.

The PROP_ENTRY() Macro

Let's look a little more closely at the syntax of the PROP_ENTRY() macro, which is given as a commented line in the code:

```
// PROP_ENTRY("Property Description", dispid, clsid)
```

The first item is the name of the property, which is used to identify the property in a **property bag**. A property bag is a mechanism whereby properties can be persisted as named items. The control is handed an IPropertyBag pointer, on which it can call the Read() method, passing the name of the property it needs to get, or the Write() method, passing the name and value of the property it wants to persist. Property bags are used to implement the <PARAM> tag in HTML, and by Visual Basic to initialize controls from (or write them to) the frm file. We will talk more about property bags later in this chapter.

The second item in PROP_ENTRY() is the DISPID of the property, and the final item is the CLSID of the property page used to initialize the property. If you specify a property page in PROP_ENTRY(), you do not need to use the PROP_PAGE() macro. If you do not have a property page for the property, then you can use CLSID_NULL.

In the following tests, we'll add to the property map all of the custom properties you previously added to the control — the Object Wizard only added the stock properties you selected. Open Prop.h and add entries for String and Number:

```
BEGIN_PROP_MAP(CProp)
    PROP_DATA_ENTRY("_cx", m_sizeExtent.cx, VT_UI4)
    PROP_DATA_ENTRY("_cy", m_sizeExtent.cy, VT_UI4)
    PROP_ENTRY("BackColor", DISPID_BACKCOLOR, CLSID_StockColorPage)
    PROP_ENTRY("Caption", DISPID_CAPTION, CLSID_NULL)
    PROP_ENTRY("ForeColor", DISPID_FORECOLOR, CLSID_StockColorPage)
    PROP_ENTRY("String", 1, CLSID_NULL)
    PROP_ENTRY("Number", 2, CLSID_NULL)
    // Example entries
    // PROP_ENTRY("Property Description", dispid, clsid)
    // PROP_PAGE(CLSID_StockColorPage)
END_PROP_MAP()
```

Next, add the following code further down in the class declaration:

```
// IViewObjectEx
    DECLARE_VIEW_STATUS(VIEWSTATUS_SOLIDBKGND | VIEWSTATUS_OPAQUE)

// IPersistStreamInit
    bool m_bInitialized;
    STDMETHOD(InitNew)()
    {
        if(m_bInitialized)
            return E_UNEXPECTED;
        m_bstrCaption = "Caption";
        m_bstrString = "String";
        m_lNumber = -99;
        m_bInitialized = true;
        return S_OK;
    }

    STDMETHOD(Load)(LPSTREAM pStm)
    {
        if(m_bInitialized)
            return E_UNEXPECTED;
        else
        {
            m_bInitialized = true;
            return IPersistStreamInitImpl<CProp>::Load(pStm);
        }
    }
```

The COM specification says that if the control is initialized with `IPersistStreamInit::InitNew()`, then `IPersistStreamInit::Load()` must return `E_UNEXPECTED`, and vice versa. This is the reason for the new variable `m_bInitialized`, and for overriding `Load()`. `InitNew()` was overridden to give the properties default values. This method is also called by `IPersistStorage::InitNew()`, so you only have to add the code in this one place.

Change the constructor to initialize this new variable:

```
CProp() : m_clrForeColor(0),
          m_clrBackColor(0xffffff),
          m_lNumber(0),
          m_bInitialized(false)
{
}
```

And finally, compile the code.

It is strange that ATL does not provide this code for you; nonetheless, you must remember to add it whenever you have a control that persists properties.

Persisting As Part Of A Compound Document

To check that this control can now persist its properties to a compound document, we will insert it into a Word document (you can also insert this control into WordPad). This test is why we made sure when creating the control that the Object Wizard marked it as `Insertable`. (As a result, the control's CLSID has the `Insertable` key in the registry.)

Note that there is a slight difference between Word and WordPad. The presence of the `Insertable` key in the component's CLSID is sufficient for the component to appear in the Insert Object dialog in WordPad, but not in Word. To see the component in Word's Insert | Object... dialog, you must add `Insertable` to the component's versioned ProgID. Open `Prop.rgs`, and make the following change:

```
HKCR
{
    Properties.Prop.1 = s 'Prop Class'
    {
        CLSID = s '{2D926FB0-5E37-11D3-89D1-00104BDC35E0}'
        'Insertable'
    }
    ForceRemove 'Insertable'
```

To test the control, run Word, and select Insert | Object.... This brings up the Object dialog, which is similar to the one you saw in the ActiveX Control Test Container. From the Create New tab, select Prop Class and then click on OK:

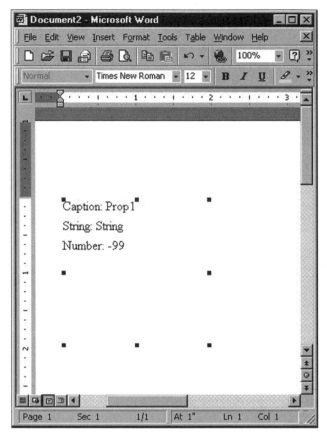

This has the default values you entered in the InitNew() method, except for the Caption property, which has changed to Prop1. (This is the case with Word 2000; if you use Word 97, Caption will retain the value you specified.) Word has called InitNew() to create a new, initialized object, but since Word 2000 allows you to script the controls placed on a document, it has named the object based on the name of the coclass, and then changed the Caption to this name.

To activate the control, you should click on it. To edit the control, you should right click on it and select **P**roperties from the context menu. You will get a dialog similar to the property box in Visual Basic:

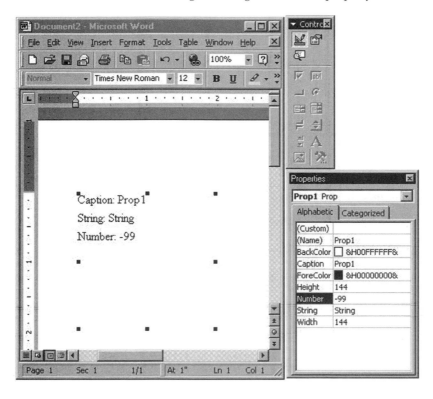

Word 97 behaves rather differently here. You should double-click on the control in order to edit it, but if you do this now you will get a dialog indicating that you cannot edit the control.

Word has read the type information for the control and added every property that it can find to the property box. However, if you change either the Number or the String property in the property box, you'll find that nothing happens — there is no corresponding change to the object in the document. On the other hand, if you close the property box and then re-open it, you will find the changes that you made will still be there. Clearly, the control is not redrawing correctly.

When you change a value in the property box, Word will write the properties to the control, but the component must be *told* to update itself. If you change the Caption or the color properties, you will find that the control *does* update itself. The answer to the problem must therefore lie in the stock properties' implementation in CStockPropImpl<>. There you will find that the IMPLEMENT_STOCKPROP() macro also calls SendOnDataChange(), which tells the container (Word) that the control's data has changed.

In addition, you must record that the control's data has changed in a flag so that when the control is asked whether it has changed at a later stage, it can check this flag. The CComControl<> base class has a flag called m_bRequiresSave that is changed by calling SetDirty(), passing true to set the flag, and false to clear it. Here are the changes you need to make:

```
STDMETHODIMP CProp::put_String(BSTR newVal)
{
    ATLTRACE(_T("String assigned to: %ls\n"), newVal);
    m_bstrString = newVal;
    SetDirty(true);
    SendOnDataChange();
    FireViewChange();
    return S_OK;
}

STDMETHODIMP CProp::put_Number(long newVal)
{
    ATLTRACE(_T("Number assigned to: %ld\n"), m_lNumber);
    m_lNumber = newVal;
    SetDirty(true);
    SendOnDataChange();
    FireViewChange();
    return S_OK;
}
```

Make a corresponding change to `InitNew()` in `Prop.h`:

```
STDMETHOD(InitNew)()
{
    if(m_bInitialized)
        return E_UNEXPECTED;
    m_bstrCaption = "Caption";
    m_bstrString = "String";
    m_lNumber = -99;
    SetDirty(true);
    m_bInitialized = true;
    return S_OK;
}
```

Now you will find that the `String` and `Number` properties can be changed, and their values will be immediately written to the control. As another test, save the document, close it, and then open the document again. When you load the file, you see the control with the values you saw when the control was saved — or do you? Actually, you're not looking at the control at all; it's just a visual representation of it. What has happened is this: when you first created the object, Word asked the control to draw itself into a metafile (it did this by calling `IDataObject::GetData()`). Essentially, what this means is that all the GDI commands used in `OnDraw()` are sent to a metafile instead of going to the screen. When you saved the document, Word saved the metafile as well. When you loaded the document from disk, Word read the metafile and 'played' the GDI commands to the area of the screen where the control should be.

Using metafiles like this is useful, because it means that Word can use them for displaying or printing, and the control does not have to be loaded and asked to draw itself. There could be a hit on performance if the control takes time to load and draw itself. The call to `SetDirty()` ensures that when the document is saved, the control will be asked for its property values because it has indicated that at some point during its lifetime the control's state has changed.

> If you are performing these tests with Word 97, the control behaves as you would expect: its properties are saved to the document, and will be used to re-initialize the control when the document is restarted. If you are using Word 2000, you will notice that there is a problem. The rest of this section is only applicable to Word 2000.

Now try and view the properties of this control. You will see something like this:

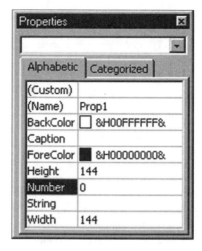

The values of Caption, Number and String are empty, and the color values are set to default values for Word. In other words, your property values do not appear to have been saved. In fact, they *have* been saved, but the control is not loading them properly. Let's review the property map again:

```
BEGIN_PROP_MAP(CProp)
    PROP_DATA_ENTRY("_cx", m_sizeExtent.cx, VT_UI4)
    PROP_DATA_ENTRY("_cy", m_sizeExtent.cy, VT_UI4)
    PROP_ENTRY("BackColor", DISPID_BACKCOLOR, CLSID_StockColorPage)
    PROP_ENTRY("Caption", DISPID_CAPTION, CLSID_NULL)
    PROP_ENTRY("ForeColor", DISPID_FORECOLOR, CLSID_StockColorPage)
    PROP_ENTRY("String", 1, CLSID_NULL)
    PROP_ENTRY("Number", 2, CLSID_NULL)
    // Example entries
    // PROP_ENTRY("Property Description", dispid, clsid)
    // PROP_PAGE(CLSID_StockColorPage)
END_PROP_MAP()
```

IPersistStreamInit::Load() is being called by Word 2000, but it fails at the entry for BackColor, and the reason why it does so is interesting. This method ultimately ends up in a call to AtlIPersistStreamInit_Load() in atlcom.h, which goes through the property map attempting to read data from the stream and initialize the appropriate component property. The process can be described with this pseudo-code:

```
DWORD dwVer = ReadFromStream();
if(dwVer > _ATL_VER)
    return E_FAIL;
while(EntriesInTheMap())
{
    if(!EntryHasAName())
        continue;
    if(IsDataEntry())
    {
        void* pData = PositionOfDataEntryInObject();
        pData = ReadFromStream();
        continue;
    }
    CComVariant var = ReadFromStream();
    CComPtr<IDispatch> pDispatch = GetControlDispatch();
    PutPropertyValueUsingDispatch(pDispatch, var);
}
```

The _cx and _cy properties are initialized successfully because they are data members of the CProp class, and they are not accessed as Automation properties. The call to initialize BackColor fails on the last line: writing the property value through the control's IDispatch pointer. The *actual* code looks like this:

```
if(FAILED(CComDispatchDriver::PutProperty(pDispatch, pMap[i].dispid, &var)))
{
    ATLTRACE2(atlTraceCOM, 0, _T("Invoked failed on DISPID %x\n"),
              pMap[i].dispid);
    hr = E_FAIL;
    break;
}
```

PutProperty() is a wrapper around a call to IDispatch::Invoke() that fails with error code DISP_E_MEMBERNOTFOUND. This is not restricted to stock properties; if you move the String or Number entries in the property map above the BackColor entry, it will still fail. A little more detective work is required.

If you run Oleview.exe and open the **Type Libraries** node, you will find that there are *two* type libraries called **Properties 1.0 Type Library**. One is the type library attached to the server for the control, but what about the other one? It's lurking in your system's Temp directory in a folder called Word8.0:

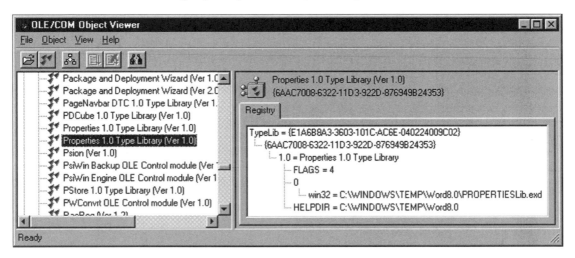

The type library has an extension of .exd. If you open it with Oleview.exe, you'll find that the IProp interface is defined as a dispinterface, but that Word has included the following properties in addition to the ones you entered:

```
[id(0x80010103), propget] single Left();
[id(0x80010103), propput] void Left([in] single rhs);
[id(0x80010104), propget] single Top();
[id(0x80010104), propput] void Top([in] single rhs);
[id(0x80010105), propget] single Height();
[id(0x80010105), propput] void Height([in] single rhs);
[id(0x80010106), propget] single Width();
[id(0x80010106), propput] void Width([in] single rhs);
[id(0x80010000), propget] BSTR Name();
[id(0x80010000), propput] void Name([in] BSTR rhs);
[id(0x80010107), propget] IDispatch* Automation();
[id(0x80010220)] void Select();
[id(0x80010228)] void Copy();
[id(0x80010229)] void Cut();
```

```
[id(0xfffffcdf)] void Delete();
[id(0x80010251)] void Activate();
[id(0x80010bc3), propget, hidden] BSTR AltHTML();
[id(0x80010bc3), propput, hidden] void AltHTML([in] BSTR rhs);
```

Word has decided to wrap your control with its own code, and this implements what Word considers are the minimal properties and methods that a control should have. Unfortunately, Word takes a rather overprotective view of the control, because it decides that only it can read or write properties through IDispatch. The interface that you get in AtlIPersistStreamInit_Load() is the IDispatch that Word implements, and although GetIdsOfNames() works and will return the correct DISPIDs for your properties, Invoke() will always return DISP_E_MEMBERNOTFOUND.

How does Word do this? It simply aggregates your control and provides its own version of IDispatch that will call your version when it wants to change your property values. The IDispatch that is used to access the properties is obtained in AtlIPersistStreamInit_Load() using this code:

```
// Declared earlier in function
CComPtr<IDispatch> pDispatch;
const IID* piidOld = NULL;

...

if (pMap[i].piidDispatch != piidOld)
{
    pDispatch.Release();
    if (FAILED(pUnk->QueryInterface(*pMap[i].piidDispatch, (void**)&pDispatch)))
    {
        ATLTRACE2(atlTraceCOM, 0,
                _T("Failed to get a dispatch pointer for property #%i\n"), i);
        hr = E_FAIL;
        break;
    }
    piidOld = pMap[i].piidDispatch;
}
```

If you don't use the PROP_ENTRY_EX() macro to specify the interface that has the property, a default of IID_IDispatch is used. The pUnk pointer is the IUnknown on your control. However, because QueryInterface() is called and the object is aggregated, the query for the property interface will be handled by the *outer object*, which will provide the overprotective version of IDispatch. You cannot make the object non-aggregatable, because if you do this Word will not create your control. The only solution is rather messy: you have to write your own loading code.

To do this, locate AtlIPersistStreamInit_Load() in atlcom.h, and copy the entire function. Paste it into Prop.cpp as a class member called CProp::IPSI_Load(). Edit the code so that the call to QueryInterface() is replaced with a call to InternalQueryInterface():

```
HRESULT CProp::IPSI_Load(LPSTREAM pStm, ATL_PROPMAP_ENTRY* pMap,
                         void* pThis, IUnknown* pUnk)
{
    ...
```

```
                if (pMap[i].piidDispatch != piidOld)
                {
                    pDispatch.Release();
                    if (FAILED(InternalQueryInterface(this, _GetEntries(),
                                                 *pMap[i].piidDispatch,
                                                 (void**)&pDispatch)))
                    {
                        ATLTRACE2(atlTraceCOM, 0,
                                _T("Failed to get a dispatch pointer for property #%i\n"), i);
                        hr = E_FAIL;
                        break;
                    }
                    piidOld = pMap[i].piidDispatch;
                }

                ...

            }
```

When this code attempts to access the IDispatch interface now, it gets its own version rather than the one implemented by Word. Call this function in the Load() method in Prop.h:

```
        HRESULT IPSI_Load(LPSTREAM pStm, ATL_PROPMAP_ENTRY* pMap,
                                         void* pThis, IUnknown* pUnk);
        STDMETHOD(Load)(LPSTREAM pStm)
        {
            if(m_bInitialized)
                return E_UNEXPECTED;
            else
            {
                m_bInitialized = true;
                return IPSI_Load(pStm, GetPropertyMap(), this, NULL);
            }
        }
```

Now when you load a document into Word 2000 that has a control on it, the control will be correctly initialized with the data held in the document. You do not need to change the corresponding IPersistStreamInit::Save() code, because it handles the saving of properties correctly.

Loading Properties From A Web Page

There is another form of persistence that we need to look at. The previous section showed how, when it is initialized, the control is passed a stream containing the values of its properties when the compound document was saved. ATL did all the work here, writing the data to the stream when the control was made persistent, and reading the data from the stream when the control was initialized. You have also seen that when a control is on a web page, you can use scripting to change the control's properties. There is, however, a third way to initialize a control, and that uses the <PARAM> HTML tag.

In this case, the control's initial data is held on the web page. When the browser loads the page, it creates a property bag object with the properties and values named on the page. This property bag object has the IPropertyBag interface, while the control itself should implement the IPersistPropertyBag interface. Like the other persistence interfaces, this has Load() and Save() methods — the browser can call the Load() method and pass it a pointer to its IPropertyBag interface. The control can now iterate through all its properties and call the IPropertyBag::Read() method for each of them, passing the name of the property. If the property bag has a value for the property, it is returned.

ATL provides support for property bags through the IPersistPropertyBagImpl<> template. To provide support, you should derive your class from this template, and add the properties that you want to initialize using the property bag to the property map. In the Properties example, you have already added the properties to the map, so all you need to do is add the new base class to the control.

Open Prop.h and derive CProp from IPersistPropertyBagImpl<>, adding IPersistPropertyBag to the COM map:

```
    public IProvideClassInfo2Impl<&CLSID_Prop, NULL, &LIBID_PROPERTIESLib>,
    public IPersistPropertyBagImpl<CProp>,
    public CComCoClass<CProp, &CLSID_Prop>
{

    ...

BEGIN_COM_MAP(CProp)
    COM_INTERFACE_ENTRY(IProp)
    COM_INTERFACE_ENTRY(IDispatch)
    COM_INTERFACE_ENTRY(IPersistPropertyBag)
    COM_INTERFACE_ENTRY(IViewObjectEx)
```

That's all the changes you need to make, so compile the project again. Next, you need to change the HTML file to use <PARAM> tags, so copy Prop.htm to Propbag.htm and change it as follows:

```
<HTML>
<HEAD>
    <TITLE>ATL 3.0 test page for object Prop</TITLE>
</HEAD>
<BODY>
    <OBJECT ID="Prop" CLASSID="CLSID:7B33B4FD-59B3-11D1-9A48-0060973044A8">
        <PARAM NAME="Caption" VALUE="Caption #1">
        <PARAM NAME="String" VALUE="String #1">
        <PARAM NAME="Number" VALUE="100">
        <PARAM NAME="BackColor" VALUE="0">
        <PARAM NAME="ForeColor" VALUE="16777215">
    </OBJECT>
</BODY>
</HTML>
```

The script code has been removed, and <PARAM> tags have been added between the <OBJECT> and </OBJECT> tags. The NAME in <PARAM> is the name of the property — the first parameter of the PROP_ENTRY() macro in the property map. The implementation that ATL uses calls IPropertyBag::Load(), passing the name of the property and a VARIANT. The vt member of this VARIANT indicates the type of the expected parameter. The browser will fill the VARIANT with the value if it's in the bag; if the value is of a different type, it will coerce it to the required type. The value 0 passed to BackColor represents black, whereas 16777215 is 0xffffff in hex, and therefore white.

To test this example, double click on `PropBag.htm` in Explorer, which will start Internet Explorer and load the page. You should see the following:

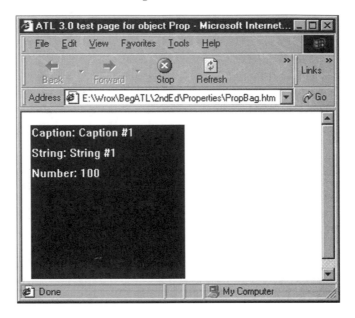

Making Object Properties Persistent

So far, the properties we've made persistent have been basic data types: integers, strings and the like. However, data is not always in this form. You may decide that you want to have an object as a property of your control, and that object may have properties of its own. In this section, you'll discover how to do this.

Since we're talking about controls that can be used in scripting languages, we can be specific and say that the object we'll create will have an `IDispatch` interface. ActiveX controls with dual interfaces have an `IDispatch` interface, so they fit the bill. Any object with an `IDispatch` interface can be exposed as an Automation property. In this example, we will create an object that has two properties — a string called `ObjString` and a `long` called `ObjNumber` — and we'll add this object as a property to the `Prop` control.

You can start by adding a new simple object to the project. On the Names page, type `PropObj` as the Short Name. Next, through ClassView, add a `BSTR` property called `ObjString` and a `long` property called `ObjNumber`.

Now add a new property to `IProp`. Make sure that the property type is `LPDISPATCH`, and call it `Obj`. After that, we need to implement the `PropObj` component, so open `PropObj.h` and add the data members for the properties at the bottom of the class:

```
// IPropObj
public:
    STDMETHOD(get_ObjNumber)(/*[out, retval]*/ long *pVal);
    STDMETHOD(put_ObjNumber)(/*[in]*/ long newVal);
    STDMETHOD(get_ObjString)(/*[out, retval]*/ BSTR *pVal);
    STDMETHOD(put_ObjString)(/*[in]*/ BSTR newVal);
```

```
private:
    CComBSTR m_ObjString;
    long m_ObjNumber;
};
```

The CComBSTR constructor will initialize the m_ObjString data member, but you still need to initialize m_ObjNumber in the CPropObj constructor:

```
public:
    CPropObj() : m_ObjNumber(0)
    {
    }
```

We want to persist the Obj property of the CProp class, so the CPropObj class will need to be derived from a persistence interface. All you need to do is add IPersistStreamInitImpl<> to the base class list:

```
class ATL_NO_VTABLE CPropObj :
    public CComObjectRootEx<CComSingleThreadModel>,
    public CComCoClass<CPropObj, &CLSID_PropObj>,
    public IPersistStreamInitImpl<CPropObj>,
    public IDispatchImpl<IPropObj, &IID_IPropObj, &LIBID_PROPERTIESLib>
```

And add this interface to the COM map:

```
BEGIN_COM_MAP(CPropObj)
    COM_INTERFACE_ENTRY(IPropObj)
    COM_INTERFACE_ENTRY(IDispatch)
    COM_INTERFACE_ENTRY(IPersistStreamInit)
    COM_INTERFACE_ENTRY_IID(IID_IPersistStream, IPersistStreamInit)
END_COM_MAP()
```

Here, the first macro states that the object supports IPersistStreamInit, while the second states that the interface implementation of the second parameter (IPersistStreamInit) also implements the interface given as the first parameter (IPersistStream). This is perfectly reasonable, since IPersistStream is vtable-compatible with IPersistStreamInit.

For this class to compile, you need to add m_bRequiresSave as a data member, because the persistence classes require it. This data member is usually provided by CComControl<>, but since we don't have this as a base class, we must add it by hand:

```
public:
    BOOL m_bRequiresSave;

private:
    CComBSTR m_ObjString;
    long m_ObjNumber;
};
```

And initialize it in the constructor:

```
    CPropObj() : m_ObjNumber(0), m_bRequiresSave(TRUE)
    {
    }
```

There is one other change you need to make to the declaration. Because this is a simple object, you don't have a property map, so we'd better add one now:

```
BEGIN_PROP_MAP(CPropObj)
    PROP_ENTRY("ObjString", 1, CLSID_NULL)
    PROP_ENTRY("ObjNumber", 2, CLSID_NULL)
END_PROP_MAP()
```

Now you can implement the property methods, so open `PropObj.cpp` and add the following:

```
STDMETHODIMP CPropObj::get_ObjString(BSTR * pVal)
{
    ATLTRACE(_T("ObjString returning: %ls\n"), m_ObjString);
    return m_ObjString.CopyTo(pVal);
}

STDMETHODIMP CPropObj::put_ObjString(BSTR newVal)
{
    ATLTRACE(_T("ObjString assigned to: %ls\n"), newVal);
    m_ObjString = newVal;
    return S_OK;
}

STDMETHODIMP CPropObj::get_ObjNumber(long * pVal)
{
    ATLTRACE(_T("ObjNumber returning: %ld\n"), m_ObjNumber);
    *pVal = m_ObjNumber;
    return S_OK;
}

STDMETHODIMP CPropObj::put_ObjNumber(long newVal)
{
    ATLTRACE(_T("ObjNumber assigned to: %ld\n"), newVal);
    m_ObjNumber = newVal;
    return S_OK;
}
```

As you can see, this is a *very* simple object. The next thing we need to do is to add support for the new property into the control, so open `Prop.h` and add a line at the top:

```
#ifndef __PROP_H_
#define __PROP_H_

#include "resource.h"       // main symbols
#include "PropObj.h"
```

At the bottom of the class, add a new member for the embedded object, and a helper method to return the values in the object:

```
public:
    CComQIPtr<IPropObj, &IID_IPropObj> m_Obj;

private:
#ifdef _DEBUG
    bool GetPropObj(CComBSTR& bstr, long* lVal);
#endif
};
```

The helper function `GetPropObj()` returns the values in the `PropObj` so that these values can be printed to the output stream under a debug build.

CComQIPtr<> is used here rather than CComPtr<> because later on we will want to initialize it using an IDispatch pointer, and the smart pointer will need to QI() the IDispatch pointer for its IPropObj interface automatically.

The last thing that needs to be done in Prop.h is to add the property to the property map:

```
    PROP_ENTRY("Number", 2, CLSID_NULL)
    PROP_ENTRY("PropObj", 3, CLSID_NULL)
    // Example entries
    // PROP_ENTRY("Property Description", dispid, clsid)
    // PROP_PAGE(CLSID_StockColorPage)
END_PROPERTY_MAP()
```

Open Prop.cpp and implement the handlers for the new property:

```
STDMETHODIMP CProp::get_Obj(LPDISPATCH *pVal)
{
#ifdef _DEBUG
    CComBSTR str;
    long num;
    GetPropObj(str, &num);
    ATLTRACE(_T("Obj returning: %ls, %ld\n"), str, num);
#endif
    return m_Obj->QueryInterface(pVal);
}

STDMETHODIMP CProp::put_Obj(LPDISPATCH newVal)
{
    // Will release any held pointer
    m_Obj = newVal;
#ifdef _DEBUG
    CComBSTR str;
    long num;
    GetPropObj(str, &num);
    ATLTRACE(_T("Obj assigned to: %ls, %ld\n"), str, num);
#endif
    SetDirty(true);
    SendOnDataChange();
    FireViewChange();
    return S_OK;
}

#ifdef _DEBUG
bool CProp::GetPropObj(CComBSTR& bstr, long* lVal)
{
    if(!m_Obj)
        return false;

    m_Obj->get_ObjString(&bstr);
    m_Obj->get_ObjNumber(lVal);

    return true;
}
#endif
```

In get_Obj(), a copy of the PropObj object, m_Obj, is returned. This is done by using the type safe QI() function we saw in Chapter 4.

In put_Obj(), a new object is passed in through an IDispatch pointer. m_Obj is a smart pointer around an IPropObj interface, so there must be a QI() going on somewhere. In fact, it is hidden: CComQIPtr<IPropObj> has an assignment operator for initializing from IPropObj pointers, and if the right hand argument is not an IPropObj pointer, then a more generic assignment operator that takes an IUnknown pointer will be used. (Any COM interface pointer created within the process can be cast to an IUnknown pointer.) In this situation, it is the latter operator that gets used, and so to initialize the object through this pointer it will have to be QI()'d for IPropObj.

The assignment releases any interfaces previously held by the m_Obj object, and since it calls QI(), this will ensure that AddRef() has been called on this pointer. There is a lot of ATL magic going on here, but as long as you're aware of the way the smart pointers work, you shouldn't get into any trouble. The rule is that the smart pointer assignment operator will release any interface in the left hand operand, assign itself the value in the right hand operand, and then AddRef() itself.

So that you can see the value of the object, you need to make the following changes to CProp::OnDraw():

```
ExtTextOut(di.hdcDraw, rc.left + 2, 2 + rc.top + 50, ETO_CLIPPED, &rc,
           OLE2T(bstrText.m_str), bstrText.Length(), NULL);

bstrText = _T("Embedded Object");
ExtTextOut(di.hdcDraw, rc.left + 2, 2 + rc.top + 75, ETO_CLIPPED, &rc,
           OLE2T(bstrText.m_str), bstrText.Length(), NULL);

bstrText = _T("   .ObjString: ");
CComBSTR str;
long num;
GetPropObj(str, &num);
bstrText += str;
ExtTextOut(di.hdcDraw, rc.left + 2, 2 + rc.top + 100, ETO_CLIPPED, &rc,
           OLE2T(bstrText.m_str), bstrText.Length(), NULL);

bstrText = _T("   .ObjNumber: ");
wsprintf(szNum, _T("%ld"), num);
bstrText += szNum;
ExtTextOut(di.hdcDraw, rc.left + 2, 2 + rc.top + 125, ETO_CLIPPED, &rc,
           OLE2T(bstrText.m_str), bstrText.Length(), NULL);

SelectObject(di.hdcDraw, hOldBrush);
```

And, of course, you need to initialize the embedded object when a new object is created:

```
STDMETHOD(InitNew)()
{
    if(m_bInitialized)
      return E_UNEXPECTED;
    m_bstrCaption = "Caption";
    m_bstrString = "String";
    m_lNumber = -99;
    CPropObj::CreateInstance(&m_Obj);
    m_Obj->put_ObjString(SysAllocString(L"ObjString"));
    m_Obj->put_ObjNumber(-999);
    SetDirty(true);
    m_bInitialized = true;
    return S_OK;
}
```

The call to CComCoClass<>::CreateInstance() on the CPropObj will create the instance and QI() for the IPropObj interface. Once that's done, the property methods are called to initialize it.

If you compile the code and test it with Word, as before, you'll see the new property items:

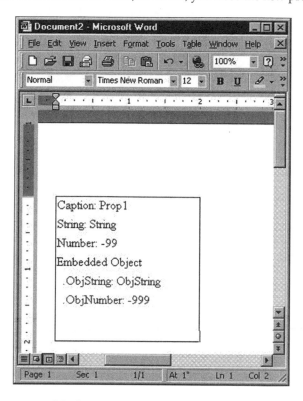

As a further test, you can save this document and then start up the DocFile Viewer (DFView.exe), which you can find in the Microsoft Visual Studio 6.0 Tools start menu folder. This allows you to look at all the storages and streams in a structured storage file. For a Word document, the appropriate storage to look in is ObjectPool:

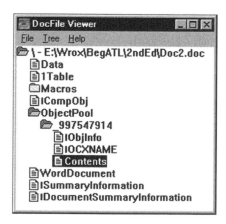

You can expand a node in the tree by double clicking on it. Within the ObjectPool is a single storage called _997547914 (the name in your pool will be different), and within that are streams pertinent to the control. Of particular interest to us is the Contents stream; double clicking on it will show you what it contains:

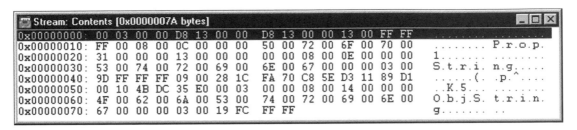

This shows that the data saved using the control's IPersistStreamInitImpl<> class includes the ObjString and ObjNumber values from the embedded object. The data at 0x5a is 0x0008, which is VT_BSTR, and this is followed by the number of bytes in the string (0x00000014 == 20 == 2 * length of string including the terminating NULL), and then the string itself. At 0x74 is 0x0003, which is VT_I4 (long), followed by -999 in hex.

What this example has shown is that objects can be added as properties to a control. All you have to do is make the property type LPDISPATCH. You have also seen that as long as the sub-object has simple properties itself (long, BSTR, float, etc.), it can be persisted. To do this, you just have to add the sub-object's properties to its own property map, and derive from IPersistStreamInitImpl<>. When you have added this new sub-object to the parent object's property map and the parent is made persistent, the code in IPersistStreamInitImpl<> will see that the property is an object and call on the sub-object's persistence interfaces. You don't have to do any special processing.

Collections

So far, our example has only used single property types: single strings, single numbers and single objects. Of course, data is rarely structured like that: quite often, there will be a variable number of items, and you'll need to be able to return all those items as one property.

For example, imagine a control that represents a business unit in a software company. Each business unit has a manager and a secretary, but may have any number of developers. You may decide to expose the manager and secretary Employee objects as properties, but what about the developers? Properties are defined at design time in the object's IDL, but at design time you do not know how many developers there will be, so you cannot expose them as Employee objects.

Instead, you must expose a single property that's an array, or **collection**, of these Employee objects. There are several ways to do this, depending on what client software you intend to support.

Problems With SAFEARRAYs

SAFEARRAYs were introduced in Chapter 5, where you saw that a SAFEARRAY is a self-describing array type that holds the size and type of each element, the number of elements, and the bounds of the array. An Automation object can have a property that is a SAFEARRAY, but it must be added as a VARIANT property; all you need to do then is copy the SAFEARRAY into VARIANT's parray member. The Universal Marshaler will read the members of the SAFEARRAY and determine how to marshal the data.

The SAFEARRAY has a pointer to the buffer of raw memory for its elements. This means that when you pass a SAFEARRAY as an [out] parameter of a method, you will need to make a copy first. If the client makes a change, it has to send the new copy in its entirety back to the object, which should then release its SAFEARRAY and make a copy of the new one. A lot of data is passed around and lots of processing has to be done. This is compounded if the method access is cross process, when the SAFEARRAY will have to be marshaled.

So, SAFEARRAYs are fine for arrays of static data — that is, data that the object knows about at one point in time and that the client will not decide to change. They are also fine for relatively small arrays. However, what happens if the property is a parts catalog containing, say, ten thousand parts? The result could be pretty disastrous, because when the client accesses the array, the whole 10,000 items will be copied into an array and marshaled to the client.

If your client is a Visual Basic application for browsing through these parts (by placing them in a list box), you will find that the application will hang for a while when the array property is accessed, even if the object is in-process. If the object is out of process, the delay could be so long that the user might think that the application has crashed.

What's required here is a method of asking the object to return, say, the first 100 items and add them to the list box. When the user attempts to scroll down beyond the end of the list, the client could then read the next 100 items, and so on. This way the user interface is updated little and often.

You could define your own methods to support obtaining data in this way (perhaps returning the subset of items in a SAFEARRAY), but it would be much nicer if a standard mechanism could be used. You won't be surprised to discover that such a mechanism already exists in COM. It's called an **enumerator**, and in the next two sections we will examine what an enumerator is. After that, you will discover how to implement a **collection** that uses an enumerator.

Enumerators

The COM documentation defines an interface called IEnumXXXX that defines the methods for an enumeration interface. In fact, this is not a real interface at all, but a template describing how an enumeration interface should look. COM does define some 'real' interfaces as well, and some useful ones are:

❑   IEnumString, which enumerates arrays of LPOLESTR strings

❑   IEnumUnknown, which enumerates arrays of IUnknown pointers

❑   IEnumVARIANT, which enumerates arrays of VARIANTs

As well as the IUnknown methods, these interfaces have four common methods. Two of these, Next() and Clone(), respectively return more enumerated items, or a copy of the enumerator. Since these have typed parameters (IEnumString::Clone() returns a double pointer to an IEnumString for example), these interfaces cannot be defined by deriving from some base interface. What is needed is a template interface, but such a thing is not possible in IDL.

You may be interested to know that macros in IDL can be handled by MIDL. You can simulate templates with some clever macro management, but we will not explore that technique here.

In the absence of templates, the COM designers have provided the IEnumXXXX interface and said, "When you design an enumerator, copy this interface and replace ELT_T with your enumerated type." Enumerator objects are not created by the system: you have to design your enumerator interface (or use one of the predefined interfaces), and implement it using your data.

```
interface IEnumXXXX : IUnknown
{
   HRESULT Next([in] ULONG celt,
               [out, size_is(celt), length_is(*pceltFetched)] ELT_T[ ] rgelt,
               [out] ULONG* pceltFetched );
   HRESULT Skip([in] ULONG celt);
   HRESULT Reset(void);
   HRESULT Clone([out] IEnumXXXX** ppenum);
};
```

As an aside, the designers could have written this interface so that Clone() would return an IUnknown pointer, and Next() would return an array of void* pointers. In that way a generic interface could be used. This is flawed, though, because the call to Clone() would have to be followed with a call to QueryInterface() to get the typed enumerator interface. Equally unsatisfactorily, a call to Next() that returned an array of void* pointers would require an additional parameter to give the size of each member of the array.

The Next() method passes a value that *requests* a number of items (in celt), and the client allocates an array large enough to return these items and passes this as the second item, rgelt; the [size_is()] attribute tells the marshaler the total size of the array. The enumerator object attempts to return the next celt items, either from the start or from the position in the array after any previous call to Next(). If it succeeds, it returns S_OK, along with the items in rgelt and the number of items in pceltFetched. If the object can return some but not all of the requested items, it will return these items in rgelt and the number of items in pceltFetched. This is the reason why rgelt has the [length_is()] attribute: it is telling the marshaler how many items in the array are valid, and so it can optimize the marshaling based on this. As a peculiarity, if Next() is passed 1 in celt then pceltFetched can be NULL because the return value of the method indicates whether the read was successful.

If the client wants to move ahead through the enumerated items without reading them, it can call Skip(), passing the number of items to skip. After several calls to Next() or Skip(), the object-maintained position in the array of items will be somewhere within the array (but there is no way that a client can find out where). To restore it to the beginning of the array, the Reset() method should be called. Finally, the Clone() method makes a copy of the enumerator, including the current position of the read pointer. Typically, you will implement this by making a **deep copy**. For example, if you are implementing an enumerator with an IEnumString interface, the Clone() method should not simply copy the array of string pointers; rather, all the strings are copied and a new array of pointers is created, and the enumerator interface on this array is returned.

How you implement an enumerator object is entirely up to you: you could allocate an array of items and return the values from that array, or you could use one of the STL containers (a popular one to use is `vector<>`).

Enumerations And Data

When you implement an enumeration object, you have two choices about the data that will be used. The first is a 'snapshot' implementation, and the second is a dynamic implementation. Which you opt for will depend on how the enumeration object will be used.

If you want to execute some aggregation function on the data at a particular point in time (for example, calculating the values of stocks in a portfolio), you will want to take a 'snapshot' (a copy) of the information. You can then peruse it at your leisure, safe in the knowledge that since you have a copy of the data, it will not be affected by any changes that are made after the snapshot was taken. To do this, the code that creates the enumerator should copy the data and use it to initialize the enumerator. The enumerator is said to **own** the data, and has the responsibility of cleaning up the data when it is destroyed.

On the other hand, you may want to show data that changes over time — cars in a parking lot, for example. In this case, when an enumerator is returned, it will have access to the *current* Car objects. As a client iterates through these objects with calls to Next(), the enumerator will reflect this. If a new car enters the parking lot, a new Car object will be added to the array that 'feeds' the enumerator, which will be apparent when the client iterates past the item's position in the enumeration. In this case, the enumerator does *not* own the data, and for each call to Next() it will attempt to access the data from its original source, ensuring that it is bang up-to-date. This is sometimes known as **lazy evaluation**. Of course, in this case the client will have to use the Car object as soon as it gets it, because the actual car that it represents could leave the parking. This COM object will still be a valid object, but the data it represents will be invalid.

ATL Enumerator Classes

Enumerator objects involve a fair amount of code, and to help you ATL provides several classes. There are two ATL classes for implementing standalone enumerator objects, CComEnum<> and CComEnumOnSTL<>. In addition, there are Impl versions of these classes (CComEnumImpl<> and IEnumOnSTLImpl<>) that are used to add an enumerator interface to an existing class.

> *The string* OnSTL *is used to identify templates that will assume the data being enumerated will be implemented in an STL container. The other classes assume that the data will be contained in a contiguous array in memory.*

The CComEnum<> template class looks like this:

```
template <class Base,
          const IID* piid,
          class T,
          class Copy,
          class ThreadModel = CComObjectThreadModel>
class ATL_NO_VTABLE CComEnum :
   public CComEnumImpl<Base, piid, T, Copy>,
   public CComObjectRootEx< ThreadModel >
{
   ...
};
```

Here, `Base` is the enumeration interface that you want to support, `piid` is the IID of that interface, and `T` is the type of the items in the enumerator object. `Copy` is a `_Copy` class that has three member functions to initialize, copy and destroy the items. As you might imagine, the methods of this class are called on each data item when the enumerator object is first called, when items are put into the enumerator object, and finally when the enumerator object is destroyed. We'll examine `_Copy` classes in the next section.

An instance of `CComEnum<>` is typically created by using it as the parameter to `CComObject<>`, which will provide its COM identity (we will see an example of this later in the chapter). If you derive your class from `CComEnumImpl<>` then your class will provide the COM identity, and a client can `QI()` your object to obtain the `Base` interface:

```
template <class Base,
          const IID* piid,
          class T,
          class Copy>
class ATL_NO_VTABLE CComEnumImpl : public Base
{
    ...
};
```

The other two classes are based on data held in an STL container. For example, you can derive your class from `IEnumOnSTLImpl<>` to add an enumerator interface with the data held in an STL container:

```
template <class Base,
          const IID* piid,
          class T,
          class Copy,
          class CollType>
class ATL_NO_VTABLE IEnumOnSTLImpl : public Base
{
    ...
};
```

In addition to the parameters of `CComEnumImpl<>`, this template contains the type (`CollType`) of the STL container that will be used. This container should be part of your class. The `CComEnumOnSTL<>` class adds a COM identity to `IEnumOnSTLImpl<>`:

```
template <class Base,
          const IID* piid,
          class T,
          class Copy,
          class CollType,
          class ThreadModel = CComObjectThreadModel>
class ATL_NO_VTABLE CComEnumOnSTL :
    public IEnumOnSTLImpl<Base, piid, T, Copy, CollType>,
    public CComObjectRootEx< ThreadModel >
{
    ...
};
```

_Copy Classes

These ATL enumerator classes are used to hold and copy many types of data, and so that they can be completely generic, the **copy policy** for the data is determined by the _Copy class. ATL provides versions that will suffice for all the common enumeration interfaces, but it is relatively easy to write your own:

ATL Class	Usage
`template <class T> class _Copy`	Shallow copy
`template<> class _Copy<VARIANT>`	Uses the `Variant*` API
`template<> class _Copy<LPOLESTR>`	Copies strings using memory from the task allocator
`template<> class _Copy<OLEVERB>`	Copies `OLEVERB` structures that contain a string member that has to be copied with memory from the task allocator
`template<> class _Copy<CONNECTDATA>`	`CONNECTDATA` contains an `IUnknown` pointer, so COM rules of copying and releasing COM pointers must be applied
`template <class T> class _CopyInterface`	COM rules must be applied when copying and releasing interface pointers

Each _Copy class has three `static` members called `copy()`, `init()` and `destroy()`, as you can see here in the definition of _CopyInterface

```
template <class T>
class _CopyInterface
{
public:
    static HRESULT copy(T** p1, T** p2)
    {
        *p1 = *p2;
        if (*p1)
            (*p1)->AddRef();
        return S_OK;
    }
    static void init(T** ) {}
    static void destroy(T** p) {if (*p) (*p)->Release();}
};
```

The `copy()` method makes a copy of the item pointed to by p2 and returns a pointer to this new item in p1. Typically, p1 and p2 will be of the same type. However, if you hold data in an STL map<> for example, then p2 will be a pointer to an item in the map<> (of type pair<>) and p1 will be the enumerated type, which will be different.

Creating Enumerators

An example of using the CComEnum<> template is shown here creating an enumerator object for VARIANTs.

```
typedef CComObject< CComEnum< IEnumVARIANT,
                              &IID_IEnumVARIANT,
                              VARIANT,
                              _Copy<VARIANT> > > EnumVar;
EnumVar* pVar = new EnumVar;
pVar->Init(...);
```

Notice that there is a space between each pair of closing brackets in _Copy<VARIANT> > >. This is to avoid confusion with the C++ right shift operator >>, which will be used if you miss out the spaces.

Take a moment to look this over. The actual enumerator code is in CComEnumImpl<>, from which CComEnum<> is derived. CComEnum<> is abstract, so to get the IUnknown methods you need CComObject<>. This takes the class for which it is providing the IUnknown methods as a parameter, and it then derives from this class. As a result, any public methods defined in CComEnum<> can be called from CComObject< CComEnum<> >. The parameters passed to the CComEnum<> template specify that the object will implement the IEnumVARIANT interface.

Before the enumerator object can be used, it has to be initialized by calling the Init() method inherited from the CComEnumImpl<> base class (CComEnumOnSTL<> has a similar method). This method is used to indicate the data that will be used to initialize the enumerator object, and to indicate who owns that data. CComEnumImpl<>::Init() looks like this:

```
HRESULT Init(T* begin, T* end, IUnknown* pUnk,
             CComEnumFlags flags = AtlFlagNoCopy);
```

begin and end are the first element and *the element after the last element* in a contiguous array of T items. The implementation relies on the fact that all of the elements are next to each other. flags determines who owns the data, and can be one of:

Flag	Description
AtlFlagNoCopy	Don't copy the data
AtlFlagTakeOwnership	Don't copy the data, but take ownership of it
AtlFlagCopy	Copy the data

These have values that are combinations of the values in CComEnumImpl::FlagBits:

Flag	Description
BitCopy	Copy data
BitOwn	Own the data

Thus, AtlFlagCopy implies ownership, and has a value of BitCopy | BitOwn.

The default value of flags in Init() is AtlFlagNoCopy, so the data is owned by another object. This other object will therefore have the responsibility of releasing the data when it is no longer needed. If you pass data to Init() with the AtlFlagCopy flag, the array is copied. If you have already allocated the array, this means that it will be allocated *twice*. To prevent this you can use AtlFlagTakeOwnership, which indicates that Init() should *not* copy the data, but puts the responsibility of releasing the data on the enumerator.

If the enumerator takes the ownership, your code doesn't have to delete the array. Note that to use `AtlFlagTakeOwnership` you must:

❑ Create the array on the heap

❑ Create the items in such a way that their resources can be released by calling `copy::destroy()`

If a user calls `Clone()`, a copy must be made of the enumerator. However, to prevent yet another copy of the data being made, `Clone()` initializes the new enumerator with the data from the creator object with `AtlFlagNoCopy`. Now, if the creator object owns the data it must live as long as the clone, since if the creator object dies before the clone it will delete the data, causing the clone's pointers to the data to be invalid. To keep the creator alive as long as the clone, `Clone()` passes the creator's `IUnknown` pointer to the clone's `Init()` method in the pUnk parameter, which caches the pointer and hence keeps a reference on its creator.

In a similar way, if you create the enumerator in an object method and the object owns the data (that is, you call `Init()` with `AtlFlagNoCopy`), you must pass the creator object's this pointer to `Init()`, to ensure that the object owning the data lives as long as the enumerator object.

There is a bug in ATL 3.0 that means **CComEnumImpl::Clone()** does not check for ownership. Instead, it checks to see if the creator *copied* the data, and if so passes its own **this** pointer to the clone. If not, it passes the cached **m_spUnk** that was set in **Init()**. If you use **AtlFlagTakeOwnership**, this check will fail, and so **m_spUnk** is passed. The check should be made for *ownership*, so the corrected code in **Clone()** should be:

```
    // If the data is a copy then we need to keep "this" object around
  hRes = p->Init(m_begin, m_end, (m_dwFlags & BitOwn) ? this : m_spUnk);
```

The array of data that the enumerator uses through `AtlFlagNoCopy` could be held as a global resource, in which case `NULL` could be used as the pUnk parameter to `Init()`. However, this presents a threading problem, because in a multithreaded server one thread could change the data in the global resource while another thread accesses the code through the enumerator. In this case, you must protect all accesses to the data from multiple threads.

`IEnumOnSTLImpl<>::Init()` looks like this:

```
  HRESULT Init(IUnknown *pUnkForRelease, CollType& collection)
```

The data must live outside of the class. An STL collection of type `CollType` will have been declared already, most likely in the class that derives from `IEnumOnSTLImpl<>`. Because of this, the `IUnknown` pointer is important to keep the enumerator alive as long as the data.

These ATL classes mean that you don't have to worry about implementing the enumerator interface methods, but this is not a solution for every problem. One such situation is where the data is not static — that is, when items may be added and removed while you're still giving access to them with the enumerator. In such a case you would have to implement your own object, as these ATL classes are not designed for such data.

Visual Basic Collections

Collections are not specific to Visual Basic, but as we saw with SAFEARRAYs, access to collections is simpler with Visual Basic than with C++, and historically they were aimed at Visual Basic programmers. Collections hold objects, and they allow you to iterate through these objects using an enumerator. What you get in addition to the enumerator are methods to add objects, remove objects, access specific objects, and get a count of the objects in the collection.

The idea of collections is to group objects together so that you can build up a hierarchy. All the Microsoft Office applications, for example, expose their objects through collections. The following figure shows some of the objects used in Excel. The convention is that collections have a name that is the plural of the objects they contain. The WorkBooks object, for example, is a collection of individual WorkBook objects:

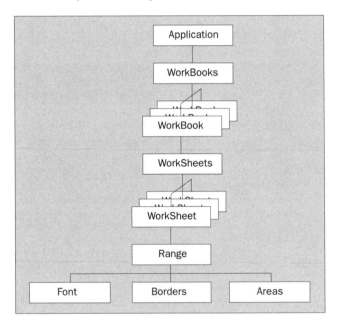

One thing that is clear from the picture above is that a collection can contain more than one object. A client using this hierarchy must be able to determine how many items there are in a collection, and then be able to access a particular object. Every collection object must provide a property called Count that returns the number of objects in the collection. It must also expose a method called Item() that gives access to a particular object in the collection, and a property called _NewEnum that returns an enumerator object. You saw enumerator objects in the last section; here they are used to iterate through all the objects in the collection.

The Item() method is quite interesting. In essence, it is passed the index of the object that the client wants to access, but this index can be anything that the collection author chooses to use as such. If the collection uses a vector (or an array) to hold the objects, the index would be a number that was the offset into that vector. Alternatively, if the collection uses a map, the index would be the key that was used when inserting the object into the map.

In Excel, for example, a `WorkSheet` objects in a `WorkSheets` collection can be accessed using either a number (between 1 and `WorkSheets.Count`) or the name of the `WorkSheet`. So if `MyAccounts` is the second sheet in the `WorkSheets` collection, then these two lines of Visual Basic code are the same:

```
WorkSheets(2).Visible = True
WorkSheets("MyAccounts").Visible = True
```

Both of these lines call the `Item()` method, which in order to enable passing both an integer and a string should take a `VARIANT` in this case. This is fine when you know which object in the collection you want to access, but what if you want to access *every* object in the collection?

One possible method would be to access the `Count` property, and then to access every object in a loop, using a counter. However, we have already seen a better way to access a whole collection: enumerators. VBA makes good use of enumerators with the `For Each` keywords, as shown in the following example, which fills the list box `List1` with the names of all the `WorkSheets` in the first `WorkBook` in the file `book1.xls`.

```
Dim ex As New Excel.Application
ex.Workbooks.Open "book1.xls"
Dim shs As Excel.Sheets
Dim sheet As Excel.Worksheet

Set shs = ex.Workbooks(1).Worksheets

For Each sheet In shs
    List1.AddItem sheet.Name
Next
```

To make this clear, the enumerator obtained by `For Each` (which calls `_NewEnum` on the collection) gives access to the objects in the collection. The above code accesses each sheet in the collection and then gets the `Name` property from each `WorkSheet` object.

Finally, collections can be filled by the object that implements them, or they may allow the user to add and remove objects. To do so, the convention is for a collection to expose two methods called — you've guessed it — `Add()` and `Remove()`. Unlike the other three items I have mentioned (the properties `Count` and `_NewEnum`, and the method `Item()`), these two methods are optional.

Writing Collections In C++

After all that theory, it's about time we had an example. We'll write a collection that can be used in Visual Basic in a moment, but first we need to examine carefully just what you need to implement in order to write a collection object.

Count

This is a read only, `long` property that returns the number of objects in the collection. The property can have whatever DISPID you choose.

Item

This method gives access to a particular item in the collection. The method must be the default method of the collection object. There is a special DISPID for the default method: `DISPID_VALUE`, which has a value of 0. The feature of default methods is that you can miss out the method name in scripts, so in Visual Basic the following two lines of code are equivalent:

```
Set shs = ex.Workbooks(1).Worksheets
Set shs = ex.Workbooks.Item(1).Worksheets
```

Item() returns a type that gives access to the specified item in the collection, but the parameter passed to the method can be any type applicable to the collection object. If the collection only gives access to items using a numeric index, Item() could take an integer; if the index is a name, then a BSTR should be used. Collections that allow both types of access should take a VARIANT as a parameter. Remember, Visual Basic will attempt to coerce the index used in the script to the type required by Item().

_NewEnum

This read-only property gives access to the enumerator object of the collection. It is usually called _NewEnum (note the underscore to prevent object browsers from showing the property), although to some extent this name is not really important, because clients that know about collection enumerators will access it directly through its DISPID, which is the standard value DISPID_NEWENUM (-4). This property should also be marked as [restricted] in IDL, which is used to mark in the type library that the property should not be accessed directly by scripting code.

The property should return a IUnknown pointer to the enumerator object that implements the IEnumVARIANT interface; the client can then QueryInterface() for this interface. The IEnumVARIANT interface is used because in general, collections can contain any type and Visual Basic expects it.

Add

This optional method allows a client to add a new item to the collection. The DISPID can be any value, and the method can take any parameters suitable for the collection. If the parameters are used to initialize a new object, that object will be added to the collection; if this is the case, the new object should be returned from Add() through an [out] parameter. Alternatively, the *client* will create an object and pass it into the Add() method using an IDispatch pointer. In both cases you can have an additional parameter that is an index indicating where in the collection to add the object, or a reference to an object after which to insert the new object.

Remove

This too is an optional method, and it allows a client to remove objects. The DISPID can be any value, and the method does not return any data. The parameter depends on the type of the objects that the collection contains.

Other Methods And Properties

As a collection object is an Automation object, you can implement any other properties and methods you want on it. By convention, MS Office exposes the following properties: Application gives access to the top level Application object, through which Office applications provide Automation; Parent is the immediate parent of the collection in the object hierarchy; and Creator is an identifier of the application that created the object.

The ATL Collection Class

ATL provides a template called ICollectionOnSTLImpl<> that, as the name suggests, will implement a collection, assuming that the data will be held in an STL container. In addition, it *adds* collection code to an existing class (there is no equivalent to CComEnumOnSTL<>). This class does not implement Add() or Remove() methods, but it does provide _NewEnum(), Count(), and Item(), implemented through IEnumOnSTLImpl<>.

You'll see an example that uses this template at the end of the chapter, and there are a number of things that you'll need to do if you want to use it in your code:

- ❑ Ensure that your object implements IDispatch — that is, it has a dual interface
- ❑ Add the read-only property _NewEnum to your class through ClassView, with a return type of LPUNKNOWN
- ❑ Add the read-only property Count to your class through ClassView, with a return type of long
- ❑ Add the read-only property Item to your class through ClassView, with the type of ItemType (see below) and a [in] parameter of type long to index on numbers
- ❑ Edit the IDL so that _NewEnum has a DISPID of DISPID_NEWENUM and Item has DISPID_VALUE
- ❑ Delete the code that ClassView adds to your .cpp and header files for these properties (leave the IDL definitions)
- ❑ Derive from an IDispatchImpl<> specialization using ICollectionOnSTLImpl<>, according to the instructions given below
- ❑ In the constructor, initialize the enumerator by adding the data to the inherited m_coll data member

The parameters of the ICollectionOnSTLImpl<> template are:

```
template <class T,
          class CollType,
          class ItemType,
          class CopyItem,
          class EnumType>
class ICollectionOnSTLImpl : public T
```

Here, T is the collection interface implemented by your class, CollType is the STL container used to hold the data and ItemType is the type of data returned by the Item property. CopyItem is the _Copy class for the data types that are held in the collection, and EnumType is a specialization of CComEnumOnSTL<> used to implement _NewEnum.

The class generated by ICollectionOnSTLImpl<> will derive from your collection interface (it needs to, because it will implement the _NewEnum, Count and Item properties of the interface). The interface must be dual (the Automation specification requires this) so your class should derive from IDispatchImpl<>. For example, if it has an interface called IDocs, you will derive it like this (we've used typedefs to make the code more readable):

```
#include <list>

typedef std::list<CComVariant> VarList;
typedef CComEnumOnSTL<IEnumVARIANT, &IID_IEnumVARIANT, VARIANT,
                      _Copy<VARIANT>, VarList> VarEnum;
typedef ICollectionOnSTLImpl<IDocs, VarList, VARIANT, _Copy<VARIANT>,
                             VarEnum> CollImpl;

class ATL_NO_VTABLE CDocs :
    public CComObjectRootEx<CComSingleThreadModel>,
    public CComCoClass<CDocs, &CLSID_Docs>,
    public IDispatchImpl<CollImpl, &IID_IDocs, &LIBID_MYOBJECTLib>
```

The collection class will have a data member called m_coll that is of the type you specify in the EnumType parameter. Your code that derives from the collection class should initialize the collection using this data member.

Example: The DeveloperCollection Object

We've talked about Visual Basic collections in previous sections. In the following example, you will see the steps needed to create a collection object and the objects that it will contain. We will use a collection of `Employee` objects called `DeveloperCollection`, following the example given in the introduction to this section.

In this example, we're modeling a company business unit that will have a manager, a secretary, and zero or more developers. In the model, each person is an `Employee` object, with a name and an employee ID, and I use a `DeveloperCollection` object to hold the developers:

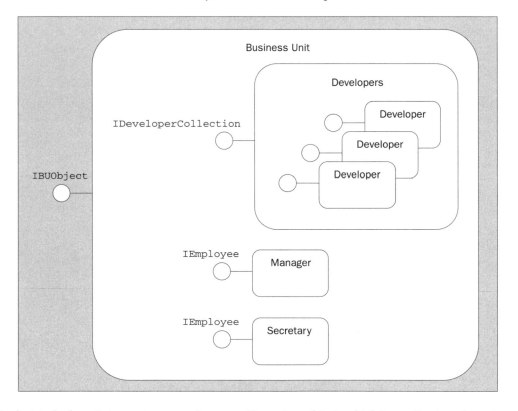

The first task, then, is to create a `DeveloperCollection` object, which is a collection of `Employee` objects.

The Employee And DeveloperCollection Objects

Start by creating a new DLL ATL COM AppWizard project called `BUObject`, and then insert a new simple object called `Employee`. This is the object that will be inserted into the business unit `DeveloperCollection` object later on.

This object really will be quite simple. It should have two properties — a `BSTR` property called `Name`, and a `long` property called `EmployeeID` — that you can add using the ClassView. Open `Employee.h` and add the following members to the bottom of the class declaration to hold the property values, and initialize the employee ID in the constructor:

```
    CEmployee() : m_lEmployeeID(0)

    ...

private:
    CComBSTR m_bstrName;
    long     m_lEmployeeID;
};
```

Next, implement the property handlers to give access to these data members, and then compile the code to make sure you haven't introduced any typing errors.

```
STDMETHODIMP CEmployee::get_Name(BSTR * pVal)
{
    return m_bstrName.CopyTo(pVal);
}

STDMETHODIMP CEmployee::put_Name(BSTR newVal)
{
    m_bstrName = newVal;
    return S_OK;
}

STDMETHODIMP CEmployee::get_EmployeeID(long * pVal)
{
    *pVal = m_lEmployeeID;
    return S_OK;
}

STDMETHODIMP CEmployee::put_EmployeeID(long newVal)
{
    m_lEmployeeID = newVal;
    return S_OK;
}
```

Our next task is to create the DeveloperCollection class that will hold Employee objects. To do this, add another simple object with the name DeveloperCollection. Use ClassView to add a read-only property called Count: make the type long and deselect the Put Function check box. Then, add another read-only property called _NewEnum and make the type LPUNKNOWN. Before dismissing the dialog, however, click on Attributes... and add the [restricted] attribute to ensure that Visual Basic users cannot access this property. Note that we can't change the DISPID to DISPID_NEWENUM here because the Wizard doesn't accept identifiers or negative numbers. You can then close both dialogs.

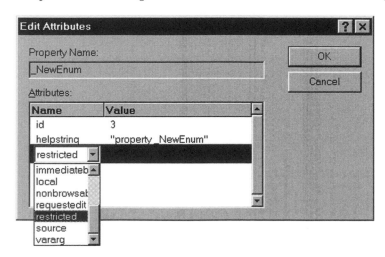

Finally, add a read-only property called Item that returns a VARIANT and has a single [in] parameter that is a VARIANT:

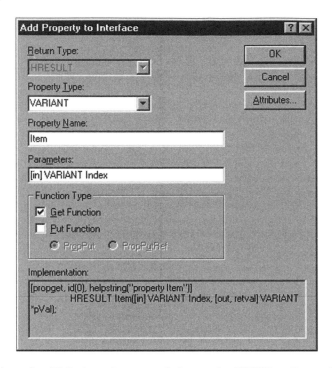

You must also click on the **Attributes...** button and change the DISPID to 0 to make this the default item. You cannot enter a symbolic name in this dialog, so you must use the actual value.

This object will have an Add() member in addition to the mandatory members. Use ClassView to add this method to the IDeveloperCollection interface. Because the client can create the Employee, the method should have an [in] parameter called IEmployee* pEmployee.

Our next task is to tidy up the IDL for the project. Since you couldn't add the required negative ID in the **Attributes** dialog, you have to amend the DISPID for _NewEnum by hand. Open the BUObject.idl file and change the DISPID of the _NewEnum property to DISPID_NEWENUM. The IDL for the interface should look something like this:

```
interface IDeveloperCollection : IDispatch
{
    [propget, id(1), helpstring("property Count")]
        HRESULT Count([out, retval] long *pVal);
    [propget, id(DISPID_NEWENUM), helpstring("property _NewEnum"), restricted]
        HRESULT _NewEnum([out, retval] LPUNKNOWN *pVal);
    [propget, id(0), helpstring("property Item")]
        HRESULT Item([in] VARIANT Index, [out, retval] VARIANT *pVal);
    [id(2), helpstring("method Add")]
        HRESULT Add([in] IEmployee* pEmployee);
};
```

The actual DISPIDs of Count and Add() do not matter, but _NewEnum must be DISPID_NEWENUM (-4) and Item must be DISPID_VALUE (0). This latter is important so that Visual Basic can access the property using square brackets.

The collection will hold values in an STL `map<>`, so open `DeveloperCollection.h` and add the following headers above the class declaration. The `pragma` is added because when you use STL containers, the symbol names used in debug builds are likely to be very large. If they are longer than 256 characters, you will get warning 4786, which we are therefore suppressing.

```
#include "resource.h"          // main symbols
#include <map>
#include "Employee.h"
#pragma warning(disable : 4786)
```

To make life easier, define the following `typedef`s just below the `#includes`:

```
typedef std::map<CComBSTR, CComPtr<IEmployee> > EmpMap;
typedef CComEnumOnSTL<IEnumVARIANT, &IID_IEnumVARIANT, VARIANT,
                    _Copy<VARIANT>, EmpMap> VarEnum;
typedef ICollectionOnSTLImpl<IDeveloperCollection, EmpMap, VARIANT,
                    _Copy<VARIANT>, VarEnum> CollImpl;
```

The items are held in a `std::map<>` as `BSTR`s and `IEmployee` pointers, so this code seems reasonable enough, but in fact it's incorrect, as you'll see in a moment. However, we'll leave it alone for now, and move on to change our class's base class to use the new `typedef`:

```
class ATL_NO_VTABLE CDeveloperCollection :
    public CComObjectRootEx<CComSingleThreadModel>,
    public CComCoClass<CDeveloperCollection, &CLSID_DeveloperCollection>,
    public IDispatchImpl<CollImpl, &IID_IDeveloperCollection,
                    &LIBID_BUOBJECTLib, 1, 0>
```

The changes here are to replace `IDeveloperCollection` with `CollImpl` and to add the version of the type library. If you compile the project now, you will get an error; the compiler will churn out a large message, but the essence of it is that the `copy()` member of `_Copy<VARIANT>` takes a `VARIANT*` and not a `std::pair<CComBSTR const, CComPtr<IEmployee> >*`. Now, the error itself is fairly straightforward, because the `copy()` method is declared like this:

```
static HRESULT copy(VARIANT* p1, VARIANT* p2) {return VariantCopy(p1, p2);}
```

But where is the `std::pair<>*` coming from? Its source is the `ICollectionOnSTLImpl<>` class's implementation of the `get_Item()` method, which looks like this:

```
STDMETHOD(get_Item)(long Index, ItemType* pvar)
{
    //Index is 1-based
    if (pvar == NULL)
        return E_POINTER;
    HRESULT hr = E_FAIL;
    Index--;
    CollType::iterator iter = m_coll.begin();
    while (iter != m_coll.end() && Index > 0)
    {
        iter++;
        Index--;
    }
    if (iter != m_coll.end())
        hr = CopyItem::copy(pvar, &*iter);
    return hr;
}
```

In other words, it creates an STL iterator, initializes it to the beginning of the map, and then iterates until it gets to the position indicated by the passed index. At this point, it copies the item using the copy() method of _Copy<VARIANT>. pvar is a VARIANT*, but each item in the map is a std::pair<> so that the map can index items using a CComBSTR. Because of this, you need to provide your own copy policy class.

Open atlcom.h and find _Copy<VARIANT>. Copy it, paste it into DeveloperCollection.h, and edit it to look like this:

```
class _CopyMapItem
{
public:
   static HRESULT copy(VARIANT* p1,
                      std::pair<const CComBSTR, CComPtr<IEmployee> >* p2)
   {
      CComPtr<IEmployee> p = p2->second;
      CComVariant var = p;
      return VariantCopy(p1, &var);
   }
   static void init(VARIANT* p) {p->vt = VT_EMPTY;}
   static void destroy(VARIANT* p) {VariantClear(p);}
};
```

Now we have the correct type of the data to copy, and code to extract the data that we wish to copy. Use this new class by replacing _Copy<VARIANT> with _CopyMapItem in the typedefs you added earlier. You'll probably also have to add a forward reference to _CopyMapItem, depending on where you placed the above code:

```
class _CopyMapItem;
typedef std::map<CComBSTR, CComPtr<IEmployee> > EmpMap;
typedef CComEnumOnSTL<IEnumVARIANT, &IID_IEnumVARIANT, VARIANT,
                     _CopyMapItem, EmpMap> VarEnum;
typedef ICollectionOnSTLImpl<IDeveloperCollection, EmpMap, VARIANT,
                     _CopyMapItem, VarEnum> CollImpl;
```

The next task is to *delete* some of the code added to the class by the Object Wizard. ICollectionOnSTLImpl<> implements get_Count(), get__NewEnum() and get_Item(), but the Object Wizard has also added these methods to the class, so they will override the base class versions. In fact, we *want* this for get_Item() (because we want to index on a VARIANT), but we want the base class implementations of the other two. Delete the declarations for get_Count() and get__NewEnum() from DeveloperCollection.h, and get rid of their respective implementations in DeveloperCollection.cpp.

At the bottom of the class, add the following private method that will be used to extract information from the employee:

```
private:
   void GetEmployee(IEmployee* pEmployee, CComBSTR& bstrName, long& pEmployeeID);
```

Open DeveloperCollection.cpp and enter the implementation for this method:

```
void CDeveloperCollection::GetEmployee(IEmployee* pEmployee,
                                       CComBSTR& bstrName,
                                       long&     pEmployeeID)
{
   pEmployee->get_Name(&bstrName);
   pEmployee->get_EmployeeID(&pEmployeeID);
}
```

Next up is the `Add()` method:

```
STDMETHODIMP CDeveloperCollection::Add(IEmployee * pEmployee)
{
    CComBSTR bstrName;
    long ID;
    GetEmployee(pEmployee, bstrName, ID);

    if(bstrName.Length() == 0)
    {
        ATLTRACE(_T("Employee %ld must have a name\n"), ID);
        return E_INVALIDARG;
    }

    ATLTRACE(_T("Adding Employee %ls (%ld)\n"), bstrName, ID);
    m_coll[bstrName] = pEmployee;
    return S_OK;
}
```

This code checks that the `Employee` object passed in has a non-empty name; this is because the `Name` property is used as the key for the entry in the STL map. The item is then added into the map with the line:

```
m_coll[bstrName] = pEmployee;
```

This is the wonderful thing about STL containers: you can insert, and access, an item in the map using the `[]` operator. The parameter on the left-hand side is the key to use when inserting an item, while the right-hand side is the item to insert. `m_coll` is a member of the `ICollectionOnSTLImpl<>` base class.

The last remaining method is a big one, which is why it's been left it until last! The `Item` property will support accessing items in two ways: by passing in an index, and by passing in a key. Enter the following implementation for `get_Item()`:

```
STDMETHODIMP CDeveloperCollection::get_Item(VARIANT Index, VARIANT *pVal)
{
    VariantInit(pVal);

    // Check to see if a number has been passed
    if(Index.vt == VT_I4)
    {
        // Use the base class
        return CollImpl::get_Item(Index.lVal, pVal);
    }

    // Check to see if a string has been passed
    else if(Index.vt == VT_BSTR)
    {
        // Indexed by name
        std::map<CComBSTR, CComPtr<IEmployee> >::iterator it;

        // Look for an item with this key
        it = m_coll.find(Index.bstrVal);

        if(it == m_coll.end())
        {
            // Can't find it
            return E_INVALIDARG;
        }
        pVal->vt = VT_DISPATCH;
        IEmployee* pEmp;
        pEmp = (*it).second;
```

```
        // Copy the item's IDispatch into pItem (also implicit AddRef())
        return pEmp->QueryInterface(IID_IDispatch,
                                    (void**) &(pVal->pdispVal));
    }

    // Unrecognised index type
    else
        return E_INVALIDARG;
}
```

Access via the key is obviously the most efficient here, since maps are designed for such access. However, the index method is provided to show you that it is possible. Notice that a QI() is made to get the IDispatch pointer when an item is found. This involves an implicit AddRef() on the interface, because when you QI() you are making a copy of the pointer. The client is required to call Release() on the pointer when it has finished with it (and Visual Basic will do this for you).

Testing The DeveloperCollection Class

Now we need to test this collection. To do that, we will use a simple Visual Basic test application. Create a new **Standard EXE** project in Visual Basic and add the following controls with the names indicated:

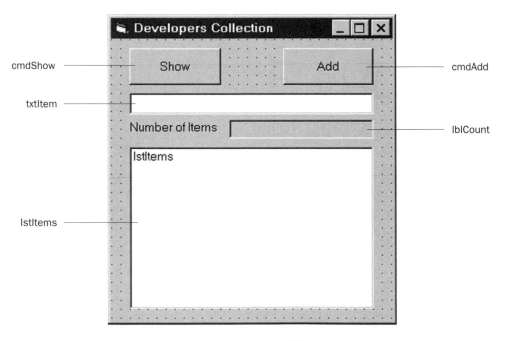

Select the Project | References... menu item, find the **BUObject 1.0 Type Library** entry, and check it. Then, add the following to the top of the code for the form:

```
Dim Devs As DeveloperCollection
Dim id As Long
```

This defines an object called Devs that should be created when the form loads. The other variable is the ID that we will use to initialize the new Employees that we add to the collection. You need to create the collection when the form loads, so add the following code:

```
Private Sub Form_Load()
    Set Devs = New DeveloperCollection
    id = 0
End Sub
```

This code uses `CoCreateInstance()` to create a new `DeveloperCollection` object. The `Devs` object has the default interface of the new object, which is `IDeveloperCollection`. Now double click on the **Add** button and add the following code to the skeleton provided:

```
Private Sub cmdAdd_Click()
    If txtItem = "" Then Exit Sub
    Dim Emp As New Employee
    id = id + 1
    Emp.Name = txtItem
    Emp.EmployeeID = id
    Devs.Add Emp
    LblCount = Str$(Devs.Count)
    txtItem = ""
End Sub
```

If there is a value in the text box, this code will add a new `Employee` to the collection using the text as the name of the `Employee`. To do this, we create a new `Employee` object (using `New`) and initialize its properties with the text in `txtItem` and the number in the global `id` variable. (This variable is incremented so that the next time **Add** is clicked, a different value is used.) This new `Employee` object is put into the collection by calling `Add`, and then the label is updated with the number of items in the collection.

Finally, double click on the **Show** button and add this code:

```
Private Sub cmdShow_Click()
    Dim Emp As Employee
    lstItems.Clear
    For Each Emp In Devs
        lstItems.AddItem Emp.Name & ", " & Str$(Emp.EmployeeID)
    Next
End Sub
```

This code uses `For Each` to iterate through the collection. Visual Basic gets the collection's `_NewEnum` property and uses the enumerator to iterate through all the items in the collection. This code just reads the name and ID of each item and adds them into the list box.

You can now run this test application and add several names to the collection by typing each one into the edit box and then clicking on **Add**. To get the contents of the collection, click on **Show**.

417

The BUObject Object

Our original specification had the `DeveloperCollection` as a property of a `BusinessUnit` object; so let's do that. The first thing you must do is close Visual Basic so that it releases the `BUObject.dll`, and then return to Visual C++. Reopen the `BUObject` project, and insert a new simple object with a short name of `BusinessUnit`.

Use ClassView to add two read/write properties called `Manager` and `Secretary` that are both of type `LPDISPATCH`. Add a third `LPDISPATCH` property called `Developers` that is read-only. Now we need to add variables to hold these properties, so open `BusinessUnit.h` and add the following private data members:

```
private:
    CComQIPtr<IEmployee> m_pManager;
    CComQIPtr<IEmployee> m_pSecretary;
    CComPtr<IDeveloperCollection> m_pDevelopers;
```

The first two of these use the `CComQIPtr<>` smart pointer, because they will be initialized with an `IDispatch` pointer in their `put_` methods. The `m_pDevelopers` member is read-only, so we do not need the automatic `QueryInterface()` supplied by `CComQIPtr<>`.

The property methods are straightforward. Open `BusinessUnit.cpp`, and add this code:

```
STDMETHODIMP CBusinessUnit::get_Manager(LPDISPATCH *pVal)
{
    return m_pManager->QueryInterface(pVal);
}

STDMETHODIMP CBusinessUnit::put_Manager(LPDISPATCH newVal)
{
    m_pManager = newVal;
    return S_OK;
}

STDMETHODIMP CBusinessUnit::get_Secretary(LPDISPATCH *pVal)
{
    return m_pSecretary->QueryInterface(pVal);
}

STDMETHODIMP CBusinessUnit::put_Secretary(LPDISPATCH newVal)
{
    m_pSecretary = newVal;
    return S_OK;
}

STDMETHODIMP CBusinessUnit::get_Developers(LPDISPATCH *pVal)
{
    return m_pDevelopers->QueryInterface(pVal);
}
```

The `get_` methods use the type safe `QueryInterface()` method to convert the smart pointer to an `IDispatch` pointer, and in the process `AddRef()` the pointer to comply with the COM rules. The `put_` methods use the overloaded `operator=()` of `CComQIPtr<>` to automatically `QI()` the passed-in `IDispatch` pointer for the `IEmployee` interface.

The code has not created any of these properties, so we need to do that when the `BusinessUnit` object is created. As so often, the best place to do this is in `FinalConstruct()`. In `BusinessUnit.h`, add this declaration after the COM map:

```
    HRESULT FinalConstruct();
```

Add this code to the top of the .cpp file so that we can access the CEmployee and
CDeveloperCollection classes:

```
#include "BusinessUnit.h"
#include "Employee.h"
#include "DeveloperCollection.h"
```

And lastly, add this code:

```
HRESULT CBusinessUnit::FinalConstruct()
{
    CComObject<CDeveloperCollection>* pDevs;
    HRESULT hr = CComObject<CDeveloperCollection>::CreateInstance(&pDevs);
    if(FAILED(hr))
        return hr;
    m_pDevelopers = pDevs;

    CComObject<CEmployee>* pEmp;
    hr = CComObject<CEmployee>::CreateInstance(&pEmp);
    if(FAILED(hr))
        return hr;
    pEmp->put_Name(CComBSTR(_T("<vacant>")));
    m_pManager = pEmp;

    hr = CComObject<CEmployee>::CreateInstance(&pEmp);
    if(FAILED(hr))
        return hr;
    pEmp->put_Name(CComBSTR(_T("<vacant>")));
    m_pSecretary = pEmp;

    return hr;
}
```

As you know, ATL classes are abstract, so we cannot create them directly. To create objects from these
classes, we need to use the CComObject<> template. Since the classes we are creating may have
FinalConstruct() methods (although they do not in this example), this code uses the static method
CreateInstance() to create instances of the objects:

```
    CComObject<CDeveloperCollection>* pDevs;
    HRESULT hr = CComObject<CDeveloperCollection>::CreateInstance(&pDevs);
```

These lines create a new DeveloperCollection COM object, and put a reference to it in pDevs. At this
point, the reference count on this object is zero, but the line

```
    m_pDevelopers = pDevs;
```

uses the CComPtr<>'s overloaded operator=(), which copies the pointer and calls AddRef() on it.

The Manager and Secretary objects are created in a similar way, except that to indicate that they have
no Employee, the Name is initialized to "<vacant>", and the EmployeeID is left with its default value of
0.

We do not need to release these objects explicitly because the destructor of the smart pointers will be
called when the BusinessUnit component is released, and smart pointer destructors release their
contained interface pointers.

Testing The BusinessUnit Class

Finally, we need to test `BusinessUnit`, for which purpose we can again use Visual Basic. Create a new Visual Basic project and add the following controls to the form:

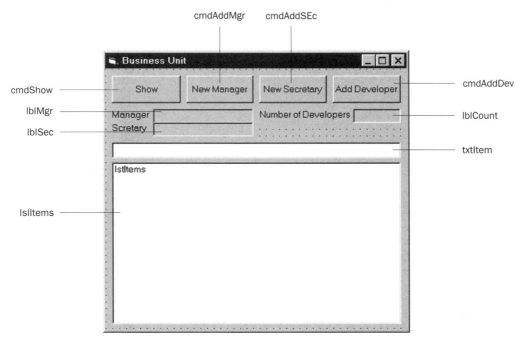

Add a reference to the **BUObject 1.0 Type Library** and, as before, add two variables to the code:

```
Dim bu As BusinessUnit
Dim id As Long
```

Add the code for `Form_Load()`:

```
Private Sub Form_Load()
    Set bu = New BusinessUnit
    id = 0
    lblCount = Str$(bu.Developers.Count)
    lblMgr = bu.Manager.Name
    lblSec = bu.Secretary.Name
End Sub
```

This creates a new, uninitialized `BusinessUnit` object. It also fills the labels with the values of the properties of this object. The next thing you need to do is add handlers for adding new developers to the collection, and changing the `Manager` and `Secretary`. So, double click on the `cmdAddMgr` button, and add these lines to change the `Manager` property:

```
Private Sub cmdAddMgr_Click()
    If txtItem = "" Then Exit Sub
    Dim emp As New Employee
    id = id + 1
    emp.Name = txtItem
    emp.EmployeeID = id
    bu.Manager = emp
    lblMgr = bu.Manager.Name
    txtItem = ""
End Sub
```

First, we check the text box to see if it has data, and if it is empty we do no more processing. Then we create a new `Employee` object and initialize its properties with the value in the text box and the `id` variable. The `Manager` member of the `BusinessUnit` object is assigned to this new object, and finally we update the display.

The `Secretary` property is handled in a similar way. Double click on the `cmdAddSec` button, and add these lines to change the `Secretary` property:

```
Private Sub cmdAddSec_Click()
    If txtItem = "" Then Exit Sub
    Dim emp As New Employee
    id = id + 1
    emp.Name = txtItem
    emp.EmployeeID = id
    bu.Secretary = emp
    lblSec = bu.Secretary.Name
    txtItem = ""
End Sub
```

Adding a new developer is similar, except that the new `Employee` must be added to the `DevelopersCollection`. Double click on the `cmdAddDev` button and add these lines to add a new developer:

```
Private Sub cmdAddDev_Click()
    If txtItem = "" Then Exit Sub
    Dim emp As New Employee
    id = id + 1
    emp.Name = txtItem
    emp.EmployeeID = id
    bu.Developers.Add emp
    lblCount = Str$(bu.Developers.Count)
    txtItem = ""
End Sub
```

Finally, add a handler to read the values from the `BusinessUnit` object. Double click on the `cmdShow` button and add these lines:

```
Private Sub cmdShow_Click()
    lblCount = Str$(bu.Developers.Count)
    lblMgr = bu.Manager.Name
    lblSec = bu.Secretary.Name
    lstItems.Clear
    lstItems.AddItem "Manager: " + bu.Manager.Name _
        + ", " + Str$(bu.Manager.EmployeeID)
    lstItems.AddItem "Secretary: " + bu.Secretary.Name _
        + ", " + Str$(bu.Secretary.EmployeeID)
    lstItems.AddItem "Developers:"
    If bu.Developers.Count = 0 Then
        lstItems.AddItem "  No developers"
        Exit Sub
    End If

    Dim emp As Employee
    For Each emp In bu.Developers
        lstItems.AddItem "  " + emp.Name + ", " + Str$(emp.EmployeeID)
    Next
End Sub
```

This code updates the labels and then adds the names and IDs of the `Manager` and `Secretary` to the list box. It then checks how many developers are in the collection, and if it is zero adds a message saying that there are no developers. If there *are* developers, it adds details of each using the enumerator accessed through the Visual Basic `For Each` statement.

421

To test the `BusinessUnit` object, run this application. You will see something like this:

Notice that the `Manager` and `Secretary` positions are both <vacant>, and the number of developers is zero. Type a name in the text box and click on **New Manager**, and the **Manager** label is updated with the new name. Do the same to add a secretary and a developer. When you click on **Add Developer**, you will find that the **Number of Developers** should increase by one.

Finally, click on **Show**, and you should find all the data entered in the list box:

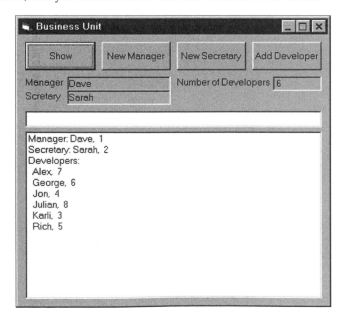

Summary

This chapter has introduced you to using properties, persisting properties, and using collections in ActiveX controls. In the first section, properties were introduced. The distinction was made between custom properties, stock properties and ambient properties, and how each should be added to a control.

After that, we discussed persistence, talking about the COM interfaces used to apply persistence and the templates that ATL provides to do most of the work for you. These templates use a property map, and the example showed how to use simple property types and objects with a property map, providing persistence with very little extra code.

Finally, the last part of the chapter introduced the methods to provide arrays or collections of data. In these last few sections we explained (and gave examples of) enumerators and Visual Basic collections.

A Full Control

The purpose of this final chapter is to wrap up all the techniques that you have seen so far. In it, you'll see the support that the ATL wizards provide for writing controls, and how to utilize this support. The example that forms a large part of the chapter illustrates most of the techniques you will use when implementing controls: message handling, drawing, property pages, and property persistence. The example also shows you how to superclass an existing Windows class.

Controls

A control is generally a visible object. Controls are *contained* by an application. The container and the control must be able to communicate with each other, so both sides expose interfaces. The container will want to tell the control to do things, notify it of events, and may also implement the control's window; while the control will want to notify the container of events so that the container can act upon them.

A visible control will need to render itself in a window, which may be created by either the control or the container. If the container creates the window, the container will use the control's interfaces to give it access to this window. When the state of the control changes, it will need to redraw itself, and hence its visual representation will change. The control will inform the container to let it know that if the container has any cached representation of the control, then that too should be updated.

Because controls have windows it means that they must be run in STAs. This also means that controls must be housed in DLLs.

Types of Control

The ATL Object Wizard gives you the option of creating several types of control, which you can see when you select the Controls category from the ATL Object Wizard:

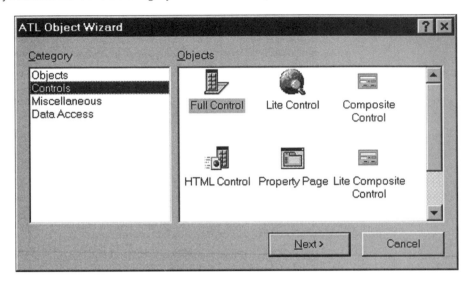

Ignoring the property page type for now, we can see that the wizard can create two versions (**full** and **lite**) of the three different types of control. These types are:

- ❑ (Basic) control
- ❑ Composite control
- ❑ HTML control

(Note that the word 'basic' does not appear in the screenshot, I'm using it here to refer to the **full control** and **lite control** types.) We'll be dealing with the basic control type in this chapter, but for completeness: a **composite control** is a control that can control (or **host**) other controls, and an **HTML control** is a control that uses a web page as its UI — and (by default) includes a DHTML page as a resource to customize this behaviour.

The difference between the full and lite versions is the number of interfaces that the wizard will add to the control. Lite controls are designed to support the minimal set of interfaces that a visual control needs to communicate effectively with Internet Explorer (and have in the past been called Internet Explorer controls for this reason). Full controls are designed to work with most containers, and provide richer functionality to the generated control.

The table below shows the interfaces provided by the wizard-generated basic controls, and which ATL class provides the implementation of that interface.

Interface	ATL Implementation Class	Supported by lite Control	Supported by full Control
IDispatch	IDispatchImpl<>	✓	✓
IViewObject	IViewObjectExImpl<>	✓	✓
IViewObject2	IViewObjectExImpl<>	✓	✓
IViewObjectEx	IViewObjectExImpl<>	✓	✓
IOleWindow	IOleInPlaceObjectWindowlessImpl<>	✓	✓
IOleInPlaceObject	IOleInPlaceObjectWindowlessImpl<>	✓	✓
IOleInPlaceObjectWindowless	IOleInPlaceObjectWindowlessImpl<>	✓	✓
IOleInPlaceActiveObject	IOleInPlaceActiveObjectImpl<>	✓	✓
IOleControl	IOleControlImpl<>	✓	✓
IOleObject	IOleObjectImpl<>	✓	✓
IPersistStreamInit	IPersistStreamInitImpl<>	✓	✓
IPersist	IPersistStreamInitImpl<>	✓	✓
IQuickActivate	IQuickActivateImpl<>	✗	✓
IPersistStorage	IPersistStorageImpl<>	✗	✓
ISpecifyPropertyPages	ISpecifyPropertyPagesImpl<>	✗	✓
IDataObject	IDataObjectImpl<>	✗	✓
IProvideClassInfo	IProvideClassInfo2Impl<>	✗	✓
IProvideClassInfo2	IProvideClassInfo2Impl<>	✗	✓

You can see that a single implementation class can support a number of interfaces when those interfaces are derived from each other. From this list you can also see that a full control can function as a lite control, since it supports all the interfaces required by IE — you can put a full control on a web page. Both control types can draw themselves and can interact with their containers. The full control provides additional persistence interfaces and support for property pages.

There are a lot of interfaces here, because the interactions between a control and its container can be pretty complicated, but ATL hides most of this complexity with its implementation classes. You have seen this already with the Prop control example in Chapter 9, review that code now to see all the code generated by ATL.

Control Implementation

ATL controls derive from CComObjectRootEx<> and CComCoClass<>, just like any other ATL COM class, but they also derive from CComControl<>. This class, and more importantly its base class CComControlBase, actually provides a lot of the power that you might think is wrapped up in the implementation classes. The following implementation classes rely on CComControlBase:

```
IDataObjectImpl<>
IOleInPlaceObjectWindowlessImpl<>
IOleInPlaceActiveObjectImpl<>
IOleObjectImpl<>
IQuickActivateImpl<>
IViewObjectExImpl<>
```

ATL 2.1 implemented the persistence interfaces IPersistStreamInit, IPersistStorage and IPersistPropertyBag with CComControlBase. This produced the unusual situation of having to derive a non-control class from CComControl<> just to get persistence functionality. This is no longer the case with ATL 3.0.

CComControlBase is a non-templated class, and implements those methods that do not depend on the type of the control. Wrapping the code for all these interface implementations into a non-template base class leads to smaller code when there are multiple controls in a module.

In addition to providing much of the implementation of a control's interfaces, CComControlBase also has some data members. These members hold:

❑ Pointers to interfaces exposed by the container

❑ The size and position of the control

❑ The control's (non-implemented) stock properties

The class also provides methods used to communicate with the container, such as retrieving the ambient properties or sending notifications.

CComControl<> is a template class derived from CComControlBase that implements methods that require access to the control's ATL class (which is the template parameter). In particular, this class implements FireOnRequestEdit() and FireOnChanged(), which require access to your control's IUnknown interface. The control can call these methods for properties marked with the [requestedit] and [bindable] IDL attributes to let the container know when the properties are about to change, or when they have changed, respectively. These methods are used when the container has passed IPropertyNotifySink interfaces to the control in order to be informed when properties change.

Composite Controls

Composite controls are made up of other controls (windows and ActiveX controls) contained on a dialog. Because of this, composite controls don't directly derive from CComControl<>, instead they derive from CComCompositeControl<> which derives from CComControl<> and CAxDialogImpl<>. This latter class is needed to allow it to host ActiveX controls on a dialog resource. The majority of a composite control's code is in CComControlBase. Because the UI is implemented by a dialog resource you don't have any drawing responsibilities. This means that the following sections on drawing are largely irrelevant to composite controls.

HTML Controls

HTML controls host the IE control. This means that they have all of the functionality of IE to navigate the Internet; render HTML and graphics; and host DocObjects (for example a Word document). You get all of this functionality for free! The IE control is hosted on a special ATL window implemented by the `CAxHostWindow` class (in `atlhost.h`); the reason why this class is used is that the IE control requires its container to support interfaces other than the normal container interfaces. In particular, this allows the container to pass an `IDispatch` interface pointer to the IE control — the so-called external dispatch interface. Scripting code hosted in the IE control can use this inteface.

Instances of `CAxHostWindow` can't be created directly, instead they are created through an instance of `CAxWindow<>` (in `atlwin.h`) which will register a special window class to host the IE control and initialise it with either HTML, a URL or with a DocObject.

The code derived from `CComControl<>` provides the control side of a control-container relationship, `CAxHostWindow` is the container side. Your code is sandwiched between the container that hosts your control and the IE control.

Because HTML controls use the IE control you can represent the UI of a HTML control with DHTML, which can be held as a resource in the control's DLL (the wizard will do this by default) or you can pass a URL to a web page. This means that your control's UI can be updated long after you control has been compiled! In general the sections in this chapter are not relevant to HTML controls.

Drawing a Control

Drawing a control is typically one of the hardest parts of its implementation, particularly since your control may need to draw itself in response to a number of different method calls or messages. For example, you need to draw the control in response to a `WM_PAINT` message, a call to `IViewObject::Draw()`, or even a call to `IDataObject::GetData()` when the container asks for a metafile representation of the control.

ATL handles one part of this for you by funneling all the drawing requests into a single method in your class called `OnDraw()`. Whenever your control needs to be drawn, ATL will make sure that `OnDraw()` is called.

`OnDraw()` is passed a reference to an `ATL_DRAWINFO` structure. This structure is not documented in the ATL help files, but you can find the definition in `AtlCtl.h`:

```
struct ATL_DRAWINFO
{
    UINT cbSize;
    DWORD dwDrawAspect;
    LONG lindex;
    DVTARGETDEVICE* ptd;
    HDC hicTargetDev;
    HDC hdcDraw;
    LPCRECTL prcBounds;
    LPCRECTL prcWBounds;
    BOOL bOptimize;
    BOOL bZoomed;
    BOOL bRectInHimetric;
    SIZEL ZoomNum;
    SIZEL ZoomDen;
};
```

The first member is the size of the structure. The rest are equivalent to their namesake parameters for `IViewObject::Draw()`. `dwDrawAspect` determines what sort of drawing will be done and will typically be `DVASPECT_CONTENT`, in other words the visual representation of the control. If the control is being asked to draw itself for a window in a container, `ptd` will be `NULL`.

If another device is used, the `ptd` and `hicTargetDev` parameters may be used to pass information about the device. A `DVTARGETDEVICE` structure is used to pass the device and driver name (for information) but also a `DEVMODE` that can be used to get information about the printer device that is being used. The `hicTargetDev` device context can be used in this case to test for the device capabilities and is provided for information purposes only.

The actual drawing should be done to the device context in `hdcDraw`. The dimensions of the window are given in the `RECTL` structure pointed to by `prcBounds`. If the drawing will be in a metafile, then `prcWBounds` will be non-`NULL` and indicates the bounding rectangle of the metafile, `prcBounds` will be within this rectangle.

The `bOptimized` flag is used to indicate whether the device context has been normalized (it's `true` if the DC has been normalized). If `bZoomed` is `true` then `ZoomNum` and `ZoomDen` give the x and y zoom ratios of the DC bounding rectangle to the natural size of the object.

Typically you will use `hdcDraw` as the device context to draw to and `prcBounds` to get the bounding rectangle. If the container uses zooming (for example changing the zoom in Word) and zooms to anything other than 100% the control must be zoomed too. You can get this zoom information in the `ZoomNum` and `ZoomDen` members.

OnDrawAdvanced()

By default, ATL also makes your drawing code simpler by setting the mapping mode of the device context to `MM_TEXT` (i.e. pixel units) and the origin of the window and viewport to (0,0). This happens in the `CComControlBase::OnDrawAdvanced()` function, which is called before `OnDraw()`.

You can override `OnDrawAdvanced()` in your own class if you want unfettered access to the device context. The easiest way to do that is to uncheck the Normalize DC box on the **Miscellaneous** tab of the Object Wizard when you create your control. When the box is checked, the wizard adds an `OnDraw()` function to the generated class; when it's unchecked, the wizard adds `OnDrawAdvanced()` instead, and you can add your drawing code to that function.

Metafiles

`CComControlBase::OnDrawAdvanced()` does not make any changes to device contexts that represent metafiles. These device contexts will be passed directly to `OnDraw()`. Typically, you'll be asked to draw into a metafile when a container calls `IDataObject::GetData()`, asking for the control to cache a metafile representation. The `CComControlBase` implementation of `IDataObject_GetData()` sets up the metafile before calling `OnDrawAdvanced()`. Some containers may also ask you to draw into a metafile device context with a call to `IViewObject::Draw()`. This is the approach taken by Internet Explorer when it requires a visual representation of a control in order to print a web page containing the control. Once again, all these requests for drawing will be passed through `OnDrawAdvanced()` to your control's `OnDraw()` function.

Windows metafiles are essentially scripts made up of GDI (Graphic Device Interface) calls. You can create a device context (DC) based on a metafile, and draw into this DC just as you would with any other. However, a metafile DC is not attached to any device, and so to see the effect of these drawing commands, you need to 'play' the metafile into the DC of an actual device. The advantage is that you can save a metafile in a disk file to play later, and once loaded in memory you can play it any number of times. Furthermore, you can scale the metafile according to the mapping mode and viewport coordinates when you play it back.

There are restrictions as to which GDI commands you can use to draw in a metafile DC. The commands are stored as tokens, so you can see what commands are possible by looking for the token definitions in WinGDI.h (search for the line #ifndef NOMETAFILE).

This means that if your drawing should be different for a metafile and a screen DC, you'll need to detect this. You can do that with the following code (bMetafile will be TRUE if the device context represents a metafile).

```
BOOL bMetafile = GetDeviceCaps(di.hdcDraw, TECHNOLOGY) == DT_METAFILE;
```

In ATL 2.1 the wizard-generated OnDraw() code used DrawText(), which is one GDI function that can't be used in metafiles. This meant that when you printed an ATL 2.1 control, your carefully positioned text did not appear. Thankfully, in ATL 3.0 the wizard now generates code that uses the metafile friendly TextOut() instead.

Sizing & Positioning Controls

There are two approaches to sizing controls: either the control will do it (autosizing) or the container will. If the container sizes the control, there are two options: content sizing and integral sizing. For integral sizing, the container passes a preferred size to the control, and the control should then resize itself. In content sizing, the container passes the control a suggested size and the control can adjust this size according to the space it thinks it should take. This communication happens when the container calls IViewObjectEx::GetNaturalExtent().

ATL controls can set the data member m_bAutoSize to true to indicate that they will autosize (and hence the control cannot be resized by the container). The default setting is false. ATL controls use content sizing, so when told to resize by the container they will return to the container their *natural size*.

An ATL control handles sizing through the methods and data members inherited through CComControlBase. The m_sizeNatural member is the size that the object thinks it is, and by default the constructor sets this to 2 by 2 inches. This is the size returned via GetNaturalExtent(). The container may not be able to show this size in its view, so the actual window size is passed to the control with IOleObject::SetExtent(). In ATL this size, the visible portion of the control, is held in CComControlBase::m_sizeExtent. Thus if you resize a control within a container, you will find that m_sizeExtent will change but m_sizeNatural will remain constant. Both of these values are held in HIMETRIC units (1 unit = 0.01mm), but they can be converted to pixels with AtlHiMetricToPixel().

In many cases, you can forget about the natural size of the control and just use the extent provided by the container. Whatever happens, the ATL_DRAWINFO::prcBounds passed to OnDraw() will always reflect the extent rather than the natural size. The natural size is only used in two cases (both when the normally false m_bDrawFromNatural is set to true). The first case is when the container has asked the object to render itself in a metafile using IDataObject::GetData(), and the second is when calculating zoom information.

The control will have some size and position within the document of the container, and the control is told of this when the container calls `IOleInPlaceObject::SetObjectRects()`. ATL stores this value in `m_rcPos`, but note that it is in the screen coordinate units of the container. You'll rarely need to use this, but it could be used if, for example, you want to create a floating modeless dialog associated with the control and position this dialog so that you can see the control.

Sizing Example

To show you how these values change, let's develop a simple control. Use Visual C++ to create a new ATL COM AppWizard project called `Extents`. Ensure that the Server Type is set to Dynamic Link Library (DLL). Now insert a new Full Control into the project using the ATL Object Wizard and give the control a short name of `Sizes`.

Open `Sizes.h` and replace the implementation of `OnDraw()` with a simple declaration, we'll implement this function in `Sizes.cpp`:

```
// in Sizes.h:
HRESULT OnDraw(ATL_DRAWINFO& di);
```

```
// in Sizes.cpp
HRESULT CSizes::OnDraw(ATL_DRAWINFO& di)
{
   RECT& rc = *(RECT*)di.prcBounds;
   TCHAR str[1024];
   wsprintf(str, _T("Natural: (%ld,%ld)"),
            m_sizeNatural.cx, m_sizeNatural.cy);
   TextOut(di.hdcDraw, rc.left, rc.top, str, lstrlen(str));
   wsprintf(str, _T("Extent: (%ld,%ld)"), m_sizeExtent.cx, m_sizeExtent.cy);
   TextOut(di.hdcDraw, rc.left, rc.top + 20, str, lstrlen(str));
   wsprintf(str, _T("Position: (%ld,%ld)-(%ld,%ld)"),
            m_rcPos.left, m_rcPos.top, m_rcPos.right, m_rcPos.bottom);
   TextOut(di.hdcDraw, rc.left, rc.top + 40, str, lstrlen(str));
   wsprintf(str, _T("rcBounds: (%ld,%ld)-(%ld,%ld)"),
            di.prcBounds->left, di.prcBounds->top, di.prcBounds->right,
            di.prcBounds->bottom);
   TextOut(di.hdcDraw, rc.left, rc.top + 60, str, lstrlen(str));
   wsprintf(str, _T("Zoomed: (%ld,%ld):(%ld,%ld)"),
            di.ZoomNum.cx, di.ZoomNum.cy, di.ZoomDen.cx, di.ZoomDen.cy);
   TextOut(di.hdcDraw, rc.left, rc.top + 80, str, lstrlen(str));
   int caps = ::GetDeviceCaps(di.hdcDraw, TECHNOLOGY);
   if (caps == DT_METAFILE)
      wsprintf(str, _T("MetaFile"));
   else
      wsprintf(str, _T("Other %ld"), caps);
   TextOut(di.hdcDraw, rc.left, rc.top + 100, str, lstrlen(str));
   MoveToEx(di.hdcDraw, rc.left, rc.top, NULL);
   LineTo(di.hdcDraw, rc.right, rc.bottom);
   MoveToEx(di.hdcDraw, rc.right, rc.top, NULL);
   LineTo(di.hdcDraw, rc.left, rc.bottom);
   return S_OK;
}
```

This simply prints out the various sizes on the control. Note that no attempt is made to ensure that the data stays within the control. If the control is smaller than 100 pixels high then some of the lower values will be clipped.

So that you can see that the control is being drawn in the values given by `prcBounds` the code also draws a line across each diagonal.

Compile the code. Now run the ActiveX Control Test Container (from the Tools menu) and from the Edit menu select Insert New Control.... In the dialog, select Sizes Class and click OK. Drag the control around the container; when you drop the control, you should find that the value given by Position will change.

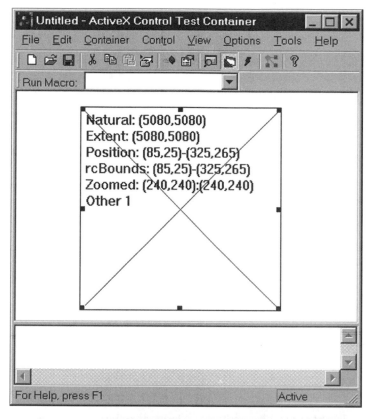

Now resize the control and watch the values.

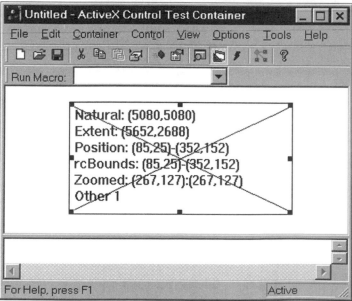

Notice that the natural size is still the same, but the other values have changed. The Other 1 value is the constant DT_RASDISPLAY, and indicates that the drawing is being done to the screen. Also note that the vertical spacing between the text lines is always the same, whatever size the control is. The diagonal lines are specifically drawn between the corners of the control, and the vertices are calculated from the control's extents.

From the Control menu select Draw MetaFile. The test container passes a metafile to your control, which will draw itself again. So that you can see what the control has put in the metafile the test container creates a window and plays the metafile in it. You should see the same values, except that MetaFile will be displayed at the bottom.

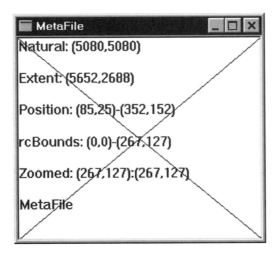

If you resize this window, you'll find that the values do not change. The reason is that the numeric values are only relevant at the time that the metafile was initailized by the control. When you resize the window, the same GDI commands will be played again, so the text does not change.

The container does note the actual size of the metafile, and any positions expressed in the GDI commands are relative to these extents. When the test container replays the metafile it uses these relative positions. This is why when you resize the window the diagonal lines will still be from corner to corner. Furthermore, the relative horizontal spacings between the text will be preserved, whatever shape you stretch the window to.

Interaction with the Container

As mentioned earlier, controls are embedded within containers. To do this they should implement the IOleInPlaceObject and IOleInPlaceActiveObject interfaces (both of which are derived from IOleWindow), so that they can receive information about their site in the container.

The first interface is used by the container to activate and deactivate the control, in particular it is used to tell the control the size and position of the control in the container's window, as we have already seen, with SetObjectRects(). This interface is implemented by CComControlBase, and exposed through IOleInPlaceObjectWindowlessImpl<>.

The second interface is quite interesting in that the container uses it to inform the control of changes in its frame and document windows. So when the container's document activates, it should call the control's OnDocWindowActivate(TRUE), which the control should use if it wants to add menus or toolbars to the container. Likewise, when the document window deactivates, the container calls OnDocWindowActivate(FALSE) so that these additional features can be removed. The ATL implementation, IOleInPlaceActiveObjectImpl<>, however, does nothing.

Windowless Controls

A control does not need to create a window of its own, instead it may allow the container to create and maintain its window. This way, if there are many controls, the container can conserve resources by giving each control access to part of its document window. This also means that a control does not need to be rectangular, since the container document will be responsible for painting the background behind the control.

These 'windowless' controls need special support from the container, which has to implement the IOleInPlaceSiteWindowless interface. If the container does not provide this support, the control can simply create its own window. An ATL control has a data member, m_bWindowOnly that can be set to true to force the control to create its own window.

Windowless controls are a relatively recent COM standard so some containers may not support them. In that case, the ATL control will create a window for itself.

The term 'windowless' is a bit misleading since these controls have still have a window, it is just that they are not responsible for creating the window. Since the 'windowless' control's window is managed by the container, a control relies on the container to forward Windows messages to it. The control must implement IOleInPlaceObjectWindowless, which derives from IOleInPlaceObject. The container can call IOleInPlaceObjectWindowless::OnWindowMessage() passing the message applicable to the control. ATL implements this method using ProcessWindowMessage(), which is provided when you add a message map to the class.

Advise Interfaces

The container typically holds much information about the control. As the user interacts with the control, its state will change, and this may mean that the information that the container has about the control will be out of date. The container can decide to ask the control to notify it of changes in the control. There are two ways that this can be done, through a connection point, or through an advise interface. Both mechanisms are used for standard communications with the container.

Connection Points

The advise interface mechanism can be seen as a lightweight version of connection points. Remember, with a connection point, a client implements a sink interface on a sink object, and connects to the control passing an interface pointer to this object for notifications from the control. This connection is made through a connection point specific to the control source interface with which the client is trying to connect. The connection point maintains an array of sink interface pointers connected to the connection point.

When the client wants to make the connection, it asks the control if it has a connection point for the source interface. If so, the connection point container in the control gives the client access to the connection point object. The client can then pass the IUnknown pointer of its sink object to the connection point object, in a method called Advise(). The connection point object holds this sink interface pointer in an internally held array. In ATL, Advise() will also do a QI() on the passed in sink interface, to get the sink interface it expects.

When the control wants to notify the connected clients, it obtains the connection point object for the source interface and can then enumerate the sink interfaces held in the connection point. The control can then call the appropriate notification method on each of these sink interfaces. As you saw in Chapter 8, you have to write this enumeration code or get the ClassView wizard to do it for you.

The advantage of this approach is that multiple clients can connect to a single control, and it means that a single control can have multiple connectable interfaces. The client can call IConnectionPointContainer::FindConnectionPoint() to determine if the control supports the connectable interface. However, the sink interface and connectable interfaces are not Microsoft defined and of course the client and control need to know about both. This means that the control will need to define the outgoing interface in its IDL (and mark it as [source]) so that the marshaling code and interface header files are generated.

IAdviseSink

An advise interface is a sink interface that the client (the container) implements. This is a Microsoft defined interface called IAdviseSink, and when compiling applications that use (or implement) this interface, you only need to have access to the interface C++ header as part of the standard SDK files. Furthermore, every machine will already have a marshaling proxy in the ole32.dll already installed and registered, which means you do not have to change your object's IDL to support advise interfaces. However, it does mean that the client is restricted in the notifications it can receive; and these are defined by the methods of IAdviseSink. Controls should support this advise interface for legacy reasons — IAdviseSink predates connection points.

A control can accept advise sinks from many clients and so to maintain these interfaces it should create a separate object, called an **advise holder**. This object is like a connection point object, but it differs in two important respects. Firstly, advise holders are created and implemented by COM. Client notification is carried out by calling on a single method of the advise holder, rather than having to enumerate all the sink interface as is necessary with connection points. The second difference is that advise holders can only manage one interface type: IAdviseSink.

COM defines two advise holders created with CreateDataAdviseHolder() and CreateOleAdviseHolder(), and accessed through the IDataAdviseHolder and IOleAdviseHolder interfaces. The first, the data advise holder, notifies clients when data (properties) change in the control. The second, the OLE advise holder, informs connected clients when the control is saved or closed.

Compare the following diagram with the equivalent in Chapter 8:

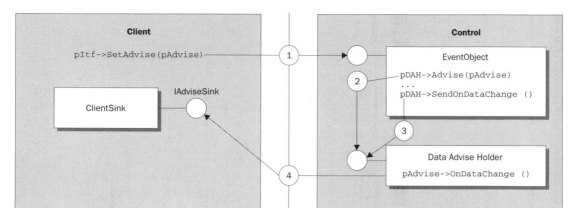

1. The client informs the control of its advise sink

2. The control adds this to its list by calling on its advise holder object (here it is a data advise holder) to save the interface pointer.

3. At some later point in time, an event occurs and the control notifies all the connected clients. To do this it calls on the data advise holder's `SendOnDataChange()` method

4. This goes through all the interface pointers that it holds and on each it calls `OnDataChange()`. The client sink object can then handle this event.

Notice the advantages of this approach. Firstly, you do not have to implement these advise holders, COM implements two for you, and when you release a holder, it will automatically release all the interfaces it holds. To notify connected clients, you do not have to enumerate all the sink interfaces, instead the holder will do this for you.

But there are problems. The main one is that only one interface is supported: `IAdviseSink`, and this restricts the events that are handled. These events are evident from the names of the methods in this interface: `OnClose()`, `OnDataChange()`, `OnRename()`, `OnSave()` and `OnViewChange()`. These methods take parameters pertinent to the event they handle, so you cannot readily use them for other events (if you implement a container for example).

ATL holds these advise holder objects using the smart pointers `m_spDataAdviseHolder` and `m_spOleAdviseHolder` in `CComControlBase`. The advise sink interfaces are registered with the control by the container calling either the `IOleObject::Advise()` or `IDataObject::DAdvise()` method. In addition to these holders, the control may be informed of an OLE advisory connection by the container calling `IViewObject::SetAdvise()`. Only a single advisory connection can be registered in this way and ATL saves this in `m_spAdviseSink`. This interface is used to notify the container of the one event not covered by the two previously mentioned advise holders: `OnViewChange()`, which is called when the view of the control has changed.

So when are these interfaces used?

The data advise holder is used by `CComControlBase::SendOnDataChange()` when properties change in the control. Note that you should call this method in the `put_` method of a property, but if the control uses a stock property, its `put_` method will be implemented by the stock property implementation macro `IMPLEMENT_STOCKPROP()`. This implementation will call `SendOnDataChange()` for you. `SendOnDataChange()` is used to make sure that the container knows that the data in the object has changed. It is used to pass the interface pointer of the control's `IDataObject` interface to the container, so that the container can use this to call the control to provide a metafile presentation.

The OLE advise holder is used by the `SendOnRename()`, `SendOnSave()` and `SendOnClose()` methods that your control code should call at appropriate times. The `m_spAdviseSink` interface is called by `SendOnViewChange()`, which is called by `FireViewChange()` when the control is inactive so that the container knows that any cached representations are invalid. If the control is active, it is merely told to redraw itself.

Site Interfaces

In addition to these `IAdviseSink` interfaces, the container can also implement other interfaces that the client can call. The control should implement `IOleObject`, and the container can call the `SetClientSite()` method to pass a pointer to its `IOleClientSite` interface. ATL holds this interface in the smart pointer `m_spClientSite`. The control can use this interface to get information about the display site in the container.

The final data member of interest for controls is `m_spInPlaceSite`. This smart pointer is valid if `m_bNegotiatedWnd` is set to true (which it is once the control is activated), and is the container's `IOleInPlaceSiteWindowless` interface pointer (or one of the base interfaces'). The control can use this interface to specify how activation is handled by the container and also to handle mouse capture and route Windows messages.

Object Wizard Options

Most of the options in Object Wizard have already been discussed in the other chapters, now let's look at the remaining options: those pertaining to controls. When you insert a control with the Object Wizard you will see, in addition to the familiar **Names** and **Attributes**, one or two new tabs. For basic controls (full or lite) you will see **Miscellaneous** and **Stock Properties**. The other types of control only have the **Stock Properties** tab.

The Miscellaneous Tab

The Miscellaneous page of the Object Wizard looks like this:

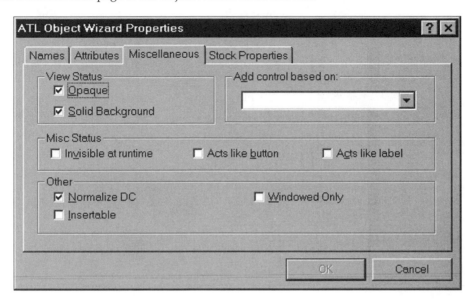

The two options in the View Status frame are inter-related. Solid Background is only enabled if Opaque is selected and indicates that the control has a solid background rather than a patterned background. Opaque means that the control draws to the entire control rectangle and will erase the background that is does not draw to. If it is not selected, it means that the control can have some transparent parts through which the container's background can be seen.

The three items in Misc Status affect the control's MiscStatus entry in the registry. The container calls IOleObject::GetMiscStatus() on the control when it is created and ATL implements this by calling the standard OleRegGetMiscStatus() function that obtains this value from the registry. Each of these check boxes sets an appropriate bit in this value.

Invisible at runtime indicates that the control is invisible when run — the control will not show in the container's window. Acts like button, means that the control's window behaves as a button, so that it can be drawn with a thick border if it is selected as the default button. Finally Acts like label, makes the control behave like a label, that is, selecting the mnemonic for the control will activate the control after it. The container decides how to interpret this bit.

The Add control based on list box allows you to base your control on an existing Windows class. There is an example of how to use this later in this chapter. Note that the drop down list box is single selection so you can base the control on just one Windows control. However, using more than one control is trivial and the example shows you how. You can also type the name of a Windows class if you want to use a class other than those that are in the list box.

We've already discussed the <u>N</u>ormalized DC option, to recap, it means that the device context is normalized so that the origin starts at (0,0). This makes the drawing code simpler. When selected, your control must implement the drawing code in OnDraw(), the normalization is carried out in OnDrawAdvanced() which calls OnDraw(). If you do not select this box, normalization will not happen and you have to implement the drawing code in OnDrawAdvanced(). Depending on your drawing code, you may get slightly better performance if you don't check this box.

In the earlier Windowless Controls section we mentioned the existance of the <u>W</u>indowed Only option, this is found here as well. If this is checked then the control *must* create its own window. The Wizard just adds m_bWindowOnly = TRUE to the constructor. Normally you will leave this unchecked so that the container will handle control windows if possible. However, if you base your control on another class this box should be unchecked because, by definition, to be based on another Windows class the control has to have a window!

Finally, Insertable allows the object to appear in the standard Insert Object dialog — it does this by adding the Insertable key in the control's CLSID registration code in the RGS file.

The Stock Properties Tab

We have already seen this tab in Chapter 8, but for completeness let's recap this page again here. Stock properties are properties implemented by the control that the container knows about. This is easiest to explain with a simple example. A container won't know what a custom property called Frequency means (is it the frequency of a sound, or the rate that something happens?), it will just know its DISPID. However, the container knows that the DISPID of -501 (DISPID_BACKCOLOR) is the color of the background of a control. If the control implements this property then its container will know that it can change the property's background color.

In addition, stock properties have certain responsibilites as far as informing containers: when stock properties are changed the container will be informed of this using the IAdviseSink and IPropertyNotifySink connection point notification mechanisms.

You can add stock properties by hand to an existing class, but, as mentioned in Chapter 8, this is a pain. The easiest way to add stock property support is through the Stock Properties tab in the Object Wizard:

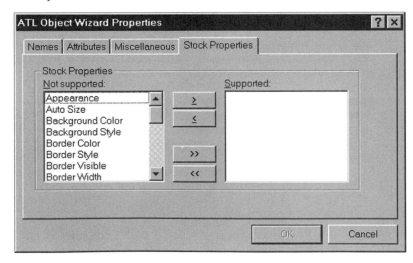

When you select one or more stock properties on this page the Object Wizard will derive your class from CStockPropImpl<> rather than IDispatchImpl<> and will add the appropriate properties to your control's dual interface.

Property Pages

Control properties can usually be set and obtained using put_ and get_ methods. Tools like VB use these methods to implement property windows where a user (programmer) can view or change an object's properties at design time. These property windows are extremely useful as they provide the user with a way of changing a control's properties without requiring any effort by the control's designer.

However, some controls may have interdependent properties, properties of some complex data type, or the control's creator may simply wish to provide a more intuitive way of setting a property than is possible via the dialogs provided by the container. In any of these situations, a property page can be used to provide an alternative (or the only) means of setting the property.

If you have any experience of using controls, you've probably seen property pages in action. Let's look at a couple of examples of the property pages used by some well known commercial controls to get an idea of the kind of things that you can do with property pages and when you'd want to make use of them for your own properties.

First, we'll take a look at the property page used by most controls that expose color properties.

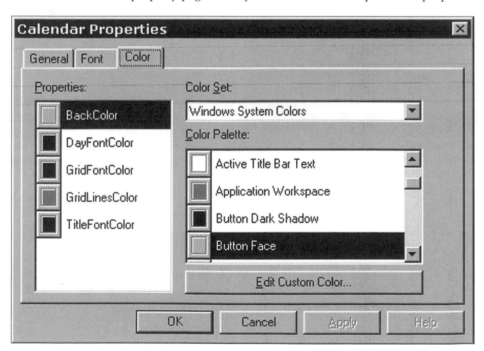

You can see that this property page provides a nice, intuitive way of setting the color value for all the different color properties supported by a control (in this case, the Microsoft Calendar control). Although colors are simple hex values that can easily be supported by any container, the property page provides a better means of setting the property. You might know that 0x000000 is black and 0xffffff is white, but most people find it pretty hard to work out the color corresponding to 0x0080ff (it's a dull orange). By providing a visual means of setting the property, and by offering choices from the standard colors and Windows system colors, the color property page is clearly an improvement on a simple hex value.

Another possible use for property pages is to provide a way of setting the properties for subobjects of your control. You can see an example of this in the Column Headers page for Microsoft's List View control, shown here:

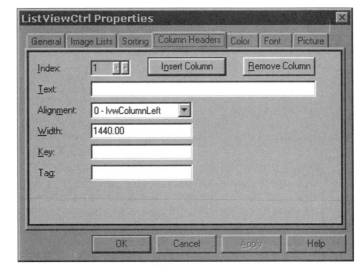

This page provides a way of creating and deleting column headers and setting each column header's properties. Each column header is a COM object provided by the List View control. Clearly property pages can be used for more than just setting top level properties on a control.

Finally, we can see how property pages can be used to group together related sets of properties. In the case of the Common Dialog control property pages shown here, all the properties are simple enough to be supported by a container's properties window. The property pages simply provide a way of separating the properties related to each of the dialogs (file, color, font, print, and help) supported by the control.

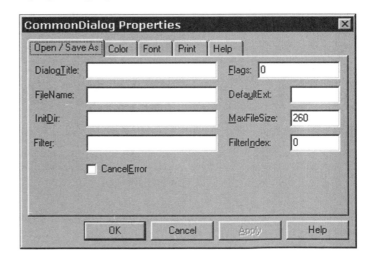

What Are Property Pages?

A property page is a COM object that implements the IPropertyPage interface. The property page is responsible for creating all the controls within the page, and for updating the properties in the control when asked to. The property page is *not* responsible for creating the dialog or even the tab that it appears in, nor is it responsible for the state of the buttons at the bottom of the dialog. Those things are the responsibility of container and its property page site.

The property page site is a COM object that implements the IPropertyPageSite interface. The property page site is provided by the container and takes responsibility for the property dialog as a whole. This enables property pages that appear in the same dialog to be written independently of each other.

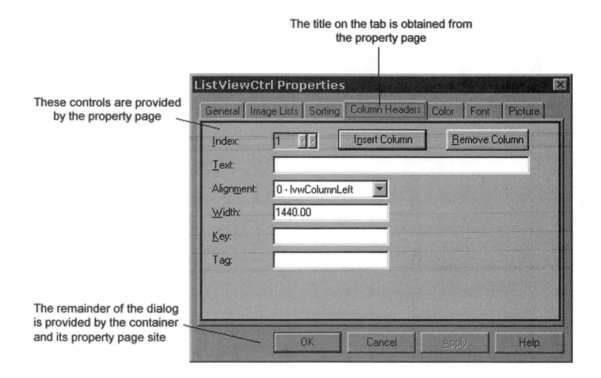

Creating a Property Page

The easiest way to create a property page is to use the ATL Object Wizard to add one to your project. Since property pages are closely associated with controls, you can find the **Property Page** item in the **Controls** group of the Object Wizard. The Wizard presents you with the familiar **Names** and **Attributes** pages to provide the standard COM settings for the property page that you're about to create, and it also provides a **Strings** page that is specific to property pages.

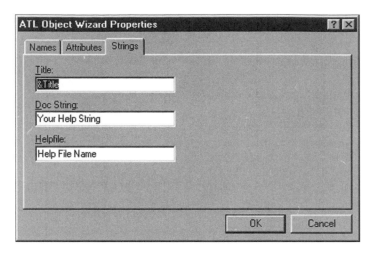

Yes, the pages used by the ATL Object Wizard itself are also COM property pages!

This information will be stored as string resources in your project and automatically returned to the container when it asks. The most important string here is the Title, which is used by the container to label the tab that it creates for your page. The Doc String can be used to describe your page, but is rarely used by containers. The Helpfile is just the name of a Windows help file for use with your page. This is only used if the page does not fully implement IPropertyPage::Help(). ATL-generated property pages implement IPropertyPage::Help() automatically.

The property page class that gets added to your project by the wizard, derives from CDialogImpl<> and IPropertyPageImpl<>. Together these classes provide 90% of the implementation that a property page needs. There are only four things that you need to do for yourself:

- ❏ Add controls to the dialog
- ❏ Initialize the page
- ❏ Tell the property page site about any changes
- ❏ Update the control

Add Controls to the Dialog

Your property pages will look pretty bare without any controls on them. You can use Visual C++'s dialog editor to add controls to the dialog resource generated by the wizard, or add some code to your class to create the controls at runtime. The types of control that you add to the page will depend entirely on the use to which you're putting your page and the types of property that you'll be adjusting.

Initialize the Page

When the property page is displayed, you'll need to initialize the page with the data from the control that it's being displayed for. You can handle the WM_INITDIALOG message to find out when the dialog has been created, and you can get the IUnknown pointer for the control whose properties the page should be setting from the m_ppUnk member of IPropertyPageImpl<>.

m_ppUnk is an array of IUnknown pointers that were passed to the property page by a call to IPropertyPage::SetObjects() (the implementation of this method is provided by IPropertyPageImpl<>). The size of this array is held in m_nObjects. The container calls SetObjects() with the IUnknown pointer of the control. You can use this pointer to query for the desired interface pointer, then use that to read the property values from the control.

Tell the Page Site About Changes

When the user changes the properties of the control via your property page, you need to tell the property page site so that it can enable the **Apply** button. You should call IPropertyPageImpl<>::SetDirty() with an argument of TRUE to indicate that something has changed. The implementation of this function handles the call to the property page site, which it does by calling m_pPageSite->OnStatusChange().

Update the Control

Finally, your page will need to update the properties of the control when told to do so by the container. The container will call IPropertyPage::Apply() when this should happen. The Object Wizard adds the following skeleton implementation of the Apply() method to your property page's class definition.

```
STDMETHOD(Apply)(void)
{
    ATLTRACE(_T("CTestPage::Apply\n"));
    for (UINT i = 0; i < m_nObjects; i++)
    {
        // Do something interesting here
        // ICircCtl* pCirc;
        // m_ppUnk[i]->QueryInterface(IID_ICircCtl,(void**)&pCirc);
        // pCirc->put_Caption(CComBSTR("something special"));
        // pCirc->Release();
    }
    m_bDirty = FALSE;
    return S_OK;
}
```

To take advantage of ATL smart pointers, this sample code should really be:

```
    for (UINT i = 0; i < m_nObjects; i++)
    {
        // Do something interesting here
        // CComPtr<ICircCtl> pCirc;
        // m_ppUnk[i]->QueryInterface(IID_ICircCtl,(void**)&pCirc);
        // pCirc->put_Caption(CComBSTR("something special"));
    }
```

But we'll ignore that oversight! The point is clear: you need to query the pointer(s) in the m_ppUnk array to get an interface that gives access to the control's properties, then copy the data from your page's controls to these properties.

This generated Apply() method is implemented inline, you may prefer to copy it into the source file, because typically you will have to change it several times. Wherever the code lies, you'll need to make sure that the header for the control's interface is included.

Relating the Page to the Control

We've seen how to code up a property page with the four simple steps outlined above, but how does the container find out from a control which property pages to display? The simple answer is that it asks it. The container will call the `GetPages()` method of the control's `ISpecifyPropertyPages` interface to get an array of GUIDs containing the property pages for that control.

ATL provides an implementation of `ISpecifyPropertyPages` in the form of the `ISpecifyPropertyPagesImpl<>` class, which is used as a base class for full controls. This class uses the information in the property map (see Chapter 9) for the control to decide what GUIDs to return in response to a call to `ISpecifyPropertyPages::GetPages()`.

This code will look through all the entries in the property map and build up an array of property page GUIDs. The property page GUIDs can appear in the map in one of three ways:

❑ As part of a `PROP_ENTRY()` macro

❑ As part of a `PROP_ENTRY_EX()` macro

❑ As part of a `PROP_PAGE()` macro

The `PROP_ENTRY()` and the `PROP_ENTRY_EX()` macros are used to provide full descriptions of a property. These descriptions can be used by a number of ATL classes including the `IPersistxxx` implementations we saw in Chapter 9, `IPerPropertyBrowsingImpl<>`, and `ISpecifyPropertyPagesImpl<>` itself. The `PROP_PAGE()` macro is used solely to provide an entry in the map to be used by `ISpecifyPropertyPagesImpl<>`.

The array will contain a single GUID for each property page specified in the map, even if it appears many times. The array will contain these GUIDs in the order that they appear in the map. Typically, this is the order that they will appear in the property dialog displayed by the container.

Full Control Example

Now that you've seen the basics of ATL controls, let's develop a control that uses most of these concepts. This example is a full control that wraps the Windows tree view and edit box common controls. The tree view will display a hierarchical view of URLs using simple names. The edit box will show the full URL for the currently selected item. Double-clicking on an item in the tree view will launch a new instance of Internet Explorer and load the URL specified by that item.

The URLs displayed in the control will be obtained from a URLs property. This property will be a SAFEARRAY of BSTRs wrapped up in a VARIANT (like the SAFEARRAY example from Chapter 5). Each string in the array will have the following form:

```
branch,url
```

branch is the branch of the tree, with sub-branches separated with forward slashes (/). The final item in the branch corresponds to the URL specified by url (which can be any URL that Internet Explorer can handle). For example, the World Of ATL sub-branch of the Wrox branch that points to http://www.worldofatl.com/ will have an entry like this:

```
Wrox/World Of ATL,http://www.worldofatl.com/
```

Notice that there is no white space around the comma.

Since we want this control to be usable from different containers including Visual Basic, we'll provide a property page, shown here, that allows the developer to add the values used to initialize the control:

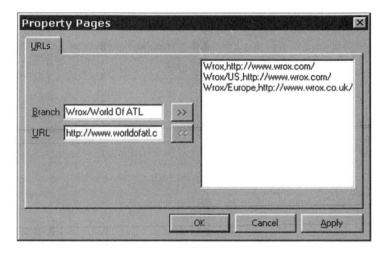

Here, I have entered the branches US and Europe on the Wrox branch, and I am about to add a new branch off the Wrox branch called World Of ATL. When I click on the >> button, the string Wrox/World Of ATL,http://www.worldofatl.com/ will be added to the list box.

We'll also need to provide persistence code for our control. The persistence code will allow the control to be used in Visual Basic and also allow us to provide values using the <PARAM> tags when the control is embedded in a web page.

Tree View Common Controls

Because we're going to be using a tree view in our control, we need to understand a little about how they work. There are several articles on MSDN that explain this in detail, but here is a potted explanation to get you started.

The tree view that you are most familiar with is the left-hand pane of the Windows Explorer, shown here.

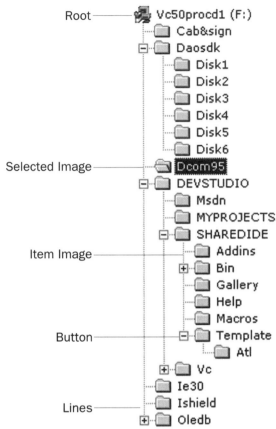

In the picture, you can see that the tree view has many branches coming off a root, in this case the root has an image of the icon for the VC++ installation program. Each item is joined to the root using lines and each item that contains child items has a button to allow you to expand or contract it. The presence of these lines and buttons isn't mandatory; the tree view control lets you set these using the window styles of the control.

Each item in the tree view example shown above is shown with a folder image. Two images are used: one when an item is selected, and another when it is not. These images are supplied by an associated image list control. When you add an item to the tree, you can specify which images in the image list to use when the item's selected and which image to use when it's not. Note that each item can have completely distinct images if you want, or no image at all.

The URLTree control should look similar to the Explorer tree, each item should have selected and non-selected images and they should be connected with lines and buttons. Compare the picture of Explorer with URLTree, and you should be able to identify the corresponding parts:

Creating a Tree View Control

If you refer back to the list of control wrappers supplied in `atlcontrols.h` (in Chapter 7), you'll see two classes we can use to help us create a tree view: `CTreeViewCtrl` and `CTreeViewCtrlEx`. The second of these two includes support for another class found in `atlcontrols.h`, `CTreeItem`. This class wraps an `HTREEITEM`.

To create a tree view in ATL, you call the `CTreeViewCtrlxx::Create()` method, using parameters as specified in the last chapter. In this example, we'll use the style parameters with a combination of these three styles:

- ❑ `TVS_HASLINES` — Lines connecting the items
- ❑ `TVS_LINESATROOT` — Root child items have lines to connect them to the root
- ❑ `TVS_HASBUTTONS` — Parent items have buttons

The `atlcontrols.h` supplied wrapper is particularly useful here. If you were just using `CWindow` there would be an awful lot of messages to learn, required every time you were to add, delete, or access items in a tree view. Sending messages to controls means using `SendMessage()` and may involve some horrible casts, which leads to ugly, unreadable code. Microsoft has also defined some macros that wrap up `SendMessage()` and the necessary casts, which we can use from ATL, but these aren't nearly as simple as using the `atlcontrols.h` wrappers. For a start, we don't have to learn about a selection of structures necessary to perform even the simplest action. All of this is hidden from us. Let's look at a few of the operations available to us, starting with adding items.

Adding Items

We can add items to a `CTreeViewCtrlxx` object using the `InsertItem()` method. This has several overloaded versions, one of which allows you to use the structures we glossed over just now, for the die-hard Win32 programmer. The easiest version to use (even though it has the most parameters!) has the following signature:

```
InsertItem(UINT nMask,
           LPCTSTR lpszItem,
           int nImage,
           int nSelectedImage,
           UINT nState,
           UINT nStateMask,
           LPARAM lParam,
           HTREEITEM hParent,
           HTREEITEM hInsertAfter)
```

449

Note that the return type of this method has been omitted. This is because this method has a different return type depending on which version of tree view object you are using. CTreeViewCtrl *returns a* HTREEITEM, CTreeViewCtrlEx *returns a wrapped version of this handle, as a* CTreeItem.

Let's examine the parameters of this method:

Parameter	Description
nMask	Determines which of the other members are valid (see below)
lpszItem	The text to display in the tree view for the item which will be created
nImage	Index in image list of image to display for the item which will be created
nSelectedImage	Index in image list of image to display when the item which will be created is selected
nState	Various state information for the item which will be created, such as if it is selected, has focus, is the target for drag and drop, or the source of a cut operation.
nStateMask	Determines which bits of nState are valid
lParam	A 32 bit value associated with the item to be created (in the example that follows we'll use this to point to the string holding the URL for the item)
hParent	The parent item, if any (note that a CTreeItem object can be used here due to its overloaded operator set)
hInsertAfter	Either the item after which to insert the new item or one of the following 'magic' values: ❑ TVI_FIRST — Inserts the item at the beginning of the list ❑ TVI_LAST — Inserts the item at the end of the list ❑ TVI_SORT — Inserts the item into the list in alphabetical order

The nMask parameter can take one or more of the following values (which can be ORed together):

Value	Meaning
TVIF_TEXT	lpszItem is valid
TVIF_IMAGE	nImage is valid
TVIF_SELECTEDIMAGE	nSelectedImage is valid
TVIF_STATE	nState and nStateMask are valid
TVIF_PARAM	lParam is valid

For example, if we wanted to create two text members in a `CTreeViewCtrlEx` object called `tvTree`, one of which is to be the child of the second, we could use the following code:

```
ATLControls::CTreeItem itmFirst, itmSecond;

itmFirst  = tvTree.InsertItem(TVIF_TEXT, _T("Item1"), 0, 0, 0, 0, 0,
                              NULL, TVI_SORT);
itmSecond = tvTree.InsertItem(TVIF_TEXT, _T("Item2"), 0, 0, 0, 0, 0,
                              itmFirst, TVI_SORT);
```

Image List Controls

As the above parameters suggest, items can have images. To do this you have to create an image list, add bitmaps into it, and associate it with the tree view. When you insert a new item, you can use the index of the bitmap in the image list as the `nImage` or `nSelectedImage` parameter of `InsertItem()`.

Image lists are another type of object that is catered for in `atlcontrols.h`, there is a class you can use called `CImageList`. There are several overloaded `Create()` methods to initialize this class, we'll use the one with the following syntax:

```
BOOL Create(int cx, int cy, UINT nFlags, int nInitial, int nGrow)
```

Where:

Parameter	Description
cx, cy	Dimensions of bitmaps in list (in pixels)
nFlags	Type of images in list (see below)
nInitial	Initial number of images in list
nGrow	Maximum number of images in list

`nFlags` can take one of the following values:

Value	Description
ILC_COLOR	Use default colours
ILC_COLOR4	Use 4-bit colour (16 colours)
ILC_COLOR8	Use 8-bit colour (256 colours)
ILC_COLOR16	Use 16-bit colour
ILC_COLOR24	Use 24 bit colour
ILC_COLOR32	Use 32 bit colour
ILC_COLORDDB	Use device dependent colour
ILC_MASK	Use transparency masks (2 entries for each bitmap)

It is common to OR the ILC_MASK value with one of the other possible values. Once an image list has been created, images can be added using the Add() method. Of course, they first have to be loaded from the module resources, which we do in a similar way to how we loaded mouse pointers into memory in Chapter 7. So, to create a new list that can contain two bitmaps of size 16x16, add these bitmaps, and use them to initialize tree view members we could use the following code:

```
ATLControls::CTreeItem itmFirst, itmSecond;
ATLControls::CImageList imgBitmaps;
HBITMAP bmpNormal, bmpSelected;
int iNormal, iSelected;

bmpNormal   = ::LoadBitmap(_Module.GetModuleInstance(),
                           MAKEINTRESOURCE(IDB_NORMAL));
bmpSelected = ::LoadBitmap(_Module.GetModuleInstance(),
                           MAKEINTRESOURCE(IDB_SELECTED));

imgBitmaps.Create(16, 16, ILC_COLOR, 0, 2);

iNormal   = imgBitmaps.Add(bmpNormal, (HBITMAP)0);
iSelected = imgBitmaps.Add(bmpSelected, (HBITMAP)0);

tvTree.SetImageList(imgBitmaps, TVSIL_NORMAL);
itmFirst  = tvTree.InsertItem(TVIF_TEXT | TVIF_IMAGE | TVIF_SELECTEDIMAGE,
                              _T("Item1"), iNormal, iSelected, 0, 0, 0, NULL,
                              TVI_SORT);
itmSecond = tvTree.InsertItem(TVIF_TEXT | TVIF_IMAGE | TVIF_SELECTEDIMAGE,
                              _T("Item2"), iNormal, iSelected, 0, 0, 0, itmFirst,
                              TVI_SORT);
```

First the images are loaded, and their handles stored in variables of type HBITMAP. These handles are used to add the images to the list, and the indexes of these images are stores in int type variables. These indexes are used when adding items to the tree view control.

Note that the image list is associated with the tree view using the SetImageList() method. The second parameter of this can either be TVSIL_NORMAL, in which case the image list will contain images for selected and unselected items, or TVSIL_STATE, where the list contains images for items in user defined states.

You may also have noticed the second parameter of the Add() method, (HBITMAP)0. This parameter is used for determining the transparency mask for images, either by specifying a separate mask bitmap or a transparent color. We're not using this here, and we use the explicit cast to avoid ambiguity between versions of the method.

Navigating the Tree

When you add items to a tree view you are returned either a handle for that item or a CTreeItem object. If you keep track of these references it is easy to obtain information about items in the tree. There are all manner of ways of navigating around the tree structure, obtaining information about various objects as you work your way through the structure. You can find the full list of these in atlcontrols.h, but let's just list a few of the commonly used ones here.

First of all, you can obtain the selected item in the tree view using the tree view `GetSelectedItem()` method. If you're using the `CTreeViewCtrlEx` object you will be returned a `CTreeItem` object, you can then use methods on that object as follows:

- ❏ `GetNextSibling()`
- ❏ `GetPrevSibling()`
- ❏ `GetParent()`
- ❏ `GetChild()`

All of which navigate in a fairly self-explanatory way, and return `CTreeItem` objects (or `NULL` if no appropriate object exists).

Once you have the item you are looking for you can get or set attributes using the data access methods of `CTreeItem`, including:

- ❏ `GetText(BSTR& bstrText)`
- ❏ `SetText(LPCTSTR lpszItem)`
- ❏ `GetImage(int& nImage, int& nSelectedImage)`
- ❏ `SetImage(int nImage, int nSelectedImage)`
- ❏ `GetState(UINT nStateMask)`
- ❏ `SetState(UINT nState, UINT nStateMask)`
- ❏ `GetData()` (returns a `DWORD`)
- ❏ `SetData(DWORD dwData)`

Note that the `GetText()` *expects a* BSTR *with a* NULL *pointer, it allocates this variable internally. It is, however, your responsibility to call* `SysFreeString()` *on the returned* BSTR *when you have finished with it.*

Notifications

When something happens to a tree view control, it will tell its container by posting a notification message to the container's window. The notification is passed as a `WM_NOTIFY` message, which ATL handles in a control's message map with the `NOTIFY_CODE_HANDLER()`, `NOTIFY_HANDLER()` and `NOTIFY_ID_HANDLER()` macros, as explained in the last chapter. The two notification messages pertinent to this example are `TVN_SELCHANGED` and `TVN_DELETEITEM`.

The first message is sent by the tree view control to its parent window when the selection moves from one item to another item, and is used to indicate the item from which the selection is moved and the item to which the selection has moved. The message also indicates how the selection changed (by a mouse click or by the keyboard). `URLTree` uses this message to get the URL associated with the new item and put the text in the edit box.

Since the `lParam` of the tree view items is used to hold a string, it means that the memory allocated for this string will have to be freed at some point when the control is destroyed, or reinitialized. This is why the `URLTree` handles the `TVN_DELETEITEM` notification. When the control is destroyed it will go through all the items and post this notification before deleting them, giving us a chance to test for the `lParam` of the item and, if necessary, free the associated buffer.

Creating the Control

We want this control to be used both in Internet Explorer and in Visual Basic, so it will have to be a full control rather than just a lite control. Here are the steps for creating the initial files:

Start Visual C++ and create a new ATL COM AppWizard project called URLTree. Ensure the **Server Type** is Dynamic Link Library (DLL).

Once the project has been generated, add a new **Full Control** to the project using the ATL Object Wizard. On the **Names** tab, give the control the **Short Name** of URLTreeView. Select the **Miscellaneous** tab and check the **Insertable** check box and from the **Add control based on** dropdown list box select SysTreeView32.

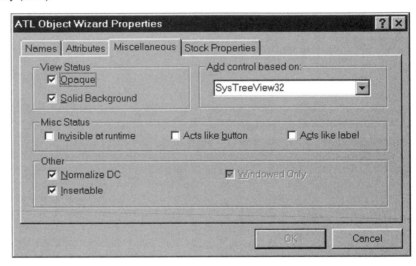

These are all the changes that you need to make so click on **OK**. (Notice that by selecting a Windows class to base this control on, the **Windowed Only** check box is disabled, this is because the control *must* be windowed.)

The URLs used in the tree control will be passed around as a VARIANT holding a SAFEARRAY of BSTRs, so you will need to add a property to hold this data. In ClassView right-click on IURLTreeView and select **Add Property....** In the next dialog, select a Property Type of VARIANT and give it a **Property Name** of URLs. Once you've OKed the dialog, ClassView should look like this:

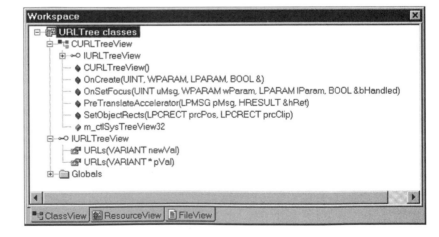

Before writing any code, let's tidy up what's been generated for us. The idea is to move code out of the header and into the implementation file. This is not strictly necessary, but it does mean that if you want to change code in the affected methods, only one source file is recompiled and not *all* the source files that include the header.

Open `URLTreeView.h` and `URLTreeView.cpp` and copy the code for `OnCreate()`, `SetObjectRects()` and the constructor from the header file and paste it into the source file.

Edit the methods that you've just added to the source file so that their header lines are as shown:

```
CURLTreeView::CURLTreeView() : m_ctlSysTreeView32(_T("SysTreeView32"), this, 1)
{
    ...
}

LRESULT CURLTreeView::OnCreate(UINT uMsg, WPARAM wParam, LPARAM lParam,
                               BOOL& bHandled)
{
    ...
}

STDMETHODIMP CURLTreeView::SetObjectRects(LPCRECT prcPos,LPCRECT prcClip)
{
    ...
}
```

Now edit the header file to remove the C++ code for these methods (leave the declaration and remember to add the semicolon):

```
CURLTreeView();

LRESULT OnCreate(UINT uMsg, WPARAM wParam, LPARAM lParam, BOOL& bHandled);
STDMETHOD(SetObjectRects)(LPCRECT prcPos, LPCRECT prcClip);
```

While you're tidying up the code, edit the property map in `URLTreeView.h` to remove the comments. The property map should look like this:

```
BEGIN_PROP_MAP(CURLTreeView)
    PROP_DATA_ENTRY("_cx", m_sizeExtent.cx, VT_UI4)
    PROP_DATA_ENTRY("_cy", m_sizeExtent.cy, VT_UI4)
END_PROP_MAP()
```

The Contained Controls

If you look near the top of the `CURLTreeView` class declaration, you will see the tree view control that we requested from the Object Wizard in the form of a `CContainedWindow` member:

```
CContainedWindow m_ctlSysTreeView32;
```

This member is initialized in the constructor to use alternative message map 1, and is created in response to the `WM_CREATE` message sent to our control's window (which is the reason that our control is windowed only, even though we didn't set that option in the Object Wizard):

```
CURLTreeView::CURLTreeView() :
    m_ctlSysTreeView32(_T("SysTreeView32"), this, 1)
{
    m_bWindowOnly = TRUE;
}
```

Currently, this code is using the basic CWindow class. We already know how to modify CContainedWindow to use the atlcontrols.h wrappers, let's modify the declaration to use CTreeViewCtrlEx, change the line in the header to read:

```
CContainedWindowT<ATLControls::CTreeViewCtrlEx> m_ctlSysTreeView32;
```

Don't forget to include atlcontrols.h *in* URLTreeView.h *now you're using its classes!*

We can also modify the constructor, as we know longer need to specify the type of control:

```
CURLTreeView::CURLTreeView() :
    m_ctlSysTreeView32(this, 1)
{
    m_bWindowOnly = TRUE;
}
```

Our control also needs an edit control, so we need to add a CContainedWindow member for it, create the control in response to WM_CREATE, and resize it and the tree control so that they don't overlap.

At the top of the class definition, add the following declaration for the edit control:

```
public:
    CContainedWindowT<ATLControls::CTreeViewCtrlEx> m_ctlSysTreeView32;
    CContainedWindowT<ATLControls::CEdit>           m_ctlEdit;
```

In the source file, add the line to initialize the contained window and set it up to use the message map with an index of 2. (Don't forget to include the comma after the initialization of the tree view object):

```
CURLTreeView::CURLTreeView() :
    m_ctlSysTreeView32(this, 1),
    m_ctlEdit(this, 2)
{
    m_bWindowOnly = TRUE;
}
```

Now add the second alternative message map to the definition for CURLTreeView:

```
ALT_MSG_MAP(1)
    // Replace this with message map entries for superclassed SysTreeView32
ALT_MSG_MAP(2)
    // Message map for edit box
END_MSG_MAP()
```

Sizing the Contained Controls

Our next task is to ensure that the controls are positioned where we want them. We want the edit control to be at the bottom of the area of the control. It should take up the whole width, but only needs to be tall enough to display a single line of text. The tree control needs to fill the remaining area of the control.

First we'll declare a member to hold the height of a line of text. We'll use this whenever we need to resize the contained windows. We'll see how to initialize it to a useful value in a while.

Add a private data member at the bottom of the class:

```
private:
    int m_tmHeight;
};
```

And initialize it to zero in the constructor:

```
    m_tmHeight = 0;
    m_bWindowOnly = TRUE;
```

Now edit OnCreate() so that both the tree view and the edit control will be created with the right size:

```
LRESULT CURLTreeView::OnCreate(UINT uMsg, WPARAM wParam, LPARAM lParam,
                                BOOL& bHandled)
{
    RECT rc;
    GetWindowRect(&rc);
    rc.right -= rc.left;
    rc.bottom -= rc.top;
    rc.top = rc.left = 0;
    rc.bottom -= m_tmHeight;
    InitCommonControls();
    m_ctlSysTreeView32.Create(m_hWnd, rc);
    rc.top = rc.bottom;
    rc.bottom = m_tmHeight;
    m_ctlEdit.Create(m_hWnd, rc, NULL,
                    WS_CHILD | WS_VISIBLE | ES_AUTOHSCROLL);
    return 0;
}
```

The RECT passed to Create() has the position of the child control as the (left, top) members (relative to the parent) and its size in the (right, bottom) members. The added line makes the tree view control smaller in height by m_tmheight. The lines for the edit control position it directly below the tree view control and makes it m_tmHeight pixels high.

Note that we've specified the window styles for the edit control explicitly, to enable the ES_AUTOHSCROLL style. This will allow the users of the control to see all the text if it doesn't fit within the area of the control without having to make room for scroll bars.

The control will be shown in a window in the container. When this window is resized, the container will call IOleInPlaceObject::SetObjectRects() to tell the control how big the window is so that it has a chance to change how it shows itself. The wizard-generated code resizes the tree view to fill the entire area of the control. Now that there's an edit control, we need to resize both of them to fit.

Add the following lines to SetObjectRects() (which is now in URLtreeView.cpp):

```
STDMETHODIMP CURLTreeView::SetObjectRects(LPCRECT prcPos,LPCRECT prcClip)
{
    IOleInPlaceObjectWindowlessImpl<CURLTreeView>::SetObjectRects(prcPos,
                                                            prcClip);
    int cx, cy;
    cx = prcPos->right - prcPos->left;
    cy = prcPos->bottom - prcPos->top;
    cy -= m_tmHeight;
    m_ctlSysTreeView32.SetWindowPos(NULL, 0, 0, cx, cy,
                        SWP_NOZORDER | SWP_NOACTIVATE);
    m_ctlEdit.SetWindowPos(NULL, 0, cy, cx, m_tmHeight,
                        SWP_NOZORDER | SWP_NOACTIVATE);
    return S_OK;
}
```

Note that the original `::SetWindowPos()` *call has been replaced by the inherited* `CWindow` `SetWindowPos()` *method for clarity.*

So far we've resized our contained windows according to the height of a line of text that will be stored in the `m_tmHeight` member. However, we haven't initialized this to a useful value yet. We need to set this member so that it represents the height of the text used in the edit control, which will be the system font. The best place to get the size of the font is when the control is sent a `WM_SIZE` message, since you will need to resize the child controls.

In the header add a handler for the message into the message map and a declaration in the class definition:

```
    MESSAGE_HANDLER(WM_CREATE, OnCreate)
    MESSAGE_HANDLER(WM_SETFOCUS, OnSetFocus)
    MESSAGE_HANDLER(WM_SIZE, OnSize)
    CHAIN_MSG_MAP(CComControl<CURLTreeView>)
ALT_MSG_MAP(1)
    // Replace this with message map entries for superclassed SysTreeView32
ALT_MSG_MAP(2)
    // Message map for edit box
END_MSG_MAP()

    LRESULT OnCreate(UINT uMsg, WPARAM wParam, LPARAM lParam, BOOL& bHandled);
    STDMETHOD(SetObjectRects)(LPCRECT prcPos,LPCRECT prcClip);
    LRESULT OnSize(UINT uMsg, WPARAM wParam, LPARAM lParam, BOOL& bHandled);
```

Add the following code to the bottom of the `.cpp` file:

```
LRESULT CURLTreeView::OnSize(UINT uMsg, WPARAM wParam, LPARAM lParam,
                            BOOL& bHandled)
{
   if (m_tmHeight == 0)
   {
      HDC hdc = m_ctlEdit.GetDC();
      TEXTMETRIC tm;
      ::GetTextMetrics(hdc, &tm);
      ReleaseDC(hdc);
      m_tmHeight = tm.tmHeight;
   }
   WORD nWidth = LOWORD(lParam);
   WORD nHeight = HIWORD(lParam);
   nHeight -= m_tmHeight;
   m_ctlSysTreeView32.SetWindowPos(NULL, 0, 0, nWidth, nHeight,
                     SWP_NOZORDER | SWP_NOACTIVATE);
   m_ctlEdit.SetWindowPos(NULL, 0, nHeight, nWidth, m_tmHeight,
                     SWP_NOZORDER | SWP_NOACTIVATE);
   return 0;
}
```

This code gets hold of the device context and through this gets information about the system font by calling `GetTextMetrics()`. The `WM_SIZE` message has the new size of the parent window and this is used to resize and reposition the child controls: the edit control's height is always the height of the system font.

Note that you could have used ClassView to add this message handler, but sometimes it is just as easy to add them by hand!

Testing the Code

Now we can compile the code and test it with the ActiveX Control Test Container. Since the control will need constant testing, we'll make the test container the executable to use to debug the control. To do this select **Settings...** from the **Project** menu, select the **Debug** tab, and click on the arrow next to the **Executable for debug session** box. From the menu, select **ActiveX Control Test Container**.

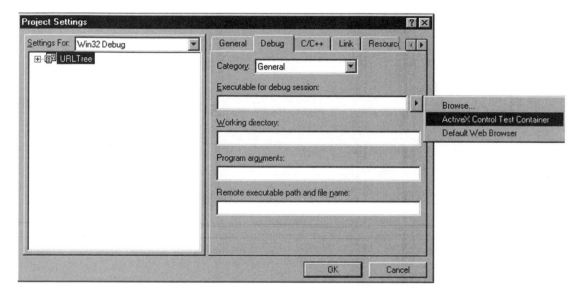

Now when you press the **Go** or **Execute Program** buttons in Visual C++, the test container will be launched and you can use it to insert a URLTreeView Class.

There's not much to see if you test the container at this stage, but you can type into the edit box at the bottom of the control, if you can find where it is — at this stage both the edit box and the tree control have no border. We will fix this in a moment.

While you are using the test container, save the session details, click on **File** and then **Save Session As** and save the session as URLTree.tcs and then close down the test container. Open the project settings once more and type URLTree.tcs as the **Program arguments** on the **Debug** tab. Now when you debug the control, it will be loaded automatically in the test container.

> *If the test container has problems opening this file you may need to change the* **Working Directory** *setting as well.*

The URLs Property

Now let's go back to the code and fix up the URLs property so that it actually stores and returns the array of strings that represents the items in the tree. We're going to store the strings in a vector internally. We'll use the vector<> class provided by the C++ standard library for this purpose.

459

First, open `URLTreeView.h` and include the vector header at the top, as well as the pragma shown below:

```
#include "resource.h"        // main symbols
#pragma warning(disable : 4530)
#include <vector>
```

The pragma turns off any warnings that the compiler will give about exception handling not being enabled. The standard library's vector<> class uses exception handling code, but by default, the ATL projects don't have exception handling enabled. This means that when you compile the code, a warning will be issued. To prevent this, you could include support for exceptions as we've discussed before, but this will increase the control size. So here we've chosen to use a pragma to ignore the warning.

At the bottom of the class, add this data member:

```
private:
    int m_tmHeight;
    std::vector<CComBSTR> m_URLs;
};
```

This is the data member that will be used to store the BSTRs. You can see that we're actually storing them as CComBSTRs so that we don't have to worry about manually freeing these strings.

Now open `URLTreeView.cpp` and add the following for `get_URLs()`:

```
STDMETHODIMP CURLTreeView::get_URLs(VARIANT* pVal)
{
    VariantInit(pVal);
    pVal->vt = VT_ARRAY | VT_BSTR;
    SAFEARRAY* psa;
    SAFEARRAYBOUND bounds = {m_URLs.size(), 0};
    psa = SafeArrayCreate(VT_BSTR, 1, &bounds);

    BSTR* bstrArray;
    SafeArrayAccessData(psa, (void**)&bstrArray);
    std::vector<CComBSTR>::iterator it;
    int i = 0;
    for (it = m_URLs.begin(); it != m_URLs.end(); it++, i++)
    {
        bstrArray[i] = (*it).Copy();
    }
    SafeArrayUnaccessData(psa);
    pVal->parray = psa;
    return S_OK;
}
```

The code is conceptually straightforward, we just create a SAFEARRAY of the same size as our stored vector and loop through, copying each BSTR from our vector into the safe array before returning it to the client.

We can do a similar thing in put_URLs(), except we do it in the reverse direction:

```
STDMETHODIMP CURLTreeView::put_URLs(VARIANT newVal)
{
    if (newVal.vt != (VT_BSTR | VT_ARRAY))
        return E_INVALIDARG;

    m_URLs.clear();
    BSTR* bstrArray;
    SafeArrayAccessData(newVal.parray, (void**)&bstrArray);

    for (int x = 0;
        x < newVal.parray->rgsabound->cElements;
        x++)
    {
        m_URLs.push_back(CComBSTR(bstrArray[x]));
    }

    SafeArrayUnaccessData(newVal.parray);
    FillTree();
    SetDirty(TRUE);
    SendOnDataChange();
    return S_OK;
}
```

First we check the type of the VARIANT passed in. If it's of the right type, we clear our vector of any existing strings, then populate it with the new strings. We call FillTree() to fill the tree control with the new array of strings. We'll implement the FillTree() function shortly. Finally, we call SetDirty() and SendOnDataChange() so that when it comes to implementing persistence code, everything will work as expected.

URLTree Tree View Code

Now we'll turn our attention to the tree view code. The tree view control should have lines and buttons, but the Wizard generated code does not create the tree view with the right styles, so edit OnCreate() so that the right styles are specified as shown below:

```
m_ctlSysTreeView32.Create(m_hWnd, rc, NULL, WS_CHILD | WS_VISIBLE |
                          WS_BORDER | TVS_HASLINES | TVS_LINESATROOT |
                          TVS_HASBUTTONS);
```

This will also add a border to the control so that we can see where it is!

Open the class header file and add the following public and private methods and data members:

```
    void FinalRelease();
private:
    void FillTree();
    ATLControls::CImageList m_hImageList;
    int m_iImage;
    int m_iSelect;
    int m_tmHeight;
    std::vector<CComBSTR> m_URLs;
};
```

Initialize the data members in the constructor:

```
m_hImageList = NULL;
m_iImage = -1;
m_iSelect = -1;
m_tmHeight = 0;
m_bWindowOnly = TRUE;
```

The m_hImageList member will hold the image list associated with the tree control, m_iImage and m_iSelect will be used to hold the index of the images within the list for the normal and selected items.

Add the following code for FinalRelease() to the .cpp file to ensure that the image list is released when the control is destroyed:

```
void CURLTreeView::FinalRelease()
{
    m_hImageList.Destroy();
}
```

We'll create the image list in OnCreate(), so add the code shown below:

```
LRESULT CURLTreeView::OnCreate(UINT uMsg, WPARAM wParam, LPARAM lParam,
                               BOOL& bHandled)
{
    ...

    m_ctlEdit.Create(m_hWnd, rc, NULL,
                     WS_CHILD | WS_VISIBLE | ES_AUTOHSCROLL);

    HBITMAP hBitmap;
    m_hImageList.Create(16, 16, ILC_COLOR, 2, 10);
    hBitmap = LoadBitmap(_Module.GetResourceInstance(),
                   MAKEINTRESOURCE(IDB_IMAGE));
    m_iImage = m_hImageList.Add(hBitmap, (HBITMAP)0);
    DeleteObject(hBitmap);
    hBitmap = LoadBitmap(_Module.GetResourceInstance(),
                   MAKEINTRESOURCE(IDB_SELECT));
    m_iSelect = m_hImageList.Add(hBitmap, (HBITMAP)0);
    DeleteObject(hBitmap);
    m_ctlSysTreeView32.SetImageList(m_hImageList, TVSIL_NORMAL);

    FillTree();
    return 0;
}
```

Here we create the image list, load two bitmaps from the resources (we'll create these in a little while), and add them to the list. Next we set the tree view to use the newly created image list. Finally, we call FillTree() to ensure that the tree is loaded as soon as the control is created.

Add the implementation of FillTree() as shown on the next page:

```
void CURLTreeView::FillTree()
{
    m_ctlSysTreeView32.DeleteAllItems();
    std::vector<CComBSTR>::iterator it;
    ATLControls::CTreeItem hRoot = m_ctlSysTreeView32.GetRootItem();
    for (it = m_URLs.begin(); it < m_URLs.end(); it++)
    {
        LPWSTR strBranch =  new WCHAR[(*it).Length() + 1];
        LPWSTR strURL;

        wcscpy(strBranch, (*it).m_str);

        if ((strURL = wcschr(strBranch, L',')) != NULL)
        {
            *strURL = 0;
            strURL++;
            TVAddItem(hRoot, strBranch, strURL, m_iImage, m_iSelect);
        }
        delete [] strBranch;
    }
    m_ctlEdit.SetWindowText((LPCTSTR)_T(""));
}
```

FillTree() empties the tree view if it has items, and then it iterates through the items in the vector and adds them to the tree with a call to TVAddItem(), a method that you'll add in a moment. Finally, it clears the text in the edit box.

Because we are using the wide character C runtime library (CRT) functions here (wcscpy() and wcschr()), you will need to add wchar.h to the list of headers at the top of the source file:

```
#include "stdafx.h"
#include "URLTree.h"
#include "URLTreeView.h"
#pragma comment(lib, "comctl32.lib")
#include <wchar.h>
```

We also need to remove the _ATL_MIN_CRT symbol from the project settings for the release builds. When this symbol is defined, it prevents the linker from linking the CRT start up code, which saves about 25Kb, but will cause link errors if you use any functions that need the start up code. To use the CRT you need to undefine this symbol.

From the Project menu select Settings... to bring up the Project Settings dialog. In the Settings For dropdown select Multiple Configurations and in the next dialog make sure that only the release build options are selected. Then click on the C/C++ tab, select Preprocessor from the Category list, and in the Preprocessor definitions box remove the reference to _ATL_MIN_CRT.

Bitmap Resources

The image list uses bitmap images, so the next thing to do is use Developer Studio's resource editor to add these images.

Click on the ResourceView tab, right-click on URLTree Resources and select Insert.... In the dialog select Bitmap and click on New. This will add a new bitmap resource to your project.

You need to resize this image so that it's 16 pixels square, so from the Vïew menu select Properties... and set both the Width and Height to 16. Also change the ID to IDB_IMAGE:

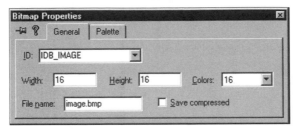

Now draw the image for a non-selected item. Here's my attempt.

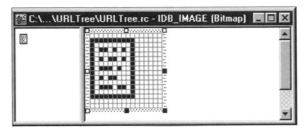

Notice that I've drawn it off-center so that when the image changes from non-selected to selected, I can make it look like an arrow has been added.

Now add another 16x16 bitmap, this time for the selected item. Give it an ID of IDB_SELECT:

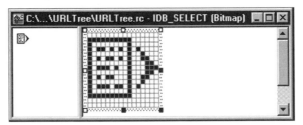

Finally, since this is a component that can be used in Visual Basic, we want a bitmap that can be used to represent the control in the toolbox. The wizard-generated registration code for the control indicates that the resource with an ID of 101 will be the image for this toolbar button. The bitmap can be seen in ResourceView in the Bitmap folder as resource IDB_URLTREEVIEW. Open this and edit it to look simlar to the other bitmaps. Notice that it is centered horizontally, and that the background is Windows background gray:

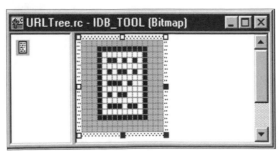

TVAddItem()

Now add the following to the header:

```
private:
    void TVAddItem(ATLControls::CTreeItem hParent, LPWSTR strBranch,
                   LPWSTR strURL, int iImage = -1, int iSelect = -1);
    void FillTree();
```

And this stub function to the source file:

```
void CURLTreeView::TVAddItem(ATLControls::CTreeItem hParent, LPWSTR strBranch,
                             LPWSTR strURL, int iImage, int iSelect)
{
}
```

You can compile the project at this stage to ensure that there are no typing mistakes. The next task is to implement TVAddItem():

```
void CURLTreeView::TVAddItem(ATLControls::CTreeItem hParent, LPWSTR strBranch,
                             LPWSTR strURL, int iImage, int iSelect)
{
    USES_CONVERSION;

    // Get a pointer to the first forward slash in the branch string
    LPWSTR ptr = wcschr(strBranch, L'/');

    // If the ptr is NULL, there are no forward slashes, so the contents
    // of strBranch must be the final item to add.
    // Once that's done, we can return from the function
    if (ptr == NULL)
    {
        // End of the string, add the item!
        TVAddItemCore(hParent, strBranch, strURL, iImage, iSelect);
        return;
    }

    // Create a string with the first part of the branch
    // and ensure that it's null-terminated
    LPWSTR strParent = new WCHAR[1 + ptr - strBranch];
    wcsncpy(strParent, strBranch, ptr - strBranch);
    strParent[ptr - strBranch] = 0;

    // Find child with the name contained in strParent
    ATLControls::CTreeItem hItem;
    hItem = hParent.GetChild();

    if (hItem == NULL)
    {
        // If there are no children, add the new item here
        hItem = TVAddItemCore(hParent, strParent, NULL, iImage, iSelect);
    }

    // Now loop through all the children and see
    // if we can find the item already in the tree
    BSTR strCmp;
    while (hItem)
    {
        strCmp = NULL;
        hItem.GetText(strCmp);
```

```
    if (lstrcmp(W2T(strParent), W2T(strCmp)) == 0)
        {
            // Here we've found the item, so we call TVAddItem() recursively
            // with the handle of the item and the latest position in the branch
            TVAddItem(hItem, ptr + 1, strURL, iImage, iSelect);
            break;
        }
    else
        {
            ATLControls::CTreeItem nextItem = hItem.GetNextSibling();
            if (nextItem == NULL)
                {
                    // If we get here, the item isn't there so we need to add it,
                    // then we can call TVAddItem() recursively
                    ATLControls::CTreeItem hNewItem = TVAddItemCore(hParent, strParent,
                                                                    NULL, iImage,
                                                                    iSelect);
                    TVAddItem(hNewItem, ptr + 1, strURL, iImage, iSelect);
                    break;
                }
            else
                {
                    hItem = nextItem;
                }
        }
    SysFreeString(strCmp);
    } // while (hItem)

    delete [] strParent;
}
```

Let's go through this code and see what it does.

This routine is recursive. Basically the idea is that strBranch has the name of the item similar to a fully qualified path name in DOS, except the items are separated by forward rather than back slashes.

The first part of the code checks for a forward slash and if there is not one present, strBranch is just the name of an item. The item can be added into the tree view under the parent given by hParent.

If there is a slash in strBranch, the code must extract the first item in the string and check to see if hParent has a child with the same name. If it doesn't then a new item is created. The method can then be called recursively with the rest of strBranch to add the item.

The while loop checks to see if hParent has a child with the name held in strParent (which is the string in strBranch up to the first slash), this is done by first calling hParent.GetChild() to get the first child of hParent (in hItem) and then calling hItem.GetText() to get the item text to compare with strParent. If the comparison fails then it calls hItem.GetNextSibling() to get the next child. This loop continues until either a child is found or there are no more children. In the second case, a new item is created. In both cases TVAddItem() is called recursively.

The tree item is actually created by the function TVAddItemCore(). Declare this function in URLTreeView.h:

```
private:
    ATLControls::CTreeItem TVAddItemCore(ATLControls::CTreeItem hParent,
                                         LPWSTR strItem, LPWSTR strURL,
                                         int iImage = -1, int iSelect = -1);
    void TVAddItem(ATLControls::CTreeItem hParent, LPWSTR strBranch,
                   LPWSTR strURL, int iImage = -1, int iSelect = -1);
```

Add the implementation to URLTreeView.cpp:

```
ATLControls::CTreeItem CURLTreeView::TVAddItemCore(
                                        ATLControls::CTreeItem hParent,
                                        LPWSTR strItem, LPWSTR strURL,
                                        int iImage, int iSelect)
{
    USES_CONVERSION;
    UINT nMask = TVIF_TEXT;

    LPTSTR newStr;
    if (strURL)
    {
        nMask |= TVIF_PARAM;
        int cbSize = wcslen(strURL) + 1;
        newStr = new TCHAR[cbSize];
        lstrcpy(newStr, W2T(strURL));
    }
    else
    {
        newStr = NULL;
    }

    if (iImage != -1)
    {
        nMask |= TVIF_IMAGE;
    }

    if (iSelect != -1)
    {
        nMask |= TVIF_SELECTEDIMAGE;
    }

    return m_ctlSysTreeView32.InsertItem(nMask, W2T(strItem), iImage, iSelect, 0,
                            0, (LPARAM)newStr, hParent, TVI_LAST);
}
```

The code is quite straightforward. It first checks to see if there is a URL associated with the item, and if so sets the mask to indicate that there will be a LPARAM parameter, which is initialized to the string. Next it checks to see if we have images before finally adding the item into the tree control.

Testing the Control

Now you can compile and test the project once more. If you use the test container, you won't see any changes since the last time (except the tree control now has a border), because the control has no data, so it will show an empty window. There is no way to send data in the right form to the control using the test container, so we'll have to use something else. In this case, we'll create a tiny Visual Basic application to send an array of strings to the control.

Start Visual Basic and select Standard EXE as the project type. From the Project menu select **Components...** and check the box next to **URLTree 1.0 Type Library**. Note that the image for the control will be added to the toolbox:

Add an instance of our `URLTreeView` control to the form. Then add the following code to the form load handler to test the control:

```
Private Sub Form_Load()
    Dim str(4) As String
    str(1) = "First Level,url1"
    str(2) = "First Level/Two,url2"
    str(3) = "First Level/Second/Three,url3"
    str(4) = "First Level/Second/Third/Four,url4"
    URLTreeView1.URLs = str
End Sub
```

Now run the project and you should see this (after expanding the branches):

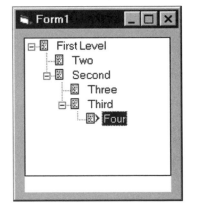

Note that the selection image automatically moves to the selected item (because that's handled by the tree control), but the URL for the item doesn't appear in the edit box. We need to add some message handlers to rectify that.

Notification Code

There are three messages that we need to handle. Two of them (TVN_DELETEITEM and TVN_SELCHANGED) are notification messages sent from the tree view to our control's main window. The third is the WM_LBUTTONDBLCLK message sent to the tree view.

The first message handler will allow us to delete the string that we're storing a pointer to in the LPARAM of each item. As the code stands at the moment, it will leak memory because we have no code to delete these strings. The TVN_DELETEITEM message will let us know when these strings are no longer needed and give us a perfect opportunity to delete them.

The second message handler will be called when the selected tree item changes. This will allow us to update the edit box with the URL for the currently selected item.

The third message will enable us to open the URL for the currently selected item in a new Internet Explorer window, when the user double-clicks on the tree view.

Again, we will add these messages by hand, so edit the message map to hook up the handlers for all three messages:

```
BEGIN_MSG_MAP(CURLTreeView)
    ...
    NOTIFY_CODE_HANDLER(TVN_DELETEITEM, OnDeleteItem)
    NOTIFY_CODE_HANDLER(TVN_SELCHANGED, OnSelChanged)
    CHAIN_MSG_MAP(CComControl<CURLTreeView>)
ALT_MSG_MAP(1)
    MESSAGE_HANDLER(WM_LBUTTONDBLCLK, OnLButtonDblClk)
ALT_MSG_MAP(2)
    // Message map for edit box
END_MSG_MAP()
```

Note that the notify handlers are in the main message map and that the double-click handler is in alternative message map 1. This is because the first two messages are sent to the control's main window, whereas the double-click message is sent to the tree view.

Now add the declarations of these handlers to the class definition.

```
LRESULT OnCreate(UINT uMsg, WPARAM wParam, LPARAM lParam, BOOL& bHandled);
STDMETHOD(SetObjectRects)(LPCRECT prcPos,LPCRECT prcClip);
LRESULT OnSize(UINT uMsg, WPARAM wParam, LPARAM lParam, BOOL& bHandled);
LRESULT OnDeleteItem(int idCtrl, LPNMHDR pnmh, BOOL& bHandled);
LRESULT OnSelChanged(int idCtrl, LPNMHDR pnmh, BOOL& bHandled);
LRESULT OnLButtonDblClk(UINT uMsg, WPARAM wParam, LPARAM lParam,
                        BOOL& bHandled);
```

The implementations need to be added to the source file as shown (we'll leave the implementation of the double-click handler aside for a while):

```
LRESULT CURLTreeView::OnDeleteItem(int idCtrl, LPNMHDR pnmh, BOOL& bHandled)
{
    NMTREEVIEW* pnmtv = (NMTREEVIEW*) pnmh;
    ATLControls::CTreeItem nItem(pnmtv->itemOld.hItem, &m_ctlSysTreeView32);
    if (nItem.GetData() != NULL)
        nItem.SetData(NULL);
    return 0;
}
```

```
LRESULT CURLTreeView::OnSelChanged(int idCtrl, LPNMHDR pnmh, BOOL& bHandled)
{
    NMTREEVIEW* pnmtv = (NMTREEVIEW*) pnmh;
    ATLControls::CTreeItem nItem(pnmtv->itemNew.hItem, &m_ctlSysTreeView32);
    m_ctlEdit.SetWindowText((LPCTSTR)nItem.GetData());
    return 0;
}

LRESULT CURLTreeView::OnLButtonDblClk(
    UINT uMsg, WPARAM wParam, LPARAM lParam, BOOL& bHandled)
{
    return 0;
}
```

In both of the notify handlers, the pnmh parameter is cast to a pointer to a NMTREEVIEW structure. This is then used to find out the item that is being deleted, or being selected, and hence to get access to its associated data.

Once again, you can compile the code. This time you can use the VB test program to verify that as you select an item, the associated URL is shown in the edit box.

Internet Explorer

The final message for which we need to write a handler is the WM_LBUTTONDBLCLICK. Add the following code to CURLTreeView::OnLButtonDblClk():

```
LRESULT CURLTreeView::OnLButtonDblClk(UINT uMsg, WPARAM wParam, LPARAM lParam,
                                      BOOL& bHandled)
{
    ATLControls::CTreeItem nItem = m_ctlSysTreeView32.GetSelectedItem();

    m_ctlEdit.SetWindowText((LPCTSTR)nItem.GetData());

    if (lstrlen((LPTSTR)nItem.GetData()) > 0)
    {
        // Create browser object
        HRESULT hr;
        CComPtr<IWebBrowserApp> pNav;
        hr = CoCreateInstance(CLSID_InternetExplorer,
                              NULL,
                              CLSCTX_ALL,
                              IID_IWebBrowserApp,
                              reinterpret_cast<void**>(&pNav));
        if (SUCCEEDED(hr))
        {
            CComVariant varZero(0);
            CComVariant varNull("");
            hr = pNav->put_Visible(true);
            hr = pNav->Navigate(CComBSTR((LPCTSTR)nItem.GetData()), &varZero,
                                &varNull, &varNull, &varNull);
        }
    }
    return 0;
}
```

The code just gets the currently selected tree item and if there's a URL associated with it, launches Internet Explorer, makes it visible and navigates to the URL specified The Navigate() method takes the URL as the first parameter. The second parameter states that a new window should be created, and the other parameters are for the target frame name, data sent with HTTP POST and HTTP headers, which we're not interested in.

So that the compiler knows about Internet Explorer, add these includes to the top of the source file:

```
#include "URLTreeView.h"
#pragma comment(lib, "comctl32.lib")
#include <wchar.h>
#include <initguid.h>
#include <exDisp.h>
```

Now compile the project. To test it, you need to change the VB code to have real URLs. The easiest thing to do (if you haven't got a permanent connection to the Internet) is create a series of files called `Url1.html`, `Url2.html`, `Url1.htm3` and `Url4.html` with the minimal HTML shown below (change the title accordingly, so you know which is which):

```
<HTML>
<TITLE>
URL1
</TITLE>
</HTML>
```

Save these in the Visual Basic project's directory and change the VB code to this:

```
Private Sub Form_Load()
    Dim str(4) As String
    str(1) = "First Level," & App.Path & "\url1.html"
    str(2) = "First Level/Two," & App.Path & "\url2.html"
    str(3) = "First Level/Second/Three," & App.Path & "\url3.html"
    str(4) = "First Level/Second/Third/Four," & App.Path & "\url4.html"
    URLTreeView1.URLs = str
End Sub
```

Notice that IE is clever enough to know that these are files on the local file system and so you do not need to give the file: protocol. Now when you run this code and double-click on an item, IE will pop up with the associated HTML file.

Persistence Code for IE

So far the control can show a hierarchy of URLs, it will show an item's URL when the item is selected, and it will launch Internet Explorer when the item is double-clicked. The control can be manipulated at runtime using the URLs property. However, it doesn't provide any way of initializing itself using design-time mechanisms such as the <PARAM> tags on a web page. This requires that the control support the IPersistPropertyBag interface, so this section will show you how to add that support.

At first sight you may think that all you need to do is derive the control class from IPersistPropertyBagImpl<> and add URLs to the property map. However, this does not work because the IPropertyBag implemented by IE does not know about arrays, so instead you will need to override the default implementation of IPersistPropertyBag::Load() to read in the data in a custom format.

The implementation of this method is not in IPersistPropertybagImpl<> as you would expect, here is the call chain:

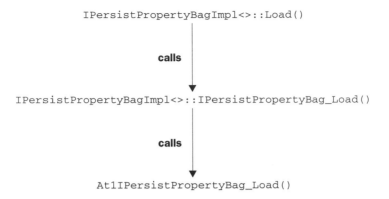

IPersistPropertyBagImpl<>::Load()

calls

IPersistPropertyBagImpl<>::IPersistPropertyBag_Load()

calls

AtlIPersistPropertyBag_Load()

The actual code appears in the global function AtlIPersistPropertyBag_Load() which again shows ATL's effort to make your code as small as possible. Having this code in a global function will ensure that one copy of the code will be in your DLL no matter how many controls in the DLL use it. The natural place to override the persistence code is in IPersistPropertyBag_Load() because this method is called by IPersistPropertyBagImpl<>::Load() like this:

```
STDMETHOD(Load)(LPPROPERTYBAG pPropBag, LPERRORLOG pErrorLog)
{
    ATLTRACE2(atlTraceCOM, 0, _T("IPersistPropertyBagImpl::Load\n"));
    T* pT = static_cast<T*>(this);
    ATL_PROPMAP_ENTRY* pMap = T::GetPropertyMap();
    ATLASSERT(pMap != NULL);
    return pT->IPersistPropertyBag_Load(pPropBag, pErrorLog, pMap);
}
```

That is, the method is called through the downcast pointer, which implies that ATL expects you to supply this method. If you don't, don't worry, because the version in IPersistPropertyBagImpl<> will be called, which is what we want to override.

The format we shall use is to read in each item as a property called Item*N* where *N* is a number. The total number of items will be in a property called noItems. Strictly speaking this should not be necessary — the code could just read in the Item*N* property incrementing *N* until the container cannot find the property — but it does give a good check.

Using this scheme, you will be able to implement a web page like this:

```
<HTML>
<BODY>
<OBJECT CLSID="...">
    <PARAM NAME="noItems" VALUE=4>
    <PARAM NAME="Item1" VALUE="First Level,c:\temp\url1.html">
    <PARAM NAME="Item2" VALUE="First Level/Two,c:\temp\url2.html">
    <PARAM NAME="Item3" VALUE="First Level/Three,c:\temp\url3.html">
    <PARAM NAME="Item4" VALUE="First Level/Four,c:\temp\url4.html">
</OBJECT>
</BODY>
</HTML>
```

Here are the steps:

Open the `CURLTreeView` class header file and add `IPersistPropertyBagImpl<>` to the list of base classes:

```
public IPersistStorageImpl<CURLTreeView>,
public ISpecifyPropertyPagesImpl<CURLTreeView>,
public IPersistPropertyBagImpl<CURLTreeView>,
public IQuickActivateImpl<CURLTreeView>,
```

Add the interface to the COM map:

```
COM_INTERFACE_ENTRY(IPersistStreamInit)
COM_INTERFACE_ENTRY2(IPersist, IPersistStreamInit)
COM_INTERFACE_ENTRY(IPersistPropertyBag)
COM_INTERFACE_ENTRY(ISpecifyPropertyPages)
```

Add the following declaration to the class definition, to override `IPersistPropertyBagImpl<>::IPersistPropertyBag_Load()`:

```
// IPersistPropertyBag
HRESULT IPersistPropertyBag_Load(LPPROPERTYBAG pPropBag, LPERRORLOG pErrorLog,
                                 ATL_PROPMAP_ENTRY* pMap);
```

In the source file, add this implementation:

```
HRESULT CURLTreeView::IPersistPropertyBag_Load(LPPROPERTYBAG pPropBag,
                                               LPERRORLOG pErrorLog,
                                               ATL_PROPMAP_ENTRY* pMap)
{
    CComVariant var;
    HRESULT hr;
    var.vt = VT_I4;
    hr = pPropBag->Read(L"noItems", &var, pErrorLog);
    if (FAILED(hr))
        return hr;
    if (var.vt != VT_I4)
        return E_INVALIDARG;

    long items = var.iVal;
    var.Clear();

    OLECHAR strParam[8];
    for (long idx = 1; idx <= items; idx++)
    {
        swprintf(strParam, L"Item%d", idx);
        hr = pPropBag->Read(strParam, &var, pErrorLog);
        if (FAILED(hr))
            return hr;
        if (var.vt == VT_BSTR)
            m_URLs.push_back(CComBSTR(var.bstrVal));
        var.Clear();
    }
    return IPersistPropertyBagImpl<CURLTreeView>::IPersistPropertyBag_Load(
                                               pPropBag, pErrorLog, pMap);
}
```

473

The first few lines of this method obtain the noItems parameter. Notice how the type of the VARIANT is set to VT_I4 before getting the parameter; this indicates to the container that it ought to try to coerce the parameter to a long type. If this coercion fails, and another type is returned, the method returns with an error.

We store the value returned in the items variable. After that the VARIANT is cleared and a loop is entered to read all the other parameters. Notice that I haven't set the type of the VARIANT to BSTR before calling Read(), Internet Explorer's implementation of IPropertyBag::Read() is clever enough to realize that the parameters are strings without any hints.

Once we've looped through all the items, we call ATL's default implementation of the Load() method so that any properties we add to the property map in the future will still be loaded.

Now compile the code. Open the URLTreeView.htm that the AppWizard generated for you in the project directory and edit it according to the following highlighted lines:

```
<HTML>
<HEAD>
<TITLE>ATL 3.0 test page for object URLTreeView</TITLE>
</HEAD>
<BODY>
<OBJECT ID="URLTreeView" CLASSID="CLSID: 83D775F8-5F9F-11D3-89D1-00104BDC35E0">
    <PARAM NAME="noItems" VALUE=4>
    <PARAM NAME="Item1" VALUE="First Level,c:\temp\url1.html">
    <PARAM NAME="Item2" VALUE="First Level/Two,c:\temp\url2.html">
    <PARAM NAME="Item3" VALUE="First Level/Three,c:\temp\url3.html">
    <PARAM NAME="Item4" VALUE="First Level/Four,c:\temp\url4.html">
</OBJECT>
</BODY>
</HTML>
```

You can now test the control by double-clicking on URLTreeView.htm in Explorer to get Internet Explorer to start up. Notice that the URLs have a full path, if you do not give a full path IE will not be able to find the HTML pages (or worse, if the URL does not start with a drive IE will not know that it should use the file: protocol).

Security Code

You may find that you get this dialog from Internet Explorer when it starts:

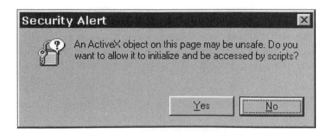

If you're using an older version of Internet Explorer, you may even find that you are unable to initialize the control if your IE options are set to a high security setting which tells IE to ignore parameters. This is designed to protect the control (and ultimately your computer) from possibly bogus values.

You have two options here. The first is to change the security settings, and the second is to mark the control safe for scripting and initialization. We'll go for the second option.

We can implement our control so that it can tell IE that it is OK for IE to read the parameters and pass them onto the control. This is achieved by implementing the IObjectSafety interface. The interface has a method, SetInterfaceSafetyOptions(), that IE will call to specify the options it is expecting the control to support.

This method has three parameters, the first is the IID of the control interface that the container is interested in, the second specifies safety options that should be supported and of these options the ones that should be enabled are given in the last parameter. These options are currently:

```
INTERFACESAFE_FOR_UNTRUSTED_CALLER
INTERFACESAFE_FOR_UNTRUSTED_DATA
```

The first means that the control will accept scripting, and the second means that the control will accept parameters. In ATL, we can support this interface by deriving our control from the IObjectSafetyImpl<> class.

> The version of this class in ATL 2.1 was flawed because it only checked for scripting options for **IDispatch**, and hence would fail for **IPersistPropertyBag**. This has been fixed in ATL 3.0.

In the class header, derive the control class from IObjectSafetyImpl<>:

```
    public IObjectSafetyImpl<CURLTreeView,
        INTERFACESAFE_FOR_UNTRUSTED_CALLER | INTERFACESAFE_FOR_UNTRUSTED_DATA>,
```

Add the interface to the COM map:

```
    COM_INTERFACE_ENTRY(IObjectSafety)
```

Compile the code and try the HTML page again. This time you won't get any warning dialogs.

Category Map

IObjectSafety is fine, but it requires that IE should run the control before it tests to see if the control can be passed untrusted data or scripted by untrusted scripts. If the control performs some costly or important initialization and then IE gets the message that the control does not want to untrusted data or scripts then the initialization will have been wasted. You have already seen the solution to this (Chapter 4): Category Maps.

When you add a category map the information is added to the registry so that IE can read this information to see if the control can be scripted or passed untrusted data. Adding a category map is simple, add this below the message map:

```
BEGIN_CATEGORY_MAP(CURLTreeView)
    IMPLEMENTED_CATEGORY(CATID_Insertable)
    IMPLEMENTED_CATEGORY(CATID_Control)
    IMPLEMENTED_CATEGORY(CATID_SafeForScripting)
    IMPLEMENTED_CATEGORY(CATID_SafeForInitializing)
END_CATEGORY_MAP()
```

I've taken the opportunity to also add the `Insertable` and `Control` categories, which allows newer containers to check for these rather than the corresponding keys in the control's CLSID entry.

Now all containers, of any type, will be able to determine if it should load the control.

Property Page

In this section, we'll add a property page for the control to allow you to change the URLs held by the control at design-time. Since the URLs property is a complex one, Visual Basic's Properties window can't handle it, so a property page will be a valuable addition to our control.

It would be possible to define a string property on the control that in its `get_` method concatenates the strings in the `m_URLs` vector (using some deliminator like '|'). This would mean that VB could show this long string and the user can then edit it. The `put_` method of the property could then parse through this string and enter the item strings into the vector.

However, such a scheme is cumbersome and it requires the VB developer to type long strings into the property box and ensure that the correct syntax is used. It would be much better if the VB developer is given a dialog to enter the data, and have the dialog code make sure that the text is correctly formatted. Such a dialog, of course, is a property page.

In Developer Studio, select **New ATL Object...** from the **I**nsert menu. In the left-hand pane select **Controls** and in the right-hand pane select **Property Page**. In the next dialog, give the page a Short Name of **URLPage** and then click on the **Strings** tab. Enter **&URLs** as the Title and clear the other edit boxes. Then click on **OK**.

This will change the IDL file to include a reference to the coclass for the property page and it will add the page to the object map. In addition to this, the wizard will add a new header and source file to the project. You will need to edit the control to use the property page, but first you need to write the property page code.

The first task is to edit the resources for the page. The IDD_URLPAGE dialog resource should be open, so add two edit boxes, two static labels, two buttons and a list box:

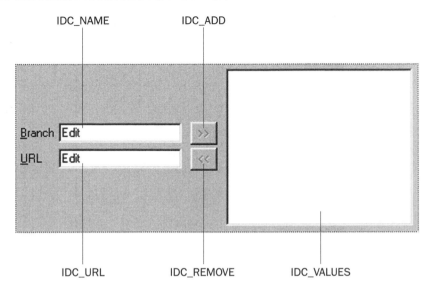

The buttons are disabled and the list box has the sort attribute turned off. The property page should work like this: the IDC_ADD button should be enabled if there is a string in the IDC_NAME edit box. When the user clicks on the IDC_ADD button, the two strings in the edit boxes should be added together separated by a comma and then this new string should be added to the list box.

When the user clicks on an item in the list box, the IDC_REMOVE button should be enabled. If the user clicks on this button, the string should be removed from the edit box, split into its constituent parts, and these new strings added to the edit boxes. There is a lot of control handling code needed here.

Before we get into the control manipulation, we can write the relatively simple functions to initialize the page with the URLs from the control when the dialog is created, and to update the control with the values from the dialog when the Apply() method is called.

Open URLPage.h, remove the Apply() method and paste it into the URLPage.cpp file. Edit the first line so that it looks like this:

```
STDMETHODIMP CURLPage::Apply(void)
{
    . . .
}
```

Add a declaration for this method in the header:

```
STDMETHOD(Apply)(void);
```

We want to initialize the controls when the page is created, so in the page's message map add the following

```
BEGIN_MSG_MAP(CURLPage)
    MESSAGE_HANDLER(WM_INITDIALOG, OnInitDialog)
    CHAIN_MSG_MAP(IPropertyPageImpl<CURLPage>)
END_MSG_MAP()
```

And add this declaration to the CURLPage class definition:

```
LRESULT OnInitDialog(UINT uMsg, WPARAM wParam, LPARAM lParam, BOOL& bHandled);
```

Also add this include at the top of URLPage.cpp:

```
#include "stdafx.h"
#include "URLPage.h"
#include "URLTree.h"
#include "atlcontrols.h"
```

And add this method:

```
LRESULT CURLPage::OnInitDialog(UINT uMsg, WPARAM wParam, LPARAM lParam,
                               BOOL& bHandled)
{
    USES_CONVERSION;
    CComPtr<IURLTreeView> pURL;
    m_ppUnk[0]->QueryInterface(&pURL);

    ATLControls::CListBox lstValues(GetDlgItem(IDC_VALUES));
    CComVariant var;

    if (SUCCEEDED(pURL->get_URLs(&var)))
    {
        if (var.vt != (VT_BSTR | VT_ARRAY))
            return 0;

        BSTR* bstrArray;
        SafeArrayAccessData(var.parray, (void**)&bstrArray);

        for (UINT x = 0;
             x < var.parray->rgsabound->cElements;
             x++)
        {
            lstValues.AddString((LPCTSTR)OLE2T(bstrArray[x]));
        }

        SafeArrayUnaccessData(var.parray);
    }

    return 0;
}
```

You've seen code like this before. It uses the type safe QueryInterface() to get the IURLTreeView interface of the control. Then it uses the get_ method of the URLs property to obtain a SAFEARRAY of strings and then loops through the array adding each string to the list box. The m_ppUnk array has the IUnknown pointers for the objects currently using the property page. For this page, we'll only support one object.

Now edit the `Apply()` method to add these lines:

```
STDMETHODIMP CURLPage::Apply(void)
{
    ATLControls::CListBox lstValues(GetDlgItem(IDC_VALUES));
    int count = 0;
    int idx = lstValues.GetCount();

    CComVariant var;
    var.vt = VT_ARRAY | VT_BSTR;
    SAFEARRAY* psa;
    SAFEARRAYBOUND bounds = {idx, 0};
    psa = SafeArrayCreate(VT_BSTR, 1, &bounds);
    BSTR* bstrArray;
    SafeArrayAccessData(psa, (void**)&bstrArray);
    BSTR str;

    while (count < idx)
    {
        str = NULL;
        lstValues.GetTextBSTR(count, str);
        bstrArray[count] = SysAllocString(str);
        SysFreeString(str);
        count++;
    }

    SafeArrayUnaccessData(psa);
    var.parray = psa;

    CComPtr<IURLTreeView> pURL;
    m_ppUnk[0]->QueryInterface(&pURL);
    pURL->put_URLs(var);

    m_bDirty = FALSE;
    return S_OK;
}
```

This code asks the list box for how many items it has and then creates a `SAFEARRAY` of the correct size. Next it asks for each of the items using an `NULL BSTR` (allocated in `GetTextBSTR()`, freed in our loop). Once the `SAFEARRAY` has been filled, the code then uses the control's `put_` method to write the data to the control.

Of course, this code is not much use at this point because you cannot add values into the list box, so we'll add code to do that now. First you need to test when data changes in the `IDC_NAME` box and use this to decide whether the `IDC_ADD` button is enabled.

Add the following in the message map

```
MESSAGE_HANDLER(WM_INITDIALOG, OnInitDialog)
COMMAND_HANDLER(IDC_NAME, EN_CHANGE, OnNameChange)
COMMAND_ID_HANDLER(IDC_ADD, OnAddItem)
```

And add these declarations to the page's class definition:

```
LRESULT OnNameChange(WORD wNotify, WORD wID, HWND hWnd, BOOL& bHandled);
LRESULT OnAddItem(WORD wNotify, WORD wID, HWND hWnd, BOOL& bHandled);
```

Copy this code into the URLPage.cpp file for OnNameChange():

```
LRESULT CURLPage::OnNameChange(WORD wNotify, WORD wID, HWND hWnd, BOOL& bHandled)
{
    ATLControls::CEdit    edName(GetDlgItem(IDC_NAME));
    ATLControls::CButton bnAdd(GetDlgItem(IDC_ADD));

    bnAdd.EnableWindow(edName.GetWindowTextLength() > 0);

    ATLControls::CButton bnRemove(GetDlgItem(IDC_REMOVE));
    bnRemove.EnableWindow(FALSE);
    return 0;
}
```

Finally add this for OnAddItem():

```
LRESULT CURLPage::OnAddItem(WORD wNotify, WORD wID, HWND hWnd, BOOL& bHandled)
{
    ATLControls::CEdit    edName(GetDlgItem(IDC_NAME));
    ATLControls::CEdit    edURL(GetDlgItem(IDC_URL));
    ATLControls::CListBox lstValues(GetDlgItem(IDC_VALUES));

    int nameSize = edName.GetWindowTextLength() + 1;
    int urlSize  = edURL.GetWindowTextLength() + 1;
    LPTSTR strName = new TCHAR[nameSize + urlSize];
    edName.GetWindowText(strName, nameSize);
    edName.Clear();
    lstrcat(strName, _T(","));
    LPTSTR strURL = new TCHAR[urlSize];
    edURL.GetWindowText(strURL, urlSize);
    edURL.Clear();
    lstrcat(strName, strURL);

    lstValues.AddString(strName);
    SetDirty(TRUE);

    delete [] strName;
    delete [] strURL;
    return 0;
}
```

This code is mostly self-explanatory. The only odd bit comes near the end. After adding the string to the list box, the **Apply** button must be enabled on the property page so that the data can be sent to the control (if required). This is done by calling IPropertyPageImpl<>::SetDirty().

Now we'll set up the code for removing items from the list. In the property page header, add the following to the message map:

```
COMMAND_HANDLER(IDC_VALUES, LBN_SELCHANGE, OnSelChange)
COMMAND_ID_HANDLER(IDC_REMOVE, OnRemoveItem)
```

Add these method declarations:

```
LRESULT OnSelChange(WORD wNotify, WORD wID, HWND hWnd, BOOL& bHandled);
LRESULT OnRemoveItem(WORD wNotify, WORD wID, HWND hWnd, BOOL& bHandled);
```

The handler for the LBN_SELCHANGE sent to the list box should enable the IDC_REMOVE button:

```
LRESULT CURLPage::OnSelChange(WORD wNotify, WORD wID, HWND hWnd, BOOL& bHandled)
{
    ATLControls::CEdit(GetDlgItem(IDC_REMOVE)).EnableWindow(TRUE);
    return 0;
}
```

The handler for clicking on the IDC_REMOVE button should extract the strings from the selected item, put them in the edit boxes and, of course, remove the item:

```
LRESULT CURLPage::OnRemoveItem(WORD wNotify, WORD wID, HWND hWnd, BOOL& bHandled)
{
    USES_CONVERSION;
    ATLControls::CEdit      edName(GetDlgItem(IDC_NAME));
    ATLControls::CEdit      edURL(GetDlgItem(IDC_URL));
    ATLControls::CListBox lstValues(GetDlgItem(IDC_VALUES));

    int idx = lstValues.GetCurSel();
    if (idx == -1)
        return 0;

    BSTR str = NULL;
    lstValues.GetTextBSTR(idx, str);
    lstValues.DeleteString(idx);

    wchar_t* ptr;
    ptr = wcsstr(str, L",");
    if (ptr)
    {
        *ptr = 0;
        ptr++;
    }

    edName.SetWindowText(W2T(str));
    if (ptr)
        edURL.SetWindowText(W2T(ptr));

    SetDirty(TRUE);
    SysFreeString(str);
    return 0;
}
```

You will need to add the following header to URLPage.cpp so that you can use the CRT functions

```
#include "stdafx.h"
#include "URLPage.h"
#include "URLTree.h"
#include "atlcontrols.h"
#include <tchar.h>
```

Now open URLTreeView.h and add this to the property map

```
    PROP_PAGE(CLSID_URLPage)
```

Note that we don't add a description for the URLs property, because ATL's persistence implementations would try to persist the property using the container's IPropertyBag interface. Many containers can't handle arrays, so we'll add our own code to persist the property later.

Now you can compile the code and test it in Visual Basic or using the ActiveX Control Test Container. You can use the property page to add and remove items from the control.

Persistence Code for Visual Basic

Now you should be able to load the control in Visual Basic and alter its properties. Try these steps:

❑ Start Visual Basic and select Standard EXE as the project type.

❑ Use the Components... item in the Project menu and add the URLTree component

❑ Add a URLTreeView control to the form and in the Properties box click on the ellipsis next to the Custom item.

Use the property page to add some items and then click on OK. The items should be added to the control.

Now save the project, close VB and then start it again, loading the project you saved. You'll find that VB issues an error saying that it can't load the control. This is because the code we provided for `IPersistPropertyBag::Load()` expects to find `noItems` in the property bag, and we haven't yet written to the code to save this information. We'll do that now.

Add the declaration for `IPersistPropertyBag_Save()` to the `CURLTreeView` class:

```
// IPersistPropertyBag
   HRESULT IPersistPropertyBag_Load(LPPROPERTYBAG pPropBag,
                                    LPERRORLOG pErrorLog,
                                    ATL_PROPMAP_ENTRY* pMap);
   HRESULT IPersistPropertyBag_Save(LPPROPERTYBAG pPropBag, BOOL fClearDirty,
                                    BOOL fSaveAllProperties,
                                    ATL_PROPMAP_ENTRY* pMap);
```

In `URLTreeView.cpp`, add the code for the `IPersistPropertyBag_Save()` method like this:

```
HRESULT CURLTreeView::IPersistPropertyBag_Save(LPPROPERTYBAG pPropBag,
            BOOL fClearDirty, BOOL fSaveAllProperties, ATL_PROPMAP_ENTRY* pMap)
{
    // First say how many items
    CComVariant var = (long)m_URLs.size();
    HRESULT hr = pPropBag->Write(L"noItems", &var);
    if (FAILED(hr))
        return hr;

    short item = 0;
    OLECHAR strParam[8];
    std::vector<CComBSTR>::iterator it;
    for (it = m_URLs.begin(); it < m_URLs.end(); it++)
    {
        item++;
        swprintf(strParam, L"Item%d", item);
        var = (*it);
        hr = pPropBag->Write(strParam, &var);
        if (FAILED(hr))
            return hr;
    }
    return IPersistPropertyBagImpl<CURLTreeView>::IPersistPropertyBag_Save(
                            pPropBag, fClearDirty, fSaveAllProperties, pMap);
}
```

Now compile the project, start up Visual Basic, select a Standard EXE as the project type and add the control as a component as you have done before. Add a new control to the form and use the property page to add items for the URLTreeView control. Close the property page and save the project.

Using a text editor, open the file for the form. Here's the result from one of my tests. I have shown only the text pertinent to the control:

```
Begin URLTREELibCtl.URLTreeView URLTreeView1
    Height          =   2895
    Left            =   960
    TabIndex        =   0
    Top             =   120
    Width           =   2895
    noItems         =   3
    Item1           =   "One/Two,url1"
    Item2           =   "One/Three,url2"
    Item3           =   "Two,url3"
    _cx             =   5106
    _cy             =   5106
End
```

Notice that the custom 'properties' have been added.

Now with VB open, run the application, what do you see? The control is empty, the values you entered on the property page are not shown, and further, when you stop the application and look at the control on the form in the VB IDE, you will see that the values have completely disappeared. Why is this?

The reason is that although `IPersistPropertyBag` is used to persist the data to a file, the VB IDE uses `IPersistStreamInit` to initialize the control when you run the VB application. VB calls `Save()` to get the state of the design time control and passes the initialized stream to `Load()` of the runtime control. When the application stops, VB reverses the process, calling `Save()` on the runtime control and then passing the stream to the design time control with `Load()`.

VB also uses this interface to serialize the state of the control when you compile a VB project. The stream that Save() should fill, is stored in the compiled EXE and when the application is run, the VB runtime will load this serialized data as a stream and call the control's Load() method.

The ATL implementation of IPersistStreamInit does not handle SAFEARRAYs, so once again you need to implement the code that the Load() and Save() methods of this interface will call. This time the data is saved to a stream, so we need to concatenate all the strings together.

In the control header, add these declarations:

```
//IPersistStreamInit
    HRESULT IPersistStreamInit_Load(LPSTREAM pStm, ATL_PROPMAP_ENTRY* pMap);
    HRESULT IPersistStreamInit_Save(LPSTREAM pStm, BOOL fClearDirty,
                                                   ATL_PROPMAP_ENTRY* pMap);
```

Implement the IPersistStreamInit_Save() method in the source file:

```
HRESULT CURLTreeView::IPersistStreamInit_Save(LPSTREAM pStm, BOOL fClearDirty,
                                              ATL_PROPMAP_ENTRY* pMap)
{
    // Add all strings together and serialize
    CComBSTR bstr = L"";
    std::vector<CComBSTR>::iterator it;
    for (it = m_URLs.begin(); it < m_URLs.end(); it++)
    {
        if (it != m_URLs.begin())
            bstr.Append(L"|");
        bstr += (*it);
    }

    bstr.WriteToStream(pStm);
    m_bRequiresSave = FALSE;
    return IPersistStreamInitImpl<CURLTreeView>:: IPersistStreamInit_Save(
                                            pStm, fClearDirty, pMap);
}
```

This iterates through all the strings in the vector and adds them together, separating each with a pipe character (|). The serialization is done right at the end where the code calls the WriteToStream() method of CComBSTR. As usual, we call the base class implementation to ensure that any properties we decide to add to the property map at a later date also get persisted.

The reverse process is just as simple. Add the following as the implementation for the IPersistStreamInit_Load() method:

```
HRESULT CURLTreeView::IPersistStreamInit_Load(LPSTREAM pStm,
                                              ATL_PROPMAP_ENTRY* pMap)
{
    m_URLs.clear();
    CComBSTR bstr;
    bstr.ReadFromStream(pStm);
    LPOLESTR ptr = bstr;
    LPOLESTR str = ptr;
```

```
    while (ptr)
    {
        ptr = wcschr(str, L'|');
        if (ptr)
        {
            *ptr = 0;
            ptr++;
        }
        CComBSTR newStr;
        newStr = str;
        m_URLs.push_back(str);
        str = ptr;
    }

    return IPersistStreamInitImpl<CURLTreeView>::IPersistStreamInit_Load(pStm,
                                                                        pMap);
}
```

Now when you compile the project, you should be able to run the VB application in the VB IDE and get the state passed correctly to the control at runtime. Further, you should also be able to compile the VB application and when you run this EXE outside of the VB IDE, you will get the items you added with the property page.

Summary

In this chapter, we've created a detailed and realistic ATL control. You've seen how to draw a control, how to base it on an existing control and how to handle messages within the control. I have also shown you how to add property pages to your control and how to make these work with VB.

These techniques were illustrated with the URLTreeView example. This control is based upon a Win32 tree view common control and an edit control. URLTreeView implements persistence interfaces to allow it to be initialized from parameters on a web page, or within Visual Basic and I have shown you how to write a property page that has interdependent controls.

Finally, much of the code for the control was concerned with making it work with VB. You have seen how VB uses IPersistPropertyBag to write the data from the control to the form's file, and how it uses IPersistStreamInit when the actual VB application is run.

And with that , our tour of the Active Template Library is complete. We hope you've found the book useful, and the examples revealing. it has been our intention throughout to provide a firm grounding in ATL, so that you can go on to choose the path that best suits you, confident that you'll be able to deal with the challenges it throws up. We'd be interested to learn whether we have been successful.

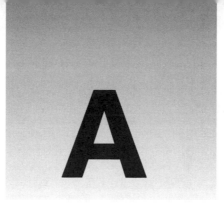

HRESULT Facility Codes

In Chapter 1, we briefly mentioned facility codes, which occupy bits 16 to 26 of HRESULTs, and are used to define groups of related return codes. The table below lists the predefined facility codes and describes what they mean:

Facility Name	Value	Description
FACILITY_NULL	0	For broadly applicable common status codes such as S_OK.
FACILITY_RPC	1	For status codes returned from remote procedure calls.
FACILITY_DISPATCH	2	For late-binding IDispatch interface status codes.
FACILITY_STORAGE	3	For status codes returned from IStorage and IStream method calls.
FACILITY_ITF	4	For most status codes returned from interface errors. The error is defined by the interface itself. The same status code returned from two different interfaces could have very different meanings.
FACILITY_WIN32	7	Used to provide a means of handling error codes in the Win32 API as an HRESULT.
FACILITY_WINDOWS	8	Used for additional error codes from Microsoft-defined interfaces.
FACILITY_SSPI	9	Security-related status codes.
FACILITY_CONTROL	10	ActiveX controls-related status codes.
FACILITY_CERT	11	Security certificate-related status codes.
FACILITY_INTERNET	12	Internet-related status codes.

The return codes that occupy bits 0 to 15 of an HRESULT are facility-specific. You can make up your own HRESULTs with the MAKE_HRESULT() macro from <winerror.h>, or break an HRESULT into its constituent parts with the HRESULT_CODE(), HRESULT_FACILITY(), and HRESULT_SEVERITY() macros.

Generally, you should only make custom HRESULTs with FACILITY_ITF, as the other facilities belong to development groups at Microsoft. It would be very unusual to need to have your own custom facility. You should use return codes in the range 0x0200–0xFFFF when constructing FACILITY_ITF HRESULTs.

Standard HRESULTs usually have a three-part symbolic name: *facility_severity_reason*, such as STG_E_FILENOTFOUND or MK_S_MONIKERALREADYREGISTERED. However, the FACILITY_NULL HRESULTs omit the NULL from their name; for example, S_OK and E_OUTOFMEMORY.

Index

Index

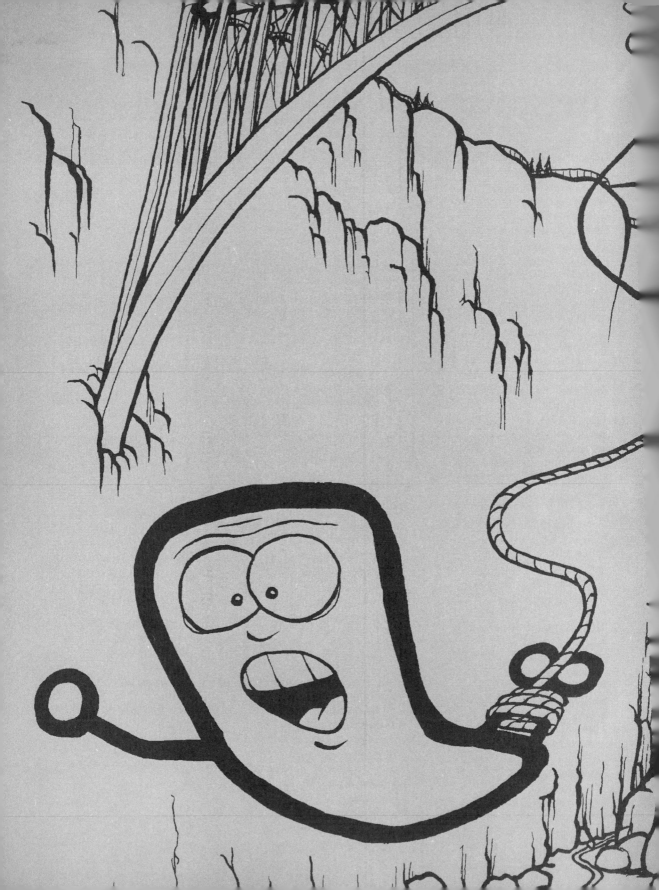

wrox
PROGRAMMER TO PROGRAMMER™

Wrox writes books for you. Any suggestions, or ideas about how you want information given in your ideal book will be studied by our team.
Your comments are always valued at Wrox.

Free phone in USA 800-USE-WROX
Fax (312) 893 8001

UK Tel. (0121) 687 4100   Fax (0121) 687 4101

Beginning ATL 3 COM Programming - Registration Card

Name _____

Address _____

_____

_____

_____

City_____ State/Region _____

Country_____ Postcode/Zip_____

E-mail _____

Occupation _____

How did you hear about this book?_____

☐ Book review (name)_____

☐ Advertisement (name) _____

☐ Recommendation _____

☐ Catalog_____

☐ Other _____

Where did you buy this book? _____

☐ Bookstore (name)_____ City_____

☐ Computer Store (name)_____

☐ Mail Order _____

☐ Other _____

What influenced you in the purchase of this book?

☐ Cover Design

☐ Contents

☐ Other (please specify) _____

How did you rate the overall contents of this book?

☐ Excellent   ☐ Good

☐ Average   ☐ Poor

What did you find most useful about this book? _____

_____

What did you find least useful about this book? _____

_____

Please add any additional comments. _____

_____

What other subjects will you buy a computer book on soon? _____

_____

What is the best computer book you have used this year?

_____

Note: This information will only be used to keep you updated about new Wrox Press titles and will not be used for any other purpose or passed to any other third party.

Check here if you DO NOT want to receive support for this ▮

wrox
PROGRAMMER TO PROGRAMMER™

NB. If you post the bounce back card below in the UK, please send it to:

Wrox Press Ltd., Arden House, 1102 Warwick Road,
Acocks Green, Birmingham B27 6BH. UK.

——— *Computer Book Publishers* ———